Medieval Russian Culture

CALIFORNIA SLAVIC STUDIES XII

Medieval Russian Culture

Edited by

Henrik Birnbaum and Michael S. Flier

UNIVERSITY OF CALIFORNIA PRESS
Berkeley   Los Angeles   London

The publication of this volume
was made possible by a subsidy from the
Center for Russian and East European Studies,
University of California, Los Angeles.

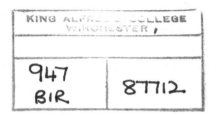
University of California Press
Berkeley and Los Angeles, California
University of California Press, Ltd.
London, England
© 1984 by The Regents of the
University of California

Library of Congress Cataloging in Publication Data

Medieval Russian culture.

(California Slavic studies ; 12)
Includes index.
1. Russian philology—Addresses, essays, lectures.
2. Russian S.F.S.R.—Civilization–Addresses, essays,
lectures. I. Birnbaum, Henrik. II. Flier, Michael S.
III. Series.
DK4.C33 no.12 [PG2025]   306′.0947   82-23866
ISBN 0-520-04938-1

Printed in the United States of America

1 2 3 4 5 6 7 8 9

For

DMITRIJ SERGEEVIČ LIXAČEV

CONTENTS

PREFACE

The publication of a volume of essays on medieval Russian culture was conceived as an appropriate forum in which specialists could present the results of current research in a circumscribed field outside the formal setting of an international conference, an alternative that has become increasingly difficult for fiscal as well as logistical reasons. A number of prominent scholars were approached for contributions—in this country as well as in Western and Eastern Europe, including the Soviet Union—and the response was most gratifying.

It is clear that an exhaustive treatment of the cultural facet of the Russian Middle Ages is beyond the scope of the present collection of fourteen essays, which represent a divergence of approach and focus. Nonetheless, each individual essay is concerned with an overall interpretation of some aspect of the Russian variety of early East European civilization rather than with the mere presentation of new data. Thus the ultimate purpose of the present volume is to examine and reassess a selection of pertinent issues in such broad subfields of early Russian civilization as cultural, intellectual, and ideological history; language, literature, and style; art in its social setting; and the practice of medicine in the monastic context of Old Rus'.

We do well to recall that the very notion of the Middle Ages as applied to Russia, or rather to the Eastern Slavs, is quite broad and is at variance with traditional European periodization: it spans the time from the beginnings of the East Slavic past in the ninth and tenth centuries through the sixteenth and (if transitional phenomena are included) even the seventeenth centuries, that is, right up to the Petrinic epoch.

Essays that were submitted in languages other than English were translated by the editors; whenever possible the authors were given an opportunity to verify the English version for accuracy. While the editors have not striven for an entirely uniform style throughout the volume, a degree of consistency—as regards transliteration, spelling norms, and the like—has been maintained. Special thanks are extended to Lori Jennings for her help in the preparation of the manuscript for publication and to Pamela Russell for producing the name index. The editors are also grateful to Randy Bowlus for his superlative composition of a difficult text.

Among the scholars most frequently mentioned on the following pages—whether in agreement or disagreement—is Academician Dmitrij Sergeevič Lixačev. Generally acknowledged as the ranking expert in the field of medieval

Russian culture today, he was among the very first scholars to be approached for a contribution to this volume, an invitation he immediately accepted, expressing great interest and expectations concerning our undertaking. Unfortunately, personal adversity has precluded his submitting an essay of his own, an essay in which he had planned to highlight and reexamine some of the crucial and, at the same time, most controversial issues of the cultural evolution of Old Rus'. The editors and other contributors wish to honor this pioneering scholar by dedicating this collection of studies to him as a modest token of their esteem.

Los Angeles   H. B.
February, 1982   M. S. F.

ABBREVIATIONS

BAN	Biblioteka Akademii nauk, Leningrad
ByzSl	*Byzantinoslavica*
ČOIDR	*Čtenija v Imperatorskom obščestve istorii i drevnostej rossijskix pri Moskovskom universitete*
GIM	Gosudarstvennyj istoričeskij muzej, Moscow
GPB	Gosudarstvennaja Publičnaja Biblioteka im. Saltykova-Ščedrina, Leningrad
IOLJa	*Izvestija Otdelenija literatury i jazyka*, Moscow
IORJaS	*Izvestija Otdelenija russkogo jazyka i slovesnosti*, St. Petersburg (Leningrad)
PDPI	*Pamjatniki drevnerusskoj pis'mennosti i iskusstva*
PL	*Patrologia Latina* (Migne)
PG	*Patrologia Graeca* (Migne)
PSRL	*Polnoe sobranie russkix letopisej*
PVL	*Povest' vremennyx let*
RIB	*Russkaja istoričeskaja biblioteka*
SbORJaS	*Sbornik Otdelenija russkogo jazyka i slovesnosti*
TODRL	*Trudy Otdela drevnerusskoj literatury*
VV	*Vizantijskij Vremennik*
ŽMNP	*Žurnal Ministerstva narodnogo prosveščenija*

Culture and Society

THE BALKAN SLAVIC COMPONENT OF MEDIEVAL RUSSIAN CULTURE

HENRIK BIRNBAUM

As is well known, there exists a vast and rapidly growing body of research about the impact of the Balkan Slavs—the Bulgarians and the Serbs—on the civilization of Old Rus'. This research not only includes the interaction that occurred between the southern and eastern segments of Orthodox Slavdom but also illuminates the role played by Byzantium in this context. The following essay is offered with the intent of synthesizing my views on the subject in line with the overall conception underlying this volume.[1]

First, a comment is called for regarding the very nature of Byzantine culture and its permeation of what D. Obolensky, following Byzantine usage, has aptly referred to as the "Byzantine Commonwealth" (οἰκουμένη). I will be concerned primarily with the East European periphery of that commonwealth and only secondarily with Byzantium proper.

When we look at Bulgaria, Serbia, and the lands of the Eastern Slavs, it is the earliest Bulgarian state, the First Bulgarian Empire, that stands out as being the closest in space and spirit to the main center of Byzantine culture, the Imperial City itself. Kievan Rus' received many of its Greek intellectual, spiritual, and artistic impulses and imports not directly from Byzantium but through the Crimean transit port of Cherson, an ancient Greek colony. Yet an immediate link between Constantinople and Kiev was

---

[1] The present essay, in addition to reviewing some new evidence, summarizes and integrates material previously discussed in two studies, based on papers presented in September 1978 at the University of Belgrade (in the context of the 8th International Conference of Slavists) and in November 1980 at Columbia University (before participants of the American-Bulgarian Conference on Bulgarian Culture, held to mark the 1300th anniversary of the foundation of the First Bulgarian Empire), respectively: "Serbian Models in the Literature and Literary Language of Medieval Russia," *Slavic and East European Journal* 23 (1979): 1-13 (Serbo-Croatian version: "Srpski uzori u književnosti i književnom jeziku srednjevekovne Rusije," *Naučni sastanak slavista u Vukove dane. Referati i saopštenja* 8 [Belgrade, 1980], 5–17); and "Bulgaria's Impact on the Culture of Old Rus'," to appear shortly in a volume of conference proceedings published by the Bulgarian Academy of Sciences (R. Lencek, ed.). In addition, some of the observations and findings reported in an earlier essay, "On the Significance of the Second South Slavic Influence for the Evolution of the Russian Literary Language," *International Journal of Slavic Linguistics and Poetics* 21 (1975): 23-50, are restated here in modified and condensed form.

also established by Grand Prince Jaroslav in the first half of the eleventh
century, as noted in the Old Russian chronicle entry for the year 1037. The
northernmost Russian gateway to foreign cultural influence was the town
of Ladoga (now Staraja Ladoga), near the estuary of the Volxov River at
Lake Ladoga. It was both the major point of entry into the early East
Slavic realm from the Varangian North and, as Obolensky has noted,
simultaneously the northernmost point to which, in terms of cultural
impact, the "Byzantine Commonwealth" extended. Specifically, this is
shown by the splendid frescoes of the Church of Saint George at Ladoga,
painted in the Byzantinesque manner.[2]

Given Bulgaria's proximity to Constantinople and the capital's highly
developed and sophisticated civilization, it is not surprising that soon after
the Slavic population south of the lower Danube had largely assimilated
their Turkic conquerors, a form of cultural precociousness evolved in the
East Balkans which implied a far-reaching Byzantinization unmatched
anywhere else among the Slavs. Nonetheless, in the other Slavic territories
where the cultural development was patterned primarily on Byzantine
models and examples—that is, in Serbia and Old Rus'—an impressive level
of education, learning, and artistic accomplishment was also attained by a
small intellectual and aesthetically inclined or skilled elite, though only
after a transitional period and in large part precisely as a result of Bulgarian mediation. It is hardly an exaggeration to claim that during the reigns
of Khan Boris (852-889) and, especially, Tsar Simeon (898-927), the Balkan
Slavic state turned into a veritable domain of Byzantine civilization. The
overt manifestation of the Bulgarian acculturation of this Byzantine model
includes the gradual substitution of the Glagolitic by the Cyrillic script (the
latter without doubt patterned on the Greek uncial characters); the shift in
cultural activities from Ohrid in the west to the new capital city of Preslav
in the east; Tsar Simeon's ambition to occupy the purple throne of the East
Roman Empire; and, finally, the various achievements of such men as Kliment of Ohrid (d. 916), Konstantin of Preslav (d. c. 910), and John
(Ioann) the Exarch (a contemporary of Tsar Simeon; no exact dates
known). Byzantium's subjugation of the First Bulgarian Empire in the
second half of the tenth century, and of the West Bulgarian (or Macedonian) rump and successor state of Tsar Samuil in the second decade of the
eleventh century, signaled the end of Bulgaria's independence as a political
entity for more than a century and a half. It did not, however, spell an end
to the flourishing hybrid of Greco-Slavic civilization that had been initiated

[2] See D. Obolensky, *The Byzantine Commonwealth: Eastern Europe, 500-1453* (New York,
1971), 354; for particulars, see esp. V. N. Lazarev, *Freski Staroj Ladogi* (Moscow, 1960).

with the Thessalonian brothers' mission among the Moravian and Panno-
nian Slavs in the second half of the ninth century; nor did it bring to a close
the activities of the successors to Methodius' disciples and associates in
West Bulgaria (Macedonia) who had resettled on the shores of Lakes Ohrid
and Prespa after the Slavic liturgy had been prohibited in Moravia toward
the end of the ninth century, following the older brother's death in 885. The
flowering of Old Church Slavic—or Old Bulgarian—writing in what has
been referred to as the "third homeland" of that language and literature,
with several extant texts dating from the eleventh and in some instances
even the late tenth century, eloquently testifies to the continuation of Slavic
literacy under Byzantine administration. Given the strikingly rapid cultural
development of Bulgaria, it seems only natural that, in addition to Greek
Byzantium itself, it would become the chief model and source of inspiration
for the other Slavic nations recently converted, or about to be converted, to
Orthodox Christianity, the Slavs of Kievan Rus' among them.[3]

It is generally agreed that Bulgaria's impact on the culture of Old Rus' took
place largely in two separate phases—an earlier one in the tenth and eleventh centuries, and a later one in the fourteenth, fifteenth, and to some
extent even the sixteenth centuries. The activities and developments unfold-
ing in the monastic community of the Holy Mountain, one of the foremost
strongholds of Eastern Christianity and a powerful link and mediator
between Byzantium and Orthodox Slavdom in the Balkans as well as in the
European East, bridged the hiatus between the two periods. Thus, literary
work, particularly the copying of Slavic manuscripts carried out in Athonite
monasteries, played a major part in the traveling of Bulgarian texts to Russia over the centuries. By the same token, Russian Church Slavic handwritten material found its way to Mount Athos where it was read, adapted, and
copied by Bulgarian and Serbian monks. No attempt will be made here,
however, to draw anything like a complete picture of the South Slavic–
Russian contacts and relations as they were established and rendered

---

[3] For an adequate survey of Byzantino-Bulgarian relations and the impact of Byzantine
civilization on Bulgaria, particularly in the crucial ninth and tenth centuries, seen from the
Byzantinist's point of view, see R. Browning, *Byzantium and Bulgaria: A Comparative Study
Across the Early Medieval Frontier* (Berkeley–Los Angeles, 1975). See also I. Dujčev, "Klas-
sisches Altertum im mittelalterlichen Bulgarien," *Renaissance und Humanismus in Mittel- und
Osteuropa*, vol. 1, ed. J. Irmscher (Berlin, 1962), 343-356; reprinted in *Medioevo bizantino-slavo*
1 (*Storia e letteratura. Raccolta di studi e testi* 102 [Rome, 1965]), 467-485. For a fairly objective Slavist assessment, see A. P. Vlasto, *The Entry of the Slavs into Christendom: An Introduction to the Medieval History of the Slavs* (Cambridge, 1970), 155-187, esp. 171-182. Many of the
relevant issues have received further treatment by Bulgarian scholars, notably in a series of
incisive studies by I. Dujčev.

productive in the larger Slavic monasteries of the Holy Mountain—Bulgarian Zograph, Serbian Hilandar, and Russian Panteleimon (also known as Rossikon)—and, presumably, in some of the smaller settlements of monks and hermits, the so-called sketes, as well. Suffice it to say that during the Middle Ages and in the following centuries, the Slavic monasteries of Mount Athos frequently seem to have housed monks from more than one Slavic country; in other words, although one particular ethnic group was predominant, members of other nationalities were welcome too, or at any rate, were tolerated. To mention just one well-known example: it may be recalled that at one time or another Hilandar not only served as the residence or retreat of such renowned Serbs as the retired grand *župan* Stefan Nemanja (who assumed the monastic name Simeon), his son Rastko—better known as Saint Sava, Serbia's first archbishop—and the monks Domentijan and Teodosije, noted for their biographic writings, but also, for some period, was the refuge of the eighteenth-century Bulgarian cleric and historian Paisij (often therefore referred to as Hilendarski) before he entered the Bulgarian Zograph Monastery. For a more comprehensive, in-depth assessment of the role of the Holy Mountain as intermediary in the spiritual interchange and literary influences among Greeks, Southern Slavs, and Russians (in the broad sense)—of particularly far-reaching consequence in the heyday of Hesychasm (briefly discussed below)—the pertinent publications by I. Dujčev, V. Mošin, and, more recently, A.-E. Tachiaos should be consulted.[4]

The earlier Bulgarian impact on Old Rus' cannot, strictly speaking, be characterized as an influence, since at that time nothing qualitatively compatible that could be affected in kind was to be found in the two major Old Russian urban communities on the banks of the Dnieper and the Volxov. This point has been made eloquently by D. S. Lixačev regarding the impact of Byzantine civilization on the Slavic world as a whole and on Old Rus' in particular. Virtually the same can be argued about the effect of thoroughly Byzantinized Bulgaria on early medieval Russia. Consequently, it may be more appropriate to refer to the Byzantine and Bulgarian cultural impact on the Kievan state of the tenth and eleventh centuries as a transplantation

---

[4] See I. Dujčev, "Le Mont Athos et les Slaves au Moyen âge," in *Le Millénaire du Mont Athos, 963-1963. Études et mélanges*, vol. 2 (Venice, 1964); reprinted in *Medioevo bizantino-slavo* 1: 487-510; V. Mošin, "O periodizacii russko-južnoslavjanskix literaturnyx svjazej X-XV vv.," in *Russkaja literatura XI-XVII vekov sredi slavjanskix literatur, TODRL* 19 (1963): 28-106, esp. 62-63, 73-74; A.-E. Tachiaos, "Mount Athos and the Slavic Literatures," *Cyrillomethodianum* 4 (1978): 1-35. These works contain, in turn, ample references to additional pertinent literature, in part by the same scholars.

of an entire range of religious, intellectual, and aesthetic values and patterns.[5] Contrary to previous contentions by some Soviet and, more surprisingly, also Bulgarian scholars (S. P. Obnorskij, P. Ja. Černyx, E. Georgiev, and others), there is actually not a shred of solid evidence to support the claim that any particular writing system was widely known and used in Rus' before the introduction and adaptation of Old Church Slavic, that is, before Old Bulgarian writing in the Cyrillic and only rarely (in a special, limited function) in the Glagolitic script. It is further not at all likely that some kind of prototype of Cyrillic—presumably some form of the Greek uncial—was in more or less regular use in pre-Christian Rus', that is to say, before Constantine-Cyril's devising of the Glagolitic alphabet, notwithstanding a few finds with brief inscriptions or incisions, notably from Gnezdovo (near Smolensk).

Yet there is some suggestion that in fact Old Bulgarian may have been used, if not on East Slavic ground, then on a few occasions earlier, in matters pertaining to the pagan rulers of the Kievan state, namely, before the conversion of Rus' to Orthodox Christianity. By this I am referring to the much discussed treaties concluded between the Varangian princes—Oleg, Igor', and Svjatoslav—and Byzantium in 911, 944, and 971, respectively. The Slavic wording of these agreements is contained in the Laurentian copy (dated 1377) of the Primary, or Nestor, Chronicle (*Povest' vremennyx let*) under the years 6420 (= 912), 6453 (= 945), and 6479 (= 971). Their language can best be characterized as Church Slavic with an admixture of some genuine East Slavic elements.[6] Although some Russists have referred

---

[5] See D. S. Likhachev, "The Type and Character of the Byzantine Influence on Old Russian Literature," *Oxford Slavonic Papers* 13 (1967): 14-32, esp. 18-20; id., *Razvitie russkoj literatury X-XVII vekov. Èpoxi i stili* (Leningrad, 1973), 20-22; O. V. Tvorogov, in *Istorija russkoj literatury X-XVII vekov,* ed. D. S. Lixačev (Moscow, 1980), 37-38. On the distinction between transplantation and influence proper, see also H. Birnbaum, *International Journal of Slavic Linguistics and Poetics* 21 (1975): 28-29.

[6] Cf. *Načalo russkoj literatury. XI – načalo XII veka. Pamjatniki literatury Drevnej Rusi,* ed. D. S. Lixačev et al. (Moscow, 1978), 46-53, 60-67, 86-88. On the language of the treaties, particularly of the two longer ones, see L. P. Jakubinskij, *Istorija drevnerusskogo jazyka* (Moscow, 1963), 89-91, 354, accounting also for previous views concerning the language of these documents, notably those by V. M. Istrin and S. P. Obnorskij. Whereas Jakubinskij was of the opinion that the treaties were translated by tenth-century Russians into Church Slavic (the East Slavic elements supposedly revealing the nationality of the translators who, however, obviously were well versed in Greek and Old Bulgarian), Istrin held the view that the treaties were translated only in the beginning of the twelfth century, probably by the compiler of the chronicle text on the basis of the Greek originals found by him in the grand-princely chancery in Kiev; this view was, consequently, not shared by Jakubinskij. Obnorskij, for his part, suggested that the first treaty was translated by a Bulgarian into Old Bulgarian (Old Church Slavic) and only subsequently adapted to Russian Church Slavic, while the second agreement would have been translated by a Russian directly into Russian Church Slavic. Generally, on

to these legal texts as evidence that East Slavic writing and/or a high level
of literacy existed in Russia even before the advent of Christianity, the Rus-
sianized Church Slavic language of these documents, now generally acknowledged, can be accounted for in at least two conceivable ways: (1) It is
due to the mixed, Old Bulgarian–East Slavic character of the language
found in the Old Russian chronicles, particularly in the *Povest'*; in that case,
the original version of the Byzantine-Russian treaties may well have been
translated into Slavic at some later date (this is the view once held by V. M.
Istrin). (2) These agreements were first drawn up by the two parties in
collaboration at the same time, in two parallel versions, one phrased in
Greek, the other in Slavic. If this was the case, the Varangian rulers of Rus'
could have availed themselves of Slavic translators and scribes from outside
their own realm, that is, of temporary residents (presumably Bulgarian clerics), given that literacy in the Slavic vernacular had not yet been introduced
in their own country.[7]

Any potential pre-Christian Bulgarian cultural impact on Old Rus', such
as the one just described, is purely hypothetical, to be sure, and thus controversial. Yet there can be little doubt about the considerable flow of Old
Bulgarian texts to Rus' after the latter's official conversion to Christianity
in 988, or about the frequent copying of Old Bulgarian manuscripts for
Kievan, Novgorodian, and other local rulers and dignitaries in Rus' as well
as outside its territory—in Bulgaria, on Mount Athos, and elsewhere.[8]
Several of the earliest, eleventh-century Russian Church Slavic texts can, as
we know, be traced to Old Church Slavic originals. This applies, in particular, to the lavishly illuminated *Izbornik Svjatoslava* of 1073, which has been
shown to be a copy, in its entirety, from a lost miscellany compiled for Tsar

---

the treaties of 911 and 944 and their significance as diplomatic documents, see now A. N.
Saxarov, *Diplomatija Drevnej Rusi. IX – pervaja polovina X v.* (Moscow, 1980), 147-180,
209-258.

[7] At the end of the earliest treaty (of 911), there is even a hint of a Slavic translator and/or
scribe by the name of Ivan; see *Načalo russkoj literatury,* 52-53, 429. Note further that in the
two earlier (and longer) treaties, there is some mention of the agreements being written on two
sets of parchment, or in two copies, suggesting the possibility of their having been worded
simultaneously in Greek and Slavic.

[8] For the exact chronology of events surrounding the baptism of Rus', see A. Poppe, *The
Political Background to the Baptism of Rus': Byzantine-Russian Relations Between 986-89*
(Washington, D.C., 1976); reprinted from *Dumbarton Oaks Papers* 30: 195-244. Obviously,
some isolated forms of Christianity and individual Christians existed in Kievan Rus' before its
official conversion. Thus, it is known that there was a Christian church in Kiev as early as the
reign of Igor; and Olga, Vladimir's grandmother, converted to Christianity at the urging of the
Byzantine emperor. It is therefore also conceivable that some minor Bulgarian effect on Rus',
in the form of a few imported Old Church Slavic manuscripts, for example, may have
occurred even before 988.

Simeon of Bulgaria.[9] The earliest dated handwritten book in Old Rus', the famous *Ostromir Evangelistary* of 1056-57 commissioned by the Novgorod *posadnik* Ostromir and, as indicated in the colophon, copied by a deacon named Grigorij, is an *aprakos* gospel of roughly the same kind as the *Codex Assemanianus* or the *Savvina Kniga* of the Old Church Slavic canonical texts—the former betraying West Bulgarian, the latter East Bulgarian provenance. The Russian Church Slavic evangelistary, exhibiting relatively few vernacular, genuinely East Slavic features, was in all probability copied and adapted from an Old Bulgarian gospel-book either in Novgorod, or, less likely, in Kiev. But other Russian Church Slavic texts, too—for example, the *Izbornik Svjatoslava* of 1076, several early gospel manuscripts, including the *Archangel Evangelistary* of 1092, and the extant portions of the *Novgorod Liturgical Menaia* (*Čet'i Minei*) of 1095-97—while written in Rus', were adapted either partially (as, for example, the 1076 miscellany) or entirely from Old Bulgarian protographs or their now-lost, earlier Russian Church Slavic copies, occasionally reaching East Slavic territory via Bohemia (as was the case, it seems, with the *Novgorod Menaia*; cf. the mention of Saint Václav in this text). In other instances, Byzantine texts, such as the learned *Chronicle of George the Monk (Hamartolos)* of the more popular *Chronicle of John Malalas*, may have passed through Bulgaria or were even first rendered into Slavic there before making their appearance in Russia, where they were subsequently copied more than once.[10] Some of these early Russian Church Slavic manuscripts are therefore only slightly more recent than their presumed Old Bulgarian counterparts. The textual tradition is even further complicated in the case of one of the more impressive literary achievements of early medieval Bulgaria, John the Exarch's *Šestodnev*, largely patterned on the *Hexaëmeron* of Saint Basil the Great. The oldest preserved manuscript of this text is a Serbian copy (dated 1263) of a Middle Bulgarian version; but several of the more recent variants, from the fifteenth, sixteenth, and seventeenth centuries, either are written in Russian Church Slavic or betray an underlying Russian Church Slavic version.[11]

---

[9] For recent research, see the volume *Izbornik Svjatoslava 1073 g. Sbornik statej*, ed. B. A. Rybakov (Moscow, 1977), esp. the contributions by B. St. Angelov (247-256), D. Angelov (256-263), È. I. Georgiev (263-272), and P. N. Dinekov (272-279).

[10] Regarding the *Chronicle of George Hamartolos*, some scholars, in particular V. M. Istrin, believed that this Greek text was first translated into Slavic not in Bulgaria but in Kievan Rus'; however, this view has been opposed by others, among them M. Weingart, N. N. Durnovo, and P. A. Lavrov. The question of the exact time and place of the original Slavic translation of the *Chronicle of John Malalas* is, if possible, even more difficult to answer. On the issues involved, see, especially, O. V. Tvorogov, *Drevnerusskie xronografy* (Leningrad, 1975), 9-20, esp. 10-11 (with nn. 6–10), 13 (with n. 19).

[11] Cf. R. Aitzetmüller, *Das Hexaemeron des Exarchen Johannes*, vol. 1 (Graz, 1958), vi-ix.

Given the undisputed facts just mentioned, the major impact of Bulgaria on early medieval Russia's literature and culture in general has long been acknowledged. This is true for Bulgarian and Russian scholars alike— among them, with only slightly different emphases, the ranking experts in the field, E. Georgiev and D. S. Lixačev.[12]

In this context it should furthermore be noted, incidentally, that Bulgaria not only provided the linguistic vehicle for transferring a rich and sophisticated body of writing to Kievan Rus', as Old Bulgarian phonology and inflectional morphology in particular were easily adapted to the sound pattern and form system of Early East Slavic; but, in addition, the Bulgarian men of letters, by having selected, absorbed, and assimilated a specific portion of the Byzantine literary legacy, largely determined, at least initially, also the kind, amount, and content of literature that would find its way to the relatively small group of readers among the Eastern Slavs. Thus, when it comes to the translated literature of Rus', including the many works adapted from Old Bulgarian, there is a considerable coincidence of specific genres and individual works between early medieval Russia and ninth- to eleventh-century Bulgaria. The preference for certain Early Christian genres and, within their framework, the particular writings selected for translation into Slavic—Old Bulgarian and/or Russian Church Slavic—need to be further examined. Yet, some general trends and broad considerations are sufficiently known and understood today. Thus, as I. P. Eremin has shown in a thoughtful essay, out of the whole range of Byzantine literature, it was virtually only the Church Fathers of the second through sixth centuries, but not the great writers of the ninth to twelfth centuries (or, in other words, the contemporaries of the *literati* in early medieval Bulgaria and Russia), that were found worthy of being translated into Slavic. The exceptions are few indeed, the *Chronicle of Hamartolos* being perhaps the most conspicuous. But most of Byzantine literature of the ninth through twelfth centuries

---

[12] See the capsulizing statements by E. Georgiev in his contribution, "Bulgarian Literature in the Context of Slavic and European Literature," in *Bulgaria, Past and Present: Studies in History, Literature, Economics, Music, Sociology, Folklore and Linguistics*, ed. T. Butler (Columbus, Ohio, 1976), 213; and by D. S. Lixačev in his "Zaključenie," summing up the collectively authored volume *Istorija russkoj literatury X–XVII vekov* (see n. 5), 447-448. In his earlier, theoretical outline, *Razvitie russkoj literatury X–XVII vekov* (see n. 5), 23-44, Lixačev defined Old Bulgarian (Old Church Slavic) literature as an "intermediary literature" (*literatura-posrednica*) which served to codify the Slavic literary legacy as it had taken shape, first in Moravia and Bohemia and subsequently in Bulgaria, Serbia, and Rus'; see also O. V. Tvorogov, in *Istorija russkoj literatury X–XVII vekov*, 38-39. However, as R. Picchio has repeatedly pointed out, equally important as the "intermediary" function of Old Bulgarian literature was its role of serving as the foundation of a viable literary system for Orthodox Slavdom as well as a "classical" (or "pattern-setting") model for this community's literary culture.

appeared in Church Slavic versions only considerably later—to be exact, in the course of the Second South Slavic Influence (see below).[13]

Two more points should be made concerning Bulgaria's qualitative and quantitative impact on East Slavic culture. The strength of Bulgarian influence was not uniform in different parts of Kievan Rus'. Though we know, of course, that various cultural centers existed in East Slavic territory during the Early Middle Ages—Kiev and Novgorod merely being the most prominent—it is not unusual to consider Old Russian culture in broad, oversimplified terms, namely, as a sort of uniform, monolithic phenomenon, an extension and variation of Byzantine civilization. Such a view no doubt has some merit as long as we recognize it for what it is—a theoretical generalization. However, it also implies a certain distortion when it comes to identifying, placing, and assessing specific details. For it is obviously no less important to be aware of the differences ascertainable among what may be termed the various cultural landscapes, or regional subcultures, within Old Rus'.[14] Thus, vestiges of Bulgaria's as well as Byzantium's cultural impact on Rus' are, by and large, stronger and more readily discernible in the South than in the North, in Kiev more than in Novgorod (where instead an additional, North European—Scandinavian and North German—foreign component is easily identified in the urban cultural pattern). This applies, incidentally, not only to literature (including oral tradition) but also to the visual arts. Thus it is only in Kiev that we find remnants of early medieval mosaics; the Russian North has nothing equivalent to offer, although its magnificent frescoes outshine even those of the East Slavic South. And whereas evidence of Bulgarian literary influences can be shown

[13] For details, see I. P. Eremin, "O vizantijskom vlijanii v bolgarskoj i drevnerusskoj litera-turax IX–XII vv.," in his collection *Literatura Drevnej Rusi. Ètjudy i xarakteristiki* (Moscow-Leningrad, 1966), 9-17. See also H. Birnbaum, *Die Welt der Slaven* 23 (1978): 194-195. In addition to the chronological selection, mention is made in the latter reference of the thematic restriction (in terms of a well-defined genre system suitable for Orthodox Christianity) as applied in the process of transposing the rich, multifaceted Byzantine literary heritage— including a variety of secular genres, in part dating back to pagan Antiquity—to the Orthodox Slavs. The particular type of selection and restriction was, it seems, first noted by the Norwegian scholar J. Børtnes in his study of the Old Russian *vita* with regard to the transplantation of literature from Byzantium to Rus'. (An English edition of Børtnes's important dissertation, so far available only in Norwegian, is in preparation; see n. 24). Cf. now also A. Issatschenko, *Geschichte* (see n. 15), 327, n. 6.

[14] For details, see my papers "Mikrokul'tury Drevnej Rusi i ix meždunarodnye svjazi," to appear in vol. 2 of the *American Contributions to the Ninth International Congress of Slavists*, ed. P. Debreczeny; and "Mestnye i xronologičeskie raznovidnosti drevnerusskoj kul'tury i ix vnutrennie i vnešnie svjazi," in the volume of essays by UCLA Slavists, *From Los Angeles to Kiev*, ed. D. S. Worth and V. Markov, to be published on the occasion of the Ninth International Congress of Slavists, Kiev, 1983. An English variant of this essay, "The Subcultures of Medieval Russia," will appear in *Viator* 15 (1984).

to have existed in Novgorod and other North Russian towns as well—to some extent transmitted through Bohemia—the general reasons why Bulgaria as well as Byzantium would have affected the South of Old Rus' more strongly (the relative geographic proximity and, in the early period, Kiev's role as capital city being merely the most obvious ones) are easily understood and need not concern us here.

Quantitatively, the Bulgarian cultural effect was felt in the literary sphere and in this sphere alone (where, however, it embraced all of religious life and related activities of man in Old Russian society). Bulgaria as such does not seem to have played any major role in the evolution of other manifestations of Christian civilization on Russian soil. In the figurative arts— architecture, mural and icon painting, book illumination, and the applied arts and crafts—and also in church music (i.e., chant), it was above all Byzantium itself and, in the later Middle Ages, Serbia, that provided the chief source of inspiration and the examples to be emulated. Thus, the few early medieval mosaics of southern Rus' just mentioned bear testimony to Byzantine, rather than to any Bulgarian, artistic skill transplanted to parts of the Kievan state.

The first Bulgarian cultural impact on Old Rus' has not stirred any major scholarly controversy as to its acknowledged significance and positive, beneficial effect. Undoubtedly, only some relatively minor points remain in need of further examination and interpretation. When it comes to the second, renewed Bulgarian impact, however, the situation is quite different. The latter forms part—indeed, some would argue, the main component—of the complex phenomenon known as the Second South Slavic Influence on Russian culture. Not only have several facets of the Bulgarian portion of this influence given rise to heated debates and contradictory explanations and evaluations, but the broader trend in civilization as well, operating in more than one direction and subsumed under this rather awkward and imprecise label (retained here only because of its wide currency), has elicited a number of controversial reactions.[15] Given this situation, I shall

---

[15] For a thorough survey and discussion of the historiography of the Second South Slavic Influence, see M. S. Iovine, *The History and the Historiography of the Second South Slavic Influence* (Ann Arbor, Mich.: University Microfilms, 1979). On the impact of Middle Bulgarian on Russian Church Slavic and its historical background, see, in particular, the important study by I. Talev, *Some Problems of the Second South Slavic Influence in Russia* (Munich, 1973); cf. my review in *Russian Linguistics* 1 (1974): 59-65. See further, Birnbaum, "Significance of the Second South Slavic Influence" (see n. 1), and, most recently, A. V. Issatschenko, "Die Rebulgarisierung der Hochsprache" (with several references to Talev's findings), in *Geschichte der russischen Sprache*, vol. 1 (Heidelberg, 1980), 211-234. Three contributions in the

focus on a few central issues while disregarding, at this point, several more marginal problems.

Thus leaving aside the very notion of the Second South Slavic Influence—which is, in fact, a misnomer[16]—it should be reiterated that the re-Slavonization—or as A. V. Issatschenko put it, the re-Bulgarization—and concomitant de-Russification of Russian Church Slavic from the late fourteenth through the fifteenth centuries cannot be viewed from one angle only. In other words, it can be considered neither a completely beneficial, progressive development (with Lixačev) nor an altogether detrimental, reactionary, and regressive factor (with Issatschenko) in the evolution of the Russian literary language. Although the strong impact of Bulgarian on the written language in Russia undoubtedly did preclude an early modernization, or Europeanization, of literary Russian, it enriched the literary language substantially, especially in its vocabulary, its phraseology, and, to some extent, its syntax, by solidifying and expanding the Church Slavic component and consequently rendering it a permanent, integral part of contemporary standard Russian.[17]

Some additional considerations regarding the Bulgarian impact on late medieval Russia were suggested by I. Talev. According to him, the Second South Slavic Influence should not be interpreted only, or even in the first place, as a consequence of the Ottoman conquest of the Balkans. The notion that there ever occurred anything like a mass exodus of Bulgarian and Serbian bookmen seeking refuge (and working possibilities) in Muscovite and Lithuanian Russia is obviously untenable. Of the two Bulgarian prelates known to us by name—Kiprian and Camblak (both of whom ended up as Russian metropolitans, the latter, although a native of Trnovo, probably of Walachian background and active also in Serbia and Moldavia; see below)—neither one came to Russia as a political refugee. Moreover, even though Middle Bulgarian manuscripts served, for the most part, as models for the standarization of the Church Slavic liturgical books in

---

volume *Bulgaria, Past and Present,* ed. T. Butler (see n. 12) discuss specific pertinent issues: I. White, "Hesychasm and the Revival of Bulgarian Literature in the Fourteenth Century," 249-254; R. Picchio, "Early Humanistic Trends in the Tŭrnovo School," 255-260; and M. S. Iovine, "Metropolitan Kiprian and the Orthodox Slavic Revival," 261-266. For a comprehensive treatment of Byzantine-Russian relations primarily in the fourteenth century, viewed from the Byzantinist's point of view, see most recently J. Meyendorff, *Byzantium and the Rise of Russia: A Study of Byzantino-Russian Relations in the Fourteenth Century* (Cambridge, 1981).

[16] See Birnbaum, "Significance of the Second South Slavic Influence" (see n. 1), 23-29.

[17] Ibid., 39-47. It should be noted, however, that Issatschenko, in his most recent treatment of this problem, took a more balanced view, acknowledging (p. 229 of his posthumous magnum opus) that "the re-Bulgarization of the standard language had both positive and negative sides for the further development of Russian and thus for the fate of Russian culture."

Russia, there is no evidence to suggest that Bulgarian handwritten material was imported on a truly large scale at that time. Such a massive transfer of Bulgarian manuscripts to Russia occurred only in the mid-seventeenth century, in connection with the church reform supervised by Patriarch Nikon. In the fourteenth and fifteenth centuries, however, most Middle Bulgarian texts were copied by Russians traveling south, during their stay at one of the monasteries of Mount Athos, in Bulgaria, Serbia, or in Constantinople. Thus it has been established, for example, that Igumen Afanasij Vysockij, a close associate of Metropolitan Kiprian, had a young monk, Vun'ko, visit the Zograph Monastery in order to copy some of the writings of Nikon of Crna Gora (also named Nikon Jerusalimac). We further know that Kiprian himself stayed both on the Holy Mountain and in Constantinople before coming to Russia, and that his alleged nephew, Grigorij Camblak, spent some time on Mount Athos and in the Imperial City before moving on to become the head of a Moldavian monastery and, later, igumen of the Dečani Monastery in Serbia.[18] In the final analysis, what counts when it comes to the Second South Slavic Influence in Russia is therefore not so much the number of persons involved in the move from one country to another within the Slavic Orthodox community, but rather the number of manuscripts, copied in various scriptoria, that were brought from the Slavic South (including the Slavic monasteries of Mount Athos) to Old Rus'.

   The standardization and unification of Middle Bulgarian, aimed at restoring the norms of the unadulterated, earliest form of Old Church Slavic (Old Bulgarian), occurred, or at any rate began, before the literary activities of the last patriarch of the Second Bulgarian Empire, Evtimij. His part in the process of standardizing the Middle Bulgarian literary language has been somewhat overrated in previous (and some current) research. As Talev has persuasively argued, the Bulgarian Church Slavic language used in the mid-fourteenth century had already acquired many of the characteristics of a supradialectal vehicle, suited to serve also as a supranational language for all Orthodox Slavs. The revision of the liturgical texts, with the purpose of reconciling them as much as possible with the linguistic standards of the first Slavic translations from the Greek, was a development whose beginnings go back to the political unification of Bulgaria under Ivan Asen II (1218-41) and, specifically, to the reintroduction of the Church Slavic liturgy as a result of the restoration of the Bulgarian patriarchate at Trnovo in 1235. The process of emendating the church books was virtually complete, at least in its initial phase, by the mid-fourteenth century, with such

[18] I. Talev, *Second South Slavic Influence* (see n. 15), 90-91, 94. On Nikon of Crna Gora, see also, e.g., D. Bogdanovič, *Istorija stare srpske književnosti* (Belgrade, 1980), 222-224.

works as the *Psalter* of 1337 and the *Gospels* of 1355-56, both associated with the name of the Bulgarian ruler Ivan Aleksandăr. Thus, at that time, the spelling rules as well as the grammatical and lexical norms had already been fairly well established. As a prolific and influential Hesychast writer and highly placed cleric, Patriarch Evtimij no doubt actively participated, and probably even took the lead, in the ongoing, continued revision of Church Slavic texts; but the notion that it was he who personally initiated and supervised an orthographic and linguistic reform is not borne out by any unequivocal evidence to that effect. Moreover, it should be noted that his own writings—mostly *vitae* of Bulgarian saints not worshiped or celebrated among the Eastern Slavs—had little impact on Russian Church Slavic literature. Any influence that he may have exerted on Russian letters could therefore have been only marginal and indirect, partly through Metropolitan Kiprian: as young men, Kiprian and Evtimij were reared together in the same Hesychast center of learning and spiritual exercise, namely, the Kilifarevo Monastery near Trnovo.

A few remarks may be appropriate here about the relationship of Middle Bulgarian and Old Serbian in view of the South Slavic influence on Russian Church Slavic writing. Of the two prominent Bulgarian bookmen that came to late medieval Russia, Kiprian had not gone through a Serbian phase. Grigorij Camblak, had, by contrast, spent some years in Serbia as igumen of the Dečani Monastery after having gone to the Holy Mountain, Constantinople, and Moldavia (where, in 1401-02, he headed the Sučava Monastery) and before continuing his travels to Lithuanian Rus'. Here he went to become metropolitan of Kiev, although he had his official residence in Novgorodok (now Novogrudok) and in the Lithuanian capital of Vilnius. A third representative of the literary facet of the Second South Slavic Influence in Russia, and the most prolific one, was a Serb—Paxomij Logofet (Pahomije Srbin, or Logotet; see below). And a fourth outstanding writer of those times and regions, Konstantin of Kostenec (Kostenečki, also called the Philosopher), never came to Russia; instead, he decided to transfer from Bulgaria to Serbia—a move of less than two hundred miles but one which, contrary to Kiprian's and Camblak's moves to Russia, was probably indeed prompted by political and safety considerations. For that reason he was not obliged to modify essentially his written language (aside from changing his general tone and style) when addressing a new, different group of readers. Thus, it is nearly impossible always to draw a sharp line between what is to be regarded as (Middle) Bulgarian and what as (Old) Serbian Church Slavic textual material.[19]

[19] See Birnbaum, "Serbian Models" (see n. 1), esp. 5-6. This consideration applies, in par-

The consistently employed stylistic technique of "word-braiding" (or "word-weaving," *pletenie sloves*) was in all likelihood not initially brought to medieval Russia from Bulgaria in the course of the Second South Slavic Influence; yet until quite recently, the origin of what was then unequivocally considered an embellishing device has often been claimed to be Bulgarian. Actually, word-braiding was systematically developed and applied to perfection during the late fourteenth century, notably in the hagiographic writings of Epifanij Premudryj, a native Russian, one of whose two extant major works has come down to us only in the reworked version of Paxomij Logofet. The ultimate source of this ornate style—the Greek term for the adorning verbiage was πλοκή—lay outside the Slavic sphere, in the heartland of Byzantium.[20] From there it seems to have spread, incidentally, not only to the Slavic provinces of the "commonwealth" (notably and earliest to Russia and Serbia) but also, in altered form and function, across the Mediterranean, to the shores of southern France, the Provence and its troubadour poets. On East Slavic soil we can find the first traces of such Byzantine stylistic influence as early as the eleventh and twelfth centuries, for example, in the famed *Slovo o zakoně i blagodati* by Metropolitan Ilarion (mid-eleventh century), in the panegyrical homilies and rhetorical prayers authored by—or attributed to—Bishop Kirill of Turov (mid-twelfth century), or even in some of the tales contained in the *Kievo-Pečerskij Paterik* (whose chronology, as far as the preserved form of this text is concerned, is more complex and at any rate covers a longer period of time).[21] As will be briefly discussed in what follows, the first more systematic and deliberate use of the device of word-braiding in Russian Church Slavic literature owes more to Serbian than to Bulgarian models.

In summary, the Bulgarian component of the Second South Slavic Influence on the writing of Old Rus', earlier considered all but exclusive, turns out on closer examination to be significant but not without competition or, for that matter, always easily isolated or identified. Even more important, it was not primarily contingent upon Patriarch Evtimij and his (the Trnovo) school's role in revising the church books of Bulgaria. Rather, the re-Bulgarization of Russian Church Slavic around the year 1400 must be seen

---

ticular, also to several texts from the Bulgarian-Serbian border town and principality of Bdin/ Vidin: see further Birnbaum, *Byzantine Studies/Études byzantines* 2 (1975): 65-66. On Grigorij Camblak, Paxomij Logofet, and Konstantin Kostenečki, see also D. Bogdanovič, *Istorija*, 204-208, 246-248, 214-218, with additional references.

[20] See Birnbaum, "Serbian Models" (see n. 1), 7-8, with further references; for details, see also the discussion below.

[21] See A. V. Issatschenko, *Geschichte* (see n. 15), 110-111, 224-226; see also below.

in the light of Metropolitan Kiprian's literary and linguistic ambitions and activities directed at reforming the orthography—and, to a lesser extent, the morphology and lexicon—of existing liturgical texts, bringing their language closer to classical Old Bulgarian (Old Church Slavic) or, at least, Middle Bulgarian, by then properly purified and archaized.

Outside the sphere of language and literature, it was Byzantium proper and Serbia that issued the new signals and impulses that reached Old Rus' in the later Middle Ages. They also provided some of the highly skilled manpower in the visual arts. Feofan Grek (or Theophanes the Greek), a prolific Byzantine painter with a refined style of his own, is known by name; many other barely identifiable or altogether anonymous Greek and Serbian icon and fresco painters can be assumed to have made substantial contributions, direct and indirect, to the adornment of a great many churches of late medieval Russia, not the least in the Russian North and particularly in and around Novgorod. In this context it may be noted that what has been said previously regarding the greater forcefulness of the Bulgarian—and, generally, the Byzantine and South Slavic—cultural impact on southern Russia as compared to the impact on the Russian North, applies, by and large, to the earlier medieval times only, that is, to the pre-Mongol period of Kievan Rus'. In the following period (or rather, periods), most of Old Rus' was first under Mongol rule, while western Russia, or what has been less appropriately called Southwestern Rus' (*Jugozapadnaja Rus'*), soon came under Lithuanian—and, subsequently, Polish-Lithuanian—administration, with its opening to the West. In particular, Novgorod and its territories (*Novgorodskaja zemlja*) were exposed to Byzantine–South Slavic cultural influence and after the rise of Muscovy in the fourteenth to fifteenth century, also the Russian lands which were under Moscow's sway.

It was Byzantium and Bulgaria that furnished the early setting for the quietist-mystical movement known as Hesychasm. After a generation or two, the movement's character, initially purely theological and religious-practical in impact, took on great political significance as well, considering that its adherents came to occupy a number of patriarchal and metropolitan sees. Gregorios Sinaites, sometimes referred to as the chief missionary of Hesychasm, had several Bulgarian followers, among them Teodosij of Trnovo, Evtimij's predecessor as patriarch of Bulgaria, and Romil Vidinski. After Gregorios' death in 1346, the monks of Paroria (which he had turned into a major spiritual center of the new movement) dispersed, and Teodosij moved to the Kilifarevo Monastery outside Trnovo. Once he had introduced the Hesychast doctrine and practice in the Bulgarian monastic community, Teodosij and his circle engaged in literary and proselytizing activities, translating many Greek texts into Middle Bulgarian. Unlike Byzantium, Bulgaria accepted and adapted to Hesychast teaching easily and thoroughly. Soon a new, Hesychast-inspired literature evolved; it not only treated Hesychast themes and individuals but also included polemical works, again mostly translated from Greek, which were directed against various heresies, Bogomilism foremost among them. The Bogomil movement, which had originated in Bulgaria and showed some similarities with early Hesychasm, was quite widespread in the Balkans at the time. It was this sort of Hesychast literature, in part in the guise of lives of saints, that culminated in Bulgaria with the writings of Patriarch Evtimij; the Bulgarian prelate's unmistakable Hesychast stamp, in style and imagery, can be said to constitute his most important contribution to the refinement of Church Slavic literature.[22]

In this developed stage, Hesychasm came to play a significant part in Russia also, from the late fourteenth through the fifteenth centuries, leaving its distinct mark in both art and literature. Bulgaria's impact can consequently be felt in these areas of religious expression as well. This is attested to by the figurative representation of the "mysticism of light" (bringing to mind the divine luminosity allegedly perceived at Mount Tabor); by the related motif of the Transfiguration, frequent in icon and mural painting of the time; and, above all, by the Hesychast facet in the biography of Saint Sergij of Radonež, as eloquently told in his *vita* by Epifanij Premudryj (reworked by Paxomij Logofet). The Russian saintly hermit was the founder of the monastery subsequently known as the Trinity-Sergius Lavra at Zagorsk, Muscovite Russia's chief Hesychast stronghold. The writings of Kiprian and Camblak, along with other, comparable literary manifestations, are further proof of the prominence that Hesychasm, imported from Bulgaria, enjoyed among the Eastern Slavs in the period of the "waning of the Middle Ages."

Altogether, Bulgaria's effect on the culture of Old Rus' was thus very significant indeed. It was strongest at the beginning of recorded Russian history and, again, in the post-Mongol period, or rather, in the period when the Mongols were no longer the predominant political and military force but merely represented a continued—and occasionally very real—threat to

---

[22] See White, "Hesychasm and Bulgarian Literature" (see n. 15), esp. 250-252. On the political facet of Hesychasm, see also G. M. Proxorov, "Isixazm i obščestvennaja mysl' v Vostočnoj Evrope," *TODRL* 23 (1968): 86-108; and J. Meyendorff, "Victory of the Hesychasts in Byzantium: Ideological and Political Consequences," in *Byzantium and the Rise of Russia* (see n. 15), 96-118.

Russian life. In the sphere of language, literature, and religious thought, primarily, Bulgaria was the chief link and mediator between Byzantium and Old Rus', the Kievan as well as the early Muscovite state. It was this opening to Byzantine civilization that made it possible for the East Slavic spiritual and intellectual community to develop its own variety of culture in close contact and cooperation with Byzantium. As a result, Old Russian culture could, in effect, turn into a full-blown extension of Byzantine civilization while preserving and adding to it its own genuine flavor.

The view just sketched would not be complete, or even properly balanced, however, without a few further comments about the specific Serbian subcomponent of medieval Russian culture. That subcomponent forms an integral part of the overall variety of medieval civilization as it evolved and flourished in Old Rus', a part in essence distinct from the Bulgarian impact.

One such Serbian influence pertains to the previously mentioned device of word-braiding (*pletenie sloves*). Several years ago, I pointed out that "the much-discussed stylistic device of so-called word-weaving ..., extremely popular in Russia during the Second South Slavic Influence ... and generally believed to have originated, on Slavic soil, in Bulgaria—specifically, in the Hesychast Trnovo School of Patriarch Evtimij—actually can be found in full bloom already some hundred years earlier in Serbia where, of course, it had developed by imitation of Byzantine examples. In this connection one should not underestimate the influence in Russia of the Serbian component of the Athonite monastic community (that is, primarily of the Hilandar Monastery) in addition to the influence coming from Serbia directly."[23] The credit for the full realization and documentation of the Serbian, rather than Bulgarian, contribution to developing and refining the device of *pletenie sloves* in the Church Slavic literature of Orthodox Slavdom belongs to the recently deceased Yugoslav scholar Malik Mulić. In a monograph summing up his previous relevant research, Mulić arrived at some significant conclusions concerning the complex set of problems pertaining to the evolution and perfection of this stylistic technique in Church Slavic writing. These conclusions can be summarized as follows:

Pletenie sloves, as a style form of medieval Slavic hagiographic (and panegyrical-liturgical) writing, and in particular in the Russian and Serbian literatures of the fourteenth and fifteenth centuries, did not constitute an

[23] H. Birnbaum, *On Medieval and Renaissance Slavic Writing* (The Hague–Paris, 1974), 317-318. The quote is from an essay, "Byzantine Tradition Transformed: The Old Serbian *Vita*," originally published in the 1969 UCLA conference volume *Aspects of the Balkans: Continuity and Change*, ed. H. Birnbaum and S. Vryonis, Jr. (The Hague–Paris, 1972), 243-284.

innovation. It was merely a Slavic adaptation of certain stylistic principles known from ancient Greek artistic (rhetorical) prose and from Old Testament Hebrew literature—the latter in its Greek translation of the Septuagint. These principles had been integrated into a new whole and found their expression in Byzantine ecclesiastic prose and poetry—homiletic, panegyrical, hagiographic, and hymnographic. *Pletenie sloves* as a stylistic mannerism in no way reflected or expressed a Hesychast, mystical-ascetic world view; on the contrary, some of the representatives of Hesychast ideology (e.g., Symeon the New Theologian) were rightly criticized by their contemporaries for their stylistic simplicity. Prominent Byzantine men of letters of the fourteenth century, Gregory Palamas among them, were more concerned with following the example of the best writers of Greek Antiquity than with continuing the tradition of the Hellenistic (so-called Asianic) rhetorical style with its emphasis on a florid manner of expression which ultimately goes back to the Σχήματα Γοργίεια (after the Greek rhetorician and sophist Gorgias and subsequently applied by the great theoreticians of rhetoric, Lysias, Demosthenes, and, especially, Isocrates and Aristotle). By the same token, this ornate style of classical Antiquity had, in later centuries, a major impact on the ranking Byzantine Christian writers, John Chrysostom, Gregory of Nazianzus (the Theologian), and Basil the Great.

As the Slavs took over the style of the Byzantine writers, they did so—as is usual when cultural models are emulated with some delay—without keeping abreast of the cultural evolution in Byzantium; their style was therefore patterned on the works of the early Byzantine authors. The reasons for this were partly political in nature and can be found within Slavic history itself. The collapse of the First Bulgarian Empire (in the late tenth and early eleventh centuries) brought to an end the "golden age" of Old Church Slavic literature. With the disintegration of the Kievan state (completed in the first half of the thirteenth century, with the advent of the Mongols), there was a cultural stagnation among the Eastern Slavs. These historical events were as significant for the Slavs as the decline of the Roman Empire and the predominance of the Christian-"barbarian" aesthetic value system of the Early Middle Ages were for the tradition of ancient classical civilization. As in the restored but politically weakened Byzantine Empire (after the Fourth Crusade and its consequences in the thirteenth century), where the representatives of a new cultural spirit and determination sought their inspiration in the models of classical Antiquity, the *literati* in the new Nemanjid state of Serbia and in the Second Bulgarian Empire turned to their own Slavic past. They adopted and adapted literary models from Kievan Rus' where Metropolitan Ilarion, Bishop Kirill of

Turov, and others once had carried on the tradition of the Ohrid and Pre-slav Schools and had further developed the legacy of Cyril-Constantine, Methodius, and Kliment of Ohrid. By taking on the literary tradition of Kievan Rus', the emerging and increasingly powerful Muscovite state of the fourteenth and fifteenth centuries not only continued the organic develop-ment of the literature of the Russian people (in the broad sense of encom-passing all of the Eastern Slavs) but also contributed politically to legit-imize the title of the Moscow sovereigns as rulers over "all of Rus'" (*vseja Rusi*).

The Psalms, read daily, provided the main literary model for the Slavic writers, the majority of whom were clerics (predominantly, monks). From the Psalter, as well as from the books of the New Testament, these authors and scribes borrowed not only individual words but also whole phrases and expressions, inserting them freely in their works. Lacking the kind of cul-tural tradition in literature that their Byzantine masters possessed, the Slavic writers were almost exclusively dependent on the Christian tradition in its Byzantine version. The Christian world view singled out certain time-honored models as both valuable and deserving of attention; hence the assessment of the ancient writers, especially those whom the Church had acknowledged among its chosen "fathers."

Hesychasm as a movement in the Orthodox monastic community existed long before the struggle between Barlaamites and Palamites, or before the arrival of Gregorios Sinaites to the Holy Mountain and to Paroria. Hesy-chast notions are, consequently, reflected also in the works of some Slavic writers of the thirteenth century, even though these notions were not yet a fully developed and consistent ideology as enunciated by Gregorios Sinaites and, in particular, by Gregory Palamas. Yet, even without such a clearly stated and elaborated theory, one can already find in the works of these Slavic writers all the basic principles of Hesychasm as the Slavic monks had come to know it before the activities of Sinaites and Palamas. It should be pointed out in this context that Hesychasm found just as much of an echo in, say, the *Kievo-Pečerskij Paterik* or in the works of the Serbian writers Domentijan, Teodosije, and Archbishop Danilo II as it did in the writings of Evtimij. However, in the Serbian writings, one finds all the characteris-tics of hagiographic literature heretofore considered innovations introduced into the Slavic *vitae* only by Evtimij.

The Serbian writers had learned *pletenie sloves* as much from the *literati* of Kievan Rus' (Ilarion, Kirill Turovskij) as from Byzantine writers. Indeed, they apparently took over the form of their literary expression both faster and to a fuller extent from their Old Russian models since here they had before them ready-made Slavic examples and patterns. Domentijan, by imitating Ilarion's style—and, it should be added, on at least one occasion, simply lifting a whole passage from Ilarion's text—also pointed out the direction that Teodosije, Danilo II, and subsequent Serbian writers would follow.

Just as Byzantium during the Palaeologan Renaissance showed a renewed interest in classical Greek culture, so did Russia, after the victory at Kulikovo in 1380 and the establishment of a new political center in Moscow, turn to the literary tradition of the Kievan period. What Antiquity had been for Byzantium, the all-but-legendary epoch of Vladimir Svjatoslavič, Jaroslav the Wise, and Vladimir Monomax meant to fourteenth- and fifteenth-century Russia. By transferring to the Muscovite territory and period the cultural traditions of Kievan Rus', the grand princes of Moscow restored the continuity of Russian statehood at the cultural level as well. Given that the Serbian writers, too, had learned from Ilarion and Kirill Turovskij and that there can be ascertained stylistic agreements between the works of the Serbian bookmen and the Russian *žitija* and *poxvaľnye slova* of Russian saints and princes—since both were influenced by Ilarion's style—why, then, could not also Epifanij Premudryj have adopted one or the other feature from the Serbian writers while he was staying and working on Mount Athos? And, moreover, why would he not have taken a look at the works of his own fellow countrymen, and learned from them, at the same time as Evtimij of Trnovo visited Constantinople and the Holy Mountain?

According to Mulić, there are two reasons for the too-great importance attributed to Evtimij and his school and for the insufficient attention given the writers of medieval Serbia for their part in developing the Slavic *pletenie sloves*. Vuk Karadžić's struggle for the vernacular language in nineteenth-century literature rendered any preoccupation with Old Slavic literature secondary among Serbian scholars, notwithstanding the fact that some important research was done at the same time, notably by Đ. Daničić. Yet, the lack of a sufficient number of specialists for this kind of work, as well as financial constraints, made any serious investigation of the old manuscripts impossible. Also, it must be remembered that Slavic philology in those days was only in its infancy and that only Russian (but not Serbian) scholars could push for and achieve some results in the collecting of and inquiry into ancient works of Slavic writing. It was, in fact, Russian philologists who first raised the question of the Second South Slavic Influence in Russian culture and who have written the fundamental studies about that phenomenon. However, the Russian philologists—spontaneously or, frequently, under the influence of the kind of thinking imposed by the

Slavophiles in nineteenth-century Russia (typified by I. S. Aksakov)—came to express, if only in a roundabout way, the official point of view of Russian foreign policy which sought to achieve for Orthodox Russia a dominant position in the Balkans and especially on the shores of the Black Sea. Russia viewed with displeasure any closer ties between Serbia and Austria; and considering the fact that Serbia did not have access to the Black Sea, Russian foreign policy was less concerned with Serbia than it was with Bulgaria. The latter's remaining in the Russian sphere of influence and guarding it, as it were, against Serbia's bad example—an issue also addressed by Aksakov—were, by the same token, very much Russia's concern.

Though not philological in nature, such were the reasons that determined A. I. Sobolevskij's position on this matter, so Mulić claims. Sobolevskij's views are also adhered to today by some Russian scholars in their treatment of the Serbian medieval writers and the mutual relations obtaining among Russian, Serbian, and Bulgarian literature. Their approach was adopted, obviously, by some Bulgarian scholars as well (e.g., I. Snegarov). On the basis of the data and examples adduced in his monograph, however, the Yugoslav Slavist arrives at the conclusion that the influences and ties between the medieval Slavic literatures were always two-directional; and the share of Serbian literature in this cultural interchange was surely not smaller, but rather greater, than that which is usually attributed to Bulgarian literature in connection with the elaboration of the stylistic device—or simply, style—of *pletenie sloves*. As a result, the claim that throughout the Middle Ages, the cultural influences between Serbs and Bulgarians always went only from east to west—or, for that matter, I would add, those between Southern and Eastern Slavs only from south to north—cannot be substantiated. Further, all indications suggest that the beginning of the style of *pletenie sloves* should be dated to a period before the establishment of the Trnovo School and should be geographically associated with the Russian (or, to be precise, East Slavic) and Serbian literary centers.[24]

[24] M. Mulić, *Srpski izvori "pletenija sloves"* (Sarajevo, 1975) (*Djela*, bk. 4. Odjelenje za književnost i umjetnost, bk. 2), esp. 95-98 ("Zaključci"). Of previous work by the same scholar, see in particular: "Srpsko 'pletenije sloves' do 14. stoljeća," "Pletenije sloves i hesi-hazam," and "Prilog pitanju ruskoga utjecaja na južnoslavenske književnosti u srednem vijeku," *Radovi Zavoda za slavensku filologiju* 5 (1963): 117-129; 7 (1965): 141-156; and 12 (1971): 21-32; further, id., "Serbskie agiografy XII–XIV vv. i osobennosti ix stilja," *TODRL* 23 (1968): 127-142. Note also that Mošin, "O periodizacii" (see n. 4), 106, points out that the literary style of word-braiding probably significantly antedates the literary activities of Patriarch Evtimij. In this context it is further worth mentioning that J. Børtnes, *Det gammelrus-siske helgenvita. Dikterisk egenart og historisk betydning* [The Old Russian life of saints. Poetic peculiarity and historical significance] (Oslo, 1975), 226, suggests that the fact that the *pletenie*

As for the impact of the Old Serbian *vita*, the hagiographic as well as the secular-biographic, on the Russian Church Slavic genre of the *žitie*, its significance is now beyond any doubt. The only related question that remains controversial is whether the Old Russian *vita* had in fact developed in some instances (namely, in some specimens of the subtype of the *knjažeskoe žitie*) into an essentially autonomous genre of secular biography, following the Serbian example, as has been claimed by some scholars (e.g., A. Stender-Petersen, D. Tschižewskij) for, say, the *Life of Prince Aleksandr Nevskij* or the *Life and Demise of Grand Prince Dmitrij Ivanovič*. Since I have stated my own position on this matter in some detail elsewhere—maintaining, with N. W. Ingham, that on East Slavic soil life-writing, when treating purely secular rulers (never mind any saintly qualities subsequently ascribed to them or even their being given the status of saints), was not quite able to free itself from the stylistic devices and compositional paraphernalia of hagiography—there is no need here to elaborate further on the subject.[25]

Next, in considering the Serbian impact on Russian Church Slavic writing, more attention should be paid to late medieval Russia's most prolific writer and its first professional, who is said to have supported himself exclusively by his pen. The reference is to Paxomij Logofet who, as his other surname indicates, was a Serb by origin. Active in Novgorod, Moscow, the Trinity-Sergius Lavra near Moscow, and the Kirillo-Belozerskij Monastery in the Russian North from roughly 1430 to the 1460s (if not longer), Paxomij had come to Russia from the Holy Mountain, probably from the then Serbian monastery of Saint Paul. He produced a quantitatively most impressive

---

sloves style, when it makes its appearance in Old Russian literature in the writings of Epifanij Premudryj, at once seems to have reached its fully developed stage may simply be due to the destruction of virtually all late-fourteenth-century Muscovite manuscripts following the sacking of Moscow by the Mongols in 1382 (i.e, only two years after the Russian victory at Kulikovo!). For some additional points of view on *pletenie sloves* and its place and origin in Russian Church Slavic writing, with a brief account of D. S. Lixačev's somewhat modified understanding of this phenomenon, see Birnbaum, "Serbian Models" (see n. 1), 7-8, 12, nn. 16-18, with bibliographic references. On some of the potentials and limitations in rendering certain characteristics of the word-braiding style in the course of translating Byzantine Greek to Slavic, exemplified by the use of the so-called *figura etymologica* in the Church Slavic (Middle Bulgarian) version of the *Life of Patriarch Kallistos* by Gregorios Sinaites, see H. Keipert, "Möglichkeiten und Grenzen der Übersetzung ins Slavische. Die Wiederholungsfiguren in der Kallistos-Vita des Gregorios Sinaites," *Slavistische Studien zum VIII. Internationalen Slavistenkongress in Zagreb 1978,* ed. J. Holthusen et al. (Cologne–Vienna, 1978), 205-217.

[25] See my "Byzantine Tradition Transformed" (see n. 23); condensed version: "Trends and traditions in Medieval Serbian Biography," in *Slavic Poetics* (festschrift for K. Taranovsky), ed. R. Jakobson et al. (The Hague, 1973), 41-48. See, moreover, "Serbian Models" (see n. 1), 8-9, 12-13, nn. 18-20.

body of writing—hagiographic, hymnographic, and panegyrical works—which, however, has generally not been considered particularly creative or innovative. Yet it must be recognized that he indeed had mastered all the technical skills that the craft of writing required at the time. In rewriting and refashioning the great Russian hagiographer Epifanij's famed *Life of Sergij of Radonež*, which was by then about half a century old and which we know only in this reworked version, he brought this piece up to the stylistic standards of the day—like his model, making ample use of word-braiding, of course. Among the other *vitae* that Paxomij rewrote was the *Life of Varlaam Xutynskij* of Novgorod. Of the at least ten hagiographic works he produced, no fewer than two (but perhaps more)—the *Life of the Novgorod Archbishop Evfimij* (1458) and the *Life of Kirill Belozerskij* (1462)—seem to be quite original, without any known sources or proto-graphs. Paxomij further wrote as many as eighteen canons, four *poxval'nye slova*, and six tales. There can be little doubt that the Serbian immigrant's "modernizing" literary activities decisively influenced the quality and course of subsequent Russian Church Slavic hagiography and panegyrical-liturgical writing. By adapting and rendering topical individual lives of saints which either had lost their appeal or had never become popular, he succeeded in revitalizing this whole major segment of Church Slavic litera-ture and its many subgenres, thus providing new models for other, future professional writers in the hagiographic and panegyrical vein. In particular, the Muscovite ecclesiastic and monastic literary community of the follow-ing, sixteenth century is much indebted to him. Generally, the Russian his-torian V. O. Ključevskij's appraisal of Paxomij, written in 1871, still retains its validity in terms of a balanced, fair judgment, notwithstanding that much otherwise seems today obsolete and arguable in Ključevskij's assess-ment of hagiographic writing and Russian Church Slavic literature as a whole. This is what the Russian historian had to say, in summary, about Paxomij: "He never manifested any significant literary talent; his thought was less flexible and inventive than Epifanij's; but he firmly established the permanent uniform methods for writing the life of a saint and for his glori-fication in church, and he provided Russian hagiography with many pat-terns of that steady, somewhat cold and monotonous style which was easy for writers endowed with only a limited amount of erudition to emulate."[26]

Some of the then new literary techniques, used or introduced by Paxomij with great virtuosity, certainly deserve mention. For example, whereas

---

[26] V. O. Ključevskij, *Drevnerusskie žitija svjatyx kak istoričeskij istočnik* (Moscow, 1871), 166. On Ključevskij's place in early research on Old Russian hagiography, see J. Børtnes, *Det gammelrussiske helgenvita* (see n. 24), 17-19.

anonymity and humility had been characteristic for most writers of previous periods—the pronounced egocentricity of Daniil Zatočnik being rather an exception—and the so-called humility topos had even become part and parcel of medieval (including earlier Russian Church Slavic) literature, the new style favored individualization and self-assertiveness, in Paxomij's case expressed in references to his own erudition and to his Serbian and Athonite background. He further excelled in emotionally motivated hyperbole and in other stylistic figures and devices implying rhetorical exaggeration, such as adorning epithets, similes, metaphors, tautologies, rhetorical questions, and exclamations. Paxomij's literary taste also found expression in his casual way of dealing with historical fact and theological "truth." For he saw his task primarily as producing readable, well-structured, if possible even entertaining, genuine fiction, not necessarily always doing justice to strict biographic accuracy or coherent, persuasive reasoning. This is the more remarkable since his works were, above all, intended for reading in monastic circles and during church service. Paxomij's abundant recourse to *pletenie sloves* may well strike us today as particularly turgid, not to say stilted, making his writing anything but enjoyable reading. Yet it should be remembered that the aesthetic effect of that mannerism was perceived quite differently by Paxomij's contemporaries, who did not necessarily share the modern reader's preference for naturalness. It was already noted that word-braiding was not at first closely associated with Hesychast doctrine and the literary practices of the Bulgarian Trnovo School, as was claimed by earlier researchers, particularly D. S. Lixačev; however, the Soviet scholar has subsequently somewhat qualified his views.[27] It must nonetheless be emphasized that Paxomij, by bringing to Russia the hagiographical style of his Serbian masters, also conveyed some of the new, Hesychast poetic mysticism to his Novgorodian and Muscovite readership. In doing so, he familiarized his audience with some of the universal or ecumenical Byzantinism concerned with sublime and broadly general topics and experiences. Thus he expanded the narrow horizons of his

---

[27] Lixačev had earlier considered Bulgaria and, especially, the alleged reforms of Patriarch Evtimij the primary source of *pletenie sloves* in Old Rus'. However, in his more recent work he acknowledges, with some qualification, the part played by Serbian models in this connection. Yet, the Soviet scholar still insists that the highly rhetorical, embellished style—*vitijstvennyj stil'*—which appeared in Russian Church Slavic literature by the fourteenth century was "closely connected with those views on language which also lay at the foundation of the Euthymian reforms." This, he claims, "is in no way contradicted by the fact that the other elements of *pletenie sloves* made their appearance long before the Euthymian reforms, and certain reform tenets [even] long before *pletenie sloves*." See D. S. Lixačev, *Razvitie* (see n. 5), 83, 88. Such an artificial chronological separation of one facet of the word-braiding style from its other consituent elements does not seem too convincing.

Russian readers, and his conception of the hagiographic *vita*—patterned on Serbian and Athonite models—became the prevailing one all over the land between the Dnieper and the far Russian North.

In addition to strictly religious writing, Paxomij also authored some secular tales—with a strong Christian Orthodox note, to be sure, often in hagiographic guise. Some of them echo Old Serbian narrative material. This applies, for example, to the medieval Serbian *Tale about the Assassination of Batu in Hungary*, written, in all likelihood, by a Serbian from the Danube region in the middle of the fifteenth century. This tale (in Serbian, *povest*) is known only from Paxomij's reworked *Story about the Martyrdom of Prince Mixail* and from later copies of that version of the same story (*skazanie*). While the historical kernel of the tale refers to the death of the Tatar khan, Batu (Batyj), in a battle with the Hungarians in 1241, Paxomij has altered the historical event by adding much legendary detail and inserting motifs otherwise found in chivalrous literature and reminiscent of the military tale. Yet, even in Paxomij's variation of the theme, this is a tale with a specific message, favoring Orthodoxy in general and Saint Sava, the Serbian archbishop, in particular. The latter's legendary mission to Hungary and the Hungarian king's alleged turning to Orthodox Christianity is told in Paxomij's *Story* (and, presumably, in its Old Serbian prototype) on the basis of Teodosije's *Life of Saint Sava*.[28]

All in all, Paxomij's dazzling style and entertaining narrative art, although not particularly original or truly creative, certainly left a mark on Russian Church Slavic writing. And, it should be added, the Serbian facet of Paxomij's impact is readily discernible, both in form and content.

As mentioned previously, Serbian influence in medieval Russian culture was not limited to literature alone. It was just as strong in the visual arts, especially in mural painting, where it was only matched, and perhaps even outshone, by the Greek impact coming directly from Byzantium, as represented, above all, by the magnificent art of Feofan Grek. While Novgorod documents, both those written on parchment and, especially, those incised on birch bark, occasionally identify an artist as being active in or near the Volxov city by the epithet "Greek" (*grek, grečin,* etc.), the identification as Serb is exceptional. Yet, there is reason to believe that Serbian fresco painters, beginning in the thirteenth century, were occasionally invited and commissioned to decorate the interiors of newly built Russian stone churches, particularly in Novgorod and its territories, which had been left

---

[28] See Bogdanović, *Istorija* (see n. 18), 248.

unscathed by any Mongol invasion and devastation and were the first to recover from the material hardships that had befallen all of Rus' with the coming of the Tatars.

The splendid frescoes of the Church of the Savior of the Transfiguration at Kovalevo just outside Novgorod are an example. These marvelous samples of Orthodox art had been destroyed in the Second World War, but their almost miraculous restoration is now nearing completion, thanks to the admirable efforts of a team of dedicated workers headed by A. P. Grekov. True, Grekov, himself an expert in art history, prefers not to share the view of most specialists—among them D. S. Lixačev and the late V. N. Lazarev, the unchallenged authority on Old Novgorodian art—who believe the Kovalevo frescoes were painted by Serbian masters or, at any rate, were decisively influenced by Serbian mural painting, probably of the South Serbian (or, possibly, the Macedonian) vein. It is, of course, quite conceivable that some wealthy patrons of the arts would have brought foreign, notably Byzantine or Serbian, masters to the North Russian boyar and merchant republic to add further to its glory and luster.[29]

From a purely artistic point of view, even more impressive were once the breathtaking murals of the Church of the Assumption (or Dormition) at Volotovo Pole near Novgorod, another victim of World War II. These lost paintings, erroneously attributed by earlier scholars to Feofan Grek, have been compared to Giotto's frescoes in the Arena Chapel in Padua, as regards both their bold composition and their emotional, expressive style. More to the point, though, the frescoes bore a striking resemblance to some of the murals of the monastery church at Sopoćani in Serbia, whose elements, previously interpreted as Italian, have more recently been viewed as reflections of Macedonian models of the eleventh and twelfth centuries. In any event, the Serbian influence on the Volotovo frescoes is now generally considered all but certain. In this context it is perhaps less important whether the North Russian frescoes were actually executed by an invited Serbian painter (or even several Serbian masters) or whether this new Serbian manner of painting—reflecting, in essence, an innovative trend within the framework of Byzantine and Byzantinesque art, comparable to Giotto's "new style"—was merely emulated on Russian soil by local artists.[30] Before

---

[29] On the Kovalevo frescoes and their restoration, see my essay, "Ancient Russian Art—Its Destruction and Restoration," in H. Birnbaum, *Essays in Early Slavic Civilization / Studien zur Frühkultur der Slaven* (Munich, 1981), 297-303, esp. 300-302.

[30] On the Volotovo frescoes, see especially M. V. Alpatov et al., *Freski cerkvi Uspenija na Volotovom pole / Frescoes of the Church of the Assumption at Volotovo Polye* (Moscow, 1977). On the Sopoćani murals (and their models), see, e.g., S. Radojčić, *Staro srpsko slikarstvo* (Belgrade, 1966), 55-70, esp. 70; further, V. J. Durić, *Vizantijske freske u Jugoslaviji* (Belgrade,

leaving this point, it should be noted that the two examples just cited are, obviously, among the most conspicuous ones illustrating Serbian influence in Old Russian art, but they are by no means isolated instances.

To conclude the discussion of the Serbian component of medieval Russian culture, I believe it reasonable to contend that, while the Serbian impact on Old Rus' undoubtedly came later than the Bulgarian influence— not before the thirteenth century (after the establishment of the Nemanjid state)—it was, in that shorter time span, of even broader scope than the Bulgarian impact, since it affected not only the language and literature of Old Rus' but also its remarkable religious art. In the period spanning the decline and fall of the Byzantine state and its immediate aftermath, Serbia became an even more multifaceted mediator and conveyer of Byzantine (and Byzantinesque) culture to medieval Russia, as compared with Bulgaria.

Finally, it may be proper to mention in closing that, in addition to the South Slavic component of medieval Russian culture which was closely associated with the common faith and liturgical practice of the Eastern Slavs, the Bulgarians, and the Serbians, there was yet another South Slavic element present on East Slavic soil. It appeared sporadically, toward the end of the Middle Ages and, again, in that transitional phase of Russian cultural history that usually still falls under the label "Old Russian" but is at times also singled out as "Middle Russian." And, just as the late medieval Bulgarian and Serbian literary influence was primarily embodied in a few personalities—Kiprian, Camblak, Paxomij—so was this additional South Slavic element represented by but a couple of men of letters.

First, I am referring here to the significant translating activities of the Croatian Dominican monk Benjamin, at what may be termed the learned court of the Novgorodian archbishop Gennadij in the last decade of the fifteenth century. As is well known, Archbishop Gennadij and his Novgorod circle, although formally remaining in the fold of the Orthodox Church—he had previously been archimandrite of the Moscow Čudov Monastery—showed considerable pro-Catholic leanings, as manifested in, among other things, his unqualified admiration for the working of the Spanish Inquisition, whose methods he tried to apply to members of the heretic sect of the Judaizers. A more positive achievement—inspired at least partly by the Catholic example but prompted also to some extent by

1974), esp. 39-41 (with pls. 26-29), 63, 211 (also available in translations into West European languages). For more discussion and references, see also J. Børtnes, *Det gammelrussiske helgenvita* (see n. 24), 171-181.

the archbishop's clash and learned competition with the humanistically inclined *židovstvujuščie*—was the completion in 1499 of the so-called Gennadij Bible, the first Russian Church Slavic Bible translation, largely based on Saint Jerome's Latin text of the Vulgate. It was in this translation project, believed to have been a collective endeavor, that the Croatian Benjamin was the leading, most instrumental coworker.

Second, another Croatian who came to exert some influence on Russian cultural life was Juraj Križanić, the seventeenth-century precursor of the Pan-Slavic idea. He spent about twenty years (1647 and 1658-77) in the Russia of Aleksej Mixajlovič, mostly under adverse conditions, exiled to Siberia. This is not the place to detail his impressive linguistic, literary, and ideological accomplishments, all aimed at bringing the Slavic peoples closer together. Suffice it to say merely that his activities occurred during a period that, although not medieval in the sense adopted in European historiography, is rightly considered transitional between medieval and modern, or rather "old" and "new," in the course of Russian history and civilization.

Given the peripheral role and ephemeral impact of Benjamin and Križanić, however, and considering further that not enough is yet known, or at any rate sufficiently clarified, about how some Croatian-Glagolitic manuscripts (in some instances, copies of earlier Czech Church Slavic texts) found their way to Russia, perhaps still in medieval times, it would certainly not be appropriate to suggest that any lasting and significant Croatian component is ascertainable in late medieval or even postmedieval Russian culture. In any event, a Croatian element in early Russian civilization would in no way be comparable, qualitatively or quantitatively, to the Bulgarian and Serbian facets of the medieval culture of Old Rus', whose content and form the two Orthodox Balkan Slavic peoples contributed to in such a decisive manner.

THE MARTYRED PRINCE AND THE QUESTION OF SLAVIC CULTURAL CONTINUITY IN THE EARLY MIDDLE AGES

NORMAN W. INGHAM

In recent times, scholarship has given considerable attention to important but controversial questions of communality and divergence in Slavic culture of the medieval and early-modern eras. Riccardo Picchio introduced the terms *Slavia orthodoxa* and *Slavia romana* to designate the two cultural communities that developed in the later Middle Ages in the wake of the confessional division of the Slavs between the Orthodox and Roman Catholic Churches,[1] and Picchio's concept and terminology are gaining currency among scholars. Much has been accomplished in redefining the nature and history of the Orthodox Slavic cultural sphere, which in certain periods behaved as a true community, that is, one where ideas and means circulated rather freely and "influences" were mutual. Better recognized today also is the fact that *Slavia orthodoxa* formed part of a greater cultural realm, that of the Byzantine "commonwealth" (Dimitri Obolensky's term). D. S. Lixačev has gone so far as to say that the culture of Old Rus' was a "transplant" from Constantinople.

The split of the Slavs into two cultural areas, Orthodox and Catholic, was real enough in the later Middle Ages; however, in the earlier period (at least until the end of the eleventh century) the situation was somewhat different. Scholars have long been aware of evidence for greater cultural intercourse at that time among the East, West, and South Slavs which seems to have transcended the incipient division of allegiance between Constantinople and Rome. But the degree to which the West Slavs entered into a Slavic cultural community in the early Middle Ages is a complex question that still awaits detailed investigation of particular cultural phenomena. The present article draws upon my long-time research into the literature of the Slavic martyred princes in order to offer what I believe is an instructive case history of cultural continuity between Bohemia and Kievan Rus' in the

---

[1] R. Picchio, "A proposito della Slavia ortodossa e della communità linguistica slava ecclesiastica," *Ricerche slavistiche* 11 (1963): 105-127.

tenth and eleventh centuries. In keeping with the purposes of this volume, I will discuss questions of theory and method as well as the substance of the matter.

Some initial comments on terminology are necessary. The customary expressions *borrowing, influence,* and *imitation* are unsatisfactory when used to describe the diffusion of cultural phenomena in this period across what are now national borders. For one thing, they may seem to imply cultural dominance or superiority of the "donor." Soviet specialists have tended to argue, where possible, for the autochthonous nature of medieval East Slavic literature, partly as a corrective to their pre-Revolutionary colleagues' stress on imported models.[2] Even if it were not for the unfortunate overtones of the terms, they should be rejected because they are imprecise and subsume quite different kinds and circumstances of interaction. R. Picchio has pointed out that *influence* fails to distinguish "general, extra-textual paradigmatic invariants from the concrete, contextual components of the literary performance."[3] He also observed—and this is a crucial point—that patterns of transmission within a cultural community are different from those between communities. Inside one sphere, cultural phenomena are shared more fully and promptly, and genuine interaction and collaboration occur. His example is the dissemination of the Renaissance-Humanistic literary system within the community of *Slavia romana* as contrasted with its later spread, in a different way (by "annexation") in *Slavia orthodoxa.* These considerations should also be kept in mind when we deal with the Slavic early Middle Ages. We should avoid such expressions as *borrowing* and *imitation* because they do not distinguish the various kinds and degrees of sharing that are possible and they appear to prejudge the question of community.

Admittedly, the term *continuity* can have its ambiguities also; but I prefer it as a neutral word that applies well where we perceive the historical evolution of a tradition. Continuity, as I use it, implies something more systematic than the transmittal of individual ideas and motifs; it involves the passing-on of a set of norms. At the same time, continuity need not entail invariability. The tradition may change in time and under new circumstances; moreover, the new features it takes on are at least equally as interesting

[2] On the attitudes of Soviet scholars toward foreign influences in the early literature, see Ju. A. Limonov in *Sovetskaja istoriografija Kievskoj Rusi* (Leningrad, 1978), 236-250; also the foreword by V. P. Adrianova-Peretc in *Bibliografija sovetskix russkix rabot po literature XI-XVII vv. za 1917-1957 gg.,* comp. N. F. Droblenkova (Moscow–Leningrad, 1961), 9-13.
[3] R. Picchio, "Principles of Comparative Slavic-Romance Literary History," in *American Contributions to the Eighth International Congress of Slavists,* vol. 2: *Literature* (Columbus, Ohio, 1978), 631.

to us as the constants. There is just such continuity and development, I would maintain, in the tradition of the prince-martyr in Bohemia and Rus'. Religious literature is no doubt our major source for Slavic written culture in the early Middle Ages. The cults of martyred rulers, as reflected in hagiographical and historical writings, provide a particularly good opportunity to investigate both diffusion and independent evolution of concepts and literary kinds. Among the Slavs this type of saint appeared first in Bohemia (Saint Wenceslas, d. 929), then in Rus' (Boris and Gleb, d. 1015), and in Serbia (Saint John Vladimir, d. 1016). Writings in Slavonic and Latin about Wenceslas (and also his martyred grandmother, Princess Ludmila) existed as early as the tenth century;[4] the first texts on Boris and Gleb date to the eleventh;[5] and a legend of John Vladimir probably was circulating at least in oral form in the eleventh, although it is represented now only by a section of the twelfth-century Latin dynastic history that scholars call *Barski rodoslov* or *Letopis popa Dukljanina.*[6]

The general type of the martyred prince or king was by no means unique to the Slavs. Saints of this kind appeared under similar historical circumstances in various European countries, and the written sources sometimes show parallels to the Slavic texts in certain respects.[7] Nonetheless, the Slavic writings—or at least those of Bohemia and Kievan Rus'—have collective features that set them apart. It is my thesis that this resulted from historical continuity and not from coincidental development. Wenceslas's martyrdom was used as a model and precedent for Boris and Gleb. The concept was further developed in Rus' and took on new and original features there. The case of the Serbian Saint John Vladimir is more problematical, and I have cited it elsewhere as a probable example of parallel development[8]—one which by contrast testifies to the continuity of the Czech-Rusian* tradition.

[4] All the early Slavonic writings on Ludmila and Wenceslas are collected in *Sborník staroslovanských literárních památek o sv. Václavu a sv. Lidmile,* ed. Josef Vajs (Prague, 1929). The main Latin works can be found in *Fontes Rerum Bohemicarum,* vol. 1 (Prague, 1873); J. Pekař, *Die Wenzels- und Ludmila-Legenden und die Echtheit Christians* (Prague, 1906); and V. Chaloupecký, *Prameny X. století legendy Kristiánovy o svatém Václavu a svaté Ludmile* (*Svatováclavský sborník,* vol. 2, pt. 2) (Prague, 1939).

[5] Texts in D. I. Abramovič, ed., *Žitija svjatyx mučenikov Borisa i Gleba i služby im,* Pamjatniki drevnerusskoj literatury, no. 2 (Petrograd, 1916).

[6] F. Šišić, ed., *Letopis popa Dukljanina* (Belgrade, 1928), 331-342.

[7] N. W. Ingham, "The Sovereign as Martyr, East and West," *Slavic and East European Journal* 17 (1973); 1-17.

[8] N. W. Ingham, "The Martyrdom of St. John Vladimir of Dioclea," in *Papers in Slavic Philology* 3, ed. R. Picchio (Ann Arbor: University of Michigan, in press).

*EDITOR'S NOTE: We have adopted the consistent spelling "Rusian" where authors have chosen to use this adjective in reference to Old Rus'.

It cannot be said that the possible connections of the martyria have been neglected. That there could be a historical tie, however slight, has always been evident to scholars. The circumstances of the deaths of Wenceslas, Boris, and Gleb are in many ways similar; and there is ample proof for the transfer of information. Wenceslas is actually mentioned in one text on Boris and Gleb (the *Skazanie*),[9] and the Sázava Chronicle refers to relics of Saints Boris and Gleb being brought to Bohemia.[10] Ludmila and Wenceslas were venerated in Rus', and writings about them are preserved in Russian manuscripts.[11] Quite a bit has been written about the possible connections of the literary traditions. The most ambitious attempt to prove that a legend of Boris and Gleb used Wenceslas as a model was included in N. N. Il'in's book of 1957.[12] A part of my own work on the subject has been published.[13] But much of the scholarship to date has concentrated on textual similarities rather than on questions of concepts and ideas. Although Il'in himself criticized the philological emphasis on verbal borrowings and attempted to show an overall similarity of the narratives, he too gave particular attention to parallel passages. Over the years since the appearance of his book, scholars have repeatedly faulted his method; and it must be said that the textual comparisons he offered are sometimes vague or involve hagiographical commonplaces.[14]

---

[9] Abramovič, *Žitija* (see n. 5), 33. The mention of Saint Wenceslas in *Skazanie*, while indicative, is not as meaningful as it might be: "[Boris] thought of the martyrdom and passion of the saintly martyr Nicetas and of Saint Wenceslas [*one MS adds*: who was killed by his brother], who were killed as he, and how Saint Barbara's murderer was her own father." Nicetas and Barbara are similar to Boris in a superficial sense, and the writer may have had only the family ties in mind in the case of Wenceslas too.

[10] *Fontes Rerum Bohemicarum*, vol. 2 (see n. 4), 251. I think it not unreasonable to speculate that some text on Boris and Gleb was known at Sázava, as it would be necessary for their cult. Church Slavonic manuscripts were subsequently lost when the language was banned.

[11] See A. V. Florovskij, "Počitanie sv. Vjačeslava, knjazja češskogo, na Rusi," *Naučnye trudy Russkogo narodnogo universiteta v Prage*, vol. 2 (Prague, 1929), 305-325; also his book *Čexi i vostočnye slavjane*, vol. 1 (Prague, 1935), 114-120.

[12] N. N. Il'in, *Letopisnaja stat'ja 6523 goda i ee istočnik (Opyt analiza)* (Moscow, 1957), 36-70.

[13] In addition to other cited articles, see my "Czech Hagiography in Kiev: The Prisoner Miracles of Boris and Gleb," *Die Welt der Slaven* 10 (1965): 166-182; and "The Litany of Saints in 'Molitva sv. Troicě,'" in *Studies Presented to Professor Roman Jakobson by his Students* (Cambridge, Mass., 1968), 121-136. The present essay summarizes the main conclusions of my as yet unpublished monograph on the Slavic prince-martyrs. It is impossible to include here all the analysis and argumentation behind each statement; and annotation has been kept to a minimum.

[14] N. K. Gudzij gave a critique of Il'in's method in his "Literatura Kievskoj Rusi i drevnejšie inoslavjanskie literatury," *Issledovanija po slavjanskomu literaturovedeniju i fol'kloristike* (Moscow, 1960), 21-23.

The most recent comparative study of the connection of Wenceslas with Boris and Gleb is the stimulating article by the historian B. N. Florja, which came out in 1978.[15] Florja rightly eschews the limited method of searching for verbal parallels and proposes that we compare significant concepts. This is a positive step; but in my opinion Florja's scope is still too narrow and his conclusions not entirely convincing. He focuses on the image of the martyred prince as a ruler and the political function of his cult, paying less attention to the religious meaning, even though the martyrological aspect is fundamental and ultimately inseparable from the dynastic-political. Florja's general conclusion is that the Czech and the Rusian traditions began differently and only later grew more alike owing to coincidental development. I will claim the opposite, that the two were quite close initially and later drifted apart.

The difficulty with Florja's procedure is that he mostly ignores the earliest texts on the saints. Unaccountably, he uses Latin sources (*Crescente fide christiana*, Gumpold's Legend), where Wenceslas is depicted as an ascetic, rather than the Slavonic works that were definitely known in Rus'. The First Slavonic Life or Legend (FSL) is almost certainly the oldest text we have about him,[16] and in it he is a nonascetic, worldly prince like Boris and Gleb in the Rusian Primary Chronicle (*Povest' vremennyx let*) and the *Skazanie*. Florja also ignores the chronicle, although it probably preserves a version of Boris and Gleb's story that is older than those of the other two principal sources, the *Čtenie* (Lection) by the monk Nestor and the anonymous *Skazanie* (Relation, History). My present essay is designed in part as a response to B. N. Florja's.

A methodological question must be discussed before I proceed. How is it possible to demonstrate a continuity of operative concepts, such as I see in the Bohemian-Rusian martyria, when quotations and close paraphrases of text passages cannot be adduced? Traditional philology has often appeared to assume that there is no genetic connection between two medieval writings unless parallel passages are evident. A colleague once remarked to me that medieval writers did not take over ideas without taking words. I have

---

[15] B. N. Florja, "Václavská legenda a Borisovsko-Glebovský kult (shody a rozdíly)," *Československý časopis historický* 26 (1978): 83-96.

[16] Such was the opinion of leading specialists earlier in this century. Miloš Weingart, for example, dated FSL before 940 (*Svatováclavský sborník* 1: 960). Some current scholars, including Florja, place FSL instead in the late tenth century and believe that a Latin work preceded it. I cannot accept this conjecture, since FSL clearly represents the initial stage of Wenceslas's cult and cannot have been influenced by a hagiographically advanced writing like *Crescente*. But even if these scholars are right about the relative chronology of the texts, it is enough for our present purposes that they consider FSL a tenth-century work.

no doubt that close textual similarities are the strongest kind of evidence, and that writers in the Middle Ages were more prone to use quotation and paraphrase than is normal in modern literary systems (which value authority less and individual expression more). Even so, we are surely doing medieval men of letters an injustice if we assume they were incapable of absorbing and adapting concepts. There is no a priori reason to suppose they could not. Perhaps we should even be more interested in the restatement or adaptation of concepts, as that is the best proof the writer thought about them, while verbatim parallels might result from mindless copying. Certainly it is more significant for the history of ideas if concepts can be studied in process of evolution. An important consideration for our purposes is the possibility that creative adaptation—which shows intimate affinity with the tradition—might be more prevalent within one cultural community than between communities. This is a conjecture that needs to be tested.

Again, how can we make a case for the transfer of ideas in a remote period of history when we do not have the help of extratextual information (such as we possess in the manuscripts of modern writers and the comments of their contemporaries) and close verbal similarities? First of all, the historical circumstances must be propitious. In the present instance, the chronology is right and the opportunity for communication is amply proved. Second, it is necessary to examine wider comparative information to be sure that the ideas under consideration do not derive from a more general source, the "literary civilization" of the time (to use Picchio's expression). Finally, we will have the strongest case if we can point not only to details but to a common *pattern* (set of norms) in the texts—a shared conceptual framework or combination of ideas. To the extent that the pattern is salient and appears from our comparative research to be unique *as a pattern*, the probability of coincidence is reduced. All of this, I maintain, can be demonstrated in the present case. We will also see that there is unusually good corroborating evidence that Kievan bookmen consciously exploited the associations of Saints Boris and Gleb with Saint Wenceslas.

The general type of the martyred ruler was preeminently a West European phenomenon and was best represented in Britain and Scandinavia. It was virtually unknown in Byzantium and was rare among the southern Slavs.[17]

---

[17] The closest Byzantine parallel is the death of the military commander Constantine Ducas, as it is described in the Life of Saint Basil the New (see my "Martyrdom of St. John Vladimir," n. 8). John Vladimir is the main Serbian example; the better-known martyr Prince Lazar died in battle against the Turks, and the circumstances do not fit the type we are considering.

One should not be surprised, then, to discover that it entered Rus' from the West. My earlier article, "The Sovereign as Martyr, East and West," while not exhaustive, gave sufficient comparative information to demonstrate that the Czech and Rusian princes belonged to the general European type and to show that some individual motifs of the Slavic writings find correspondences in the West (probably by coincidence). Now we must consider the pattern of common traits in the Bohemian and Rusian martyria that sets them apart as a distinct subgroup. The shared features are fundamental and systematic; they include a narrative schema and a set of basic concepts.

The historical circumstances were quite analogous to begin with, and this fact was not lost on Rusian writers. Each of the three princes, Wenceslas, Boris, and Gleb, was murdered treacherously by his own brother in a struggle for power. In the larger scheme of things, Wenceslas' grandmother, Saint Ludmila, was readily seen as a counterpart and predecessor to Saint Olga, great-grandmother of the Kievan martyrs; and the story of Ludmila's martyrdom had some traits in common with those of the princes.[18] There was a historical parallel too, although not as strong a one, between Wenceslas's father, Prince Vratislav (who was not canonized) and the Kievan martyrs' father, Saint Vladimir. The sainthood of the princely martyrs was viewed as having the same significance in Bohemia and in Rus'. It marked the culmination of the first period of Christianity and showed God's favor and the coming of age, as it were, of the nation. The canonized members of the dynasties also provided national saints and protectors.

Let us begin with the narrative structure of the early texts about the princes (the First and Second Slavonic Lives, *Crescente fide christiana*, and Christian's Legend of Wenceslas; the chronicle, *Skazanie*, and *Čtenie* about Boris and Gleb). We can identify an impressive sequence of story elements that are common to most or all of them:

1. A brother of the saint conspires with evil men, holding stealthy meetings with them, and plans to kill the saint.
2. The murderer uses deceit and cunning, pretending to love his brother but enticing him to a place where he can be trapped.
3. The saint is warned about the fratricide but rejects the warning (either from disbelief or out of principle).
4. The site of the murder is away from the prince's own territory, and he is virtually undefended.

---

[18] I do not have space here to deal with Princess Saint Ludmila as a predecessor to the martyred princes. See, *inter alia*, R. O. Jakobson, "Russkie otgoloski drevnečešskix pamjatnikov o Ljudmile," in *Kul'turnoe nasledie Drevnej Rusi. Istoki, stanovlenie, tradicii* (Moscow, 1976), 46-50.

5. The killing takes place in the morning, after the saint's activities of the night before have been described.
6. He usually has time to pray (and attend Matins).
7. The murder is done as though from ambush; the victim is suddenly surrounded by several men, who close in on him by stages.
8. The saint does not resist his attackers. (This essential fact must be examined further.)
9. He is stabbed to death, the actual killing being done by henchmen, not by the brother himself.
10. The body is mistreated and/or neglected.
11. The slaughter and robbery of the saint's followers take place immediately.
12. The remains of the saint are retrieved and entombed with appropriate honors.
13. Divine vengeance is visited upon the murderers, who suffer "evilly" for their crime.

In this skeletal list of narrative elements, I have included only the murder plot itself, omitting other possible similarities. Note that many of these shared features are not incidental or trivial motifs but functional elements of the story. The essential narrative lines of the martyria are the same to a surprising degree.

There is always a possibility that some details of the parallel may have resulted from a coincidence of fact. Part of the similarity certainly derived from what I call the *iconic* aspect of the martyria, that is, the attempt to portray the martyr as the image of the betrayed and crucified Christ. Thus, for example, the meetings of conspirators correspond to the plot against Jesus; attendance at Mass symbolizes the Last Supper; the stabbing represents Christ's spear-wound (more about the iconic principle later). But many of the narrative elements are more individual and cannot be explained away by biblical allegory or as inevitable in the murder of a prince or king; consider particularly points (1) through (5). And what is decisive is the fact that taken together as a pattern, as a narrative schema, they are unique. The closest non-Slavic analogue I have found, that of Saint Magnus of Orkney, by no means includes all of these features. Neither does the story of the Serbian saint John Vladimir. Even if the striking similarity of Wenceslas's fate with that of the Rusian princes resulted entirely from coincidence—which is very improbable—it would be obvious to Kievan bookmen, who could then use Wenceslas as a precedent.

N. N. Il'in went too far when he claimed, on the basis of a comparison of narrative components, that the legend of Boris and Gleb is no more than a

literary reworking of the Wenceslas legend.[19] Without independent historical evidence, we cannot get at the facts and determine how much the
account of Boris and Gleb's deaths was altered to make it conform to a
hagiographical model.[20] As remarkable as the similarity of narrative lines
is, it does not by itself prove that the Bohemian texts were a source. I am
concerned in this paper to probe more deeply—to the level of operative
concepts. Here the continuity is not the rather superficial one of story but
goes to the ideational core of the martyria.

It ought to be obvious that the most basic conceptual aspect of the literature of the martyrs is precisely the martyrological—the nature of the martyrdom in Christian terms. Yet B. N. Florja, among others, largely ignores
this central issue. Like D. S. Lixačev before him,[21] Florja concentrates on
the political meaning of the Slavic martyria, divorcing that from the martyrological in a way alien to the medieval mind. To the extent that Florja deals
with religious questions, he confines himself to remarks on asceticism, concluding that Wenceslas was depicted as an ascetic saint while Boris and
Gleb were not. Even this is a misleading statement, because the Czech
prince is not an ascetic at all in the First Slavonic Life, and the extreme
piety of the Kievan brothers in *Čtenie* verges on a monkish ideal (although
they do not actually carry on ascetic practices).[22] In any case, asceticism is
not the mark of a martyr qua martyr. Sacrifice for the faith or for essential
Christian values is the martyr's claim to sainthood.

My discussion of martyrology will center around these important themes:
the righteous prince as an innocent sufferer; Christian nonresistance; and
the imitation of Christ's Passion. While I examine them separately here,
they are parts of one conception of martyrdom, and they are also bound up
with the political implications which I will consider subsequently.

---

[19] Il'in, *Letopisnaja stat'ja 6523 g.* (see n. 12), 53.

[20] A few scholars (notably Il'in) have gone so far as to claim that the whole story of Boris
and Gleb's killing by their brother Svjatopolk is a fabrication by writers loyal to Prince Jaroslav, and that it was really the "righteous" Jaroslav—the supposed avenger of Boris and
Gleb—who had them put to death. This provocative inference may well be correct, but it
cannot be accepted as historical fact as long as it is based only on a tortured reading of an
enigmatic Norse saga. If the martyrdom of Boris and Gleb were a complete fiction drawing
upon that of Wenceslas, we might expect an even greater similarity with the Czech legends
than we actually find.

[21] D. S. Lixačev, "Nekotorye voprosy ideologii feodalov v literature XI–XIII vekov,"
TODRL 10 (1954): 87-90.

[22] D. Tschiževskij believed that some of Wenceslas' ascetic practices were "echoed" instead
in the *Life of Saint Theodosius*, composed by the same Nestor who wrote *Čtenie*. See Tschiževskij's *Kleinere Schriften*, vol. 2: *Bohemica* (Munich, 1972), 40-54.

Because the Slavic princes could not be said to have died in the manner of traditional martyrs, that is, refusing to abandon the Christian faith (a pagan opposition was introduced only in the more fantastic legends of Wenceslas), a different rationale had to be advanced for recognizing them as Christian martyrs. An important element at the early stage was the idea of the prince as a righteous man who is innocently slaughtered and thereby becomes identified with Christ and his martyrs. The scriptural passage giving authority for associating martyrs with the innocent sufferers of the Old Testament is Matt. 23:29-35. It ends: "Therefore I send you prophets and wise men and scribes, some of whom you will kill and crucify, and some you will scourge in your synagogues and persecute from town to town, that upon you may come all the righteous blood shed on earth, from the blood of innocent Abel to the blood of Zechariah the son of Barachiah."[23] Christ himself was shown in the Gospels as a righteous victim. The idea was, of course, known to writers of martyria, but it is not prominent in works on martyred rulers in general. The theme of righteousness and innocent death is one of the most important connecting links between the tradition of Wenceslas and that of Boris and Gleb.

It is an essential element in the Rusian concept of the *strastoterpec*, the passion-sufferer.[24] Despite G. P. Fedotov's contention, this type of saint was not original with the Kievans; it had an immediate model in Saint Wenceslas, particularly in the First Slavonic Life. FSL emphasizes the righteousness of the victim as a major justification for considering him a saint. *Pravednyi* 'just, righteous' is the adjective most often applied to him in place of the expected *blažennyi* 'blessed' or *svętyi* 'saint' (which never appear). Innocence is a theme running through FSL; Boleslav is tricked into killing his brother Wenceslas who is "without guilt," as Wenceslas earlier had mistakenly exiled his mother without cause.[25]

The Primary Chronicle's account of Boris and Gleb likewise stresses the righteousness of the princes and their guiltlessness at death, while the murderers are "law-breakers" who practice injustice or unrighteousness

---

[23] In biblical and rabbinical literature, this type was usually exalted for his guiltlessness and not expressly for his moral purity; but it was a small step from innocent man to righteous man in the positive sense. See A. Descamps, *Les justes et la justice dans les Evangiles et le christianisme primitif hormis la doctrine proprement paulinienne*, Universitas Catholica Lovaniensis, *Dissertationes*, ser. 2, vol. 43 (Louvain, 1950), 51. In *Čtenie*, Gleb refers to the death of Zechariah (Abramovič, *Žitija* [see n. 5], 13).

[24] *Strastotrъpьcь* occurred in Old Church Slavonic as a calque for the Greek ἀθλοφόρος. However, in early Kievan usage it seems to have been reserved for martyrs of the type of Boris and Gleb, who were not Christian martyrs (*mučenici*) in the traditional sense.

[25] My thematic analysis of FSL is given in a forthcoming paper. We will see that one East Slavic redaction of FSL confuses the plot.

(*nepravda*). The assassins are quick to spill blood unjustly (*bez pravdy*—a phrase added by the chronicler to his source in Prov. 1:16).[26] When Prince Jaroslav decides to seek revenge against Svjatopolk, he reiterates the double concept of innocence and righteousness: "Zane bez viny prolьja [Svjatopolk] krovь Borisovu i Glěbovu pravednuju."[27]

In Judeo-Christian tradition, the first righteous victim was Abel, killed by his brother Cain out of jealousy that God accepted only Abel's sacrifice (Gen. 4). The theme of Cain and Abel, not in itself usually pertinent to martyria, plays an extensive role in the Czech and Kievan works. An analogy with the two sons of Adam would naturally suggest itself when the saint's murderer is his own brother; but it probably is not a coincidence in this case when we consider that it was introduced by FSL and is part of a pattern of ideas suggested by that source.

The First Slavonic Life does not mention Abel and Cain by name; but there can be no doubt that the miracle of the blood that refuses to enter the ground was meant to recall the "innocent blood of Abel" which cried out to the Lord for justice. In Judaic tradition Abel's blood was believed to remain on the surface of the ground.[28] Just so did the Rusian composer of the *Prologue* entry on Wenceslas understand the miracle, because he added (if indeed this was not in the Bohemian source): "For [the prince's blood] cried out to God like Abel's against Boleslav."[29] The motif is explicit in later works about Wenceslas. Christian's Legend (late tenth century) gave prominence to it and called Boleslav a second Cain (*alter Cayn*), just as Svjatopolk is *vtoryi Kainъ* in both *Čtenie* and *Skazanie* (the phrase is probably a coincidence).[30]

The Rusian Primary Chronicle took up the theme of Cain and Abel. Svjatopolk is compared to Cain (rather than Judas, as expected in a passion) just before each of the two murders. We have already seen that Jaroslav mentions the righteous blood of his brothers that has been spilled. Later he stands on the very spot where Boris was killed, raises his arms to the heavens, and intones: "The blood of my brother calls out to Thee, Lord! Avenge the blood of this righteous one, as Thou didst avenge the

[26] *Povest' vremennyx let*, vol. 1, (hereafter *PVL*) ed. V. P. Adrianova-Peretc (Moscow-Leningrad, 1950), 90.
[27] For [Svjatopolk] without guilt [or, without cause] spilled the righteous blood of Boris and Gleb, *PVL*, 96.
[28] *Theologisches Wörterbuch zum Neuen Testament*, vol. 1 (Stuttgart, 1949), 7; L. Ginzberg, *The Legends of the Jews*, vol. 5 (Philadelphia, 1909), 140.
[29] Vajs, *Sborník* (see n. 4), 67.
[30] Pekař, *Wenzels-und-Ludmila-Legenden* (see n. 4), 113; Abramovič, *Žitija* (see n. 5), 9, 32.

blood of Abel."[31] In subsequent texts on Boris and Gleb, especially *Ska-zanie*, the analogy with the two sons of Adam becomes associated with an important new idea, that of brother-love. I will return to this subject when discussing political ideology.

A final point to be noted here is that the righteousness of the Bohemian and Rusian princes (their positive moral quality before God) is established largely by their charitable activity. Twice the FSL prominently lists the good deeds of Wenceslas, which are partially based on the "six acts of mercy" of the Gospels. This is the ideal of a perfect Christian prince and may have its roots in the Byzantine concept of the ruler's *philanthropia*.[32] Nestor, in writing his *Čtenie*, developed the idea of charitableness into a major theme, contrasting the *miloserdie* 'mercifulness' of Vladimir, Boris, and Gleb, with the *nemiloserdie* 'unmercifulness' of Svjatopolk. With respect to philanthropy, the sainted Rusian princes once again find a fore-runner in Prince Wenceslas.[33]

Nonresistance in the face of violent death is an important trait of the Rusian legends and one aspect of what G. P. Fedotov saw as Boris and Gleb's practice of *kenosis*, the humble "emptying" of the self in imitation of Christ.[34] Willing submission to the martyr's fate is, of course, the norm rather than the exception in Christian martyrdoms generally. But it is probably true that what we may call the "heroic" variant (where the saint triumphantly acts out a scenario of martyrdom prepared by God and dis-plays superhuman powers of endurance) is more common in conventional *passiones* than is the humble and pathetic. Kenotic nonresistance, in which the martyr submits quietly and humbly, becoming a passive sufferer, is the more striking in the case of soldier saints who are capable of defending themselves but refuse out of Christian principle. There are examples among sainted rulers such as Edmund, Magnus, and John Vladimir, as I have shown elsewhere. Fedotov wrongly believed the Rusian concept of nonre-sistance to be original and unique. The writers on Boris and Gleb found their immediate source of inspiration in the legends of Saint Wenceslas, who also died unresisting and for similar reasons. Fedotov was right only in the sense that the Rusian tradition emphasized the kenotic or pathetic

---

[31] *PVL*, 97.

[32] A. P. Vlasto, *The Entry of the Slavs into Christendom* (Cambridge, 1970), 266.

[33] Some scholars have attempted to portray the philanthropy of the Rusian princes, and Vladimir Monomax in particular, as an original idea; but it certainly was not. This subject is worth a separate study.

[34] For Fedotov's theories, see his books *Svjatye drevnej Rusi (X–XVII st.)* (Paris, 1931) and *The Russian Religious Mind*, vol. 1 (Cambridge, Mass., 1946).

possibilities. (This is more like the legend of Wenceslas' grandmother, Saint Ludmila, who died humbly and unresisting, a helpless victim.)

In the First Slavonic Life, it is true, the Czech prince does not willingly allow himself to be killed; he puts up a defense and tries to escape. But it is significant that he spares his attacker, his brother Boleslav, after overcoming him. In refusing to fight back, he foreshadows the Wenceslas of the Second Slavonic Life (SSL) and other works, who practices nonresistance and willingly sacrifices his life.

The situation in SSL strongly anticipates the Primary Chronicle and *Skazanie* accounts of Boris (Gleb is more helpless; only in the stylized *Čtenie* does he also make a decision for nonresistance). Wenceslas has a *druzhina* (troop of men) with him but expressly refuses to use them to defend himself. On the eve of his murder, he jousts with his men in the courtyard and says to them: "On horseback with you Czechs, could I not find our enemies? But I don't want to!"[35] This is a thinly veiled reference to the conspiracy against him which, as the author assures us repeatedly, Wenceslas knows all about. Boris closely imitates this behavior when he dismisses his druzhina and consigns himself to his fate. The authors' point is the same: here is a strong warrior prince with soldiers at his command who nonetheless deliberately shuns violence upon principle. Nothing speaks more eloquently for a prince-martyr's nonresistance than Wenceslas' simple words: "No ne xoštju" (But I don't want to). During the night he prays, "knowing that his death is coming and ready to endure it willingly." The key word *voleju* 'willingly, voluntarily' has no correspondence in Gumpold's Latin text; it has been added in the Slavonic version.[36]

In other respects Wenceslas in SSL is quite unlike Boris. He is an ascetic prince who achieves a heroic martyrdom rather than a humble one. Nonetheless, the principle of nonresistance is clear, and the circumstances are more similar to those of Boris's death in the chronicle and *Skazanie* than could be expected from the common tradition of Christian martyria. Very important is the fact that in SSL Wenceslas declines to employ force because it would be against his own brother. Having disarmed Boleslav, he says, "Do you see, brother, the source of your cruelty could turn against you! For what keeps me from becoming the spiller of my brother's blood? But I do not wish that from my hands, brother, your blood seek accounting of me at the Last Judgment.[37] Similarly, Boris in the chronicle is motivated by

---

[35] Vajs, *Sborník* (see n. 4), 108.

[36] Ibid., 110. It is always possible that the word *voleju* was added by an East Slavic copyist. This would not diminish the importance of the passage, as it would only show that the scribe understood the association with Christ's sacrifice.

[37] Ibid., 11-12.

a desire not to harm his brother, telling the druzhina: "Far be it from me to
raise my hand against my elder brother; if my father has died, let him be in
my father's place."[38] In *Skazanie* Boris is concerned that he could not
escape God's judgment if he used violence against Svjatopolk; and in
Čtenie also he fears judgment if he opposes his brother.[39]

Thus the theme of nonresistance, whose first significance is martyrological (the martyr submits on Christian principle and in imitation of Christ), is
a connecting thread in the tradition of Bohemian and Kievan martyrs; and
what makes this particularly distinctive is its combination with the principle of right behavior toward a brother. The Rusian accomplishment was
the elaboration of the kenotic aspect. We will explore later the differing
shades of political meaning that the theme takes on.

Innocence and nonresistance are, in the greater context, substantive
components in the martyr's imitation of Christ. What I term the *iconic*
concept is the idea that the martyr's death in its external circumstances
duplicates the Passion and that by reenacting Christ's fate he becomes identified with him, that is, becomes his image (εἰκών). An allegory of the Passion has been employed in martyria since the earliest centuries of the
Church. To apply it to accounts of murdered rulers required finesse on the
part of medieval writers, because, if the saints did not die for the Christian
faith, a theological significance to the allegory might be hard to find. Even
so, the iconic principle does appear in works on the sainted kings of the
West. Perhaps nowhere is it as skillfully developed, however, as in the
First Slavonic Life of Saint Wenceslas, which systematically parallels Wenceslas' life, as well as his death, with the Gospels. In his summary at the
end, the author calls attention to this fact and consciously offers the iconic
as an argument for recognizing the Czech prince as Christian martyr: "In
truth his suffering equalled the suffering of Christ and the holy martyrs."[40]

As Ludolf Müller showed, the biblical allegory was important too in the
chronicle's tale of Boris and Gleb (and subsequently in *Skazanie*). Contrary
to Müller's contention, however, the allegory is not carried out as thoroughly and meaningfully as in FSL.[41] Only Boris's death scene is really
constructed this way in the chronicle; and having him recite the Good Friday psalms is a more superficial device than working an allegory into the
whole story.

---

[38] *PVL*, 90.
[39] Abramovič, *Žitija* (see n. 5), 10, 30.
[40] Vajs, *Sborník* (see n. 4), 19.
[41] In *Zeitschrift für slavische Philologie* 27 (1959): 310-311.

As it happens, we possess proof that Wenceslas's martyrdom was interpreted in eleventh-century Rus' in just the way I have described. A liturgical office of the Czech saint, probably composed in Rus' (or possibly in
Bohemia), is included in the Menaeum extant from the years 1095-97 (the
oldest documentary evidence for knowledge of Wenceslas among the East
Slavs). The first ode of the Canon contains these key words: "Vladyčьnemъ
strastjamъ, slavьne, upodobni sja, jako agnę neporočьno, bes pravьdy ubi-
vaemь; těmь sъ liky m(u)č(e)n(i)kъ, bo(go)bl(a)ž(e)ne, nyně vesiliši sę."[42]
The lines state concisely but unambiguously the theological justification for
viewing ˙Wenceslas as a Christian martyr: his passion took the form of the
Lord's sufferings (the iconic principle), and he was an innocent and righteous man (the immaculate lamb) slaughtered without guilt. The Rusian
author showed that he grasped the martyrological foundations of FSL very
well. Even should it be proved that the Canon was composed in Bohemia,
the interpretation was available for Kievans to read and hear.

Another verse of the Canon demonstrates understanding of the Abel and
Cain analogy: "Lьstiju prelukavago drevle očьrьvlena bys(tь) zemlja bra-
toubiistvьnoju rukoju; nyně že krъvьju okroplь sja, bl(a)gouxanija žьrъtvu
x(risto)vi prinošaetь."[43] The death of righteous Abel prefigured the sacrifice
of the martyr Wenceslas.

If the martyrological concepts are not unique to the Slavic tradition
when considered one at a time, the pattern that they enter into is not common to martyria of rulers. One cannot fail to see that the Rusian bookmen
had in Wenceslas a ready-made precedent and model for the prince-martyr.
They could find, especially in the First Slavonic Life (which they knew and
understood), a solution to the problem of how to portray as a Christian
martyr a secular prince who was not killed for the faith but for political
reasons. The answer they found was to show him as a righteous and charitable ruler who was killed though he was guiltless, who practiced nonresistance, and whose death in its circumstances formed an allegory of Christ's
Passion.

---

[42] O glorious one, you likened yourself to the Lord's sufferings, being killed like a pure
[immaculate] lamb unjustly; for this, o blessed of God, you now rejoice with the choirs of
martyrs. V. Jagić, *Služebnye minei za sentjabr', oktjabr' i nojabr' v cerkovno-slavjanskom perevode po russkim rukopisjam 1095-97 g.*, Pamjatniki drevnerusskogo jazyka, no. 1 (St. Petersburg, 1886), 213-222. I quote from the edition of the Canon in Vajs, *Sborník* (see n. 4),
137-145. Certain scholars, notably Josef Vašica, have thought the Canon was composed in
Bohemia rather than in Rus'.

[43] In ancient times the ground became red through the temptation of the most wicked
[devil] and by a fratricidal hand; and now, being sprinkled with blood it bears a fragrant
sacrifice to Christ. Vajs, *Sborník* (see n. 4), 144.

Let us now turn to that aspect to which B. N. Florja gave particular attention, the political. I would maintain, in contrast to his observation, that the
political images of the princes, like the saintly, started out quite similarly
and diverged only later. In the earliest versions of their stories (especially
the First Slavonic Life, the Primary Chronicle, *Skazanie*) they were all portrayed as exemplary rulers, not as otherworldly saints, and their deaths
were caused by a brother's political aspiration to the throne rather than by
their defense of the faith as such. We should remember also that the *philanthropia* of the princes has political as well as religious meaning; it makes
them ideal rulers. Later—as Florja correctly points out—Wenceslas was
turned into an ascetic (a role that programmatically conflicts with his secular functions); and the tradition of Boris and Gleb took on another political coloring when they were held up to the living princes as an example of
loyalty to the hierarchy of elder and younger brothers.

    True, the dynastic situations were from the beginning somewhat differ-
ent, and that is reflected in details of the literature. Wenceslas was the elder
son and legitimate heir who had already been on the throne several years;
the conspiracy to replace him with his younger brother Boleslav was a
usurpation. By contrast, the murderer Svjatopolk was the eldest son and
might be thought of as the rightful successor. But on closer examination the
circumstances are not so unalike. Rus' did not recognize the principle of
primogeniture, and because Svjatopolk's taking of the throne was accompanied by deception and violence (he treacherously killed off his brothers
to assure his position), his succession has the appearance of illegitimacy.
This is all the more true when the sources state he was not Vladimir's own
son and hint that the christianizer of Rus' favored Boris as his successor.[44]
It is possible that these last two points are unhistorical; they tendentiously
serve to justify Jaroslav's revenge against the evil fratricide. What we
should notice is that they have the side effect of making Svjatopolk look
more like the usurper Boleslav than he otherwise would.

    Another significant parallel between the First Slavonic Life of Wenceslas
and the texts on Boris and Gleb is that the murderer acts partly out of the
mistaken belief that he is in danger from his victim and must defend himself. This was explicit in the archetype of FSL, where the plotters incited
Boleslav by telling him the lie that Wenceslas meant to kill him. That this
twist was understood in Rus' is proved by Redaction *M* and the *Prologue*.[45]

---

[44] Historians have long speculated that Boris was meant as successor. See, e.g., A. Pres-
njakov, *Knjažoe pravo v Drevnej Rusi. Očerki po istorii X–XII stoletij* (St. Petersburg, 1909),
31-32.
[45] Vajs, *Sborník* (see n. 4), 22, 66.

A misapprenhension of the brother's intent also figures in Svjatopolk's motivation, although the idea is not expressly developed in most of the texts because the purpose was to depict Svjatopolk as a villain by nature. Boris, who is especially loved by the people and is his father's favorite, is returning to Kiev with an army loyal to him. Svjatopolk can only view this as a threat that requires preemptive action. In Nestor's *Čtenie*, it is brought out explicitly that Svjatopolk believes Boris is plotting to take the throne.[46]

All of this brings us to a more profound thematic parallel that makes the differences of familial relationships pale in significance. *Younger brother Boris refuses to commit the very act of revolt against an elder brother that Boleslav perpetrates.* The Czech murderer provides, with regard to political ideology (and religious as well), a negative example for the Rusian princes that complements the positive precedent of Wenceslas and is perhaps even more salient. Boris finds himself in the legal and moral dilemma that Boleslav faces—threatened by his older brother (or so Boleslav is led to believe in FSL) and urged by advisors to oppose him and seize the throne. But Boris rejects the counsel that the young Czech prince took, and thereby he avoids the latter's transgression. The contrast between Boleslav and Boris is meaningful in a way that cannot have failed to impress Kievan writers concerned with the proper relations of younger and older brothers.[47]

We should keep in mind that if we attempt, with our modern viewpoint, to separate out the "political" elements from the religious in the literature of the princes, we risk anachronism. Nothing shows this danger more clearly than the theme of brotherly love, to which we now come.

Brother-love (*bratoljubie*) is probably the most distinctive and attractive feature that evolved in the Rusian literature of the *strastoterpcy*. On the religious side, it offers something profound that is lacking in nearly all legends of Wenceslas—a positive Christian virtue which the saint dies serving. And brotherly love was also given a political meaning; it was used to characterize the proper subordination of "younger brothers" (less senior members of the dynasty) to "elder brothers" and the reciprocal responsibility of seniors towards the younger princes. In other words, the Christian principle of *philadelphia* was made in the chronicle and elsewhere (*Čtenie*)

---

[46] Abramovič, *Žitija* (see n. 5), 7.

[47] To the extent that Boris's act is a renunciation of political power, he has a forerunner in the Wenceslas of SSL who wants to give up his princedom, although Wenceslas' motive is very different—to become a monk (Vajs, *Sborník* 106). Closer to Boris and Gleb is Wenceslas' grandmother Ludmila's vain attempt to assure her murderess that she has no desire to rule: "Regnare ego nolo neque ullam potestatis tue particulam habere volo" (*Fuit in provincia Boemorum*, in Chalupecký, *Prameny X. století* [see n. 4], 472).

to justify a "feudal" hierarchy within the Rurikid dynasty. The political side
was described well by D. S. Lixačev; but we should not lose sight of the
religious foundation which is inseparable from it. The princes could not be
venerated as martyrs for the political aspect of their actions, as Lixačev
implied; and the two moralities, Christian and political, were treated as one
by medieval writers.

The New Testament source used by the Rusian bookmen was the First
Epistle of John: "... Whoever does not do right is not of God, nor he who
does not love his brother. For this is the message which you have heard
from the beginning, that we should love one another, and not be like Cain
who was of the evil one and murdered his brother. And why did he murder
him? Because his own deeds were evil and his brother's were righteous....
Any one who hates his brother is a murderer, and you know that no murderer has eternal life abiding him" (3:7-15).[48] At 4:18 the Epistle repeats
words of Christ that are paraphrased in the Primary Chronicle: "There is
no fear in love, but perfect love casts out fear.... If any one says, 'I love
God,' and hates his brother, he is a liar; for he who does not love his
brother whom he has seen, cannot love God whom he has not seen. And
this commandment we have from him, that he who loves God should love
his brother also."

In the Primary Chronicle and *Skazanie* of Boris and Gleb, Christ's commandment to love one's brothers (fellow men) is applied literally to brothers in the flesh. This was natural in that John mentions Abel and Cain,
who were indeed brothers; and in the Rusian kinship system, even one's
cousins were called brothers. Svjatopolk is a Cain, a brother-hater and fratricide. Boris proves that he is the opposite by refusing to use violence
against Svjatopolk; and Boris and Gleb give a touching example of *bratoljubie* with their affection and devotion for each other. Describing Gleb's
reunion with his older brother in heaven, the chronicler wrote: "He
received the [martyr's] crown, entered into the heavenly abodes, and saw
his beloved brother and rejoiced with him in indescribable joy which they
attained through their brother-love. How fine and how beautiful it is for
(two) brothers to live together [Ps. 132(133):1]." The concept of brotherly
love, briefly touched upon in the chronicle, is developed into an important
theme in *Skazanie* and extends to their love for their father and even for
Svjatopolk. It is not only an attractive character trait but a Christian ideal
that gives deep meaning to their deaths. They are not martyrs simply for

---

[48] The *Parimejnik* text on Boris and Gleb identifies the author of the sentiments as John the
Theologian, i.e., Evangelist (Abramovič, *Žitija* [see n. 5], 116).

the form of their demise; they die obeying a basic Christian commandment. The political meaning of the sacrifice would appear to be secondary. *Philadelphia* as such is not a theme in the literature of Saint Wenceslas, where the prince has no brother-companion in his martyrdom. We are told variously that he treats Boleslav well as a brother and does not wish to do him harm or see him damned to hell; but nowhere in the legends is it stressed that he loves him. The tradition of Wenceslas, as we have seen, took a different religious path; it turned him into an ascetic saint and invented an unhistorical pagan opposition in order to justify calling him a martyr for the faith (both of these elements are absent, however, from FSL).

Nonetheless, we should not follow B. N. Florja in denying any similarity of political ideals at the beginning of the two "cycles" of legends. The First Slavonic Life foreshadows the theme of familial loyalty, despite Florja's assertion that it deals with the revolt of vassals against their feudal lord instead of the mutual obligations of princely brothers.[49] A disruption of familial bonds is signaled by the scriptural epigraph to the Life: "Brother will rise up against brother, and son against father, and those of [a man's own] household [will be] his enemies." The quotation from Matt. 10:21 has been significantly altered by changing the first verb and switching the order of *father* and *son*, with the result that the idea of rebellion against familial authority is better conveyed.

FSL strongly makes the point that Wenceslas is the elder brother and Boleslav should be under him. Wenceslas is called "the first-born son";[50] and when he takes the throne, Boleslav "nača podъ nimъ xoditi" (began to be subordinated to him). In their dialogue they address each other as "brother." All of this calls attention to their relationship and the nature of Boleslav's crime, as, of course, does the allusion to Cain and Abel. The reason Florja thought to find a different concept in FSL is that Wenceslas is called "lord" (*gospodinъ*); but this is part of the elaborate analogy with Christ. Curiously, it was a Kievan scribe who underlined the other interpretation by adding to the crimes of the murderers: "they killed their prince."[51]

The Second Slavonic Life of Wenceslas, deriving as it does from Bishop Gumpold's Latin legend, is a more conventional *vita et passio*. Yet even here readers would find reminders that Boleslav's crime is revolt against an elder brother who is the legitimate sovereign. Their father designates Wenceslas his successor, and Chapters 15 and 17 repeatedly mention that

---

[49] Florja, "Václavská legenda" (see n. 15), 87n.
[50] Vajs, *Sborník* (see n. 4), 14.
[51] Ibid., 18.

Boleslav is the "younger brother." SSL expands upon the brothers' dialogue and has Wenceslas answer the invitation with the epigrammatic: "Radostь bratьnja radostь božia estь."[52] The entry on Saint Wenceslas for September 28 in the Kievan *Prologue* makes the point that Prince Wenceslas had "two brothers *under him*" (more later about the second brother). Clearly, the dynastic priority of elder brothers was a principle implicit in the legends of the Czech prince, and Kievan bookmen took note of that. But it was in Rus'—with its proliferation of princes and lack of primogeniture—that the concept of brotherly love was elaborated in both its religious and its political meaning.

The best proof of the intimate connections of Wenceslas's tradition with that of Boris and Gleb is one that has not attracted much attention, although most of the facts were pointed out long ago. I refer to the reverse effect that the Rusian legends had on the Czech ones in Kiev—namely, that Kievan bookmen altered texts about the Bohemian prince in the spirit of those on the native saints. While not all the sources are contemporary, they show convincingly that the Kievans were aware of the analogy and were ready to make use of it.

The Vostokov Redaction of the First Slavonic Life (discovered in Russia and named for its editor) has it that Wenceslas was warned by the conspirators that Boleslav intended to kill him[53]—while in the original of FSL, they untruthfully told Boleslav that Wenceslas harbored such designs against *him* (we have seen that Redaction *M* and the *Prologue* preserve the correct reading). This is clearly a redactional change on the part of an East Slavic scribe, due either to a misunderstanding or an attempt to make the situation more consistent with the story of Svjatopolk (who is not told a false rumor about Boris or Gleb). Another detail is the phrase *i bezakonija moja* (and my transgressions) apparently added to Boleslav's confession in the Rusian version.[54] "Sins and transgressions" was a common phrase in Orthodox writings; but we should recall that *bezakonie* (lit. lawlessness) is an important term used to describe Svjatopolk's behavior in the Primary Chronicle.

The explicit comparison of Boleslav to Svjatopolk interpolated in Redaction *M* of FSL leaves no doubt of conscious analogy: "At the same time the devil, who from the beginning has hated humankind, sowed wicked thoughts in the heart of Boleslav and incited him against his brother, just

---

[52] A [or, My] brother's joy [celebration] is God's joy. Ibid., 108.
[53] Ibid., 15.
[51] Ibid., 20, 28.

like the accursed Svjatopolk, who plotted wickedness against his brothers in his heart. He [Svjatopolk] killed his brothers and took power alone in the Rusian land, not knowing the vengeance of God—that the servants of God do not carry swords for nought but for the destruction of the unfaithful. Just so [did] these wicked counsellors and devils who plotted wicked things in their hearts together with Boleslav against the blessed prince Wenceslas."[55]

The Rusian *Prologue* (*Synaxarion*; a collection of short texts about the saints to be read on their feast days) has, under September 28, an entry on Wenceslas's passion that was composed perhaps in the thirteenth century or at the very end of the twelfth.[56] It shows not only comparison but adaptation. To begin with, the title (as in the Rusian redactions of FSL) emphasizes the saint's worldly position, which is like that of the Rusian princes: "The Passion of St. Wenceslas, Czech Prince."[57] The text opens with a summary of the dynastic situation, as do sources on Boris and Gleb: "It is appropriate to know first the patrimony and throne of the saintly martyr Wenceslas. He was the son of Vratislav, Czech prince, having under him two brothers, Spytignev and Boleslav." In no other work do we hear of the supposed brother Spytignev (the name is rather that of Wenceslas's uncle), and he is forgotten later in this same entry. A misunderstanding is unlikely here; the addition of the second brother appears to be a deliberate redactional change. It serves to enhance the parallel to the Kievan situation, since Svjatopolk had two younger brothers who were the particular objects of his attention, Boris and Gleb.

As Serebrjanskij pointed out, the characterization of Boleslav, "bě bo jazykomъ lstivymъ" (for he was deceptive of tongue), not found in any Bohemian source, is a reminiscence of words applied to Svjatopolk. Some manuscripts of the *Prologue* have the evil advisors tell Boleslav, "a my tobě prijaemъ" (and we wish you well), which echoes Svjatopolk's question to his henchmen: "Prijaete li mi vsěmъ serdcemь?" (Do you wish me well with all your hearts?). We have noted that *Prologue* explains the meaning of the blood that will not enter the ground for three days: it cries out to God for justice like the blood of innocent Abel. This proves that the Rusian compiler understood the symbolism implicit in FSL; but he may well have had in mind, too, the elaboration of the Abel theme in the Rusian Primary Chronicle.

---

[55] Ibid., 24.
[56] See the introduction by N. Serebrjanskij in Vajs, *Sborník*, 47-63. M. Weingart also discussed the *Prologue* texts at length in *Svatováclavský sborník*, vol. 1 (Prague, 1934), 939-950.
[57] Vajs, *Sborník*, 65.

Serebrjanskij cited other similarities between the September 28 passage
and the literature of Boris and Gleb, but most of these are vague or commonplaces. He may be right, however, that the *Prologue* omits Boleslav's
repentance out of a desire to identify him with the unrepentant Svjatopolk.
The *Prologue*'s entry of March 4 on the Translation of Wenceslas's relics
does mention Boleslav's change of heart, as a prerequisite to the removal.[58]
However, this entry was probably written by a different compiler at a different time. The Translation, incidentally, is less interesting for our present
purpose. One manuscript of it calls Boleslav the *older* brother, very possibly
because the scribe was thinking of Svjatopolk.

The cited facts prove that Kievan bookmen were very much aware of the
close parallel between the Czech and Rusian saints. More than that, in the
Prologue they enhanced the similarity, reshaping Wenceslas's legend to correspond with Boris and Gleb's. This must have been done deliberately,
since the changes form an obvious pattern. Serebrjanskij and Weingart
both wondered why Wenceslas's legend was altered in Rus' at all, as this
was an unusual proceeding. The explanation can only be that the identification with Wenceslas was an operative one; he was an already-canonized
saint of the same type as Boris and Gleb and could serve as precedent in a
doubtful case of martyrdom. The rationale for deeming him a Christian
martyr, particularly in FSL, was taken as a starting point by Kievan historians and hagiographers, and an effort was made to establish parallels in
details of the legends. A corollary to my argument is the fact that other
early Czech saints, Prokop (Procopius) and Vojtěch (Adalbert) attracted
much less interest in Rus' than Wenceslas (and his martyred grandmother
Ludmila). Chronology had something to do with this (Prokop was not
canonized until 1204); but we can now see another reason—these saints
were not valuable as models.

It is understandable that the Czech prince-martyr Wenceslas, of all modern foreign saints, was given so much attention in Rus' in the eleventh and
twelfth centuries. Why, then, did his cult fade in later times? The schism of
the Churches certainly affected veneration of Western saints; and there
were apparently no relics of Wenceslas in Rus' that could bring about cures,
while the shrine of Saints Boris and Gleb at Vyšgorod had become a much-
frequented place of pilgrimage. Their cult was encouraged by the princely
family and the local church because of the prestige it brought. But the
decline of Wenceslas's cult in the later period was almost a predictable
result of the role it had played. Once the Czech prince was no longer

---

[58] Ibid., 67.

needed as model and justification for the Rusian cults, he naturally became overshadowed by the well-established and popular native saints of the same kind, the *strastoterpcy* Boris and Gleb.

We have seen that the close association of the early literature on the Bohemian and Kievan martyred princes is apparent in a common narrative schema, a set of martyrological concepts, and to some extent in what we now call political ideology. The similarities are not superficial but are fundamental elements of the story and its conceptual framework; and taken together they form a pattern that is distinctive and unique. It stands out by comparison with the martyria of non-Slavic martyred rulers and even with that of the Serbian saint John Vladimir. Furthermore, there is direct evidence of interaction; Kievan writers exploited the analogy in reverse by amending texts on Wenceslas. We cannot escape the conclusion that the original impetus came from the Bohemian legends.

Returning to my opening remarks, I prefer to speak of a continuity of tradition in this case rather than of an influence, for I perceive one living tradition that was shared by Rus' and evolved there in its own way. Rusian writers treated the conceptual system as their own. They did not just "borrow" ready-made formulations; they absorbed ideas and freely reshaped them. They continued some themes and developed others whose seeds they found in the Bohemian texts. Their original contributions were major ones: the kenotic brand of nonresistance; the combined religious and political principle of brother-love.

There was no reciprocal impact of the Kievan legends on the later ones of Wenceslas, as one might expect in a cultural community. That was precluded by the abolition of Church Slavonic as a liturgical language in the Czech lands (at the end of the eleventh century). Such an impact would have been unlikely in any case because—Florja is right about this—Wenceslas's image evolved along different lines. In the religious aspect, he came to be portrayed as an ascetic, and in the political, as the *rex perpetuus* of the Czech kingdom.[59] A like conception of the prince-martyr, begun in Bohemia and continued in Kievan Rus', became clearly differentiated. But the extent and nature of the initial sharing speak for a considerable degree of cultural interaction between the Czechs and East Slavs in the early Middle Ages.

[59] See D. Třeštík's lengthy treatment of Wenceslas' political image in his *Kosmova kronika: Studie k počátkům českého dějepisectví a politického myšlení* (Prague, 1968), 183-231.

MONASTIC MEDICINE IN KIEVAN RUS'
AND EARLY MUSCOVY

RUSSELL ZGUTA

Until the early eleventh century, the practice of medicine among the Eastern Slavs was largely in the hands of folk healers. Known by a variety of names, these professional healers—who, according to some, also doubled as pagan cult leaders — were a common fixture in every community.[1] It appears that by the mid-eleventh century there had also evolved a distinct secular medical tradition in Kievan Rus' about which, unfortunately, we know very little.[2] With the introduction of Christianity in 988, both the folk and secular traditions gave way, in theory if not in practice, to monastic medicine.[3]

In the early Middle Ages scientific medicine found a modest refuge in the monasteries of the West. From the very beginning of monasticism, certain monks were entrusted with the care of the sick. It was not, however, until the founding of the monastery of Montecassino by Saint Benedict of Nursia

This publication was supported in part by NIH Grant LM 03163 from the National Library of Medicine and by funds from the Research Council of the University of Missouri, Columbia, which I gratefully acknowledge. My sincere thanks also to Muriel Heppell for making available to me her M.A. thesis "The Kievo-Pechersky Monastery from Its Origins to the End of the Eleventh Century" (University of London, 1951).

[1] Still unsurpassed as a comprehensive study of Russian folk medicine is G. I. Popov's *Russkaja narodnobytovaja medicina* (St. Petersburg, 1903). Among the most common names for healers were *znaxar', vorožej, koldun, čarodej, volxv, zelejnik, kudesnik*; see R. Zguta, "Witchcraft and Medicine in Pre-Petrine Russia," *Russian Review* 37 (1978): 440. Regarding the healer's role as cult leader, see L. I. Min'ko, "Magical Curing (Its Sources and Character, and the Causes of Its Prevalence)," *Soviet Anthropology and Archeology* 12 (1973): 5.

[2] The evidence for this secular medical tradition can be found in the *Russkaja Pravda*: "If [a man injures a man, and the injured man] is smeared with blood or is blue from bruises, he needs no eyewitness [to prove the offense]; if there is no mark [of injury] upon him, let him produce an eyewitness; if he cannot, the matter ends there. If he is not able to avenge, he receives 3 *grivna* for the offense and the physician his honorarium" (G. Vernadsky, trans., *Medieval Russian Laws* [New York, 1969], 27, art. 2). Since monks accepted no compensation for their services and the folk healers were outlawed, it is difficult to identify the physicians in question.

[3] Even though Vladimir the Saint, in his Church Statute (*Ustav*), tried to proscribe the folk healers, they continued to serve the medical needs of the majority of the people until relatively recent times. See S. V. Juškov, ed., *Pamjatniki russkogo prava*, vol. 1: *Pamjatniki prava Kievskogo gosudarstva X–XII vv.*, ed. A. A. Zimin (Moscow, 1952), p. 238, art. 7.

in 529 that a genuine interest in medicine was awakened in the cloisters of Western Europe. At Montecassino, medicine was taught and practiced, medical texts were collected, copied, and preserved, and the teaching of medicine was spread by the Benedictines to other monasteries, most notably to Fulda in Germany. Quite independent of the Benedictines, important monastic medical centers were also established by Irish missionary monks in Switzerland, at Saint Gall and Reichenau, and in Italy, at Bobbio.[4]

In the East, beginning with the fourth century, monasticism had become less and less isolationist and more responsive to human needs. Under the influence of Basil the Great, it became more firmly rooted in the Christian commitment to charity, or *philanthropia*, which was directed at the less fortunate of society, including the aged, the infirm, the blind, the crippled, the wounded, the insane, and the dying.[5] As a result, Eastern monastic medicine evolved more rapidly, was better developed, and became more sophisticated than monastic medicine in the West. This is already evident by the year 375, when Basil the Great included a hospital and leprosarium in the group of institutions he opened in Caesarea in Syria.[6]

Between the years 400 and 403, Saint John Chrysostom, following Basil's example, built a number of hospitals in Constantinople.[7] No doubt the most important of these, from a medical standpoint, were the hospital and related institutions attached to the great monastery known as Pantocrator. Endowed and founded by the Byzantine Emperor John II Komnenos (1118–1148) and his wife Irene in 1136, the Pantocrator was "one of the great and splendid monasteries" of the period. The Pantocrator actually had two hospitals, a small six-bed unit for sick monks, and a much larger facility for the sick and poor of the city.[8]

An examination of the *Typikon*, or constitution, of the Pantocrator, drawn up by its founder, provides a rare glimpse into the day-to-day operations of this remarkable institution.[9] It contained fifty beds, divided into

---

[4] On monastic medicine in the West, see D. Riesman, *The Story of Medicine in the Middle Ages* (New York, 1935), 17–27; also, A. Castiglioni, *A History of Medicine*, trans. E. B. Krumbhaar, 2nd ed. (New York, 1947), 288–299.

[5] D. J. Constantelos, *Byzantine Philanthropy and Social Welfare* (New Brunswick, N.J., 1968), 3, 89.

[6] O. Temkin, "Byzantine Medicine: Tradition and Empiricism," *Dumbarton Oaks Papers* 16 (Washington, 1962), 111. See also J. D. Thompson and G. Goldin, *The Hospital: A Social and Architectural History* (New Haven, 1975), 10.

[7] Constantelos, *Byzantine Philanthropy* (see n. 5), 155.

[8] P. S. Codellas, "The Pantocrator, the Imperial Byzantine Medical Center of 12th Century A.D. in Constantinople," *Bulletin of the History of Medicine* 12 (1942): 395–396.

[9] A. Dmitrievskij, *Opisanie liturgičeskix rukopisej*, vol. 1: *Typika* (Kiev, 1895), 682–702 (Greek text). A description of the section of the *typikon* dealing with the administration of the hospi-

units or wards of ten beds each. Two units were set aside for medical patients, and one each for surgery, gynecology, and ophthalmology. Each unit also contained a bed for emergency cases, and six others for extremely ill or bedridden patients. In addition, there was a separate psychiatric ward, primarily for the treatment of epilepsy as well as other mental disorders, an outpatient clinic, and a home for the totally disabled aged.[10] A professional staff of thirty-five men and women, including physicians' assistants and nurses, were assigned to the hospital.[11] Clergymen constituted almost the entire staff.

Various support facilities, of both a medical and nonmedical nature, were also included in the complex. There were two churches, one for male, the other for female, patients. There was a pharmacy with a professional staff of six, a library housed in a separate facility with its own personnel and copyists, baths for hydrotherapy, a kitchen bakery, a mill, a laundry, and a cemetery.[12]

The method of treatment was basically that prescribed by Galen. It was not uncommon, however, for the staff physicians to write their own methods of treatment. In this connection, it should be pointed out that the Pantocrator also housed what may be described as an unofficial medical school, staffed by a single instructor or professor. Students in the school were required to attend lectures on anatomy, physiology, and the theories of disease. In addition, they received clinical experience in the various units of the hospital itself.[13]

Shortly after the introduction of Christianity in Kievan Rus', monasticism began to take firm root among the Eastern Slavs. In fact, between the mid-eleventh and the mid-thirteenth century, some seventy monasteries were founded in the Kievan lands.[14] In its structure and broad outlines, Kievan monasticism was thoroughly Byzantine, "an offshoot," in the words of Dimitri Obolensky, "of Athonite monasticism."[15] By the late tenth century there was already some infiltration of East Slavic monks into Athonite

tal can be found in I. V. Bezobrazov's "Materialy dlja istorii Vizantijskoj imperii," *ŽMNP* 254 (November, 1887): 71-73.

[10] Codellas, "The Pantocrator" (see n. 5), 398-401.
[11] Constantelos, *Byzantine Philanthropy* (see n. 5), 174.
[12] Codellas, "The Pantocrator," 404, 406, 409-410.
[13] Ibid., 402-404, 409-410.
[14] An excellent general overview of Russian monasticism can be found in I. Smolitsch's *Russisches Mönchtum: Entstehung, Entwicklung und Wesen, 988-1917* (Würzburg, 1953). For the Kievan period, see R. P. Casey, "Early Russian Monasticism," *Orientalia Christiana Periodica* 16 (1953): 372-423. See also E. Golubinskij, *Istorija russkoj cerkvi*, vol. 1, pt. 2 (Moscow, 1904), 566.
[15] D. Obolensky, *The Byzantine Commonwealth: Eastern Europe, 500-1453* (London, 1971), 298.

monasteries. Even earlier, Athos had become a center of Slavic literary activity, with Bulgarian monks engaged in the transcription and translation of Greek manuscripts into Slavonic.[16] Sometime before the year 1016, monks from Kievan Rus', with the assistance, according to legend, of Vladimir the Saint himself, acquired a cloister of their own on the Holy Mountain, identified in the sources as the Monastery of Xylourgou.[17] A deed of purchase, dated 1013, shows that the community grew rapidy in size and expanded.[18] According to V. Mošin, it was at this early stage in the evolution of the Xylourgou monastery that the Blessed Antonij, the founder of Kievan monasticism, twice visited Athos and took his monastic vows there.[19] An inventory of the monastery's possessions, made in 1142, lists over forty books—an indication of the important role that Athos would play as a conduit of Byzantine culture into the East Slavic world. In 1169 the Rus' acquired a second monastery, that of Saint Panteleimon, which had originally been owned by Thessalonian monks, and henceforth made that their principal center.[20] There is no evidence of any organized medical activity at either of the Rus' monasteries on Athos.

The beginnings of monasticism in Kievan Rus' itself are obscure. The Primary Chronicle, in an entry for the year 1051, recounts at length the early history of the famed Pečerskij Monastery near Kiev. It is apparent, however, that this was not the first monastery founded on Kievan soil. Both the Primary Chronicle, in the same 1051 as well as in an earlier (1037) entry, and Metropolitan Ilarion, in his *Sermon on Law and Grace*, allude to the existence of monasteries before 1051.[21] Unfortunately, no further details

[16] Casey, "Early Russian Monasticism" (see n. 14), 407. Also, V. Mošin, "Russkie na Afone i russko-vizantijskie otnošenija v XI–XII vv.," *ByzSl* 9 (1947-1948): 57.

[17] M. V. Levčenko, *Očerki po istorii russko-vizantijskix otnošenij* (Moscow, 1956), 465. See also Casey, "Early Russian Monasticism" (see n. 14), 407.

[18] Levčenko, *Očerki*, 465.

[19] Mošin ("Russkie na Afone" [see n. 16], 60) dates Antonij's first visit to 1015, shortly before Vladimir's death, and the second to sometime before 1051.

[20] *Akty russkago na Svjatom Afone monastyrja sv. velikomučenika i celitelja Pantelejmona* (Kiev, 1873), 55-57. See also A. Solov'ev, "Histoire du monastère russe au Mont-Athos," *Byzantion* 8 (1933): 219. On the role of Athos, see G. Il'inskij, "Značenie Afona v istorii slavjanskoj pis'mennosti," *ŽMNP*, n.s., vol. 18, pt. 2 (November, 1908): 11. On the monastery of Saint Panteleimon, see P. Charanis, *Social, Economic and Political Life in the Byzantine Empire: Collected Studies* (London, 1973), 67-68.

[21] S. H. Cross and O. P. Sherbowitz-Wetzor, trans. and eds., *The Russian Primary Chronicle: Laurentian Text* (Cambridge, Mass., 1953), 137, 139-142. M. Heppell contends that there is evidence to suggest that the Pečerskij Monastery may have actually been founded as early as 1031, rather than 1051 as is commonly assumed; cf. "The 'Vita Antonii,' a Lost Source of the 'Paterikon' of the Monastery of Caves," *ByzSl* 13 (1952): 50 et passim. For Ilarion's sermon,

are known pertaining to the earliest stage in the evolution of monasticism in Kievan Rus'. Not so with respect to the Pečerskij Monastery. In addition to a number of both lengthy and short entries in the Primary Chronicle,[22] there is also a collection of documents known as the *Kievo-Pečerskij Paterik*. Similar to other collections in the same genre, the *Pečerskij Paterik* is not the work of a single author but a synthesis of both written and oral traditions accumulated between the mid-eleventh and late thirteenth century and ultimately attributed to the three Pečerskij monks, Nestor, Simon, and Polikarp.[23] Along with providing valuable insights into the ecclesiastical history of the period, the *Pečerskij Paterik* is the single most important source for the history of monastic medicine in Kievan Rus'. Of the thirty-eight Discourses that constitute it, eight contain information on medicine.

As is abundantly clear from a variety of sources, the Eastern Slavs embraced Christianity with a fervor characteristic of the convert. Much like in Byzantium, the emphasis in Kievan Rus' was on the Christian virtue of charity toward the underprivileged, particularly the sick and the dying.[24] The evidence for this can be found in a number of places. In Vladimir's Church Statute, for example, the sick and those caring for them, both individuals and institutions, were placed under the direct legal protection of the Church. Vladimir also stipulated that such institutions as the hospital be maintained by means of a tithe. According to the chronicles, the bishop of Perejaslavl', Efrem, established in 1091 a number of hospitals (*bol'nicy*) to provide free medical care for the sick of his eparchy. These hospitals, according to Mal'cev, were patterned after those in Byzantium, where Efrem had lived for a total of eighteen years.[25]

The care of the sick, then, was from the very beginning one of the normal functions of the Pečerskij Monastery.[26] In fact, very early in the history

---

see J. Fennell and D. Obolensky, eds., *A Historical Russian Reader* (Oxford, 1969), 13; Smolitsch, *Russisches Mönchtum* (see n. 14), 54-55.

[22] These are found under the years 1051, 1072-1075, 1089, 1091, 1096, and 1107-1110.

[23] Casey, "Early Russian Monasticism" (see n. 14), 381-383.

[24] Sokolovskij, "Blagotvoritel'nost' v drevnej Rusi," *Trudovaja pomošč'* 6 (1901): 53-56. With specific reference to the Pečerskij Monastery, see L. K. Goetz's *Das Kiever Höhlenkloster als Kulturzentrum des vormongolischen Russlands* (Passau, 1904), 165-181.

[25] On Vladimir's stipulations, see Juškov, *Pamjatniki russkogo prava* (see n. 3), p. 246, arts. 12, 15. See also A. F. Mal'cev, "O malorusskix 'spitaljax,'" *Trudy Poltavskoj učenoj arxivnoj kommissii* 4 (1907): 4. On Efrem's hospitals, see *PSRL*, vol. 9: *Letopisnyj sbornik, imenuemyj Patriaršeju ili Nikonovskoju letopis'ju* (St. Petersburg, 1862), 116; and A. F. Mal'cev, "Sv. Efrem Perejaslavskij—stroitel' pervyx bol'nic v Rossii," *Trudy Poltavskoj učenoj arxivnoj kommissii* 1 (1905): 41-42. See also M. D. Grmek, "La medicine byzantine et les peoples slaves," *XVIIᵉ Congrès international d'histoire de la medicine* 1 (Athens, 1960), 344-348.

[26] Casey, "Early Russian Monasticism" (see n. 14), 415.

of the monastery it became necessary to build a separate facility to house the large number of the sick and infirm who flocked there. In the Life of Saint Feodosij, written by the monk Nestor, we read that "he [that is Feodosij, abbot from 1062 to 1074] built a dwelling [*dvor*] close to his monastery, and a church dedicated to the holy protomartyr Stephen, and here he ordered the beggars, the blind, the lame, and the sick to stay, and gave them according to their need from the monastery, and from all that belonged to the monastery he gave a tenth part."[27] To what extent this facility actually resembled a hospital, we do not know. Judging, however, from the description of its patient-inmates, one is tempted to compare it to the hospice-hospitals prevalent in the West during the Middle Ages. Like some of the larger Western monasteries, the Pečerskij also had a separate infirmary reserved for the sick monks of the community.[28]

The medical facilities of the Pečerskij Monastery were expanded in the early twelfth century. Prince Svjatopolk Davidovič of Černigov, known in religion as Nikolaj Svjatoša, took monastic vows there in 1106.[29] Shortly thereafter he also established a hospital (*bol'nica*), staffed by a trained physician, which ultimately became the nucleus of the Bol'ničnyj Monastery. Although part of the Pečerskij complex, the Bol'ničnyj was, until the eighteenth century, an autonomous cloister headed by its own abbot who, however, was subordinate to the Pečerskij archimandrite.[30] While there are no further details in the sources regarding Svjatoša's hospital, there is evidence to suggest that the practice of medicine continued to be an important function of the monastery and that there was more than one facility set aside for that purpose. A charter of privileges granted the Pečerskij Monastery by Andrej Bogoljubskij in 1159 specifically singles out "those in the hospitals (*bol'nicy*)" in its enumeration of the people to whom the privileges are extended.[31]

As for the kind of medicine practiced in the monastery, as well as the state of medical knowledge in Kievan Rus' in general, we turn, once again, to the *Pečerskij Paterik* for clues. One is struck, first of all, by the intense rivalry between the professional court physicians and the physician-monks on the one hand, and the phsyician-monks and folk healers, or *volxvy*, on the

[27] K. I. Abramovič, ed., *Kievo-Pečerskij Paterik*, new German ed. with introd. by D. Tschiževskij (Munich, 1963), 57.

[28] Thompson and Goldin, *The Hospital* (see n. 6), 20; Abramovič, *Kievo-Pečerskij Paterik*, 181.

[29] Cross and Sherbowitz-Wetzor, *The Russian Primary Chronicle* (see n. 21), 203.

[30] Evgenij, Metropolitan of Kiev and Galicia, *Opisanie Kievopečerskoj Lavry* (Kiev, 1847), 32-33.

[31] Ibid., 166-167. The charter is reproduced in full on pp. 162-168.

other. Two prominent court physicians, one Syrian, the other Armenian, are introduced as adversaries of the physician-monks. The classic confrontation takes place between the monk Agapit and the Armenian. Agapit, who had been a disciple of Antonij, founder of the Pečerskij Monastery, was renowned both for his sanctity and his skill as a physician. The Armenian, who served as court physician to the Kievan prince Vsevolod Jaroslavič (1078-1093), was equally celebrated for his healing abilities. His fame rested in part on his mastery of prognosis. In the best Hippocratic tradition, he was able to predict accurately the course and outcome of a disease, particularly in the case of a fatally ill patient. After a certain high-ranking individual had been told by the Armenian that he had but eight days to live, he was brought to the monastery. Here he was treated by Agapit who administered a potion of cooked herbs which he had himself frequently ingested. The patient recovered immediately. The Armenian's reputation was tarnished while Agapit's fame was spread even wider. The Armenian tried several more times to outwit and outpractice the monk but to no avail. Their medical rivalry finally reached a climax when Vladimir Monomax, then prince of Černigov, became ill (allegedly in the year 1093). The Armenian was summoned from Kiev but failed to effect a cure. Then Agapit was sent for. Since the latter had taken a vow never to leave the monastery, he sent Vladimir a special potion by messenger which cured the prince of his unspecified illness. The Armenian finally admitted defeat and asked the monk about his potent herbal medicines. His own, he conceded, though imported from Alexandria, were no match for Agapit's.[32]

The rivalry between the physician-monks and the folk healers was no less intense than that between the monks and the court physicians. One of Kiev's wealthier residents was afflicted with leprosy. After he had sought a cure in vain from the pagan *volxvy*, he came to the Pečerskij Monastery where he was washed with water from the tomb of Saint Feodosij. This only exacerbated his condition. The stench from his body had become so strong now that people shunned him and he was forced to remain indoors, in quarantine. In desperation he went to see Alimpij, a Pečerskij monk who was also an accomplished painter of icons. The latter smeared his face with the chalk, or lime, that he used in his painting and then administered the Eucharist to him. Finally, he told him to go and wash the lime off his face with water. The man's unsightly sores soon disappeared and he was told to

---

[32] Abramovič, *Kievo-Pečerskij Paterik* (see n. 27), 128-133. The basis for the Armenian's prognostic skill was apparently his ability to take and correctly interpret the pulse of patients, as he did in the case of Agapit himself when the latter had become ill.

go and show himself to the priests, who would confirm and certify the cure and, presumably, lift the quarantine.[33]

In addition to leprosy and several unspecified illnesses, the diseases mentioned in the *Pečerskij Paterik* as being treated in the monastery are epilepsy, fever, urinary obstruction, and kidney dysfunction. The prevailing mode of therapy was herbal.[34] This was often accompanied, as might be expected, by a liberal dose of prayer. Hydrotherapy, in the form of the *banja*, or steam bath, was also common, particularly in the treatment of chronic conditions such as gout and rheumatoid arthritis.[35] There are no references either to phlebotomy (bloodletting) or surgery of any sort.

As for the sources of medical knowledge available to the Pečerskij monks, there was, first of all, the *Izbornik Svjatoslava* (1073), a work of encyclopedic scope containing, among other things, medicohygienic and dietetic advice as well as a section on medical botany.[36] Another early source of medical information was the so-called "Theology of Saint John Damascene." Translated into Old Bulgarian (Old Church Slavonic) by John, Exarch of Bulgaria, it gained steadily in popularity from the tenth century on. In addition to astronomical knowledge, Damascene's writings contain references to the four basic elements in nature and their corresponding humors in the human body. Also written by John, exarch of Bulgaria, was the *Šestodnev* (*Hexaëmeron*) which, though primarily a theological tract, contains sections on human anatomy, physiology, and *materia medica*. It should be noted that the *Šestodnev* borrows freely from such classical writers as Aristotle, Dioscorides, Theophrastos, Hippocrates, and Galen.[37] A fourth Byzantine source, popular in Kievan Rus' from the early eleventh century, was the *Fiziolog* (*Physiologos*), a collection of fantastic bird and animal stories with a liberal dose of medicobiological information.[38]

---

[33] Ibid., 174-175.

[34] In this connection, see the interesting essay by M. Rowell, "Russian Medical Botany before the Time of Peter the Great," *Sudhoffs Archiv* 62 (1978): 339-358.

[35] X. Schaffgotsch, "The Russian Steam Bath," *CIBA Symposium* 12 (1964): 93.

[36] The 1073 version of the *Izbornik* was published in a facsimile edition in St. Petersburg in 1880 by the Obščestvo ljubitelej drevnej pis'mennosti. A different version, dating from 1076, was published by V. S. Golyšenko et al., *Izbornik 1076 goda* (Moscow, 1965).

[37] The "Theology" was published in *ČOIDR*, 1877, bk. 4; the *Šestodnev* was published in *ČOIDR*, 1879, bk. 3. On classical borrowings from the latter, see N. A. Bogojavlenskij, *Drevnerusskoe vračevanie v XI–XVII vv. Istočniki dlja izučenija istorii russkoj mediciny* (Moscow, 1960), 19.

[38] A. Karneev, *Materialy i zametki po literaturnoj istorij "Fiziologa,"* Izdanie Imperatorskogo obščestva ljubitelej drevnej pis'mennosti i iskusstva, no. 92 (Moscow, 1890).

With the dawn of the so-called Mongol period in the mid-thirteenth century, there is a shift of both political power and population from the
Kievan lands in the south to the Muscovite lands in the northeast. During
this turbulent period Russian medicine was, with the exception of folk medicine, largely in the hands of monks. Not a single name of a secular physician can be found in the contemporary sources.[39] Illustrative of the high
esteem in which the clergy was held for its medical expertise is an entry in
the chronicles for the year 1357. An envoy from Sarai arrived in Moscow
with an urgent plea from the Tsaritsa Taidula, the wife of the khan, for
Metropolitan Aleksej to come and cure her of a disease of the eyes from
which she had been suffering for the past three years. Aleksej went and
successfully treated the woman who, in gratitude, sent him home "with
great honor" and, presumably, fitting compensation.[40] Why did the tsaritsa
specifically ask for Aleksej? According to F. Dörbeck, the metropolitan
"enjoyed the reputation of being a good ophthalmologist,"[41] a conclusion
that Dörbeck does not document but which, on the surface at least,
appears plausible in light of what we know about Aleksej's career. In 1353,
a year before his elevation to the highest ecclesiastical office, the Byzantine
patriarch summoned him to Constantinople where he remained for the next
two years.[42] With his apparent interest in medicine, it is not at all unlikely
that Aleksej, during his stay in Constantinople, would have availed himself
of the opportunity of visiting and perhaps even studying at the famed
Pantocrator hospital which boasted, as was noted earlier, a separate oph-
thalmological unit.

Since the Horde, generally speaking, assumed a benevolent attitude
toward the Church and its institutions, they grew and prospered.[43] New
monasteries sprang up in rapid succession, eventually becoming the spiritual and intellectual centers of medieval Muscovy. Among the most illustrious of these were the Trinity-Sergius Monastery, some forty miles north-
east of Moscow, and the Kirillo-Belozerskij, located deep in the forests of
the Beloozero region, approximately three hundred miles north of Moscow.
In addition to their many other important contributions to the cultural
history of Muscovite Russia, both institutions were also actively engaged in

[39] M. Ju. Laxtin, *Medicina i vrači v Moskovskom gosudarstve v do-Petrovskoj Rusi, Učenye zapiski Imperatorskogo Moskovskogo universiteta, Medicinskogo fakul'teta* 10 (Moscow, 1907), 8.
[40] *PSRL*, vol. 8: *Prodolženie letopisej po Voskresenskomu spisku* (St. Petersburg, 1859), 1.
For additional details, see E. Golubinskij, *Istorija russkoj cerkvi*, vol. 2, pt. 1 (Moscow, 1917),
374-375.
[41] F. Dörbeck, "Origin of Medicine in Russia," *Medical Life* 30 (1923): 225.
[42] Golubinskij, *Istorija russkoj cerkvi* (see n. 40), vol. 2, pt. 1: 177ff.
[43] G. Vernadsky, *The Mongols and Russia* (New Haven, 1953), 165, 377-379.

the practice of medicine and served as modest depositories of medical knowledge.

The Trinity-Sergius Monastery was founded by the illustrious Sergij (Sergius) of Radonež in the mid-fourteenth century. Epifanij the Wise, in his biography of Sergij written in 1418, records the early history of the monastery. Unfortunately, Epifanij's account contains only one general reference to medicine. In his description of the division of labor in the community, he notes that Sergij "appointed to each brother his duties, one to be cellarer, others to be cooks and bakers, another to care for the sick," and so forth.[44] As was true of the Kievan monasteries, so too in the Muscovite cloisters: the care of the sick was high on the priority list of daily duties.

Although direct evidence is lacking regarding the nature and scope of medical activity in the Trinity-Sergius Monastery before the mid-sixteenth century, it is possible to draw some suggestive inferences on the basis of the monastery's excellent library holdings. According to A. V. Gorskij, the library was founded by Saint Sergij himself. From its modest beginnings in the late fourteenth century, it grew and increased its holdings rapidly. The most significant period of growth occurred in the first half of the fifteenth century, while Nikon (1392–1428), Savva (1429–1432), and Zinovij (1432–1443) were abbots. As the colophons of many of the early manuscripts attest, a large proportion of the library's books came from Mount Athos were they were transcribed or translated from the Greek into Church Slavonic.[45]

There are a number of manuscripts in the Trinity-Sergius collection that are of general interest to the medical historian. Among the oldest is a late twelfth– to early thirteenth-century *sbornik* containing part of an early herbal. There are five copies of the *Paleja* (known also as the *Tolkovaja Paleja*), the earliest of which is dated 1406. In addition to being an exposition of biblical history, the *Paleja* offers some unusual explanations of natural phenomena, human embryology, anatomy, as well as information culled from sundry herbals and lapidaries. The *Šestodnev*, already popular in Kievan times as a source of medical knowledge, as we have seen, is well represented in the library. The collection also includes a copy of the *Pčela*, containing quotations and adages from the Church Fathers as well as from the ancients. Of some seventy chapters into which the *Pčela* is divided, four

---

[44] S. A. Zenkovsky, ed., *Medieval Russia's Epics, Chronicles, and Tales,* rev. ed. (New York, 1974), 281.

[45] *Opisanie slavjanskix rukopisej biblioteki Svjato-Troickoj Sergievoj Lavry, ČOIDR,* 1878, pt. 1, bk. 2, sec. 3; see also, ibid., 1879, pt. 3, bk. 2: 141.

are devoted to hygiene and medicine, with the most interesting entitled "On Physicians."[46]

Of special interest, from the standpoint of medicine and science in general, are a number of shorter manuscripts incorporated into some of the library's larger miscellanies, or *sborniki*. Thoroughly secular and, in some instances, even non-Christian in spirit and content, these scientific and pseudoscientific tracts are a stark reminder that the Muscovite monasteries, at least the more prominent ones, were by no means intellectual backwaters. A fifteenth-century anthology of selected writings of Saint John Damascene, for example, also contains short treatises on the following: bloodletting, the twelve signs of the zodiac, the phases of the moon, the relationship bewteen illness and astrology, and the "Galinovo na Ipokrata" (Galen on Hippocrates), a terser overview of Galen's physiology and of what is essentially the classic humoral theory of disease. A second fifteenth-century *sbornik* contains, in addition to medical and astrological works identical to those found in the Damascene anthology, an excerpt from Menander Protector, the sixth-century Byzantine historian, and the *Gromnik*, an astrological tract attributed to the Byzantine Emperor Heraklios. A *sbornik* from the beginning of the sixteenth century explores such topics as thunder and lightning, meteors, the oceans, and the creatures of the land, sea, and air.[47]

Whether these medical, scientific, and pseudoscientific texts were read and studied is a moot question. One cannot be certain, also, to what extent they provided the theoretical basis for the practice of medicine in the Trinity-Sergius Monastery. The fact that there was more than one copy of the treatises on bloodletting, theory of disease, and critical days would seem to indicate that they were in some demand, which perhaps reflects on the kind of medicine practiced at the monastery in the fifteenth and sixteenth centuries.

There is no mention in the early sources of any special medical facilities at the monastery until 1552. That year, according to the so-called Short Chronicle of the Trinity-Sergius Monastery, "they erected a hospital (*bol-*

[46] On the *sbornik*, see ibid., 1878, pt. 1, bk. 2: 19, no. 12. On the *Paleja*, see ibid., 45-46, no. 38. The *Paleja* was published in the Izdanie Obščestva ljubitelej drevnej pis'mennosti, no. 93 (St. Petersburg, 1892). The *Šestodnev* had ten complete and two fragmentary copies; see *Opisanie slavjanskix rukopisej, ČOIDR*, 1878, pt. 2, bk. 4: 124-126, nos. 375-384; also 95, no. 317; and 1878, pt. 1, bk. 2: 30, no. 15. On the *Pčela*, see ibid., 1879, pt. 3, bk. 2: 127-128, no. 735; also, V. Semenov, ed., *Drevnjaja russkaja Pčela, po pergamennomu spisku* (St. Petersburg, 1893), esp. "On Physicians," 316-320.

[47] On these three works, see *Opisanie slavjanskix rukopisej* (see n. 45), 1878, pt. 1, bk. 2: 159-160, no. 177; ibid., 169-171, no. 762; and ibid., 186-187, no. 769.

nica) at the Sergius Monastery, as well as a stone cell...."[48] Because of the ambiguous placement of the modifying adjective, there is some confusion as to whether or not the hospital was built of stone or wood. The most recent scholarship, based largely on archeological evidence and painstaking reconstruction of the original buildings, has established that the 1552 structure was wooden.[49] Apparently, by 1635 this building was no longer standing, for in that year a new stone hospital with an adjacent tent-roofed church was begun. Completed two years later, this new hospital was relatively large and was divided into four units or wards.[50]

The Short Chronicle does not make clear for whom the hospitals, both the earlier and later ones, were intended. Gorskij maintains that they were restricted to old and infirm monks of the cloister. While the latter may have indeed been admitted into the hospital and cared for as patients, it should also be remembered that most monasteries maintained separate facilities for the aged and infirm on the one hand and for the sick on the other.[51] This distinction between a hospital (*bol'nica*) and rest home or almshouse (*bogadel'nja*) was preserved at the Trinity-Sergius Monastery. Writing in the mid-seventeenth century, the monk Simon Azarin describes how under the archimandrite Dionisij (1610–33), the monastery intensified its efforts on behalf of the sick and the poor. An appalling number of people had fallen victim to the military chaos and suffering spawned by the Time of Troubles. Taking the initiative, the monks of the Trinity-Sergius Monastery went out and brought many of the sick, wounded, and the abused to the monastery. Some were placed in the hospital, others in the almshouses.[52]

While in Western Europe, it was the urban monasteries that served as a focus of intellectual activity during the Middle Ages, by contrast, the monasteries of medieval Russia with the greatest intellectual impact were those located in the remote and sparsely populated regions of the North.[53] It was in this tradition that the Kirillo-Belozerskij Monastery, located some three

[48] A. Byčkov, "Kratkij letopisec Svjatotroickija Sergievy Lavry," *Letopis' zanjatij Arxeografičeskoj kommissii* 3 (St. Petersburg, 1865), 21 in the Appendix.

[49] Byčkov assumes that it was of stone; ibid., no. 48. A. V. Gorskij, in his history of the monastery, likewise refers to the hospital as a stone building; see his *Istoričeskoe opisanie Svjato-Troickija Sergievy Lavry, ČOIDR*, 1878, bk. 4: 7. For archaeological evidence, see I. V. Trofimov, *Pamjatniki arxitektury Troice-Sergievoj Lavry* (Moscow, 1961), 82.

[50] Byčkov, "Kratkij letopisec" (see n. 48), 26; Trofimov, *Pamjatniki arxitektury*, 82, illus. 69-72.

[51] Gorskij, *Istoričeskoe opisanie* (see n. 49), 27. Also, Trofimov, *Pamjatniki arxitektury* (see n. 49), 82.

[52] S. Azarin, "Kniga o novojavlennyx čudesax prepodobnogo Sergija. Tvorenie kelarja Simona Azarina," *Pamjatniki drevnej pis'mennosti* 70 (1888): 22.

[53] A. N. Kirpičnikov and I. N. Xlopin, *Velikaja gosudareva krepost'* (Leningrad, 1972), 9.

hundred miles north of Moscow, evolved and gained fame as a center of learning and scholarship. Very early it had become a major literary center, producing its own literary style and form of book illumination.[54] In addition to its founder, Kirill, the monastery had, over the years, boasted a number of other prominent literary figures. Among the more illustrious of these were the two monks Efrosin and Gurij Tušin, the latter also serving as abbot briefly in 1484. Efrosin wrote an early version of the well-known epic *Zadonščina* and "a host of other literary, medical, and natural-scientific works." Gurij Tušin wrote, in addition to many religious works, "Proročestva ellinskix mudrecov," which draws heavily on such classical Greek writers as Plato, Aristotle, Homer, Euripides, Pythagoras, and others.[55]

The founder of the Kirillo-Belozerskij Monastery was a scion of a prominent boyar family. He was ordained a priest and then entered the Simonov Monastery in Moscow. Becoming dissatisfied with life there, he left for the North, at the age of sixty, with several other monks. In 1397 he founded his own monastery in a forest midway between the old towns of Vologda and Beloozero. A well-read and learned man, Kirill had engaged in literary activity, both writing and translating, while still at the Simonov Monastery. Eleven original manuscripts and four miscellanies, or *sborniki*, are ascribed to him.[56]

As was true of the Trinity-Sergius Monastery, so too with the Kirillo-Belozerskij: the earliest evidence of interest in medicine can be found in its library. Kirill and his successors were bibliophiles who made a conscious effort to acquire books and manuscripts, not necessarily restricted to religious topics. According to Rozov, between the fifteenth and seventeenth centuries the monastery's library had few rivals in Russia. In the history of Russian bibliography, the Kirillo-Belozerskij Monastery has the distinction of being the first to compile a complete, annotated catalog of its library holdings. This was in the late fifteenth century. Another significant development, dating from the mid-seventeenth century, if not earlier, was the

---

[54] This was characterized by simple geometric ornamentation, reminiscent of North Russian wood and stone carving. N. N. Rozov, "Rukopisi iz Kirillovskogo kraevedčeskogo muzeja," *Trudy Gosudarstvennoj publičnoj biblioteki imeni M. E. Saltykova-Ščedrina* 1, no. 4 (1957): 285.

[55] On Efrosin, see Kirpičnikov and Xlopin, *Velikaja gosudareva krepost'* (see n. 53), 207. On Tušin, see N. A. Kazakova, *Očerki po istorii russkoj obščestvennoj mysli* (Leningrad, 1970), 270.

[56] Kirpičnikov and Xlopin, *Velikaja gosudareva krepost'* (see n. 53), 19-21. Also, N. N. Rozov, "Iz istorii Kirillo-Belozerskoj biblioteki," *Trudy Gosudarstvennoj publičnoj biblioteki imeni M. E. Saltykova-Ščedrina* 9, no. 12 (1961): 178-179. A detailed description of his eleven original manuscripts can be found in Arximandrite Varlaam's "Obozrenie rukopisej sobstvennoj biblioteki Kirilla Belozerskogo," *ČOIDR*, 1890, bk. 2: 1-69.

establishment of branch libraries at several key sites, including at the larger of the monastery's two hospitals.[57] This branch medical library was probably the first of its kind in Russia.

Kirill himself apparently had a more than casual interest in medicine, for the earliest known version of the "Galinovo na Ipokrata" is attributed to him. It is included in one of the four *sborniki* that he is credited with compiling. The Kirillo-Belozerskij copy of this Galenic medical tract has been dated 1424. It is said to have been transcribed by Kirill from an existing Slavonic translation of unknown provenance but, presumably, traceable to Mount Athos. The same *sbornik* also contains an essay on the development of the human embryo as well as several other pieces of a purely scientific rather than a medical nature.[58]

Since it was the largest institution of its kind in the entire region, the Kirillo-Belozerskij Monastery could be expected to maintain medical facilities commensurate with its size. Not only did it have to provide medical care for its own growing community of monks, it had also to minister to the needs of the large peasant population on its estates.[59] It should thus come as no surprise that by the 1530s the monastery supported four hospitals, one of which was specifically set aside for laymen. There was, in addition, a separate almshouse which accommodated eleven individuals, for whose upkeep the tsar had set aside funds from his own local estates.[60] Nothing is known about these medical facilities other than that they were all wooden and thus fell easy prey to the fire that destroyed much of the

[57] Rozov, "Iz istorii Kirillo-Belozerskoj biblioteki," 177, 185-186. Also, Rozov, "Rukopisi iz Kirillovskogo kraevedčeskogo muzeja" (see n. 54), 285. The annotated catalog, which contains 212 entries, was published together with an interpretive essay and extensive explanatory notes by N. Nikol'skij as *Opisanie rukopisej Kirillo-Belozerskogo monastyrja sostavlennoe v konce XV veka* (St. Petersburg, 1897).

[58] On the attribution to Kirill, see Bogojavlenskij, *Drevnerusskoe vračevanie* (see n. 37), 32. The text of the "Galinovo na Ipokrata" was published by L. F. Zmeev in his *Russkie vračebniki* (St. Petersburg, 1896), 242-245. For further descriptions of the tract, its dating, transcription, and general contents, see Rozov, "Iz istorii Kirillo-Belozerskoj biblioteki" (see n. 56), 180; also, Bogojavlenskij, *Drevnerusskoe vračevanie* (see n. 37), 32. The *sbornik*'s scientific pieces deal with geography, the four elements in nature, and natural phenomena such as thunder, lightning, clouds, and the morning star. Excerpts from some of the scientific pieces can be found in S. P. Sevyrev, *Poezdka v Kirillo-Belozerskij monastyr'*, vol. 2 (Moscow, 1850), 23-25.

[59] In 1584 the community numbered 200 monks; in 1601 the figure had reached 773; Kirpičnikov and Xlopin, *Velikaja gosudareva krepost'* (see n. 53), 35. By the mid-seventeenth century the monastery had become the fifth largest landowner in Russia, surpassed only by the Trinity-Sergius Monastery, the Romanovs, the Morozovs, and the Patriarch. It owned 3,854 *dvors*, inhabited by some 20,000 peasants; ibid., 34-35.

[60] On the monastery hospitals, see N. Nikol'skij, *Kirillo-Belozerskij monastyr' i ego ustrojstvo do vtoroj četverti XVII veka, 1397-1625*, vol. 1, pt. 1 (St. Petersburg, 1897), 29. On the almshouse funding, see *RIB* 2 (St. Petersburg, 1875), col. 31, no. 30, cols. 32-33, no. 32.

monastery in 1557. After the fire, the four smaller hospitals were amalgamated into a single larger structure, which in 1643 was one of the first
wooden buildings to be converted into stone.[61]

Recently restored, this larger monastery hospital, as distinguished from a
smaller one built in 1730, measures 35 by 17.5 meters. A relatively low
building with a sloping roof, it is divided into two large wards, each meas-
uring 220 square meters. Separating the two wards is a wide corridor of
5.35 meters. A series of small but well-placed windows provide ample light
and ventilation. The interior is spartan and functional.[62] A year after the
completion of the hospital, a stone, tent-roofed church, dedicated to Saint
Evfimij, was built adjacent to it.[63] It is not known if admission and treatment were restricted to the monastic community. The arrangement of the
two wards, however, might suggest that half of the hopsital was set aside
for monks, the other half for laymen.

Judging from the location of the two Kirlilo-Belozerskij hospitals, in
secluded corners of the monastery compound, one would have to conclude
that rest and quiet were basic to the prevailing mode of therapy.[64] Unlike at
the Trinity-Sergius Monastery, there are no surviving treatises on bloodletting from the Kirillo-Belozerskij library. This, coupled with the absence of
surgical instruments, would seem to rule out the practice of surgery by the
Kirillo-Belozerskij monks.[65] It should be noted, however, that while to date
only a few surgical instruments have been unearthed by Russian archeolo-
gists, surgery, called *rezanie* or *xytrost' železnaja*, had evolved as a separate
branch of medicine as early as Kievan times.[66] By the late fifteenth century
barber-surgeons, or *krovopuski*, were common fixtures in the Novgorod
region.[67]

Like its Byzantine prototype, East Slavic monasticism was firmly rooted
in the Christian virtue of charity, particularly as it pertained to the poor
and the sick. Given the philanthropic emphasis, it was quite natural for the
monasteries of Kievan Rus' and Muscovite Russia to take a leading role in

---

[61] Kirpičnikov and Xlopin, *Velikaja gosudareva krepost'* (see n. 53), 35, 103.

[62] Ibid., see fig. 2.

[63] Ibid., 104, see fig. 3.

[64] See fig. 2 for the location of both hospitals.

[65] A ban on surgery by clerics would have been consistent with the Church's traditional
attitude toward the shedding of blood. For an excellent reevaluation of the Church's attitude
toward surgery in medieval Europe, see D. W. Amundsen's "Medieval Law on Medical and
Surgical Practice by the Clergy," *Bulletin of the History of Medicine* 52 (1978): 22–44.

[66] N. A. Bogojavlenskij, "Značenie dannyx arxeologii pri izučenii istorii otečestvennoj mediciny," *Sovetskoe zdravooxranenie* 27 (1963): 66.

[67] B. A. Rybakov, *Remeslo drevnej Rusi* (Moscow, 1948), 558.

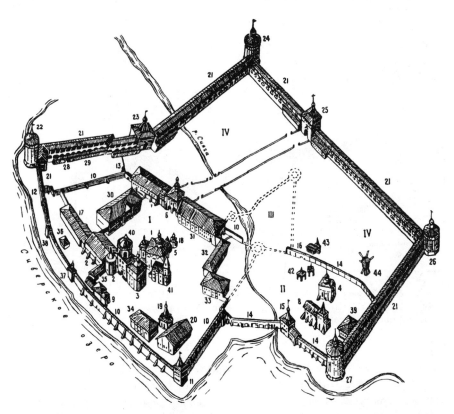

Fig. 1.   View of the Kirillo-Belozerskij Monastery with the large and small hospitals (nos. 20 and 39, respectively) in lower foreground. From A. N. Kirpičnikov and I. N. Xlopin, *Velikaja gosudareva krepost'* (Leningrad, 1972). Reprinted with permission.

Fig. 2.   Restored exterior wall of the larger Kirillo-Belozerskij hospital. From A. N. Kirpič-nikov and I. N. Xlopin, *Velikaja gosudareva krepost'* (Leningrad, 1972). Reprinted with permission.

Fig. 3.   Artist's reconstruction of the larger Kirillo-Belozerskij hospital with Church of Saint
Evfimij. From A. N. Kirpičnikov and I. N. Xlopin, *Velikaja gosudareva krepost'* (Leningrad,
1972). Reprinted with permission.

the practice of medicine. They built hospitals after the Byzantine fashion
and read some of the Greek medical texts in translation, but they also
relied on native *materia medica* and the *banja*, or steam bath, for basic
therapy. The result was an amalgamated medical tradition, one which
would endure well into the seventeenth century and beyond.

In conclusion, we may ask: What do the sources examined here suggest?
First, that there was a genuine monastic medical tradition in Kievan Rus'
and early Muscovy, one which, though admittedly not as sophisticated or
"scientific" as the Byzantine, compares favorably to what obtained in the
West; second, and more significant, that the life of the mind in the Kievan
and Muscovite monastery was not quite as sterile or one-dimensional as
has frequently been alleged. In light of this, it is perhaps time for a
thoughtful and probing overall reevaluation of the intellectual history of
medieval Russia, with particular emphasis on the legacy of the monasteries.

ON THE SO-CALLED
CHERSONIAN ANTIQUITIES

ANDRZEJ POPPE

In seventeenth- and eighteenth-century inventories, from large and small churches all over Russia as well as from private and public collections and museums, there are some cult objects of different ages and provenances, especially icons and crosses, that are described as "Korsunian." The adjective *Korsunian* suggests that these objects originated in Cherson (the Korsun' of the Old Rusian sources). It has been known for a long time, however, that most of them cannot, in fact, be Chersonian in origin. A strong conviction has evolved nevertheless that the adjective *Korsunian* originally referred to those cult objects brought to Rus' from Cherson (as we are told by the Primary Chronicle for the year 989, recording the baptism of the Rusian prince Vladimir) and was later applied to some Old Rusian precious cult objects that were distinguished by their artistic value and were archaic in origin.

The last observation, not entirely unfounded, derives from the fact that beginning in the seventeenth century, the clergy sought Korsunian cult relics for their churches. This cult was further promoted by antiquarians who found support in scientific works that assigned to Cherson an exceptional role regarding artistic influences on Rusian art of the tenth to thirteenth centuries.[1] Twentieth-century data, mainly archaeological, make it possible to ascertain that Cherson did not, in fact, exert the influences ascribed to it on the culture, the art, or even the artistic handicrafts of Kievan Rus'. It turns out that more than ten pectoral crosses with Slavonic inscriptions from excavations in Cherson, earlier regarded as proof of the production of local workshops for the market of Rus', should rather be connected with the migration of the Rusian population that fled there from the Mongol invasion in the middle of the thirteenth century.[2]

Translated from the Polish by Henrik Birnbaum.

[1] N. P. Kondakov, *Russkie klady* (St. Petersburg, 1896), 42-43, 46-47.
[2] G. F. Korzuxina, "O pamjatnikax 'korsunskogo dela' na Rusi (Po materialam mednogo lit'ja)," *VV* 14 (1958): 129-137. A. L. Jakobson, "Russko-korsunskie svjazi XI–XIV vv.," *VV* 14 (1958): 117-128, considered that in the early medieval period the cultural and economic ties of

In opposition to N. Kondakov, who linked Chersonian influences with
pre-Mongolian Rus', A. Sobolevskij was prepared to date the influx of
"Chersonian" objects into Rusian lands to the thirteenth and fourteenth
centuries. According to Sobolevskij, after 1204, when direct contact between
Rus' and Byzantium ceased, Cherson and other Crimean towns such as
Sugdaia and Caffa began furnishing cult objects. The artistic products of
various origins which thus found their way to Rus' began to be called "Korsunian."[3] This hypothesis is derived from the age determinations of many
"Korsunian antiquities," mainly icons.

The essence of the matter rests, nonetheless, not only with the age of the
relics themselves (some of which did originate in the eleventh century) but
also with the circumstances under which they began to be called "Korsunian," circumstances that are so far unclear. The sources do not corrob-
orate G. F. Korzuxina's claim that as the genuine "Korsunian" icons and
other cult objects brought to Rus' from Cherson in 989 were exhausted,
local ones were substituted and the old designation transferred to them.[4]

In seeking an answer to this question, one should take into account all
Old Rusian references to "Chersonian" objects as well as the oldest objects
referred to as "Korsunian" themselves.

The Icon of Saint Nikolaj Zarazskij "from Cherson"

Apparently one of the earliest, if not the most ancient, references to a
"Korsunian" cult object is found in the cycle of Rjazan' stories about Saint
Nikolaj Zarazskij, the first of which relates the story about the bringing "of
the miracle-working icon of the great miracle-worker Nikolaj Korsunskij
Zarazskij from the renamed city of Cherson, into the land of Rjazan'" in

---

Kievan Rus' stretched directly to Constantinople, bypassing Cherson or using it as a transition
point. His suggestion that Cherson became the center of constant economic and cultural ties
with Rusian lands beginning in the thirteenth century is not very convincing, especially since
Nogaj's capture of the city in 1299 terminated the flourishing urban life of Cherson; see below
n. 3, and J. Smedley, "Archeology and the History of Cherson: A Survey of Some Results and
Problems," *Arxeion Pontou* 35 (1979): 172-192.

[3] A. I. Sobolevskij, "Dva slova o 'korsunskix predmetax,'" *Novgorodskaja cerkovnaja starina. Trudy Novgorodskogo cerkovnoarxeologičeskogo obščestva* 1 (Novgorod, 1914), 63-65.
From the thirteenth century on, Surož-Sugdaia became the center of Russo-Crimean trade
relations, which is indicated by the spreading of this city's name throughout the entire
Crimean Peninsula (the merchants trading with the Crimea were called "Surožane"; the Sea of
Azov was called "Surožean" in Rus'). See the article surveying the basic literature on the subject, D. Andrews, "Moscow and the Crimea in the 13th to 15th Centuries," *Arxeion Pontou* 35
(1979): 261-281. Following A. Sobolevskij, we would expect the imported cult objects in Rus'
to be called "Surožean" and not "Chersonian."

[4] Korzuxina, "O pamjatnikax" (see n. 2), 137.

1225.[5] Nonetheless, the complicated literary history of this cycle—parts of which were formed at different times but which were copied as a single entity in the manuscript tradition known to us—does not sufficiently support the accepted fourteenth-century dating of the primary text.[6] Doubts are raised not by the fact that the two most ancient manuscripts from among the more than seventy extant copies belong to the end of the sixteenth century (since a significant hiatus between the compilation of a work and its earliest copy is quite common in the Old Rusian tradition), but by the fact that, clearly, the reconstructed history of the literary life of this text, attested in eleven versions, belongs essentially to the seventeenth to eighteenth centuries, with marks even of the second half of the sixteenth century found in the most ancient of them, the so-called basic version.[7] The year 1560, indirectly recorded in the *Lineage of the Servants of the Miracle-worker Nikola Zaraskov*,[8] probably points to the composition of the cycle of stories about Nikolaj Zarazskij as a single entity, while the question about the time of the compilation of its constituent parts remains open. Of these parts, the primary and most ancient is generally considered to be the well-known *Tale of Batu's Destruction of Rjazan'*. It opens with the report of Batu's invasion of the land of Rus' in the twelfth year after bringing the miracle-working icon of Saint Nikolaj from Cherson. The accepted dating of this tale rests on the premise that the traces of influence upon it from subsequent literary works are later insertions.[9] It is noted, in particular, that the lament of the Rjazan' prince Ingvar' over the demise of all the people close to him and the destruction of Rjazan' had as its source the lament of the widowed princess in *The Tale of the Life and Passing of Grand*

[5] *Voinskie povesti drevnej Rusi* (Moscow–Leningrad, 1949), 249.

[6] It is accepted that the two initial tales of the cycle be considered the basic ones: the previously mentioned *Transference of the Icon of Saint Nikolaj* and the military *Tale About Batu's Destruction of Rjazan'*; see *Istoki russkoj belletristiki* (Leningrad, 1970), 284-285, 287. In the opinion of the author of this section, L. A. Dmitriev, the first tale is older than the second and their merger took place in the first half of the fourteenth century. N. V. Vodovozov's attempt —in an article and subsequently in his *Istorija drevnerusskoj literatury* (Moscow, 1958), 112-116—to ascribe authorship of both tales to Evstafij, the literary participant in the transference of the icon to Rjazan' and the son of the Chersonian priest Eustaphios, must be considered odd.

[7] The literary history of the writing has been clarified thanks to the thorough textual study and publication of all its versions by D. S. Lixačev, "Povesti o Nikole Zarazskom. Teksty," *TODRL* 12 (1949): 257-406. The cycle was also published in nearly complete form (based on a few manuscripts) in *Voinskie povesti* (see n. 5), 9-29, 243-255.

[8] Lixačev, "Povesti," 302, 322; *Voinskie povesti*, 253.

[9] Lixačev, "Povesti," 258-264. Cf. J. Fennell and A. Stokes, *Early Russian Literature* (Berkeley–Los Angeles, 1974), 88-96; cf. the English translation of the *Tale* in *Medieval Russia's Epics, Chronicles and Tales*, ed. S. A. Zenkovsky (New York, 1974), 198-207.

Prince Dmitrij Ivanovič, Tsar of Rus'.[10] But as has been convincingly shown, the latter tale is a work composed in the late 1440s.[11] In the *Tale of the Destruction of Rjazan'* there also appear traces of influence from the *Tale of the Capture of Constantinople in 1453*, based on the notes of an eyewitness to the actual event and available in a reworked version from the beginning of the sixteenth century.[12] More complicated is the relationship between the *Tale of the Destruction of Rjazan'* and the Chronicle's *Tale of the Invasion of Moscow in 1382 by Toxtamyš*, found in a short version from the beginning of the fifteenth century and in an expanded one from the middle of the same century.[13] An incisive explanation of the twofold influence of the *Tale of the Destruction of Rjazan'* on the text of the story about Toxtamyš's invasion of Moscow derives from a presumption about the primacy of the first in relation to the latter.[14] However, textual parallels also render conceivable an opposite and less complicated single influence; it is therefore easier to assume that the more expanded story about the invasion by Toxtamyš (in the Fourth Novgorod Chronicle) influenced the *Tale of the Destruction of Rjazan'*. This is all the more plausible as the latter undoubtedly used a chronicle compilation in which the tale of the invasion by Toxtamyš occurs on an equal footing with the *Tale of the Life and Passing of Grand Prince Dmitrij Ivanovič.*

A conclusion about the late—no earlier than the second half of the fifteenth century—compilation of the *Tale of the Destruction of Rjazan'* would be premature. Yet the suggestion that it belongs to the first half of the fourteenth or even to the end of the thirteenth century remains an

---

[10] V. P. Adrianova-Peretc, "Slovo o žitii i prestavlenii velikogo knjazja Dmitrija Ivanoviča, carja rus'skago," *TODRL* 5 (1947): 94-95; D. S. Lixačev, "Literaturnaja sud'ba Povesti o razorenii Rjazani Batyem v pervoj četverti XV veka," in *Issledovanija i materialy po drevnerusskoj literature. Sbornik statej* (Moscow, 1961), 16-20; id., *Tekstologija* (Moscow–Leningrad, 1962), 254-258.

[11] M. A. Salmina, "Slovo o žitii i o prestavlenii velikogo knjazja Dmitrija Ivanoviča, carja rus'skago," *TODRL* 25 (1970): 81-104; M. F. Antonova, "Slovo o žitii i o prestavlenii velikogo knjazja Dmitrija Ivanoviča, carja rus'skago," *TODRL* 28 (1974): 140-154; W. Vodoff, "Quand a pu être composé le Panégyrique du grand-prince Dmitrii Ivanovich, tsar' russe?" *Canadian-American Slavic Studies* 13, nos. 1-2 (1979): 82-101.

[12] M. N. Speranskij, "Povesti i skazanija o vzjatii Car'grada turkami," *TODRL* 10 (1954): 136-165; Ja. S. Lur'e, *Ideologičeskaja bor'ba v russkoj publicistike konca XV–načala XVI veka* (Moscow–Leningrad, 1960), 355-356.

[13] A short account in the chronicle compilation of 1408, expanded in that of 1448. See M. A. Salmina, "Povest' o našestvii Toxtamyša," *TODRL* 34 (1979): 143-151. Cf. Ja. S. Lur'e, *Obščerusskie letopisnye svody XIV–XVI vv.* (Leningrad, 1976), 65-66.

[14] Lixačev, "Literaturnaja sud'ba" (see n. 10), 11-16; also id., *Tekstologija* (see n. 10), 249-252 (cf. the correspondences cited there).

unreliable hypothesis and requires more weighty proof.[15] The proposed attempt to reconstruct the ancient text of the *Tale* might play an important role here.[16] Such a reconstruction requires the removal of all texts recognized as insertions in the original and the exclusion of all later stylistic and linguistic phenomena, traces of Turkic influence which, incidentally, are clearly related to the fifteenth and sixteenth centuries.[17] But would these measures not violate the composition and thematic unity of the work? The *Tale of the Destruction of Rjazan'* in its present form is an artistic work, and although it deals with an important historical event, it is not very historical.[18] Moreover, the factual aspect of the event in the *Tale* is not only insufficiently illuminated but is simply confused. Attempts to make out the genealogy of the Rjazan' princes present in the *Tale* are futile since the author has simply invented several personages while indiscriminately copying others from the chronicles and then forcing them to perish at the hand of Batu's hordes, while in reality they died earlier than 1237 or continued to flourish in subsequent decades.[19] None of these genealogical distortions seem to be the "epic" inexactitudes of an artistic work that arose two to three centuries after the events described. The early dating of the *Tale* as a work of the time when the sons and grandsons of the Rjazan' princes

[15] The basis of the *Tale* is the contemporaneous chronicle account about Batu's destruction of Rjazan', which is most fully reflected in the Synodal copy of the First Novgorod Chronicle under the year 1238; see D. S. Lixačev, "K istorii složenija Povesti o razorenii Rjazani Batyem," *Arxeografičeskij ežegodnik za 1962* (Moscow, 1963), 48-51. J. L. I. Fennell, "The Tale of Batu's Invasion of Northeast Rus' and its Reflexion in the Chronicles of the Thirteenth-Fifteenth Centuries," *Russia Mediaevalis* 3 (1977): 65-66, also favors the Rjazan' chronicle as a source. In the opinion of A. G. Kuźmin, *Rjazanskoe letopisanie* (Moscow, 1965), 154-165, the particular *Story of Batu's Destruction of Rjazan'*, compiled by a contemporary of the events, appears to be the source of all the chronicle versions as well as of the *Tale*. The author's view that the *Tale of Nikolaj Zarazskij* should be dated at the beginning of the sixteenth century is undoubtedly interesting; however, his assertion that the *Story* is to be identified with the *Tale* without subsequent additions, and the attribution of the motif of the icon's transferral from Cherson to the text of the thirteenth century, reinforce the hypothetical nature of this assumption.

[16] See D. S. Lixačev, "Obščie principy rekonstrukcii literaturno-xudožestvennyx tekstov" in *Tekstologija slavjanskix literatur* (Moscow, 1973), 131-137.

[17] See A. S. Demin, "Èlementy tjurkskoj kul'tury v literature drevnej Rusi XV-XVII vv.," in *Tipologija i vzaimosvjazi srednevekovyx literatur Vostoka i Zapada* (Moscow, 1974), 321.

[18] According to the apt remark of A. S. Orlov, *Geroičeskie temy drevnej russkoj literatury* (Moscow–Leningrad, 1945), 107.

[19] Cf. Lixačev, "Povesti' (see n. 7), 261, and also his commentary in *Voinskie povesti* (see n. 5), 284ff. It should be pointed out that the genealogy of the Rjazan' princes, established in the 1540s, is based on the chronicle tradition and completely ignores the genealogical legend of the *Tale of Batu's Destruction of Rjazan'*; see the edition of family registers of the sixteenth century by A. N. Bočkareva and M. E. Byčkova in *Redkie istočniki po istorii Rossii*, vol. 2 (Moscow, 1977), 80.

lived—the princes who were contemporaries of the invasion of Batu—raises
doubts that up to now have not been satisfactorily answered.

The first part of the cycle, which is dedicated specifically to the history of
the miracle-working icon of Saint Nikolaj, belongs to the characteristic
migrant motifs of medieval literature: transferring the sacred relics from the
ancient cult site to the new. It is impossible to attribute its compilation to a
time near to the imaginary event, that is, to the thirteenth century, because
of the legendary quality of the main personages of this tale—including the
new guardians of the icon, the Rjazan' appanage prince Fedor Jur'evič and
his wife Evpraksija, "from the royal family"—who were completely unknown to the chronicles. In a completely undefined, unclear fashion, the
Tale and the *Transference of the Icon of Saint Nikolaj* speak of the new
location of the icon "within the boundaries of the Rjazan' land, in the
appanage of the faithful prince, Fedor Jur'evič of Rjazan'," but the district,
that is, the domain, of this prince is not named. Evpraksija, along with her
infant son, was said to have thrown herself out of the church built by
Prince Fedor Jur'evič (Saint Nikolaj of Cherson) when she learned that her
husband had perished in a battle with the Tatars. The two hurtled (*zarazi-
šasja*) to their deaths and therefore, "the great miracle-worker Nikolaj is
called Zaraskij."[20] The author of the *Transference* indicates the old location
of the icon in Cherson, in the middle of the city near the Church of the
Holy Apostle James, in which the "autocrat and grand prince of all Rus',
Vladimir Svjatoslavič of Kiev" was baptized. The reference to the Church
of Saint James as the place of Vladimir's baptism is secondary in relation
to that of the account of the Primary Chronicle and appears in the version
of the *Life of Vladimir*, compiled no earlier than the second half of the
fourteenth century.[21] The designation of Anastas Chersonian as bishop of
Cherson seems to be a later addition. This office was assigned to Anastas
only in the very latest adaptations of the expanded *Life of Saint Vladimir*,
belonging already to the sixteenth century.[22] At any rate, the glorification

---

[20] *Voinskie povesti* (see n. 5), 10, 17, 249, 252f.; see also below, nn. 41, 42.

[21] The most ancient preserved manuscript copy of the *vita* from the 1470s (corresponding to
a lost manuscript of 1414, known in a copy from the beginning of the nineteenth century) has
been published by A. A. Zimin, "Pamjat' i poxvala Iakova mnixa i žitie knjazja Vladimira po
drevnejšemu spisku," in *Kratkie soobščenija Instituta slavjanovedenija* 37 (1963): 72-75. From
the middle of the fifteenth century, the Church of Saint James (the existence of this church in
Cherson is not known) also appears in the chronicle accounts about the baptism of Rus'. See
the Fourth Novgorod and First Sophia Chronicles, *PSRL* 4, pt. 1, sec. 1 (1915): 82; 5, pt. 1
(1925): 66. The Novgorodian linguistic features of the manuscripts of 1414 and the 1470s also
point to the Novgorodian origin of this detail.

[22] The West Russian version according to the manuscript of the second half of the sixteenth
century. See, "Sbornik Belorusskij Čudova Monastyrja. Bibliografičeskie materialy A. I.

of Anastas as bishop began no earlier than the end of the fifteenth century and in all probability was only introduced in the first half of the sixteenth century.[23] Finally, the reference to the Greek emperors—"Vasilej, Kostjantin Porfienitos, the Orthodox"—in the *Transference of the Icon of Saint Nikolaj* clearly shows the influence of the listing of Byzantine emperors, "the tsars, ruling in Constantinople, who are orthodox and heretics," a listing that appeared in Rusian chronicles and chronographs beginning with the middle of the fifteenth century.[24] The hellenized form of the record

---

Popova," ed. M. Speranskij, *ČOIDR*, 1889, bk. 3: 35-39. In the Moscow version, this *vita* is known in a manuscript copy from the seventeenth century and according to its stilted exposition is defined as a stylistic reworking of no earlier than the middle of the sixteenth century; see N. I. Serebrjanskij, "Drevnerusskie knjažeskie žitija. Obzor redakcij i teksty," *ČOIDR*, 1915, bk. 3: 62-65, nos. 7, 21-25. It seems that the advancement of the "man named Anastas" to the office of bishop of Cherson took place gradually, which is even noticeable in the inconsistency of the citations in the later reworkings of the *Life of Saint Vladimir*; the Moscow version more consistently represents Anastas as holding the office of bishop. In the Commission manuscript of the First Novgorod Chronicle (see *Novgorodskaja pervaja letopis' staršego i mladšego izvodov*, ed. A. N. Nasonov and M. N. Tixomirov [Moscow–Leningrad, 1950], 165) he is referred to as a priest for the first time. At any rate, the ascribing of the priesthood to Anastas is a fact of the fifteenth century since the Fourth Novgorod Chronicle notes it (*PSRL* 4, pt. 1, sec. 1 [1950]: 91), but in its protograph, i.e., in the chronicle compilation of 1448, judging by the First Sophia Chronicle traceable to the same protograph, Anastas was not yet a priest. Anastas' priesthood is noted by such manuscripts of the second half of the fifteenth century as the Ermolin Chronicle and the Moscow Chronicle of 1479; also some of the chronicles of the sixteenth century continue to call Anastas a priest (see the Voskresenie Chronicle, *PSRL* 7 [1856]: 313). but it is characteristic that the priesthood of Anastas is unknown to the Nikon Chronicle compilation of the 1520s and 1530s.

[23] A. A. Šaxmatov considered that Anastas was a priest, but honoring him as a bishop "seems to be in connection with the significance which this Chersonian acquired among the clergy of the Church of the Tithe" ("Korsunskaja legenda o kreščenii Vladimira," in *Sbornik posvjaščennyj … V. I. Lamanskomu*, pt. 2 [St. Petersburg, 1908], 1109, 1064). In connection with this observation by Šaxmatov, Serebrjanskij wrote that the reports of the episcopal office of Anastas in the *Life of Saint Vladimir* "if not completely arbitrary, are in any event based on sources of dubious antiquity and extremely low value" ("Drevnerusskie knjažeskie žitija," 75ff.). In reality, Anastas was not even a cleric but a secular figure, a steward of the prince's church (the Church of the Tithe) in Kiev. See L. Müller, *Zum Problem des hierarchischen Status und der jurisdiktionellen Abhängigkeit der russischen Kirche vor 1039* (Köln–Braunsfeld, 1959), 42-47; A. Poppe, *Państwo i kościół na Rusi w XI w.* (Warsaw, 1968), 46-48; id., "The building of the Church of St. Sophia in Kiev," *Journal of Medieval History* 7 (1981): 24, 55, nn. 47-49. The groundlessness of A. Šaxmatov's attempt ("Korsunkaja legenda," 1029–1153, particularly the reconstruction, 1143ff.) to recover the ancient form (second half of the eleventh century) of the so-called Chersonian legend, i.e., the *Tale of the Life of Saint Vladimir*, by adducing later reworkings of the *Life* (where, incidentally, Anastas is named as a bishop), has been persuasively proven by Serebrjanskij, "Drevnerusskie knjažeskie žitija," 43-81. However, even Šaxmatov himself recognized the precariousness of his reconstruction: "The restoration of the *Tale of the Baptism of Vladimir* leads us into the sphere of suppositions and guesswork" ("Korsunskaja legenda," 1137).

[24] See O. V. Tvorogov, *Drevnerusskie xronografy* (Leningrad, 1975), 28, 118.

Porfienitos instead of the usual *Porfirogenit,*[25] shown along with the adapted form *Cherson* for the Old Rusian *Korsun',* focuses attention on the attempts at erudition characteristic of Russian bookmen of the fifteenth and sixteenth centuries.

At any rate, it is absolutely impossible to recognize all these data about Vladimir's baptism in Cherson as a later insertion in the *Transference of the Icon of Saint Nikolaj.* For here lies the essence of the story: to show that the transference concerned not merely the miracle-working icon of Saint Nikolaj but an icon topographically connected with the great event that gave rise to Orthodox Rus'.

The only text of the cycle of tales about Nikolaj Zarazskij that lends itself to a more exact dating is the so-called *Kolomnian Episode,* a story about the transferral in 7021 of the miracle-working icon of Saint Nikolaj to the town of Kolomna, about the icon's later theft, and the miraculous tracking down of its frame.[26] On the basis of the mention of Prince Jurij, the brother of Vasilij III, who was considered the heir to the throne of Moscow until the birth of Ivan IV on August 25, 1530, the chronological boundaries of the compilation of the Kolomnian story have been reliably established as being between 1513 and 1530.[27] This dating can presumably be made more precise by taking into account the role ascribed in this story to Bishop Mitrofan of Kolomna, who is described as flourishing.[28] The theft of the frame apparently took place at the beginning of 1515.[29] Nothing is noted in the story about the miraculous return of the icon to its old place in the district of Rjazan'. The second Kolomnian story, which was compiled later, also relates this event to the time of Bishop Mitrofan.[30] At

---

[25] Cf. the list of the Byzantine emperors in the Nikon Chronicle, *PSRL* 9: 20; *PSRL* 12: 82.

[26] Lixačev, "Povesti" (see n. 7), 346-348; *Voinskie povesti* (see n. 5), 253-255. The reason for the transferral—the devastating incursion of the Tatars onto Rjazan' soil—is supported by the chronicle reports for October of 7021 (cf. *PSRL* 28 [1963]: 347), i.e., the fall of 1512, and not of 1513 as is usually recounted, disregarding September as the beginning of the year.

[27] V. L. Komarovič, "K literaturnoj istorii Povesti o Nikole Zarazskom," *TODRL* 5 (1947): 65.

[28] Mitrofan was appointed bishop on February 1, 1506, and left the post because of illness in June 1518; see *PSRL* 13: 5, 29.

[29] According to the Kolomnian story, the theft occurred two years and fifteen weeks after the icon was brought to Kolomna, and the frame was "missing" for five weeks; see *Voinskie povesti* (see n. 5), 254. At that same time (1513-14), a church was built in the name of Saint Nikolaj Zarazskij for the miracle-working icon by order of the grand prince. The existence of this church, along with its keeping by the tsar's treasury, is supported by the cadaster of 1577-78. See *Piscovye knigi XVI v.,* sec. 1, ed. N. B. Kalačev (St. Petersburg, 1872), 301, 306.

[30] Lixačev, "Povesti" (see n. 7), 348ff. The precise dating of the icon's return on the third Sunday of Lent (the Veneration of the Cross), March 9, indicates a later provenance (the middle or second half of the sixteenth century) of this story. Both of these events occurred in a

any rate, the *Kolomnian Episode* was recorded before 1528–1531—when the construction of the stone fortress and church in honor of Saint Nikolaj Zarazskij was begun and completed.[31]

Great significance must be attached to the complete absence of any reference to the Chersonian origin of the miracle-working icon of Saint Nikolaj in the *Kolomnian Episode* of 1515–1528. He is called here the miracle-worker Nikolaj Zarazskij, and never the miracle-worker Nikolaj of Cherson, although the latter appellation does appear in both of the primary tales of the cycle (it occurs in the *Tale of the Destruction of Rjazan'* and is dominant in the *Transference of the Icon of Saint Nikolaj*). This nonmention is all the more revealing since, as is clear in both Kolomnian stories, there were attempts to keep the miracle-working icon in Kolomna, not allowing it to return to its "old site," which was, after all, not within the boundaries of the Kolomnian diocese, but in the eparchy of Rjazan'. The very attempt to retain the sacred relic, additionally justified by the ever-present danger of Tatar raids, is completely understandable, but concealing the Chersonian genealogy of the miracle-working icon, thus providing more of a basis for Kolomna's ownership of the sacred relic, would be completely incomprehensible. Analysis of the Kolomnian story leads to the conclusion that the miracle-working icon of Saint Nikolaj Zarazskij was already known and worshiped in Kolomna in the second decade of the sixteenth century but that the legend about its Chersonian origin was unknown.

The challenge I have directed at the currently prevailing opinion inevitably leads to the question of when the cult of the Zarazskian miracle-working icon originated. The fact that the icon, which has been preserved to the present day, is a painting of the early sixteenth century does not answer the question, since the presumed original Zarazskian icon could have been lost and replaced. But neither is there substantiation for the assumption that the iconographic type, already known among Russian icons of the fourteenth and fifteenth centuries (which represent Saint Nikolaj standing erect in bishop's robes, the Gospels in his left hand and blessing with his right), had been called Zarazskian from the very beginning—that is, since the thirteenth century, under the influence of the cult of the Zarazskian icon of the

---

year when Easter fell on April 6. In the sixteenth century this could only have been 1539, 1550, 1561, or 1577. The icon's return occurred at the latest in 1531, when the construction of the Zarazskij fortress was completed.

[31] The Chronographic Chronicle of 1451–1551 records for the year 7036: "In the same year the grand prince founded a stone borough on the Osetr and in it the stone church of the miracle-worker Nikolaj Zarazskij," *PSRL* 22 (1911): 521; cf. S. O. Šmidt, "Prodolženie xronografa redakcii 1512 goda," *Istoričeskij Arxiv* 7 (1951): 283. For the completion of the construction in 1531, see *PSRL* 8: 278; *PSRL* 13: 58; *PSRL* 20: 412.

saint which was supposed to have begun at that time[32] The most ancient icon, which is inscribed "Nikolae Zarajski," belongs to the very end of the sixteenth century.[33] The fact that the depiction of Nikolaj with outstretched arms was in no way called "Zarazskian" in Moscow in the first quarter of the sixteenth century is verified by the extensive record of 1524 on the reverse side of the recently restored icon "of the holy and great miracle-worker Nikola," dated to the beginning of the fourteenth century.[34] It would be more correct to conclude that it was not the miracle-working icon

---

[32] Cf. V. I. Antonova, "Moskovskaja ikona XIV veka iz Kieva i Povesti o Nikole Zaraj-skom," *TODRL* 13 (1957): 375-392. Antonova's assertion about the composition of the ancient form of the *Tale About Nikolaj Zarazskij* at the end of the thirteenth or beginning of the four-teenth century forms the initial premise of her erroneous reconstructions. On the iconography of Saint Nikolaj with outstretched arms, see È. S. Smirnova, *Živopis' Velikogo Novgoroda serediny XIII—načala XV veka* (Moscow, 1976), 195-197, 201-203. It has been shown quite persuasively that the question of identifying this iconography as Zarazskian remains open; cf. G. V. Popov and A. V. Ryndina, *Živopis' i prikladnoe iskusstvo Tveri XIV–XVI v.* (Moscow, 1979), 348, no. 3. There is also reason to doubt Antonova's assertion that the original depic-tion of Saint Nikolaj Zarazskij, i.e., the icon which was brought to Kolomna in 1512, was *v dejanijax*, that is to say, that the depiction of Saint Nikolaj in the middle was framed by scenes from the life and miracles of the saint. From the Kolomnian stories it follows that soon after the miracle-working icon was transferred to Kolomna, a copy was made that was eventually housed in the Kolomna Church of Saint Nikolaj Zarazskij. According to V. Antonova, this icon is presently located in the Tret'jakov Gallery; see V. I. Antonova and N. E. Mneva, *Katalog drevnerusskoj živopisi*, vol. 2 (Moscow, 1963), 162-64, no. 557. But is this really the same icon? In a detailed description of the icons of the Kolomna Church of Nikolaj Zarazskij from 1577-78, four icons depicting Saint Nikolaj are enumerated. The first in the description must be regarded as a copy of the miracle-working icon, distinguished by an abundance of gold and silver pendants (votive offerings), while no such ornamentation is mentioned for the second icon, described as *s dejaniem*; see *Piscovye knigi XVI v.* (see n. 29), 306.

[33] Cf. Antonova, "Moskovskaja ikona," 378, no. 3; Smirnova, *Živopis' Velikogo Novgoroda*, 196. I note the use of the new form *Zarajski(j)*, which appears only at the end of the sixteenth century, instead of the old form *Zarazski(j)*. Antonova's assertion (pp. 380-384), with reference to the Nikon Chronicle, that a church named for Saint Nikolaj Zarazskij had already existed in Moscow in 1471 must be ascribed to a pure misunderstanding, since this chronicle notes only that the metropolitan met the grand prince "with crosses near the church" (this is the way it reads in the majority of the manuscripts, but in one it reads, "near the great church," i.e., the cathedral, see *PSRL* 12: 141). Even if it is agreed that the Church of Saint Nikolaj *v sapožkax* is intended here, there is still no indication that in the fifteenth or sixteenth century it was called by the name of Nikolaj Zarazskij.

[34] Antonova, "Moskovskaja ikona," 375ff. See further, Antonova and Mneva, *Katalog drev-nerusskoj živopisi*, vol. 1 (see n. 32), 78-80, no. 13. Considering that the icon represents the "Zarazskian" iconographic type of the saint, Antonova tries to prove the Kievan origin of this icon and on the same grounds to explain the national (Kievan), and not Byzantine (Cherson-ian) sources of the worship of the icon of Saint Nikolaj Zarazskij. Without discussing this line of thinking there, we note that Antonova's opinion that the restoration of the icon in 1524 was connected "with an intensification of interest in the *Tale About Nikolaj Zarazskij*," is com-pletely unsubstantiated, since neither the icon-reverse inscription of 1524 nor the subsequent extensive inscriptions about the renovations in 1656 and 1691 mention that the icon depicts the miracle-worker Zarazskij.

of Nikolaj Zarazskij that gave rise to the spread of this iconographic type in Rusian lands, but the reverse: that the spread of depicting the bishop-saint standing up, blessing and teaching (the Gospels), occurred before the appearance of the local Zarazskian cult with a representation of this type.

The issue of where the cult was initially located has not been settled. As noted above, the tales of Nikolaj Zarazskij do not pinpoint the location of the miracle-working icon, referring only to the "land of Rjazan'." It is noteworthy that even from the *Kolomnian Episode* it follows only that the miracle-working icon was located in the Church of Nikolaj Zarazskij "na Rjazani," that is, on Rjazanian soil, before its transfer to Kolomna in the fall of 1512.[35] A town or population referred to as Zarazsk or Zarajsk did not yet exist at this time; claims ascribing the founding of Zarazsk to the twelfth or thirteenth century, apart from a reference to a tale about Nikolaj Zarazskij, are insufficient evidence. According to innumerable cita-tions in the sources from the sixteenth to seventeenth centuries—including such official documents as military records, beginning with the building of the stone fortress in 1528-1531—the town continually, throughout the six-teenth and into the seventeenth century, bore the name "Nikolaj Zarazskij," sometimes with the elucidation "on the Osetr," especially in the early period.[36] That this name was derived from the fact that the fortress was built on the site of a *pogost* (i.e., a parish church with a cemetery), where the church named for Saint Nikolaj had stood, seems convincing.[37] Until

---

[35] Lixačev, "Povesti" (see n. 7), 346ff.; *Voinskie povesti* (see n. 5), 253 ff. Rjazan' is named in this story not in the sense of a city but in the accepted sense of the land or principality of Rjazan'. For this usage, see the Testament of Grand Prince Ivan III of 1504, in *Duxovnye i dogovornye gramoty velikix i udel'nyx knjazej XIV–XVI vv.* (Moscow–Leningrad, 1950), no. 89, pp. 357 ff.; see also p. 473 (the deed of 1539).

[36] See the index in *Razrjadnaja kniga 1475–1598*, ed. V. I. Buganov (Moscow, 1966). Here, beginning with October 1531, the fortress-town "Nikolaj Zarazskij" (by the end of the century the form "Zarajskij" also appears) is mentioned 44 times. It is interesting that in the first reference of 1531, this borough is called "on the Osetr with Nikola" (ibid., 81). In the duty-books of 1594–1597 it is named "gorod Nikoly Zarazkogo" or simply "Nikolaj Zarazskij" or "Nikolaj" (see *Piscovye knigi Rjazanskogo kraja*, vol. 1, no. 1 [Rjazan' 1898], 157-158). And in the seventeenth century, the town officially continues to be called Nikolaj Zarazskij (see *Razrjad-nye knigi 1550–1636*, no. 2, [Moscow, 1976], 254); but from the end of the sixteenth to the beginning of the seventeenth century, "the Zarazskij (Zaraskov, Zarajskij) borough" comes into use; cf. *PSRL* 14: 28, 29, 89, 99, 107; 31 (1968): 152; *Pamjatniki russkoj pis'mennosti XV–XVI vv. Rjazanskij kraj* (Moscow, 1978), 80. In the 1627 source (known only from the manuscripts of the 1670s and 1680s), "the borough of Zaraesk (Zarazesk)" and "the borough Zarajskij" are mentioned; see *Kniga bol'šomu čertežu* (Moscow, 1950), 120-122.

[37] M. N. Tixomirov, *Rossija v XVI stoletii* (Moscow, 1962), 402. A. G. Kuz'min, *Rjazanskoe letopisanie* (Moscow, 1965), 87, 173, indicated with good reason a later origin of the town of Nikolaj Zarazskij but mistakenly suggested that in the 1530s the new name Nikolaj Zarazskij appeared, replacing the old name Osetr. Yet, citing the single chronicle reference to the city

1528 there had been neither fortifications nor a town there, and "none of the archaeological materials known to us from the city of Zarajsk permits us to speak about its antiquity."[38] This assertion has forced one investigator to pose the legitimate question: "Can the tale itself, closely connected by its subject matter with this town, be related to such an early time," that is, to 1225?[39] In answering this question negatively, one must, however, note that the legend in the cycle of tales about Nikolaj Zarazskij does not at all reflect an attempt to interpret the town's appellation, Zarazsk. Yet this is often proposed,[40] if only because in the sixteenth century, when this legend undoubtedly already existed, there was no town with precisely that name. The legend does attempt to interpret the church and miracle-working icon's designation "Zarazskian" as being prior to the designation "Chersonian."[41] Only a later chronographic variant (c. 1599) of the *Tale of the Destruction of Rjazan'* (a reworking of the basic version) attempts to explain the legend topographically. It mentions that the place where the church had stood, from which the princess and her son had hurled themselves, began to be called Zaraz.[42] Considering the meaning of this word as 'steep slope, precipice, ravine', it seems reasonable to assume that this attempt at an explanation was based on the topography of the site selected for the fortress "Nikolaj Zarazskij."

The Zarazskian fortress was built on a high, steep, hilly bank of the Osetr River and was, moreover, protected on all sides by gullies and ravines.[43] But before this, the wooden church of Saint Nikolaj had stood

---

Osetr under the year 1541 in the so-called Book of the Reign (*PSRL* 13: 434; cf. *PSRL* 34: 174), Kuz'min did not take into account the fact that the town Osetr, instead of the river Osetr, appeared here as a result of the unsuccessful abridgement of one and the same text: "the Crimean tsar came ... to the Osetr to the borough Nikolaj Zarazski," *PSRL* 13: 138.

[38] A. L. Mongajt, *Rjazanskaja zemlja* (Moscow, 1961), 238.

[39] Lixačev, *Tekstologija* (see n. 10), 544ff.

[40] Cf. Kuz'min, *Rjazanskoe letopisanie* (see n. 37), 173.

[41] The *Tale of the Destruction of Rjazan'*, reporting the burial of prince Fedor, his wife Evpraksija and son in the church "of the great miracle-worker Nikolaj of Cherson," gives the following explanation: "And because of this may the great miracle-worker Nikolaj be called Zarazskij: because the faithful princess Evpraksija, along with her son, Prince Ivan, had flung herself to her death (*sama sebe zarazi*)," *Voinskie povesti* (see n. 5), 17. The same text repeats verbatim the *Transference of the Icon*, ibid., 253. Cf. Lixačev, "Povesti" (see n. 7), 287, 300, 328, 341.

[42] *Voinskie povesti* (see n. 5), 25; Lixačev, "Povesti" (see n. 7), 353: "And whence derived the place name Zaraz: because it was there that princess Evpraksija and her son had hurtled to their death (*zarazisja*)." In an abridged chronographic redaction of about 1661, the form Zarazsk already appears; see ibid., 273, 357.

[43] V. V. Kostočkin, *Russkoe oboronitel'noe zodčestvo* (Moscow, 1962), 83–84. Settlements named Zaraz are known in the district of Moscow, Rjazan' and Tula; see V. A. Nikonov, *Kratkij toponimičeskij slovar'* (Moscow, 1966), 145. According to the cadaster of 1578–79,

there, and, because of its location either on the *zaraz* 'steep bank' of the river, or among the *zarazy* 'ravines', began to be called *Zarazskian*. The *Kolomnian Episode* of 1515–1528 has only a reference to the Church of Nikolaj Zarazskij within the Rjazan' Land. That this mention is simultaneously an indication of the site location (c. 40 km from Kolomna) becomes evident only after the building of the fortress that acquired the name Nikolaj Zarazskij. Consequently, even before the *Kolomnian Episode* of 1512, this church began to be famous for its miracle-working icon. The icon's cult had a local and limited character, which is shown by the remote placement of the parish cemetery and the wooden church. All of this also speaks in favor of the recent date of this cult. However, the first known manifestation of the icon's miracle-working power occurred in Kolomna in 1515. Hospitable Kolomna's attempt to retain the icon, and Vasilij III's attention to it—he ordered a stone church to be built in Kolomna in the name of Nikolaj Zarazskij—added a new dimension to the cult. The Muscovite grand prince continued to promote the development of the cult of the miracle-working icon. While his decision to build a stone fortress on the Osetr, protecting the southern approaches to Moscow, was dictated by military considerations, it is also true that a spiritual bulwark was purposefully raised against the Tatar threat, and thus the stone church was built along with the fortress in the name of the protector-saint, prepared to house his miracle-working icon—a palladium in the struggles with the Tatars.[44] Pilgrimages by the sovereign raised the miracle-working icon to the level of a statewide sacred relic of Muscovy: in March of 1533, Vasilij III made a

---

several toponyms are known in the neighboring Kašira district: Zaraz, Zarazy, Zarazskoe Pole; see *Piscovye knigi XVI v.*, sec. 2 (Moscow, 1877), 1389, 1404, 1406, 1411, 1416.

[44]Saint Nikolaj was widely worshiped as the patron of the Rusian land. By the fifteenth century, the cult of Saint Nikolaj of Možajsk the miracle-worker already embodied the idea of the bishop-protector. Antonova's suggestion ("Moskovskaja ikona" (see n. 32), 386) that the cult of Nikolaj Zarazskij gave birth to the iconography of the image of Nikolaj of Možajsk (with a sword and town church in his outstretched hands) is unsubstantiated, even though the Možajsk cult is older than that of Zarazskij. The description of the icons located in the churches of Kolomna in 1577—the city where, in the second decade of the sixteenth century, the miracle-working icon of Nikolaj Zarazskij was located and the Church of Saint Nikolaj Zarazskij was built—bears witness to the fact that the spread of the cult of this miracle-working icon (as attested by the practice of making copies from this icon) did not begin immediately. But of more than thirty icons of Saint Nikolaj from various churches, not one is called "Zarazskian," while four icons of Nikolaj of Možajsk are mentioned in the various churches of Kolomna; see *Piscovye knigi XVI v.* (see n. 29), sec. 1, 306, 319-320, 331. It is interesting that in Kazan', where the icons were received from all over Russia, including many donations from the tsar, the registers of 1566 make no mention of a Zarazskian copy, although they do note the icon of the saint-bishop of Možajsk among the icons of the Church of Saint Nikolaj Ratnyj; P. Zarinskij, *Očerki drevnej Kazani preimuščestvenno XVI veka* (Kazan', 1877), 106.

pilgrimage to Nikolaj Zarazskij, followed in August of 1550 and in June of 1556 by Ivan IV, and in May of 1562 by Tsarevich Fedor.[45] The miracle-working icon of Saint Nikolaj Zarazskij had no Chersonian pedigree in the initial period of its worship. But the necessity of ascribing to it a worthy genealogy began to ripen from the moment that Vasilij III raised it to the rank of state sanctuary.[46] The origin of the legend about the Chersonian ancestry of the icon and its literary manifestation must be related to a time after 1531.[47] The addition of the icon to the sacred relics traceable to the days of the baptism of the first Christian ruler of Rus' has something in common with the ideopolitical program of the Muscovite descendants of the Rurik dynasty. But the very thought of such a genealogy could not have arisen in isolation and must be connected with the interest in the Chersonian sacred relics that began to appear in Rusian lands, primarily, as we shall see, in Novgorod. It is not by accident that the legend about the travel of the icon directed attention to that city: the icon was brought from Cherson onto the soil of Rjazan' by way of Novgorod where, remaining for "many days," it bore witness to itself "by great miracles."

[45] *Razrjadnaja kniga* (see n. 36), 129, 158; *PSRL* 8: 22; *PSRL* 13: 68, 341. But in those years the Zarazskian icon had undoubtedly not yet achieved the level of worship that the Možajsk icon, or even the miracle-working icon of Saint Nikolaj of Vjatka (Velikoreck, Vjatka) had attained. In 1555 the latter was transferred to Moscow, where it remained for more than a year and was restored by Metropolitan Makarij himself. At that same time, "many icons of him were made in his measure and likeness." The tsar even built a wooden church in honor of Nikolaj of Vjatka and established a stone side-chapel in the name of the same saint in the Church of Vasilij Blažennyj, which was being built as a monument to the Kazan' victory. See *PSRL* 13: 254–255, 273, 320.

[46] Antonova has noted that the Chersonian theme was developed in detail only in the sixteenth century during a reworking of the tales about Nikolaj Zarazskij in connection with the revival of his military cult and in keeping with the general direction of the Russian historical conception ("Moskovskaja ikona" [see n. 32], 379, 392). This quite vaguely formulated thought about a "detailed elaboration"—suggesting that in its rudimentary form, the Chersonian episode is older than the sixteenth century—was indicated by a a desire "to prove the original Rusian (Kievan) sources of the cult of the Zarazskian icon to those who have a predilection for Byzantinism." But Antonova's chronological considerations regarding the cult of Saint Nikolaj Zarazskij are unacceptable. The Zarazskian cult is actually a genuinely Rusian phenomenon which, however, began at the earliest in the beginning of the sixteenth century.

[47] The dating of the Chersonian tradition of the Zarazskian icon substantiated here is consonant with the opinion of an outstanding expert on the Old Russian manuscript legacy, K. F. Kalajdovič: "The doubtful tale about its [the Zarazskian icon's—A.P.] transfer from Cherson in 1224 is not corroborated by ancient evidence: perhaps the beginning of this tale is no older than Makarij's Great Minei-Čeři ...," i.e., the middle of the sixteenth century; K. F. Kalajdovič, *Pis'ma k A. F. Malinovskomu ob arxeologičeskix issledovanijax v Rjazanskoj gubernii* (Moscow, 1823), 73.

The "Chersonian Doors" from Magdeburg

The western façade of the Novgorod Cathedral of Saint Sophia is adorned by Romanesque bronze doors, which for centuries were referred to as Chersonian. The doors were manufactured in a Magdeburg casting workshop in 1153 by order of Alexander, bishop of Płock. No later than the first months of 1154, the doors were dispatched to their destination on the Vistula. They left Płock under unknown circumstances and at an undetermined time. However, after mysterious travels, the doors found their way to Novgorod in good condition, where, in the mid-fifteenth century, the Slavo-Cyrillic inscriptions were engraved on them.[48]

How the doors acquired the name Chersonian is one of the remaining puzzles connected with their fate. It is worthwhile investigating how the work of a twelfth-century Romanesque workshop in Magdeburg was attributed a provenance from Cherson, a Crimean possession of the Byzantine Empire.

As early as the eighteenth century, attention was drawn to the discrepancy between the name of the doors and their appearance;[49] yet, their traditional epithet continued to be maintained in the colloquial language of the Novgorodians and in Russian literature. According to one theory, the adjective *Chersonian* was applied to the doors as a definition used for Old Rusian precious cult objects, distinguished by their artistic value and archaic origin.[50] The answer that the doors received this name "either from its archaism or by misunderstanding"[51] does not seem to be satisfactory

---

[48] For details about the Rusian inscriptions on the doors, see A. Poppe, "K istorii romanskix dverej Sofii Novgorodskoj" in *Srednevekovaja Rus'. Sbornik pamjati N. N. Voronina* (Moscow, 1976), 191-200. On the time of manufacture and some iconographic questions, see id., "Some Observations on the Bronze Doors of St. Sophia in Novgorod," in *Acta Universitatis Upsaliensis*, 1981, fig. 19, 407-418. A major study of the doors by the present author is in preparation. The basic work on the art problems remains that of A. Goldschmidt, *Die Bronzetüren von Novgorod und Gnesen* (Marburg a/L, 1932), 1-26, tables 1-70.

[49] One of the first to mention it was the historian and traveling tutor to the son of the Earl of Pembroke, William Coxe, *Travels into Poland, Russia, Sweden and Denmark*, vol. 1 (London, 1784), 452.

[50] F. Adelung, *Die Korssunschen Türen in der Kathedralkirche zur heiligen Sophia in Novgorod* (Berlin, 1823), 99-100; Sobolevskij, "Dva slova o 'korsunskix predmetax'" (see n. 3), 59-60, 65.

[51] Kondakov, *Russkie klady* (see n. 1), 4-5. S. A. Beljaev believes that the name Chersonian was attributed to the Romanesque bronze doors because of a misunderstanding; cf. "Korsunskie dveri Novgorodskogo Sofijskogo sobora," in *Drevnjaja Rus' i Slavjane* (Moscow, 1978), 300-310. Here, the author used the name Chersonian for the doors with copper plates, whose flower cross (*crux florida*) is the central decorative element. From the seventeenth century on, these doors were set up in the arch of the cathedral that separates the side chapel of the Nativity of the Mother of God from the Porch of the Martyrs. Recognized as a monument of

either. In seeking an answer, one should follow the fate of the doors after they were already in the portal of the Novgorod Cathedral.

The Third Novgorod Chronicle under the year 1450 records: "In the year 6958 the vestibule of Saint Sophia by the Chersonian Gates (*u korsunskix vrat*) was covered with paintings by order of Archbishop Evfimij."[52] This, however, cannot be considered the oldest reference to the doors. The fresco redecoration of the western chapel was assuredly based on an older record, while the mode of localization "by the Chersonian Gates" clearly reveals a later interpolation; in all probability, it was made by the compiler of this chronicle, which was composed shortly after 1673.[53] In the thirteenth to

---

Byzantine handicraft, they were dated from the eleventh or twelfth century even at the end of the nineteenth century (I. I. Tolstoj and N. P. Kondakov). Drawing on comparative evidence, Beljaev made an artistic analysis of the doors and proposed dating them to the second half of the eighth through the first half of the ninth centuries. However, in light of known material, such precise dating of the doors seems premature, especially if we bear in mind the doors with the blossoming crosses of the eleventh century from Amalfi, Mt. Athos, Atrani, and Salerno from the beginning of the twelfth century; see M. E. Frazer, "Church Doors and the Gates of Paradise: Byzantine Bronze Doors in Italy," *Dumbarton Oaks Papers* 27 (1973): 147-162, pls. 1, 4, 11, 14, 15. The doors from Novgorod seem to be closer to the doors from Italy than to those of the sixth century from the Hagia Sophia. Moreover, a certain impression of secondary accretion is produced: the simplicity of the panel composition with its blossoming crosses combines with the rich ornamentation of their borders. A more definite dating of the Byzantine doors from Novgorod is of substantial significance for the determination of their early fate. If they are a work of the eleventh century, then their appearance in Novgorod in connection with the construction of the Cathedral of Saint Sophia (1050) is tied to the prince's order in the Byzantine workshop. With the earlier dating, it would be more reasonable to propose that these doors are really a trophy from the Chersonian campaign of Vladimir in 989. But one way or another, these doors ended up in Novgorod in the eleventh or twelfth century. Even recognizing the merit of Beljaev's initial, thorough study of this artwork, I cannot, however, agree with his suggestion that these doors were called Chersonian from the very beginning; nor can I accept that they were located until the seventeenth century inside the entrance of Saint Sophia at the western vestibule, transmitting the name Chersonian to the latter. In Beljaev's opinion, the transference of these doors in the seventeenth century in connection with the liquidation of this doorway led to the Romanesque doors becoming the major doors into the cathedral, and in turn, the name Chersonian was carried over to them from the name of the vestibule (ibid., 307). Even though this is a logical explanation, in light of the data presented here, it is historically incorrect. The Byzantine, not to mention the Chersonian, origin of these doors was completely forgotten, and not to be recalled even at the height of the demand for Chersonian antiquities in the seventeenth century when a Chersonian genealogy was ascribed to clearly local wares.

[52] *Novgorodskie letopisi* (the so-called Second and Third Novogord Chronicles) (St. Petersburg, 1879), 273; ibid., 210. Under the year 1299, the reference to the Chersonian vestibule consitutes a definite interpolation in comparison with a corresponding text not only in chronicles compiled in the fourteenth and fifteenth centuries (First Novgorod Chronicle [see n. 22] 330) but also toward the end of the sixteenth century. See the Second Novgorod Chronicle in *Novgorodskie letopisi*, 24; *PSRL* 30 (1965): 188.

[53] Cf. S. N. Azbelov, *Novgorodskie letopisi XVII veka* (Novgorod, 1960), 95ff.

sixteenth centuries, the location of the western chapel was defined as follows: "to the side of the Bishop's court" or "to the west." In addition, the
seventeenth-century compiler employed the term *vrata* 'gates' instead of
dveri 'doors,' though these two terms were distinguished in the language of
Old Rus' up to the sixteenth century.

In an extensive description of two processions that took place on
December 8 and 15, 1499—a description rich in topographical details—the
author, who undoubtedly participated, twice noted that Archbishop Gennadij stopped before the cathedral entrance at the side of his court (i.e., to
the west), "sprinkled holy water on the vestibule and church doors," and
blessed the participants of the procession.[54] Because of the detailed nature
of this report, one can safely conclude that at the end of the fifteenth century, a more precise appellation of the doors had not become accepted,
although the legend surrounding them must have already begun to take
shape. The oldest trace of such a legend is contained in Herberstein's narrative. Looking at the "copper church doors," he heard that they had been
brought from Greece many centuries ago as a trophy from conquered
Cherson.[55] Thus, in 1517, a tradition existed in Novgorod that made it
possible to call the doors Chersonian. The fact that Herberstein was shown
the bronze doors manufactured in Magdeburg and was told the legend pertaining to them follows indisputably from two further testimonies: a
Swedish one of 1616 and a Syrian one of 1655.

Jacob de la Gardie, the commander of the Swedish units occupying
Novgorod, answered the Swedish chancellor, Count Axel Oxenstierna, on
March 4, 1616, on the advisability of sending back the doors of Sigtuna,
now found in Novgorod. For political reasons he advised against the confiscation of "these doors which lead to the main temple of the metropolitan, and which the Russian assure me were brought as a gift from
Greece."[56] Thus, he heard the same story that the imperial ambassador had

---

[54] See the Second Novgorod Chronicle, *PSRL* 30: 152-154.

[55] In his autobiography (preserved in manuscript), Herberstein, describing his stay in
Novgorod in April of 1517, reports: "Da liess man mich sehen ain kupferene khirchtur, die aus
Griechenlanndt solte gebracht sein worden vor viell hundert Jaren, Alls man aus derselben
gegenndt gezogen, unnd ain Stat, die sy Corsun nennen, belegert." See *Fontes Rerum Austria-
carum, Scriptores*, vol. 1 (Vienna, 1855), 117. Cf. id., *Rerum Moscoviticarum Commentarii*
(Basel, 1557), 75, and the German translation: *Beschreibung Moskaus der Hauptstadt in Russland samt des Moskowitischen Gebietes 1557*, selections translated by H. Picard (Graz, 1966),
71. In the essay, Herberstein notes that the Novgorodians brought a bell along with the doors
from Cherson.

[56] A. Oxenstierna, *Skrifter och brefvexling*, vol. 1 (Stockholm, 1893), 94. The creator of the
Sigtuna legend of our doors was the Swedish pastor Martin Aschaneus, who was convinced that
during his stay in Novgorod in 1614 he had discovered the gates that were once carried away

been told a hundred years earlier, with the exception that his informers, most likely the cathedral clergy, omitted for good reasons the part of the tradition regarding wartime booty. When Makarios, patriarch of Antioch, visited Novgorod in 1655, however, there was no need to hide this information. His son, Archdeacon Paul of Aleppo in Syria, who accompanied him, wrote about the Novgorod Cathedral as follows: "It possesses immense wonderful doors of two wings of yellow copper; on the doors human figures and similar subtleties of art are represented. They say that the ruler of this town, around 700 years ago, led an expedition against the country of the Serbs and Greeks.... He proceeded to Cherson, conquered it, destroyed it and brought from there these doors along with other objects and great ancient, magnificent Greek icons which have survived to this day."[57]

That both Herberstein and Paul of Aleppo uncritically repeated this local tradition despite having seen the doors with their own eyes gives one food for thought. After all, Herberstein was one of few people able to read both the Latin and Slavic inscriptions on them. Paul of Aleppo, although he wrote in Arabic, knew Greek and could have observed that Greek inscriptions were lacking. One must assume that both were entertained as honored guests, surrounded, but also constrained, by their hosts' hospitality, and did not have enough time to take a closer look at the relics. The stories of the hosts must also have been extremely convincing. Even at the beginning of the nineteenth century, when the question of the doors' genealogy was better known, a German traveler saw in them "the entire Greek hierarchy from the sacristan to the patriarch in contemporary costumes of the period and the Greek court in figure bas-reliefs with inscriptions."[58]

The first source calling the doors Chersonian is the so-called Second Novgorod Chronicle, a compilation preserved in a manuscript from the end of the sixteenth century. The extensive description of the procession with the icon of "Our Lady of Vladimir" on Sunday, June 22, 1572, was the work of an eyewitness. Tsar Ivan IV (the Terrible) was staying in Novgorod and participated in this procession, which wended its way toward the

---

from Sigtuna. Aschaneus even aroused the interest of King Gustavus Adolphus in this matter. The hypothesis that the doors found their way from Magdeburg to Novgorod through the Swedish town of Sigtuna cannot be substantiated. It was aptly criticized by O. Almgren in 1912 but still finds support. Cf. recently again I. P. Šaskoľskij, *Boŕba Rusi protiv krestonosnoj agressii na beregax Baltiki XII–XIII vv.* (Leningrad, 1978), 94-104. For details on the Sigtuna legend, see my study in preparation (see n. 48).

[57] "Putešestvie Antioxijskogo patriarxa Makarija v Rossii opisannoe ego synom arxidiakonom Pavlom Aleppskim," *ČOIDR,* 1898, bk. 4: 70.

[58] D. Raupach, *Reise von St. Petersburg nach dem Gesundbrunnen zu Lipezk am Don* (Breslau, 1809), 33.

cathedral and reached the Chersonian Doors.[59] During the ceremony in front of the cathedral entrance the tsar, surrounded by church and lay dignitaries, stood before the Romanesque doors looking at the religious scenes on them. What is noteworthy is that two years earlier, Ivan IV had taken other church doors—manufactured in 1336 by order of Archbishop Vasilij— from Novgorod to his residence near Moscow. These "gilded bronze doors," somewhat smaller than the Romanesque ones, had adorned the cathedral's southern portal until 1570; this was the southern chapel, also called "golden."[60] The evidence from 1570 and 1572 makes it possible to reject the assumption that the name "Chersonian Doors," originally ascribed to the 1336 doors, was transferred to the bronze Romanesque doors from Magdeburg. That the Chersonian Doors were considered a special ornament of the archepiscopal cathedral is shown by the fact that a proper decorational frame was provided for them in the fifteenth or sixteenth century. The western façade at that time was not covered with white plaster as it was in 1439 when Archbishop Evfimij "whitewashed the entire Sophia Church." In 1528 Makarij, then archbishop of Novgorod, "ordered the icon painters to cover the wall of Saint Sophia with frescoes above the doors through which he himself entered from the west and to paint the Holy Trinity higher up, but Saint Sophia, the Divine Wisdom, and the image of the holy face of Our Lord Jesus Christ [i.e., the Veronica—A.P.] lower down, and two archangels on both sides; and the archbishop himself entering and leaving the cathedral prayed here." We learn from this contemporary record, moreover, that "there had also been a painting on this site earlier, but only one image of the Pantocrator—a bust, occupying practically the entire site where the frescoes are painted now—however, it had been destroyed because of age."[61] The image of Christ Pantocrator placed

---

[59] *Novgorodskie letopisi* (see n. 52), 103; *PSRL* 30: 161. The Novgorodian Saint Sophia *Pontifical* of c. 1630 also indicates that during major church celebrations, ceremonies took place in front of the Chersonian Doors; see "Činovnik Novgorodskogo Sofijskogo sobora," ed. A. Golubcov, *ČOIDR*, 1889, bk. 2: 166, 183, 205.

[60] Beginning with the record of 1336 in the First Novgorod Chronicle, there is much that speaks for the fact that these doors, ordered by Archbishop Vasilij, were originally intended for the main (western) entrance. This possibility was not considered here because it is believed that the western portal of Saint Sophia had already been decorated with the Romanesque bronze doors in the fourteenth century. In any event, the doors that were executed in 1336 could be found in the doorposts of the southern chapel some time after 1411. See V. N. Lazarev, "Vasil'jevskie vrata 1336 g." in his book *Russkaja srednevekovaja živopis'* (Moscow, 1970), 181-183, 189-190. For illustrations of these doors, see also *Alexandrov*, ed. A. Rogov (Leningrad, 1979), 60-65, ill. 47-59.

[61] Second Sophia Chronicle, *PSRL* 6 (1853): 285, and the Novgorod Chronicle, Dubrovskij manuscript, *PSRL* 15, pt. 1, sec. 3 (1929): 546; cf. N. E. Andreev, "Mitropolit Makarij kak dejatel' religioznogo iskusstva," *Seminarium Kondakovianum* 7 (Prague, 1935), 234, reprinted in

on the external wall and hence exposed to the destructive effects of weather must have been made only after 1439, most likely around 1450, when the western chapel was decorated with paintings by order of Archbishop Evfimij. This decoration was preceded in 1439 by the renovation and gilding of the tombstones located here—those of the cathedral's founder, Prince Vladimir (d. 1052), and of his mother, connected with the inception of their cult.[62] These dates are not too remote from the time when the Cyrillic inscriptions were etched on the doors. It is therefore reasonable to assume that the installation of the Romanesque doors in the cathedral's portal was connected with the redecoration of the western chapel.

It should be emphasized here, once again, that the author of the passage from the Chronicle quoted above, writing immediately after 1528, used the description "doors ... to the west" although he must have known the legend about their Chersonian origin. It would seem that at this time the name Chersonian Doors had not yet gained acceptance. But a few decades later it came to be the colloquial name among the Novgorodians for the western gates of the cathedral.

The middle of the fifteenth century could be considered the defiinite *terminus post quem* for the rise of the tradition that was to justify the name Chersonian for the bronze doors. These new doors, unusual for Novgorodian religious art, were placed in the portal of Saint Sophia during the work of restoration on the western chapel undertaken in 1439–1450.

The decision to adorn Saint Sophia, which was the heart of the Novgorod Republic, with the Romanesque doors, betokened no lack of awareness of the doors' Western provenance, if only because of the Latin inscriptions. After all, Latin was not unknown in Novgorod;[63] the author of the

---

his *Collected Studies in Muscovy: Western Influence and Byzantine Inheritance* (London, 1970), no. 4.

[62] First Novgorod Chronicle (see n. 22), 420; *PSRL* 30: 118. A. S. Xorošev ("Iz istorii boŕby Novgoroda protiv Moskvy. Mestnye kanonizacii 30–40-x XV v.," *Vestnik Moskovskogo universiteta*, 1971, no. 6: 59ff.) considers that the establishment of the commemoration of the cofounder of Saint Sophia Cathedral—a symbol of Novgorod's independence—also had its own anti-Muscovite, political motivation.

[63] The lively trade and diplomatic relations with their frequent conflicts, particularly with the Hansa and Livonia, and their permanent representatives in Novgorod (the German and Gotland factories; the Catholic church) promoted contact between the Novgorodians and the "Latins" as well as familiarity with Western Europe. See, for example, N. A. Kazakova, *Russko-livonskie i russko-ganzejskie otnošenija. Konec XIV–načalo XVI v.* (Leningrad, 1975), 85-123; A. L. Xoroškevič, *Torgovlja Velikogo Novgoroda s Pribaltikoj i Zapadnoj Evropoj v XIV–XV vv.* (Moscow, 1963), 5-31. It should also be emphasized that the Novgorod archbishop Evfimij II (1429–1458) was known for his patronage of the arts, numerous building projects, and contacts with the West; see V. N. Lazarev, *Iskusstvo Novgoroda* (Moscow–Leningrad, 1947), 134ff. J. Raba, "Evfimij II., Erzbischof von Gross-Novgorod und Pskov. Ein Kirchen-

Rusian inscriptions was able to read and translate them, at times with an exaggerated literalness. At the end of the fifteenth century, attempts were even made to teach Latin more broadly at the archepiscopal court and in the monasteries.[64] Hence, it cannot be said that the competent church hierarchy was ignorant either at the time the doors were being put up or later when they began to be associated with Cherson. Nevertheless, from the moment the church leaders decided to expose the doors to public view, a question arose concerning how to define the nature of their iconography from the point of view of the Orthodox canon. The religious and symbolic content of the bas-reliefs did reach through Italy to Byzantine patterns. Only in the treatment of one of the subjects did they differ essentially from representations proper to Byzantine art.[65]

Before it was decided to place the Romanesque doors in the main portal of Saint Sophia, the archbishop and the cathedral clergy had to agree that their iconography accorded with the tradition of Orthodox representation. The Cyrillic inscriptions then etched on the doors were a visible expression of this *imprimatur* of the church authorities.[66]

---

fürst als Leiter einer weltlichen Republik," *Jahrbücher für Geschichte Osteuropas* 25 (1977): 166-172; also A. V. Ryndina, "Novgorod i zapadnoevropejskoe iskusstvo XV veka (o nekotoryx izdelijax xudožestvennogo remesla iz raskopok Gotskogo dvora)," in *Drevnerusskoe iskusstvo. Zarubežnye svjazi* (Moscow, 1955), 240-251. It should be noted that Raba's attempt in the above-mentioned article to divide up the activity of Evfimij II into two periods, one when he was innovative in his perception of Western art (1429-1437), and a second, when he became a traditionalist, is grossly oversimplified. The political vacillations of Evfimij did not find such an impudent and direct reflection in his cultural policy. Any reference to his commission to build a church on "the old base" as an expression of his traditionalism is entirely unfounded. In Old Rusian church architecture, the use of old foundations was normal.

[64] A. O. Sedel'nikov, "Očerki katoličeskogo vlijanija v Novgorode v konce XV–načale XVI veka," *Doklady AN SSSR*, 5th ser., 1929, no. 1: 16-19. On the "Latinism" of the Gennadij circle, see Lur'e, *Ideologičeskaja bor'ba* (see n. 12), 266-283. See also J. L. Wieczynski's summarizing survey, "Archbishop Gennadius and the West: The Impact of Catholic Ideas upon the Church of Novgorod," *Canadian–American Slavic Studies* 6 (1972): 374-389.

[65] I refer to the bas-relief of the enthroned Christ between the Apostles Peter and Paul—a composition strongly emphasizing Peter's primacy, derived from the *traditio legis*. This scene and its reinterpretation in Novgorod as a special variant of the Deësis composition, is discussed in my unpublished study (see n. 48).

[66] The decision of the Stoglav Church Council of 1551 spelling out the requirements for an icon painter and emphasizing the responsibility of church authorities, established the earlier, particularly Novgorodian, practice as a general rule. Questions dealing with denomination, i.e., the inscription of the icons, were also debated at the Council. See G. Ostrogorsky, "Les décisions du 'Stoglav' au sujet de la peinture d'images et les principes de l'iconographie byzantine," *L'art byzantine chez les Slaves. Recueil Th. Uspensky*, vol. 1 (Paris, 1930), 393-411; Andreev, "Mitropolit Makarij" (see n. 61), 237-242. The superscripts explaining the image depicted are its essential component and were perceived as "the image of the voice" and "the soul of the icon," since only an image that is attested by name becomes an icon in the proper sense of the

Thus, once the subject of the doors was recognized as Orthodox, as being in accordance, in the terms of that time, with the "Constantinople mode" and "old Greek patterns," they began to be considered by many as a work of Greek masters, that is, as a Byzantine relic. Thanks to Herberstein, it is known that in 1517, and certainly for some time before that, the doors were perceived in Novgorod as a trophy brought from Cherson. This perception was possibly based on the reference to "four copper icons" among the loot brought from Cherson by Prince Vladimir, noted in the mid-fifteenth-century manuscript of the Novgorod Chronicle under the year 986.[67] The expression *icon* also had the broader meaning of any image, any figural representation and, hence, one should consider the Novgorod correction of the original record as very ingenious. The doors with their subject matter—a kind of iconostasis—fully deserve, in the eyes of a Christian of medieval Rus', the name of "copper icon." It was only a matter of time before the Novgorod cleric or lay person began to associate the doors, before which he prayed upon entering and leaving the cathedral, with the legend of their having been brought from Cherson: to call them Chersonian on an everyday basis, in accordance with a point of view felt to be so important then. The end of the fifteenth century saw the formation of the tradition itself, while the name Chersonian Doors became permanent during the second half of the subsequent century.

---

word. Without an inscription it cannot be an icon, since worship is equally related to the image and the name. The right of appellation—i.e., the assertion of the auto-identity (*samo-toždestvo*) of the person depicted, and the furnishing of inscriptions on an icon—belongs to the Church and is carried out under the supervision of the bishop or even with his participation in important cases. See P. A. Florenskij, "Ikonostas," in *Bogoslovskie Trudy* (Moscow, 1972), 111ff., 137; B. Uspensky, *The Semiotics of the Russian Icon* (Lisse, 1976), 11, 24, n. 25.

[67] First Novgorod Chronicle (see n. 22), 156; this reading also occurs in some later manuscripts, ibid., 548; *PSRL* 30: 36. The original record in the Primary Chronicle refers to "four bronze horses," i.e., the *quadriga*; cf. *PSRL* 1: 116; *PSRL* 2: 101; *The Russian Primary Chronicle: Laurentian Text,* trans. and ed. S. H. Cross and O. P. Sherbowitz-Wetzor (Cambridge, Mass., 1953), 116. Evidently the text did not convey much to the person transcribing it in the middle of the fifteenth century; believing that his predecessor accidently omitted the letter *i*, he filled in the gap, changing *koni* to *ikoni*. The tendency toward this erroneous reading can be seen in the Laurentian manuscript of 1377, *PSRL* 1: 116 (*koně* to *ikoně*). It would be simpler to suggest that in Novgorod during the second half of the fifteenth century, there remained a remote recollection about the importation of Byzantine (Chersonian) doors at the dawn of Christianity (see n. 51). But such a situation should be recognized as implausible when the memory of the object is not associated with the object itself, which was not only preserved but even continued to function in full view in one of the apertures of Saint Sophia.

The "Chersonian" Shrines between Novgorod and Moscow

There is no need to examine all references to Chersonian religious art-works or every relic designated as Chersonian.[68] All those I have examined lead me to conclude that the attribution Chersonian originally appeared in Novgorod, with the oldest references belonging to the second half of the fifteenth or, rather, to the turn of the sixteenth century. Further references appear sporadically during the sixteenth century, while in the seventeenth, the number greatly increases. While sources contemporaneous with Ivan the Terrible indicate that he confiscated three icons considered to be of Chersonian origin, the seventeenth-century report of the Third Novgorod Chronicle creates the impression that at that time innumerable "valuable Greek, i.e., Chersonian icons" were carried away from Novgorod and its environs.[69]

To explain why the Chersonian shrines appeared so late and primarily in Novgorod, it is worth taking a closer look at the oldest references to these relics as well as at the objects themselves. Such a review reveals how very gradually the conviction emerged concerning their origins in Cherson, Greece, or Constantinople, and how only with time the label Chersonian became permanently connected with its object.

When recording the "peculiar signs" that foretold the fall of the Novgorod Republic in 1471, the chronicle written in Moscow in late 1490 mentions that "in the Church of Our Savior, in the Xutyn' Monastery (near Novgorod), the Chersonian bells rang by themselves."[70] This tale of a requiem for Novgorod had to appear, then, no earlier than after the final defeat (in 1478), since the record in the Stroev Manuscript of the Fourth

---

[68] For example, the famous *Mstislav Evangelistary* of 1115–1117 was acknowledged as a Chersonian article. Its binding, as is apparent from the colophon, was completed in Constantinople by order of the prince and has been preserved to the present day with significant changes and additions made in the sixteenth century; see I. I. Tolstoj and N. P. Kondakov, *Russkie drevnosti* 5 (St. Petersburg, 1897), 532; 6 (St. Petersburg, 1899), 159. The name Chersonian was also attributed to the Church of "Fiery Gilding" by a Russian workshop at the end of the fifteenth century; see *The Dormition Cathedral in the Moscow Kremlin*, ed. M. P. Alpatov (Moscow, 1971), 17, 50.

[69] *Novgorodskie letopisi* (see n. 52), 341, 399–400.

[70] The text about the Chersonian bells is absent from the Muscovite chronicle compilation of the early 1490s (*PSRL* 25 [1949]) but is present in the chronicle compilation from the very end of the 1490s found in the Simeon Chronicle (*PSRL* 18 [1913]: 224), Vologda–Perm' Chronicle (*PSRL* 26 [1959]: 279), Nikanor Chronicle (*PSRL* 27 [1962]: 128) and chronicle compilations of 1497 and 1518 (*PSRL* 28 [1964]: 121, 230). The Chersonian bells in Xutyn' are also mentioned in the compilations from the first half of the sixteenth century. See *Iosafovskaja letopis'* (Moscow, 1957), 62; *Nikonovskaja letopis'* (*PSRL* 12 [1901]: 124), *Voskresenskaja letopis'* (*PSRL* 8 [1859]: 158). Of later manuscripts, see *Novgorodskie letopisi* (see n. 52), 305.

Novgorod Chronicle, running through the year 1477, is satisfied with a more modest listing of these prophecies and does not mention the Chersonian bells.[71] As to their number, opinions must have differed, since in 1517 Herberstein was told of one bell that had been brought with the doors as a trophy from Cherson.

A Chersonian bell was also reported in Pskov, a center closely connected with Novgorod. In this case it is possible to determine the chronological period of the legend's origin. The Pskov Chronicle compiled in 1547 tells us that in 1518 Pskov received from the Muscovite ruler a new bell "in place of the previously removed Chersonian bell which was used to call the town assembly." The extensive *Tale of the Occupation of Pskov,* written after the events of 1510, contains a detailed description of the confiscation of the assembly bell, but the author says nothing about its genealogy or age, although he tells of the despair and tears of the Pskovians.[72] Thus, the tradition was born somewhere between 1510 and 1547.

The Chersonian icon of the Mother of God appears in the *Vision of Sacristan Aaron of Saint Sophia*: spending the night in the church, the sacristan, a monk Aaron, awoke and saw a procession from the vestibule to the altar of former Novgorodian archbishops, who then sang for a whole hour in front of the "Chersonian icon of the most pure Mother of God." When Archbishop Evfimij heard about what had happened from Aaron, he interpreted the vision as follows: "God will not leave this place thanks to the prayers of its archbishops."[73] An inscription recently discovered on the

---

[71] *PSRL* 4 [1848]: 128; *PSRL* 4, pt. 1, sec. 2 [1925]: 446.

[72] *Pskovskie letopisi,* vol. 1, ed. A. N. Nasonov (Moscow, 1941), 94ff., 100; ibid., vol. 2 (1955), 224, 255. On the copy of 1547, see A. Nasonov, "Iz istorii pskovskogo letopisanija," *Istoričeskie zapiski* 18 (1946): 260-268. On the history of Pskovian chronicle writing in the sixteenth century and its anti-Muscovite tendency, see N. E. Andreev, "O xaraktere Treťej Pskovskoj letopisi," in *The Religious World of Russian Culture. Russia and Orthodoxy: Essays in Honor of Georges Florovsky,* vol. 2 (The Hague-Paris, 1975), 117-158.

[73] *Aaron's Vision* is included in the Novgorod Chronicle, Dubrovskij MS, under the year 6966 (1458) immediately following the report of the death of Archbishop Evfimij (*PSRL* 4, pt. 1, sec. 2: 491) and in the Third Novgorod Chronicle in the version of c. 1673 (according to the manuscripts of the eighteenth century and the Pogodin MS, no. 1416 from the end of the seventeenth century; see *Novgorodskie letopisi* (see n. 52), 271; *PSRL* 3: 239). Thanks to the obliging help of I. P. Šaskoľskij, Leningrad, and Ja. N. Ščapov, Moscow, we have at our disposal the unpublished text of the "Vision" from two manuscripts: (1) one from the mid-seventeenth century belonging to the Leningrad division of the Institute of History of the Soviet Academy of Sciences, N. P. Lixačev Coll., no. 294, fol. 47v–48v; and (2) one from c. 1540, a miscellany of the Lenin Library, Volokolamsk Coll. (F. 113), no. 659, fol. 357–357v; cf. also the notes on these manuscripts by L. A. Dmitriev, *Žitijnye povesti russkogo severa kak pamjatniki literatury XIII–XVII vv.* (Leningrad, 1973), 171-174. I am also indebted to Ja. N. Ščapov for the reference to the copy made by P. Stroev in 1816 from MS no. 196 of the Savvin-Storoževskij Monastery coll. (Rumjancev 39/1, fol. 12v). Its text is very close to the

lower frame of one of the icons of the iconostasis in the Cathedral of Saint Sophia, which tells about the painting of icons by the monk Aaron in 6946 (1438) by order of Archbishop Evfimij, provides a good reason to identify the sacristan monk Aaron with the icon-painter monk Aaron.[74] The story about *Aaron's Vision* must have been composed long after his participation in icon painting had been forgotten; in order to explain Aaron's presence in the cathedral at night, he was made a sacristan, which he could, in fact, have become at a later time. But by the same token, the text has preserved an interesting detail: when he saw the archbishops' procession, Aaron, "lying on his bed, overcome by great fear, did not dare to awaken his associates." This detail, completely superfluous from the standpoint of the *Vision*, becomes understandable if we consider that the monk Aaron was an icon painter and was conducting work at that time in the cathedral along with his partners, who, like himself, were icon painters. Such artistic artels were commonplace, as was the practice of spending the night in a building of the church while working. During these years Archbishop Evfimij was in fact restoring and redocorating the Cathedral of Saint Sophia.

The observations referred to above (n. 73) regarding the composition of the Volokolamsk Collection Manuscript 659 and the indirect connection between the *Vision* and the cycle of Novgorodian legends suggest that the *Vision* was recorded in the last quarter of the fifteenth century[75] It must be added that *Aaron's Vision* remains indisputably connected with the cult of Archbishop Evfimij; evidence of his worship, apparent in the last decade of the fifteenth century, was established by Evfimij's successor, Archbishop Iona (1458–1470), when he ordered the *vita* of his predecessor to be written

---

Volokolamsk MS 659. Comparing the known manuscripts, I conclude that the Volokolamsk MS 659 has preserved the most precise, original wording. The Dubrovskij MS from the very end of the sixteenth century suffers in its characteristic mechanical omission and simultaneous addition (copied from Novgorodian chronicles of the fifteenth century), placing the vision in the year 6946 (1438). The late sixteenth-century manuscript connects the vision with the subsequent renovation of the tombstones of Prince Vladimir and his mother and the establishment of their commemoration on October 4. The text, included in the Third Novgorod Chronicle (without noticeable omission), shares a common protograph with the Dubrovskij MS. The wording of the *Vision* in Lixačev no. 294 is clearly secondary in relation to Dubrovskij's protograph, disseminated as it was in the verbose style of the end of the sixteenth and the seventeenth centuries and remade into a narration by Aaron himself (conducted in the first person) and late at night on the 3rd of October, 6846.

[74] See V. V. Filatov, "Ikonostas Novgorodskogo Sofijskogo sobora" in *Drevnerusskoe iskusstvo. Xudožestvennaja kul'tura Novgoroda* (Moscow, 1968), 65-68; È. S. Smirnova, "Ikony 1438 g. v Sofijskom sobore v Novogorode" in *Pamjatniki kul'tury. Novye otkrytija. Ežegodnik 1977* (Moscow, 1977), 215-224.

[75] V. I. Ključevskij, *Drevnerusskie žitija svjatyx kak istoričeskij istočnik* (Moscow, 1871), 161-164; Dmitriev, *Žitijnye povesti* (see n. 73), 171-173.

by Paxomij Logofet.[76] This *vita* was compiled in the 1460s.[77] The cult of
Evfimij which arose thereafter undoubtedly stimulated the oral, and later
written, record of the *Vision*. There are, however, no data that permit a
closer determination of the time of the *Vision*'s literary treatment.[78] Perhaps
it was written only in the sixteenth century: *Aaron's Vision* did not exist in

[76] E. E. Golubinskij, *Istorija kanonizacii svjatyx v russkoj cerkvi, ČOIDR*, 1903, bk. 2: 82.

[77] Ključevskij, *Drevnerusskie žitija svjatyx* (see n. 75), 153-156; V. Jablonskij, *Paxomij Serb i ego agiografičeskie pisanija* (St. Petersburg, 1908), 17ff., 80-83. On the *Life* with miracles added as late as the sixteenth century, see *Pamjatniki starinnoj russkoj literatury*, ed. G. Kušelev-Bezborodko (St. Petersburg, 1872), 16-26; there is, however, no allusion to *Aaron's Vision*. The *Life* is usually dated c. 1460, when Paxomij was in Novgorod; but during the term of office of Archbishop Iona (1458–1470), he could have visited this city more than once; living in Moscow, Paxomij remained in constant contact with the Novgorod prelate, and therefore it is more correct to date the *Life of Evfimij* over a broader period.

[78] A reference to the *terminus post quem* for such a literary treatment may be contained in *Aaron's Vision*. Deserving of attention is the report that "the already deceased archbishops entered the church from the vestibule through the former church doors and went to the holy altar; the church doors opened to them by themselves" (Volok. 659, fol. 357). Ascertaining which doors this passage may refer to holds a decisive significance for further conclusions. First of all, we must exclude the enticing possibility that the story was referring to the doors at the main outside entrance to the cathedral, i.e., those doors that were replaced by the Romanesque bronze doors, since the procession did not accidentally begin from the western vestibule where several burial sites of Novgorodian bishops were located. The reference may have been to the inside doors leading into the actual cathedral since such doors separating the vestibule from the church proper existed even at the beginning of the seventeenth century (cf. "Činovnik Novgorodskogo Sofijskogo sobora [see n. 59], 210, and Beljaev, "Korsunskie dveri" [see n. 51], 307). But considering the context, which indicates that the procession set off to the altar with the undoubtedly closed Royal Doors (Gates of Paradise), it is more likely that the story has in mind only these doors. Calling them "Church" (*cerkovnye*), and not "Royal" (*tsarskie*), Doors does not preclude such an interpretation of the text since a general designation of the Royal Doors as "Church" Doors was known to have existed (cf. I. I. Sreznevskij, *Materialy dlja slovarja drevnerusskogo jazyka*, vol. 1 [St. Petersburg, 1893], 648). If this is the case, then the designation of the doors as "former" acquires a special meaning in comparison with the chronicle's information that Archbishop Makarij in 1528 ordered that "Royal Doors into Saint Sophia be constructed, because the former doors had long since become dilapidated, no longer beautiful" (*PSRL* 6: 284; 4, pt. 1, sec. 3 [1929]: 545). The designation of the doors as "former" could be attributed to the author of the literary wording of the oral *Vision*, which must, then, be dated to the time shortly after 1528 when the impression of the construction of new "Royal Doors" was still fresh. The possibility of such a later dating of the written version of the *Vision* remains, however, a hypothesis that requires further verification. The later inclusion of *Aaron's Vision* in the practice of the Church is indicated by the *Pontifical* of the Novgorod Cathedral of c. 1630, thus registering a liturgical practice that arose in the sixteenth century, probably around the time of Makarij, i.e., before 1542. In the *Pontifical* under October 4 (ibid., 41), the day that coincides with the requiem in memory of *Aaron's Vision*, there is no mention of the vision although the appearance of the saintly Novgorodian Archbishop Ioann to Archbishop Evfimij is noted. As a result, October 4 was established as an annual day of requiem in memory of all the Novgorod bishops. Evfimij's vision itself, the so-called *Tale of the Tomb of Saint Ioann of Novgorod*, was compiled in the 1470s. See Dmitriev, *Žitijnye povesti* (see n. 73), 160-169.

the chronicle compiled in Novgorod shortly after 1491, but judging by the
Dubrovskij manuscript, it was already included in the Archbishops' Chronicle of Novgorod, compiled between 1542 and 1548, containing information
through the year 1539.[79] At any rate, by the end of the fifteenth century, at
least an oral tradition about *Aaron's Vision* was alive in Novgorod, a tradition containing a reference to an icon in front of which the dead archbishops prayed. This reference must have been topographically concrete and
comprehensible to every Novgorodian, since there was more than one icon
of the Mother of God in Saint Sophia. Therefore, lacking other distinguishing marks, the reference to this icon of the Mother of God as Chersonian
must be interpreted as being initially inherent in the tradition. Evfimij's
interpretation of Aaron's vision—that God would not leave Novgorod
because of the prayers of its holy archbishops—was topical after the events
of 1471, on the eve of the last attempt to defend the city-state's independence at the end of the 1470s, and continued to sound encouraging and
comforting even after 1478.

The icon of Our Lady of Cherson, to which *Aaron's Vision* referred, is in
all probability the very same one that is located in Novgorod's Saint
Sophia to this day. This huge icon (173 centimeters in height) in the basic
tier of the iconostasis is painted in several coats (the uppermost coat is
from the nineteenth century) and, judging by the frame, belongs to the
twelfth century. It represents a type of Hodegetria, similar to other Chersonian icons, one from Toropec, dating from the twelfth or thirteenth century, and the other from the Annunciation Cathedral of the Moscow
Kremlin, dating from the end of the thirteenth century. However, these
oldest icons had no influence on the shaping of the iconographic type of
Our Lady of Cherson; the latter was formed only in the sixteenth and seventeenth centuries on the basis of one of the variants of the Virgin
Glykophilousa.[80]

[79] The Dubrovskij MS belongs to the very end of the sixteenth century, but there is no
basis for suggesting that it was supplemented while being copied, i.e., after the 1540s. True, the
Vision does not appear in the Academy MS which reflected this chronicle compilation (cf.
PSRL 4, pt. 1, sec. 2: 463-470), which A. Šaxmatov explains through the abridgement of a text
identical with the Dubrovskij MS. Nor is it contained in the MS of the Archive Collection
(*CGADA* F. 181, no. 20/253); but this is for another reason, since in this MS the chronicle
compilation of 1539 is represented as beginning with 1479. See A. A. Šaxmatov, "O tak
nazyvaemoj Rostovskoj letopisi," *ČOIDR*, 1904, bk. 1: 50-66, 163-177. On the chronicle
compilation of 1491 and 1539, see also A. N. Nasonov, *Istorija russkogo letopisanija* (Moscow,
1969), 354ff., 465-470; and Lur'e, *Obščerusskie letopisi* (see n. 13), 135, 169, 177, 190, 252ff.

[80] See Tolstoj and Kondakov, *Russkie drevnosti* 6 (see n. 68), 155; cf. N. P. Kondakov,
Ikonografija Bogorodicy, vol. 2 (Petrograd, 1915), 207; Antonova and Mneva, *Katalog*, vol. 2 (see
n. 32), 263; O. S. Popova, *Iskusstvo Novgoroda i Moskvy pervoj poloviny četyrnadcatogo veka. Ego*

Two more icons from the Novgorod Cathedral of Saint Sophia, both of which have been preserved and described as Chersonian, deserve mention: the Savior enthroned (with a finger pointing to an open Gospel) from the end of the fourteenth or the beginning of the fifteenth century; and Peter and Paul from the eleventh or twelfth century. The first of these icons inspired the author of the *Tale of the Miraculous Appearance of the Image of the Savior to Manuel, the Greek Emperor*. We find out from this tradition, which arose in Novgorod in the first quarter of the sixteenth century, that "this icon was in Constantinople before the baptism of Vladimir and was painted by Manuel, the Greek emperor."[81]

At the time this asynchronism might not have been shocking, but the reference to Manuel I Komnenos, an emperor with theological ambitions, was not accidental. A concise interpretation of the symbolic nature of the picture reveals the author's true aim: to condemn the infringement of the Church's judicial immunity by a secular ruler. Recalling the rights of the *sacerdotium* and the duties of the *imperium* was very topical in view of the increasing interference of the Muscovite ruler in Novgorod's church affairs.

The Novgorod chronicler, writing about these two icons being taken to Moscow in 1561 and their subsequent return in 1572, says nothing about their Chersonian derivation.[82] But the seventeenth-century editor clearly interpolates the text, "the icon ... of Peter and Paul ... almost entirely covered with silver," by adding "Chersonian."[83] This icon has been preserved and dates to the eleventh century; its silver frame is a local twelfth-century product, as is shown by the Old Rusian inscriptions. Both icons must have been particularly distinguished among the others of the Novgorod Cathedral since the author, writing in the 1530s, names them, stating

svjazi s Vizantiej (Moscow, 1980), 168ff. For a photograph of the Novgorodian icon and of Our Lady of Cherson and remarks about them, see N. Mneva and V. Filatov, "Ikona Petra i Pavla Novgorodskogo Sofijskogo Sobora," in _Iz istorii russkogo i zapadnoevropejskogo iskusstva_ (Moscow, 1960), 86 n. 13, 92 n. 27, 97; and Smirnova, _Živopis' Velikogo Novgoroda_ (see n. 32), 65, 153.

[81] _Novgorodskie letopisi_ (see n. 52), 183; V. G. Brjusova and Ja. N. Ščapov, "Novgorodskaja legenda o Manuile care grečeskom," _VV_ 32 (1971): 85-102, text 103, ill. 1. In V. Brjusova's opinion, the icon was painted in Novgorod after a model of a Greek icon of the eleventh to thirteenth centuries.

[82] Second Novgorod Chronicle, _PSRL_ 30: 174-192. Here the chronicler—an eyewitness to the event—describes these icons simply as the "basic, old" ones, i.e, the icons long since belonging to the regular (basic) tier of Saint Sophia's iconostasis. On their return, it was not noticed that the icon of the Savior was a copy, but the question came to light in the seventeenth centry. At any rate, it was perhaps considered improper to doubt the tsar's gesture.

[83] Cf. _Novgorodskie letopisi_ (see n. 52), 93, 117, 347. For photographs of the silver frame, see A. N. Svirin, _Juvelirnoe iskusstvo Drevnej Rusi XI–XVII vekov_ (Moscow, 1972), 46-69, nos. 17, 18.

that Archbishop Makarij "recommended that the icons in Saint Sophia be arranged according to a determined order ... also the Constantinopolitan icons of Our Most Merciful Savior ... and of the Holy Apostles Peter and Paul."[84] Thus, the icons, which by the seventeenth century and perhaps a bit earlier were consistently being called "Chersonian," are here labeled "Constantinopolitan."

There is one more Chersonian icon with an interesting history. This is an Annunciation depicted in a rarely encountered iconographic version with the Child descending to the Virgin's womb. It is the so-called Ustjug Annunciation, a twelfth-century icon from the Saint George Monastery near Novgorod, at present in the Tret'jakov Gallery.[85] Taken to Moscow at the turn of 1553, it was soon the object of disputes being waged at that time on the permissibility of various iconographic representations from the Orthodox point of view. Among the participants of the discussion were the former archbishop of Novgorod and, after 1542, metropolitan of Moscow, Makarij, as well as the priest Silvester, brought in from Novgorod. These two had recruited to Moscow numerous icon painters from Novgorod and Pskov who hastened the development of a new tendency in church art and aroused the opposition of conservative circles.

Both sides, however, invoked tradition. In the dispute with Chancellor Ivan Viskovatyj, who protested against certain departures from the canon in the composition of the Annunciation (among them "Latin sophistication"), Metropolitan Makarij, referring to the icon brought from Novgorod, explained that "it was painted in Cherson and brought from there 500 years ago or more." In other statements, Makarij constantly invoked the tradition of the Eastern Church, citing "Constantinopolitan" or "Greek painting" as the

---

[84] *PSRL* 6: 285. Cf. Mneva and Filatov, "Ikona Petra i Pavla" (see n. 80), 81-102; V. N. Lazarev, *Novgorodian Icon-Painting* (Moscow, 1969), 6, pl. 1. In the works cited here, the proposed dating of this monumental icon of Peter and Paul on a limewood panel (236 × 147 cm) from the middle of the eleventh century, which would make the painting of the icon coincide with the date of the building of Novgorod's Saint Sophia, does not sound convincing, particularly since there is no way to distinguish the palette of an eleventh-century artist from that of a twelfth-century one. Moreover, a substantial detail—the lack of traces of paint on the wide (17 cm each) borders—indicates that from the very beginning the icon was intended for framing. The silver setting of the locally executed frame has been preserved on the icon. This frame may be dated from the 1120s, although according to the paleographic characteristics one could certainly speak loosely about the twelfth century. There are no grounds for suggesting that the first frame was replaced in such a relatively short period of time, all the more since it has become clear in the course of restoration that while the faces, hands, and feet of the apostles were touched up several times (the oldest coat is from the fifteenth century), the areas covered by the frame were never retouched.

[85] Antonova and Mneva, *Katalog*, vol. 1 (see n. 32), 54-57, pl. 20; Lazarev, *Novgorodian Icon-Painting*, 9, pl. 6.

obligatory model. He expressed pride in the fact that the Novgorod Saint Sophia was adorned with paintings by "authentic Greek painters" and emphasized that he recommended "that the painting be done according to old Greek patterns." Similarly Silvester, in defending the orthodoxy of the composition of the icon of Saint Sophia—the Divine Wisdom—indicated that it was a copy of a Greek icon contemporaneous with the building of the Novgorod Cathedral, and thus from the middle of the eleventh century. And then, generalizing, he stated: "And in all Rus' what is painted on walls and on icons is Greek and Chersonian painting while the works of the local painters are also based on these models."[86]

It can be seen that in the dispute about the iconographic and theological content in religious art, the label "Chersonian" was used as an equivalent for "Constantinopolitan" or "Greek." This dispute also unambiguously stated that Rusian iconography was derived from that tradition of painting initiated by the icons brought from Cherson by Saint Vladimir, the baptizer of Rus'. They found their way to the temples of Kiev and Novgorod, and after the destruction of Kiev were preserved only in Novgorod; it becomes evident that the proper guardian of Orthodox tradition is the Novgorodian Church. Thus, it is obvious that the confiscation of the Chersonian icons in Novgorod, ordered by Ivan IV and supported and inspired by Muscovite Church circles, formed part of the program aimed at guaranteeing the spiritual primacy of Moscow.[87]

There is no doubt that the dispute taken up in the early fifties of the fifteenth century in Moscow was a continuation of the countless opposing tendencies in religious art that had already come to the surface much earlier in Novgorod. Makarij himself, as archbishop of Novgorod (1526–1542), as well as his eminent predecessors in this post such as Gennadij (1482–1503) and Evfimij II (1429–1458), did not refrain from Western influence. The Novgorodian church hierarchy tolerated the penetration of "Latin" motifs into religious

---

[86] See the notes on the questioning of chancellor (dumnyj d'jak) I. Viskovatyj in *ČOIDR*, 1858, bk. 2: 3, 11, 13, 21; cf. N. E. Andreev, "O dele d'jaka Viskovatogo," *Seminarium Kondakovianum* 5 (Prague, 1932), 197-241, reprinted in *Studies in Muscovy* (see n. 61); "Mitropolit Makarij" (see n. 61), 227-244. L. Ouspensky, "Rol' Moskovskix cerkovnyx soborov XVI veka v cerkovnom iskusstve," in *Messager de l'Exarchat du Patriarche Russe en Europe Occidentale* 64 (Paris, 1968), 217-250.

[87] The fashionability of Chersonian icons and other objects of church art also appeared in the Grand Duchy of Lithuania in the sixteenth century. A legend arose about the expedition of Prince Olgerd to Cherson in 1363 and the bringing back, among other numerous icons, of the icon of Our Lady of Ostra Brama. It was even claimed that the Gniezno Doors came from Cherson via Kiev. Cf. *Drzwi Gnieźnieńskie*, vol. 1 (Warsaw, 1956), 109. The interest in Chersonian objects in the Ukraine and Belorussia requires examination. It seems to be linked with the aspirations of the Orthodox Church in the Jagiellonian states.

iconography, particularly those that enriched its theological-didactic content;[88] but when disputes or doubts arose it favored the new, while simultaneously emphasizing—as was still done by the Novgorodian priest Silvester in Moscow—that Novgorodian religious art took a determined stand on the basis of the canons of Orthodox Christianity and that its origin was immaculately Byzantine.

Thus, in the case of debatable subjects of iconography, the attestation by ecclesiastical authorities that this was a "Greek," "Constantinopolitan," or "Chersonian" painting signified the assertion of Orthodox iconographic tradition. The Byzantine canon in iconography was binding to such a degree that when the Pskovian icon painter invoked "Greek patterns" c. 1502, this swayed the opinion of Gennadij, the archbishop of Novgorod and Pskov.[89]

The history of the Novgorod Republic in the fifteenth century, its political downfall in 1471–78, and the intensification of its intellectual and artistic life that subsequently followed, explain why it was precisely in Novgorod that the need arose for religious art with a Chersonian pedigree. In the fifteenth century and in the first half of the sixteenth, Novgorod, thanks to its lively contacts with Western Europe, was not only under the influence of the latter but itself undertook the initiative for assimilating the achievements of the world of Latin culture. Indeed, during the last decade of the fifteenth century, the Dominican Benjamin worked at the court of Saint Sophia on a translation and codification of the full text of the Bible.[90] In spite of obvious contacts with

[88] An informative example of the influence of Western art as well as a Latin commentary on the subject is furnished by the Apocalypsis icon of c. 1500, whose iconography transcends the framework of Byzantine tradition. Cf. Y. Christe, "Quelques remarques sur l'Icone de l'Apocalipse du maître du Kremlin à Moscow," in *Izograf* 6 (Belgrade, 1975), 54-67, and 14 plates. For the same icon in color, see M. V. Alpatov, *Early Russian Icon Painting* (Moscow, 1974), pls. 159-162. The influence of the Gothic model on the Novgorodian icon "The Mother of God with the Child Enthroned" has been convincingly shown by M. Alpatov in "Eine abendländische Komposition in altrussischer Umbildung," in *Byzantinische Zeitschrift* 30 (1929): 623-626. The author dates the icon from the second half of the 15th century, while V. Lazarev (*Iskusstvo Novgoroda* [see n. 63], 118), on the basis of the icon's coloring, dates it from the first half of the fifteenth century. The presence of Saint Sergij of Radonež among the figures on the border would contradict this dating, if not for the assumption that this figure was added later; cf. Antonova and Mneva, *Katalog*, vol. 1 (see n. 32), no. 49, 111, ill. 59.

[89] See the letter of Dmitrij Gerasimov (who had been one of the members of the Gennadij circle) to the Pskov governor M. G. Misjur̃-Munexin (after 1510, in *Pribavlenija k tvorenijam sv. otcov* 17 (1859): 190 ff; cf. N. Andreev, "Inok Zinovij ob ikonopočitanii i ikonopisanii," *Seminarium Kondakovianum* 8 (1936): 272 ff., reprint in *Studies in Muscovy* (see n. 61). On the identity of the letter's author, see Lur̃e, *Ideologičeskaja bor̃ba* (see n. 12), 484, n. 270.

[90] On the study of the translation itself, see the works of G. Freidhof and his contribution in the present volume; cf. A. D. Sedel̃nikov, "K izučeniju 'Slova kratka' i dejatel̃nosti dominikanca Veniamina," *IORJaS* 30 (1925/26): 205-225. This "Slovo kratko," written at the request of Archbishop Gennadij by a Catholic author, was directed against the encroachment (of the

Catholic countries, however, Novgorod was far from "falling into the Latin heresy." Yet it was precisely this accusation that served as a pretext for the 1471 expedition that deprived Novgorod of its independence.[91] The Novgorodian Church was thrust into a stance of constantly having to prove its fidelity to the principles of Orthodoxy and of defending its position, including property, against the secularization attempts of the Muscovite authorities.[92] In losing the political struggle with Moscow, Novgorod did not neglect the ideological confrontation, justifying its rights to spiritual supremacy. An entire cycle of tales that arose during the last decades of the fifteenth century and the first half of the sixteenth served this purpose.[93] These tales stressed that for

---

Muscovite authorities) on church property; see also Lur'e, *Ideologičeskaja bor'ba* (see n. 12), 225-228. On the variety of cultural relations, see the article dedicated essentially to Novgorod by N. Angermann, "Kulturbeziehungen zwischen dem Hanseraum und dem Moskauer Russland um 1500, *Hansische Geschichtsblätter* 84 (1966): 20-48. See also H. Birnbaum, "Die Hanse in Novgorod," in *Festschrift für Dietrich Gerhardt* (Marburg, 1977), 28-35; id., "Lord Novgorod the Great: Its Place in Medieval Culture," *Viator* 8 (1977): 249-254.

[91] In M. N. Pokrovskij's apt estimation (*Izbrannye proizvedenija*, vol. 1 [Moscow, 1966], 226), the subjugation of Novgorod was perceived by Moscow as a crusade against apostates from Orthodoxy. On the history of the fall of the Novgorod state, see L. V. Čerepnin, *Obrazovanie russkogo centralizovannogo gosudarstva v XIV–XV vv.* (Moscow, 1960), 855-874; J. Raba, "The Fate of the Novgorodian Republic," *The Slavonic and East European Review* 45, no. 105 (1967): 307-323. The most thorough research in recent times—by V. N. Bernadskij, *Novgorod i Novgorodskaja zemlja v XV veke* (Moscow–Leningrad, 1961), 265-313—is not always sufficiently critical regarding the pro-Muscovite sources. This is undoubtedly due to the influence of a conscious interpretation of the subjugation-annexation of Novgorod "in light of the main political task of the epoch—the completion of the unification of Great Russia" (ibid., 7, 9ff., 308). On the tendentiousness of the Muscovite chroniclers, see the substantive remarks on the sources by Ja. S. Lur'e, "K istorii prisoedinenija Novgoroda v 1477-1479 g..," in *Issledovanija po social'no-političeskoj istorii Rossii. Sbornik statej pamjati B. A. Romanova* (Leningrad, 1971), 89-95.

[92] On the "Slovo kratko," directed toward the defense of church property, see n. 90. It is not by accident that in the struggle with the "heretics," or rather, with those whom it was convenient to accuse of heresy (for example, the "Nonpossessors"), the church circles of Novgorod headed by Archbishop Gennadij represented themselves as the fervent champions of Orthodoxy, assuming the duty of uprooting any type of "heresy," not only among their own but in Moscow as well, in the environment of the sovereign himself. The relationship to tradition (and the perception of innovations in the spirit of truly Orthodox tradition), including icon painting, undoubtedly formed a substantial part of the ideological battle around the vital issues of that time. On the role of Novgorod in the struggle with the Novgorod–Moscow "heresy," see Lur'e, *Ideologičeskaja bor'ba* (see n. 12), 75-203; E. Hösch, *Orthodoxie und Häresie im alten Russland* (Wiesbaden, 1975), 68-72; cf. also F.v. Lilienfeld, "Die 'Häresie' des Fedor Kuricyn," *Forschungen zur osteuropäischen Geschichte* 24 (1978): 39-60.

[93] In *Drevnerusskie žitija svjatyx* (see n. 75), 162, V. Ključevskij writes: "In our history there are not many epochs which would have been surrounded by a swarm of poetic tales as the fall of Novgorodian liberty. It seemed that 'Lord Novgorod the Great,' feeling its life's pulse weakening, transferred its thoughts from Jaroslav's Court, where its voice had fallen silent, to Saint Sophia and other local shrines, calling forth from them the legends of olden times." On

centuries Novgorod, after Kiev, had occupied the first place in Rus'. The "Muscovites" were scoffed at because they had accepted the faith of Christ later, and they were reminded of the blows they had suffered in 1170 from the Novgorodians, supported by the Holy Virgin.[94] Material and written proofs were invoked as testimony that Novgorod was the legitimate heir to the heritage of Constantinople-Cherson-Kiev. For this purpose, some of the icons and other cult objects were now given a Chersonian origin, that is, were associated with the beginnings of Christianity in Rus'. The premise for this was furnished by the well-known record of the Primary Chronicle of 988 concerning the icons and other church objects transported from Cherson to Kiev. The interpretation that something of this fell to Novgorod's lot was facilitated by the list of the Novgorodian bishops, composed only at the beginning of the fifteenth century, naming Joachim of Cherson as the first archbishop of Novgorod. This was then interpolated by the Novgorod Chronicle into the story about the baptism of Rus'.[95] The chronicler gave

Novgorod's literature of the second half of the fifteenth through the first half of the sixteenth century, see the comprehensive section by D. S. Lixačev in *Istorija russkoj literatury*, vol. 2, pt. 1 (Moscow–Leningrad, 1946), 368-389. In recent times there has been a tendency to avoid an isolated treatment of Novgorod's literature from the time when Novgorod lost its independence. The story about the miracle "in the city of Cherson" during the harvest feast on the occasion of the holiday of Saints Koz'ma and Damian, compiled in Novgorod (the oldest MS is from the threshold of the sixteenth century), must be attributed to the time when Cherson became fashionable and the notion of it became, to a certain degree, an epic designation. See M. N. Speranskij, "'Korsunskoe' čudo Koz'my i Damiana," in *IORJaS* 1, no. 1 (1928): 358-375. The author's attribution of the compilation of this story to the fourteenth century seems too early in light of the considerations expressed in the present paper.

[94] A literary rewriting of the *Tale about the Sign from the Icon of the Mother of God* from the middle of the fourteenth century is attributed to the middle or second half of the fifteenth century. This legend acquired a clearly anti-Muscovite character during the period of the fall of Novgorod. For the manuscript tradition, see Dmitriev, *Žitijnye povesti* (see n. 73), 95-148. The icon known in several copies from the second half of the fifteenth through sixteenth centuries, depicting the "Battle of the Novgorodians with the Suzdalians," appears to be a representation of this struggle; see Lazarev, *Novgorodian Icon-Painting* (see n. 84), 35ff., pls. 51-53. Cf. also A. Florow, "Le 'Znamenie' de Novgorod. Évolution de la légende," *Revue des études slaves* 24 (1948): 67-81; 25 (1949): 45-72; D. S. Lixačev, "Ideologičeskaja bor'ba Moskvy i Novgoroda v XIV–XV vekax," in *Istoričeskij Žurnal*, 1941, no. 6: 43-56.

[95] First Novgorod Chronicle (see n. 22), 160, 163, 473, 551. The date of the listing of the Novgorodian bishops and archbishops is based on the results of the study of the listing of *posadniks* by V. L. Janin, *Novgorodskie posadniki* (Moscow, 1962), 14-44. On the first Novgorodian bishop, see A. Poppe, *Państwo i kościół na Rusi w XI w.* (Warsaw, 1968), 162ff. V. G. Brjusova ("Russko-vizantijskie otnošenija serediny XI veka," *Voprosy istorii*, 1972, no. 3: 51-62) has tried to prove that the "Chersonian antiquities" appeared in Novgorod as the result of the campaign and capture of Cherson in 1044. She cites, among other things, the evidence of the Primary Chronicle that all the icons, crosses, and church vessels taken from Cherson were handed over by Vladimir to the Kievan Tithe-Church of the Mother of God. But the hypothesis about the campaign of 1044 is based merely on an uncritical interpretation of legendary

Joachim the cognomen "of Cherson," concluding that the first Novgorodian bishop must have descended from those "Chersonian priests" who were brought into Rus' by Vladimir as mentioned in the Primary Chronicle. It is no wonder, then, that when during the last decades of the fifteenth and the beginning of the sixteenth centuries, material proofs had been gathered and enumerated regarding Novgorod's role as the second spiritual capital of Rusian Christianity after Kiev, the doors of Novgorod's Saint Sophia, considered a Byzantine work, found their way to this list as one of the first items.

The first tradition about the Chersonian sacred shrine preserved beyond the confines of Novgorod—namely, the miracle-working icon of Saint Nikolaj Zarazskij—undoubtedly arose under the influence of the legend about the Chersonian heritage of several Novgorodian "antiquities." It may have been one of the last attempts by the Rjazan' princes who had lost all their independence,[96] to furnish evidence following Novgorod's example, of a direct God-given connection, without Moscow's mediation, between Rjazan' Christianity (and the Rjazan' princes) and the sources of the Christian statehood in Rus'. But even if the cult of the miracle-working icon had been conceived in this fashion, in statu nascendi it was imitated and included in the service of all-Russian ideas as a spiritual bulwark on the southern border of the Muscovite state, which was endangered by the Tatar invasions.

In the end, a simple conclusion can be drawn: the tradition about the sacred "Chersonian antiquities," preserved through the centuries in Russia, appeared no earlier than the second half of the fifteenth century during an ideological confrontation with Moscow, when Novgorod invoked its famous past and its right to be the guardian of Orthodoxy in Russian Christendom. Thus, all the "authentic" Chersonian antiquities received their pedigree beginning at that time.

In Russian ecclesiastic circles of the sixteenth century, the definition of a religious iconographical object as "Chersonian" became synonymous with "Greek" or "Constantinopolitan," that is, as being in accordance with the Orthodox canon. At the same time, the designation "Chersonian" gave concrete historical expression to the Byzantine tradition that began for Rus', according to the Primary Chronicle, with the baptism of its ruler— isoapostolos Vladimir—in Cherson.

---

material from the sixteenth and seventeenth centuries. Also highly uncritical is the attempt to ascribe to the trophies of 1044 those Novgorodian objects of church art, for which the appellation "Chersonian" had become established.

[96] At any rate, before 1521, when the last Rjazan' prince fled to Lithuania; see A. A. Zimin, "Feodaľnaja znať Tverskogo i Rjazanskogo velikix knjažestv i Moskovskoe bojarstvo konca XV–pervoj treti XVI veka," Istorija SSSR, 1973, no. 3: 134-42.

SUNDAY IN MEDIEVAL RUSSIAN CULTURE: *NEDELJA* VERSUS *VOSKRESENIE*

MICHAEL S. FLIER

> ... *i prazdnikъ subotě presta, a nedĕli blagodatь dana bystь vъskresenia radi, i carstvuetъ uže vъ dnexъ nedĕlja, jako vъ tu vъskrese Xristosъ iz mertvyxъ. Věnčaimъ Caricju dnemъ, bratie ...*[1]
>
> — Kirill Turovskij

When Kirill Turovskij extolled the transfer of grace from the Jewish Sabbath to Christian Sunday in his twelfth-century sermon for Thomas Sunday, he could not have foreseen the replacement several centuries later of *nedelja*, the inherited Slavic word for Sunday, by *voskresenie*. The latter originally signified only resurrection and was frequently used in reference to the Resurrection of Christ. Since the Resurrection occurred on a Sunday, the indexical link between Sunday and *voskresenie* 'resurrection' (hereafter V/r) is clear. Nonetheless Kirill might have been surprised to learn that the change from *nedelja* 'Sunday' (hereafter N/S) to *voskresenie* 'Sunday' (hereafter V/S) was not the result of any official edict, secular or religious. To this day the Russian Orthodox Church retains *nedelja* as the official Church Slavic designation for Sunday.[2]

The research on this paper was partially supported by a grant from the UCLA Committee on Research. In textual citations the written date is enclosed in angle brackets < >; the date of the manuscript (in case it differs from the former), in square brackets [ ], e.g., a chronicle entry under the year 1412 in a sixteenth-century copy would be <1412> [MS 16th c.].

[1] ... and Saturday ceased to be a holiday, while Sunday was granted grace because of the Resurrection, and it is Sunday that reigns over the days, since it was on that very day that Christ resurrected from the dead. Brethren, let us crown the Empress of Days ... (from Kalajdovič 1821: 19).

[2] *Nemecko-latinskij i russkij Leksikon kupno s pervymi načalami russkogo jazyka k obščej pol'ze* (St. Petersburg, 1731) lists V/S as the general Russian word for Sunday; *Slovar' Akademii Rossijskoj, po azbučnomu porjadku raspoložennyj* (henceforth *SAR*), 6 vols. (St. Petersburg, 1806–1822) notes that N/S is the Church Slavic word for Sunday, and V/S is the Russian form. *Polnyj pravoslavnyj bogoslovskij ènciklopedičeskij slovar'* (St. Petersburg, 1913), 566, incorrectly assigns V/S to the lexicon of the Church from the sixteenth century on; in fact, V had a slightly different meaning (see below). The distinction in spelling between V/r (*voskresenie*) and V/S (*voskresen'e*) was apparently introduced in the second half of the nineteenth century; *SAR* (1806–1822) has identical spelling for both; Ja. Grot distinguishes them (*Filologičeskie razyskanija*, 4th ed., exp. [St. Petersburg, 1899], 894).

Such popular innovation in a word class as basic as the days of the week is unusual for an already Christianized society with an elaborated liturgical terminology, including, for instance, *Nedelja Vaij* 'Palm Sunday', *Nedelja Pravoslavija* 'Orthodoxy Sunday'. The change of N/S to V/S is not comparable to the loan translations made by the heathen Germanic tribes in adopting the Roman seven-day calendar (*Dies Solis* > *Sun's Day, Dies Jovis* > *Thor's Day* or *Thunder's Day,* etc.); nor is it analogous to the renaming and redividing of the months following the French Revolution (September 22 to October 21 > *Vendémaire*, October 22 to November 20 > *Brumaire*, etc.). Furthermore, it is a change unique to Russian as compared with the other Slavic languages.

It is quite remarkable that there is not a single study that attempts to document and explain the replacement of N/S by V/S. The handbooks and other scholarly literature dealing directly or indirectly with the Russian calendar do not offer much insight.

Vasmer and Trubačev note without further comment that V/S developed from the phrase *den' voskresenija* 'Day of the Resurrection',[3] while others consider V/S to be original. In a discussion about the days of the week in Old Russian, for example, A. S. L'vov cites the following passage to document the early use of V/S:[4]

> I došedъ velika d͞ne. Vskr͞snьja po obyčaju. praznova[vъ] světlo. vpade vъ bolěznь....[5]
>
> *Lavr. let.* <1074> [MS 1377]

This passage concerns the death of Feodosij Pečerskij and follows a detailed terminological description of important feast days and weeks of the Great Fast. The chronicler here refers not simply to a Sunday, but to Easter, the "Great Day of the Resurrection." In Old Russian the elliptical *Velikъ dьnь* frequently replaces *Pasxa* 'Easter'; compare Ukrainian *Velykden'*, Belorussian *Vjalikdzen'* 'Easter'.

J. Jungmann and G. Schreiber see a link between Russian V/S and the occasional Greek use of *'Αναστάσιμος ἡμέρα* 'Sunday', lit. Resurrection Day, as if V/S had existed in the Old Russian lexicon since the baptism of

---

[3] M. Vasmer, *Ètimologičeskij slovar' russkogo jazyka*, vol. 1, trans. and exp. O. N. Trubačev, ed. B. A. Larin (Moscow, 1964), 357. Cf. also *Ètimologičeskij slovar' russkogo jazyka*, vol. 1, ed. N. M. Šanskij (Moscow, 1963), 171.

[4] A. S. L'vov, "Vyraženie ponjatija vremeni v 'Povesti vremennyx let,'" in *Russkaja istoričeskaja leksikologija*, ed. S. G. Barxudarov et al. (Moscow, 1968), 29.

[5] And having reached Easter, he celebrated radiantly according to custom and then fell ill....

Rus'.[6] Actually Old Russian had a precise calque of the Greek phrase, namely, *vъskrъsьnyi dьnь*. And, *nota bene*, the Greek equivalent of Old Russian V/r, ἀνάστασις, is *never* used to designate Sunday and thus could not serve as a model for the Russian innovation.[7] E. Fraenkel's assumptions about the antiquity of V/S betray a lack of familiary with Old Russian:

> Nur die Russen nennen ihn [den Sonntag] nach der Auferstehung des Herrn als *voskresenije*. Dass aber auch bei ihnen einmal *nedělja* im Sinne 'Sonntag' EXISTIERT HAT [emphasis mine—MSF], folgt aus der von ihnen mit den übrigen slav. Völkern geteilten Bezeichnung des Montags als *ponedělinik* 'Tag nach der *nedělja*'.[8]

These few examples show that the change N/S > V/S has not been viewed as a particularly troublesome issue. But if one carefully distinguishes circumlocution (*den' voskresenija* 'Day of the Resurrection') from appellation (*voskresenie* 'Sunday'), then the change is not at all straightforward. In point of fact, we are dealing with a development of complex origin, one that involves elements of Slavic prehistory as well as the distinctive evolution of social, political, and religious institutions in Muscovite Rus'. An extensive analysis of this wide-ranging topic will be undertaken in a separate monograph currently in preparation. In the present study, I will examine the relevant philological data and attempt to identify the nonlinguistic factors germane to the emergence of V/S in Russian.

The corpus upon which this study is based comprises hundreds of published documents of varied content from the eleventh to seventeenth centuries—chronicles, epistles, sermons, diplomatic reports, private correspondence, juridical texts, inventories, deeds, wills, bills of credit, proclamations, liturgical texts and tracts—texts that are likely to contain precise days and dates or that deal with Sunday specifically. A fairly clear pattern of development emerges from these documents, a pattern which leads me to believe that the selection is representative. In tracing the development of *voskresenie* I have taken the written date of the text at face value for the most part, even if the manuscript is a much later copy. There is no evidence of any

---

[6] Jos. A. Jungmann, "Beginnt die christliche Woche mit Sonntag?" *Zeitschrift für katholische Theologie* 55, no. 4 (1931): 610; G. Schreiber, *Die Wochentage im Erlebnis der Ostkirche und des christlichen Abendlandes* (Cologne–Opladen, 1959), 39. Cf. N. M. Nikol'skij, "Xristianskie prazdniki," *Izbrannye proizvedenija po istorii religii* (Moscow, 1974), 208; originally published as second part of *Evrejskie i xristianskie prazdniki, ix proisxoždenie i istorija* (Moscow, 1931).

[7] See W. H. Lampe, ed., *A Patristic Greek Lexicon* (Oxford, 1961), 121-124.

[8] E. Fraenkel, "Griechisches, Lateinisches und Baltisch-Slavisches, pt. 1: Zu griechischen Inschriften," *Indogermanische Forschungen* 40 (1922): 95.

attempt on the part of later scribes to substitute V/S for older N/S, even in seventeenth- and eighteenth-century copies.

Voskresenie, nedelja and their derivatives in Old Russian

One cannot hope to have a clear understanding of the interaction of *voskresenie* and *nedelja* without first establishing their place in the Old Russian lexicon. The word *vъskrъsenie* itself was introduced into Old Russian from Church Slavic to designate resurrection from the dead. It is used most frequently in two basic senses: (1) resurrection in general and (2) the Resurrection of Christ.

> Věrui **vъskreseniju** mrъtvyixъ i žizni buduštaago věka ...[9]
>
> *Izb. 1076* f44v, 4-6

> Vъ Suḇ Velikuju slovo stḡo grigorija antioxiiskaago na sḏoje i spšьnoje pogrebenije i **vъskrъsenije** ḡa našego iṡ xā.[10]
>
> *Usp. sbor.* f239v, 17-22 [MS 12-13th c.]

As noted above, Old Russian has two phrases correlated with V/r used to refer to the Resurrection of Christ in two extended temporal senses: (1) Easter Day and (2) Sunday. The phrases are *dьnь vъskrъsenija* 'Day of the Resurrection' and the derivative *vъskrъsьnyi dьnь* 'Resurrection Day'. The former is often modified by *Xristova* 'of Christ' or *Gospodnja* 'of the Lord'.

> Slovo na Svjatuju Pasxu vъ světonosnyj **denь Vъskresenia Xristova** ...[11]
>
> Kirill Turovskij <12th c.> [MS 1535]

> I poide na nja vъ **denь vъskresenia**, iulja vъ 15 ...[12]
>
> *Pskov. II let. Sinod.* <1253?>, f157v, 16 [MS end 15th c.]

> Otъ ... **vъskrěsьnaago dьne** do novyja nedělja vьsju nedělju vъ čṟkvaxъ prěbyvati ...[13]
>
> *Kormč. kn. Efrem., Prav. Trul.* 66 [MS c. 1100]

> Vъprašalъ bo esi: ašče estь podobno vъ **denь vъskresnyj**, eže estь nedělja, zaklati li volъ, li ovьnъ, ili pticju ...[14]
>
> Feodosij Pečerskij, *Vprošenie Izjaslava* <11th c.>

[9] Believe in the resurrection of the dead and in life everlasting ....

[10] The sermon of Saint Gregory of Antioch for Good Saturday on the holy and salvatory Entombment and Resurrection of Our Lord, Jesus Christ.

[11] A sermon for Holy Pascha on Easter Day (lit. the Radiant Day of the Resurrection of Christ) ... (from Kalajdovič 1821: 10).

[12] And he marched out against them on Sunday, July 15.

[13] From ... Easter (lit. Resurrection Day) to Thomas Sunday (lit. New Sunday) one should spend the entire week in church ... (cited in I. I. Sreznevskij, *Materialy dlja Slovarja drevnerusskogo jazyka.* 3 vols. and suppl. [St. Petersburg, 1893–1912], 2: 381).

[14] For you have asked whether it is appropriate to slaughter an ox or a ram or a fowl on Resurrection Day, that is, Sunday ... (from Makarij 1856: 213).

It should be emphasized that neither *dьnь vъskrъsenija* nor *vъskrъsьnyi dьnь* is used as a neutral designation for Sunday, equivalent to *nedělja*; both retain the religious connotations of the Resurrection.

Old Russian *vъskrъsenie* is also used as a metonym for Easter; in such cases V is almost always modified by *Xristovo* or *Gospodne*.

> ... v njaže d͞ni očistivšisja d͞ša prazdnujetь světlo na **Vskr̄snь̆e Gͦsͭne** veseljaščisja o Bͦzě.[15]
>
> *Lavr. let.* <1074> [MS 1377]

It is important to distinguish V in the metonymic usage from V in the other constructions discussed so far. The metonym alone has inherent value as a calendrical unit without *dьnь*. I will symbolize such metonymic instances of V as V/R and gloss them as 'Resurrection', one of the designations for Easter; compare *Pasxa, Velikъ dьnь*. It is noteworthy that V/R, unlike the circumlocutions from V/r, cannot designate Sunday.

Old Russian *nedělja* has two basic meanings, "Sunday" (N/S) and "week" (hereafter N/w). Unlike the circumlocutions in V/r which designate Sunday, N/S is a neutral term. Religious connotations are a function of context rather than inherent lexical value. For this reason it is important to distinguish four contexts in which N/S functions in varying degrees of specificity, two general and two specific.

In *general* contexts N/S designates Sunday as distinct from other days of the week. Two subtypes can be isolated: (1) *indefinite* (N/S-ind)—Sundays as a class, expressed by N/S in the singular or plural, and (2) *appellational* (N/S-app)—Sunday as the name of a day of the week.

> ... i jadь ixъ bě rъžanъ xlěbъ tъkmo ti voda vъ subotu že ti vъ **nedělju** sočiva vъkušaxutь.[16] (N/S-ind)
>
> *Usp. sbor.* f35g, 28–31 [MS 12th–13th c.]

> ... a pojutъ [svjaščenici] po **neděljamъ** ...[17] (N/S-ind)
>
> *Blagoslovennaja gramota Mitropolita Filippa Pskovičamъ* <1471> [MS 16th c.]

> Vъ to že lěto pride Novugorodu knjazь Svjatoslavъ Olgovicь [*sic*]
> ... měsjacja ijulja vъ 19 ... vъ **nedělju**[18] (N/S-app)
>
> *Nov. I let. Sinod.* <1136> [MS 13th–14th c.]

---

[15] ... having purified itself during those days [of the fast], the soul celebrates radiantly on Easter Day (lit. the Resurrection of the Lord), rejoicing in God.

[16] ... and their food consisted solely of rye bread and water on Saturday (Saturdays in general) and on Sunday (Sundays in general) they would eat some lentil gruel.

[17] ... and [the priests] sing on Sundays ... (*AIst*, no. 283, p. 520).

[18] In that same year Prince Svjatoslav Oľgovič came to Novgorod ... on Sunday ... July 19.

In *specific* contexts, N/S designates Sundays as distinct from one another. In this diacritic usage, N/S must be modified by an adjective, pronominal adjective, or nominal complement (in general contexts N/S usually occurs without modification). Two subtypes can be isolated: (1) *absolute* (N/S-abs)—a particular holiday that always falls on a Sunday, and (2) *definite* (N/S-def)—a particular Sunday (or Sundays), often identified by its chronological position relative to a holiday (especially Easter), a fast, or an interfast period (*mjasoědъ*).

> Toja že vesne, mesjaca aprilja 21, v **nedelju Fominu**, priexaše [*sic*] ...
> posly pskovskyja.[19] (N/S-abs)
>
> > *Pskov. III let. Stroev.* <1471> [MS 1560s]

> [Knjazь velikij Vasilej Ivanovičъ] ... na Moskvu priěxalъ vъ **nedělju
> 5-ju posta**, marta 17.[20] (N/S-def)
>
> > *Sof. II let. Arx.* <1510> [MS 1518?]

It is in specific contexts that N/S is often ascribed religious connotations.

The phrase *nedělьnyi dьnь*, lit. Sunday Day, Do-nothing Day (= Sabbath?), is derived from *nedělja* and is used to designate Sunday; compare *četvъržьnyi dьnь* 'Thursday', *pjatъčьnyi dьnь* 'Friday', *subotьnyi dьnь* 'Saturday, Sabbath Day'.

> ... čto estь zlo togo ne tvorit[i] vъ **dnь nedělnyi** nikogda že ...[21]
>
> > *Slovo ... o dnii rekomomъ nedělě,*
> > *Paisiev. sbor.* f47v [MS late 14th–15th c.]

The distinction between general and specific contexts proves to be important in characterizing the status of the circumlocutional designations for Sunday derived from both V and N: they may be used only in general contexts. Collocations like the following are impossible: *dьnь vъskrъsenija Gospodnja Vaii* 'Palm Sunday', *Fominъ vъskrъsьnyi dьnь* 'Thomas Sunday', *pjatyi nedělnyi dьnь po Pascě* 'the fifth Sunday after Easter.' The functions and connotations of V, N, and their derivatives are compared in Table 1.

This table shows that V/R and N/S are, for all intents and purposes, in complementary distribution: V/R cannot be used to designate Sunday and always has religious connotations, while N/S is rarely used to designate Easter and has religious connotations only in context. It is the derivatives of V and N alone that can contrast in the general contexts of Sunday, but most typically with a difference in connotation.

[19] The same spring, on Thomas Sunday, April 21, the Pskovian emissaries ... arrived.
[20] [Grand Prince Vasilij Ivanovič] ... arrived in Moscow on the fifth Sunday of the fast, March 17.
[21] ... never do anything evil on Sunday ... (from Gaľkovskij 1913: 81).

TABLE 1

FUNCTIONS AND CONNOTATIONS OF V, N, AND THEIR DERIVATIVES

CONSTRUCTION	EASTER	SUNDAY abs	SUNDAY def	SUNDAY ind	SUNDAY app	RELIGIOUS CONNOTATIONS
V/R	+	-	-	-	-	⊕
V-derivatives	+	-	-	+	+	⊕
N-derivative	-	-	-	+	+	O
N/S	(-)	+	+	+	+	O

+ = *occurs*
(-) = *negligible occurrence*
- = *does not occur*
⊕ = *inherent*
O = *contextual*

The homonymic status of *nedelja* in Old Russian

Before examining the development of *voskresenie*, we must anticipate and refute the notion that the existence of homonymy (*nedelja* 'Sunday' N/S versus *nedelja* 'week' N/w) was responsible for the replacement of N/S by V. The best evidence we have, of course, is the preservation of the homonymous relationship in Russian Church Slavic and modern Serbian.[22] The

---

[22] It is not clear whether Slavic in general had a special word for "week" before *nedělja*. The periphrastic *tъ(že) dьnь* 'the same day' is apparently used fairly early to denote the recurrence of a particular day in the weekly cycle, hence a "week." Fraenkel ("Griechisches, Lateinisches, und Baltisch-Slavisches" [see n. 8], 96-97) and P. Skok ("La semaine slave," *Revue des études slaves* 5 [1925]: 21-22) incorrectly limit its use to Slavs of the Latin rite: it is found in Old Russian texts as well as a substitute for *nedělju* 'for a week'. The phrase is eventually reanalyzed as a declinable noun and replaces *nedělja* as the primary designation for week in the Latin-oriented Slavic languages, and in Ukrainian and Belorussian through Polish influence: Polish *tydzień*, Czech *týden*, Slovak *týždeň*, Lower Sorbian *tyźeń*, Upper Sorbian *tydźeń*, Slovene *téden*, Croatian *tjedan*, Ukrainian *tyžden'*, Belorussian *tydzen'*. N/w is rarely used in Polish, but it serves as a secondary designation for "week" in Ukrainian and Belorussian. In Czech it is a permissible alternative to *týden* in the plural (the gen. pl. is *neděl* vs. the gen. pl. of Sunday *nedělí*); it exists in the singular in the phrase *s neděle* 'next week'. In Upper Sorbian it is regularly used in the dual and plural, i.e., in those contexts in which it is least likely to contrast with Sunday.

Bulgarian patterned *sedmica* 'week' after the Greek neologism ἑβδομάς; cf. Late Latin *septimana*. It is the primary designation for "week" in modern Bulgarian and Macedonian but has only marginal status in Serbian, which still prefers *nèdelja*. *Sedmica* made its way into Russian through Bulgarian and is currently used in Russian Church Slavic as an alternative for *nedělja*.

reasons are fairly clear: the contexts in which N/S and N/w appear are nearly complementary. In Old Russian, N/S occurs most frequently after the prepositions *vъ* (N/S-app) and *po* (N/S-ind), while N/w is found in the prepositionless accusative (*nedělju* 'for a week'), after numerals (*pjatь nedělь* 'five weeks', in the prepositionless genitive (*vъ sredu vъrbьnyja nedělja* 'on Wednesday of Palm Week', lit. Willow Week), and after the preposition *na* (*na syropustьnoi neděli* 'during Cheesefast Week').

There are syntactic contexts, however, in which it is impossible to disambiguate N without extralinguistic information or additional discourse. Thus *strastьnaja nedělja* is not ambiguous because it refers only to Holy Week (lit. Passion Week); there is no Holy Sunday. But *vъrbьnaja nedělja* can refer either to Palm Week or Palm Sunday. The first citation below is ambiguous without information provided by the second:

> Po vъsja že d̄ni s̄tyixъ mjasopuščь s̄tyi o̅cь našь Feodosii otxožaše vъ s̄tuju svoju peščeru ide že i čьstьnoje tělo jego položeno bystь. tu že zatvorjaše sja jedinъ do **vrьbьnyja nedělja**.[23]

> I vъ pjatъkъ toja **nedělja** vъ godъ večerьnjaja prixožaaše kъ bratii.[24]
>
> *Usp. sbor.* f37g, 14–24 [MS 12th–13th c.]

The reference to Friday of "that week" resolves the ambiguity of *vrьbьnyja nedělja* in favor of Palm Week. Cases of unresolved ambiguity are extremely rare.

N/S and N/w coexist as homonyms in the written language well into the seventeenth century; they are still the norm for Kotošixin in 1667.[25] This situation must be kept in mind as we turn our attention to the development of *voskresenie* in the spoken language.

---

[23] Throughout all the days of the holy meatfast, our holy father Feodosij would go off to his holy cave, where his venerable body has also been laid to rest, and there he would shut himself off alone until Palm Week/Sunday.

[24] And on Friday of that week he would come to the brethren at Vespers.

[25] Pennington glosses two occurrences of V in Kotošixin as 'Sunday', when they actually refer to Resurrection-Sunday (Sunday as a church holiday) or Easter (Kotošixin 1667 [1980]: 432):

> ... i postavljati kutiju po vsja dni, kromě **voskresenija** i bolšixъ praznikovъ.   (f28v)
>
> ... and *kutija* (ritual food in commemoration of the dead) is to be offered every day except Resurrection-Sunday and the major feasts.

> ... vъ novoe lěto, sentjabrja vъ 1 denь; na **Světloe Xristovo Voskresenie** ...   (f34v)
>
> ... at the New Year, September 1; at Easter (lit. the Bright Resurrection of Christ) ...

The development of *voskresenie* in Middle Russian

The study of the replacement of N/S by V/S in Russian is complicated by the fact that the written documents at our disposal are, for the most part, not representative of the spoken language. The consistent use of N/S in the majority of sixteenth- and seventeenth-century chronicles, letters, and official documents belies the colloquial ubiquity of V/S confirmed by foreign visitors to Muscovite Rus' in the late sixteenth and early seventeenth centuries: André Thevet in Moscow, 1586; Tönnies Fenne in Pskov, 1607; and Richard James in Archangel and Xolmogory, 1618–19.[26] The dictionaries and wordlists that they have provided show *voskresenie* at the very conclusion of its development, however, after it has replaced *nedelja* in the appellational function of Sunday.

It should come as no surprise that there is such disparity between the spoken and written designations for Sunday in Middle Russian. The replacement of N/S by V/S is not of the type *grad* > *gorod* or *lanita* > *ščeka*, that is, a simple exchange of a Church Slavic word and a corresponding Russian one. As we shall see below, the earliest innovations in V did not have the simple meaning "Sunday" and were therefore inappropriate as substitutes for N/S in most instances. Be that as it may, the fact that we find no dated evidence of V having replaced N/S before the sixteenth century need not dissuade us from assigning the initial stages of this development to the late fifteenth century.

Despite the paucity of written evidence from the sixteenth century concerning the innovative use of *voskresenie*—some forty instances in all, most dated after 1530—the functional and chronological distribution of the new forms is striking. With one apparent exception (see below) no instances of V used in the appellational function are found in Russian texts before the seventeenth century (but cf. V/S in Thevet 1586 [in Boyer 1905: 37]). This fact of distribution suggests that the first innovations with V had not severed their metonymic association with resurrection per se; compare *dьnь vъskrьsenija, vъskrьsьnyi dьnь*. The earliest and most numerous instances of new collocations with V occur in an absolute function to designate two church holidays, Orthodoxy Sunday and Palm Sunday. I have symbolized such cases V/R and glossed them as 'Resurrection', thereby suggesting that their model was the metonym *Voskresenie Xristovo* (or *Gospodne*) 'Resurrection of Christ' (= Easter) and that initially they did not designate Sunday in the new names for these two Paschal holidays. Later innovations with V

---

[26] Boyer 1905: 37; Fenne 1607 (1961), 1: 35; 2: 22; James 1618–19 (1959): 123, 381, respectively.

occur in other specific and general contexts with religious connotation, an indication that V has been extended to all Sundays qua religious holidays. Such cases are symbolized V/RS and glossed as 'Resurrection-Sunday'. By the beginning of the seventeenth century, the religious connotations of V/RS appear to fade, resulting in V/S, a word capable of opposing N/S in all written contexts, secular as well as religious (see Table 2).

TABLE 2

OCCURRENCE OF V/R, V/RS AND V/S IN CONTEXTS
PREVIOUSLY RESERVED FOR N/S

Context		- - - - - - - - - - - - - -*Time* - - - - - - - - - - - - ->			
		I	II	III	IV
Specific	Absolute	N/S	V/R	V/RS	V/S
	Definite	N/S	N/S	V/RS	V/S
General	Indefinite	N/S	N/S	V/RS	V/S
	Appellational	N/S	N/S	V/RS	V/S

Stage I is representative of Old and Middle Russian up to the sixteenth century. Stage II is seen in the *Razrjadnaja kniga 1475–1598*, while Stage III is characteristic of a few sixteenth-century chronicles and the *Stoglav* of 1551. Stage IV is representative of usage in the Petrinic Age. Church documents of the sixteenth century occasionally reflect Stages II or III, but for the most part preserve the conservative Stage I.

Although Table 2 is based on written evidence alone, it has implications for the development of V in the spoken language as well. It is clear that the formula N/S > V/S is inadequate as a representation of the means by which V/S eventually came to replace N/S as the designation for Sunday. The chronological progression from specific to general (V/R > V/RS > V/S) implies a concurrence of V and N/S which allowed V to extend into an ever greater number of contexts previously reserved for N/S and its circumlocutional substitutes. The secularization of *voskresenie* as V/S—the final stage of the development—provided the proper conditions for V/S to compete with and ultimately replace N/S as the basic name for Sunday.

As noted above, the earliest written attestions for V/R refer to two specific holidays: Synod Resurrection (*Sbornoe/Sobornoe voskresenie*), a popular name for Orthodoxy Sunday (*Nedelja Pravoslavija*), and Willow Resurrection (*Verbnoe voskresenie*), a popular name for Palm Sunday (*Nedelja Vaij*).

Synod Resurrection is first attested in an early sixteenth-century promissory note from the Rjazan' region:

> se az, Jurьe ... syn Podyvnikov, zanel esmi, gospodine, u Alekseja u [Koži ...]ina syna dva rublja deneg ot **Sobornogo v[oskresenьja]** na god.[27]
>
> <1514/15> *Dokladnaja zaemnaja služilaja kabala Jurija Podьivnika* [MS end 17th c.]

Willow Resurrection is first attested in an early sixteenth-century promissory note from Bežeckij verx, an area some 150 miles north–northwest of Moscow:

> Se az Vasilei Dmitreev s(y)nъ Petrova zanjal esmi u Fedora u Ivanova s(y)na Mičjurina dva rublja moskovskim(i) d(e)ngami ot **Verbnovo voskresen(ь)ja** do **Verbnovo voskresen(ь)ja** ...[28]
>
> <1524/25> *Zakladnaja kabala Vasilija Dmitrieva syna Petrova[-Mikulina] Fedoru Ivanovu synu Mičjurina* [MS 1641]

These earliest attestations of V/R antedate by seventy-two and twenty-two years, respectively, the earliest occurrences of Synod Resurrection and Willow Resurrection cited in *Slovar' russkogo jazyka XI–XVII vv.* (henceforth *SRJ XI–XVII*).[29] A number of examples of both can be documented in the sixteenth and seventeenth centuries, primarily, but not exclusively, from business documents, which would be less subject to the prescriptive norms of the written language.[30]

The first examples of V/RS in a definite function date from the 1530s. In these cases V/RS is preceded by an ordinal number.

---

[27] I, Jurij, Podyvnik's son, have borrowed, my lord, from Aleksej [Koža, ...]'s son, two rubles in currency on Synod Resurrection for one year (in *ASÈISVR* 3, no. 380, pp. 395-396). The portions in square brackets are interpolations of the original publisher Juškov in 1898. There is no question that the *v* after *Sobornogo* in the defective text should be read as *voskresenie*, since the older name of the day was *Sobornaja nedělja*.

[28] I, Vasilij Dmitriev, Petrov's son, have borrowed from Fedor Ivanov, Mičjurin's son, two rubles in Moscow currency from Willow Resurrection to Willow Resurrection (in *ARG*, no. 241, p. 242).

[29] Ed. S. G. Barxudarov et al. 9 vols. to date. (Moscow, 1975-).

[30] *Sbornoe voskresenie*: <1542> [MS late 16th–early 17th c.] in *Nov. II let. Arx.*; <1543> in *ASob* 1, no. 198, p. 177; <1554> in *ASob* 1, no. 240, p. 257; <1556> in *AIst* 1, no. 165, p. 318; <1559> [MS 16th c.] cited in Sreznevskij, *Materialy*, vol. 3 (see n. 13), 650; <1559/60> [MS 1680s] in *PRPRK*, no. 75, p. 111, <1565> [orig.?] in *AIst* 1, no. 174, p. 336; <1587> cited in *SRJ XI–XVII* 3: 42; <1611> [MS 17th c.] in *Pribavl. Pskov. let. A*, 54, and in *RK* [MSS 1556-1604] s.a. <1550, 1555, 1556, 1576, 1578, 1579>; *Verbnoe voskresenie*: <c. 1535> [MS 16th c.] in *PRPRK*, no. 66, p. 103; <1545> in *ASob* 1, no. 205, p. 184; <1547> cited in *SRJ XI–XVII* 2: 81; <1590> [MS beg. 17th c.] in *DopAIst* 1, no. 135, p. 218; <1611> [MS 17th c.] in *Pskov. III let. Okonč. Arx.* 2; <1653> cited in *SRJ XI–XVII* 3: 42 and in *RK* [MSS 1556-1604] s.a. <1550, 1551, 1558, 1576, 1578, 1579, 1586>.

... arxiepiskopъ Makarij ... blagoslovi osnovanie gradu, měsjaca maija
vъ 3 denь, vъ **pjatoe voskresenie** po Pascě.[31]

Otryvok let. po Vosk. Novoierus.
<1534/35> [MS 1553?]

In this chronicle text, all instances of the general functions of Sunday are
expressed by N/S, such as in <1535, 1552>. There are attestations of
V/RS-def. in documents (some original) from the mid–1530s on.[32]

I have found one example of V/RS in a definite, deictic function; it is
modified by the pronoun *to* and refers to an instance of V/RS-def in the
preceding sentence.

... byti bylo vam u korolja v **pervoe voskresenie** sego Petrova mjaso-
edu.... I gosudarju našemu, korolju, v **to voskresenie** ženitisja.[33]

Statejnyj spisok I. M. Voroncova
<1567> [MS 2nd half 16th c.]

In this same text the appellational function of Sunday is expressed by
N/S.[34]

The *Stoglav* of 1551 provides a variety of expressions for Sunday in an
indefinite function with plural constructions (all page references are from
Stoglav 1551/1863 [MS mid-16th c.]):

Da vo ustavě že pisano po **neděljamъ** pěti otъ vozdviženija čestnago
kresta do syrnyja neděli: "xvalite imja Gospodne.[35]

(133)

po **voskresnymъ dnemъ** i po gospodskimъ prazdnikomъ i velikimъ svjatymъ na večerni.[36]

(56)

---

[31] ... Archbishop Makarij ... blessed the foundation of the town on May 3, on the fifth
Resurrection-Sunday after Easter.

[32] Ordinal number + *voskresenie*: <1535> in *AOtn* 1, no. 45, pp. 47, 48, 50; <1542> in *Nov.
II let. Arx.* [MS late 16th–early 17th c.]; <1543> *DopAlst* 1, no. 32, p. 34; <1552> in *Otryvok
let. po Vosk. Novoierus.* [MS 1553?]; <1564> and <1565> in *Prodolž. Aleks.-Nevsk. let.* [mid-
17th c.]; <1567> [2nd half 16th c.] in *PRP XVI–XVII*, 36, and in Gorskij 1841/1879 [MS
1533–47], 23 (2x).

[33] ... you were to have appeared before the king on the first Resurrection-Sunday of this
Peter interfast period (the period between the Great Fast and the Apostolic Fast when meat
may be eaten).... And our lord, the king, is to marry on that Resurrection-Sunday (from *PRP
XVI–XVII*: 36).

[34] *PRP XV–XVII*: 7.

[35] And it is written right in the *Typikon* that "Praise the name of the Lord ..." is to be sung
on Sundays from Exaltation of the Venerable Cross to Cheese Sunday.

[36] ... on Resurrection Days (= Sundays) and feast days of the Lord and the major saints at
Vespers.

Po vsěmъ sobornymъ cerkvamъ po **vsja voskresenija** i po vsja vladyčni prazdniki i Bogorodični i pročimъ svjatymъ egda pojutъ slavoslovie ...[37]

(143)

Po vsěmъ gradomъ i po vsěmъ cerkvamъ sobornymъ ... čtoby po vsja dni molebny pěli i božestvennyja liturgii služili po **vsja voskresenija**, takože i po vladyčnymъ prazdnikomъ i po bogorodičnymъ i svjatyxъ velikixъ o zdravii blagočestivago carja.[38]

(147)

In both of the passages with V/RS, the Resurrection-Sundays are totalized as a set of religious holidays, on a par with the feast days of the Lord, the Mother of God, and the major saints. The effect of the quantifier *vsja* 'all' is to blur the distinction between indefinite and definite.[39] The inclusion of V/RS in the *Stoglav* is testimony to the status that the word had achieved by the mid-sixteenth century in the highest echelons of church and state: as is well known, the *Stoglav* was the collaborative effort of Metropolitan Makarij (1542–1563) and Tsar Ivan IV (1533–1584).

The earliest attestation of V/RS-ind in a singular construction occurs in a liturgical and dietary code from the Troice-Sergiev Monastery compiled between 1533 and 1547. N/S is used as the standard term for Sunday, but the heading makes a distinction between *obyčnyja dni* 'ordinary days' and *Vladyčni prazdniki, vъskresenia, prazdniki Svjatyxъ* 'feast days of the Lord, Resurrection-Sundays, feast days of the saints'. In the section devoted to the Lenten period, V/RS is used after ordinal numerals except for one occurrence in the indefinite function:

Črezъ vse že gověnie vъ **Voskresenie** pojutъ večernju vъ cerkvi: Gospodi vozzvaxъ Tebě.[40]

Vъ Troicy Sergievě monastyrě obixodъ bratckoj ěstьe
[MS 1533–47]

I have not found other instances of V/RS-ind in the singular. One quite early attestation noted by Klibanov in passing turns out to be a misinter-

[37] In all cathedral churches on all Resurrection-Sundays and all feast days of the Lord, and the Mother of God and the rest of the saints, when the Doxology is sung ...

[38] In all cities and in all cathedral churches ... prayer services should be sung daily and the Divine Liturgy should be celebrated on all Resurrection-Sundays, as well as on the feast days of the Lord and the Mother of God and the major saints for the health of the pious tsar.

[39] Cf. M. S. Flier, *Aspects of Nominal Determination in Old Church Slavic* (The Hague–Paris, 1974), 167ff.

[40] And throughout the entire fast "Lord, I have cried out to Thee" is sung on Resurrection-Sunday in church during Vespers (from Gorskij 1841/1879: 22).

pretation.[41] In the verdict of the Synod of 1490, Klibanov finds a passage which he interprets as an accusation that the heretics have honored Saturday more than Sunday: "čli subbotu pače voskresenьja." A closer examination of the actual text, however, reveals that the author (writing on behalf of Metropolitan Zosima) accuses the heretics not of honoring Saturday more than Sunday but of Judaizing by honoring the Sabbath more than the Resurrection of Christ. The relevant passage is followed immediately by a reference to the Resurrection and the Ascension.

> A vsi este čli subotu pače **vъskresenia Xristova**. A inii ot vas **vъskre-senьju Xristovu** i ego svjatomu vъznesenьju ne verujut.[42]
>
> <Oct. 1490> *Sobornyj prigovor i poučenie protiv eretikov*
> [MS late 15th c.]

The first attestation of V/RS in an appellational function appears in the logistical plans for the controversial second marriage of Grand Prince Vasilij III and Princess Elena Glinskaja in Moscow in 1526.

> Lěta 7034 (1526), Janvarja vъ 21 denь, vъ **Voskresenьe**, velikij knjazь Vasilij Ivanovičъ povelělъ byti bolьšemu narjadu dlja svoej, velikago knjazja, svadьby.[43]
>
> *Svad'ba vtoraja Vasilija Ioannoviča*
> <1526> [MS 1624]

One might be tempted to view this attestation not as V/RS, but as V/S, an early sixteenth-century solecism representing the intrusion of vernacular usage into the written language. Favoring this analysis is the fact that the scribe clearly has difficulty adhering to written convention and lapses into dialectal forms on occasion. We find traces of *akan'e* (*kalači* and *kolači*, *karavaj* and *korovaj*), the loss of the unstressed suffix vowel in the infinitive (*zažečь* and *zažeči*, *bytь* and *byti*), and unusual infinitive innovation (*idtitь*, *prijtitь* alongside *idti*). Such infinitives are characteristic of Rjazan' dialects and are widespread in official documents of the seventeenth century,[44] but occur in the sixteenth century as well. Nevertheless, the fact that V is capi-

---

[41] A. I. Klibanov, *Reformacionnye dviženija v Rossii v XIV–pervoj polovine XVI vv.* (Moscow, 1960), 238.

[42] And you have all honored the Sabbath [celebrated by the Jews on Saturday] more than the Resurrection of Christ [celebrated by the Christians on Sunday]. And others of you do not believe in the Resurrection of Christ and in His Holy Ascension ... (from N. A. Kazakova and Ja. S. Lur'e, *Antifeodal'nye eretičeskie dviženija na Rusi XIV–načala XVI veka* [Moscow–Leningrad, 1955], 383).

[43] In the year 1526, on January 21, on Resurrection-Sunday, Grand Prince Vasilij Ivanovič has commanded that there be a great ceremony for his, the grand prince's, wedding (from Saxarov 1849, pt. 2, sec. 6: 38).

[44] A. I. Sologub, "Formy infinitiva v russkix govorax," *IOLJa* 28, no. 4 (1969): 353.

talized (highly unusual for ordinary days of the week, including N/S, but not unusual for V/RS) and occurs in the context of marriage, one of the seven sacraments of the Church, makes the reading "Resurrection-Sunday" more likely. All the other attestations of V/RS make reference to religious holidays, fasts, interfast periods, or the nuptial day (note the use of V/RS in this context in the diplomatic report [MS 1567] cited above). The occurrence of *Voskresenie* 'Resurrection-Sunday' instead of *nedělju* 'Sunday' (found in four other marriage documents from the same 1624 MS) may actually represent an unsubtle attempt to lend Christian legitimacy to a royal marriage that was, strictly speaking, in violation of Orthodox tradition and practice; on November 28, 1525, Vasilij had divorced Solomonija, his wife of twenty years, for failing to produce an heir, had banished her to a nunnery, and had married Elena Glinskaja less than two months later. Metropolitan Daniil sanctioned or was forced to sanction the second marriage and actually presided at the ceremony.[45]

The first attestation of V/S-app is in the entry for 1615 in a Pskov chronicle covering the years 1493?–1650. The secular context permits the reading V/S instead of V/RS.

> Ijulja vъ 30 denь, v **voskresenie**, rano na 1-m času, nikomu ne věduščǔ, obъjavilsja korolь Gustaf Adolьfъ Svěiskii.[46]
>
> *Pskov. III let. Okonč. Arx. 2* <1615> [MS 17th c.]

This text, written in different hands, exhibits various stages in the development of the designation for Sunday: <1510> *vъ nedělju* 'on Sunday', <1611> *vъ 5-ju nedělju posta* 'on the fifth Sunday of the fast', *v Verbnoe voskresenie* 'on Willow Resurrection'.

From 1620 on, V/S-app is the norm in the *Vesti-Kuranty*: out of thirty-five occurrences of Sunday in the appellational function from 1620 to 1648, five show N/S and are traceable to one or two emissaries. The two occurrences of Sunday in the indefinite function in the same texts are expressed by V/S.[47] The nearly universal use of V/S-app in seventeenth-century diplomatic reports is in sharp contrast to the exclusive use of N/S-app in reports from the late sixteenth century.[48]

---

[45] Cf. E. Golubinskij, *Istorija russkoj cerkvi*, vol. 2: *Period vtoroj, Moskovskij*, pt. 1 (Moscow, 1900), 731-732.

[46] Early, during the first hour after midnight on Sunday, July 30, without anyone knowing, the Swedish king Gustavus Adolphus appeared.

[47] Cf. *VK* 1600–39, *VK* 1642–44, *VK* 1645–48 with indexes.

[48] *PRP XVI–XVII*: <1567> [MS 2nd half 16th c.], 7; <1570> [MS 2nd half 16th c.], 91, 99; <1582/83> [MS late 16th c.], 104.

A review of the chronology of the earliest attestations of V reveals an orderly pattern of development from specific to general and religious to secular in the *written* language: V/R (1514–15), V/RS (1526), V/S (1615). Since we know from foreign sources that V/S was already a fact of the spoken language by 1586—twenty-nine years before the earliest written attestation—we must look to the fifteenth century to discern the sources of V/R itself. This view is supported by independent textual evidence.

Vasmer reconstructs the prototype *O of a medieval Russian-Byzantine Greek phrasebook on the basis of four extant manuscript copies (copy A [late 15th–early 16th c.],[49] copy B [mid–16th c.], copy C [17th c.], copy D [mid–16th c.], and after a careful philological analysis assigns *O to the fifteenth century.[50] The phrasebook contains a section devoted to the days of the week and selected holidays. The Russian for Sunday is *nedělja*, but Palm Sunday is listed as *verbnoe vъskresenie* 'Willow Resurrection'.[51]

The juxtaposition of *nedelja* and *Verbnoe voskresenie* in a fifteenth-century phrasebook provides additional evidence that V/R emerges first in the absolute function. Furthermore it suggests that the initial innovation is precisely *Verbnoe voskresenie*. We find support for this view from a 1590 dietary code for the Troice-Sergiev and Tixvin Monasteries.[52] Menus are provided for all Sundays (*vo vsjakuju nedělju*) and weekdays, and then for all holidays, month by month. The Troice-Sergiev code has *vъ nedělju*

---

[49] On the basis of a paleographic comparison Nikoľskij (1896) suggests a common origin for copy A of the phrasebook and a late fifteenth-century *Horologion* located in the Kirill Belozerskij Library. The *Horologion* belonged to Nil Sorskij's teacher, Paisij Jaroslavov; Nikoľskij assumes that he owned the phrasebook as well and is inclined to date it to the late fifteenth, rather than early sixteenth, century. Vasmer ("'Reč' tonkoslovija grečeskogo'—pamjatnik srednegrečeskogo jazyka XIII v.," *VV* 14 [1909]: 447) links copy B with Vassian Patrikeev and conjectures that enlightened members of the Trans-Volga elders may very well have studied Greek from the Russian-Byzantine Greek phrasebook.

[50] Vasmer 1922: 138.

[51] Ibid., 14. As luck would have it, the Russian citation for Palm Sunday in copy A is *verb . . .* (apparently the text is spoiled); copy B has *verbnoe vъskr̄snie*, copy D has *verьbonosie*, lit. Willowbearing, and copy C has *vxodъ vo ieȓslmъ*, lit. the Entry into Jerusalem. On the basis of shared errors and other features, Vasmer posits a common prototype *K₁ for copies A, B, and D juxtaposed to *K₂, represented by copy C (1922: 4–10). He prefers the reading in copy B to that of copy D (*contra* P. K. Simoni, "Pamjatniki starinoj russkoj leksikografii po rukopisjam XV–XVII stoletij," *IORJaS* 13, no. 1 [1908]: 205) for the prototype *O without comment. His choice can be justified on two counts: (1) the first four letters of the citation in B are identical to those in A, while D has an inserted ь, apparently reflecting the pronunciation [r']; and (2) the citation *verbonosie* in D is a slavish imitation of the Greek ἡ βαϊοφόρος and is out of keeping with the original intent of the phrasebook, to provide Cyrillic renditions of the Greek preceded by Russian Church Slavic glosses, many of which are abbreviated. The form *verbo-nosie* is not otherwise attested in the Old Church Slavic, Russian Church Slavic, or Middle Russian lexicons; it appears to be the product of sixteenth-century Hellenization.

[52] *DopAIst* 1, no. 135, pp. 215–228.

Sobornuju and *vъ Verbnoe voskresenie* for Orthodoxy Sunday and Palm Sunday, respectively,[53] while the Tixvin code has the more conservative *vъ nedělju pervuju posta, sirečъ, Pravoslavija* 'on the first Sunday of the Fast, i.e., of Orthodoxy' and *vъ nedělju Cvětnuju* 'on Flower Sunday' for the same two holidays.[54]

On the basis of the evidence presented so far, I propose the following developmental hierarchy for *voskresenie* in the extended usage:

DEVELOPMENTAL HIERARCHY FOR *VOSKRESENIE*

1.	V/R	*Voskresenie Xristovo*	'Resurrection of Christ' (= Easter)
2.	V/R	*Verbnoe voskresenie*	'Willow Resurrection' (= Palm Sunday)
3.	V/R	*Sbornoe voskresenie*	'Synod Resurrection' (= Orthodoxy Sunday)
4.	V/RS	Resurrection-Sundays as a class of religious holidays with a status analogous to that of the feast days of the Lord, the Mother of God, and the major saints	
5.	V/S	Sunday in all functions	

To understand why Palm Sunday might stimulate the initial extension of V/R to Willow Resurrection—an innovation that eventually leads to the replacement of N/S by V/S—we must analyze the function of that holiday and of Sunday in general within the framework of the Orthodox calendar.

Sunday and the Orthodox Calendar

Medieval Russians regulated their personal lives according to the holidays and fasts of the Orthodox calendar. Peasants, for example, were permitted to settle their accounts and leave their masters (*otkazat'sja*) once a year, a week before and after Saint George's Day in the fall. The ecclesiastical tariff (*sbornoe*) was collected from churches and monasteries twice a year, at Christmas and on Saint Peter's Day. Events in the chronicles were often dated not only by month and day but by temporal proximity to a major feast day (for example, on Tuesday of the second week after Easter, on Thursday after Annunciation Day) or to a fast, since fasts in medieval Rus' were observed at a level of severity and frequency unknown in the West. Consider Giles Fletcher's impression of Muscovite fasting practices towards the end of the sixteenth century:

> Besides their fastes on Wednesdayes, and Fridayes throughout the whole yeere, (the one because they say Christ was solde on the Wednes-

---

[53] Ibid., pp. 217, 218.

[54] Ibid., p. 225.

day, the other because he suffered on the Friday) they haue foure great
Fastes, or Lentes euery yeere.... In their great Lent for the first weeke,
they eate nothing but bread and salt, and drinke nothing but water,
neither meddle with anie matter of their vocation, but intende their
shriuing and fasting only.[55]

In addition to their purely chronological function, certain days and
weeks of the year were associated with particular rituals, superstitious customs, weather forecasts, and the like. Many of these popular beliefs date
from pre-Christian times and were either grafted onto events of the church
calendar or maintained separately. Such practices were continually condemned by the Church. It is in the context of pagan custom and Christian
celebration that we must consider the status of Palm Sunday as a source of
linguistic innovation.

The Orthodox calendar is best understood in terms of cycles—yearly,
weekly, daily. The yearly cycle is regulated by the *Menaion* (*Mineja*),
a twelve-volume liturgical work with hymns for each of the 366 days of
the calendar year, including the fixed feasts, fasts, and commemorations
of the saints. In the yearly calendar, there are twelve major feasts (*dva-
nadesjatye prazdniki*) and Easter (see Table 3). The church year begins on
September 1.[56]

The fixed parts of the daily cycle are set down in the *Horologion* (*Časo-
slov*). In accordance with the Jewish pattern, the Orthodox day begins at
sundown. It should be noted that the celebration of the Divine Liturgy of
the Eucharist is independent of the daily cycle. Nevertheless, the liturgy
may be celebrated no more than once per day by the same priest at the
same altar. If the *Stoglav* of 1551 is indicative of medieval Russian practice,

[55] Giles Fletcher, *Of the Russe Commonwealth* (1591), facsimile ed. with variants, ed.
Richard Pipes (Cambridge, Mass, 1966), f104v. Besides the four great fasting periods—the
Great Fast, the Apostolic Fast, the Dormition Fast, and the Christmas Fast—and Wednesday
and Friday fasts, there are fasts on separate feast days: more than half the year altogether. On
these days meat and all dairy products (eggs included) are not permitted. During Lent even
fish is prohibited, and on certain days xerophagy (restriction to dry, unboiled vegetable foods)
must be observed; cf. Makarij, *Istorija russkoj cerkvi*, vol. 8 (St. Petersburg, 1877), 322-323; E.
Golubinskij, *Istorija russkoj cerkvi*, vol. 1: *Period pervyj, Kievskij ili Domongol'skij*, pt. 2, 2nd
ed., rev. and exp. (Moscow, 1904), 462ff.; G. P. Fedotov, *The Russian Religious Mind*, vol. 1:
Kievan Christianity: The 10th to the 13th Centuries (New York, 1946/1960), 184; T. Ware, *The
Orthodox Church*, rev. ed. (Middlesex–New York, 1980), 306-307.

[56] I. N. Božerjanov (*Kak prazdnoval i prazdnuet narod russkij Roždestvo Xristovo, Novyj god,
Kreščenie i Masljanicu* [St. Petersburg, 1894], 42ff.) suggests that the Russian Church began
the New Year on March 1, while the civil year began on September 1, in accordance with
Byzantine Church and civil tradition. In 1342 Metropolitan Feognost proposed that both the
ecclesiastical and civil years begin on September 1; this proposal was reaffirmed at the Synod
of 1505.

TABLE 3

THE TWELVE MAJOR ORTHODOX FEASTS AND EASTER

8 Sep	*Roždestvo Presvjatoj Bogorodicy*	Nativity of the Mother of God
14 Sep	*Vozdviženie Kresta Gospodnja*	Exaltation of the Cross (Holy Cross)
21 Nov	*Vvedenie vo xram Presvjatoj Bogorodicy*	Presentation of the Mother of God in the Temple
25 Dec	*Roždestvo Xristovo*	Christmas
6 Jan	*Kreščenie Gospodne*	Theophany (Epiphany)
2 Feb	*Sretenie Gospodne*	Hypapante (Candlemas)
25 Mar	*Blagoveščenie Presvjatoj Bogorodicy*	Annunciation
M O V A B L E	*Vxod Gospoden' vo Ierusalim*	Palm Sunday
	PASXA	**EASTER**
	Voznesenie Gospodne	Ascension
	Pjatidesjatnica (Troica)	Pentecost (Whitsunday)
6 Aug	*Preobraženie Gospodne*	Transfiguration
15 Aug	*Uspenie Presvjatoj Bogorodicy*	Dormition (Assumption)

the liturgy was celebrated at the very least on Sundays and major feasts.

It is the Paschal and derivative weekly cycles that provide the variable parts (propers) for each week and thus have the greatest impact on the thematic development of the Orthodox message throughout the year. These cycles are dominated by Easter, the most important day of the Orthodox year. Easter in effect stands apart from the calendar, since it determines its place each year according to the rhythms of nature rather than a particular date.[57] In the mind of the faithful, Easter is simultaneously the climax and the beginning of the Orthodox year, governing the place and function of its own set of dependent feasts and reifying itself liturgically every Sunday, the Day of the Resurrection.[58] The weekly cycles

[57] In the Orthodox Church, Easter falls on the Sunday after the first full moon following the vernal equinox (March 21), unless that Sunday would precede or coincide with the Jewish Passover. In that case, the Eastern Church, unlike the Roman Catholic Church and Protestant Churches, postpones Easter until the following Sunday.

[58] After the Council of Nicaea (A.D. 325), Easter became firmly established as the great Sunday par excellence and Sunday itself came to be called a weekly Easter (H. Dumaine, "Dimanche," in *Dictionnaire d'archéologie chrétienne et de liturgie*, vol. 4, pt. 4, ed. F. Cabrol and H. Leclerq (Paris, 1920), 907; cf. W. Rordorf, *Sunday: The History of the Day of Rest and Worship in the Earliest Centuries of the Church* [Philadelphia, 1968], 17, n. 7); prior to this time

are regulated by three liturgical books: the *Triodion* (*Postnaja Triod'*) contains the propers for the ten-week period preceding Easter; the *Pentekostarion* (*Cvetnaja Triod'*), for the eight-week period following Easter; and the *Oktoechos* (*Oktoix*), for the weeks of the remaining, non-Paschal period.[59]

Using Easter as a point of departure, we note that the Sundays and weeks in Eastertide are *retrospective*, that is, they are identified in part by their position after Easter and Sunday, respectively. Thomas Sunday is the First Sunday *after* Easter, the Sunday of the Myrrhophores is the Second Sunday *after* Easter, and so forth. The name of each week is taken from the Sunday that heads it (thus Thomas Week, the Week of the Myrrhophores, etc.) or from the position of the week relative to Easter (thus the Second Week after Easter, the Third Week after Easter, etc.). The outlook remains retrospective after the Paschal cycle ends with the Sunday of All Saints. The Sundays and weeks that follow are identified in part by their position after Pentecost and Sunday, respectively. The Sunday of All Saints is the First Sunday *after* Pentecost, the Sunday of All Saints Radiant in the Russian Land is the Second Sunday *after* Pentecost, and so on. The weeks, if named at all, are designated according to the name of the dominant Sunday, or more frequently, according to their position relative to Pentecost; thus the Week of All Saints is the Second Week *after* Pentecost. This retrospective pattern continues until the end of the Thirty-fourth Week after Pentecost.

The Lenten portion of the Paschal cycle begins with the Sunday of the Publican and the Pharisee, a day that stands outside the established series of weeks in isolation (see fig. 1; Sundays are symbolized by squares, the weekdays by circles).

At this point the ecclesiastical view of the week becomes *anticipatory*: Monday is the first day of the week and Sunday is the last day or climax of the week. The shift in attitude towards the order of the days of the week is prompted by the need for the faithful to prepare themselves physically, mentally, and spiritually for the joyous celebration of the Resurrection of Christ. Each week in the Lenten period anticipates Sunday, the Day of the Resurrection, just as the entire Lenten period itself anticipates Easter: thus Meatfast Week anticipates Meatfast Sunday; Cheesefast Week, Cheesefast Sunday; Synod Week, Synod Sunday; and Palm Week, Palm Sunday. Once

there was no universally accepted date or day for Easter (M. H. Shepherd, *The Paschal Liturgy and the Apocalypse* [Richmond, 1960], 41ff.).

[59] The use of the *Oktoechos* hymns during the Paschal cycle is determined by the *Triodion* and the *Pentekostarion*.

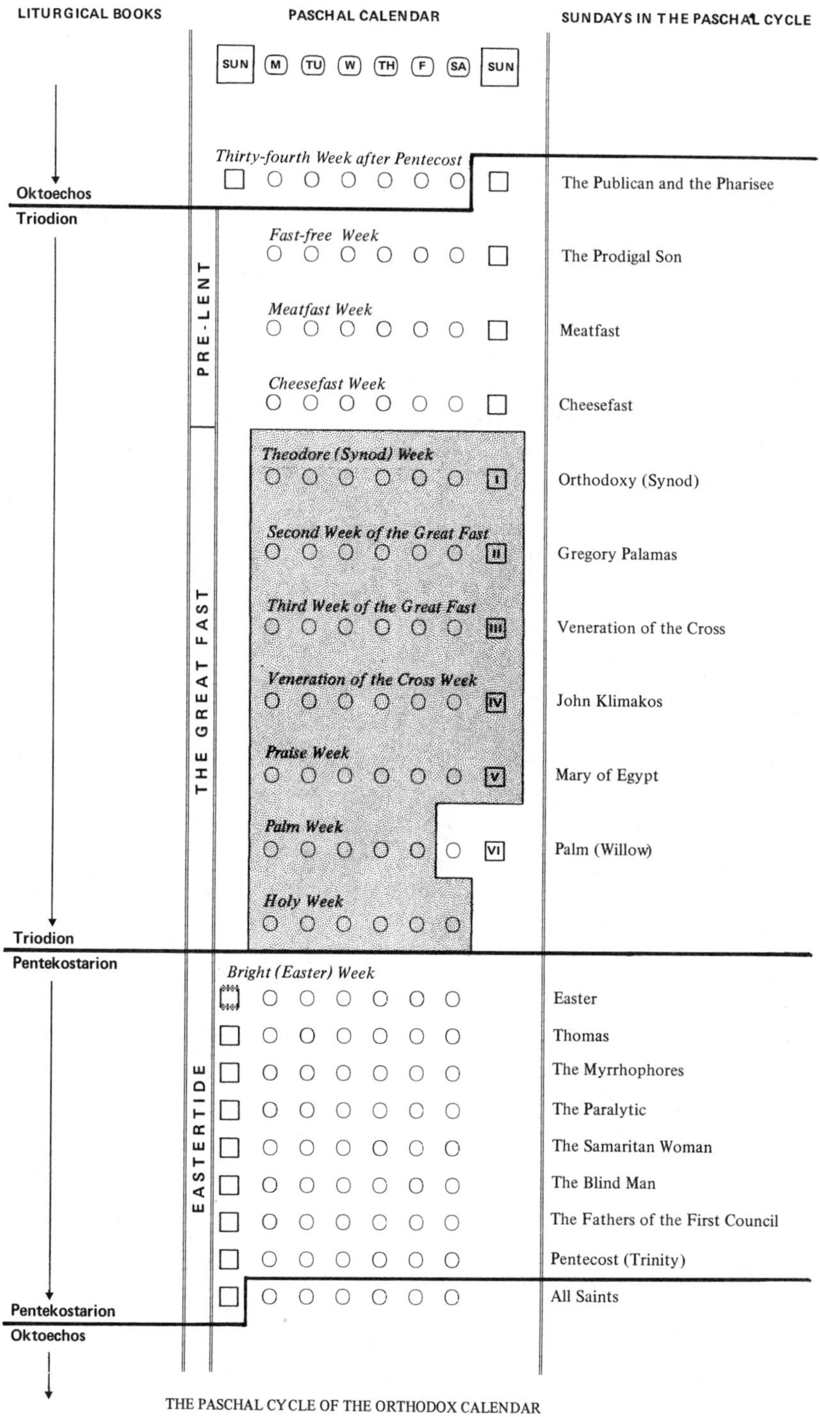

LITURGICAL BOOKS
PASCHAL CALENDAR
SUNDAYS IN THE PASCHAL CYCLE
SUN
M
TU
W
TH
F
SA
SUN
Thirty-fourth Week after Pentecost
The Publican and the Pharisee
Oktoechos
Triodion
Fast-free Week
The Prodigal Son
Meatfast Week
Meatfast
Cheesefast Week
Cheesefast
PRE-LENT
Theodore (Synod) Week
I
Orthodoxy (Synod)
Second Week of the Great Fast
II
Gregory Palamas
Third Week of the Great Fast
III
Veneration of the Cross
Veneration of the Cross Week
IV
John Klimakos
Praise Week
V
Mary of Egypt
THE GREAT FAST
Palm Week
VI
Palm (Willow)
Holy Week
Triodion
Pentekostarion
Bright (Easter) Week
Easter
Thomas
The Myrrhophores
The Paralytic
The Samaritan Woman
The Blind Man
The Fathers of the First Council
Pentecost (Trinity)
All Saints
EASTERTIDE
Pentekostarion
Oktoechos

THE PASCHAL CYCLE OF THE ORTHODOX CALENDAR

Fig. 1.

Easter is reached, the retrospective pattern is reintroduced and Sunday takes its customary position as the head of the week.[60]

The seasonal switch of Sunday from first to last day of the week is not without significance, for it is during the Lenten period that the ecclesiastical view of the week with Sunday last coincides with the popular view of the week, a synchronization that facilitates the interaction of Christian and popular traditions. It is beyond the scope of the present inquiry to show that *nedelja* was the last day of the popular week in medieval Rus', but two points may be made in passing. First, as the weekly day of rest, Sunday, the Christian Sabbath, would be viewed in practical terms as a reward for six days of labor, hence, as the end and not the beginning of the week. Second, the distinctive double designation of Slavic *nedělja* as "Sunday" and "week" finds its source in the Jewish and derivative Greek models in which "Saturday" (*šabbāt* and σάββατον) is also used to designate "week." In both the Slavic and Jewish-Greek models, the *last* day (Sabbath) is used as an index of the passage of seven days, a week.[61] With this in mind we will assume that during the Lenten period, the ecclesiastical and popular weeks were identical.

In figure 1, one can see that the Lenten period actually divides into the three-week pre-Lent period of preparation and the seven-week Great Fast (*Velikij post*), indicated by shading. The Great Fast consists of the Fast of the Forty Days (*Velikaja četyredesjatnica*) and the Fast of Holy Week (*Post Strastnoj sedmicy*). Although Palm Saturday and Palm Sunday are part of Palm Week and technically within the fasting period, they are not considered part of the Great Fast, but serve rather as a bridge between the two major fasts of Lent. A brief examination of the prescribed patterns for fasting, hymnody, and liturgy illustrates the special status of these two days within the *Triodion* cycle (see figs. 2a, 2b, 2c).

The gradual development towards abstinence in the pre-Lent period ends with Cheesefast Week, popular *Maslenica*, when no meat is permitted but dairy products and fish are allowed. The first days of the Great Fast serve as an abrupt change leading to the usual Lenten xerophagy; only Saturdays

---

[60] It is equally possible to view the first two weeks of the *Triodion* cycle as retrospective vis-à-vis Sunday, thus, the Week of the Publican and the Pharisee (the Sunday of the Publican and the Pharisee plus the next six days) and the Week of the Prodigal Son (the Sunday of the Prodigal Son plus the next six days). In the context of fasting, however, this second week is anticipatory, since all the days of Meatfast Week anticipate Meatfast Sunday, the last day before Easter that meat *may* be eaten (i.e., Meatfast Sunday anticipates the meatfast).

[61] L. V. Čerepnin, *Russkaja xronologija* (Moscow, 1944), 33; W. Havers, *Neuere Literatur zum Sprachtabu*, Akademie der Wissenschaften in Wien, Philosophisch-historische Klasse, Sitzungsberichte 233, no. 5 (Vienna, 1946), 141.

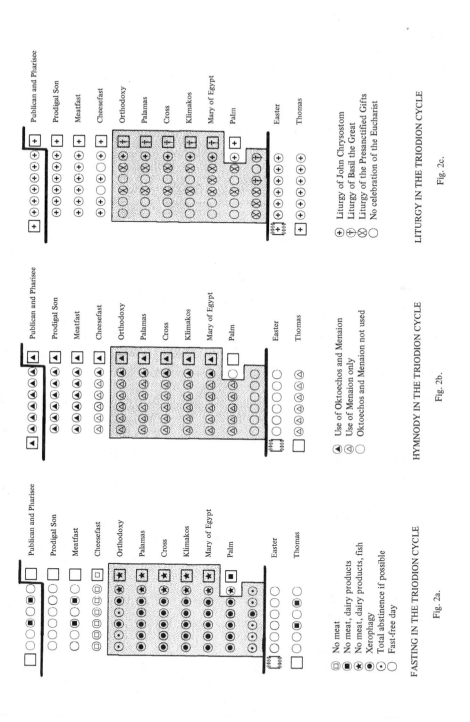

FASTING IN THE TRIODION CYCLE

Fig. 2a.

▢ No meat
▣ No meat, dairy products
✦ No meat, dairy products, fish
● Xerophagy
⊙ Total abstinence if possible
○ Fast-free day

HYMNODY IN THE TRIODION CYCLE

Fig. 2b.

◀ Use of Oktoechos and Menaion
◁ Use of Menaion only
○ Oktoechos and Menaion not used

LITURGY IN THE TRIODION CYCLE

Fig. 2c.

⊕ Liturgy of John Chrysostom
✛ Liturgy of Basil the Great
⊗ Liturgy of the Presanctified Gifts
○ No celebration of the Eucharist

Publican and Pharisee
Prodigal Son
Meatfast
Cheesefast
Orthodoxy
Palamas
Cross
Klimakos
Mary of Egypt
Palm
Easter
Thomas

and Sundays are less severe. Except for Annunciation Day, when it happens to fall within the fasting period, Palm Sunday is the only day in Lent on which fish is allowed, a mark of distinction that presages the arduous Fast of Holy Week (see fig. 2a). The abstinence from food is mirrored in the patterns of hymnody and liturgy.

In figure 2b, we note that the *Oktoechos*, which contains the hymns based on one of eight tones (melodies), one for each week of an eight-week cycle, is limited in use to Saturdays and Sundays after the second week of the Lenten period until the Sunday of Mary of Egypt, after which it is set aside until the Monday of All Saints Week. The hymns of the *Menaion* are sung throughout the Lenten period until the end of the Fast of the Forty Days, Palm Friday, after which the *Menaion* is set aside until the Monday of Thomas Week. Thus Palm Saturday and Palm Sunday are isolated by the hymnodic pattern as well.

The celebration of the liturgy shows a redistribution during the Lenten period (see fig. 2c). The normal liturgy, that of Saint John Chrysostom, which may be celebrated daily during the first two weeks of the *Triodion* cycle, is proscribed for Cheesefast Wednesday and Friday and is limited to Saturdays during the Great Fast. On Wednesdays and Fridays, the Liturgy of the Presanctified Gifts is performed after Great Vespers.[62] The Liturgy of Saint Basil, somewhat longer than the normal liturgy, is celebrated every Sunday of the Great Fast until Palm Sunday, when the Liturgy of Saint John Chrysostom is reintroduced, thus marking Palm Sunday as the only Sunday during the fast when the normal liturgy may be celebrated.

The isolation of Palm Sunday in the *Triodion* cycle is anticipated by a paradoxical switch that marks Palm Saturday. The joyful Resurrection service for Sunday is performed at Matins on Saturday, a change that is especially striking because Saturday in the Lenten period in addition to being a day of preparation for the Day of the Resurrection is a day for commemorating death. Except for Theodore Saturday and the fifth—of the Akathistos—Saturdays in the Lenten period are days of universal commemoration of the dead who await the general resurrection following the Second Coming. But it is precisely Palm Saturday that symbolizes the fulfillment of that expectation, since it is on this day that the Orthodox Church celebrates the resurrection of Lazarus.

> All Saturdays of the liturgical year receive their meaning from two decisive Saturdays: that of Lazarus' Resurrection, which took place in this world and is the announcement of the common resurrection; and

---

[62] A. Schmemann, *Introduction to Liturgical Theology* (Portland, Me., 1966), 30; id., *Great Lent: Journey to Pascha* (Crestwood, N.Y.: St. Vladimir's Seminary, 1974), 55ff.

that of the Great and Holy Sabbath of Pascha when death itself was transformed and became the "passover" into the new life of the New Creation.[63]

The key to understanding the emergence of *Verbnoe voskresenie* is to be found in the special relationship between Lazarus Saturday (*Lazareva subbota*), as the day is more commonly called, and Palm Sunday.[64] All the weekdays of Palm Week are devoted thematically to Lazarus and Christ's activities in Bethany,[65] that is, to the forthcoming encounters between Christ and Death, first in the death of Lazarus, then in his own death on Good Friday. Aside from the resurrectional hymns that link the Sunday services of Lazarus Saturday with Palm Sunday, the festal troparion of the general resurrection, which is sung only on Lazarus Saturday and Palm Sunday, recurs throughout the services for both days.[66]

> Obščee voskresenie prežde Tvoeja strasti uvěrjaja,
> iz mertvyxъ vozdviglъ esi Lazarja, Xriste Bože:
> Těmže i my, jako otròcy pobědy znamenija nosjašče,
> Tebě poběditelju smerti vopiemъ:
> osanna vъ vyšnixъ, blagoslovenъ Grjadyj vo imja Gospodne.[67]

Birkbeck's description (hyperbolic though it may be) of the Palm Sunday Vigil (Great Vespers, Matins, and the First Hour) on Saturday evening in Moscow in 1897 conveys the effect of the message:

> The sight which met our eyes baffles description. All the chandeliers both in the nave and in the galleries round the church were lit. The "palms," which in Russia as in England consist of boughs of budding willow, had just been distributed, and every worshipper in the vast building, which is calculated to hold over 5000, and which was packed

---

[63] Schmemann, *Great Lent*, 69.

[64] Besides the normal designation for Palm Sunday in the Orthodox Church—Κυριακὴ τῶν βαΐων—the Patriarchate of Jerusalem also uses Κυριακὴ τοῦ Λαζάρου 'Lazarus Sunday' (N. Nilles, *Kalendarium Manuale Utriusque Ecclesiae Orientalis et Occidentalis*, vol. 2: *Complectens mobilia totius anni festa* (Oxford–Paris, 1897), 202; F. Cabrol, "Lazare (Samedi et Dimanche de)," in *Dictionnaire d'archéologie chrétienne et de liturgie*, vol. 8, pt. 2, ed. F. Cabrol and H. Leclerq (Paris, 1929), 2086-2088.

[65] John 11: 1-45.

[66] On Lazarus Saturday it is sung towards the beginning (three times) and end (twice) of the Matins service, at the Hours and the Divine Liturgy, and at Great Vespers (twice) and Matins (three times) services of the Palm Sunday Vigil on Saturday evening. On Sunday it is sung at the Hours and the Divine Liturgy.

[67] Giving us before Thy Passion an assurance of the general resurrection, Thou hast raised Lazarus from the dead, O Christ our God. Therefore, like the children, we also carry tokens of victory, and cry to Thee, the Conqueror of death: Hosanna in the highest; blessed is He that comes in the Name of the Lord (translation from the Greek by Mother Mary and Archimandrite Kallistos Ware, *The Lenten Triodion* [London–Boston, 1978], 476).

from end to end, had his branch with a lighted taper fastened in the middle of it.... To describe the liturgical features of the service would take too long; but the *troparion* for the day is so remarkable for the skill with which it sets forth the connection of the feast of the previous day with the day itself, as well as with the Resurrection which is of course commemorated on every Sunday of the year, that I cannot forbear from quoting it.[68]

As regards the connection between the Saturday and Sunday of Palm Week, we note that by the late fifteenth century the calendrical metonym V/R was used not only to designate Christ's Resurrection (= Easter Sunday), *Voskresenie Xristovo*, but Lazarus' Resurrection (= Lazarus Saturday) as well, *Voskresenie Lazarevo*. The latter is found in the fifteenth-century Russian-Byzantine Greek phrasebook and in a liturgical-dietary code from the Troice-Sergiev Monastery dated 1467–74.[69] *Voskresenie Lazarevo* is not an innovation of the type *Verbnoe voskresenie*, however, but simply the extension of an existing metonymic pattern constrained in reference to a specific resurrection of the past and thus bereft of the possibility of further development as a calendrical unit; compare a similar constraint on *Voskresenie Xristovo* itself, thus 'the Resurrection of Christ' (= Easter), but not 'Christ Resurrection-Sunday' or 'Christ Sunday'. The developmental hierarchy based on the innovation *Verbnoe voskresenie* refers to Sundays as cyclical commemorations of Easter Day, but one level removed from the actual Day of the Resurrection itself. It is the *innovations* in V/R that eventually develop into V/RS and V/S. Even though *Voskresenie Lazarevo* is not part of the hierarchy itself, its very presence reflects the thematic progression of the various patterns of the *Triodion cycle*—fasting, hymnody, liturgy, Gospel readings—as they build towards a climax at the end of Palm Week.

A thematic nexus of resurrection—the resurrection of Lazarus, the general resurrection, Palm Sunday as a Day of the Resurrection, the impending Resurrection of Christ—binds Lazarus Saturday and Palm Sunday together as a concentrated period of joyful expectation between the Fast of the Forty Days and Holy Week, a period whose resurrectional bond with Easter Sunday is ultimately expressed through *Verbnoe voskresenie*, the Willow Resurrection. Defined, as it were, in *human* terms through the resurrection of Lazarus and the promise of the general resurrection, *Verbnoe voskresenie* emerges as a fitting complement to *Voskresenie Xristovo*, the Resurrection of Christ, a day defined in terms both human and divine.

[68] W. J. Birkbeck, *Birkbeck and the Russian Church* (essays and articles, 1888–1915), coll. and ed. A. Riley (London–New York, 1917), 130-131.
[69] Vasmer 1922: 14; Gorskij 1841/1879: 8.

The functional similarity of the two Sundays flanking Holy Week—Palm Sunday and Easter Sunday—is underscored by their inherent duality. Palm Sunday serves simultaneously as the end of Palm Week and the beginning of Holy Week, the Lord's Entry into Jerusalem,[70] while Easter functions as the climax of Holy Week—in which all the days from Monday through Saturday are called "Great"—hence *Velik den'* 'Great Day', and the beginning of Bright Week, hence *Svetloe Voskresenie Xristovo* 'the Bright Resurrection of Christ'. Within the framework of the Orthodox calendar, the innovative extension of V/R from *Voskresenie Xristovo* to *Verbnoe voskresenie* finds strong motivation.

Even though Lazarus Saturday and Palm Sunday are isolated by the Orthodox calendar in general and by the *Triodion* cycle in particular, we do well to recognize that the scheme considered above presents the Orthodox message in its ideal form. It is generally assumed that in both quantitative and qualitative terms, medieval Russian practice in the large cathedral church with its capacity for great pomp, circumstance, and spectacle was a far cry from that found in the impoverished parish church, removed from direct episcopal supervison.[71] Furthermore there is no basis for assuming that medieval Russians were such experts in liturgical matters that they understood the underlying significance of every ritual, hymn, or prayer they might encounter. In fact, their comprehension of Russian Church Slavic must have been inversely proportional to the complexity of syntax and the abstruseness of the church lexicon. But even the most backward, simple peasant could not have been oblivious to the general course of the fast, the loss of hymnal variety, and the introduction of a somber tone into the services of the Lenten period. The ever-increasing focus on the theme of death and resurrection that crystallizes at the end of Palm Week was clearly understood as the innovation *Verbnoe voskresenie* itself testifies.

Voskresenie and the Russian Folk Tradition

Although the sources of resurrection and renewal expressed by V can be found in the teachings of Orthodoxy, the actualization of the new combinations was apparently possible only if the religious meaning behind them

---

[70] In liturgical texts, Lazarus Saturday and Palm Sunday are described as the "beginning of the Cross" and are to be understood in the context of Holy Week (A. Schmemann, *Holy Week: A Liturgical Explanation for the Days of Holy Week* [Crestwood, N.Y.: St. Vladimir's Seminary, 1971], 3).

[71] P. Znamenskij, *Učebnoe rukovodstvo po istorii russkoj cerkvi*, 2nd ed., rev. (St. Petersburg, 1904), 24-188; Golubinskij, *Istorija russkoj cerkvi* (see n. 55), vol. 1, pt. 2: 343-384; vol. 2: *Period vtoroj, Moskovskij*, pt. 2 (1910): 404-442.

reverberated in the Russian folk tradition. Thus it is no accident that the first innovation in V occurs during the period when the ecclesiastical and popular weeks coincide with Sunday as the last day. But we have only discerned the ecclesiastical underpinnings for *Verbnoe voskresenie*; we must turn to the Russian folk tradition for a complete understanding of this significant innovation and its derivative progeny.

Palm Sunday. Like many church holidays, Palm Sunday has a number of designations in Russian: *Vxod Gospoden' vo Ierusalim* 'the Lord's Entry into Jerusalem', *Nedelja Vaij* 'Palm Sunday', *Cvetnaja nedelja* 'Flower Sunday', *Cvetonosnaja nedelja* 'Flower-bearing Sunday', *Verbnica* 'Willowtide', and *Verbnaja nedelja* 'Willow Sunday'. But there is no *Voskresenie Vaij* 'Palm Resurrection', *Cvetnoe voskresenie* 'Flower Resurrection', and so on—only *Verbnoe voskresenie*. This restriction is due to the special place of the willow (*verba*) in Old Russian culture.

The willow was revered among the ancient Slavs as a symbol of spring renewal and health; in general terms, the willow, especially the male pussy willow with its distinctive cottonlike catkins, is a common harbinger of spring in Northern Europe because it is among the first trees to bud in the new season. The willow was used by the Russians as an instrument of well-being and enrichment. The catkins were eaten to ward off fever and sore throats (the sap contains salicin, a common ingredient in pain relievers). Sick children were bathed in water containing willow branches. Fields were commonly sprinkled with broken willow branches to guarantee a good harvest. A willow branch thrown against the wind was thought to ward off an approaching storm. It was obligatory to strike cattle with willow branches on Saint George's Day, April 23, before the first cattle drive into the fields.

Birkbeck's description cited earlier attests to the important role that the willow played in the rituals of Palm Sunday. The branches were broken off and gathered on Lazarus Saturday—according to an old saying "Svjatoj Lazar' za verboj lazil."[72] They were blessed during a special ceremony at Matins as part of the Palm Sunday Vigil: the willow branch was an appropriate substitute for the palm branch in a climate in which the latter was unobtainable. After returning home with the sanctified branches, the faithful would place a few in or behind the icon case (*božnica*) as a token of health and then perform a characteristic ritual with the rest. Members of the family would lightly strike one another as part of a ritual beating while intoning a chant, for example:

---

[72] Saint Lazarus has clambered after the willow.

Ne ja b'ju, verba b'ët
črez nedelju Velik den';
Buď zdorov, kak voda,
Buď bogat, kak zemlja.[73]

Similar chants have been noted by folklorists:

Verba xlëst, bej do slëz,
Verba krasna, bej naprasno,
Verba bela, bej za delo.[74]

In the evening the catkins were cooked with kasha and eaten (verbnaja kaša).[75] The link between the "palms" of Palm Sunday and the willow was the result of a convenient marriage of church symbolism and pagan custom. As a sign of spring renewal and health, the willow branch was an opportune source for the symbolism of Palm Sunday: the association of the ritual beating with willow branches and the scourging of Christ during the Passion scarcely requires mention. It is not unlikely that the very term Verbnica existed in pre-Christian times to refer to a period—Willowtide?— during which the rites of spring involving the willow were celebrated.[76] The use of this word for a week-long period is noted in the dialects.[77] With the introduction of Christianity, Verbnica came to be associated with Palm Sunday alone. The term Verbnaja nedelja appears to be a later derivative;[78] it is not found in Old Church Slavic texts. Vrьbnica (or Vrьbnicy = Palm Week?)[79] occurs only in the Euchologium Sinaiticum and the Codex Suprasliensis.[80]

---

[73] It is not me beating, the willow beats, Easter Day is in a week. Be healthy like the water, be rich like the earth.

[74] Willow crack!—beat to tears; willow red—beat without cause; willow white—beat with cause.

[75] See Ènciklopedičeskij slovar' (Leipzig–St. Petersburg, 1890–1907), s.v. verba; A. Ermolov, Narodnaja sel'skoxozjajstvennaja mudrost' v poslovicax, pogovorkax i primetax, vol. 1: Vsenarodnyj mesjaceslov (St. Petersburg, 1901), 109; V. K. Sokolova, Vesenne-letnie kalendarnye obrjady russkix, ukraincev i belorusov XIX–načalo XX v. (Moscow, 1979), 97ff.

[76] Sokolova (Vesenne-letnie kalendarnye obrjady [see n. 75], 101) suggests the likelihood of many more rituals keyed to this period of the yearly cycle and cites the South Slavic, especially Serbian and Bulgarian, maidens' holiday celebrated on Lazarus Saturday with rituals involving willow branches (Serbian Lazarice, Bulgarian Lazaruvane). Cf. S. Kulišić, P. Ž. Petrović, N. Pantelić, Srpski mitološki rečnik (Belgrade, 1970), 191-192.

[77] Slovar' russkix narodnyx govorov, vol. 4, ed. F. P. Filin (Moscow–Leningrad, 1969), 122.

[78] The oldest attestation seems to be Nestor's Žitie Feodosija, written before 1093. In the Izbornik of 1073 Palm Sunday is termed prazdьnikъ vьrbьny 'willow holiday'.

[79] See L. Sadnik and R. Aitzetmüller, Handwörterbuch zu den altkirchenslavischen Texten (Heidelberg, 1955), 154.

[80] Slovník jazyka staroslověnského, vol. 1 (Prague, 1959), 223.

The more common terms are *Cvětьnaja nedělja, Cvětonosьnaja nedělja* and *Cvěty* (cf. Serbo-Croatian *Cvêti* 'Palm Sunday', lit. Flowers, Flowertide).[81] The apparent reason that V/R does not extend to the flower terms for Palm Sunday is that flowers played a minimal role in both the Palm Sunday rituals and in pre-Christian vernal rites: the brilliant hues of seasonal flowers appear quite late in the Russian spring.[82] *Verbnoe voskresenie*, however, resonates in both the church and pagan calendars as a mark of spiritual and physical rebirth.

Orthodoxy Sunday. At first glance the extension of V/R from Willow Resurrection to Orthodoxy Sunday is puzzling. As the first Sunday of the Great Fast (see fig. 2a) following a six-day period of severe abstinence, Orthodoxy Sunday does stand out as a special day, but not so much as to warrant the term *Resurrection*. But Orthodoxy Sunday is also the one day each year when the faithful reaffirm their commitment to Orthodoxy during a special Office of Orthodoxy (*Čin Pravoslavija*) celebrated after the liturgy. The Office of Orthodoxy was brought to Russia in the late fourteenth century by Kiprian, a Bulgarian monk who had spent his early years at Mount Athos and had come to Russia in the 1370s to assume the position of metropolitan. The existing turmoil in church-state relations delayed his absolute claim to the title Metropolitan of All Russia until 1390, but his zealous leadership in correcting and codifying existing religious practices established him as one of the primary figures of the Orthodox Slavic revival in Russia.[83]

Before Kiprian, the first Sunday of the Great Fast had simply been a day in commemoration of Moses, Aaron, David, and Samuel.[84] His decision to establish Orthodoxy Sunday in the Russian Paschal cycle was not an idle

[81] The official *Vxod Gospoden' vo Ierusalim* never seems to have enjoyed much popularity, even in an abbreviated form *Vxod*; cf. the universally accepted *Vvedenie* (*vo Xram Presvjatoj Bogorodicy*) 'Presentation (of the Virgin in the Temple)', *Uspenie* (*Presvjatoj Bogorodicy*) 'Dormition (of the Virgin)', and so forth.

[82] The ritual of blessing the flowers on Palm Sunday seems to have originated in the Latin-oriented countries of the south and then spread north. F. V. Mareš ("Nedělja cvětьnaja, květná nedĕle, 'dominica in Palmis,'" *Slavia* 25 [1956]: 258-259) is probably correct in assuming that Cyril and Methodius added the flower terms for Palm Sunday to the Old Church Slavic lexicon only after arriving in Moravia, where they were already in use.

[83] I. Mansvetov, *Mitropolit Kiprian v ego liturgičeskoj dejatel'nosti. Istoriko-liturgičeskoe issledovanie* (Moscow, 1882); M. S. Iovine, "Metropolitan Kiprian and the Orthodox Slavic Revival," in *Bulgaria Past and Present: Studies in History, Literature, Economics, Music, Sociology, Folklore and Linguistics*, ed. T. Butler (Columbus, 1976), 261-266; J. Meyendorff, *Byzantium and the Rise of Russia: A Study of Byzantino-Russian Relations in the Fourteenth Century* (Cambridge, 1981), 119-126, 197ff.

[84] Mansvetov, *Metropolit Kiprian* (see n. 83), 81, n. 3.

one; the Strigoľnik heresy that had flared up in Novgorod in the mid-fourteenth century and spread to Pskov demanded a strong response from the Church. The Office of Orthodoxy or *Synodikon* (*Sinodik*) was appropriate, since it had been conceived as an antiheretical affirmation of the faith.[85] The Office was celebrated in the presence of the higher clergy, which gathered as a synod (*sъborъ*) at the episcopal churches, whence the popular name of the day, Synod (*Sbor*) or Synod Sunday (*Sbornaja nedelja*), the latter from the fifteenth century on. The emphasis on the cyclical renewal of the faith is apparent in the opening proclamation:

Dolžnoe kъ b͞gu lětnoje bl͞godarenie vonь že dn͞ь vosprijaxomъ B͞ьju cьrkovь, so obьjavleniemъ bl͞gočstivyxъ velěnii i v razvraščenie zlobьnyxъ nečstii. Proročьskimь poslědujušče gl͞mъ ap͞slъskimъ že poučenijemь novinujuščesja i evaggelьskimь spisaniemь priložьšesja obnovlenija dn͞ь prazdnuimь.[86]

The Office had been reworked several times over the centuries before it was translated into Russian Church Slavic.[87] Although the translation itself is clumsy, at times almost incomprehensible, the last part of the ceremony must have made a profound impression on those in attendance, for it is here that the heroes and villains of Orthodoxy are enumerated and alternately praised three times to eternity (*věčnaja pamjatь*) or anathematized three times to eternal damnation (*anafema* or *da budutь prokljati*). That this ceremony was still effective after the fourteenth century is evident from the fact that names of Novgorod and Muscovite heretics from the late fifteenth-early sixteenth centuries were subsequently added to the list of the damned.

The aspect of reaffirmation and renewal thematically links the first and last Sundays of the Lenten period, Orthodoxy Sunday and Palm Sunday,[88]

---

[85] The Office of Orthodoxy was first celebrated in Constantinople in 842 on the first Sunday of the Great Fast to commemorate the ultimate triumph of Regent Empress Theodora and Emperor Michael III over Iconoclasm and other heresies. It was written by Methodios, the patriarch of Constantinople, on the basis of the protocols of the anti-Iconoclast Seventh Ecumenical Council of Nicaea (787).

[86] The obligatory annual thanksgiving to God, on which day we have accepted God's Church by proclaiming pious commands and casting away malicious impieties. Following the words of the Prophets, renewing ourselves through the teachings of the Apostles, and having applied ourselves through the Gospel Writ, let us celebrate a day of renewal (from Petuxov 1895: 10).

[87] Ibid., 3-7.

[88] Since the addition of the Office of Orthodoxy to the liturgy made for a very long ceremony, Kiprian preferred to use the Liturgy of Saint John Chrysostom instead of the longer Liturgy of Saint Basil, which is customary for Sundays in the Lenten period (*AIst* 1, no. 11, p. 19). The use of the shorter liturgy links Orthodox Sunday and Palm Sunday as well. And judging from the writings of Nikon Černogorec, it was apparently the practice in the fourteenth and fifteenth centuries for the laity to be permitted fish on three days during the Lenten

but we must again turn to the folk tradition to find the native Russian element in the equation that sees the actualization of *Sbornoe voskresenie* 'Synod Resurrection'.

Like Palm Sunday, Orthodoxy Sunday has a number of designations: *Nedelja Pravoslavija/Nedelja Pravoslavnaja* 'Orthodoxy Sunday', *Sbornaja nedelja* 'Synod Sunday'. But there is no innovation *Voskresenie Pravoslavija* or *Pravoslavnoe voskresenie* 'Orthodoxy Resurrection'—only *Sbornoe (Sobornoe) voskresenie* 'Synod Resurrection'. Apparently the synodal aspect of this Sunday—a time of gathering together—was part of the Russian tradition long before the introduction of Orthodoxy Sunday. The convening of the synod on the first Sunday of the Great Fast signaled the beginning of the week-long Synod Market or Fair (*Sbornaja jarmanka/jarmarka*).[89] The aspect of community (*sobornost'*), then, unites Orthodoxy Sunday, the gathering of the faithful, and Palm Sunday, the gathering in expectation of the general resurrection. Although the thematic unity explains the restriction of the innovation to *Sbornoe voskresenie*, there is a more profound factor that binds these two Sundays together.

It is commonly assumed that the Old Russian year began on March 1 (the March year), but that the East Slavs were well aware of the Byzantine tradition of beginning the year on September 1 (the September year) and tried to adapt their own chronicle calculations to the latter.[90] After a detailed study of units of time and time calculation in the Laurentian and I Novgorod chronicles, however, Stepanov concludes, contrary to popular opinion, that the Russian New Year began not *on* March 1, but *around* March 1 (circa-March year), falling sometimes before, but most often after, the beginning of March.[91] The reason for this movable New Year is that the Russian calculation was based on a lunar, and not solar, year. Since the lunar and solar calendars do not coincide (an average month of 29.5 days × 12 months = 354 days for a lunar year versus 365.25 days for a solar year), it was necessary to have an intercalated thirteenth month every three years

---

period other than Palm Sunday: Orthodox Sunday, Veneration of the Cross Sunday, and Annunciation Day (March 25), yet another point held in common between the two Sundays; see Mansvetov, *Metropolit Kiprian* (see n. 83), 186ff, esp. 195.

[89] Cf. Saxarov 1849, pt. 2, sec. 7: 98; Ermolov, *Vsenarodnyj mesjaceslov* (see n. 75), 106; V. Dal', *Tolkovyj slovar' živogo velikorusskogo jazyka*, 4 vols. 3d ed., rev. and exp. J. Baudouin de Courtenay (St. Petersburg–Moscow, 1903–1909), vol. 4: 43-44.

[90] Old Russian chroniclers, especially from Novgorod and Pskov, also used units from the Roman calendrical system; see Ja. N. Ščapov, "Drevnerimskij kalendar' na Rusi," in *Vostočnaja Evropa v drevnosti i srednevekov'e*, ed. L. V. Čerepnin (Moscow, 1978), 336-345.

[91] N. V. Stepanov, "Edinicy sčeta vremeni (do XIII veka) po Lavrentievskoj i I-j Novgorodskoj letopisjam," *ČOIDR*, 1909, bk. 4, sec. 3: 1-74.

so that the months would not become too far removed from their appropriate seasons.[92] Stepanov suggests that in actual practice the Russians began their New Year with the first full moon following the twelfth full moon of the "preceding year," unless that moon occurred more than one lunation before the vernal equinox or the weather was inappropriate for a celebration of spring. In that case, they would intercalate a thirteenth month and begin the year with the next full moon.[93]

He calculates the dates for the earliest vernal full moon over the nineteen-year lunar cycle using the chronicle years 6639–6657 (1131–1149) and compares them with the dates of Easter. A striking pattern emerges from the data: the occurrences of the vernal full moon, the sign of the Old Russian New Year, cluster around two periods in the Paschal cycle—the second week and the juncture of the six and seventh weeks of the Great Fast. Within the Christian context of fasting, the beginning of the New Year had to be transferred to the Sundays flanking these periods, namely, to Orthodoxy Sunday and Palm Sunday.[94] These two pivotal Sundays, with their focus on resurrection and renewal, amplify the cyclical renewal of the folk year at both of its possible junctures: Synod Resurrection thus serves as the appropriate derivative complement to Willow Resurrection.[95]

Cheesefast Sunday and Thomas Sunday. Two more Sundays must be mentioned in connection with the emergence of *Verbnoe voskresenie* and *Sbornoe voskresenie*. A popular term for Cheesefast Sunday, the eve of the Great Fast and the last day of *Maslenica*, is *Proščenoe* (*Proščaľnoe*) *voskresenie* 'Forgiveness (Farewell) Resurrection'. In Northern Russia, a popular name for Thomas Sunday, the first Sunday after Easter, is *Raduničnoe voskresenie* 'Radunica Resurrection' (derived from *radunica*, etymology unclear). Both appear to be well established in the folk tradition, but neither is well documented in the texts.[96] Without pursuing the matter here, I will

---

[92] Stepanov (ibid., 50) cites a passage by Kirik, author of the I Novgorod Chronicle, which indicates a familiarity with this system of reckoning years; see R. A. Simonov, *Kirik Novgorodec* (Moscow, 1980), 32-45, 58-89.

[93] Stepanov, "Edinicy sčeta vremeni" (see n. 91), 51. He also speculates (ibid., 48-49) that the reckoning of time by the full moon to determine the beginning of the New Year must have been borrowed, most probably from the Jews in the Diaspora, who used a lunar-solar calendar.

[94] Ibid., 52; id., "K voprosu o kalendare Lavrentievskoj letopisi," *ČOIDR*, 1910, bk. 4, sec. 3: 4, 36.

[95] The first full moon *after* the vernal equinox—the Paschal moon—would be assigned to Palm Sunday, since Easter follows it on the next Sunday. The first full moon *before* the vernal equinox—the pre-Paschal moon—would be assigned to Orthodoxy Sunday.

[96] B. O. Unbegaun notes the occurrence of *Raduničnoe voskresenie* in a North Russian (Vologda region) document from 1607 ("Remarques sur l'ancien calendrier russe," in *Selected Papers on Russian and Slavonic Philology* [Oxford, 1969], 126).

note simply that in a Christian context Cheesefast Sunday and Thomas Sunday reflect the themes of repentance and faith in the Resurrection, respectively. In folk tradition the two days are connected with a cult of ancestor worship. Both *Proščenoe voskresenie* and *Raduničnoe voskresenie* may be analyzed as hierarchical extensions of *Verbnoe voskresenie* and *Sbornoe voskresenie* by virtue of their association with renewal of the faith, ancestor worship, and the general resurrection.

The extension of V/R from *Verbnoe voskresenie* to certain Sundays and not others in the Paschal season attests to the strength of the *dvoeverie*, the dual faith, well into the medieval period of Russian history. The five points that comprise the hierarchy of what might be called the Resurrection Cycle represent a syncretism of two separate, but partially overlapping, belief systems, the Orthodox Christian and the pagan Russian. The focal point of both is the beginning of spring, the annual period of renewal signaled by the interaction of the lunar and solar cycles—the full moon and the vernal equinox—the period when equilibrium is restored between day and night. The dominant tonalities of the hierarchy—the Resurrection of Christ and spring—stimulate the faith and expectation that band these Resurrection days together in a unity of purpose (see fig. 3).

The Resurrection Cycle in Its Historical Context

The determination of the Christian and pagan sources of the Resurrection Cycle leads naturally to the question of when and why the cycle arose in the first place. The most likely time for the innovation *Verbnoe voskresenie*, the catalyst for the rest of the hierarchy, is the fifteenth century, one of the most fateful and turbulent periods of Russian history when the religious, social, and political institutions of the Russian lands were forged together as components of a single, absolute monarchy dominated by Moscow. The linguistic facts as we know them speak for the fifteenth century as well: Vasmer dates the phrasebook with *Verbnoe voskresenie* to this period; Synod Resurrection could have developed only after the introduction of the Office of Orthodoxy by Kiprian, who assumed sole authority of the Church in 1390; and the earliest dated attestation of innovation outside the phrasebook is from 1514–15. The Resurrection Cycle can be understood only in the framework of the fifteenth century and the roles played by the Church, the State and the philosophy of the times.

The Russian Church underwent a number of changes in the late four-teenth–early fifteenth centuries as a result of the influx of Balkan church-men during the decline of the Byzantine Empire and the subjugation of the

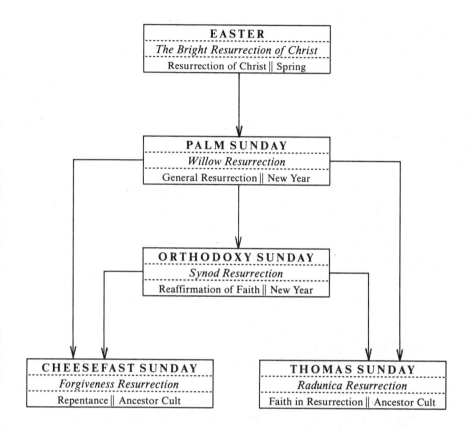

THE HIERARCHY OF THE RESURRECTION CYCLE

Fig. 3.

Serbian and Bulgarian kingdoms by the Turks. These men professed a deep belief in the destiny of Eastern Orthodoxy to vanquish the power of the Latin heretics on the one hand, and the pagan infidels on the other. Moscow would provide the leadership in this crusade as the last great bastion of Orthodoxy. Most were aligned theologically with the antischolastic Hesychasts and favored a strong alliance between Church and State to root out heresy and contend with apocalyptic forebodings that had germinated in the Balkans.[97] Metropolitan Kiprian, already mentioned in connection with Orthodoxy Sunday, was one of the most influential of the religious figures who migrated to Russia from the Balkans. Two of his accomplishments have a direct bearing on the crucial linkage of Lazarus Saturday and Palm Sunday: (1) the institution of the Jerusalem Rule and (2) the addition of rituals to the Palm Sunday celebration.

Both the Studite and Jerusalem Rules (*Ustavy*) or *Typika* govern liturgical practice and monastic discipline in the Eastern Church. The latter began to replace the former in Constantinople in the twelfth century. This reform filtered into Russia in the thirteenth century but was not systematically carried through until the terms of Kiprian (1390–1406) and Fotij (1408–31).[98] Although the differences between the two are not substantial, the Jerusalem *Typikon* prescribed a stricter, monastic code for the daily and festal practices of the Church. Of especial interest here is the establishment of the "All-Night" Vigil (*Vsenoščnoe bdenie*), which combined the services for Vespers, Matins, and the First Hour on the eve of all Sundays and major feasts. Although the institution of this practice was left up to the individual churches, its ultimate establishment had the net effect of elevating the status of Sunday even higher and of binding Saturday and Sunday more closely together, since the Sunday Vigil occurs Saturday evening.[99] The Vigil for Palm Sunday was undoubtedly in place by the end of Kiprian's term as metropolitan.

The ritual Procession on the Ass (*Xoždenie* [or *Šestvie*] *na osljati*), which imitates Christ's triumphant entry into Jerusalem, was apparently instituted together with the Jerusalem *Typikon* during Kiprian's time.[100] After the Matins service on Saturday evening, at which the willow branches were blessed, a tub containing ceremonial willow branches decorated with flowers and fruit was transported to a spot at some remove from the church as part of a procession of icons. After the singing of appropriate hymns, the ranking church authority (in Moscow the metropolitan himself) was seated on an ass (actually a horse disguised as an ass) and was led back to the church by the leading secular figure (in Moscow the grand prince) while those in attendance shouted hosannas and threw their coats in the path of

[97] Cf. J. H. Billington, *The Icon and the Axe: An Interpretive History of Russian Culture* (London, 1966), 56-57.

[98] Golubinskij, *Istorija russkoj cerkvi*, vol. 1, pt. 2 (see n. 55), 350ff.; ibid., vol. 2, pt. 1 (see n. 45), 329-331; ibid., vol. 2, pt. 2 (see n. 71), 428ff.; Meyendorff, *Byzantium* (see n. 83), 122-124.

[99] Stepanov's studies of the early chronicles ("Edinicy sčeta vremeni" [see n. 91], 4-22) suggest that the secular day began at sunrise, and not at sunset as did the ecclesiastical day. Thus liturgical Sunday began on the evening of secular Saturday.

[100] Golubinskij, *Istorija russkoj cerkvi*, vol. 1, pt. 2 (see n. 55), 378-379.

the procession.[101] The concentration of the most important ritual activities of Lazarus Saturday and Palm Sunday on Saturday served to unite both days in the minds of the faithful as a continuous celebration of the general resurrection and the impending Passion and Resurrection of Christ (see n. 64). The ubiquitous willow branch was the primary symbol of that unity.

The second third of the fifteenth century is marked by the Greek Orthodox capitulation to the Latin Church at the Council of Florence and Ferrara in 1438–39. The union of East and West was ultimately rejected by the Russians, who imprisoned its adherent, Metropolitan Isidor (a Greek by birth) on his return to Moscow in 1441. In 1448 a synod of bishops convened in Moscow and elected its own metropolitan without counsel from Constantinople, thus establishing the autocephalous Russian Church. The capture of the Byzantine capital by the Turks in 1453 was viewed by the Russians as fitting punishment from God for the Greek betrayal of Orthodoxy. The notion of a New Rome, which had taken seed in Serbia and Bulgaria a century before, was brought to Moscow by the Balkan churchmen: Moscow was destined to take up the fallen banner of Christianity as the Third Rome. Ivan III, who succeeded his father as grand prince of Moscow in 1462, assumed the trappings of the Byzantine imperium: the titles *autocrat* and *tsar,*[102] the double-headed eagle and scepter, and the elaborate court ceremonial. The dynastic link was sealed in 1472 by his marriage to Sophia Palaeologue, the niece of the last Byzantine emperor. Muscovite messianism was validated by the so-called gathering of the Russian lands. One by one, voluntarily or through battle, the Russian principalities fell under the sway of Moscow: Jaroslavl' (1463), Rostov (1474), Novgorod (1478), Tver' (1485), parts of Western Russia (1500–1503), Pskov (1510), Smolensk (1514) and Rjazan' (1520), the last three during the reign of Vasilij III (1505–1533). Full independence from the Golden Horde was achieved in 1480.

The decline of Byzantium and the rise of Moscow in the fifteenth century was interpreted not only in political and ecclesiastical terms but in chiliastic ones as well. The eschatological presentiments that had colored Russian thought after the mid-thirteenth century Tatar invasions were reactivated by the Balkan churchmen at the end of the fourteenth century and intensified as the cataclysmic events of the fifteenth century unfolded.

A Christian interpretation of the End Times had been fashioned in the first centuries of the Church on the basis of Jewish apocalyptic writings

---

[101] This ceremony is noted by Fletcher (*Russe Commonwealth* [see n. 54], f105r); cf. Saxarov 1849, pt. 2, sec. 7: 98; Makarij, *Istorija*, vol. 8 (see n. 55): 66-67.

[102] The title *tsar* became official only in 1547 during the reign of Ivan IV.

(especially the Prophets and the Psalms), the Book of Revelation and the Epistles.[103] Since one day in the sight of God was equivalent to one thousand years (Ps. 90:4), the myth of the Creation was projected in millennial terms over the course of human history: the first six thousand years would be followed by the Second Coming, when Christ would reign over the earth for another one thousand years together with the Christian martyrs, who would be resurrected from the dead for this purpose, the so-called first resurrection (Rev. 20:4–6). The completion of the seven thousand years was to be followed by the general resurrection of the dead and the Last Judgment. Those not inscribed in the Book of Life would be cast into eternal fire, while the righteous would share life anew in the New Jerusalem, a heaven on earth (Rev. 20:11–15, 21:1–8). Another interpretation postponed the Second Coming and the Last Judgment until the year 7000, but predicted a one thousand–year reign of the Antichrist before the expiration of human history (Hippolytos, Kyprianos, Methodios of Patara, Ephraim the Syrian). It was primarily the latter interpretation that took hold in Rus'.[104]

One of the most powerful means of communicating the message of the Last Judgment was the Byzantine iconostasis, which evolved on Russian soil into a multitiered sanctuary screen that reached its full development in Moscow in the fourteenth–fifteenth centuries.[105] The central focus of the iconostasis is the Deësis above the Royal Doors, the depiction of Christ at the Last Judgment flanked by the Mother of God and John the Baptist as intercessors. The procession of figures on either side (archangels, apostles, Church Fathers, and martyrs)—the čin—directs the eye of the observer towards the center, inviting contemplation of the Church's final promise and of humanity's ultimate test.

The popular collections like *Zlatoust* and *Izmaragd* contained numerous sermons concerned with the End of the World, sermons which placed emphasis on repentance and fasting, strict avoidance of pagan ritual and ancestor worship, and a special veneration of Sunday as the Day of the Resurrection. Several sermons in fact condemn a particular cult of Sunday

[103] See J. A. MacCulloch, "Eschatology," in *Encyclopedia of Religion and Ethics*, vol. 5, ed. J. Hastings (New York, 1925), 373-391; N. Cohn, *The Pursuit of the Millennium*, rev., exp. ed. (New York, 1970), 19-36.

[104] N. Rudnev, *Rassuždenie o eresjax i raskolax byvšix v russkoj cerkvi so vremeni Vladimira Velikogo do Ioanna Groznogo* (Moscow, 1838), 103-104; G. P. Fedotov, *The Russian Religious Mind*, vol. 2: *The Middle Ages: The Thirteenth to the Fifteenth Centuries*, ed. J. Meyendorff (Cambridge, Mass., 1966), 86.

[105] See K. Onasch, "Identity Models of Old Russian Sacred Art," this volume; A. Voyce, *The Art and Architecture of Medieval Russia* (Norman, Okla., 1967), 217ff.

that involves the worship of an idol (*bolvan*),[106] identified in one of them as *Nedělja*:

> Slov[o] istolkovano mudrostьju ot stx̄ъ ap̄lъ i prrkъ i ōсь о tvari i о dnii rekomomъ nedlě jako ne podbaet k̄rstьjanom klanjatis nedlě ni celovat jeja zane tvarь estь.[107]
>
> *Slovo ... o dnii rekomomъ nedělě, Paisiev. sbor.*
> f47v [MS late 14th–15th c.]

This same sermon decries pagan rituals, idol worship and sacrifices performed on Sunday in lieu of church attendance, and makes a forceful attempt to distinguish the Resurrection of Christ and the day *nedělja*:

> Ašče li vo inyja dni čto zlo tvorjatь da ... prixodjašče vъ c̄rkvь pomoljatьsja o gresěxъ svoixъ čajušče ot ḡa proščenija i klanjajuščisja voskrsnьju x̄vu a ne dni neděli.[108]
>
> *Ibid.*

---

[106] Although a cult of Sunday may very well have existed in Kievan and Muscovite Rus'—as evidenced by the frequent mention of pagan rituals on Sunday in the sermons from the twelfth to sixteenth centuries (see Kalajdovič 1821; Tixonravov 1863; Arxangel'skij 1888–90; Gal'kovskij 1913; E. V. Aničkov, *Jazyčestvo i Drevnjaja Rus', Zapiski Istoriko-filologičeskogo fakul'teta Imperatorskogo Sankt-Peterburgskogo universiteta* 117 [St. Petersburg, 1914]), a specific veneration of Saint Nedelja, as found in the Balkans and Southwestern Rus', has yet to be proved for Russia proper. Saint Nedelja represents the confounding of Saint Anastasia, who was martyred at Sirmium c. 303/4 during the reign of Diocletian, and the personification of Resurrection Day; cf. Άναστάσιμος ἡμέρα. Saint Nedelja (or Nedel'ka) is often linked with Saint Paraskeva (Pjatnica) in apocryphal tales in which Sunday and Friday (and sometimes Wednesday) interact with human beings as intercessors. Except for the mention of Nedělja worship in this sermon (included in the twelfth to thirteenth century *Finland Fragments* (see Sreznevskij 1876: 31-32) and the late–fourteenth to early–fifteenth–century *Paisievskij sbornik*, her name never appears. It is quite possible that this sermon was Kievan in origin or was brought to Rus' from Bulgaria, hence the reference to Nedělja. The tales that feature Nedělja and Pjatnica in Bulgarian versions show Nedělja replaced by the Virgin Mary in corresponding Russian versions; see A. Veselovskij, "Opyty po istorii razvitija xristianskoj legendy 2: Berta, Anastasija i Pjatnica," *ŽMNP* 189 (1877): 186-252, esp. 194ff. Rites associated with (A)Nastasija and Paraskeva-Pjatnica, however, are well known on Russian soil; see, e.g., the *Stoglav* 1551/1863: 138-139; cf. Fedotov, *The Russian Religious Mind*, vol. 1 (see n. 55), 358; *Enciklopedija Leksikografskog Zavoda*, vol. 4 (Zagreb, 1966–1969), 493; Kulišić et al., *Srpski mitološki rečnik* (see n. 76), 210, 257-258; Golubinskij, *Istorija russkoj cerkvi*, vol. 1, pt. 2 (see n. 55), 855-856; B. A. Uspenskij, *Filologičeskie razyskanija v oblasti slavjanskix drevnostej. Relikty jazyčestva v vostočnoslavjanskom kul'te Nikolaja Mirlikijskogo* (Moscow, 1982), 106, 134-138.

[107] A sermon interpreted on the basis of wisdom from the Holy Apostles and Prophets and Fathers about the creature and the day called *Nedělja*, since it is not fitting for Christians to worship *Nedělja* nor to kiss her, inasmuch as she is a creature (from Gal'kovskij 1913: 78).

[108] And if they do something evil on other days, then ... arriving at the church, they should pray for their sins, asking forgiveness of the Lord and worshiping the Resurrection of Christ and not the day *nedělja* (ibid., 80).

The week is treated as a metaphor for the seven millennia; *nedělja* is
characterized in eschatological terms as the Eighth Day, for the Eighth
Millennium will have no end.

The sermons of Grigorij Camblak, metropolitan of Kiev (1415–1419),
enjoyed great popularity in Muscovite Rus'.[109] His sermon on Palm Sunday
bears witness to the fifteenth-century focus on the relationship of Lazarus
and the End Times:

> Paky Spasъ vъ Ierusalimъ vъsxoditъ i paky čudesa. Paky vъskresenia
> uvěrenie, paky merьtvii vъstajutь. No ne jakože vdovyja syna vъskresi,
> tako i Lazarja. Onago bo abie umerša i iz grada iznosima otъ odra
> vъzdviže: sego že četverodnevna i smerdjašča iz groba vъzva slo-
> vomъ.... Egože i my nyně sъ otroky, jako poběditelja smerti, vspě-
> vaemъ; jako Carju i Bogu našemu, poklanjaemsja—spodobiti nasъ i
> tridnevnomu svoemu vъskreseniju, vъ vtoroe že Ego prišestvie dostojny
> sъtvoritъ nasь srěsti Ego na oblacěxъ....[110]

Camblak's obvious reference to the Palm Sunday troparion, his emphasis
on the uniqueness of Lazarus' resurrection (as compared with the mere
raising of the widow's son in Nain [Luke 7:11–15]) and his allusion to the
Second Coming and the general resurrection are striking when viewed
against the common concern for the End Times found in the fifteenth
century.

So convinced was the Orthodox Church that the world would come to an
end with the advent of the Eighth Millennium in the year 7000 that the
Greek Paschal tables (πασχάλια) used to compute the date of Easter and
correlated holidays only provided calculations up to the year 7000.[111] It is
quite likely that in the last quarter of the fifteenth century, discussion of the
Apocalypse must have intensified dramatically. By Byzantine reckoning,
the world had been created 5,508 years before Christ; therefore the year
7000 would begin on 1 September 1492.

Contributing to the sense of impending doom, a new heresy had flared
up in Novgorod in the late 1470s and spread to Moscow by the mid-

[109] Fedotov, *The Russian Religious Mind*, vol. 2 (see n. 104), 25.

[110] Once again the Savior goes up to Jerusalem and once again the miracles. Once again the assurance of the resurrection, once again the dead rise up. But not like the widow's son He raised,
but like Lazarus. For He raised the former from his deathbed just after he had died and had been
taken out of the city; but the latter, dead four days and stinking, He called forth from the grave
with a word.... So now with the children do we sing the praises of Him as the Conqueror of death;
as Emperor and our God do we worship [Him], that He might favor us with His three-day resurrection as well, that he might make us worthy of meeting Him in the Heavens at his Second Coming (cited in Makarij, *Istorija russkoj cerkvi*, vol. 5 [Moscow, 1886], 431-433).

[111] "Drevnie russkie pasxalii na os'muju tysjaču let ot sotvorenija mira," *Pravoslavnyj
Sobesednik*, 1860, no. 3: 333-334.

1480s.[112] The heretics—the so-called Judaizers—shàred many of the views of the Strigol'niki: they were opposed to excessive ritual and neither believed in resurrection, prayers for the dead, nor in the Eighth Millennium and the Last Judgment. In fact, the heretic Aleksej, an archpriest from Novgorod, even taunted Archbishop Gennadij about the Eighth Millennium in 1489: "Preidut tri leta, končaetsja sedmaja tysjača, i my, dej, togda budem nadobny."[113]

It is in this climate of heightened fear, superstition, and religiosity that *Verbnoe voskresenie*—the icon of the general resurrection—was born. Towards the end of the fifteenth century the theme of resurrection, specifically the general resurrection, was in the air. The Orthodox campaign against the heretics led by Abbot Iosif of Volokolamsk and Archbishop Gennadij of Novgorod must have elicited a strong reaffirmation of the faith—especially among the illiterate masses—a commitment to the notion of resurrection and the efficacy of prayers for the dead. The remaining portions of the Resurrection Cycle hierarchy emerged shortly thereafter.

When the Last Judgment failed to materialize in 1492, a number of commentaries (*skazanija*) on the end of the Seventh Millennium appeared. Those opposed to the Church accused the patristic writers of lying and the current ecclesiastics of practicing deceit, while apologetic texts cited other authorities who claimed that it was not for mankind to know when the End Times would come.[114]

Once 1492 had passed, the original motivation for the Resurrection Cycle was obscured. The innovation V/R was dissociated from the specifically human orientation of the Cycle—Palm Sunday and the promise of the general resurrection—and was extended instead from Easter, the Bright Resurrection of Christ, to all Sundays of the year as a mark of their special status as Days of the Resurrection, Resurrection-Sundays (V/RS). Even after this change, the proper names of the four Paschal holidays remained the same: *Verbnoe voskresenie, Sbornoe voskresenie, Proščenoe voskresenie, Raduničnoe voskresenie,* but no *Cvetnoe voskresenie, Pravoslavnoe voskresenie,* and the like. The final stage in the development of V was reached with the loss of the original association of form and spiritual function:

[112] Kazakova and Lur'e, *Antifeodal'nye eretičeskie dviženija* (see n. 42), 109, 148.

[113] Three years will go by, the seventh millennium comes to an end and then indeed it will be our turn (cited in ibid., 134).

[114] See ibid., 388-414 for the texts. It is quite possible that the millennial crisis in Russia was responsible for the "official" change of the New Year from March to September 1, the feast day of Simeon the Stylite; cf. Čerepnin, *Russkaja xronologija* (see n. 61), 27; Unbegaun, "L'ancien calendrier russe" (see n. 96), 123; S. I. Selešnikov, *Istorija kalendarja i xronologija,* ed. P. G. Kulikovskij (Moscow, 1977), 164.

V/RS was reinterpreted as V/S, merely an appellation for the last day of the secular week. At this point the holiday names were reinterpreted as well: Willow Resurrection-Sunday > Willow Sunday, Synod Resurrection-Sunday > Synod Sunday, and so on. The distinction between V/S and N/S was at first a stylistic one, the former representative of the spoken language, the latter, of the written language. The colloquial-written opposition of V/S and N/S appears to have been valid by the second half of the sixteenth century. By 1700, N/S had begun to fade into obsolescence as a native Russian word,[115] but was retained in the Russian lexicon as a functional Slavonism; cf. N/S in Russian Church Slavic.

Voskresenie 'Sunday' as a Uniquely Russian Development

In the preceding discussion I have attempted to isolate each of the factors that contributed to the ultimate realization of *voskresenie* 'Sunday' in Russian. Any one of these factors in isolation would not have had the same effect. The rise and fall of *voskresenie* is a uniquely Russian phenomenon, the product of a particular constellation of elements—spiritual, ecclesiastical, social, political, historical—that permitted the necessary associations to be made.

It is unlikely that V/S could have developed anywhere besides Muscovite Rus'. Slavs of the Latin rite were excluded from this possibility by virtue of the fact that the Resurrection does not enjoy the absolute central position in the Western Church that it does in the Eastern Church. As for Slavia Orthodoxa, the Serbs and the Bulgarians, with their special reverence for Saint Nedelja, were not likely to replace *nedelja* as the designation for Sunday. Furthermore, all the non-Russian Orthodox Slavs were under foreign domination, hardly an appropriate setting for the fulfillment of expectation. In fifteenth-century Muscovy the timing was optimal. The late fourteenth–early fifteenth century Orthodox revival and chiliastic philosophy found echoes in the native Russian tradition. It took only the emergence of Moscow as the Third Rome, the resurrector of fallen Christianity, to provide the catalyst for a popular response on the eve of the Apocalypse: *Verbnoe voskresenie* and the Resurrection Cycle.

In the last analysis, the fate of *voskresenie* reflects the secularization of Russian spirituality itself after the consolidation of the Muscovite state: Resurrection-Sunday gives way to Sunday and *voskresenie* descends to the purely secular level, replacing *nedelja*. Sacred is transformed into profane as Muscovy moves towards the Time of Troubles.

---

[115] Dal' (*Tolkovyj slovar'*, vol. 2 [see n. 89], 1345) notes N/S in some South Russian dialects.

SOURCES

AIst 1	*Akty istoričeskie, sobrannye i izdannye Arxeologičeskoj Komissiej.* Vol. 1 (1334–1598). St. Petersburg, 1841.
AOtn 1	*Akty otnosjaščiesja do graždanskoj raspravy drevnej Rossii.* Vol. 1 *(1432–1699 gg.).* Compiled and edited by A. Fedotov-Čexovskij. Kiev, 1860.
ARG	*Akty russkogo gosudarstva 1505–1526.* Compiled by S. B. Veselovskij, edited by L. V. Čerepnin et al. Moscow, 1975.
Arxangel'skij 1888–90	Arxangel'skij, A. S. *K izučeniju drevne-russkoj literatury. Tvorenija otcov cerkvi v drevne-russkoj pis'mennosti.* 4 vols. St. Petersburg-Kazan', 1888–1890.
ASÈISVR	*Akty social'no-èkonomičeskoj istorii Severo-Vostočnoj Rusi konca XIV–načala XVI v.* 3 vols. Compiled by I. A. Golubcov, edited by B. D. Grekov and L.V. Čerepnin. Moscow, 1952–1964.
ASob 1	*Akty, sobrannye v bibliotekax i arxivax Rossijskoj Imperii Arxeografičeskoj Èkspediciej Imperatorskoj Akademii Nauk* (with supplements). Vol. 1 (1294–1598). St. Petersburg, 1836.
Boyer 1905	Boyer, Paul. *Un vocabulaire français-russe de la fin du XVIᵉ siècle extrait du Grand Insulaire d'André Thevet.* Paris, 1905.
DopAIst 1	*Dopolnenija k Aktam Istoričeskim, sobrannye i izdannye Arxeografičeskoj Komissiej.* Vol. 1. St. Petersburg, 1846.
Fenne 1607/1961	*Tönnies Fenne's Low German Manual of Spoken Russian—Pskov 1607.* Edited by L. L. Hammerich et al. 2 vols. Copenhagen, 1961.
Gal'kovskij 1913	Gal'kovskij, N. *Bor'ba xristianstva s ostatkami jazyčestva v drevnej Rusi.* Vol. 2: *Drevne-russkie slova i poučenija, napravlennye protiv ostatkov jazyčestva v narode.* Moscow, 1913.
Gorskij 1841/1879	"Istoričeskoe opisanie Svjato-Troickoj Sergievy lavry sostavlennoe po rukopisnym i pečatnym istočnikam ... v 1841 godu." Compiled by A. V. Gorskij with supplement by Archimandrite Leonid. *ČOIDR*, 1879, bk. 2, sec. 2.
Izb. 1076	*Izbornik 1076 goda.* Edited by V. S. Golyšenko et al. Moscow, 1965.
James 1618–19/1959	*Russko-anglijskij slovar'-dnevnik Ričarda Džemsa (1618–1619 gg.).* Edited by B. A. Larin. Leningrad, 1959.
Kalajdovič 1821	*Pamjatnik rossijskoj slovesnosti XII veka.* Edited by K. Kalajdovič. Moscow, 1821.
Kotošixin 1667/1980	Kotošixin, Grigorij. *O Rossii v carstvovanie Alekseja Mixailoviča: Text and Commentary.* Edited by A. E. Pennington. Oxford, 1980.
Lav. let.	*Polnoe sobranie russkix letopisej.* Vol. 1: *Lavrent'evskaja letopis'.* 2nd ed. Leningrad, 1926–1928.
Makarij 1856	Makarij. "Sočinenija Prepod. Feodosija Pečerskogo v podlinnom tekste." *Učenye zapiski vtorogo otdelenija Imperatorskoj Akademii Nauk* 2, no. 2 (1856): 193–224.

148   MICHAEL S. FLIER

Nikoľskij 1896   Nikoľskij, N. K. *Reč' tonkoslovija grečeskogo. Russko-grečeskie razgovory XV–XVI vekov* (Pamjatniki drevnej pis'mennosti, no. 114). St. Petersburg, 1896.

Nov. I let. Sinod.   *Novgorodskaja pervaja letopis' staršego i mladšego izvodov. Novgorodskaja pervaja letopis' staršego izvoda, Sinodaľnyj spisok.* Edited by A. N. Nasonov and M. N. Tixomirov. Moscow–Leningrad, 1950. Pp. 15–100.

Nov. II let. Arx.   *Polnoe sobranie russkix letopisej.* Vol. 30: *Novgorodskaja vtoraja (Arxivskaja) letopis'.* Moscow, 1965. Pp. 147–205.

Otryvok let. po   *Polnoe sobranie russkix letopisej.* Vol. 6: *Sofijskie letopisi. Otryvok
Vosk. Novoierus.   letopisi po Voskresenskomu Novoierusalimskomu spisku.* St. Petersburg, 1853. Pp. 277–315.

Petuxov 1895   Petuxov, E. V. *Očerki iz literaturnoj istorii Sinodika.* Pamjatniki Obščestva ljubitelej drevnej pis'mennosti, no. 108. St. Petersburg, 1895.

Pribavl. Pskov. let. A   *Polnoe sobranie russkix letopisej.* Vol. 5: *Pskovskie letopisi. Pribavlenija A (Sneg. II, Obol. II, Arx. XXV).* St. Petersburg, 1851. Pp. 51–73.

Prodolž. Aleks.-Nevs. let.   *Polnoe sobranie russkix letopisej.* Vol. 29: *Prodolženie Aleksandro-Nevskoj letopisi.* Moscow, 1965. Pp. 315–355.

PRP XVI–XVII   *Putešestvija russkix poslov XVI–XVII vv.* Edited by D. S. Lixačev et al. Moscow–Leningrad, 1954.

PRPRK   *Pamjatniki russkoj pis'mennosti XV–XVI vv. Rjazanskij kraj.* Compiled by S. I. Kotkov and I. S. Filippova, edited by S. I. Kotkov. Moscow, 1978.

Pskov. II let. Sinod.   *Pskovskie letopisi.* Vol. 2: *Pskovskaja vtoraja letopis', Sinodaľnyj spisok.* Edited by M. N. Tixomirov. Moscow, 1955. Pp. 9–69.

Pskov. III let. Okonč.   *Pskovskie letopisi.* Vol. 2: *Okončanie Arxivskogo vtorogo spiska
Arx. 2   (Pskovskoj treťej letopisi).* Edited by M. N. Tixomirov. Moscow, 1955. Pp. 251–290.

Pskov. III let. Stroev.   *Pskovskie letopisi.* Vol. 2: *Pskovskaja treťja letopis', Stroevskij spisok.* Edited by M. N. Tixomirov. Moscow, 1955. Pp. 78–250.

RK   *Razrjadnaja kniga 1475–1598.* Edited by M. N. Tixomirov and V. I. Buganova. Moscow, 1966.

Saxarov 1849   Saxarov, N. *Skazanija russkogo naroda,* pt. 2, sec. 6: *Russkie narodnye svaďby;* sec. 7: *Russkaja narodnaja godovščina (Narodnyj dnevnik—Narodnye prazdniki i obyčai).* St. Petersburg, 1849.

Sof. II let. Arx.   *Polnoe sobranie russkix letopisej.* Vol. 6: *Sofijskie letopisi. Sofijskaja vtoraja letopis', Arxivskij spisok.* St. Petersburg, 1853. Pp. 119–276.

Sreznevskij 1876   Sreznevskij, I. I. *Svedenija i zametki o maloizvestnyx i neizvestnyx pamjatnikax.* Vols. 41–80. St. Petersburg, 1876.

Stoglav 1551/1863   *Stoglav.* Edited by D. E. Kožančikov. St. Petersburg, 1863.

Tixonravov 1863   Tixonravov, Nikolaj. *Pamjatniki otrečennoj russkoj literatury.* 2 vols. St. Petersburg–Moscow, 1863.

Usp. sbor.	Uspenskij sbornik XII–XIII vv. Edited by S. I. Kotkov et al. Moscow, 1971.
Vasmer 1922	Vasmer, Max. Ein russisch-byzantinisches Gesprächbuch. Beiträge zur Erforschung der älteren russischen Lexikographie. Leipzig, 1922.
VK 1600–39	Vesti-Kuranty 1600–1639 gg. Edited by S. I. Kotkov et al. Moscow, 1972.
VK 1642–44	Vesti-Kuranty 1642–1644 gg. Edited by S. I. Kotkov et al. Moscow, 1976.
VK 1645–48	Vesti-Kuranty 1645–1646, 1648 gg. Edited by S. I. Kotkov et al. Moscow, 1980.

Aside from the texts listed above (and the volumes or collections in which they are found), the following texts were examined and found to contain no instances of V/R, V/RS or V/S:

Akty feodaľnogo zemlevladenija i xozjajstva XIV–XVI vv. Edited by S. V. Baxrušin and L. V. Čerepnin. 2 vols. Moscow, 1951, 1956.

Akty otnosjaščiesja do juridičeskogo byta drevnej Rusi. 3 vols. and index. St. Petersburg, 1857–1901.

Domostroj po Konšinskomu spisku i podobnym. Edited by A. S. Orlov. 2 vols. Moscow, 1908, 1910.

Duxovnye i dogovornye gramoty velikix i udeľnyx knjazej XIV–XVI vv. Moscow–Leningrad, 1950.

Gramoty Velikogo Novgoroda i Pskova. Edited by S. N. Valk. Moscow–Leningrad, 1949.

Ioasofskaja letopis'. Edited by M. N. Tixomirov and A. A. Zimin. Moscow, 1957.

Pamjatniki diplomatičeskix snošenij drevnej Rusi s deržavami inostrannymi. Vol. 1. St. Petersburg, 1851.

Pamjatniki russkogo prava. Vol. 3 (XIV–XV vv.); Vol. 4 (XV–XVII vv.). Edited by L. V. Čerepnin. Moscow, 1955, 1956.

Polnoe sobranie russkix letopisej. Vols. 2–4, 7–8, 11–13, 25–28, 31–34.

Xoženie za tri morja Afanasija Nikitina 1466–1472 gg. Edited by B. D. Grekov and V. P. Adrianova-Peretc. Moscow–Leningrad, 1948.

UNRESOLVED ISSUES IN THE HISTORY OF THE IDEOLOGICAL MOVEMENTS OF THE LATE FIFTEENTH CENTURY

JAKOV S. LURIA

The period from the late 1470s through the first five years of the sixteenth century occupies a special place in the history of the social thought of Old Rus'. This is the period of the heretical "storm," as it was called by contemporaries, a time when debates about belief went on among "monks and laymen" (*inoki i mirskie*) everywhere—"in the home, on the road and in the marketplace as well' (*i v domax i na putjax i na toržiščix*).[1] Even if one assumes that the picture of universal debates drawn by the most prominent "denouncer of heretics," Iosif Volockij, was somewhat exaggerated by him in the heat of battle, the indisputable fact remains that polemical literature connected with the heresy appeared over a period of no less than one quarter of a century. The first such work, the epistle of Iosif Sanin in defense of the depiction of the Trinity in icons, was written before 1479, when Iosif was installed as abbot of the Volokolamsk Monastery; the last were completed only after the condemnation of the heretics by the Council of 1504.

Two decades ago scholars were especially interested in the ideological struggle of the late fifteenth and early sixteenth centuries. The most important sources for the history of the Novgorod-Moscow heresy were published precisely during this period: the epistles of Iosif Volockij,[2] works by A. A. Zimin, A. I. Klibanov, the present author, and others working on this subject.[3] Interest in this problem waned in the years following. Historians

Translated from the Russian by Michael S. Flier.

[1] "Poslanie igumena Iosifa Volockogo episkopu Nifontu Suzdal'skomu," in N. A. Kazakova and Ja. S. Lur'e, *Antifeodal'nye eretičeskie dviženija na Rusi XIV–načala XVI v.* (Moscow–Leningrad, 1955), 429; *Prosvetitel'*, 3rd ed. (Kazan', 1896), 45.

[2] A. A. Zimin and Ja. S. Lur'e, eds., *Poslanija Iosifa Volockogo* (Moscow–Leningrad, 1959).

[3] A. A. Zimin, "O političeskoj doktrine Iosifa Volockogo," *TODRL* 9 (1953), 159–177; A. I. Klibanov, *Reformacionnye dviženija v Rossii v XIV–pervoj polovine XVI v.* (Moscow, 1960); Ja. S. Lur'e, *Ideologičeskaja bor'ba v russkoj publicistike konca XV–načala XVI v.* (Moscow–Leningrad, 1960). For a survey of the literature on the heretical movements for the period up to 1970, see E. Hösch, "Sowjetische Forschungen zur Häresiegeschichte Altrusslands. Methodische Bemerkungen," *Jahrbücher für Geschichte Osteuropas*, n.s., vol. 18 (1970): 279-312.

turned their attention instead to the ideological movements of the first half of the sixteenth century (especially to the Nonpossessor movement [*nestja-žatel'stvo*]), the works of Maksim Grek, and the political struggle during the reign of Ivan the Terrible. Nonetheless, investigators made a number of individual observations during this period on works of the late fifteenth and early sixteenth centuries, observations that are significant for the history of social thought. Therefore it is quite appropriate to sum up the results of recent findings and take note of remaining issues.

One particular circumstance has exerted considerable influence on the historical investigation of the heretical movements of the late fifteenth and early sixteenth centuries. "Jewish sophistry" was the accusation leveled against the heretics by the "denouncers" in the polemics of the late fifteenth century; this accusation acquired particular significance during the execution of heretics after 1504. In Russian historical literature from the late eighteenth and nineteenth centuries, the heresy came to be called the "Judaizer heresy." This name, which is absent in the sources (Iosif Volockij called the teaching he denounced "novojavivšajasja eres' novgorodskix eretikov" [the newly arisen heresy of the Novgorod heretics], but did not use the term *židovstvujuščie* 'Judaizers'), has become so firmly rooted in the historiography that it frequently slants the study of the sources according to its history.

Broadly speaking, these sources can be divided into two major categories: works opposing the heresy to a greater or lesser degree, and works associated with the heretics themselves. The extreme tendentiousness of the sources in the first category is obvious, since they were typically written with the primary aim of denouncing and destroying the heretics; while they are unquestionably important for studying the activity of the denouncers themselves, they offer little in the way of characterizing the heretical teachings. One obviously cannot pick and choose, selecting the evidence that seems probable and rejecting that which seems less probable. One must proceed instead from some sort of general methodology for studying obvious, extremely tendentious sources (traces of actual polemics, evidence

---

Unfortunately I have not been able to consult E. Hösch, *Orthodoxie und Häresie im alten Russland* (Wiesbaden, 1975). Other articles indirectly touching upon the problem of the heresy should be noted as well: H. Birnbaum, "On Some Evidence of Jewish Life and Anti-Jewish Sentiments in Medieval Russia," *Viator* 4 (1973): 225-255; C. J. Halperin, "Judaizers and the Image of the Jew in Medieval Russia," *Canadian-American Slavic Studies* 9 (Summer 1975): 141-155. In addition, two more articles of a compilatory nature (which are not based on an independent study of the sources) may be cited: J. Allerhand, "Die Judaisierenden in Russland," *Kairos*, n.s., vol. 21 (1979): 264-272; J. Juszczyk, "O badaniach nad Judaizantyzmem," *Kwartalnik historyczny* 76 (1969): 111-151.

contradicting the general tendency of the work, etc.).[4] Especially promising for the study of the heretics' ideology is the utilization of their own works or literature at their disposal. But it is easy to become trapped in a vicious circle in studying such literature and utilizing works indirectly connected with the subject matter at hand—by relying on evidence that does not treat the Novgorod-Moscow heresy of the late fifteenth and early sixteenth centuries per se but rather treats contemporary East European Jews or Judaizers.

This type of logically vicious circle can be found in the works of A. I. Sobolevskij and other authors who introduced so-called *Judaizer literature* as a scientific term referring to translations of Jewish works that had currency in Russian literature of the fifteenth and sixteenth centuries; investigators viewed these works as new and authentic sources for the history of the Russian "Judaizer heresy." All these translations, however, were done in Western Rus', and their connection with the Novgorod-Moscow heresy of the late fifteenth and early sixteenth centuries was assumed solely on the basis of the fact that the heretics were condemned for "Judaizing."[5]

In a recently published book, Russell Zguta declares *Secreta Secretorum* (often called *Aristotelevy vrata* in the literature) to be a monument of the "Judaizers' political ideology" on the very same grounds.[6] He is surprised at my "objection to including the *Aristotelevy vrata* in the body of the literature traditionally identified with the Judaizer movement," and he explains such an objection solely by the fact that *Aristotelevy vrata* was not mentioned in the well-known list of books which "u eretikov vse estь" (all are

---

[4] Cf. Ja. S. Lur'e (J. Luria), "Problems of Source Criticism (with reference to Medieval Russian documents)," *Slavic Review* 27 (March 1968): 13–16; "O nekotoryx principax kritik istočnikov," in *Istočnikovedenie otečestvennoj istorii* 1 (Moscow, 1973), 94–96. I have defined works not exhibiting traits of actual polemics as *denunciatory*. A. A. Zimin does not consider this term to be very cogent (especially in its application to the indictment of the Council), but he does admit that "the difference between these kinds of sources is great." See A. A. Zimin, "Trudnye voprosy metodiki istočnikovedenija drevnej Rusi," in *Istočnikovedenie. Teoretičeskie problemy* (Moscow, 1969), 445; cf. *Voprosy istorii*, 1962, no. 11: 151.

[5] A. I. Sobolevskij, *Perevodnaja literatura Moskovskoj Rusi XVI–XVII vv.* (St. Petersburg, 1903), 409–413, 419–423, 423–428. Cf. V. P. Zubov, "Vopros o 'nedelimyx' i beskonečnom v drevnerusskom literaturnom pamjatnike XV v.," in *Istoriko-matematičeskie issledovanija* 3 (Moscow, 1950), 427; *Očerki russkoj kul'tury XVI v.*, pt. 2 (Moscow, 1977).

[6] R. Zguta, "The 'Aristotelevy vrata' as a Reflection of Judaizer Political Ideology," in *Jahrbücher für Geschichte Osteuropas*, n.s., vol. 26 (1978): 1–10. Concerning *Secreta Secretorum*, see Sobolevskij, *Perevodnaja literatura Moskovskoj Rusi*, 419–428; M. Speranskij, "Iz istorii otrečennyx knig, pt. 4: Aristotelevy vrata ili Tajna Tajnyx," *PDPI* 171 (1908), and "'Aristotelevy vrata' i 'Tajna Tajnyx,'" *SbORJaS* 101, no. 1 (Leningrad, 1926), 15–18 (in this last work, which Zguta did not take into account, the identification of *Secreta Secretorum* with the *Aristotelevy vrata* forbidden by the *Stoglav* is placed in doubt).

THE IDEOLOGICAL MOVEMENTS OF THE LATE FIFTEENTH CENTURY 153

in the hands of the heretics), cited by Archbishop Gennadij in a 1489 epistle. In disagreeing with me, Zguta indicates that this list "is by no means exhaustive and cannot be traditionally identified with the catalogue of works attributable to the Judaizers."[7] Of course, this is absolutely correct, but the list cited by Gennadij does give us at least some basis for deciding which books the heretics possessed; and even evidence of this sort relating to *Secreta Secretorum* and most fifteenth- and sixteenth-century translations from the Hebrew is lacking. The only additional argument cited by Zguta in favor of linking *Secreta Secretorum* with the Novgorod-Moscow heresy is that the ideology of that work corresponds to the political ideology of the heretics, "which focused on furthering the centralization of the autocratic state"; the author sees features of the same ideology in the *Tale of Dracula,* possibly written by Fedor Kuricyn, leader of the Moscow heretics. This connection seems very doubtful, however. The *Tale of Dracula* is not a publicistic work but a fictional one; it is hardly possible to define its ideology unambiguously. In any case, it cannot in any way be considered an apotheosis of Dracula's centralized power.[8] It is even more difficult to identify the ideology of the heretical movement as a whole—including that of the Novgorod and Moscow group of heretics—with the ideology of a centralized state. At any rate, to ascribe *Secreta Secretorum* to the literature of the Novgorod-Moscow heretics on the basis of such remote analogies hardly seems possible, especially because this work, as noted by Zguta himself, is almost exclusively preserved in the West Russian manuscript tradition.[9] Even in Zguta's case, the chief argument for assigning this translated work to the literature of the heretics is apparently the representation of the heresy as "Judaizing," based on the account by Iosif Volockij.[10]

---

[7] Zguta, "The 'Aristotelevy vrata,'" 6–10. The author incorrectly ascribes to me the view that *Logic* and *Šestokryl,* as distinct from *Secreta Secretorum,* can be "assumed to have originated with the sectarians." I have never thought that *Logic* and *Šestokryl* were translated or written by the late fifteenth-century Novgorod-Moscow heretics, granting only that they utilized these works (judging by Gennadij's statements). Even this assumption seems doubtful to me now (see below, pp. 155–7).

[8] This state of affairs is noted in my book, to which Zguta makes reference (Lur'e, *Ideologičeskaja bor'ba* [see n. 3], 395–402) and also in *Povest' o Drakule* (Moscow–Leningrad, 1964), 42–58.

[9] Zguta, "The 'Aristotelevy vrata'" (see n. 6), 3–4; cf. Sobolevskij, *Perevodnaja literatura Moskovskoj Rusi* (see n. 5), 419–420; Speranskij, "Iz istorii otrečennyx knig (see n. 6), 76, 117. As seen in the study by W. F. Ryan, "A Russian Version of *Secreta Secretorum* in the Bodleian Library," *Oxford Slavonic Papers* 12 (1965): 43–48, the late sixteenth-century Russian copy brought to England by Christopher Borough goes back to a West Russian original.

[10] In this regard it is characteristic that the author consistently depicts the history of the heresy according to the *Enlightener* (more precisely, according to its retelling in an article by G. Vernadsky; see Zguta, "The 'Aristotelevy vrata'" (see n. 6), 4–5; cf. G. Vernadsky, "The Heresy of the Judaizers and the Policies of Ivan III of Moscow," *Speculum* 8 [1933]: 436–454).

Similar logic is found in a recent study by G. M. Proxorov of a work he translated, the *Dialogue* of Gregory Palamas "s xiony i turki" (with the Chions and the Turks). The *Dialogue* is an account of a dispute (1354) of Archbishop Palamas, who had fallen into Turkish captivity, with Turks and certain "Chions." This latter term has been variously explained as referring to Turkish sailor-preachers, Muslim apologists, and finally Judaizers. Proxorov subscribes to the last point of view in defining *Chion* as "Karaite." According to him, the very appearance of this work in Rus' is evidence that the late fifteenth-century Novgorod-Moscow heretics were "Karaites," or Judaizers. But even if one accepts the proposition that the Chions were Judaizers, the fact remains that the *Dialogue* was translated into Russian no later than the first half of the fifteenth century (the period of the oldest copies); Proxorov even assigns the Slavonic translation to the fourteenth century.[11] It obviously follows from this that it cannot serve as a source for the history of the late fifteenth- and early sixteenth-century heresy and in no way supports the biased and nonauthentic testimony of the *Enlightener* and other denunciatory works on the nature of the heresy.

The testimonies of the denouncers provide no basis for ascribing to the heretics any works connected with Judaism, but their concrete statements about literature that enjoyed currency among the heretics definitely warrant attention. Such statements are to be found in the epistles of Gennadij, archbishop of Novgorod, in the late 1480s, before the first council against the heretics in 1490. Gennadij wanted to confer with the renowned northern church dignitaries Paisij Jaroslavov and Nil Sorskij concerning the list of books owned by the heretics (already noted above), which Gennadij cited in his epistle to Ioasaf, the former archbishop of Rostov. The books he enumerated were not heretical: the discussion concerned biblical books (the Prophets, Genesis, Kings, Proverbs, and Ecclesiasticus); works of a theological, didactic, and ecclesiastical-polemic nature (*Sylvester—Pope of Rome*; *Athanasios of Alexandria*; the *Discourse Against the Recent Heresy, Bogomilism* by Presbyter Kozma; the *Epistle of Patriarch Photios to Boris, Prince of Bulgaria*; *Dionysios the Areopagite*) and only two works that cannot be assigned to this group: *Menander* (sayings of the classical playwright Menander) and the anonymous *Logic*.[12] In a desire to broaden our percep-

[11] G. M. Proxorov, "Prenie Palamy 's xiony i turki' i problema 'židovskaja mudrstvu-juščix,'" *TODRL* 27 (1972): 438.

[12] Kazakova and Lur'e, *Antifeodal'nye eretičeskie dviženija* (see n. 1), 320. The *Logic* mentioned by Gennadij is usually identified with the *Logic* of Maimonides al-Ghazali, translated in Western Rus' and preserved in sixteenth-century Russian manuscripts (cf. Lur'e, *Ideologičeskaja bor'ba* [see n. 3], 194–195). It should be noted that even this identification is controversial, since it is based solely on the name of the work mentioned by Gennadij.

tion of the heretics' sphere of interests, investigators have noted other pronouncements of Gennadij, citing as relevant for the Novgorod heretics, for example, his comments that "nynešnie židova eretičeskoe predanie drьžatь, psalmy Davydovy ili proročьstva isprevraščali po tomu, kak im eretici predali—Akila i Simmax i Feodotion."[13] Thus they assume that "the Novgorod heretics utilized the interpretations of the Psalter of David and the prophecies about Christ by the ancient Greek heretics (Aquila, Symmachos, and Theodotion), abrogating the interpretations established in the patristic literature."[14] But Gennadij's statement does not concern the Novgorod heretics at all. In his epistles, the Novgorod archbishop discusses a question of extreme concern for his contemporaries, namely, the impending End of the World (which was supposed to occur in the year 7000/1492, according to officially accepted opinion in the Greek Orthodox world), and in this connection he analyzes the chronological systems of different peoples—*židova, latyna, tatarove* (Jews, Latins, Tatars). His discussion concerns *nynešnie židova*, the actual Jews themselves (in Lithuania and other states) and the *eretičeskoe predanie* of Aquila, Symmachos, and Theodotion (second to third centuries A.D.), which had nothing whatsoever to do with the Novgorod heresy of the late fifteenth century.[15]

Disturbing thoughts about the End of the World prompted Gennadij to turn to a medieval astronomical work translated from the Hebrew in Western Rus'—*Šestokryl* (Gk. Ἑξαπτέρυγον). As Gennadij noted in two epistles, *Šestokryl* had stirred his interest because he had learned from it that according to the Jewish calendar only 5,228 years, and not 7,000 (less a few years), had passed since the Creation of the World as reckoned by the Greeks and Slavs:

> Da i Šestokryl esmi učil togo dnja, i obretox v nem eresь: čisla postavleny ot Adama 200 i 70 i 6 devjatьnadesjatnicь! Nyne idetь šestaa devjatьnadesjatnica, po čemu židova leta čtut. Ino to učinili na prelestь xristianьskuju. Xotjatь rešči: leta xristianьskago letapisca skratišasь, a naša prebyvajut.... Ino te čisla, čto postavleny: 276 devjatnadesjatnicь, let budetь ot Adaama do sex mest 5000 i 200 i 28....[16]

---

[13] The Jews of today maintain a heretical tradition; they have distorted the Psalms of David or the Prophets in accordance with the way that the heretics Aquila, Symmachos and Theodotion have handed them down to them.

[14] A. S. Orlov, *Drevnjaja russkaja literatura XI-XVI vv.*, 2nd ed. (Moscow-Leningrad, 1939), 218.

[15] Ibid., 319. Cf. Lur'e, *Ideologičeskaja bor'ba* (see n. 3), 191.

[16] And I was also studying the *Šestokryl* the other day and I found heresy in it: the calendar provided is 276 nineteen-year [lunar] cycles from the time of Adam! Currently the sixth cycle is in progress, according to the way the Jews reckon years. But they have set this up to deceive Christians. They wish to say, "The years of the Christian chronograph have been cut short, while ours endure...." But according to the calendar provided, 276 cycles, there would be 5,228 years from the time of Adam to the present....

Here, as we see, the discussion does not concern the Novgorod heretics at all, but rather the Jews themselves. But in the process of proving that the End of the World would not occur in 1492, did the Novgorod heretics not utilize argumentation based on calculations in the Jewish calendar and *Šestokryl*? At first glance, such a conclusion seems likely: when comparing the Jewish and Byzantino-Slavic calendars, Gennadij mentions the years which "u nas ukrali eretici židovьskimi čisly" (the heretics stole from us by using the Jewish calendar).[17] It is precisely this reference that has permitted scholars (the present author included) to place *Šestokryl* among the readings of the heretics, despite the fact that Gennadij did not specifically include this book among those they had.[18]

Recently, however, the English scholar J. Howlett cast doubt on this view in her dissertation on Russian heretical movements.[19] Even if one concludes that in speaking about the "stolen" years, Gennadij has in mind the Novgorod heretics (and not the ancient ones like Aquila, Symmachos, and Theodotion), it is absolutely impossible to confirm that the reference to *židovskie čisly* 'the Jewish calendar' belongs to the heretics themselves and was not reconstructed for them by Gennadij when he was attempting to discover why the heretics did not believe in the imminent End of the World and even remained hopeful about the year 1492, which was fast approaching. Judging by the tales about the End of the Seventh Millennium, the actual reason for the heretics' disbelief in the End of the World was their lack of faith in the patristic tradition (Ephraim the Syrian and others), which only noted (unlike the biblical texts) that the last year of the Earth's existence was 7000. As for Gennadij, the notion of the relativity of chronological systems was so utterly foreign to him that he explained the differences in calendars by the fact that some peoples have more years and some have fewer as punishment for their sins, especially heresy. He also refers in a different place to the years "stolen" by the heretics, in this case referring not to the Jewish calendar, but to the Latin one: "Da i to mi sja mnit: odnova budut eretici u nas ukrali let! Zaneže u latyny našego bolši osmiju lety."[20] Thus it is apparently unjustified to include *Šestokryl* (and other

---

[17] Kazakova and Lur'e, *Antifeodal'nye eretičeskie dviženija* (see n. 1), 311, 318.

[18] Lur'e, *Ideologičeskaja bor'ba* (see n. 3), 186–187; cf. J. Luria, "L'hérésie dite de judaisants et ses sources historiques," *Revue des études slaves* 45 (1966): 64, n. 3. See also Proxorov, "Prenie Palamy" (see n. 11), 357–358.

[19] Howlett's work (the author kindly provided me with her conclusions) is not yet published, and I am thus unable to set forth its argumentation.

[20] And it even seems to me that at one time the heretics must have stolen years from us, because the Latin calendar has eight years more than ours. Kazakova and Lur'e, *Antifeodal'nye eretičeskie dviženija* (see n. 1), 319. Actually the difference between the Russian and Western

Jewish cosmographic and astronomical works) in the "literature of the heretics."

The *Laodicean Epistle*, written by the prominent Moscow heretic Fedor Kuricyn, belongs to the group of works actually asociated with the late fifteenth-century Russian heretics and thus able to serve as source material for the history of the heresy. It is divided into three parts: (1) philosophical sayings composed in such a way that each of them begins with the same word that ends the previous one, making up some ten lines of verse; (2) *litoreja v kvadratax* 'cryptogram in squares'—tables consisting of forty squares, each containing two letters of the alphabet and grammatical commentary on them; and (3) Kuricyn's signature, encoded in numbers (which apparently explains why the manuscript has survived).[21] Most investigators have no doubts about the organic connection of the three parts. An exception is F. Kämpfer, who has drawn attention to the fact that one late fifteenth- or early sixteenth-century fragment of the work contains only the first part (the verses) and has suggested that the name "Laodicean Epistle" be reserved for the philosophical discourse in verse; the remaining parts of the work are the product of later additions that appeared in the manuscript tradition. This suggestion merits investigation, but it must be said that if we accept it (and admit that the oldest copy represents the original tradition of the work, without heading, without the cryptogram in squares, without Kuricyn's signature), then not only do we have no basis for calling the philosophical part "Laodicean Epistle," we also have no right to use it as a source for the history of the fifteenth-century Novgorod-Moscow heresy. All that links the work with the heresy is the signature of Kuricyn, "prevedšij Laodikijskoe poslanie" (who translated the *Laodicean Epistle*); if the poem existed independently at the beginning of the fifteenth century and was joined together with the cryptogram in squares and Kuricyn's signature later on, then it tells us as little about the character of the heretical movement as the translations from the Hebrew texts mentioned above.[22]

---

reckoning of eras was 5,508 years, but in Rus' it was reckoned theoretically that 5,500 years had transpired from the "Creation of the World" to the "Birth of Christ," hence the discrepancy of eight years.

[21] Ibid., 265–276.

[22] F. Kämpfer, "Zur Interpretation des 'Laodicenischen Sendschreibens,'" in *Jahrbücher für Geschichte Osteuropas,* n.s., vol. 16 (1968): 66–69. R. Stichel has come to this "inescapable" conclusion by assuming the original, independent existence of the poem and Kuricyn's signature. He suggests that Kuricyn translated an epistle of John Damascene to the bishop of Laodicea; cf. R. Stichel, "Zur Bedeutung des altrussischen 'Laodicenischen Sendschreibens,'" *Zeitschrift für slavische Philologie* 40, no. 1 (1978): 134–135.

Kämpfer's proposal is not supported by manuscript tradition, however. Of course, the structure of the oldest copy does not prove anything in and of itself; most of the copies contain all three elements of the text: the second oldest copy of the work (GPB Q I. 1468, first quarter of the sixteenth century) includes, in addition to the verses, an introduction to the grammatical table and Kuricyn's signature. Moreover, the tripartite composition is characteristic of both types of the work that have survived (the Paschal and the Grammatical—they differ in the latter's containing a text of grammatical commentary in the table). Thus the basic—tripartite— structure of the work was determined before its division into types. Consequently we have no basis for doubting that the *Laodicean Epistle*, a fragment of which (together with some secondary readings) was preserved in a late fifteenth- or early sixteenth-century manuscript, contained not only a philosophical part but a grammatical part as well, and was actually linked with the "načalьnik moskovskix eretikov" (the leader of the Moscow heretics [in the words of Gennadij])—Fedor Kuricyn.[23]

What facts on the nature of the heresy can be drawn from this work? In recent years the *Laodicean Epistle* has attracted the attention of several non-Russian scholars. In an analysis of the philosophical part of the work (the verses), J. Fine, the above-mentioned F. Kämpfer, and J. Maier see traces of Judaism (according to Fine, specifically Talmudic features in the construction of the verses, in the reference to *zagrada* 'enclosure'—*ograda* 'fence', etc.). D. Freydank and J. Haney, on the contrary, connect this work with the Greco-Byzantine tradition; Freydank, in fact, sees this connection first and foremost in the cryptogram in squares, the grammatical part of the *Laodicean Epistle* (similar to the tradition of Dionysius Thrax), while Haney includes the philosophical part as well (influence of Plato and Neoplatonism).[24]

In recent years the German scholar F. v. Lilienfeld has written several works on the *Laodicean Epistle* as a source for the history of late fifteenth-century social thought.[25] Lilienfeld begins her analysis with the cryptogram

[23] J. Luria, "Zur Zusammensetzung des 'Laodicenischen Sendschreibens,'" in *Jahrbücher für Geschichte Osteuropas*, n.s., vol. 17 (1969): 161–169.

[24] J. Fine, "Fedor Kuricyn's 'Laodikijskoe Poslanie' and the Heresy of the Judaizers," *Speculum* 41 (1966): 500–504; Kämpfer, "Zur Interpretation" (see n. 22), 62–66, 69; J. Maier, "Zum jüdischen Hintergrund des sogenannten 'Laodicenischen Sendschreibens,'" in *Jahrbücher für Geschichte Osteuropas*, n.s., vol. 17 (1969): 1–12; D. Freydank, "Der 'Laodicener-brief' (Laodikijskoe poslanie). Ein Beitrag zur Interpretation eines altrussischen humanistischen Textes," *Zeitschrift für Slawistik* 11 (1966): 355–370; J. V. Haney, "The Laodicean Epistle: Some Possible Sources," *Slavic Review* 30 (1971): 832–842.

[25] F. Lilienfeld, "Ioann Tritemij i Fedor Kuricyn (O nekotoryx čertax rannego Renessansa na Rusi i v Germanii)," in *Kul'turnoe nasledie drevnej Rusi. Istoki. Stanovlenie. Tradicii*

in squares, which she views as a cryptographic key (Kuricyn shares an interest in cryptography with the German humanist and cryptographic expert Johannes Trithemius) and as an indication of Kuricyn's cabalistic interests. She views as cabalistic the naming of a number of letters as "tsars" (**а, н, ω, ю**), the assignment of a particular meaning to the first letter of the alphabet, **а** (*načalo čelovek* 'beginning of mankind', *samoderžec* 'sovereign'), the terms *obšče estestvo* 'common essence', *rodstvo* 'kinship' associated with the letters **ѣ, ь, ѧ** (Lilienfeld links them with the notions "matter, being" and "form" used in the Cabala), the very system of squares of the cryptogram (the "mysticism of squares" in the Cabala), and so on. At the outset Lilienfeld leaves open the question of the origin of this cabalism —Judaic, Hermetic-Platonic, or Christian. In her last work on the "heresy of Fedor Kuricyn," Lilienfeld also directs her inquiry at the introduction to the *Laodicean Epistle*, the philosophical discourse in verse. In the author's view, the introduction as a whole does not diverge from the Orthodox Christian world view and even includes quotations from authors who were popular in the Russian monastic tradition. The sole exception is the phrase *Mudrosti sila farisejstvo žitelьstvo*, which appears to Lilienfeld to be incompatible with Christian tradition. It is just this positive mention of the Pharisees that prompts her to admit the possibility that the introductory portion of the *Laodicean Epistle* (as opposed to the cryptogram in squares which had a different provenance) was translated from a Hebrew original.

Lilienfeld's observations are very important, but as the author herself admits, a great number of issues remain unresolved. If Kuricyn's interest in alphabetic mysticism and even in the Cabala is indeed possible for a man of the fifteenth century who was somehow affected by Renaissance influences (for example, during a stay at the court of Matthias Corvinus in Hungary), then his familiarity with Hebrew and European cabalistic literature would be extraordinary for Muscovite Rus'. The Old Russian translations from Hebrew that have come down to us bear West Russian features; apparently most of them were done in Western Rus'.[26]

(Moscow, 1976), 116–123; see further id. "Das 'Laodikijskoe poslanie' des grossfürstlichen D'jaken Fedor Kuricyn," in *Jahrbücher für Geschichte Osteuropas*, n.s., vol. 24 (1976): 1–22; id., "Über einige Züge des Frühhumanismus und der Renaissance in Russland und Deutschland. Johannes Trithemius und Fjodor Kuritsyn," *Jahrbuch für fränkische Landesforschung* 36 (1976): 23–35; id., "Die 'Häresie' des Fedor Kuricyn," in *Forschungen zur osteuropäischen Geschichte* 24 (1978): 39–64.
[26] Apparent exceptions are the translations of a medieval Jewish Psalter commissioned by Ivan III and Metropolitan Filip (1464–1473) but done by a certain Fedor the Jew in the West Russian language (M. N. Speranskij, "Psaltyr' židovstvujuščix v perevode Fedora evreja," *ČOIDR*, 1907, bk. 2, pt. 2: 41) and certain additions to the Academic Chronograph, appar-

But the *Laodicean Epistle* is of an entirely different nature: there are no
West Russian traits in it whatsoever, and if we are actually dealing with a
translation from the Hebrew, then we must assume that it is a unique case
of a translation done by a Muscovite. In her search for Hebraisms in the
text of the *Laodicean Epistle*, Lilienfeld points to such phrases as *prorok
nakazanie* 'the teaching of the prophets' (in the BAN copy, 4.3.15; in all
other varieties and copies these words are absent) and *farisejstvo žitelьstvo*
(thus in texts of both the Paschal and Grammatical type; in the BAN copy
žitie farisejsku), seeing in them a reflection of Hebrew grammatical construction, which the Russian translator attempted to render but without
success. Nevertheless, in the Old Russian translations from the Hebrew
known to us, such phrases—fairly common in Old Russian—are not found
and can scarcely be considered as Hebraisms.[27]

Lilienfeld views the words *mudrosti sila — farisejstvo žitelьstvo* as reflecting the Judaic character of the original, especially because *farisejstvo* is
presented here in a positive context. But even this argument is not very
persuasive. It is not clear that the term *farisejstvo* in the *Laodicean Epistle*
has a completely positive meaning; Klibanov has proposed a different reading of the same line: *"Mudrosti — sila, farisejstvo — žitel'stvo"* (i.e., only the
external regulation of life—πολιτεία).[28] Besides, we know of a positive reference to the Pharisees in the medieval Russian translation of George
Hamartolos by a Russian author, a contemporary of Kuricyn: the deadliest
enemy of the heretics, Gennadij of Novgorod, when condemning the
ancient Sadducees, wrote that

> saddukei ubo otmetaxusja vъskresenija mertvyx, i ni angela, ni duxa imejaxu;
> farisei že oboja ispovedaxu. No po farisejax mnogoe božestvennoe pisanie
> svidetelьstvuet, i ot prorok, i ot apostol, i ot svjatyx otecь; saddukeem že —
> ni edino ot nix.[29]

---

ently going back to some Jewish source; cf. N. A. Meščerskij, "K voprosu o sostave i istoč-
nikax Akademičeskogo xronografa," *Letopisi i xroniki, Sbornik statej 1973 g.* (Moscow, 1974),
217–219.

[27] Lilienfeld, "Die 'Häresie'" (see n. 25), 50. For examples of Hebraisms in Old Russian
translations, see N. A. Meščerskij, "K voprosu ob izučenii perevodnoj pisьmennosti kievskogo
perioda," *Uč. zap. Karelo-finskogo Ped. In-ta* 2, no. 1 (Petrozavodsk, 1955), 209–210; id. (ed).
Istorija Iudejskoj vojny Iosifa Flavija v drevnerusskom perevode (Moscow–Leningrad, 1958),
140–141, 147–148. Lilienfeld also indicates that "die vielen Nominalsätze ohne Kopula 'ist'
mache sich hebräisch ebensogut wie altrussisch," but it is clear that such examples can in no
way serve as evidence of reliance on a Hebrew original (in light of the common omission of
the copula "estь" in fifteenth-century Russian texts).

[28] Klibanov, *Reformacionnye dviženija v Rossii* (see n. 3), 68.

[29] For the Sadducees rejected the resurrection of the dead and had neither angel nor spirit;
the Pharisees, however, confessed both. But many of the Divine Scriptures bear witness

A number of writers, J. Fine and J. Maier among them, have interpreted the reference to the Pharisees in the *Laodicean Epistle* as proof of the heretics' Judaic views. But it is Maier who noted that the term *farisejstvo*, used in the New Testament and in Josephus Flavius, was almost unknown to Jews of the Middle Ages; to translate the term *farisejstvo* in the Middle Ages, they did not use the word *pārûš* (etymologically related to the word *farisejstvo*), but other terms instead.[30] If, as Lilienfeld assumes, Fedor Kuricyn had before him a Hebrew text with the word *pārûš, pərūšîm*, why did he translate it as *farisejstvo*? How was this Hebrew term translated into other languages in the Middle Ages? In general, what is known about direct translations of Hebrew cabalistic literature in the fifteenth century? Why was Kuricyn's work called the *Laodicean Epistle*, a name clearly associated with the Greek and Christian tradition (cf. the apocryphal Pauline epistle to the Laodiceans)?

Additionally, it should be noted that the definitions of letters in the cryptogram in squares (*carʹ, samoderžec,* and so forth), which Lilienfled interprets as cabalistic terms, had, in a number of instances, the sense of specific scientific terminology (vowels and consonants, endings of different substantival genders, the ability of a letter to *sʹvrʹšatʹsja* independently—to form its own syllable, etc.). In the *Discourse on Letters,* another grammatical tract closely linked to the *Laodicean Epistle,* the author notes in his characterization of *zvatelʹnye* 'vowels' that "svobodnyja polnyja glasy samoderžny imejut vostjagnovenie, po sebe pritjagajut drugyja glasy skudny i soglasujut s nimi...."[31]

Of course, it is entirely possible that the commentary on the cryptogram, like the introduction to the *Laodicean Epistle*, was polysemous, even consciously ambiguous in nature; but to understand the connection this work had with cabalistic and mystical literature of the late Middle Ages, one must trace the reflection of this literature in the Greek and East European

---

according to the Pharisees: the Prophets, the Apostles and the Holy Fathers as well; but as concerns the Sadducees—not a single one of them. *RIB* 6: *Pamjatniki drevnerusskogo kanoničeskogo prava*, ed. A. S. Pavlov, pt. 1 (St. Petersburg, 1908), col. 815. The Pharisees are mentioned in a positive context as well in the medieval Russian translation of the Hamartolos Chronicle: V. M. Istrin, *Knigi vremen'nyja i obraznyja Georgija Mnixa. Xronika Georgija Amartola* 1 (Prague, 1920), 233–234; cf. Stichel, "Zur Bedeutung des altrussischen 'Laodicenischen Sendschreibens'" (see n. 22), 135.

[30] Maier, "Zum jüdischen Hintergrund" (see n. 24), 1, 7–8.

[31] Independent, full, sovereign sounds have [the force of] attraction; they attract other poor sounds to themselves and give voice together with them.... V. Jagić, "Rassuždenija južnoslavjanskoj i russkoj stariny o cerkovnoslavjanskom jazyke," in *Issledovanija po russkomu jazyku* (St. Petersburg, 1885–1895), 659; cf. Klibanov, *Reformacionnye dviženija v Rossii* (see n. 28), 82.

tradition, which is more or less close to that of Rus'. For Lilienfeld's interesting proposals to be convincing, we must establish the intermediate links
between the cabalistic works she has noted and Old Russian literature.

Certain secondary formulations of Lilienfeld stemming from her observations on the *Laodicean Epistle* are even less convincing. Thus in connection with her conjecture about the possible astrological interests of the
heretics, she turns to the question of Zaxarija Skara of Taman', with whom
Ivan III conducted negotiations in 1481–1500 (concerning his arrival in
Rus') and whom a number of scholars have identified as the legendary
Sxarija in the *Enlightener,* who had supposedly lured the Novgorodians into
židovstvo in 1471. Despite documentary evidence attesting to the Italian
origin and Catholic faith of Zaxarija Skara-Gujgursis (Guixulfis) of Taman',
Lilienfeld is inclined to identify him as Zaxarija ben-Aron Ga-Kohen,
whose astronomical manuscript is noted by Brutskus, and she asserts that
Zaxarija Skara was called *knjaz' Tamanskij* (in the correspondence with
Ivan III) only in the metaphorical sense in accordance with "Jewish Renaissance usage." But Brutskus says nothing about the Kievan Zaxarija Ga-
Kohen except that in Kiev in 1468 he copied—only copied!—the astronomical manuscript of Al-Fergan translated by Jakov Anatoli (unfortunately Brutskus did not indicate the catalogue number of this manuscript in
his encyclopedia entry); thus the identification of Ga-Kohen with Zaxarija
. Skara-Gujgursis from the Black Sea littoral rests solely on the coincidence
of the rather common name, Zaxarija.[32]

Based on her study of the *Laodicean Epistle,* Lilienfeld is prompted to
raise anew the question of the connection between the Novgorod-Moscow
heretics (the Judaizers) and those translations from the Hebrew that had
currency in Russian literature of the fifteenth and sixteenth centuries.[33] But

---

[32] B(rutskus, J.), "Judaisierende" in *Encyclopaedia Judaica,* vol. 9 (Berlin, 1930), cols.
520–522. The Saltykov-Ščedrin Public Library collection contains a fragment of an astronomical work (*On spheres*), copied by Zaxarija ben-Aron Ga-Kohen somewhat earlier, in 1454
(GPB, Firkovič collection I, Evr. I. 355). I am grateful to L. Vil'sker for bringing this work to
my attention; cf. I. Guljand, *Kratkoe opisanie matematičeskix, astronomičeskix i astrologičeskix
evrejskix rukopisej* (St. Petersburg, 1866), 14–15. If Brutskus' observations are correct, then it
is obvious that the Saltykov-Ščedrin Public Library has another manuscript by the same
writer. In his bibliography Brutskus cites an article by S. Cinber, "Avraam Krymskij i Moisej
Egipetskij" (*Evrejskaja Starina* 11 [Leningrad, 1924]), but this article contains no mention of
Zaxarija Ga-Kohen. In subscribing to Brutskus' point of view, Lilienfeld does not render his
opinion accurately: the idea that the title "Prince of Taman'" referred to Zaxarija Gujgursis in
the metaphorical sense does not belong to Brutskus, but to another scholar, V. I. Ogorodnik
(see *Sbornik statej v čest' D. A. Korsakova* [Kazan', 1913], 52–75; cf. also Lur'e, *Ideologičeskaja
bor'ba* [see n. 3], 131–133).

[33] Lilienfeld writes, "Dass ein grosser Teil dieser Übersetzungsliteratur nichts mit den
'Judaisierenden' gemein habe, nehme ich J. Luria ... nicht mehr ab; ich habe es ihm lange

as I have already noted, there is no evidence that the heretics used this literature. A reexamination of this question seems premature at the present time.

The antiheretical movements are as important as the Novgorod-Moscow heresy itself for characterizing Russian social thought of the late fifteenth and early sixteenth centuries. Historiographic tradition usually makes a sharp distinction between the two directions in Orthodox thought of the late fifteenth century: the Nonpossessor movement (*nestjažateľstvo*) and Josephism (*iosifljanstvo*). Although the polemics of the Nonpossessors against Iosif Volockij are linked with the early sixteenth-century monk and publicist Vassian Patrikeev, scholars are sure that the initiator of these polemics was the North Russian monastic figure, Nil Sorskij, whom Vassian considered his teacher. To a considerable degree, this view of Nil Sorskij stems from liberal Slavophile criticism and historiography of the last third of the nineteenth century (O. Miller, V. Žmakin), which found its conceptual precursors in the "moral-liberal" direction of Nil Sorskij and the Trans-Volga elders. Nil Sorskij is credited with criticism of church literature, the idea of freedom for the serfs, and tolerance of the heretics. In actual fact, these claims have never been supported by the sources. On the contrary, we know that in his epistle to Ioasaf, Gennadij, preparing for battle against the heretics, solicited the aid of the Kirill elders Paisij Jaroslavov and Nil Sorskij. At no time did Nil ever speak out publicly against the execution of the heretics; he expressed his hostile attitude towards them directly in his *Legend of the Life of the Holy Fathers*: "Lžeimenityx že učitelej eretičeskaja učenia i predania i vsja proklinaju jaz i suščii so mnoju, i eretiki vsi čjuži nam da budut."[34] Only Vassian Patrikeev

geglaubt (Lilienfled, "Die 'Häresie'" [see n. 25], 59, n. 135). Such a formulation of the question (even if the discussion concerns the "belief" in a colleague's conclusions) strikes me as odd. As the Greek poet Epicharmos said: "νᾶψε καὶ μέμνασ' ἀπιστεῖν· ἄρθρα ταῦτα τᾶν φρενῶν." (Be sober. Learn not to believe. In that lies the principles of intellect; Polyb. XVIII, 40, 4).

[34] I and those with me curse the heretical teachings and traditions and everything associated with these so-called teachers; and may they all be alien to us. *Nila Sorskogo Predanie i Ustav*, with introd. by M. S. Borovkova-Majkova (St. Petersburg, 1912), 3. In a strange way, even this direct statement against the heretics has been viewed in the literature as evidence of "broad tolerance" shown by Nil and his adherents, the Trans-Volga elders—for here Nil "said not a word about the execution of the apostates"—or as proof of the fact that "Nil was forced to certify in writing his complete acceptance of all the church dogmas repudiated by the heretics" because of the similarity of his methodology with that of the heretics; cf. M. S. Borovkova-Majkova, "Nil Sorskij," in *Istorija russkoj literatury*, vol. 2, pt. 1 (Moscow–Leningrad, 1946), 320; Proxorov, "Prenie Palamy" (see n. 11), 359. But it would have been surprising if, in his confession of faith, Nil had spoken not only of his hostility towards the heresy but also about

spoke out against excessive cruelty to anyone connected with the heresy (but only after the smashing defeat of the heresy in 1504), and in doing so never once cited the authority of Nil Sorskij.

Despite the insufficiently argued but constantly repeated historiographical view of the contradictions between Nil's critical direction and Josephism, the link between the literary traditions of Nil and Iosif, the Josephites' high esteem for the *bogoduxovnovennye pisanija* 'God-inspired writings' of the *revniteľ svjatyx otecь* 'zealot of the Holy Fathers', Nil Sorskij, has already been noted in the literature.[35]

New studies of the manuscript tradition have produced convincing affirmation of the close ties between the two most prominent church writers of the late fifteenth century. For our purpose, the most important observations concern the oldest copy of the *Enlightener* from Iosif's time, now housed in the collection of the Saltykov-Ščedrin Public Library in Leningrad (GPB, Sol. no. 326/346). This manuscript is a "deed for the soul" (*vklad po duše*) for the benefit of the Iosif Volokolamsk Monastery, donated by the renowned Josephite monk and copyist Nil Polev in 7022 (1514). The dedication by the Volokolamsk monk Nil Polev, which is preserved on the manuscript, shows unequivocally that Polev participated in its creation and that it was completed before 1514 (*terminus ante quem*). But it says nothing about the earliest dating of the manuscript (*terminus a quo*), nor about the possible group of copyists.

A study by B. M. Kloss and G. M. Proxorov of manuscript Sol. no. 326/346 and those with similar handwriting shows that only the beginning part, including the dedication and Iosif Volockij's *Monastic Rule*, is written in Nil Polev's hand. The text of the *Enlightener* was copied by others, the largest part in a hand found in a number of hagiographical collections with

---

measures to combat the heretics; it would be just as strange to view Nil's declaration against the heretics as forced and showing the similarity of his views and those of the heretics. In his *Sermon on Law and Grace,* Ilarion wrote "... Ni posledovaxom lžuumu koemu proroku, ni učenija eretičeskaja deržim" (Neither have we followed any false prophet, nor do we maintain heretical teachings), (*Pamjatniki duxovnoj literatury vremen vel. knjazja Jaroslava I. Pribavlenija k tvorenijam sv. otcov,* pt. 2 [Moscow, 1844], 251), but this in no way suggests the similarity of his views and heretical ones. When indicating that the Trans-Volga elders "machten sich dafür stark, 'Häretiker' zu bekehren und zu gewinnen, statt sie zu verfolgen und körperlichen Strafen auszuliefern," Lilienfeld refers to the argumentation of Iosif Volockij against anonymous opponents in epistles to Nifont and Mitrofan and in the *Epistle on Observing the Verdict of the Church;* see Lilienfeld, "Die 'Häresie'" (see n. 25), 59, n. 129 (the citation is taken from my book). But there is no basis for thinking that in these works Iosif is polemicizing with Nil Sorskij and the Trans-Volga elders.

[35] M. S. Borovkova-Majkova, "K literaturnoj dejateľnosti Nila Sorskogo," *PDPI* 177 (1911): 7; Luŕe, *Ideologičeskaja boŕba* (see n. 3), 312–314.

ispravlenija or *perepisi* by Nil Sorskij. Nil's most reliable autograph is a collection from the Volokolamsk Monastery (deposited, like the *Enlightener*, in 1514), known to nineteenth-century specialists, which disappeared and was only recently brought to light (State Literature Museum MS no. 126). The entire text up to folio 253v is written in one hand, and on folio 253v there is a notation (by Nil Polev): "V sej knige do zde perepisi starca Nila, ošelnika Sъrьskyja pustyni, iže na Beleezere."[36] By comparing the State Literature Museum manuscript and the GPB, Sol. no. 326/346 manuscript, we find that the text of folios 47–51v, 67–103v and 215–287v of the oldest copy of the *Enlightener* is written in the same hand, that of "starecь Nil, ošelnik Sъrьskyja pustyni."[37]

The first redaction of the *Enlightener* was anonymous, but the name of its author—Iosif Volockij—was already included in the second (fifteenth or sixteenth "actual") redaction. It is extremely important to establish once and for all that a good part of the manuscript of this work brought to Iosif's monastery in his lifetime (Iosif died in 1515) was written in the hand of Nil Sorskij. What is important here is not simply that it clarifies the date of the writing of the manuscript—before 1508, the year of Nil Sorskij's death—and the place where it was written—the Kirill Monastery or the nearby Beloozero sketes, where Nil Polev and Nil Sorskij lived at the time; more important is the active participation of the Sorka hermit in the writing of the book. What evidence do we have to indicate that Nil played such a role? As one of the most authoritative church figures, to whom Gennadij had turned for assistance against the heretics as early as 1490, Nil Sorskij, by the beginning of the sixteenth century, had already written his fundamental works: *Chapters of Instruction* (*Monastic Rule*), and *Tradition*. In no way can he be seen as a mere professional copyist, ready to copy any text on demand. Manuscript Sol. no. 326/346 was no *kelejnyj sbornik*, in which a compiler might copy out for himself interesting passages (even those inimical to his own view). This was a ceremonial copy, with elegantly decorated headpieces, clearly intended for some extraordinary purpose. What kind of purpose might this have been? I have already had occasion to

---

[36] The copying up to here in this book is by the elder Nil, hermit of the Sorka wilderness at Beloozero.

[37] V. M. Kloss, "Nil Sorskij i Nil Polev—'spisateli knig,'" in *Drevnerusskoe iskusstvo. Rukopisnaja kniga*, no. 2 (Moscow, 1974), 150–167; on the State Literature Museum copy no. 126, ibid., 167, n. 48; G. M. Proxorov, "Avtografy Nila Sorskogo," in *Pamjatniki kul'tury. Novye otkrytija. Ežegodnik 1974 g.* (Moscow, 1975), 37–54. The articles by Kloss (except n. 48) and Proxorov were written before the discovery of Nil's volume in the State Literature Museum; for this reason it was necessary to resort to more complex and indirect means to attribute the texts in Sol. 326/346 and other manuscripts to the hand of Nil Sorskij.

mention that the initial redaction of the *Enlightener*—which contains (in contradistinction to the epistle to Nifont used in it) a discussion of the *pagubnaja burja* 'disastrous storm' as an event of the past (*toliko bystъ smuščenie v xristianex* [so great was the confusion amongst Christians])— must have been written after the heretical "storm" had already passed but before the executions of the heretics, condemned at the Council of 1504; otherwise the author would have mentioned these executions, as he did in the later, expanded version of the *Enlightener* (fifteenth discourse). Thus the time between 1502, when the patrons of the heresy at the court of Ivan III were stripped of influence and incarcerated, and the Council of 1504, is the most likely period for the writing of the original eleven-discourse redaction of the *Enlightener* found in Sol. 326/346.[38] Hence it is highly plausible that in its original form the *Enlightener* was intended for the Council of 1504 as documentation for indictment.[39] But if this is so, is copy Sol. 326/346 not the official copy especially prepared for the Council? Should we not assume that it was produced not only before 1508 but even before 1504? This is only speculation, of course. In any case, it is clear that we are dealing with a specially prepared text of the work which was appropriately kept by Iosif in his monastery.

Nil Sorskij's participation in the production of this copy bears testimony above all to his complete sympathy with what he wrote. Which parts of the *Enlightener* are written in Nil Sorskij's hand? There are three sections: (1) the first half of the introductory *Story of the Recent Heresy*, including the legend of Sxarija, especially damaging to the fate of the heretics (an indictment for apostasy, punishable by death); (2) the first and second discourses, which were closely associated with it; and (3) the second half of the seventh discourse and the eighth, ninth, and tenth discourses (concerning the End of the World and patristic writings).[40]

These are the most important sections of the *Enlightener*. Especially worthy of attention is the seventh discourse, also entitled "Story" (*Skazanie*), concerning the worship of different objects—icons, the cross, churches, and the like. It is precisely the second part of the seventh discourse, written in Nil Sorskij's hand, that contains the "fundamentally revolutionary teaching" already noted by M. A. Djakonov—that tsars

---

[38] The GPB copy Sol. 326/346 contains the thirteenth through sixteenth discourses of the *Enlightener* as well, but they are written in a seventeenth-century hand on different paper and interpolated after the fact (cf. Kazakova and Lur'e, *Antifeodal'nye eretičeskie dviženija* [see n. 1], 458 n. 4, 461).

[39] Lur'e, *Ideologičeskaja bor'ba* (see n. 3), 100–105, 421.

[40] Kloss, "Nil Sorskij i Nil Polev" (see n. 36), 150–167; Proxorov, "Avtografy Nila Sorskogo" (see n. 36), 52.

should only be obeyed "telesne" (in body), and not "duševne" (in spirit), and that if a tsar is "ne božij sluga, no diavolь, i ne carь, no mučitelь," then "ty ubo takovogo carja ili knjazja da ne poslušaeši, na nečestie i lukavьstvo privodjašče tja, ašče mučitь, ašče smertьju pretitь!"[41] No less significant is the ending of the discourse which states that the teaching mentioned above "lučši bo estь věnca careva—toj bo v ad svedet, a sija v žiznь věčnuju vvedetь."[42] This ending appears to have been excessively radical even to the editors of the *Pravoslavnyj sobesednik*, who published the *Enlightener* as a supplement in the second half of the nineteenth century: in the preface it was stated that "those articles" of the work "inappropriate to the program of our journal will be omitted," and excluded this passage (up to the words "... v ad svedet") in the Kazan' editions of 1857–1904.[43]

As we have seen, Nil Sorskij had no quarrel with these statements, and he copied them in his own hand. But did he only copy them? Was his role in the production of the *Enlightener* limited to being one of the copyists of the official copy of the book?

The seventh discourse has a rather complex history. It existed apart from the *Enlightener* as the second—central—of three discourses on icons added to the *Epistle to an Icon Painter* (*Poslanie ikonopiscu*, all three of these discourses were put into the *Enlightener* in a different order: the first became the fifth; the third became the sixth; and the second became the seventh discourse of the *Enlightener*). A comparison of the texts added to the *Epistle to an Icon Painter* with the texts in the *Enlightener* shows that the former were original and the latter, secondary.[44] But who is to be credited with writing the *Epistle to an Icon Painter* and the discourses on icons? Like the first redaction of the *Enlightener,* this work was anonymous. But M. S. Borovkova-Majkova has even pointed out that the *Epistle to an Icon Painter* was itself not original: except for a mention of the "Novgorod heretics," described as appearing "now," and a reference to the discourses to follow, the entire text corresponds to the *Epistle from a Church Elder to a Certain Brother* found in a number of collections and apparently belonging to Nil

---

[41] ... not a servant of God but of the Devil, and not a tsar but a tormentor ... [then] ... you must therefore not obey such a tsar or prince, who brings you to dishonor and wickedness, even if he tortures you or threatens you with death! *Prosvetitel'* (see n. 1), 287. Cf. M. D'jakonov, *Vlast' moskovskix gosudarej* (St. Petersburg, 1889), 92–96.

[42] ... for it is better than a tsar's crown, for that will lead you to hell, while this will lead you to life eternal. GPB, Sol. 326/346, 1. 247. Cf. Kazakova and Lur'e, *Antifeodal'nye eretičeskie dviženija* (see n. 1), 360.

[43] *Prosvetitel'* (see n. 1), 331. Cf. ibid., 25.

[44] Kazakova and Lur'e, *Antifeodal'nye eretičeskie dviženija* (see n. 1), 320–373; cf. Lur'e, *Ideologičeskaja bor'ba* (see n. 3), 112–114.

Sorskij. The very genre of the epistle supports this attribution, inasmuch as it is addressed from an "elder" to a "brother," who requests teaching for the "benefit of the soul"—such were the epistles from Nil Sorskij to the elder German and Gurij Tušin.[45] In their very structure, the manuscript copies containing the epistle are also connected with Nil's tradition: GPB, Sol. no. 1489, sixteenth century; and GIM, Uvar. no. 1846 (754) (718), seventeenth century (Borovkova-Majkova's publication of the epistle is based on the latter). Nil Sorskij's *Epistle to Vassian Patrikeev* comes directly after the *Epistle from a Church Elder to a Certain Brother*, then follows the *Response of the Kirill Elders*, apparently belonging to Vassian Patrikeev and directed against Iosif Volockij. One copy of the *Epistle from a Church Elder to a Certain Brother* actually contains an epistle from Iosif Volockij to Prince Jurij Ivanovič Dmitrovskij.

A comparison of the *Epistle from a Church Elder to a Certain Brother* and the *Epistle to an Icon Painter* suggests that the former is primary and the latter, secondary (the interpolations concerning the heresy and the heretics clearly interrupt the flow of text in the teaching for a "certain brother"). But if the *Epistle to a Certain Brother* belongs to Nil Sorskij and the *Epistle to an Icon Painter*, to Iosif Volockij, then one is led unavoidably to assume a diverse and complex correlation of both authors' works: during the writing of the *Epistle to an Icon Painter*, Iosif utilized Nil's *Epistle to a Certain Brother*; then the three discourses from the *Epistle* were included in the *Enlightener*, while Nil for his part copied part of one of these discourses together with other sections of the *Enlightener*. But is it not more plausible to assume that the collaboration of both authors was more straightforward and direct? Is it not more likely that the two leading church figures of the late fifteenth century acted as coauthors?

Who wrote the *Epistle to an Icon Painter* together with the discourses on icons—Iosif Volockij or Nil Sorskij? Researchers have noted the clear echoes of Hesychast ideas in this work;[46] Hesychast views were more typical of Nil than of Iosif, although similar ideas were not unknown to Iosif either. The reference to the Old Testament story about the appearance of the three angels (the Old Testament Trinity) to Abraham by the oak of

---

[45] Borovkova-Majkova, "K literaturnoj dejatel'nosti Nila Sorskogo" (see n. 35), 4–12. A comparison of the *Epistle from a Church Elder to a Certain Brother* and an anonymous epistle from the collection GPB, Q.XVII.50 by Borovkova-Majkova (pp. 7–8) is not convincing because the latter epistle cannot be attributed to Nil Sorskij (cf. Lur'e, *Ideologičeskaja bor'ba* (see n. 3), 301–303.

[46] N. K. Golejzovskij, "'Poslanie ikonopiscu' i otgoloski isixazma v russkoj živopisi na rubeže XV–XVI vv.," *VV* 26 (1965): 231–238; id., "'Poslanie ikonopiscu' Iosifa Volockogo i ego adresat Dionisij," cand. diss. synopsis (Moscow, 1970), 23.

Mamre connects the first discourse on icons (the fifth discourse in the *Enlightener*) with Iosif Volockij's epistle on the Trinity; a number of passages in the second discourse (seventh discourse in the *Enlightener*) coincide with Iosif's *Monastic Rule*.[47]

After analyzing the argumentation in defense of the veneration of icons enunciated in the discourses of the *Epistle to an Icon Painter*, L. A. Uspenskij suggests that "this work is a compilation, belonging not to one, but two authors, as evidenced by disagreement on certain issues." He notes disagreement in the third discourse on icons in which it is said that "božii čeloveci" in the Old and New Testaments "ne sutь videli božestvenago estestva i nevidimyx veščej, no v sěnex, i v obrazax, i v gadaniix, potrěb radi nekotoryx kažema veledarovaniem božiim. Ne javljaetsja ubo, eže estь, no jako ne možetь vidjaj videti."[48] Such a formulation of the issue justifies "any representation of the Divine," outside the constraints of prophetic visions and sensual phenomena. But in the second discourse on icons (the seventh discourse in the *Enlightener*), the sources of icon painting are sharply delimited:

> Ašče bo i neopisana estь božestvom svjataa i vsemoguščaa i životvorjaščaa Troica, no obače mnogymi obrazy bogoglasny i vsečestnyi proroci že i pravednicy o toj prorekoša; Avraamu že čjustveno i v čelovečьstemь podobii javisja.[49]

Moreover, Uspenskij sees essential stylistic differences between the second and third discourses on icons: the contents of the second are set down in laconic, accurate form; in the third, they are presented with pathos and

---

[47] Lur'e, *Ideologičeskaja bor'ba* (see n. 3), 215–216, 221, 255–256; Golejzovskij, "'Poslanie ikonopiscu' i otgoloski isixazma," 231.

[48] The men of God ... did not see the Divine Being and invisible things, but rather things made apparent for the sake of certain needs by the grace of God in the form of shadows, images, and mysteries. Therefore it is not the case that what exists does not appear, but that he who sees cannot see.

[49] For even if the Holy and Almighty and Life-giving Trinity is not described by the Divine, the God-praising and honorable prophets and the righteous have foretold it nonetheless in many forms; it appeared perceptibly to Abraham in human guise. Kazakova and Lur'e, *Antifeodal'nye eretičeskie dviženija* (see n. 1), 372, and 336 (these words in the second discourse are not written in Nil Sorskij's hand, but a reference to them is given later in the text written by Nil; cf. 356). It is worth noting that the same two points of view on the depiction of "nevidimoe božestvo i besplotnye" are found in the sixteenth century as well, in the disputes between I. M. Viskovatyj and Sylvester (who had the support of Metropolitan Makarij). Cf. N. E. Andreev, "O dele d'jaka Viskovatogo," *Seminarium Kondakovianum* 5 (Prague, 1932); reprinted in N. E. Andreyev, *Studies in Muscovy*, sec. 3 (London, 1970).

verbosity. Thus he concludes that they were written by two different authors.[50]

The stylistic differences between the second and third discourses are suggestive of the differences between Nil and Iosif as writers. Hence the textual observations concerning the *Enlightener* and its sources lead to the same proposition as the paleographic evidence—that Nil Sorskij participated directly in the creation of this work. In an epistle to Ioasaf, former archbishop of Rostov, in 1489, Gennadij, archbishop of Novgorod, requested that he enlist the aid of the most prominent church figures in Northern, Trans-Volga Rus' in the struggle against the heresy, Paisij Jaroslavov and Nil Sorskij. Now, one can conceive of the consequences of this request: the collaboration of Iosif and Nil on the *Epistle to an Icon Painter* and the discourses on icons,[51] and the participation of Nil Sorskij in the writing of the *Enlightener*. How was this collaboration carried out in concrete terms? I have already noted that the manuscript of the *Enlightener* written by Nil Polev and Nil Sorskij (Sol. 326/246) was apparently produced in the North, in a place adjacent to the Kirill Belozerskij Monastery. Does this imply that when Nil Polev left for "Отець Nil" at "Belo Ozero" with Iosif's blessing,[52] he took with him the materials for a book in preparation, or had contact been established even earlier by other means? Were the sections of the *Enlightener* written in Nil Sorskij's hand the fruit of his own creation, or do his handwriting and his authorship not necessarily coincide? We are not in a position to answer all these questions as yet. But Nil Sorskij's patent sympathy for Iosif Volockij's denunciations, his close participation in the writing of antiheretical literature, especially the *Enlightener*, are obvious.

[50] L. A. Uspenskij, "Isixazm i rascvet russkogo iskusstva," ch. 3, *Vestnik Russkogo Zapadno-Evropejskogo Patriaršego Èkzarxata,* 1967, no. 60: 23, n. 23; id., "Rol' moskovskix soborov XVI v. v cerkovnom iskusstve," ibid., 1968, no. 4: 225, n. 19. Cf. G. V. Popov, *Živopis' i miniatjura Moskvy konca XV – načala XVI v.* (Moscow, 1975), 131–133, n. 24.

[51] The dating of the *Epistle to an Icon Painter* and the discourses on icons is complicated by the fact that in one of the copies (Sof. no. 1474) only Archpriest Aleksej is accused of heresy, which indicates the period before the condemnation of his associate Denis and other heretics at the Council of 1490, while in another, Aleksej, Denis, and Fedor Kuricyn are accused, which indicates the early sixteenth century. On the subject matter of the discourses concerned with the question of the veneration of icons that was raised at the council against the Novgorod heretics in 1490, see Lur'e, *Ideologičeskaja bor'ba* (see n. 3), 112–114; Golejzovskij, "'Poslanie ikonopiscu'" (see n. 46), 29–30.

[52] "Žitie prep. Iosifa Volockogo, sostavlennoe neizvestnym" *ČOIDR,* 1903, bk. 3, pt. 2: 20. Cf. Lur'e, *Ideologičeskaja bor'ba* (see n. 3), 313.

The examples enumerated above do not, of course, exhaust the list of controversial and unresolved issues in the history of the ideological movements of the late fifteenth century. But even these few examples show that in the study of the history of social thought in Old Rus', the investigator must overcome the peculiar phantoms of historiography, the views of late nineteenth- and early twentieth-century historians (O. Miller, V. Žmakin, A. Sobolevskij, and others) which often appear as conjecture or simple guesses and turn into historiographical commonplaces. A historian who repudiates these phantoms must remind his readers again and again that there is no evidence of them in the sources.

And, as I have tried to show here, a reexamination of the manuscripts and a critical analysis of known sources allow us to uncover new, important facts of the history of the fifteenth-century ideological battle. The recent attention paid to such an important and puzzling work as the *Laodicean Epistle* by scholars from different countries must be viewed in a very positive light. And while the question of the sources for the heretical literature and possible foreign influences on it (and on the ideological movements of Old Rus' in general) is important and interesting, it cannot be decided a priori. It is essential that the search continue for instances of full coincidence of Russian and non-Russian texts and that the direct sources of Old Russian translated works be established.

Art and Architecture

IDENTITY MODELS OF OLD RUSSIAN SACRED ART

KONRAD ONASCH

Jako že v mirotvorenii reče bog: sotvorim čeloveka po obrazu našemu i po podobiju. Egda tako sozdan pervyj čelovek, nosja obraz božij v sebe i narečen v dušu živu, to po čto ty nyne zaziraeš blagoobraznym i živopodobnym personam svjatyx i zavidueš bogodarovannej krasote ix ...
— *Iosif Vladimirov, Russian icon painter of the seventeenth century*[1]

Toward the end of the tenth century, when Grand Prince Vladimir Svjato-slavič of Kiev (d. 1015) accepted Christianity in its Byzantine form both for himself and for his emerging feudal state in a typical medieval mass baptism, approximately a century and a half had elapsed since the Iconoclastic strug-gle had shaken the foundations of the Byzantine state and civilization. The significance of this development for art, culture, theology, and philosophy (including aesthetics) is sufficiently known and therefore needs no further discussion.[2] My present concern, the problem of the image (in its broadest sense), viewed from a particular perspective, will provide a point of departure for approaching the topic of identity models of Old Russian sacred art.

The positive models that imitate life and enrich human experience by the process referred to as *identification* are important for the individual, for society, and for their interaction. We are dealing here with a complex phe-nomenon which perhaps can be summed up by the capsule formulation: "to recognize and acknowledge oneself." Perceptible identifying signs are of great significance for the cohesion and stability of groups, associations, and

Translated from the German by Henrik Birnbaum and Rebecca Ziegler.

[1] When God created the world, He said, "Let Us make man in Our image and in Our like-ness." Since the first man was thus created, bearing the image of God and given a living soul, why do you regard with contempt the well-shaped, lifelike persons of the saints and why do you envy them their God-given beauty? From the "Poslanie nekoego izugrafa Iosifa k carevu izu-grafu i mudrejšemu živopiscu Simonu Fedorivičiu," in E. S. Ovčinnikova, *Drevnerusskoe iskus-stvo* (Moscow, 1964), 9–61 (the quotation is on p. 59).

[2] K. Wessel, "Bild," in *Reallexikon zur byzantinischen Kunst*, vol. 1 (Stuttgart, 1966), 616–662. From the extensive literature, I will quote here only the following: A. Grabar, *L'Iconoclasme byzantin. Dossier archéologique* (Paris, 1957); L. W. Barnard, *The Graeco-Roman and Oriental Background of the Iconoclastic Controversy* (Leiden, 1974); *Iconoclasm: Papers Given at the Ninth Spring Symposium of Byzantine Studies* (Birmingham, 1977).

societies. When the relationship between these signs and groupings loses its immediacy and intensity or ceases to exist altogether, this usually signals a profound crisis in society as a whole. Conventional symbols, signs, rites, and images that are no longer understood lose their value as identity models. Society slowly turns to a new convention with its own semiotics, which is accepted by some but rejected by others.

Compared to most religious communities of late Antiquity and to the Roman state, the Church commanded an unusually effective identification mechanism, which is captured by the classic formula of Ignatius of Antioch (d. 107): "Wherever *the bishop* appears, there is also *the congregation*; just as if *Jesus Christ* were there, so also the *universal Church* is there."[3] The early Church did not need material orientation patterns and identifying signs. In that period of church history, it was still a purely spiritual process that the bishop, as Christ's "imitator," would recognize himself in Christ and likewise see himself "confirmed" by Him in a canonical sense; the congregation would view the bishop in the same way. Although the bishop at that time still lacked any special insignial representation, he himself, his priestly office, and the Eucharist, which only he could celebrate, symbolized the unity of the congregation, founded by Christ in the one Flesh and Blood.[4] When the Church was legalized by Constantine I and, from an exclusive community, became a Church of the people, it had increasingly to avail itself of material means for representing its internal and external identity. Particularly significant was the introduction of images of the bishop and of Christ, the latter patterned on the image of the emperor.[5] The "pictorial agreement" between imperial and ecclesiastic imagery flourished in the age of Justinian I.[6]

The pictorial program of the Church initially emerged as dogmatic information[7] at the same time as the first fully developed form of Byzantine

[3] Ep. ad Smyrnaeos 8.1; italics added. *PG* 5: 713. Cf. Cyprian of Carthage: "Unde scire debes episcopum in ecclesia esse et ecclesiam in episcopo, et, si qui cum episcopo non sit, in ecclesia non esse" (*PL* 4: 406).

[4] Ignatius of Antioch, Ep. ad Philadelphenses 4. *PG* 5: 700. Cf. Cyprian: "Si Christus Iesus Dominus et Deus noster ipse est summus sacerdos Dei Patris, et sacrificium Patri se ipsum obtulit, et hoc fieri in sui commemorationem praecepit, utique ille sacerdos vice Christi vere fungitur, qui id quod Christus fecit imitatur et sacrificium verum et plenum tunc offert in ecclesia Deo Patri, si sic incipiat offerre secundum quod ipsum Christum videat obtulisse" (*PL* 4: 385).

[5] See now H. G. Thümmel, "Kaiserbild und Christusikone," *ByzSl* 39 (1978): 196–206; K. Wessel, "Kaiserbild," in *Reallexikon* (see n. 2), vol. 3: 722–863.

[6] K. Onasch, "Einige soziologische Aspekte der Ikonenmalerei," *Theologische Literaturzeitung* 93 (1968): 321–332.

[7] C. Ihm, *Die Programme der christlichen Apsismalerei vom 4. Jahrhundert bis zur Mitte des 8. Jahrhunderts* (Wiesbaden, 1960); Wessel, "Bildprogramm," in *Reallexikon* (see n. 2), vol. 1:

hymnography—the *kontakion*—appeared. In its structure and content the latter was based on the homiletics of the Church Fathers.[8] These texts and their intellectual condensation in turn served as basic models for the imagery of the visual arts, as a result of which a common "language" gradually developed.[9] With the Hagia Sophia in Constantinople as "sacred image" ("sakrale Schaubühne," A. M. Schneider), Byzantine liturgy reached its first high point.[10] The term *cel'nost'*, a central notion of nineteenth-century Russian philosophy, is particularly suited to characterize the way in which the liturgy integrates the passive and the active, creative powers of man. It found its expression in an appropriate aesthetics.[11]

The image in the broad sense can be conceived of as a complex abstract model for ecclesiastic and imperial identities, as well as for their various interrleationships. It is easy to understand why Iconoclasm questioned this system of evaluative and behavior-determining models of church and state, in an attempt to replace it with a new one. This, however, would have implied a cultural revolution with unpredictable consequences.[12] It was characteristic of the rigorous spiritual utopianism of the Iconoclasts that they aimed at reducing the full pictorial representations to mere outlines and, in particular, at eliminating saints as immediate, perceptible representatives of an ethical universe. Provoked by them, the Iconodules developed a system for identifying relationships that distinguished between a chain of protoimage (*Urbild*)—

662–690; V. N. Lazarev, "Sistema živopisnoj dekoracii vizantijskogo xrama IX–XI vekov," in *Vizantijskaja živopis'* (Moscow, 1971), 90–109.

[8] In general, E. Wellesz, *A History of Byzantine Music and Hymnography,* 2nd ed. (Oxford, 1961), 179–197. But see also K. Mitsakis, "The Hymnography of the Greek Church in the Early Christian Centuries," *Jahrbücher der österreichischen Byzantinistik* 20 (Vienna–Cologne–Graz, 1971), 31–49; S. S. Averincev, *Poètika rannevizantijskoj literatury* (Moscow, 1977), 102ff, 210–220.

[9] The unity of image and hymn text has already been pointed out by Ju. Olsuf'ev, *Zametki o cerkovnom penii i ikonopisi kak vidax cerkovnogo iskusstva v svjazi s učeniem cerkvi* (Tula, 1918). See also K. Onasch, *Die Ikonenmalerei. Grundzüge einer systematischen Darstellung* (Leipzig, 1968), 151–198; B. Uspensky, *The Semiotics of the Russian Icon* (Lisse, 1976).

[10] H.-J. Schulz, *Die byzantinische Liturgie. Vom Werden ihrer Symbolgestalt* (Freiburg i.B., 1964); K. Onasch, "Der Funktionalismus der orthodoxen Liturgie. Grundzüge einer Kritik," *Jahrbücher für Liturgie und Hymnologie* 6 (1961): 1–48.

[11] V. V. Byčkov, *Vizantijskaja èstetika* (Moscow, 1977); Lazarev, "Vizantijskaja èstetika," in *Vizantijskaja živopis'* (see n. 7), 194–199; G. Mathew, *Byzantine Aesthetics* (London, 1963); A. Michelis, *Esthétique de l'art byzantin* (Paris, 1959); P. Florenskij, "Xramovoe dejstvo kak sintez iskusstv," *Makovec. Žurnal Iskusstv* 1 (1922): 28–32; id., "Ikonostas," in *Bogoslovskie Trudy* 9 (1972). On the notion of *cel'nost* in modern art theory, see A. A. Mixajlova, "Xudožestvennyj obraz kak dinamičeskaja celostnost'," *Sovetskoe iskusstvoznanie* 71 (1976): 222–257.

[12] See n. 1, and, also, V. M. Polevoj, *Iskusstvo Grecii. Srednie veka* (Moscow, 1973), 115–137.

depiction (*Abbild*)—recipient, constituting "photographic" identities, as it were, which they rejected, on the one hand, and a relationship of ascertainable analogies, which they favored, on the other.[13]

Theological considerations among the Iconodules, which also influenced the aesthetics of the subsequent period, resulted in a rearrangement of the imagery. This found its expression in a restructuring of the pictorial program as well as in a firmer control of artistic activities by the bishops (who essentially remained suspicious of the image).[14] It aimed at keeping the sensitive identity mechanism intact.[15] Moreover, the reorientation toward classical models after the period of Iconoclasm created the precondition, at least initially, for a stable and effective, that is, clear and structured, imagery in Byzantine sacred painting. This imagery was transplanted to Kievan Rus' after a remarkable prehistory and at a significant juncture of its further evolution.

After the mass baptism in the Dnieper, Christianity gained strength only slowly, to begin with, and mostly in the towns of the feudal principalities; even here it encountered difficulties, as in Novgorod, for example, In the vast expanses of the *Russkaja zemlja*, Christianity prevailed only gradually over the centuries. Similarly, the transplantation and assimilation of Byzantine culture was a complex process, as exemplified by Old Russian architecture.[16]

Concerning the image as a medium of emotive and cognitive behavior patterns—the former primarily in the liturgy—the following can be stated: In the large town churches—above all, in the Cathedral of Saint Sophia in

---

[13] See the data adduced by Wessel in the work cited in note 2. For some basic thoughts on analogy, see J. M. Lotman, *Vorlesungen zu einer strukturalen Poetik* (Munich, 1972), 22–54. See further Onasch, *Ikonenmalerei* (see n. 9), 18–28, esp. n. 18.

[14] Answering an inquiry of mine, Cyril Mango advised me that we can assume that the bishops controlled church painting as early as Byzantine times; to be sure, we know of no sources to support this. In Russia, such control is corroborated in the *Stoglav* of 1551; cf. Onasch, *Ikonenmalerei*, 125ff. H.-G. Beck, *Die Fragwürdigkeit der Ikone,* Sitzungsberichte der Bayerischen Akademie der Wissenschaften, Philosophisch-historische Klasse, no. 7 (Munich, 1975).

[15] Here we are dealing with a problem that is still awaiting its resolution, at least insofar as the icon (in the broadest sense) is concerned. We speak of the dogmatic information of the icon, and this is the crux of the problem: while information implies innovation, dogma must always consider innovation a disruption. The minute changes in the iconographic canon, discernible only to the expert, clearly indicate this field of tensions. The church hierarchy had to be protected from innovations in the media of its dogmatic information, if these media— ecclesiastic chant and painting—were to be effective identifiers. This dialectic corresponds to that of cultic image versus artistic image in the icon. The intention of protecting the church hierarchy and its media from disruption by innovations must have been conceived as utopian, given the pragmatic dynamics of the medieval art of the Eastern Church.

[16] V. N. Lazarev, "Vizantija i drevnerusskoe iskusstvo," in *Vizantijskoe i drevnerusskoe iskusstvo* (Moscow, 1978), 211–221.

Kiev[17]—the pictorial program took on the function of the post-Iconoclastic ornamental system of the ninth century; the devout individual engaged in prayer was analogically related to the imperceptible, noetically conceived Church by way of a sequence of saints, arranged according to a vertical hierarchy, which extended down from the Pantocrator in the dome and connected the heavenly with the earthly Church.[18] Just as the images were viewed as a visible depiction of their imperceptible prototype according to the principle of similarity (ὁμοίωμα), so the chant of the earthly church choir was conceived as an "echo" (ἀπήχημα) of the heavenly song of the angels, following the writings of Pseudo-Areopagite.[19] Consequently, problems of hymnology, the second most important medium of ecclesiastic teaching, were much discussed in Old Rus'.

The Old Russian Chronicle, in its famous description of mass celebrated in the Hagia Sophia of Constantinople,[20] has not only left us with a lively impression of that liturgy but has also given us an invaluable insight into the aesthetic notions of Kievan Rus'—their intensity and their comprehensive *cel'nost'*. This must not be disregarded in the study of the Old Russian pictorial program.[21] With all the means of artistic-optical and acoustic illusionism available from Byzantium, an experience of security in a holy cave of light was generated, an experience separated by eons from the evil reality of earthly life outside the closed, mighty gates of the cathedral.

---

[17] G. N. Logvin, *Sofija Kievskaja* (Kiev, 1971); Lazarev, "Freski Sofii Kievskoj," in *Vizantijskoe i drevnerusskoe iskusstvo* (see n. 16), 65–115.

[18] See n. 13, with a reference to Lotman. By identities we mean analogous interrelations and not perfect, static congruences. This is comparable to hagiographic semantics, where *podobie* and not *toždestvo* characterizes the relationship between the saint and Christ. This, in turn, corresponds to ὁμοουσία 'identity of substance' versus ὁμοίωσις 'likeness of substance' in pictorial theology. It is only the latter of the two notions that describes the interdependence between the noetic prototype and its "aesthetic" image (εἰκών). Thus, Byzantine aesthetics also yields a differentiated system of analogous identities when it comes to the hierarchical-societal connections of the image. For the philosophical-aesthetic foundations, see R. Roques, *L'Univers Dionysien. Structure hiérarchique du monde selon le Pseudo-Denys* (Paris, 1954); H. Goltz, *Mesiteia. Zur Theorie der hierarchischen Sozietät im Corpus Areopagiticum* (Erlangen, 1974). If one is to view a society defined in terms of Areopagitic συμμετρία, εὐταξις, ἀναλογία, etc., as an intact social order, then any heretic community must seem defective; see also n. 43.

[19] Cf. Roques (see n. 18), Index. On ἀπήχημα as formula of intonation in Byzantine choral chant, cf. Wellesz, *History of Byzantine Music* (see n. 8), 304.

[20] *PVL*, vol. 1 (Moscow, 1950), 74–75.

[21] Cf. K. Onasch, "Zur ästhetischen Theorie der Bildprogramme der Sophienkirchen in Kiev und Ochrid," lecture read at the Colloquium of the Association international d'études sud-est européennes, Moscow and Kiev, 23–27 January 1978; id., "Zur Deutung des Kirchengebäudes in den byzantinischen Liturgiekommentaren," in *Byzantinischer Kunstexport*, ed. H. L. Nichel (Halle [Saale], 1978), 301–308.

However, the image of the identifier reveals itself in all its complexity of reception and impact in an artistic sphere combining Byzantine and Old Slavic religious concepts, which G. K. Vagner aptly and intriguingly labeled "genre."[22] The images of patrons are of particular interest as models for ethical-social behavior. In accordance with the hierarchically structured pyramid of medieval feudal society, they range from the "saints militaires" of the ruling elite down to the patrons of trade, agriculture, and cattle raising venerated by merchants and peasants.

Among the former, Saints George and Demetrios of Salonika are known from a multitude of Old Russian art objects to have been name-patrons of Jaroslav Mudryj and Izjaslav. In general, the heroic-epic genre was an identity preserve for the princes, whose personified symbolization obliged them to make their own sacrifice for Rus'.[23] The national patronage of the first martyrs of Rus', Boris and Gleb,[24] was an admonition directed at the princes in the face of the devastating internecine wars, similar in a sense to that of Vladimir Monomax's letter to Oleg: "Let us not bring disaster upon the Russian land."[25] By hagiographically stylizing two tragic human fates (compare in a similar vein Saint Václav of Bohemia and his grandmother, Saint Ludmila)—two carriers of the moral norm, removed from history—a model was created not only for the ethics of politics but also for all relationships between people. This is attested by the great number of princely churches dedicated to Boris and Gleb, monuments of large-scale as well as small-size art, including icon painting.[26]

Without entering here into a discussion of other significant means of identifying the people, the state, and the Church of Old Rus' (among which the *pokrov* is of particular interest),[27] I now turn to some patrons loosely connected with the lives of the ordinary people, hence particularly linked with "life itself." Here, too, I shall select only a few of the many examples.

---

[22] G. K. Vagner, *Problema žanrov v drevnerusskom iskusstve* (Moscow, 1974).

[23] Ibid., 126–134.

[24] È. S. Smirnova, "Otraženie literaturnyx proizvedenij o Borise i Glebe v drevnerusskoj stankovoj živopisi," *TODRL* 15 (1958): 312–327.

[25] *PVL* (see n. 20) 1: 164.

[26] A. V. Poppe, "O roli ikonografičeskix izobraženij v izučenii proizvedenij o Borise i Glebe," *TODRL* 22 (1966): 24–45; M. X. Aleškovskij, "Russkie glebo-borisovskie ènkolpiony 1072–1150 godov" in *Drevnerusskoe iskusstvo* (Moscow, 1972), 104–125; cf. L. Müller's edition of *Die altrussischen hagiographischen Erzählungen und liturgischen Dichtungen über die Heiligen Boris und Gleb* (Munich, 1967), based on the earlier edition of D. I. Abramovič.

[27] See the literature in È. S. Smirnova, *Živopis' Velikogo Novgoroda. Seredina XIII–načalo XV veka* (Moscow, 1976), 222–257. On the history of iconography, cf. also Ch. Belting-Ihm, *"Sub matris tutela." Untersuchungen zur Vorgeschichte der Schutzmantelmadonna* (Heidelberg, 1976).

Patronage was one of the most important integrating phenomena, not only in the Church but also in medieval society as a whole; the patron of a particular profession is usually discernible from the corresponding hagiographic texts. This is the case, for example, with the ἀνάργυροι, whose patronage was furthered by the social destitution of the medieval masses.[28]

Without the text of the *vita*, the pictorial representation of the patron saint could not be understood—particularly so since the iconography of figures in the Eastern Church resorted to many symbols. Instead, one used as a reading device the marginal row of pictures (*klejma*), which provided a selection from the *vita*. The *klejma* furnished much more bibliographical information about the patron saint; in other words, it was much closer to "life itself" than the considerably idealized central picture of the saint.[29]

Nevertheless, the complex relationship between the patron, the individuals or objects benefiting from his protection, and the whole tradition (frequently going back to pre-Christian times) suggests that, underlying the overt hagiographic message, one should look for a subtext or "cryptogram" whose context is ethnographic and religious-historical in character. Deciphering it provides insights into social identities, whose ideal models permit us to take a direct look at the ethical behavior of people many centuries ago. A few examples: The figure of Saint George is pragmatically ambivalent in its social profile. He was not only the elitist image of the ideal ruler but also the patron of the peasants of northern Russia in their struggle against the inexorable forces of nature, the "illuminator" (*prosvetitel'*) and carrier of culture and, as such, the friend of the wolf (a "diplomatic friendship" benefiting the peasants).[30] Behind and beneath the *vita* and the icon of the great woman martyr Parasceve-Pjatnica, with its *klejma*, is concealed the pre-Christian Finnic patron of domestic activities—spinning and weaving—and of trade; here the "antagonism of affinity" between the Finnic deity Mokoš and the ascetic Christian woman martyr is worth noting.[31]

In this way, as a result of the vitality of the indigenous Slavic population within the framework of a syncretism of two coexisting faiths (*dvoeverie*), a

[28] A. Müsseler, "Ärzte, heilige," in *Lexikon der christlichen Ikonographie* (henceforth *LChI*), vol. 5 (Rome–Freiburg–Basel–Vienna, 1973), 255–259.

[29] Vagner, *Problema* (see n. 22), 193ff. See also B. A. Uspenskij, *Poètika kompozicii* (Moscow, 1970); German ed. (Frankfurt am Main, 1975), chap. 7.

[30] E. Lucchesi Palli, "Georg," in *LChI* (see n. 28), vol. 6 (1974), 365–373; O. Loorits, *Der Heilige Georg in der russischen Volksüberlieferung Estlands* (Berlin, 1955); G. L. Malickij, *Sv. Georgij v oblike starca v russkoj narodnoj legende i skazke* (Moscow, 1915).

[31] K. Onasch, *Ikonen* (Berlin, 1961), 352–353; V. V. Filatov, "Rjazanskaja ikona 'Paraskeva-Pjatnica,'" in *Sovetskaja arxeologija* 1 (1971): 173–190; Ju. Lotman and B. Uspenskij, "Die Rolle dualistischer Modelle in der russischen Kultur," *Poetica* 9 (1977): 7–8.

number of patrons of field and cattle survived up to the nineteenth century.[32] Their frequently dialectical relationship with the dogmatic-ascetic notions of the Church finds its expression in the magnificent thirteenth-century icon, Evan (i.e., John Klimakos), George, and Blasius[33] (fig. 1). The distance between the patron saints George and Blasius, on the one hand, both associated with the harsh daily life of the North Russian peasants, and the tall figure of the Early Christian ascetic on the other hand, who reaches toward heaven and is removed from all earthly things—a distance that seems to contain a certain hidden irony—becomes somewhat clearer in its nonhagiographic subtext if we point to this ascetic figure's iconographic affinity with the Old Russian, or rather, Old Slavic *kumiry* (see, further, n. 35).

A very complex cryptogram must be deciphered in the representation of Saint Nicholas (Nikolaj, Nikola, Mikula, etc.).[34] It indicates that the worshiper in front of certain Nikola icons would not always identify with the Christian saint, or, at any rate, would not have his thoughts focused on the Christian alone.[35] This is evident from representations of the Deësis—one of the most important means of integration in the teaching of the Orthodox Church. In a Deësis icon of the sixteenth century, John the Forerunner is replaced by Nikola. In the upper space of a Pskov icon, the Nativity of the Mother of God from the first half of the fourteenth century, the Mother of God is not on the right of Christ, as usual,[36] but on his left, while her

[32] G. L. Malickij, *Drevnerusskie kul'ty sel'skoxozjajstvennyx svjatyx po pamjatnikam iskusstva* (Moscow, 1915); È. S. Smirnova, *Živopis' Obonež'ja* (Moscow, 1967); id., *Živopis' Velikogo Novgoroda* (see n. 27); M. A. Reformatskaja, *Severnye pis'ma* (Moscow, 1968).

[33] Smirnova, *Živopis' Velikogo Novgoroda* (see n. 27), 157–160. Cf. Onasch, *Ikonenmalerei* (see n. 9), 42ff, and Vagner, *Problema* (see n. 22), 188ff.

[34] B. A. Uspenskij, "Kul't Nikoly na Rusi v istoriko-kul'turnom osveščenii," *Semiotika kul'tury. Trudy po znakovym sistemam* 10 (Tartu, 1978), 86–140.

[35] The dialectic of the transfer of Old Slavic *numina* and their personifications into Christianity can perhaps be sufficiently defined by the notion of "adaptive antagonism"; in other words, their reception must always be viewed against a background of situational conflict. Thus, for example, the moral demands of Saint Parasceve-Pjatnica (cf. n. 31) are directed against the Old Slavic sexual freedom of women (see below, Dittrich). The *dvoeverie* is here matched by an ambiguity of the identifiers. This is shown by the icon in figure 1 where Klimakos very much resembles an Old Russian idol. From an aesthetic point of view, this has an ironic effect (as an expression of marking, in a superior fashion, the distance from the religious past?). For the religious data, see e.g., V. K. Sokolova, *Vesenne-letnie kalendarnye obrjady* (Moscow, 1979); B. A. Rybakov, "Jazyčeskoe mirovozrenie russkogo srednevekov'ja," *Voprosy istorii* 1 (1974); N. Gal'kovskij, *Bor'ba xristianstva s ostatkami jazyčestva v drevnej Rusi, Zapiski Moskovskogo arxeologičeskogo instituta* 18 (1913); Z. R. Dittrich, "Zur religiösen Ur- und Frühgeschichte der Slaven," *Jahrbücher für Geschichte Osteuropas* 9 (1961): 481–510.

[36] Regarding right and left on the icon, see Uspenskij (n. 9), Index under "Right" and "Left"; id., "'Left' and 'Right' in Icon Painting," *Semiotica* 13, no. 1.

Saints Evan (= Ivan, John), Georgij (George), and Vlasij (Blasius). Second half of thirteenth century, School of Novgorod; Russian State Museum, Leningrad. (From K. Onasch, *Icons*, 2nd ed. [New York, 1969], pl. 27, pp. 357–358.) Reprinted with permission.

Fig. 1

normal place is taken by Nikola[37] (fig. 2). And finally, in another Pskov icon, the Resurrection of Christ (Descent into Hell) from the fourteenth century,[38] Nikola occupies the place of Christ, with the Mother of God on his right and George on his left; this composition not only reminds us that Nicholas was assessed as a ὑπεράγιος already in Byzantine hagiography but it also recalls the Russian proverb: "Once God dies, let Saint Nikola be our God" (*Svjaty Mykolaj Bogom bude, jak Bog umre*).[39]

The rich ethnological-religious material cited by B. A. Uspenskij conveys an insight into the protective functions of such Christian saints as Nikola, Parasceve-Pjatnica, Vlasij, and the Archangel Michael. These functions pertain to the self-understanding, stability, and (as in the case of merchants)[40] the potential social organization of certain professional groups (peasants, fishermen, traders, housewives, and so forth). In addition, the saints perform life-related functions and aid in extreme situations (dying, emergency at sea for Nikola, protection of marriage for Parasceve-Pjatnica, and others).[41] Such spheres of activity and their patrons can be traced back to pre-Christian society: the equivalent functions can be found in the deities Perun, Mokoš, and Veles.

This points to the individual's and society's basic need for self-identification and to the necessity of establishing corresponding ideal images. Old Rus' also had nonecclesiastical ideals—for example, the heroes (*bogatyri*) performing their own tasks. The function of personal "identifiers" of the Church was to protect the medieval feudal state (doubtless in a sort of "iconic concordat") against regressive tendencies of pagan society (cf. the several uprisings of the *volxvy*),[42] as well as against dangerous influences

---

[37] For the following, see Uspenskij, "Kul't Nikoly" (n. 34), 87–88; Onasch, *Ikonen* (see n. 31), pl. 65.

[38] A. Ovčinnikov and N. Kišilov, *Živopis' drevnego Pskova* (Moscow, 1971), pl. 27.

[39] Uspenskij, "Kul't Nikoly" (see n. 34), 100ff.

[40] K. Onasch, *Gross-Nowgorod. Aufstieg und Niedergang einer russischen Stadtrepublik* (Leipzig–Vienna–Munich, 1969), 71ff. on the Church of Saint Parasceve-Pjatnica as the patron saint of the *zamorskie* and the Church of John the Forerunner as the patron of the Guild of Saint John with its commercial court in Novgorod.

[41] See also V. L. Janin, "Patronal'nye sjužety i atribucija drevnerusskix xudožestvennyx proizvedenij," in *Vizantija, Južnye Slavjane i Drevnjaja Rus'. Zapadnaja Evropa. Iskusstvo i kul'tura. Sbornik statej v čest' V. N. Lazareva* (Moscow, 1973), 267–271; Onasch, *Ikonen* (see n. 31), pl. 44, 366ff.

[42] *PVL, s. a.* 1024 and 1071. Whether the account *s. a.* 1071 points to Bogomil influences has not yet been definitely proven. See E. Hösch, *Orthodoxie und Häresie im alten Russland* (Wiesbaden, 1975), 54; id., "Zur Frage balkanischer Hintergründe altrussischer Häresien," *Saeculum* 27 (1976): 240. Here, as in other cases, a dualist world view blends with religious, partly non-Christian folklore, as was pointed out by Gal'kovskij (see n. 35). An example is the relationship between Nikola and the Archangel Michael, of Bogomil provenance, as has been

Roždestvo Bogorodicy, The Nativity of the Mother of God. Fourteenth century, School of Pskov; Collection Korin, Moscow. (From K. Onasch, *Icons*, 2nd ed. [New York, 1969], pl. 65, p. 374.) Reprinted with permission.

Fig. 2

coming from the dualist-defect models of society.[43] I shall return later to the culmination of this function and to its decline.

In the fourteenth century, one of the most impressive monuments of ecclesiastic teaching[44] came into existence—the iconostasis—(fig. 3). The structure alone, the thematic "programming" of this liturgical feature of architecture, which formed a functional unit with the iconic program of the whole church interior, not only made the Old Russian icon screen into a source of information but into a very important means of cognition as well. Because it included the sphere of human experience, it had the character of *cel'nost'* applicable to all facets of man's life.

The iconostasis, organized along both vertical and horizontal coordinates, is no less than a pictorial "Summa Theologiae" of the Eastern Church, an iconic representation of the conceptual-imperceptible cosmos, in line with the iconic theology of Byzantium. The theological edifice implicit in the full-fledged icon screen is focused on the *vertical.* It consists of the following icons, moving from top to bottom:[45] (1) the *Troica* as point of departure for the "economy of salvation" through the Holy Trinity; (2) the Mother of God of the Sign (*znamenie*) as the symbolic figure of the ongoing incarnation of the salvation process, below which is the festival tier (*prazdničnyj jarus*)[46] cutting through the *vertical* from one end to the other, as a pictorial manifestation of the Logos turned man. The *vertical* continues with (3) the Deësis (Christ in Judgment, with the Mother of God on his right and John the Forerunner on his left, both in the positin of intercession), which is central to the overall composition of the iconostasis.[47] Below the Deësis and above the Holy (or Royal) Gates is (4) the depiction of the Last Supper. On the Gates themselves are (5) the Annunci-

---

shown by Uspenskij ("Kul't Nikoly," 34, 93ff.): the Archangel Michael played an important part among the heretics.

[43] K. Onasch, "Zur Frage der Hierarchie in der Bogomilenkirche," in *Studien zum Menschenbild in Gnosis und Manichäismus*, ed. P. Nagel, (Halle [Saale], 1979), 211–222.

[44] On the iconostasis, see e.g., V. N. Lazarev, "Tri fragmenta raspisnyx epistilev i vizantijskij templon," *VV* 7 (1967): 161–196; L. V. Betin, "Ob arxitekturnoj kompozicii drevnerusskix vysokix ikonostasov" in *Drevnerusskoe iskusstvo* (Moscow, 1970), 29–56; id., "Istoričeskie osnovy drevnerusskogo vysokogo ikonostasa," ibid., 57–72; M. Chatzidakis, "Ikonostas," in *Reallexikon* (see n. 2), vol. 3: 326–353; P. Müsseler, "Ikonostasis," in *LChI* (see n. 28), vol. 6 (1974): 578–582.

[45] The iconostasis did not yet carry a *Troica* in its uppermost tier in the time of Rublev.

[46] The icons of the festival tier were removed beforehand ("recalled" as dogmatic information) and placed on a pulpit before the iconostasis. Their content could provide material for sermons. Such small-sized icons were referred to as *tabletki*; cf. V. N. Lazarev, *Dvustoronnie tabletki iz Sobora Sv. Sofii v Novgorode* (Moscow, 1977).

[47] J. Myslivec, "Proisxoždenie 'Deisusa,'" in *Vizantija* (see n. 41), 59–63; Th. v. Boggyay, "Deesis," in *Reallexikon* (see n. 2), vol. 1: 1178–1186.

General scheme of the Iconostasis.

Fig. 3

ation, above, and (6) either the four evangelists or the two liturgical Church Fathers, John Chrysostom and Basil. This vertical is supplemented by the following *horizontal* tiers: (1) the ancestors of Christ; (2) the prophets, usually beginning with David and Solomon; (3) the Mother of God and John, followed by the archangels, by Peter and Paul, the two liturgical fathers, and by other saints. All figures along the vertical are in the position of intercession. As a result, the concave silhouettes have an aesthetic effect that mellows the rigorous intellectual concentration of the central axis.

There is a close connection between church dogma and the pastoral intent of the icon screen's overall arrangement, an intent made manifest by the intercession. God's love for man, represented by the economy of salvation and the Incarnation, does not abandon us even in the face of Christ's Judgment. The central component is the Deësis; its above-mentioned iconographic modifications point to fluctuations (*šatanija*) in the faith within the ecclesiastical community, which is to say that it is no longer necessarily identical with the dogma. Thus, the Old Russian iconostasis, a highly developed identity model of religion, world view, and aesthetics, represents the total integrity or *cel'nost'* of a specific medieval group and the larger society of which it forms a part.

The basically pragmatic character of such models and their complex social interrelations suggest, however, that it was precisely the ideal character of the iconostasis that must be understood (in terms of feedback) as a reaction against certain events in the broader social context. The icon is not a self-contained monad; rather, because it represents a specific sign system based on convention, it is dependent on changes in conventional social behavior. This dialectic corresponds to the double character of the icon as a cult image, determined by tradition, and as an artistic work, naturally conditioned by shifting cultural motivations. Put differently, modifications and, even more so, innovations in the iconographic canon must be interpreted less as manifestations of artistic creativity, let alone spontaneity (given the strict rules applied to this art form by the Church), than as nervous reactions to particular provocations from outside the sphere of aesthetics. One finds examples of this not only in the high iconostasis as it emerged at the juncture of the fourteenth and fifteenth centuries but, above all, in the treatment of the theme of the Trinity in religious painting.

There is a characteristic nonartistic indicator for the intensified treatment of this central Christian theme in the period indicated: the increase in Trinity consecrations. While tenth-to-thirteenth-century Rus' only had eight or nine churches and monasteries of the Holy Trinity, there were twelve of them in the fourteenth, fifteen in the fifteenth, and thirty-four in the sixteenth century. Monasteries of the Holy Trinity were founded primarily in territories where nonconformist or even heretical movements appeared. [48] It is not by chance that among them was the Trinity-Sergius Monastery outside Moscow with its famous local icon, the *Troica* by Andrej Rublev.

Before turning to this most outstanding artwork of the Russian Late Middle Ages, however, I shall discuss another icon of the Trinity which, though less internationally famous than the *Troica*, better illustrates the problem at hand. The Fatherhood (*Otečestvo*) (fig. 4)[49] emerged toward the end of the fourteenth and the beginning of the fifteenth centuries in the Novgorod area and in the city of Novgorod itself.[50] The iconography of the *Otečestvo* depicts the anthropomorphic, rather than the angelomorphic, type of *Troica*. Composed in accordance with the structural type of the Mother of God with the Child on her lap, the *Otečestvo* represents the "within-each-other" model known in the East since the tenth and eleventh centuries. By contrast, the "next-to-each-other" or σύνθρονος type (in its oldest manifestations, however, in "binitarian" form) was becoming widespread around 830, primarily in France, concurrently with an increase in Trinity consecrations and masses, which was a reaction against Neo-Arian movements.[51]

Ever since the eleventh century—and during a "dark" period even earlier—this central Christian dogma had been the target of attack from dualistically oriented anti-Trinitarians who had nothing in common with classic Arianism: in the West, the Cathars, in the East, the Bogomils.[52] In

---

[48] K. Onasch, "Andrej Rublev: Byzantinisches Erbe in Russischer Gestalt," *Akten des XI. Internationalen Byzantinischen Kongresses, München, 1958* (Munich, 1960), 427–29; L. S. Retkovskaja, "O pojavlenii i razvitii kompozicii 'Otečestvo' v russkom iskusstve XIV–XVI vekov," in *Drevnerusskoe iskusstvo* (Moscow, 1963), 235–262 (esp. 250).

[49] Onasch, *Ikonen* (see n. 31), pl. 24.

[50] Retkovskaja, "O pojavlenii" (see n. 48); V. N. Lazarev, "Ob odnoj novgorodskoj ikone i eresi antitrinitariev," in id., *Russkaja srednevekovaja živopis'* (Moscow, 1970), 279–291; Smirnova, *Živopis' Velikogo Novgoroda* (see n. 27), 324–336; Vagner, *Problema* (see n. 22) 200; see also R. Hamann-MacLean, *Grundlegung zu einer Geschichte der mittelalterlichen Monumentalmalerei in Serbien und Makedonien*, vol. 2 (Giessen, 1976), 47–55, with heretofore virtually unnoticed data. As in the case of *pokrov* (see Belting-Ihm, "*Sub matris tutela*," n. 27), the legal implications should not be overlooked with regard to the *Otečestvo*; see A. Papadopoulos, "Essai d'interprétation du thème iconographique de la Paternité dans l'art byzantin," *Cahiers archéologiques* 18 (1968): 121–136.

[51] G. Schreiber, *Die Wochentage im Erlebnis der Ostkirche und des Christlichen Abendlandes* (Cologne–Opladen, 1959), 37–52 and Index under "Arianismus" and "Dreifaltigkeit."

[52] On the Cathars, see A. Borst, *Die Katharer* (Stuttgart, 1953); M. Loos, *Dualist Heresy in the Middle Ages* (Prague, 1974); J. Duvernoy, *Le Catharisme: La religion des Cathares* (Toulouse, 1976). Of the rich literature on the Bogomils, the following, in addition to Borst and Loos (see above) deserve particular mention: D. Angelov, *Bogomilstvoto v Bălgarija*, 3rd ed. (Sofia, 1969); D. Obolensky, *The Bogomils* (Cambridge, 1948); H.-Ch. Puech and A. Vaillant, *Le Traité contre les Bogomiles de Cosmas le Prêtre* (Paris, 1945).

Otečestvo, The Fatherhood. Fourteenth century, School of Novgorod; Tretyakov Gallery, Moscow (From K. Onasch, *Icons,* 2nd ed. [New York, 1969], pl. 24, pp. 355–356.) Reprinted with permission.

Fig. 4.

the thirteenth century, at the height of the controversy between the Catholic Church and the Cathars, the pictorial model subsequently (after Luther) called the Mercy Seat (*Gnadenstuhl*) came into being.[53] The representation of God the Father with the crucified Christ (or the Man of Sorrows) in his arms must have appeared to the dualist-Docetic heretics as an insult to their religious notions, as an assault on their self-identification. Their "identifier" was the Docetic incorporeal Christ in an impassible, unreal body, who therefore could not logically be depicted materially. The lack of a concrete image is, by the same token, reflected in the defective social order of these late Manichaean groups—in the deep gap, the social hiatus between the *electi* with their elitist hierarchy and rigorous conformist attitude, and the masses of the ordinary believers, entrusted only with subordinate tasks by the elite. The elite withheld the ultimate secrets of the heresy from the common believers, a heresy with which they alone could fully identify.[54]

Contrary to the angelomorphic type, the iconography of the *Otečestvo*, with only a minimum of aesthetic options, has a theological foundation: the Ancient of Days with his long white beard and hair (cf. Dan. 7:9ff.) holds the boyish Emmanuel on his lap (cf. Isa. 7:14; Matt. 1:23), who in turn holds a disk with a dark center, from which the Third Person of the Trinity flies in the form of a dove. In this, Emmanuel, the Second Person, signifies the preexistent Logos, distinct from the Father even before his Incarnation, while at the same time represented as of one being in and with the Ancient of Days. Yet God the Father, who cannot be represented, may only be perceived through his Son. For that reason, his halo, like Emmanuel's, shows a cross. In the evolutionary history of the two iconographic types, those of the Ancient of Days and of Emmanuel, there are stages of convergence (portraying Emmanuel as a young man with discernible beard) as well as differentiation (showing the Second Person beardless or as a boy), which ultimately prevails in the eleventh century. Emmanuel now remains youthful and beardless.[55]

This peculiar shifting relationship between Emmanuel and the Ancient of Days goes back to the literary topos of the "child/old man" (παιδάριον-γέρων, *puer-senex*) known already to Early Christian literature.[56] Its Gnostic-

---

[53] *LChI* (see n. 28), vol. 1: 535–536.

[54] See note 43.

[55] On the iconography of the Ancient of Days and Emmanuel, see Wessel, "Christusbild," in *Reallexicon* (see n. 2), vol. 1: 1008ff., 1029; Lucchesi Palli, *LChI* (see n. 28), vol. 1: 390ff., 394ff.

[56] Onasch, *Ikonenmalerei* (see n. 9), 161ff; id., "Ketzergeschichtliche Zusammenhänge bei der Entstehung des anthropomorphen Dreieinigkeitsbildes der byzantinisch-slavischen Orthodoxie," *ByzSl* 31 (1970): 229–243, esp. 233–236.

Docetic meaning is readily palpable. Thus, for example, the earthly Christ appears in the Acts of John at times as a rather bald man but with a full beard descending, and at other times as a downy-cheeked youth.[57] No wonder the Bogomils in the Balkans used these *topoi* for their dualistic-Docetic Christology.[58]

There can hardly be any doubt that the earliest, as yet binitarian, Eastern images of the Fatherhood must have been the institutional Church's response to provocation from the heretics. This is borne out by the fact that their first appearance as well as the formation of their definitive trinitarian model, including the Holy Spirit, falls into the period of the first anti-Bogomil writings (Kozma Presviter, between 969 and 972; Euthymios Zigabenos between 1081 and 1118) and an increased interest in the teachings of the heretics among the Byzantine intelligentsia. It is certainly conceivable that such images were used in sermons against the heretics for the purpose of reintegrating the latter into the Christian community. Instead of a "hypostase unique et changeante" with vague, sometimes pantheistic contours,[59] these images or icons graphically demonstrated both the unity of the Trinity and, by the same token, the distinctive features (ἰδιώματα) of the three Persons in their relation to one another (though not in their being).

One must not overlook the fact, however, that the issue of the intra-Trinitarian relationship played an important role during this same period in the controversy about the Latin *filioque* in Byzantium. The Greek formula, prevailing from the twelfth century onward, that the Holy Spirit proceeded only from the Father and not from the Son also (*filioque*), yet *per filium*

---

[57] Ibid., 235.

[58] Ibid., 232: "Zunächst sollen sie gelehrt haben, dass der 'himmlische Vater dreigestaltig sei und aus verschiedenen Personen bestehe' ... Sie glaubten, dass der Vater, mit dem sie den Sohn und den heiligen Geist vereinigten 'anthrōprosōpon' sei. Ihr Gott sei 'körperähnlich und ein Monstrum (sōmatoeidē tina kai teratomorphon Theon) und rein in der Idee existierend.' Dieser Sohn und Geist in sich vereinigende Vater habe sich von 5500–5533 der Weltära zu einem 'triprosōpon' aufgelöst, um danach wieder zu einem 'monoprosōpon' zu werden, obwohl wesenhaft 'asōmaton,' doch eben 'anthrōpomorphon,' d.h. der Inkarnation fähig"; 233: "Sie sagen, dass sie oftmals nicht nur im Traum, sondern auch im wachen Zustand *den Vater wie einen Greis mit langem Bart* (hos geronta bathygeneion) sähen, *den Sohn wie einen bärtigen Mann*, den heiligen Geist aber wie einen unbärtigen Jüngling" [emphasis mine—K.O.] following the account of Euthymios Zigabenos. Lazarev has expressed his agreement with my views, albeit with some hesitation; see now, with some additions, I. Dujčev, "Literatur und Kunst gegen 'Ariana Haeresis' in Südosteuropa," *Slovo* 25/26 (Festschrift J. Hamm) (1976) 203–211. I am currently preparing a longer study, "Iconography and the History of Heresy," in which I intend to develop the topic more fully, including some facets only briefly touched upon here.

[59] Puech and Vaillant, *Le Traité* (see n. 52), 179, 8.

(διὰ υἱοῦ),[60] was precisely what could find its anti-Latin defense in the Fatherhood motif, given the many contacts between East and West. However, the Fatherhood's early binitarian representations were of little interest in this context.

When the *Otečestvo* was painted in Novgorod, Bogomilism no longer constituted an immediate danger for church and state, even though its lasting traces still elicited reactions in religious folklore.[61] Nor was *filioque* the subject of heated disagreements among different Christian groups in a city where Latin sympathizers and the Orthodox with their respective church services had lived side by side for several generations. Moreover, it remains controversial to this day whether there existed any anti-Trinitarianism in Novgorod and in Russia in general during the period under consideration.[62] Thus, the transfer of the heretofore unknown pictorial motif to Russia from the South Slavic area must have occurred ad hoc. As an identity model, it can have been claimed by the official Church only for a specific situation which must have been similar to that prevailing in the Balkans. However, when attempting to verify this, one encounters virtually insurmountable difficulties, at least as regards the Novgorod *Otečestvo*. To begin with, the decipherment of the Trinitarian text does not cause any difficulties if one proceeds from the assumption that a Latin-type representation of God the Father, prohibited in the East, is to be interpreted in the Orthodox fashion.[63]

Information on the accessory figures seems equally important. The Stylites in the Early Christian-Syrian tradition, like the seraphim on the arms of the throne (see Isa. 6:2), were considered sentries at the Throne of the Trinity.[64] The figure in the lower right corner, presumably representing the patron saint of the sponsor, suggests two possible interpretations—both

---

[60] H.-G. Beck, *Kirche und theologische Literatur im byzantinischen Reich*, Munich, 1959; 2nd ed. 1977), Index under "Filioque."

[61] See n. 42.

[62] The existence of anti-Trinitarianism as early as the end of the fourteenth century is assumed by N. A. Kazakova, "Ideologija strigol'ničestva," *TODRL* 15 (1958): 116, and by Lazarev, "Ob odnoj novgorodskoj ikone" (see n. 50), 290ff.; A. I. Klibanov, *Reformacionnye dviženija v Rossii v XIV–pervoj polovine XVI vv.* (Moscow, 1960), 165, and now also the present writer take a critical attitude toward this view. See further, Hösch in his studies listed in n. 42. It should be mentioned that not all criticism leveled against the theological dogma in the narrow sense can be labeled anti-Trinitarianism.

[63] The fact that the type "Ancient of Days" is here denoted with *Oč'* (= Father) in the legend could be explained as being due to Western influence. The Orthodox painter immediately corrected this by means of the nimbus with a cross on it and the abbreviation "IC XC" (= Jesus Christ) on the shoulders of the Father-figure.

[64] Cf. Onasch, *Ikonen* (see n. 31), 356ff.

interesting. Whether seen as Thomas or Philip,[65] he appears in a New Testament passage (John 14) that played a great role in Byzantium. The composition of the *Otečestvo* corresponds to Christ's reply to Philip, in which the "within-each-other" type is unequivocally recorded in this Scripture (John 14:10; "Do you not believe that I am in the Father and the Father in me?"; cf. also John 1:18). Perhaps the verse, "He who has seen me, has seen the Father" (John 14:9) has some anti-Bogomil significance,[66] particularly in view of the Orthodox interpretation mentioned in note 63. Of considerable theological relevance, moreover, is verse 28, chapter 14 of the Gospel according to John: "the Father is greater than I," a passage that still occupied the minds of the Byzantines in the twelfth and even the thirteenth centuries.[67] Verse 26, where Christ says that the Father sends out the Holy Spirit in his name, must also have been taken into account. The theological considerations and controversies pertaining to the Trinity were also a part of Hesychasm,[68] which was known in Russia at the time that the Novgorod *Otečestvo* was painted.[69] Should the figure of the patron saint be Thomas,

---

[65] Thus O. I. Podobedova according to Smirnova, *Živopis' Velikogo Novgoroda* (see n. 27), 235.

[66] When the *strigol'niki* are accused of "lifting up their eyes from the ground to the sky, (there) calling God the Father (*ot zemli k vъzduxu zrjašče, boga otca sobe naricajušče*; N. A. Kazakova and Ja. S. Lur'e, *Antifeodal'nye eretičeskie dviženija na Rusi XIV–načala XVI veka* [Moscow–Leningrad, 1955], 254, cf. 66), this immediately recalls the viewing of the Bogomils, referred to in n. 58; neither case signals any particular anti-Trinitarianism. Our icon responds to this with the text of John 14:9.

[67] Beck, *Kirche und theologische Literatur* (see n. 60), 622–629.

[68] Cf. J. Meyendorff, *Introduction à l'étude de Grégoire Palamas* (Paris, 1959), 296, which characterizes the relationship between the three hypostases of the Trinity as "mutual penetration" ("compénétration," Gk. περιχώρησις) on the basis of common ἐνέργεια. This theological conception of Palamas, which he borrowed from John Damascene, no doubt finds its expression in the type of the anthropomorphic Trinity icon rather than that of the angelomorphic. On Palamas' theology of the Trinity, see Meyendorff, ibid., 300ff. Likewise, it is possible to establish a connection between our icon-type and Palamas' pneumatology, since he has the "exit" (Gk. ἐκπόρευσις) of the Holy Spirit occur from the Father "through the Son, and if he so wishes, from the Son" (ibid., 315). This theological statement can be better expressed in the icon of the Fatherhood of the Eastern type. Yet it is remarkable that this type developed at the same time that Hesychasm reached its intellectual maturity; in this context, the controversy concerning the *filioque* of the Western Church played an important role (ibid., 311–317). Also Iosif of Volokolamsk's Chalcedonian formula; "... sego radi edinogo boga ispovedati, a ne tri: ni bo otlučenni suť drug ot druga ... no vkupe otec i syn i svjatyj dux *drug v druze* neslitne i nerazdeľne vmeščajutsja" (because of this, one must confess one God, and not three: for they are not separated from each other; rather the Father, the Son and the Holy Spirit are contained *in each other* together, distinct and not divided; Retkovskaja, "O pojavlenii," [see n. 48], 246, emphasis by Retkovskaja) should be considered in assessing the *Otečestvo*.

[69] G. M. Proxorov, "Isixazm i obščestvennaja mysľ v Vostočnoj Evrope v XIV v.," *TODRL* 23 (1968): 86–109; id., *Povesť o Mitjae. Rus' i Vizantija v èpoxu Kulikovskoj bitvy* (Leningrad,

however, other equally intriguing associations suggest themselves—as when, in John 14:6, Christ tells Thomas that nobody comes to the Father but through Him. Along with John 14:26 ("the Holy Spirit, sent out by the Father, will teach everything"), this sentence can aid in reading our icon not only starting with the Father but also backwards, beginning with the Holy Spirit. The well-known role of Thomas in chapter 20 of the Gospel according to John, with its anti-Docetic orientation, suffices to single out this particular figure in the overall information function of the *Otečestvo*.

If the *Otečestvo* reflects the self-understanding of the official Church, that is, its identification with the central dogma of the Trinity (as represented here by the intra-Trinitarian relationship), it is much more difficult to find a specific addressee whose counteridentity is discernible. By the same token, it would be wrong, if only because of the control of the Church over one of its most important and efficient information media, to attribute this peculiar compositional schema, suddenly imported from the Balkans, to artistic ambitions or merely to preoccupation with the Trinity dogma within the Church itself. To be sure, the first anti-Trinitarian tendencies among the nonconformists can be ascertained only in the second half of the fifteenth century.[70] However, in this context, one must not disregard another consideration: the church hierarchy was a very sensitive organism, so that a violation of the ethical or dogmatic norm in one part of the structure could shake the whole. In his epistle to the Pskov congregation of 27 June 1427, Metropolitan Fotij links the names of Areios Makedonios, Nestorios, and Seuerios with anti-Trinitarian heresies for the first time.[71] In contrast to Iosif of Volokolamsk, he makes no reference to such deviations in Pskov. More clearly than in his earlier pastoral epistles or in the work of Stefan of Perm', Fotij expresses the view here that any doubt in the one God must have as its consequence the rejection of the clergy according to the Orthodox conception instituted by God, and vice versa.[72]

1978); J. Meyendorff, *Byzantine Hesychasm: Historical, Theological, and Social Problems. Collected Studies* (London, 1974).

[70] See the literature quoted in n. 62. For the sources of the anti-Trinitarianism of the Judaizers, cf. Kazakova and Lur'e, *Antifeodaľnye eretičeskie dviženija* (see n. 66). See also the comprehensive study by Th. M. Seebohm, *Ratio und Charisma. Ansätze und Ausbildung eines philosophischen und wissenschaftlichen Weltverständnisses im Moskauer Russland* (Bonn, 1977).

[71] Kazakova and Lur'e, *Antifeodaľnye eretičeskie dviženija* (see n. 66), 252.

[72] "... eže edinago boga delo bysť, to i velikomu bož'ju svjaščenstvu delo vručeno bysť, iže grexi čelovečʼskija praščati" (... any issue concerning the one God, was also an issue entrusted to the great God's priests, for whom it is to forgive the sins of man. Ibid.).

The famous *Troica* by Andrej Rublev (fig. 5) is also noteworthy in this context, given some of the characteristics of its composition.[73] Painted only a short time after the Novgorod *Otečestvo,* it depicts the angelomorphic type of the Trinity icon. Furthermore, Rublev has removed from the Philoxenia type (cf. Gen. 18) all epic and superfluous or redundant elements and has thus created a picture with extraordinary thought concentration, a "dogmatic telegram," as it were. Central to the picture is not only the intra-Trinitarian relationship of the three divine figures, as in the case of the *Otečestvo,* but also the process of salvation which the three agree upon in their "silent conversation." With the help of inverted perspective and circular composition,[74] the viewer looks into the depths of the triune Divinity as it sacrifices itself for mankind in the symbol of the Lamb. Here, in Christ's sacrificial death, according to the theologian of Hesychasm, Gregory Palamas, Trinity became "accessible à l'homme d'une façon immédiate, directe et intime," just as "concorporalité" is attainted in the Eucharist.[75] While the *Otečestvo,* despite its anthropomorphic schema, remained a more or less abstract "pictogram," the same does not apply to Rublev's angelomorphic icon, its "telegram" style notwithstanding.

If in this context we regard the *Troica* as dogmatic information, with due consideration to the pragmatic character of all such dogmatic information[76] and the mechanisms of feedback as part of its social function, the following can be noted:[77] the Trinitarian hagiographic stylization of Sergij of Radonež and the antiheretic writings of Stefan of Perm' and of Fotij suggest that the addressees of the *Troica* were the *strigol'niki* of early fifteenth-century Pskov who showed radical characteristics. It can be assumed that in Moscow these and other nonconformist or even heretical groups were known not only to Metropolitan Fotij but also to a number of other people. The sources show that while the *strigol'niki* did not, in fact, embrace dualist

---

[73] Onasch, *Ikonen* (see n. 31), pls. 99–102. For the following, see id., "Kunst und Gesellschaft im Modell der Dreieinigkeitsikone Andrej Rublevs," in *Beiträge zur byzantinischen und osteuropäischen Kunst des Mittelalters,* ed. H. L. Nickel (Berlin, 1977), 19–32.

[74] On the inverted perspective, cf. Uspensky, *Semiotics* (see n. 9), 62, fig. 2. On the circle schema, see A. A. Tic, "Nekotorye zakonomernosti kompozicii ikon Rubleva i ego školy," in *Drevnerusskoe iskusstvo* (Moscow, 1963), 22–53, esp. 49ff. H. Goltz, "Studien und Texte zur slavischen Kirchenvätertradition. Zur Tradition des Corpus Areopagiticum Slavicum," Theol. Diss. B (Halle [Saale], 1979), 78–118, publishes the work by Theodore Pediasimos, "Why nimbs should be painted above the heads of the saints" in the Old Russian original with German translation. The author cautions against drawing any hasty conclusions from such philosophical-theoretical writings regarding any relations between the Areopagites and Rublev.

[75] Cf. Meyendorff, *Grégoire Palamas* (see n. 68), 216, 225, 247.

[76] See n. 15.

[77] Extensive data in my article cited in n. 73.

Troica, The Trinity (also The Old Testament Trinity or The Hospitality of Abraham). Painted in 1411 by Andrej Rublev; Tretyakov Gallery, Moscow. (From K. Onasch, *Icons,* 2nd ed. [New York, 1969], pl. 98, p. 386.) Reprinted with permission.

Fig. 5

world view, they did combine a Donatist attitude with rigorous biblicism[78] and with the characteristic lay elements that emerged during the High Middle Ages; they thus vigorously protested against the clergy's exclusive claims to represent Christianity.[79] In terms of cumulative feedback aimed at destroying systemic stability,[80] they polemicized against the morally corrupt clergy's usurpation of the means of salvation through the Trinity, made manifest in the Eucharist. In view of what has been previously mentioned, this attitude implied a serious attack on one of the most important identity models of the church hierarchy, represented in the Eucharist and by the bishop (viewed as the imitator of Christ). The hierarchy of bishops therefore reacted with repressive measures. Rublev's *Troica* was a response to this provocation from the heretics. It shows Christ, as the Second Person of the Trinity, blessing his own sacrifice—represented by the bishop as the proper celebrant.

In transforming this message into art, Rublev shows himself as the sovereign artist that he was. The nonplacative and unapologetic nature of his art made the worshiper before his *Troica* identify himself as purified, enlightened anew through the grace of baptism, one body with Christ; the worshiper could thus find his own identity in front of this icon. The *Troica* was a classic example of what can be called the internalization of a dogma by a disciple in the process of identification. It may be proof of this view that in the controversy between Iosif of Volokolamsk and the anti-Trinitarian Judaizers, icons of the angelomorphic Trinity-type similar in composition to Rublev's *Troica* (though not that icon itself) were used to indict the heretics.[81]

---

[78] Cf. Seebohm, *Ratio und Charisma* (see n. 70), 170–179, with reference to the Waldensian hypothesis advanced by Popov. It still seems the most plausible to me as regards the early *strigol'niki*, except that they lacked the impulse of the poor wandering preachers. For a critical discussion of the Hussite hypothesis, see ibid., 184ff; also n. 79 below.

[79] J. Matthes, *Religion und Gesellschaft. Einführung in die Religionssoziologie*, 2nd ed. (Hamburg, 1969), 33–35, shows that the strengthening of the laity triggered the first criticism of religion.

[80] Onasch, "Kunst und Gesellschaft" (see n. 73), 31–32.

[81] Cf. Kazakova and Lur'e, *Antifeodal'nye eretičeskie dviženija* (see n. 66), 120. However, the *Troica* on the miniature there is not by Rublev. Still, this is not really important, since Iosif of Volokolamsk must have thought of the angelomorphic type when writing both his *Prosvetitel'* (see the account given by Seebohm, *Ratio und Charisma*) and his epistle to Vassian. But he must also have known the anthropomorphic type; see n. 68. It remains an open question whether Iosif's addressees were anti-Trinitarians as we know them one or two generations later, or whether they were representatives of the previously mentioned laity whose educated rationalism, as elsewhere in Europe, soon led to the crystallization of outspoken anti-Trinitarianism; see also n. 87 below. From the by now ample literature on Rublev's *Troica*, only the following titles will be mentioned here: V. N. Lazarev, "'Troica' Andreja Rubleva," in

It is interesting to note that both types of the Trinity were painted, and not only separately, but to an increasing degree, on one and the same object or building. This is true of two sacred linens associated with the Trinity-Sergius Monastery.[82] One, commissioned by Sophia Palaeologue, the spouse of Ivan III, was possibly designed to defend her Orthodoxy against her political adversary, Elena Vološanka, who was considered a heretic.[83] The other one, dated 1525 and commissioned by Vasilij III and his first wife Solomona Saburova, also displays both types of the Trinity, with God the Father carrying the additional inscription "Lord Sabaoth" (*Gospod' Savaof*). Incidentally, in 1526, Vasilij sent Solomona, who was infertile, to the Pokrov Monastery in Suzdaľ. In the middle of the sixteenth century, the main gates of the Trinity-Sergius Monastery were adorned with the angelomorphic and anthropomorphic types of the Trinity.[84] The sixteenth century had particular problems concerning the image of the Trinity as an identity model.

It is certainly not by chance that the crisis of the church hierarchy and its identity was connected with the two just-mentioned types of the Orthodox Trinity. This crisis began in the sixteenth century. Supplanting the earlier compositions, which were simple and had only a minimum of figures, were now representations with many figures, constituting complex theological pictorial synopses. Though prohibited by the *Stoglav* of 1551, they were patterned on the "Summa Theologiae Orthodoxae" of the iconostasis. The decipherment of their text—in contrast to that of the iconostasis—requires adequate theological knowledge.

A good example of this new art is the four-part icon of the Cathedral of the Annunciation in the Moscow Kremlin, painted in the mid-sixteenth century.[85] It exhibits the following four themes: "God rested on the seventh

---

id., *Russkaja srednevekovaja živopis'* (see n. 50), 292–299; id., *Andrej Rublev i ego škola* (Moscow, 1965); M. V. Alpatov, ed., *Andrej Rublev i ego škola* (Moscow, 1971); M. V. Alpatov, *Andrej Rublev* (Moscow, 1972); V. A. Plugin, *Mirovozzrenie Andreja Rubleva* (Moscow, 1974); N. A. Demina, *Andrej Rublev i xudožniki ego kruga* (Moscow, 1972); G. I. Vzdornov, "Novo-otkrytaja ikona 'Troicy' iz Troice-Sergievoj Lavry i 'Troica' Andreja Rubleva" in *Drevnerusskoe iskusstvo* (Moscow, 1970), 115–154 (important also for the history of the iconography of the Trinity motif); J. A. Lebedewa, *Andrei Rubljow und seine Zeitgenossen* (Dresden, 1962).

[82] Retkovskaja, "O pojavlenii," (see n. 48), 252–254; N. A. Majasova, *Drevnerusskoe šiťe* (Moscow, 1971), 21ff.

[83] Regarding the case of Elena Vološanka, see Hösch, *Orthodoxie* (see n. 42); Kazakova and Luŕe, *Antifeodaľnye eretičeskie dviženija* (see n. 66); and Seebohm, *Ratio und Charisma* (see n. 70), Index, with partly controversial views.

[84] Retkovskaja, "O pojavlenii" (see n. 48), 252.

[85] Ibid., 256ff.; N. E. Mneva, in *Istorija russkogo iskusstva*, vol. 3 (Moscow, 1955), 578–580 (German ed. [Dresden, 1959], 210–214).

day" (*Poči bog v den' seďmyj*); "the only-begotten Son" (*Edinrodnyj Syne*); "Come all and adore the trihypostatic God" (*Priidite ljudie triipostasnomu božestvu poklonimsja*); and "in the tomb according to the flesh" (*Vo grobe plotski*). Without entering into the details of this intellectually complex and concentrated pictorial synopsis, it should at least be pointed out that the general topic of salvation is treated markedly in the spirit of a Trinitarian theology, and it is not the angelomorphic but the anthropomorphic schema that is used in several variations. "God rested ..." shows God the Father holding Christ, hanging on the cross and covered by cherubim's wings—in other words, the previously mentioned Mercy Seat. The "only-begotten Son" shows God the Father in an aureole holding the nimbus containing the youthful Son seated on the cherubim throne. In "Come all ..." three beams emanate from God the Father (as in the Ancient of Days) toward the Annunciation, the Nativity, and the Baptism of Christ. "In the tomb ..." shows the binitarian "next-to-each-other" type known from the West, beneath the symbol of the Holy Spirit, the dove, in an octagonal star, behind the opened Gates of Paradise.

Such paintings demonstrate the significance of the icon's function as a factor of identification and stability, both for the church hierarchy and, at least in the sixteenth century, also for parts of society at large. The well-known protest of State Secretary Viskovatyj against the complexity of mul-tifigure compositions overburdened with many scenes,[86] as well as against the "sophistic Latin tradition" (*suemudroe latynskoe predanie*), which, as we have seen, is evident, suggests that a large group of Orthodox believers were disturbed by such pictures. As Viskovatyj combined personal Ortho-doxy with the lay self-assertiveness of the well-educated contemporary, his protest was also directed against the authoritarian attitude of the episco-pate in its dealings with the traditional iconography. The state secretary was forced to recant.

Although the church hierarchy was able to rebut Viskovatyj's attack, it could not stand up against the assault on this iconographic "innovation" expressed by Matvej Baškin and Feodosij Kosoj in their nonconformist, if

---

[86] In addition to Mneva, *Istorija* (see n. 85), see with regard to Viskovatyj's case, A. A. Zimin, *I. S. Peresvetov i ego sovremenniki* (Moscow, 1958), 170–172, 716–179; here the com-plex relations between Viskovatyj and the heretics, especially Baškin, are shown. Still impor-tant is N. Andreev, "O dele ďjaka Viskovatogo," *Seminarium Kondakovianum* 5 (1932): 191–242 (reprinted in *Studies in Muscovy: Western Influence and Byzantine Inheritance* [Lon-don, 1970], sec. 3, 47–98). Cf. Hösch, *Orthodoxie* (see n. 42), 140–142. Also valuable, not least because of its iconographic material, is F. I. Buslaev, "Dlja istorii russkoj živopisi XVI veka," in *Sočinenija*, vol. 2 (St. Petersburg, 1910), 286–343.

not outright heretical, views.[87] Feodosij in particular espoused anti-Trinitarian tenets, which were quite common at that time, along with an anti-
clerical stance. During the Synod of 1553–54, Baškin's and Feodosij's
deviant views, as well as Viskovatyj's protest (of early 1554) were dealt
with. Feodosij's critic, Zinovij of Oten', pointed out that anti-Trinitarianism
logically led to a rejection of the entire salvation process, of Christ's divinity, of Mary's everlasting virginity, and of the veneration of saints and
icons. Against this background, the four-part icon in the Cathedral of the
Annunciation in the Kremlin can be conceived of as the pictorial counter-
argument given by the Synod. The "emphasis on the nature of God as the
point of departure for the processes which take place within God" can be
considered the essence of Zinovij's Trinitarian teaching.[88]

Seen in this light, the use of the anthropomorphic type in this icon
becomes meaningful, since it is more appropriate for Trinitarian teaching
than the angelomorphic would be. Possibly, the Western Mercy Seat and
the "next-to-each-other" type of the Father may have seemed to Makarij
and the Synod like a useful loan from the Latin pictorial treasury, in view
of the anti-Trinitarian sentiments that infiltrated Russia from the West via
Poland-Lithuania. This would be in keeping with Zinovij's rather restrained
anti-Latin position. Yet, such a montage of heretofore unknown pictorial
elements must have been more difficult for the Orthodox believer to identify with in his faith. The consequences of the flaws of identification that
such compositions implied became apparent in Feodosij's and Viskovatyj's
conduct: people either ceased to identify with the dogma (as did Feodosij)
or they embraced conformity (the course chosen by Viskovatyj). Moreover,

[87] The annotated source material can be found in Zimin, *I. S. Peresvetov* (see n. 86). Cf.
further the studies by Klibanov, *Reformacionnye dviženija* (see n. 64) and Hösch, *Orthodoxie*
(n. 42), the respective Indexes; I. Smolitsch, *Russisches Mönchtum. Entstehung, Entwicklung und
Wesen* (Würzburg, 1953), 312–315. On Polish anti-Trinitarianism, see St. Kot, *Socianism in
Poland: The Social and Political Ideas of the Polish Antitrinitarians in the Sixteenth and Seventeenth Centuries*, 2nd ed. (Boston, 1957). On the personality of Budny, important (although to
different extents) for Kosoj and Artemij, see id., "Szymon Budny: Der grosse Häretiker
Litauens im 16. Jh.," in *Studien zur älteren Geschichte Osteuropas*, vol. 1 (Graz and Cologne,
1956), 63–118. On the history of anti-Trinitarianism in general, see particularly D. Cantimori,
Italienische Häretiker der Spätrenaissance (Basel, 1949); here chap. 34 is relevant, treating
Fausto Sozzini's activity in Transylvania and Poland. An example of the confrontation with
anti-Trinitarianisim in Poland-Lithuania can be found on an icon in the Cracow National
Museum, showing both types of the Trinity; see J. Kłosińska, *Ikony*, no. 1 (Cracow, 1973),
64–66.

[88] R. M. Mainka, *Zinovij von Oten', ein russischer Polemiker und Theologe der Mitte des 16.
Jhs.* (Rome, 1961), 191, 218; Andreev, "Inok Zinovij Oten'skij ob ikonopisanii i ikonopočitanii," *Seminarium Kondakovianum* 8 (1936): 259–278 (reprinted in *Studies in Muscovy* [see n.
86], sec. 6, 259–278).

Feodosij was only one of many anti-Trinitarians in Russia—one who had attracted attention—as can be seen from the interlocutors of Zinovij.

Metropolitan Makarij's "cybernetic" control of such an important identity model as icon painting affected both the clergy and the late feudal society at large, which was associated with it by many militant interests partly held in common.[89] This informational sphere of the Church, extending to all of society, had to change once the relationship between church and state was radically modified. The division of the realm into *Zemščina* and *Opričnina*, the fall of Metropolitan Filip, and other events during the time of Ivan IV show that the change had gradually started already in Ivan's reign.

The seventeenth-century believer's relationship to the icon and the image in general was marked by strong ambivalences. For the wealth and ever more politically influential merchant class of the cities, images now constituted a sort of "comfort for the soul," a feature that one can note in the Western motifs found in the frescoes of churches in Moscow, Jaroslavl', Vologda, and elsewhere, This feature of "comfort" also applies to the small icons painted in the exquisite miniature technique of the so-called Stroganov School, which signaled a religious intimacy previously unknown in this form. While this closeness, spiritual as well as social, had its own tradition—thinking of Silvestr's sixteenth-century *Domostroj* viewed against the background of the artist's workshop—in the seventeenth century, such precious icons increasingly assumed the function of status symbols.

At the same time, among broad segments of the population who could not afford the valuable Stroganov icons, the demand for cheap icons grew. As a result, the quality of icons diminished, and they now became a mass product and hence a mere devotional souvenir. Parallel to this and contrary to the directives of the Oružejnaja Palata and the Office of Icons of the Holy Synod, there developed in the painters' villages of Ivanovo, Palex, and Xoluj an independent and self-conscious painting activity whose

---

[89] Cf. 1 Cor. 12:28. For κυβέρνησις and κυβερνήτης in patristic literature, see G. W. H. Lampe, *A Patristic Greek Lexicon*, vol. 1, no. 2 (Oxford, 1964), 784. On episcopal "cybernetics" concerning icons, see Onasch, *Ikonenmalerei* (see n. 9), 125. For a comprehensive presentation of sixteenth-century icon painting, with due consideration given to contemporary heresies and societal problems, including the case of Viskovatyj, see O. I. Podobedova, *Moskovskaja škola živopisi pri Ivane IV. Raboty v moskovskom Kremle 40-x – 70-x godov XVI v.* (Moscow, 1972). See also L. Uspenskij, "Rol' moskovskix soborov XVI v. v cerkovnom iskusstve," in *Vestnik Russkogo Zapadnoevropejskogo Patriaršego Ėkzarxata* 64 (Oct.–Dec. 1968): 217–250; id., "Bol'šoj moskovskij sobor i obraz Boga-Otca," ibid. (Apr.–Sept., 1972): 78–79. On Makarij, see Andreev, "Mitropolit Makarij kak dejatel' religioznogo iskusstva," *Seminarium Kondakovianum* 7 (1935): 227–244 (reprinted in *Studies in Muscovy* [see n. 86], sec. 4, 227–244) and id., "Ioann Groznyj i ikonopis' XVI veka," *Seminarium Kondakovianum* 10 (1938): 185–200 (reprinted in *Studies in Muscovy* [see n. 86], sec. 5, 185–200).

multifigured icons, crowded with scenes, are now among the most costly examples of this ancient art form in its final phase. The joy of epic breadth, the close realistic detail, and the emotional scenery, particularly in the *klejma*, betray the painter's intimate knowledge of his subject matter—a form of artistic intimacy always and everywhere characteristic of popular art. In this context belong also the printed icons and the well-known popular picture sheets with religious themes (*lubki*), in which the populace easily recognized its everyday worries, needs, longings, and difficulties. Long before them, the unusually attractive *severnye pis'ma*, original, variegated, and close to everyday life, had displayed a kind of primitive realism, so that the North Russian peasants, fishermen, and seafarers could find in them the miracles of their daily toil as well as those of their nature-bound holidays. By contrast, the world of the icons, removed from reality as it was, only seemingly coincided with this everyday world.

As the icon becomes more intimate, we feel, at the same time, an increasing spiritual distance from it; initially, at least, this distance must not be mistaken for estrangement. The icon's function of portrayal developed into the iconlike portrait—the independent artistic sphere that primarily served to depict and identify high church dignitaries and the tsar and his family and soon turned into full-fledged oil painting. Icon painting was only one of several subjects taught at the remarkable art institute in the workshops of the Oružejnaja Palata of the Moscow Kremlin. In this all-Russian art academy, Western motifs were represented, as were Western aesthetic views and concepts, which led to a reorientation of the classical Byzantine iconic theology and a modification of the iconographic canon. In this functional framework of depiction, the previously mentioned "iconic concordat" between church and state remained in effect, as illustrated by the well-known large icon *Bogomater' Vladimirskaja "Nasaždenie Dreva Rossijskago Gosudarstva"* by Simon Ušakov from 1668.[90] Peter I, together with Catherine and a high prelate (Feofan Prokopovič? Stefan Javorskij?) is shown under the *pokrov* of the Mother of God in a Baroque Ukrainian icon from as late as the eighteenth century.[91] But it was Peter who cancelled this concordat by abolishing the separate *Ikonnij Prikaz* of the Oružejnaja Palata and subordinating its functions to the Most Holy Governing Synod, the new collective church leadership that had replaced the Patriarchate. This made the separation of ecclesiastic and secular painting definitive.

It is characteristic that a parallel development can be found in the second most important means of conveying Christian teaching: the ecclesiastic

---

[90] Onasch, *Ikonen* (see n. 31), pl. 133, 402ff.

[91] I. Grabar', ed., *Istorija russkogo iskusstva*, vol. 6 (Moscow, n.d.), 473, 475ff.

chant. As was mentioned above, structurally it was closely connected with pictorial representation. Such a complex phenomenon as *xomonija*—the artificial vocalization of formerly reduced vowels in chant—shows clearly that the text and melody of a hymn were not considered sacrosanct. Rather, the hymn was regarded as a historically developed form, which could therefore be considered from a critical point of view. As early as the sixteenth century, attempts were made in Novgorod to supplement the classical system of neumes—which functioned remarkably well but always remained only approximative—with a notation indicating absolute tones. The next step was to replace the old Byzantine-Slavic cheironomic notational system of neumes by linear notation, which itself replaced homophony with the polyphony of the *partesnoe penie*. This somewhat progressive evolution was considerably furthered by the brotherhoods (*bratstsva*) in the Ukraine and Belorussia, with their strong lay component. As was the case in icon painting, a separation between the Moscow synodal choir (succeeding the *patriaršie pevčie ďjaki* after the abolition of the patriarchate in 1721) and the *gosudarevi pevčie ďjaki* (subsequently the *Peterburgskaja pridvornaja pevčeskaja kapella*) occurred here, too.

However, the Church experienced its deepest identity crisis in the schism of the Old Believers (*staroobrjadci*) in the seventeenth century. This is not the place to discuss its origin, which was motivated not only by the evolution of piety but also by canonistic considerations. The confrontation between the Church and the followers of the archpriest Avvakum took place, to a large extent, in the realm of painting and chant. Likewise, the genre of classic hagiography suffered a major crisis as a result of Avvakum's autobiography. The new mode of painting, in the minds of many, had violated the hitherto prevalent analogous identity structure of *podobie* (ὁμοίωσις, cf.k Gen. 1:26), the resemblance between man and God the Creator. This can be seen from the quotation cited in this essay's epigraph, from the pamphlet of Iosif Vladimirov, who represented this style against Pleškovič, the defender of the old, conservative art. Many could no longer identify with, or see their faith confirmed in, the icons of the new school.

Conversely, large groups of society could no longer understand the language of the ancient icon painting. With its decline, one of the basic prerequisites of medieval sacred art had been given up—its ubiquity—that is to say, its teaching, which had been understood everywhere within its informational sphere and by all parts of the church hierarchy and by society at large. Likewise, the historical "ubiquity," the continuity of tradition, was eliminated when the Synod of 1666-67 annuled the *Stoglav* of 1551. This annulment rendered directives regarding icon painting immaterial, to the extent that they had not been already weakened by Makarij. As the archpriest Avvakum stated: "Old Rus' no longer exists."

The epoch of Old Russian icon painting and sacred art in general, with its impressive achievements, only touched upon here, long ago became history. What has remained is an aesthetic-ethic model of a multifaceted art which can inspire in more ways than one beyond its immediate religious motivation.

THE CHURCHES OF NOVGOROD:
THE OVERALL PATTERN

NIKOLAI DEJEVSKY

For nearly five centuries, from the early eleventh to the fifteenth centuries, Novgorod was the most consistent and prolific center of culture in medieval Russia. The men of Novgorod left a lasting mark on every form of culture, from various genres of literature to painting and applied arts and crafts. A surprisingly large number of these works have survived, scattered mostly in museums and libraries outside Novgorod itself. The modern city of Novgorod does retain one type of cultural monument, however, which could not, as all others, be removed from the city or transferred from the exact place where medieval man created it. These are the medieval churches of Novgorod, more than forty of which still stand in the city and its immediate environs: many more are known from written sources, and the remains of a fair number have been located through archaeological excavation. The surviving churches provide a veritable inventory of builders' craft and architectural style: they show that medieval Novgorod was a leading center of Russian ecclesiastical architecture, which flowered there as fully as any other form of high culture.

The churches of Novgorod have been studied extensively since the middle of the nineteenth century. Successive generations of Russian and Soviet scholars have investigated these buildings, producing a voluminous body of published scholarship, largely in the form of articles in various specialized journals and series.[1] Unfortunately, most of these works are

[1] See particularly Archimandrite Makarij, *Arxeologičeskoe opisanie cerkovnyx drevnostej v Novgorode*, pt. 1 (Moscow, 1860); D. Prozorovskij, *Novgorod i Pskov po letopisnym dannym, Zapiski otdelenija russkoj i slavjanskoj arxeologii russkogo arxeologičeskogo obščestva* 4 (1887); various articles by P. L. Gusev published in the *Vestnik arxeologii i istorii*, St. Petersburg, at the turn of the century, particularly 1900–1903; M. K. Karger's many articles in *Sovetskaja arxeologija* and *Kratkie soobščenija Instituta istorii materiaľnoj kuľtury* (later ... *Instituta arxeologii*) from the 1950s to the 1970s and his *Novgorod Velikij* (Leningrad-Moscow, 1961, and many subsequent editions), the single comprehensive, if general, survey of Novgorodian architecture; V. M. Štender's many articles in the last-named two journals since the 1960s and in the serials *Drevnerusskoe iskusstvo* and *Pamjatniki kuľtury. Novye otkrytija* since the 1970s; and V. L. Janin's articles in various journals and collections during the 1970s, the most impor-

quite specialized. Architectural historians have devoted separate studies, largely stylistic or techincal, to individual churches; archaeologists have written at length about excavating particular ruins, often concentrating overmuch on the minutiae of their digs; and art historians have dwelt on frescoes, with scant regard for how these were arranged to suit worship in the church for which they were commissioned. Neither the architectural historian, nor the archaeologist, nor the art historian has looked much beyond his own discipline or individual buildings at the overall pattern of Novgorod's churches. Indeed, only recently have some attempts been made to explore the social significance of Novgorod's ecclesiastical topography; regrettably, none has considered the same pattern as material for the history of religion and worship. In recent decades, S. N. Orlov has produced a number of ambitious mappings of Novgorod's medieval churches, which include both extant churches and those whose existence or location have been confirmed through cartography or excavation.[2] Orlov's maps, useful as they are in the absence of others, suffer from being strictly cumulative, rather than historical in purpose. All known churches are plotted there, but no chronological, stylistic, or historical differentiation is made between them, nor are any unifying generalizations or inferences drawn. Extensive mappings are indeed the way to tap the full potential of ecclesiastical topography for cultural history, but to be meaningful they must be both specific and controlled. The present study is a first attempt of this kind.

My purpose has been to map all the churches built in Novgorod during the eleventh and twelfth centuries and to consider how this pattern helps to understand the city's early development.[3] The period chosen is important for being the formative one in Novgorod's history; by the end of the twelfth

---

tant being reprinted in his *Očerki kompleksnogo istočnikovedenija* (Moscow, 1977). The following journals are most important for articles concerning Novgorodian architecture: the prerevolutionary ones are *Vestnik arxeologii i istorii* (St. Petersburg), *Sbornik Novgorodskogo obščestva ljubitelej drevnosti*, and *Trudy Novgorodskogo cerkovno-arxeologičeskogo obščestva*; the Soviet ones are *Novgorodskij istoričeskij sbornik*, *Sovetskaja arxeologija*, *Kratkie soobščenija Instituta arxeologii* (formerly ... *Instituta istorii material'noj kul'tury*), and *Arxitekturnoe nasledstvo*.

[2] S. N. Orlov, "K topografii Novgoroda X–XVI vv.," *Novgorod, k 1100–letiju goroda* (Moscow, 1964), 264–285; id., "K topografii istoričeskix kamennyx zdanij drevnego Novgoroda," *Učenye zapiski Novgorodskogo pedagogičeskogo instituta* 1, no. 1 (1965): 53–71; id., "Topografija Novgoroda X–XII vekov," *Problemy arxeologii* 2 (festschrift for M. I. Artomonov) (Leningrad, 1978), 194–200.

[3] This study is a reworking of chapter 2 of my doctoral thesis, "Novgorod in the Early Middle Ages: The Rise and Growth of an Urban Community" (Oxford, 1977). For my earlier observations on the same theme, see "Novgorod: The Origins of a Russian Town," *European Towns: Their Archaeology and Early History*, ed. M. W. Barley (London, 1977), 391–403.

century the city had attained political and ecclesiastical autonomy from Rus', a status it was to enjoy until the late fifteenth century, and the built-up urban body of the city had taken its lasting shape. It is perhaps useful to summarize these landmarks in Novgorod's early history before turning to the churches of the time.

Novgorod is now believed to have begun when three closely neighboring settlements united into a single community towards the end of the tenth century.[4] One of these settlements grew into the Slavenskij *konec* (borough) by Novgorod's market place on the Torgovaja *storona* of the river Volxov (fig. 1). The other two gave rise to the Nerevskij and Ljudin *koncy* on the opposite Sofijskaja *storona* of the river. Between the latter two *koncy,* the citadel of Novgorod, commonly callead the *Detinec,* appeared at the end of the tenth century. The citadel served as the town's hub, connecting directly with the two *koncy* on the left bank and commanding the bridge that linked the Sofijskaja *storona* with the market place and the Slavenskij *konec* on the right bank. By the late twelfth century, the new Plotnickij *konec* took shape on the northern edge of the Slavenskij, and within a half-century the Zagorodskij *konec* appeared inland of the citadel, adjoining both the Nerevskij and Ljudin *koncy.* The built-up urban mass of Novgorod thus merged into a circular conglomerate bisected neatly by the Volxov. By the late fourteenth or early fifteenth century, a single town wall was completed, encircling fully the continuous urban body formed by the five *koncy.*

Until the 1120s Novgorod remained a politically integral, if far-removed, part of the Kievan state: the princedom of Novgorod was indeed the second most important Rurikid seat after the grand princedom in Kiev itself. From the 1130s onward, however, princely authority diminished sharply in Novgorod, largely as a result of the growing feud between the Mstislaviči, Oľgoviči, and Rostislaviči—which affected the Novgorod seat directly. Simultaneously, Novgorod's indigenous local officials (especially the *posad-niki,* or mayors, but also the *tysjackie* and *sotskie*) rose to prominence in the city's government. These officials functioned in close concert with the city's *veče* apparatus, a many-tiered system of administrative assemblies extending from small ones representing single streets to *konec* assemblies and finally to the central city assembly. This complex system of representative city government, which was to remain unaltered through Novgorod's independence, was functioning with reasonable efficiency and predictability by the mid-twelfth century. It allowed the Novgorodians to pick and

    [4] V. L. Janin and M. K. Aleškovskij, "Proisxoždenie Novgoroda. K postanovke voprosa," *Istorija SSSR,* 1971, no. 2: 32–61; V. L. Janin, "Vozmožnosti arxeologii v izučenii drevnego Novgoroda," in his *Očerki kompleksnogo istočnikovedenija* (Moscow, 1977), 213–229.

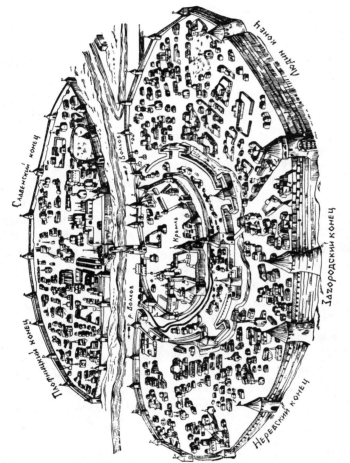

Fig. 1

Pictorial plan of Old Novgorod as shown on a late seventeenth-century Icon of the Sign

choose which princes they wanted and thus limited the real authority of the latter essentially to that of an appointed military governor. Similarly, the *veče* system was also central to the selection of Novgorod's prelates (bishops until the mid-century and archbishops from 1167 on) from the middle of the twelfth century and of the town's archimandrite, who presided over Novgorod's many abbots.[5]

Thus, by the end of the twelfth century both Novgorod's urban body and administrative structure had taken the form they would retain during the city's entire period of independence. Bearing this in mind, one can appreciate why it is so important to map the development of Novgorod's ecclesiastical topography during the formative eleventh and twelfth centuries. This exercise will reveal much about social, economic, and religious changes during this period.

Novgorod's architectural history before the twelfth century is sketchy indeed. The city's greatest and most venerated church, the Cathedral of Saint Sophia, was built between 1045 and 1050; it was erected within the citadel as soon as that fortified district was expanded in 1044 (fig. 2).[6] This cathedral must certainly have replaced an earlier one: indeed, a late source claims that the original cathedral was erected in 989, when Novgorod was supposedly baptized.[7] The location of that first cathedral is controversial, but it most probably was very near to the surviving eleventh-century one. The same late source declares that a stone church dedicated to Saints Joachim and Anna was already standing near the cathedral when the later one was going up in the 1040s. An eighteenth-century source cited by a nineteenth-century local historian mentions three churches supposedly built in the *koncy* in 1092,[8] but there is no mention of this in medieval sources, nor have archaeological excavations corroborated the claim. Thus, only the cathedral of Saint Sophia is definitely known to have stood in

---

[5] On Novgorod's system of government, see V. L. Janin, *Novgorodskie posadniki* (Moscow, 1962), and his "Problemy social'noj organizacii Novgorodskoj respubliki," *Istorija SSSR,* 1970, no. 1: 44–54; and *Očerki kompleksnogo istočnikovedenija* (see n. 4).

[6] This and all following dated information will be found in the corresponding annual entries of the Novgorod First Chronicle (*Novgorodskaja pervaja letopis'*, ed. A. N. Nasonov [Moscow-Leningrad, 1950]), unless otherwise footnoted. Information on the extant and some excavated churches is at present most conveniently assembled in Karger's *Novgorod Velikij*, but this will soon be superseded by G. M. Štender and A. I. Komeč's forthcoming substantial study of Novgorod's architecture.

[7] The Novgorod Second Chronicle in *Novgorodskie letopisi*, ed. A. F. Byčkov (St. Petersburg, 1879), 2.

[8] Makarij, *Arxeologičeskoe opisanie* (see n. 1), 181, 186f, 550–551.

Fig. 2

Plan of the Novgorod Citadel (Detinec)

1. Cathedral of Saint Sophia
2. Saint Sophia bell cot
3. "Little house by the bell cot"
4. Palace of Facets
5. Bell tower
6. Archbishop's Palace
7. Lixud Seminary
8. Metropolitan's Chambers
9. Nikita Chambers
10. Millennium Monument
11. Chancery (Public Administration) building
12. Church of Saint Andrew Stratilates
13. Church of the Intercession
14. Church of the Entry into Jerusalem
15. Palace Tower
16. Savior Tower
17. Prince's Tower
18. Kukuj Tower
19. Intercession Tower
20. Saint John Chrysostom Tower
21. Metropolitan Tower
22. Theodore Tower
23. Vladimir Tower

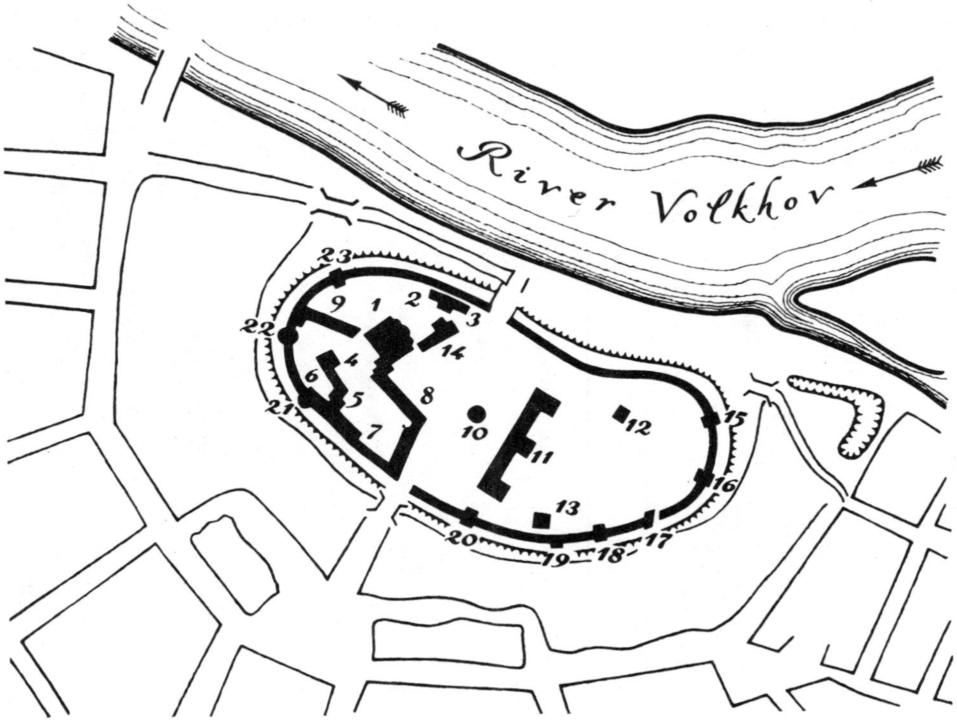

eleventh-century Novgorod, and it seems likely that the smaller Church of Saints Joachim and Anna stood nearby, both sheltered within the citadel. The first years of the twelfth century gave notice of how prolific the century would be in terms of church building in Novgorod. In 1103 a large stone church dedicated to the Assumption was completed at Gorodišče, the princely suburban residence situated just three kilometers south of the city on the Volxov (fig. 3). By 1105 a church dedicated to Saint Elijah (Il'ja) was standing on the northern periphery of the Slavenskij *konec* (fig. 4). Another one, dedicated to John the Baptist, was standing on the edge of the market place in the same *konec* in 1108.[9] In 1113 the great stone Church of Saint Nicholas, the second largest in Novgorod after the Sophia, was completed, also adjacent to the market. A new church dedicated to Saint Theodore the Tyro was completed in 1115 just north of the Slavenskij *konec*. The first of Novgorod's suburban monasteries, the Antonov (named after its enigmatic founder Antonij Rimljanin), dedicated to the Nativity of the Virgin, was established in 1117; it was situated about two kilometers north of the market on the Torgovaja *storona*.[10] The other great suburban monastery, the Jur'evskij, dedicated to Saint George, was founded in 1119 some four kilometers south of Novgorod where the river Volxov flows from Lake Il'men'.

The ecclesiastical topography of Novgorod that developed over the first quarter of the twelfth century is distinctive. All the churches known to have been built within the town during this period appeared in the Slavenskij *konec* on the Torgovaja *storona*. Two churches, those of c. 1108 and 1113, directly adjoined the market place and were commissioned by great patrons: the former was built by Bishop Nikita and the latter by Mstislav Vladimirovič, then prince of Novgorod. The lesser churches on the *konec* periphery were probably both private foundations: that of 1115 was commissioned by a certain Vojgost, who was neither prince nor prelate, while the anonymous builder of the 1105 church must have been of similar station. The fact that both prince and bishop chose to build major churches by the market indicates that this was Novgorod's social center at the time. By the same token it may be supposed that Vojgost and the unknown builder of c. 1105 were both natives of the Slavenskij *konec* and had

[9] Janin, *Novgorodskie posadniki* (see n. 5), 88–89f.

[10] On Antonij and his *žitie*, see V. Ključevskij, *Drevnerusskie žitija svjatyx kak istoričeskij istočnik* (Moscow, 1971), 306–311; K. Onasch, "Zur Vita Antonijs 'des Römers,'" *Orbis Scriptus* (festschrift for D. Tschižewskij) (Munich, 1966), 581–585; A. A. Vasil'ev, *The Goths in Crimea* (Cambridge, Mass., 1936), 137–138; and M. N. Tixomirov, "O častnyx aktax v drevnej Rusi," *Istoričeskie zapiski* 17 (1945): 238-239.

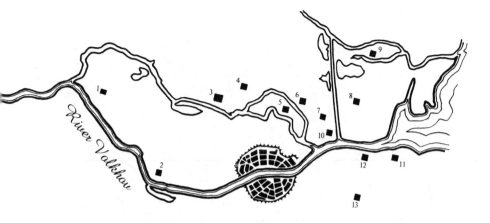

Fig. 3

Plan of the environs of Novgorod

1. Xutynskij Monastery of the Transfiguration
2. Derevjanickij Monastery
3. Church of the Assumption on Volotovo Field
4. Church of Our Savior in Kovalevo
5. Monastery of Saint Cyril
6. Church of Saint Andrew in Siteckij Monastery
7. Church of Our Savior on Neredica Hill
8. Church of Saint Michael in Skovorodksij Monastery
9. Church of Saint Nicholas in Lipno
10. Church of the Annunciation in Gorodišče
11. Church in Peryn Monastery
12. Jur'evskij Monastery
13. Church of the Annunciation at Arkaži
14. Syrkov Monastery
15. Vjažišče Monastery

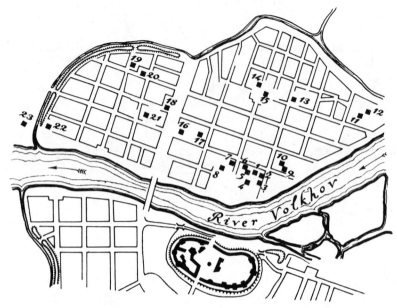

Fig. 4

Plan of Market Side (Torgovaja storona)

1. Church of Saint Nicholas in Yaroslav's Court
2. Church of Saint Procopius
3. Church of the Myrrhophores
4. Gatehouse of the Trading Mart
5. Church of Saint Parasceve-Pjatnica in Market Square
6. Church of the Dormition (Assumption) in Market Square
7. Church of Saint George in Market Square
8. Church of Saint John the Baptist in Opoki (in Market Square)
9. Church of Saint Michael on Mixajlova Street
10. Church of the Annunciation in Vitkov Lane
11. Church of Saint Elijah in Slavno
12. Church of Saints Peter and Paul in Slavno
13. Church of the Apostle Philip on Nutnaja Street
14. Church of Our Savior on Elijah Street
15. Cathedral of the Virgin of the Sign
16. Church of Saint Demetrios of Salonika on Slavkova Street
17. Church of Saint Clement on Ivorova Street
18. Church of Saint Theodore the Tyro
19. Church of the Nativity of the Virgin in Mixalica
20. Church of the Assembly of the Virgin
21. Church of Saint Nicetas (Nikita)
22. Church of Saints Boris and Gleb in Plotniki
23. Church of Saint John the Theologian in Radokovici

probably amassed the wealth necessary to build churches from market activity. The two great monasteries of 1117 and 1119 can also be seen as indirect indicators of the importance of trade for Novgorod at that time. Both monasteries were situated on the Volxov's bank, and both likely served as fortified strongholds commanding the river's southern and northern approaches to Novgorod. These pious foundations must certainly have played a vital role in safeguarding the water highway on which the city's market depended. Medieval Russian monasteries are generally known to have served as strategic fortresses, even when they were simultaneously renowned centers of learning and worship.

The second quarter of the twelfth century saw the pattern of church building in Novgorod change gradually. Initially, building was concentrated, as previously, in the market place. In 1127 the church of John the Baptist was rebuilt in stone by Prince Vsevolod Mstislavič of Novgorod.[11] In 1133 the same prince founded two new wooden churches by the market: one was dedicated to Saint George and the other to the Dormition. Vsevolod had the latter church rebuilt in stone soon thereafter; this construction was prolonged, lasting from 1135 to 1144. This record of church building permits us to acknowledge in Prince Vsevolod the first dedicated patron of church building in Novgorod known from surviving records. His churches were all by the market, and this seems to indicate that the princes of Novgorod were just as much involved with trading as were the townsmen themselves.

The 1130s yield the earliest evidence of church building on the Sofijskaja *storona* outside the citadel (fig. 5). A certain Irožnet, probably a boyar or a merchant, built a church dedicated to Saint Nicholas in the Nerevskij *konec* during 1135–36. Also in 1136 we find first mention of the already existing Monastery of the Resurrection, located just south of the Ljudin *konec*. The Nunnery of Saint Barbara within the same *konec* is likewise mentioned as existing in 1138.

The 1140s witnessed a great multiplication of churches on the Sofijskaja *storona*. In 1146 the wooden Church of Saints Boris and Gleb was built in the citadel, and another dedicated to Saints Cosmas and Damian was erected in the Nerevskij *konec*. In 1148 we find first mention of the Church of the Image Not Made by Hands standing just south of the citadel in the Ljudin *konec*. A similar first mention dated 1148 records the existence of

---

[11] This later became the patronal church and headquarters of the *Ivanovo sto* merchant guild, the best-studied of Novgorod's guilds. See A. I. Nikitskij, *Istorija èkonomičeskogo byta Velikogo Novgoroda* (St. Petersburg, 1893), 17–20, and N. L. Podvigina, *Očerki social'no-èkonomičeskoj i političeskoj istorii Novgoroda Velikogo v XII–XIII vv.* (Moscow, 1976), 97–99.

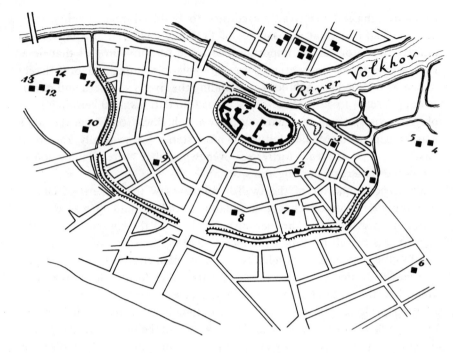

Fig. 5

Plan of the Sophia Side (Sofijskaja storona)

1. White Tower
2. Church of Saint Blasius on Volosova Street
3. Church of the Holy Trinity on Redjatina Street
4. Church of the Persuasion of Thomas
5. Church of Saint John the Almsgiver
6. Church of Saints Peter and Paul on Sinič'ja Hill
7. Ruins of the Church of the Nativity of the Virgin in the Tithe Monastery
8. Church of the Twelve Apostles
9. Church of Saint Theodore the Tyro on Ščirkova Street
10. Church of the Holy Trinity in the Monastery of the Holy Spirit
11. Church of Saints Peter and Paul in Koževniki
12. Church of the Intercession in Zverin Convent
13. Church of Saint Simeon in Zverin Convent
14. Church of Saint Nicholas the White

the Zverin Convent situated just north of the Nerevskij *konec*. The same year marked the foundation of the Panteleimon Monastery a few kilometers south of the Ljudin *konec*. As for the Torgovaja *storona*, only two church constructions are recorded there during the 1140s. The first of these was a rebuilding in 1146 of the Church of Saint Elijah (first mentioned in 1105), situated on the northern edge of the Slavenskij *konec*; the other, in the same year, was the erection close by of a new wooden church dedicated to Saints Peter and Paul. Existing records unfortunately mention none of the patrons who commissioned the churches of the 1140s. One can, nevertheless, surmise that these were not great lords, but individual townsmen; the repeated mention of new churches being wooden structures suggests that the patrons were not wealthy enough to afford stone ones.

The topographical distribution of church building evened out during the 1150s, with new constructions recorded on both *storony* with about equal frequency. In 1151 a new church dedicated to Saint Basil appeared in the Ljudin *konec*, and another to Saints Constantine and Helen was built in the Nerevskij *konec*. In 1152 we find first mention of the existence of the Church of the Archangel Michael near the market on the Torgovaja *storona*. The founders of these three churches are unknown, but such information becomes more common from the mid-1150s onward. In 1154 Bishop Nifont of Novgorod had a church dedicated to Saint Sabbas (Sava) built in the Nerevskij *konec*. In 1156 a merchant corporation engaged in overseas trade (*zamorskie kupcy*) erected a church of Saint Parasceve-Pjatnica next to the market. As for the monasteries, 1153 marked the foundation of the Dormition Monastery by Arkadij, a wealthy Novgorodian who became its first abbot (and later the town's bishop), and after whom it became widely known as the Arkaž Monastery; its location was some three kilometers south of the Ljudin *konec*. These foundations of the 1150s reveal that church building patronage took many different forms in Novgorod, with commercial wealth (whether individual or corporate) underlying many of these pious undertakings. The 1160s and 1170s provide more illustrations of this diversity.

Another merchant corporation, the *ščecincy* (apparently merchants specializing in trade with Stettin[12]) commissioned a new church in 1165; this was dedicated to the Trinity and was located on the bank of the Ljudin *konec*. Most of the corporation's members must have lived in this *konec*: the market place in which they operated was almost directly across the river from their church. Also in 1165 a new Church of Saint Nicholas was

---

[12] St. Alexandrowicz, "Stosunki handlowe polsko-ruskie do roku 1240," *Zeszyty naukowe Uniwersytetu A. Mickiewicza*, no. 14, *Historia*, no. 3 (Poznań, 1958), 62–63.

constructed at the princely residence at Gorodišče, and first mention appears of the already existing Church of Saint Blasius in the Ljudin *konec*. In 1167 a major rebuilding was undertaken of the Church of Saints Boris and Gleb in the citadel. The new church was a very large stone building, and the patron was a certain Sotko Sytinic (= Sytinič). This Sotko is generally believed to have been an extremely wealthy merchant who probably inspired the epic cycle about Sadko *bogatyj gost'* of the Novgorodian *byliny*.[13] Sotko's church was completed in 1173. His rebuilding of an existing church heralded a period of frequent similar rebuildings over the last quarter of the twelfth century.

The next church mentioned in sources after Sotko's was, however, the new Church of Saint James, founded by an unnamed patron in the Nerevskij *konec* in 1172. In 1175 three previously existing churches are mentioned for the first time: they are those of Saint Michael, Saint James, and the Ascension, all located along Prussian Street on the inland northern periphery of the Ljudin *konec*. These three churches burned in a great fire, and the first-named of them was rebuilt in 1176 by *posadnik* Mixail Stepanec. In the same year, a certain Moisej Domanežic (= Domanežič) commissioned a church dedicated to the Decollation of John the Baptist inland of the citadel, then an unincorporated territory which would later become the Zagorodskij *konec*. Moisej is otherwise unknown, but we can safely assume that he was a well-to-do townsman.

Little monastic construction is reported during the 1160s and 1170s. In 1162 we have first mention of the existence of the Pentecost Monastery on the northern edge of the Nerevskij *konec*. In 1166 a stone gate chapel was built at the Jurevskij Monastery. The year 1170 saw the foundation of the Annunciation Monastery very near the Arkaž Monastery south of the Ljudin *konec*. This was a notable undertaking by two brothers, one being the then archbishop of Novgorod Iľja (prelate from 1165 to 1186) and the other his brother and subsequent successor Gavriil.[14] Iľja and Gavriil gave lasting care to their creation; in 1179 they jointly commissioned the monastery's main church to be rebuilt in stone. The brothers' joint building patronage was not restricted to this monastery. As we shall see, they are also known to have commissioned the rebuilding of a parish church in 1184.

The 1180s were marked by extensive rebuildings of existing churches, together with a few new foundations. In 1181 alone, five rebuildings are

[13] See A. N. Veselovskij, 'Byliny o Sadke," *ŽMNP* 1886, no. 11: 276–280, and M. Speranskij, *Russkaja narodnaja slovesnost'* (Moscow, 1917), 280–294.
[14] See my thesis, "Novgorod in the Early Middle Ages" (see n. 3), 137–162.

reported: these were of the Churches of Saint George by the market, Saints Cosmas and Damian, and Saint Sabbas in the Nerevskij *konec*, Saint James on Prussian Street, and the Archangel Michael near the market in the Slavenskij *konec*. In the same year two already existing churches are mentioned for the first time, these being those of Saint John (founded at an unspecified time by a certain Erevša, otherwise unknown) and the Nicaean Fathers, both somewhat inland of the market. Both burned in 1181; the former was rebuilt in the same year and the latter in 1182. In 1183 a new church dedicated to Saint Evpatij was constructed inland of the Slavenskij *konec* by a certain Rjad'ko together with his brother—another case of brotherly patronage after that of Il'ja and Gavriil. Two established churches were rebuilt in 1184; one was that of John the Baptist by the market, which Il'ja and Gavriil rebuilt jointly, while the other was that of Saint Blasius in Ljudin *konec*, where Il'ja was originally a parish priest. It is more than likely that the latter rebuilding was likewise the work of the cleric brothers, although the sources do not state so specifically. The first known instance of corporate patronage by a group of residents occurs in 1185; in that year the inhabitants of Luke's Street (*lukincy*) in the Ljudin *konec* jointly commissioned the stone Church of Saints Peter and Paul just south of their *konec*. The construction was completed in 1192. An even more complicated patronal corporation was organized in the same year to initiate a rebuilding of the Church of the Ascension on Prussian Street: a group of eighteen individuals, headed by a certain Miloneg, who held the rank of *tysjackij,* jointly financed the reconstruction of this church in stone.[15] Their church was completed in 1191. Another Prussian Street church was modified in 1189 when the one of Saint Michael had a chapel built onto it: this addition was dedicated to Ananias, Azariah, and Michael (the three youths of the fiery furnace) and the prophet Daniel.[16]

There is but one report of monastic construction during the 1180s, this also a rebuilding. In 1180 Semen Dybučevic (= Dybučevič), a boyar of Novgorod, had the main church of the Dormition Monastery south of the Ljudin *konec* replaced with a new stone building. Semen was presumably an especially wealthy boyar among those of the Ljudin *konec*.

---

[15] Miloneg is mentioned as builder in the Novgorod First Chronicle, but the other eighteen patrons are listed in that church's eighteenth-century *sinodik*; see S. N. Azbelev, "Razvitie letopisnogo žanra v Novgorode v XVII v.," *TODRL* 15 (1958): 258–259. The *sinodik* mentions no Miloneg but does contain the name Michael: this Michael may very well be *posadnik* Michael Stepanec (who built the nearby Church of Saint Michael in 1176), and Miloneg a distorted or alternative form of his name.

[16] Makarij, *Arxeologičeskoe opisanie* (see n. 1), 184–185.

The 1190s were distinguished by a mixed pattern of church building, with an almost equal number of rebuildings and new foundations. Two major rebuildings marked the year 1191. The Church of the Image Not Made by Hands, first mentioned in 1148, was rebuilt by *posadnik* Vnezda Nezdenic (= Nezdenič, governed 1189–1204), brother of the earlier *posadnik* Miroška. The wealth of the Nezdenic family clearly underwrote this reconstruction. Commercial wealth appears to have permitted the simultaneous rebuilding of the Church of Saint Parasceve-Pjatnica by the market. The patrons there were two Novgorodian brothers, one the boyar Konstantin, the other unnamed. The brothers were most probably members of the overseas merchant corporation that founded the church in 1156 and would rebuild it yet again in 1207. Konstantin was an energetic builder and was to found a new monastery in 1196, that time jointly with his "name-brother" (*bratennik*). Also in 1191, Archbishop Gavriil constructed a new church dedicated to the Purification inside the episcopal palace situated within the citadel. In 1194 the old Church of Saints Peter and Paul south of the Slavenskij *konec* was rebuilt by a certain Živoglož; this building was wooden, so the man's wealth was probably not great enough for a stone successor. In the same year, boyar Rodoslav Danilovič erected a new church dedicated to Saint Philip on the inland eastern edge of the Slavenskij *konec*. The year 1195 marked the rebuilding of the Church of the Exaltation of the Cross in the Ljudin *konec*. It was first mentioned a year before, when the then existing building burned. In the same year there were two more rebuildings, one of the Church of Saint Basil in the Ljudin *konec* (first mentioned in 1151), and the other of a previously unknown church of Saint Demetrios, north of the market.[17] A major rebuilding of the old Church of Saint Elijah north of the Slavenskij *konec* was begun in 1198 by a certain Erevša; the new stone building was finished in 1202. This patron was probably an exceptionally wealthy man, as certainly was boyar Prokša Malyševič, who commissioned the last Novgorodian church built in the twelfth century. In 1199 Prokša's church dedicated to the Forty Martyrs was begun in the Nerevskij *konec*; it was completed by his son Vjačeslav in 1211.

Monastic construction intensified somewhat during the last decade of the twelfth century, in contrast to the preceding ones. The great Xutynskij Monastery was founded in 1192 some five kilometers north of Novgorod on the Volxov. It was dedicated to the Transfiguration by the venerated

[17] The Novgorod First Chronicle describes the church as *Nezdricyna*. This personal possessive adjective may derive from the name Nezdreča, which belonged to a boyar whose home was ransacked in 1118 (see the same chronicle). The Church of Saint Demetrios may have been originally by him or one of his sons.

monk Varlaam (previously a wealthy townsman), its founder, and came to serve as Novgorod's river forepost north of the Antonov Monastery on the Volxov's east bank.[18] New churches were built in 1194 and 1195 in the Resurrection Monastery south of the Ljudin *konec*: the first was a gate chapel dedicated to Saint John the Compassionate, while the second was a stone replacement for the main church commissioned by Archbishop Martirij. The Monastery of Saint Cyril was founded in 1195 a few kilometers inland of the Slavenskij *konec*; the joint patrons were the boyar Konstantin and his name-brother Dmitr—the first recorded instance of laymen bound by a spiritual bond acting as copatrons. The first woman patron is mentioned in 1197, when Poljužaja Gorodšinica, daughter of *posadnik* Žiroslav, founded the Abbey of Saint Euthemia on the northern riverbank periphery of the Plotnickij *konec* (the new borough directly north of the Slavenkskij *konec*). In 1198 the Transfiguration Monastery was established at Neredica, some three kilometers southeast of the Slavenskij *konec*. Its main church, soon to be decorated with exquisite frescoes, was begun simultaneously. The patron was Jaroslav Vladimirovič, prince of Novgorod, whose residence at Gorodišče was nearby. In 1199 the same prince's wife founded the Abbey of the Nativity (commonly called Mixalica) on the inland verge of the Plotnickij *konec*. This must have been a grand foundation, with the main church in stone and the first abbess a *posadnik's* wife.

Church building and rebuilding continued at an essentially even pace, without notable interruptions, for the duration of Novgorod's history. However, that pace was never to match the frequency and extent seen in the twelfth century. The topographical pattern of church building that crystallized during that century permits the following observations about Novgorod's urban development during the formative century of its history:

The first third of the twelfth century. Between 1103 and 1135, a total of nine churches are known to have been erected in Novgorod. All of them were on the Torgovaja *storona*, with seven clustered around the market place. The known patrons included princes, a bishop, and lesser townsmen. The first great patron of church building was active in this period; he was Prince Vsevolod Mstislavič, who commissioned four churches next to the market between 1127 and 1134. The pattern of ecclesiastical construction over this period shows clearly that the market was Novgorod's vital center. There can be no doubt that the construction of churches around this place was made possible by the wealth amassed there by the patrons. Nearly all

---

[18] On Varlaam and his *žitie*, see L. A. Dmitriev, *Žitijnye povesti russkogo Severa kak pamjatniki literatury XIII–XVI vv.* (Leningrad, 1973), 3–95.

the known patrons of this time were princes and a bishop, so it seems that
these lords were deeply and profitably involved in Novgorod's commerce
from an early time.

   The second third of the twelfth century. Over this period construction
increased on the Sofijskaja *storona*, while that on the Torgovaja *storona*
declined sharply. Only three new constructions are reported on the market
side, while nine new churches appear on the Sofijskaja *storona*. Most of the
latter were built in the decade between 1146 and 1156. This shift should
not, however, be taken as a sign of any diminution in the connection
between patronage and trade. Indeed, commercial patronage of church
building took a new form in the 1150s and the 1160s: sponsorship by merchant corporations, first by the *zamorskie kupcy* in 1156 and then by the
ščecincy in 1165. If the first group built their church next to the market
where they traded, the second positioned theirs in a residential area on the
river's opposite shore—probably where most of the corporation's members
had their homes. Thus, patronage made possible by wealth accumulated in
trade resulted in new churches appearing far from the market place. We
may well wonder how many churches built on the Sofijskaja *storona* by
now-forgotten patrons were the work of men grown wealthy through trade
on the Torgovaja *storona*. Of those known, one was almost certainly a very
wealthy merchant; this was Sotko Sytinic, who commissioned the Church
of Saints Boris and Gleb in the citadel to be rebuilt in 1167, making it one
of the grandest in the town.

   The last third of the twelfth century. The distribution of new construction
became essentially even between the two *storony* in this period. The overall
pace of building increased, but more than half the work was devoted to
rebuilding old churches rather than founding new ones: of the thirty-four
mentioned over this period, nineteen were rebuildings. Of the new foundations, most were located farther away from the built-up residential centers
than before. The increasing number of rebuildings may reflect a growing
concern for improvement among patrons or a growing desire to replace old
architectural style with new (though none of the rebuildings survives to
provide real evidence of changing tastes). Alternatively, it is quite possible
that Novgorod was growing inward as well as outward, that the built-up
area was becoming more concentrated, and that less and less space was left
for new churches within the *koncy*. As for patronage, new forms of this
institution emerged. Brothers repeatedly appear as joint patrons, the most
illustrious being Archbishop Il'ja together with his brother and successor,
Gavriil. Spiritual brothers could also be joint founders, as were Konstantin
and Dmitr. Residential corporations were formed specifically to build

churches in their *koncy* or even in their streets: the most remarkable of these was the group of eighteen who jointly built the Church of the Ascension between 1185 and 1191. Finally, aristocratic women came forth as patrons of abbey building in the 1190s. By and large, however, the patrons of the last third of the twelfth century were native Novgorodians of non-aristocratic station, men who had apparently accumulated by commercial endeavor the wealth necessary for patronage.

To conclude, the topography of Novgorod's twelfth-century churches permits us to discern two main forces at work in the town during that century. First, it seems quite clear that the wealth that made possible the proliferation of churches was generated through trade. The initial concentration of church construction around the market place attests to this, as does the later patronage by merchant corporations of churches both near the market and in residential areas. Indeed, the practice of joint residential patronage followed chronologically after the commercial kind and may well have been modeled on the latter. Second, the institution of patronage became widespread among the townsmen and took a great variety of forms. Only during the century's early part were great lords the most frequent patrons; thereafter the native townsmen were most commonly the patrons. This changing pattern seems to indicate that by the middle of the century wealth was becoming sufficiently distributed to allow a great many individuals and groups to undertake the costly venture of patronage. The various forms that patronage took clearly reflect considerable flexibility in terms of social organization and enterprise. Having discerned these two main forces within twelfth-century Novgorod, we can see that commercial enterprise and pious patronage went hand in hand. The wealth accumulated by Novgorodians in successful trading and the organizational flexibility learned in the process must ultimately explain why church-building patronage became so widespread an expression of piety, quite probably bordering on a civic custom. The history of Novgorod after the twelfth century, when written sources become more abundant and topography proportionately less important, must be seen in the light of the twelfth-century background to which the town's churches give witness.

Language and Literature

TOWARD A SOCIAL HISTORY OF RUSSIAN

DEAN S. WORTH

Our contemporary knowledge, such as it is, of the origins and development of the Russian literary language grew only gradually out of medieval grammatical treatises and the controversies involving Trediakovskij, Lomonosov, and Sumarokov in the eighteenth century and Šiškov and Karamzin and their followers in the early nineteenth.[1] The more or less scientific study of this topic began only with Vostokov in the twenties of the last century.[2] Most of the literature of the past century and a half has dealt with the respective roles of indigenous and imported elements in the formation of what eventually became a national standard language. The two best-known views of this matter, associated with the names of Šaxmatov and of Obnorskij, are that the standard language arose from the gradual Russification of Slavonic, and from the gradual Slavonicization of Russian, respectively. This is, of course, a historiographic oversimplification: in fact, Šaxmatov's views can be traced back to Vostokov and were developed by

---

[1] On the manuscript tradition see above all V. Jagić, *Codex slovenicus rerum grammaticarum. Rassuždenija južnoslavjanskoj i russkoj stariny o cerkovno-slavjanskom jazyke* (Berlin, 1896); for an occasionally different view of some of these MSS, see D. S. Worth, *The Origins of Russian Grammar: Notes on the State of Russian Philology Before the Appearance of Printed Grammars*, UCLA Slavic Studies, vol. 5 (Columbus, Ohio, 1983). The principal historiographic surveys are S. K. Bulič, *Očerk istorii jazykoznanija v Rossii*, vol. 1 *(XIII v.–1825 g.)*, *Zapiski Istoriko-filologičeskogo fakul'teta Imperatorskogo S.Peterburgskogo universiteta* 75 (St. Petersburg, 1904); E. F. Karskij, *Očerk naučnoj razrabotki russkogo jazyka v predelax SSSR, SbORJaS* 101, no. 1 (Leningrad, 1926); P. S. Kuznecov, *U istokov russkoj grammatičeskoj mysli* (Moscow, 1958); V. V. Vinogradov, "Russkaja nauka o russkom literaturnom jazyke," *Rol' russkoj nauki v razvitii mirovoj nauki i kul'tury*, vol. 3, pt. 1, *Učenye zapiski Moskovskogo gosudarstvennogo universiteta* 106 (Moscow, 1946), 22–147; id., "Osnovnye problemy obrazovanija i razvitija drevnerusskogo literaturnogo jazyka," *Issledovanija po slavjanskomu jazykoznaniju* (Moscow, 1961), 4–113 (and as a preliminary brochure for the Fourth International Congress of Slavists, Moscow, 1958); V. D. Levin and A. D. Grigor'eva, "Vopros o proisxoždenii i načal'nyx ètapax russkogo literaturnogo jazyka v russkoj nauke XIX v.," *Učenye zapiski Moskovskogo gorodskogo pedagogičeskogo instituta imeni V. P. Potemkina* 51, *Kafedra russkogo jazyka*, no. 6 (Moscow, 1956), 257–291.

[2] A. X. Vostokov (v. Osteneck), *Rassuždenie o slavjanskom jazyke, služaščee vvedeniem k Grammatike sego jazyka, sostavljaemoj po drevnejšim onogo pis'mennym pamjatnikam* (St. Petersburg, 1820).

Maksimovič, K. S. Aksakov, and partially by Sreznevskij,[3] while a somewhat more tenuous intellectual thread leads back from Obnorskij via
Lamanskij to Nadeždin in the 1830s.[4] Various combinations and modifications of the Šaxmatov and Obnorskij positions are found in the work of
Jakubinskij, Unbegaun, Vinogradov, Issatschenko, Filin, Uspenskij, Hüttl-
Folter, and many others.[5] A great deal of valuable and stimulating work has
been done—so much so, in fact, that one is all the more surprised at the
almost total lack of agreement about basics: we have not been able to

[3] Ibid.; and id., *Russkaja grammatika, po načertaniju sokraščennoj grammatiki, polnee izlo-
žennaja* (St. Petersburg, 1831); M. A. Maksimovič, *Polnoe sobranie sočinenij*, vol. 3 (Kiev,
1880), passim; K. S. Aksakov, *Lomonosov v istorii russkoj literatury i russkogo jazyka* (Moscow,
1846); I. I. Sreznevskij, *Mysli ob istorii russkogo jazyka i drugix slavjanskix jazykov* (St. Petersburg, 1849-1850). A. A. Šaxmatov's views, which show little originality, can be found in his
Kurs istorii russkogo jazyka (St. Petersburg, 1910-1911); *Očerk sovremennogo russkogo literaturnogo jazyka*, 4th ed. (Moscow, 1941); *Očerk drevnejšego perioda istorii russkogo jazyka,*
Ènciklopedija slavjanskoj filologii, no. 11, ed. V. I. Jagič (St. Petersburg, 1916); "Russkij
jazyk, ego osobennosti. Vopros ob obrazovanii narečij. Očerk osnovnyx momentov razvitija
literaturnogo jazyka," *Istorija russkoj literatury do XIX v.,*, vol. 1, ed. A. E. Gruzinskij
(Moscow, 1916), reprinted as a supplement to his *Očerk sovremennogo russkogo literaturnogo
jazyka*, 4th ed. (Moscow, 1941), 223-224.
[4] N. I. Nadeždin, "Evropeizm i narodnosť," *Teleskop* 31, no. 1 (1836): 5-60; no. 2 (1836):
206-264; id., "Mundarten der russischen Sprache," *Jahrbücher der Literatur* (Vienna, 1841),
181-240; V. I. Lamanskij, *Slavjanskoe žitie sv. Kirilla kak religiozno-èpičeskoe proizvedenie i
kak istoričeskij istočnik* (ŽMNP 346 [1903]: 345-385; 347 [1903]: 136-161; 348 [1903]: 350-388,
350 [1903]: 370-405; 351 [1904]: 137-173). Obnorskij himself once held views close to those of
Šaxmatov; cf. "K istorii slovoobrazovanija v russkom literaturnom jazyke," *Russkaja reč'*, n.s.,
no. 1 (Petrograd, 1927), 75-89, and came to his later views in a series of studies in the thirties
and forties, summed up (with certain modifications) in his *Očerki po istorii russkogo jazyka
staršego perioda* (Moscow-Leningrad, 1946). These and other works will be discussed in detail
in our study, *The Historiography of Literary Russian*, in prep.
[5] See such representative works as, e.g., L. P. Jakubinskij, *Istorija drevnerusskogo jazyka,*
ed. and with foreword by V. V. Vinogradov (Moscow, 1953); B. O. Unbegaun, "Proisxoždenie
russkogo literaturnogo jazyka," *Novyj žurnal* 100 (1970): 306-319; id., "The Russian Literary
Language: A Comparative View," *The Modern Language Review* 68 (1973): xix-xxv; V. V.
Vinogradov, *Očerki po istorii russkogo literaturnogo jazyka XVII-XIX vv.,* 2nd ed. (Moscow,
1938); id., "Osnovnye voprosy i zadači izučenija istorii russkogo jazyka do XVIII veka,"
Voprosy jazykoznanija, 1969, no. 6: 3-34; A. V. Issatschenko, "Vorgeschichte und Entstehung
der modernen russischen Literatursprache," *Zeitschrift für slavische Philologie* 37 (1974):
235-274; id., *Mythen und Tatsachen über die Entstehung der russischen Literatursprache*, Öster-
reichische Akademie der Wissenschaften, Philosophisch-historische Klasse, Sitzungsberichte,
vol. 298, no. 5 (Vienna, 1975); F. P. Filin, *Istoki i sud'by russkogo literaturnogo jazyka* (Moscow,
1981); B. A. Uspenskij, *Istorija russkogo literaturnogo jazyka. Proekt prostrannoj programmy*
(Moscow, n.d. [= 1973, typescript]), and cf. his paper in this volume; G. Hüttl-Worth/Folter,
"Roľ cerkovnoslavjanskogo jazyka v razvitii russkogo literaturnogo jazyka. K istoričeskomu
analizu i klassifikacii slavjanizmov," *American Contributions to the Sixth International Congress
of Slavists, Prague, 1968, August 7-13* (The Hague-Paris, 1968), 95-124; id., "Spornye problemy izučenija literaturnogo jazyka v drevnerusskij period," in *Beiträge österreichischer Slavisten
zum VII. Slavistenkongress, Warschau 1973* (*Wiener Slavistisches Jahrbuch* 18 [1973]), 29-47.

define the object under investigation (the Russian literary language, *russkij literaturnyj jazyk*) to one another's satisfaction, nor have we found a conceptual framework within which reasonable scholars might look at the same facts and come out with (at least) similar conclusions. In this paper, I shall examine some of the reasons for this backward state of our art and propose a framework that might, perhaps, help to eliminate some of the problems that have faced us so far.

The list of important but unanswered questions about the linguistic situation in medieval Russia is a long one. For example: How much literacy was there before 988? Were Church Slavonic and Russian two languages or one? Do juridical texts reflect the spoken language? Was there a spoken koine in Kiev? If so, was it Church Slavonic? Are birchbark letters part of a "literary language"? How much did Bulgarian and Serbian really affect Russian in the fifteenth and sixteenth centuries? Is the concept of diglossia applicable to medieval Russia? There is no shortage of published opinions about these and similar matters, but there is a noticeable shortage of convincing evidence, and it is by no means always clear just what sort of evidence might be available. In my opinion, there are two major reasons for this; that is, there are two persistent weaknesses that have troubled the study of literary Russian almost since the beginning, and especially in the past several decades.

The first problem is connected with the semantically slippery term *Russian literary language,* which means different things to different people. For some, it is not too far from *language of literature* and includes, above all, works of some aesthetic content, which eliminates a good many secular and some religious works from the subject under investigation.[6] For others, the term includes almost anything preserved in written form—for example the Novgorod birchbark letters—giving rise to such dubious labels as the *èpistoljarnyj stil' drevnerusskogo literaturnogo jazyka,*[7] a term that leads one to wonder whether, for instance, the famous pre-Christian mustard-pot (if that is what it was) inscription *Gorušnja (čaša)* is an example of the *èpigra-*

---

[6] E.g., "Xotja 'delovoj jazyk' imel, nesomnenno, ves'ma bol'šoe značenie v kul'turno-istoričeskom razvitii Kievskogo gosudarstva, on tem ne menee ne vxodil v sistemu literaturnogo jazyka ètoj èpoxi." A. I. Gorškov, *Istorija russkogo literaturnogo jazyka* (Moscow, 1961), 43.

[7] See, for example, A. I. Efimov, *Istorija russkogo literaturnogo jazyka. Kurs lekcij* (Moscow, 1957), 51–52. Efimov refers to legal language as the "dokumental'no-juridičeskij stil' (drevnerusskogo literaturnogo jazyka)," ibid., 57. V. D. Levin and V. V. Vinogradov opposed this view.

fičeskij stiľ drevnerusskogo literaturnogo jazyka.[8] Some Soviet scholars take it for granted that their Kievan ancestors had a *literaturnyj jazyk*—as if to be without one were a sign of cultural impoverishment—but seldom take the trouble to define it. In the first twenty-two pages of the generally sober and reasonable discussion in F. P. Filin's newest book, for example, the term *russkij literaturnyj jazyk* occurs sixty-three times but is never defined.[9] The only clear definition of *literary language*, by A. V. Issatschenko ("normalized, polyvalent, stylistically differentiated, obligatory for all") is clearly not applicable to the prenational period,[10] but no better one has been proposed.

This is no mere terminological quibble, but a conceptual problem of some importance. The very existence of an Old Russian Literary Language—that entity, in terms of which all other entities and processes are defined and evaluated—has never been proved. If there was such an entity, why, after two hundred years of scholarship, do we have no description of it? We find syntactic descriptions of charters, of chronicles, of various genres,[11] but no Syntax of the Old Russian Literary Language. We have lists of phonetic and morphological Slavonisms and their East Slavic counterparts, but no Phonology or Morphology of this literary language. In the absence of a Grammar of Old Literary Russian, simple caution would suggest that this entity may be an anachronistic projection of the present into the past. Note that to deny the existence of a literary language in Kievan Rus' is in no way to disparage the social or cultural level of Kievan society. Factually, nothing is changed; we still have the same texts (some religious, some secular; some aesthetic, some utilitarian; some interesting, some dull) and the same problems (literacy, intermingling of Slavonic and autochthonous elements, genre systems, etc.). If the term *Old Russian Literary Language* cannot be provided with a specific definition, a content based on the incontrovertible evidence of the texts themselves, this term should be abandoned, and we should get about our business of describing what does exist:

[8] Of the literature on this artifact, see, e.g., D. A. Avdusin and M. N. Tixomirov, "Drevnejšaja russkaja nadpis'," *Vestnik AN SSSR*, 1950, no. 4: 76; P. Ja. Černyx, "K voprosu o gnezdovoj nadpisi," *IOLJa* 9, no. 5 (1950): 401; R. O. Jakobson, "Vestiges of the Earliest Russian Vernacular," *Word* 8 (1952) (= *Slavic Word* 1), 350–351.

[9] F. P. Filin, *Istoki i suďby russkogo literaturnogo jazyka* (Moscow, 1981), 3–25.

[10] A. V. Issatschenko, "Kakova specifika literaturnogo dvujazyčija v istorii slavjanskix jazykov?," *Voprosy jazykoznanija*, 1958, no. 3: 42.

[11] E.g., V. I. Borkovskij, *Sintaksis drevnerusskix gramot. Prostoe predloženie* (Lvov, 1949); E. Istrina, *Sintaksičeskie javlenija Sinodaľnogo spiska I-oj Novgorodskoj letopisi, IORJaS* 24 (1919), 26 (1921), and separately (St. Petersburg, 1923); *Sravniteľno-istoričeskij sintaksis vostočnoslavjanskix jazykov. Tipy prostogo predloženija*, ed. V. I. Borkovskij (Moscow, 1969), and other vols. in this series.

the sermons, the legal texts, the correspondence, the chronicles and tales, and so forth. Only when we know to what extent the phonology, the inflection and derivation, the syntax, and the lexicon of these several genres coincide, will we be able to discuss on a reasonable and factual basis whether or not it makes sense to speak of a single linguistic entity that might be called the Old Russian Literary Language. But that time is not yet close, and until it arrives, we would do well to forget the concept of an Old Russian Literary Language and speak, instead, of the *social history of Russian* (on the meaning of this term, see below).

The second weakness that has recurred throughout the historiography of this topic is more subtle, but perhaps still more pernicious. This is the tendency to equate a series of descriptive dichotomies that are, in fact, by no means always commensurable. Taken by themselves, these dichotomies are of obvious importance: Church Slavonic versus East Slavic, religious versus secular texts, written versus spoken language, normalized versus non-normalized language, literary versus practical use of language, and so forth. The actual content of each of the two opposing terms within each dichotomy changes in time, and the textual evidence suggests that in most cases there exists a continuum rather than a polarized opposition, but the dichotomies are nonetheless of considerable value as a series of frames within which to discuss the textual facts. However, even the best scholars have tended at times to equate these several dichotomies, so that "Slavonic" comes to equal "literary," "normalized," "prestigious," "religious," and so forth, while "East Slavic" ("Old Russian") is equated with "non-literary," "non-normalized," "secular," and the like. Examples of such unjustified equations are legion; I shall adduce only two.

In 1950 Boris Unbegaun wrote that "epic poety, lyric songs and fairy tales were oral literature, and so could only be expressed in colloquial Russian," which Unbegaun himself defines as the language of "legal documents, diplomatic correspondence and private letters."[12] Almost everything in this assertion must be challenged. Above all, it is clearly inaccurate to lump together such disparate genres as the oral epic and the birchbark letters, the fairy tale and the *gramoty,* under *any* single label, "colloquial" or other. In addition, our knowledge of "oral literature" is entirely inferential for the older periods, and what we can infer about the language of, say, the epic poem (fixed syllabic length, dactylic clausulae, syntactic repetition, stable epithets, etc.) is anything but colloquial. Legal documents are highly

---

[12] B. O. Unbegaun, "Colloquial and Literary Russian," *Oxford Slavonic Papers* 1 (1950): 26–36.

formulaic (*kuda soxa xodila, a poslusi na to ...*, et al.), and so are some parts of private correspondence (*piši mne, gosudare, o svoem mnogoletnem zdorov'e*, etc., in seventeenth- and eighteenth-century letters). Diplomatic correspondence is more or less colloquial, depending on the taste of the correspondent and the complexities of his subject matter.[13] Such coarse equations lead us nowhere.

More recently, Boris Uspenskij writes that "Primenitel'no k jazykovoj situacii Drevnej Rusi, delo idet o suščestvovanii literaturno obrabotannogo (normirovannogo) cerkovnoslavjanskogo jazyka i literaturno ne obrabotannogo (nenormirovannogo) jazyka drevnerusskogo."[14] This equation of "Slavonic" with "normalized" and "literary" is difficult to support with textual evidence. Both Hilarion and Serapion of Vladimir wrote in flawless Church Slavonic, but Hilarion's *Slovo o zakone i blagodati* is *literaturno obrabotano*, that is, "literary" in the sense that it deliberately employs rhetorical devices (most notably, antithetical parallelism) with an aesthetic and not merely a conative goal; the *Slovo* is a poetic work in Roman Jakobson's sense,[15] while Serapion's more modest efforts, although no less literate, are much less literary. Within Old Russian (in the narrow sense, that is, in works with a zero or minimal Slavonic component), one finds a wide range of literary and nonliterary works, from the heroic epic on the one hand to the birchbark letters on the other. The *Russkaja Pravda* was neither Slavonic nor literary, but it was certainly normalized (otherwise it could hardly have been passed on from generation to generation in the preliterate period), while even the Psalm translations, which were certainly Slavonic and presumably literary, show a wide degree of variation, that is, of nonnormativeness, at least in their vocabulary.[16] Furthermore, it should not be forgotten that any discussion of normalization before the sixteenth century is based entirely on inference; there is no textual evidence, before that time, that the concept of normative grammar was known to the scribes. Similarly, there is no evidence that these scribes had the sense that Slavonic and

---

[13] Of the six diplomatic reports published in *Putešestvija russkix poslov XVI–XVII vv. Statejnye spiski* (Moscow–Leningrad, 1954), for example, that of the envoy Elčin to Georgia shows substantially more use of Slavonisms than the others. On the language of these texts, see D. S. Worth, "Slavonisms in Russian Diplomatic Reports 1567–1667," *Slavica Hierosolymitana* 2 (1978): 3–12.

[14] B. A. Uspenskij, "K voprosu o semantičeskix vzaimootnošenijax sistemno protivopostavlennyx cerkovnoslavjanskix i russkix form v istorii russkogo jazyka," *Wiener Slavistisches Jahrbuch* 22 (1976): 94.

[15] Roman Jakobson, "Closing Statement: Linguistics and Poetics," *Style in Language*, ed. T. A. Sebeok (Cambridge, Mass., 1960), 353–358.

[16] On this and related questions, see the rich material in L. P. Žukovskaja, *Tekstologija i jazyk drevnejšix slavjanskix pamjatnikov* (Moscow, 1976).

Old Russian were two internally coherent and mutually opposed entities. Even this most basic of dichotomies may well turn out to be an anachronism, a projection into the past of a dualism that came into existence only in the late seventeenth and eighteenth centuries. The widespread tendency to portray the history of "literary Russian" as a centuries-long duel between Slavonic and native elements might have its roots in the oft-quoted dictum of Ludolf, "Adeoque apud illos dicitur, loquendum est Russice [et] scribendum est Slavonice."[17] This passage is generally quoted out of context, and one has only to read the grammar itself to discover how much more complex things were for Ludolf himself. Ludolf certainly had a clear view of some of the important genetic differences between Slavonic and Russian: he adduces such contrasting pairs as *golova/glava, odin/edin, xočet/xoščet,* and *pravda/istina.* Nonetheless, his illustrative examples and his descriptive text are full of genetic Slavonisms: *glava, edinorodnyj, sreda, drevo, umrĕti, vlasť, sladko,* quite aside from the many biblical citations, which naturally abound in forms like *ašče, xoščet, blagočestie, telesnie slasti,* and *prosvĕščajuščij,* so that one has to assume a substantial degree of interpenetration of Slavonic and autochthonous elements. The role of Ludolf's grammar in the historiography of Russian has yet to be studied.[18]

The problem posed by these descriptive dichotomies is extremely complex. With the possible exception of normative/non-normative, they really seem to exist, but the extent to which they overlap (i.e., the extent to which Slavonic = prestigious = written, etc.) varies from genre to genre at any given time, and from one time to another in any given genre. If, as seems to be the case, these dichotomies are an essential part of our conceptual framework, then we can only hope to utilize them cautiously and without undue generalization.

Problems such as those just mentioned make it desirable to find a methodological framework independent of the notion of a literary language and flexible enough to help avoid equating the several descriptive dichotomies just discussed. Such a framework might be sought in what I shall call *the social history of Russian.*[19] Such a history differs from regular language

[17] B. O. Unbegaun, *Henrici Wilhelmi Ludolfi Grammatica Russica, A. D. MDCXCVI* (Oxford, 1952).

[18] Scholars often forget that Ludolf's grammar was intended both as an introduction to Slavonic and as a grammar of Russian, a fact that is already clear from its full title: *Grammatica Russica quae continet non tantum praecipua fundamenta Russicae linguae, verum etiam manuductionem quandam ad grammaticam Sclavonicam.*

[19] I have chosen this term, somewhat reluctantly, over *sociolinguistic history of Russian,* since the latter might imply a Labovian precision alien to this field.

history in that it emphasizes the social role of linguistic forms, and it differs
from the *istorija russkogo literaturnogo jazyka* in that it is not restricted to
those developments that eventually resulted in a standard national language. In what follows I shall provide an outline sketch of what is meant
by "social history of a language," and then show how such a history is
illustrated by the specific case of Russian. Such a topic would obviously fill
at least one whole book; the most that can be given here is a survey, for
purposes of discussion. Of necessity, such a survey must deal in broad and
unprovable generalizations. These are, of course, no substitute for detailed
works on the texts themselves, but one can at least hope that these generalizations will provide a conceptual and methodological framework within
which such detailed textual work can profitably be pursued.

To speak of the social history of a language implies the existence of a
sociolinguistic system consisting of three components. On the one extreme,
there is the *social structure* of the given society, as this structure develops
through time, that is, a *social history*. This social history—including economic and intellectual history and the like—may but need not impinge on
linguistic history at any given time. On the other extreme, there is the *linguistic structure* of the society, which also develops through time; that is,
there is a *linguistic history*. Linguistic history, too, may but need not impinge on social structure at any given point in time. Mediating between
social and linguistic history, serving, as it were, as the interface connecting
these two systems, is the third component, a *system of genres*. The genre
system is society's way of utilizing linguistic structures; it is what enables
language to serve social needs. Each genre fulfills a social function (cult,
aesthetic, legal, etc.), and is therefore a fact of social history, but each genre
also has its own linguistic form, its own functional style, and is therefore
also a fact of linguistic history. It is here, in the form/function relationships
of the genre system, that social and linguistic structures interact. It is here
that history and language impinge upon each other, and the history of these
impingements is, precisely, the social history of the language.

It is clear from these definitions that the social and linguistic components
of the social history of a language will be far narrower than either social or
linguistic history taken separately. Only those facts of social history that
affect the types, varieties, and interrelations of genres (and which, therefore, necessarily involve language, namely the functional styles of these
genres) will be part of the social history of the language. Similarly, only
those facts of linguistic history that affect the efficiency of the genre system
(that is, which help or hinder the ways in which language fulfills its social
purposes) will be dealt with in this social history of language. In the case of

Russian, for example, the victory of 1380 is irrelevant to this topic, but the consolidation of the Ukraine into the Muscovite state in 1667 was important, since it accelerated the influx of Ukrainians to Moscow and thus the interaction of the southwestern and northeastern varieties of Church Slavonic. The fact that some Russian dialects developed seven- or six-vowel systems had no discernible effect on the social use of language, but the so-called $e \rightarrow o$ change led to high- and low-style doublets in the eighteenth century and still affects the freedom of rhyme choice in our own day.

The social history of a language can perhaps best be viewed as a dialectic process between those forces that tend toward stability, towards equilibrium in the form/function relationships of the genre system, and those that are disruptive, which tend to an imbalance in these relationships, thus lowering the social efficiency of the system. I take it as axiomatic that any society, left to its own devices (that is, not subject to disruptive influences from without or to overly rapid internal linguistic development), tends toward a state of sociolinguistic equilibrium, toward a state of rest in which there has been time to work out a system of genres (each with its functional style) adequate to the social purposes at hand. Linguistic forms and their social functions are in a state of relative equilibrium. This equilibrium is, however, disrupted by external or internal developments that render the language inadequate to the social tasks of the society, either by the creation of new or hybrid genres for which no adequate functional style has yet evolved, or by internal linguistic developments rendering a formerly adequate functional style archaic or otherwise stylistically unsuited to its task. Such was the situation, for example, when external events led to the introduction of drama to Moscow in the late seventeenth century, at which time there existed no lyric style adequate to the expression of emotion and passion. The result was such love scenes as the following interchange between Holophernes and Judith:

> Holophernes: O! sadisja, pobeditelnico xrabrosti moeja, obladatelnico serdca moego! Sadisja vozle mene, da jasi i pieši so mnoju, veseljaščesja. Ibo, jako ty edina moe nepobědimoe velikodušie obladala esi, tako imaši milosť moju sama, ni črez kogo že inogo, soveršenno upotrebljati.
> Judith: Ej, gospodine moj! Az vozveseljusja userdstvenno; nikogda že ešče takoj česti vosprijax.[20]

---

[20] Holophernes: Sit thyself down, O conqueress of my valor, O possessor of my heart! Sit thyself down next to me, that thou mayest eat and drink with me, that we might rejoice. For since thou alone hast taken possession of my invincible magnanimity, so thou thyself shall enjoy my favor completely, without any intermediary. Judith: Ah, my lord! I shall rejoice most fervently; never before indeed did I receive such honor. (A scene from the drama "Komedija iz

The social inadequacy of this mishmash of Slavonic and vernacular elements is obvious, but it took Russian a century and a half to get from this point to Puškin's "Ja vas ljubil ...," that is, to work out a functional style adequate to this lyric purpose. A similar disequilibrium was created after the 1917 revolution, when the proletarian writers introduced dialect and substandard forms into preexistent genres, and it took all the authority of a Gor'kij to remind them that Russian writers were supposed to write in Russian, not in "Nižegorodian."[21] In both cases, the disruption of the form/function equilibrium called into being counterforces which worked to restore the previous balance.

Disruption caused by internal linguistic developments has been less frequent, at least in the history of Russian, than that caused by external historical events. The Russification of the originally imported Old Church Slavonic, that is, the creation of a Russian Church Slavonic which had evolved away from the original Greek models, had—at least in the righteous eyes of those engaged in the *ispravlenie knig*—rendered the cult language inadequate to its sacred purposes. The gradual loss of the aorist and its replacement by the copula-less *l*-participle had partially destroyed the stylistic unity of diplomatic treaties by the end of the thirteenth century, as evidenced by Alexander Nevskij's treaty with the Teutonic Knights, which starts out with traditional aorists but then slips into the more natural participial past.[22] And, of course, many of the elements of the Lomonosovian high style were "high" not because of Slavonic origin, but because they were formerly good Old Russian forms which, becoming archaic, had turned into "functional Slavonisms," to use Avanesov's term.[23] The contribution of internal linguistic developments to sociolinguistic disequilibrium is considerable, but its role is, nonetheless, far less significant than that of external events. Regardless of whether the disruptive force came from without or from within, however, the response of the sociolinguistic system is to restore balance, by whatever internal and/or imposed means are available: a new truncated vocative develops, at least in the *a*-declension, to replace the original lost vocative (*mam! Son'! Len!*); elaborate participial or gerundial embedding develops to render the complexities of scientific prose;

---

knigi Iudif'," or "Olofernovo dejstvo," first staged in February 1673; cf. *Pervye p'esy russkogo teatra*, Rannjaja russkaja dramaturgija XVII–pervoj poloviny XVIII v., vol. 1, [Moscow, 1972], 447).

[21] A. M. Gor'kij, "O jazyke," cited in Gorškov, *Istorija* (see n. 6), 190.

[22] Jakubinskij, *Istorija drevnerusskogo jazyka* (see n. 5).

[23] R. I. Avanesov, "K voprosam periodizacii istorii russkogo jazyka," *Slavjanskoe jazyko-znanie. VII Meždunarodnyj s"ezd slavistov. Varšava, avgust 1973 g. Doklady sovetskoj delegacii* (Moscow, 1973), 5–24.

foreign words, calques, or semantic loans are borrowed to fill in the native lexicon; and so forth. All of this occurs either spontaneously (or, at least, without an apparent cause) or by deliberate intervention of authority figures (Maksim Grek, Peter the Great, Lomonosov, et al.). The sociolinguistic system moves toward its natural state of equilibrium.

Such an outline sketch is obviously highly schematic and simplistic; actual sociolinguistic situations are far more complex. For one thing, the very changes in functional style or in the social utilization of genres that serve to bring form and function into harmony can themselves create new imbalances, new tensions which demand their own resolution. The newly introduced Christian cult demanded a functional style adequate to the liturgy, hagiography, and so forth that came with this new belief; the need was filled by a massive influx of South Slavic, largely Greek-calqued vocabulary and syntax foreign to all but a few of the inhabitants of medieval Rus', and this influx of foreign elements took centuries to be assimilated. Similarly, under Peter the Great, the new science and technology demanded a vocabulary missing from Russian; the gap was filled by a flood of Europeanisms (foreign words, calques, semantic loans),[24] but these masses of new words created whole sets of semantically overlapping and stylistically inchoate terminologies which, again, took decades to sort out. After the October Revolution, Russian was filled with acronyms for the hundreds of newly created social institutions, to such an extent that some literature of the period is hardly comprehensible to the nonspecialist.[25] Most of these were eliminated from literary usage, so that today's reader hardly has to worry about more than an occasional *KPSS* or *MGU*. In each such case, and in countless others, the perceived need to respond to some sociolinguistic imbalance was itself the impetus that created new imbalances.

Times of equilibrium and times of disruption do not succeed each other in simple chronological alternation. Disruption in one part of the system may accompany perfect balance elsewhere. For example, lexical barbarisms are a source of annoyance to some authorities,[26] but other parts of the

---

[24] G. Hüttl-Worth, *Die Bereicherung des russischen Wortschatzes im 18. Jhd.* (Vienna, 1956); id., *Foreign Words in Russian: A Historical Sketch, 1550–1800.* University of California Publications in Linguistics, no. 28 (Berkeley–Los Angeles, 1963).

[25] On the language of this period, see R. Jakobson, *Vliv revoluce na ruský jazyk* (Prague, 1921); A. Mazon, *Lexique de la guerre et de la révolution en Russie (1914–1918).* Bibliothèque de l'Institut français de Petrograd, no. 6 (Paris, 1920); A. M. Seliščev, *Jazyk revoljucionnoj èpoxi. Iz nabljudenij nad russkim jazykom poslednix let (1917–1926),* 2nd ed. (Moscow, 1928).

[26] E.g.: "K čemu govorit' 'defekty', kogda možno skazat' nedočety ili nedostatki ili probely?" — V. I. Lenin, *Sočinenija* 30: 274, cited by Gorškov, *Istorija* (see n. 6), 190. Needless to say, *defekt* and its derivatives are now accepted items of the Soviet vocabulary.

linguistic system appear to be functioning smoothly. Orthography, phonology, morphology, syntax, and the lexicon do not respond to external stimuli with the same speed or the same force, as seen, for example, in the fact that the orthographic response to the so-called Second South Slavic Influence was rapid but ephemeral, compared to the much slower but longer-lasting changes in the derivational system.[27] One has to conclude that, although individual cases of disturbance and re-equilibrium may be seen as cases of excitation and subsequent entropic development, the system as a whole cannot be characterized as teleologically entropic; the sociolinguistic system does not "perfect itself" (*usoveršenstvovat'sja*), to use a term encountered occasionally, it does not develop toward a single final goal of inert uniformity, of perfect balance between linguistic form and social function. Rather, this system shows a continuing dynamic interplay of innovation and preservation, occurring simultaneously but not in synchrony in various parts of the system. The social history of a language is a self-generating and self-renewing *dialectic of form/function interrelations.*

Such, then, in bare outline form, is the conceptual framework within which I would propose to examine the social history of a language. Let us now turn, in equally cursory form, to the social history of the Russian language. I shall deal here only with a few of the major external events that caused disruption in the sociolinguistic system.

In a thousand years of language history, there are two, perhaps now three, developments of overwhelming significance for the Russian language. The first of these was the Christianization and Byzantinization of East Slavic culture in the tenth and subsequent centuries. The second was the secularization and Europeanization (or de-Byzantinization) of Russian culture in the seventeenth and, especially, in the eighteenth centuries. In addition, we can discern the workings of a third great change in our own day, although we are still *in medias res* and cannot see too clearly: the "technicalization" and internationalization of Soviet civilization. Other events, such as the founding of the Kievan state by Scandinavian merchants and warlords in the ninth century, the quarter-millennium of "Tatar yoke," or the revolution of 1917, major as they were as purely historical events, had relatively insignificant results as far as the language was concerned (a few dozens of loanwords in the first two cases, numerous but ephemeral

---

[27] On the latter, see H. Keipert, *Die Adjektive auf -telьnъ. Studien zu einem kirchenslavischen Wortbildungstyp.*, vol. 1, Veröffentlichungen der Abteilung für slavische Sprachen und Literaturen des Osteuropa-Instituts (Slavisches Seminar) an der Freien Universität Berlin, no. 45 (Wiesbaden, 1977).

acronyms and some changes in journalistic style in the third). The three major developments, and especially the first two, have much in common. They are cosmopolitan, in that they draw Russia (in the oldest period, Rus') into contact with other and largely non-Slavic civilizations, which were more advanced technically and more sophisticated culturally (this is less obviously so in the case of technicalization, given the generally high level of Soviet technology). In the cases of Christianization and secularization, the main source of sociolinguistic disequilibrium was the sudden influx of new genres, the prestige of which was guaranteed by the ruling authorities and which drew with it an equally sudden flood of foreign language forms in which to express these new genres: Church Slavonic and barely disguised Byzantine Greek in the oldest period; Polish, Ukrainian, and West European during the second. In the technicalization of our own day, the influences are English or, perhaps better, international and pseudoclassical. In addition to these parallels among the two or three major external developments affecting Russian, there were, of course, a great many differences, especially in the number and types of new genres introduced, and in the degree of homogeneity or disparity among the functional styles in which these genres were expressed.[28]

To lend a bit more substance to this rather bare frame, we shall look in more detail at the sociolinguistic situation in Kievan Rus'. It goes without saying that only a portion of any description of Kievan Rus' can actually be based on textual evidence, and the evidence itself is often open to more than one interpretation. For the preliterate period, one must operate entirely by inference, except for a few rare non-Slavic sources (Photios, Al-Masudi, et al.). However, most of the statements below refer to well-known facts or, where inferential, are based on documented though later situations and typologically reasonable generalizations.

All serious problems in the early social history of Russian are connected with the Kievan (in the broad sense) response to Christianization. It is reasonable, therefore, to begin this survey with the sociolinguistic situation present on the eve of this momentous event. The first thing to be said is that Christianization was not in fact an event, but a process, and a lengthy one at that. Missionary activity had been going on for over a century prior to the official Christianization in 988, certainly directly from Byzantium, as

---

[28] According to one view, the creation of a national standard language was due primarily to the increasing linguistic homogeneity of the genre system as it developed through time; cf. D. S. Worth, "Was There a 'Literary Language' in Kievan Rus'?," *The Russian Review* 34 (1975): 1–9.

we know from Photios and Constantine Porphyrogenitos,[29] and probably via Bohemia in Novgorod as well (cf. the Glagolitic graffiti on the walls of the Sophia Cathedral and the fact that mass was celebrated there in honor of Saint Václav).[30] Vladimir's grandmother Olga had converted to Christianity some decades before her grandson, unless this is an apocryphal event based on the parallel with the Ludmila-Václav legend in Bohemia.[31] This missionary activity must have brought a certain, albeit limited, degree of literacy to the Eastern Slavs, although the actual evidence for such literacy is tenuous: we know that at least one grave was marked with the name of the deceased and of the then ruling prince (although we have no idea in what language this marking was written);[32] there is one apparently pre-Christian pot inscribed in Cyrillic;[33] and the earliest East Slavic treaties with Byzantium (911, 944) seem to have been recorded in something close to Old Church Slavonic, judging by the manuscript preserved nearly half a millennium later.[34] One can assume, conversely, that the still-mysterious črъty i rězy, said by Černorizec Xrabr to have been used for divination, were in all probability neither Glagolitic nor Cyrillic; it is hard to imagine terms like "slashes and cuts" being used for an alphabet like Glagolitic, in which curves and circles play such a role, and Cyrillic of course would have

[29] F. Dvorník, *Les Slaves, Byzance et Rome au IXe siècle,* Travaux publiés par l'Institut d'études slaves, no. 4 (Paris, 1926; 2nd ed., Hattiesburg, Miss., 1970), 143 ff.; id., *The Slavs: Their Early History and Civilization* (Boston, 1956), 197.

[30] On the epigraphy, see A. A. Medynceva, *Drevnerusskie nadpisi Novgorodskogo Sofijskogo sobora. XI–XIV veka* (Moscow, 1975).

[31] N. K. Nikoľskij, "K voprosu o sledax moravo-češskogo vlijanija na literaturnyx pamjatnikax domongoľskoj èpoxi," *Vestnik AN SSSR,* 1933, nos. 8–9: 5–18; more recently, N. Ingham, "Czech Hagiography in Kiev: The Prisoner Miracles of Boris and Gleb," *Die Welt der Slaven* 10, no. 2 (1965): 166–182; id., "The Sovereign as Martyr, East and West," *Slavic and East European Journal* 17 (1973): 1–17.

[32] The report, from Ibn-Faldan, is described in I. I. Sreznevskij, *Drevnie pamjatniki russkogo pis'ma i jazyka* (St. Petersburg, 1882), 34. For an optimistic view of the extent to which writing was used by the pagan East Slavs, see D. S. Lixačev, "Istoričeskie predposylki vozniknovenija russkoj pis'mennosti i russkoj literatury," *Voprosy istorii,* 1951, no. 12: 30–54. Lixačev, like many Soviet scholars, never questions the meaning of *Rus';* e.g., when Al-Masudi reports on a Russian temple with an inscription in the wall, Lixačev seems to take it for granted that this was an East Slavic edifice, in spite of the fact that all available evidence indicates that the term referred exclusively to Scandinavians in this early period; any writing seen in this temple was more probably Runic than Glagolitic or Cyrillic (incidentally, if ever a writing system fitted the description črъty i rězy, it was Runic).

[33] See n. 8 above.

[34] S. P. Obnorskij, "Jazyk dogovorov russkix s grekami," *Jazyk i myšlenie* 6–7 (1936): 79–103; I. S. Svjencickyj, "Pytannja pro avtentyčnisť dohovoriv Rusi z hrekamy v X vici," *Voprosy slavjanskogo jazykoznanija,* vol. 2 (Lvov, 1949), 103–122; especially, B. A. Larin, "Dogovory russkix s grekami," in his *Lekcii po istorii russkogo literaturnogo jazyka (X–seredina XVIII v.)* (Moscow, 1975), 24–52.

been recognized as such by Xrabr himself. In any case, we can assume that at least a small number of Eastern Slavs were conversant with (Old) Church Slavonic before 988. At the same time, one should not forget that the dichotomy Slavonic/East Slavic had very little meaning at a time when written language was used mostly for marking pots, spindles, and gravestones with their owners' or inhabitants' names. It might not be too far from the truth to infer from this scant evidence that some of the Eastern Slavs were literate in the sense of being able to read and write, but that—with the possible exception of the two treaties, knowledge of which was surely restricted to the princely court—writing was used only for primitive purposes. It was a situation in which some people may well have been literate, but few if any had any cultural breadth. The use of writing for simple needs was in no way disruptive; it was only after 988 that Byzantine culture flooded Kievan Rus'.

As far as indigenous East Slavic is concerned, everything one can say lies in the realm of guesswork. However, comparative-historical evidence leads one to assume the existence of such folk genres as the heroic epic, probably the lament (although the comparison of Serbian with Russian is less fruitful than in the case of the epic),[35] and perhaps the fairy tale. The existence of an orally codified legal code inherited from Common Slavic can hardly be denied, although this codex was first written down in the early eleventh century and is actually preserved only from the late thirteenth. Evidence for other codified speech forms (other "functional styles") is slimmer; among them one can mention the ambassadorial and military formulae assumed by Lixačev.[36] Finally, it would be odd if there had been no incantations connected with the pagan cult, but there is no direct evidence about them at all.

All of this available evidence—and there is not much of it—justifies the assumption that pre-Christian Kievan Rus' was in a state of sociolinguistic equilibrium. There were relatively few codified genres (the epic, the legal code, perhaps religious incantations); to the extent Slavonic forms appeared at all, in the early treaties, they could hardly have constituted a functional style. The sociolinguistic equilibrium of a relatively stable pagan society could not have been upset much, if at all, by the first stirrings of missionary activity and the few rare instances of writing.

What happened with the official Christianization of the Kievan state by Vladimir in 988 is well known. The previous balance of form and function

---

[35] R. Jakobson, "Studies in Comparative Slavic Metrics," *Oxford Slavonic Papers* 3 (1952): 21–66.

[36] D. S. Lixačev, *Vozniknovenie russkoj literatury* (Moscow–Leningrad, 1952), 90ff.

was destroyed by the sudden appearance of a dozen or so hitherto unknown genres: tetra- and aprakos-gospels, the Psalter, various liturgical texts (with and without musical notation), canon law, hagiography, sermons, patristic writings of all sorts, and a variety of secular types such as history (John Malalas, George Hamartolos; Josephus Flavius), natural history (bestiaries, geographical descriptions), and fictional tales (Digenis Akritas, Akir Premudryj, Varlaam and Joasaphat, et al.). These came partly from Byzantium itself, partly from the older Middle East, and they were written largely or even entirely in Church Slavonic, which in its syntax and derivational structure was patterned largely on Greek, although its phonology and morphology did not differ significantly from those of the Eastern Slavs. Literacy appears to have spread fairly rapidly, at least among the upper clergy and the ruling family, the women of which could also read and, at least to some extent, write (Anna Jaroslavna). Delighted at having been included into the Christian family and thus becoming part of world history,[37] Kievan scribes began a whole spate of literary activity: the princely archives, oral legend, and borrowed church history were combined into the first Russian chronicle, the legal codex was amended and set down in writing, church orators composed their own original sermons, and monks began a local hagiography (Antonij Pečerskij [?], Feodosij Pečerskij, Boris and Gleb) and, for the first time, business transactions could be recorded on parchment (the *Mstislavova gramota* of c. 1131 is the oldest preserved princely charter, but there must have been others before it; the oldest complete birchbark letter from the Nerev End in Novgorod may date from as early as 1025, and in any case no later than 1096).[38] Only the pagan poetic and religious genres, recognized as anti-Christian by the organized Church, were kept in the realm of oral transmission—a fact that is understandable enough in the case of religious incantations, though the complete absence of recorded *stariny* until the seventeenth and eighteenth centuries remains a mystery.

The result of this sudden outburst of literary activity was a large and heterogeneous group of genres, some more or less pure, some mixed, some written in straight Church Slavonic, others in nearly pure East Slavic vernacular (which is, incidentally, not to be equated in all cases with the

---

[37] Dm. Tschiẑewskij, *Geschichte der altrussischen Literatur im XI–XIII Jahrhundert. Kiever Epoche* (Frankfurt a/M., 1948), 105ff.

[38] *Gramota* no. 246, published by A. V. Arcixovskij and V. I. Borkovskij, *Novgorodskie gramoty na bereste (iz raskopok 1956–1957 gg.)* (Moscow, 1963), 67–69; for the latest dendrochronological table, see A. V. Arcixovskij and V. L. Janin, *Novgorodskie gramoty na bereste (iz raskopok 1962–1976 gg.)* (Moscow, 1978), 5.

spoken language of the time; the legal code, for example, was almost certainly archaic), and many in one or another mixture of the two. Here were the origins of the centuries-long tension between Church Slavonic and native elements, a tension that was to be more or less resolved only in Puškin's time. To try to classify genres by their language is a risky business, mostly because the preliminary work has yet to be done. In particular, the evaluation of Slavonic and East Slavic doublets has really only begun, and even then, primarily for the so-called phonetic Slavonisms.[39] Really close attention to conditioning factors produces surprising results, for example, that the choice of *azъ* versus *jazъ* is conditioned by the syntactic environment,[40] or that in certain chronicle segments the gen.-acc. *ego* must be considered a Slavonism, compared to the neutral *i.*[41] Another problem lies in the fact that so many of our texts are preserved only in much younger copies, often after the so-called Second South Slavic Influence, so that the textual data are of uncertain value (as is well known, Šaxmatov reconstructed the *Igor' Tale* with *trat* forms, while Jakobson tends to assume that *torot* may have been original).[42] Finally, a major problem lies in the concept of "genre" itself: we may speak blithely of a "system of genres," but it remains to be proved that there really were objectively definable genres, in the linguo-social sense in which we use the term (one is hard put to find common linguistic elements in Hilarion and Luka Židjata), not to mention the problem of proving that they formed a system.[43] Only after a great deal of preliminary work has been done will we know enough, not only about the obvious phonetic (*trat/torot*, etc.) and morphological (gen.sg.fem. -*ę/-ě*, etc.) Slavonisms but also about derivational patterns, syntactic embedding procedures, element order (subject–verb–object/verb–subject–object, etc.),

[39] G. Hüttl-Folter, "Zur Sprache der Nestorchronik: Russisch-kirchenslavisch–altrussische lexikalische Wechselbeziehungen," *Zeitschrift für slavische Philologie* 41, no. 1 (1980): 34–57.

[40] D. S. Worth, "Vernacular and Slavonic in Kievan Rus'," *Slavonic Literary Languages: Essays Honouring Robert Auty and Anne Pennington* (Oxford–Los Angeles, forthcoming).

[41] Emily R. Klenin, "The Genitive-Accusative as a Slavonicism in the Laurentian Manuscript: The Problem of Text Segmentation," *American Contributions to the Ninth International Congress of Slavists, Kiev, September 7–14, 1983*, vol. 1: *Linguistics*, ed. Michael S. Flier (Columbus, Ohio, 1983), 161–170.

[42] *La geste du Prince Igor'. Epopée russe du douzième siècle*. Texte établi, traduit et commenté sous la direction d'Henri Gregoire, de Roman Jakobson et de Marc Szeftel, assistés de J. A. Joffe, Annuaire de l'Institut de philologie et d'histoire orientales et slaves, no. 8. (New York, 1948). Jakobson retains Slavonic readings where these are used in a twelfth-century sense, but adds the East Slavic forms, as possibly original, in parentheses.

[43] On the genre system of Kievan Rus', see R. Jagoditsch, "Zum Begriff der 'Gattungen' in der altrussischen Literatur," *Wiener Slavistisches Jahrbuch* 6 (1957/58): 113–137; D. S. Lixačev, (inter alia) "Žanry i vidy drevnerusskoj literatury," in his *Razvitie russkoj literatury X–XVII vekov. Èpoxi i stili* (Leningrad, 1973), 49–62.

clause length, and so on, to begin using the term *system* with any real content. Nonetheless, even our present preliminary knowledge may allow us to risk a few generalizations.

One can tentatively assume the existence of three groups of genres in Kievan Rus', with three different degrees of linguistic stability and, consequently, three different degrees of blending of autochthonous and Slavonic elements (bearing in mind that the latter were assimilated rather early; by the thirteenth century it makes no sense to speak of Slavonisms as "foreign" or "imported"; they were merely elements of a particular group of functional styles). On the extremes, one has those genres, both indigenous and imported, that had already existed in well-codified form before the introduction of Christianity to Kiev. On the Slavonic side, these were the Bible itself (the New Testament, the Psalter, perhaps some more of the Old Testament), some liturgical works, and some patristic literature. These genres, which had in most cases already lived through a hundred-year-long Slavonic tradition in Moravia, Bohemia, and Bulgaria-Macedonia, were transplanted to Kiev as well-established forms, with well-established functional language styles, and as such, they were very nearly immune to penetration by East Slavic elements (except for minor phonetic adjustments such as *žd* → *ž* and *-tъ* → *-tь*). The same was probably true, though we have no evidence, of those indigenous genres with a long East Slavic tradition, namely, the legal code and the folk genres referred to above, which were too well established, and in some cases too prestigious, to be affected in any substantial way by Church Slavonic.[44] On each of the extremes, then, we find a group of well-codified genres with a high degree of functional specialization and a correspondingly strong resistance to any linguistic incursions from the opposite extreme.

In a second group of genres, the situation was somewhat more fluid. This occurred when the given genre had not existed as such in codified form before the advent of Christianity, or when the genre itself, being less directly connected with the revealed word of God, was by definition less firmly codified. In such cases the scribe, who had no ready-made model to follow, was more free to pick and choose from both Slavonic and native forms, as his sense of stylistic appropriateness dictated. His choices were to

---

[44] The Slavonisms in the *Russkaja Pravda*, noted by A. M. Seliščev in a 1941 article published only in 1957 ("O jazyke Russkoj Pravdy v svjazi s voprosom o drevnejšem tipe russkogo literaturnogo jazyka," *Voprosy jazykoznanija,* 1957, no. 4: 57–63), are not numerous and are more likely to have been added by the scribe of the 1282 *Kormčaja* (at a time when the interpenetration of Slavonic and East Slavic had been under way for three hundred years) than to have been in the original eleventh-century text.

a large extent determined by his subject matter: new genres tended to imitate the language of those genres whose subject matter they most closely resembled. Documents of a juridical nature (*gramoty*, treaties, political agreements) tended to use a language close to that of the *Russkaja Pravda*, but with a freer admixture of Slavonic, especially in opening and closing formulae (*Se az M'stislav* ...). Sermons and semihagiographic works like the chronicle account of the murders of Saints Boris and Gleb tended to use a heavily Slavonicized language imitative of the preexistent Christian genres, but they showed a freer range of variation in their use of indigenous elements than did the latter (*Stopolkъ že ... posylaja k Borisu glše· jako s toboju xočju ljubovь iměti ... Stopolkъ že pride nočьju Vyšegorodu ...*, etc.).[45]

Finally, there was a third group of genres which evolved primarily in East Slavic territory, although not entirely without Byzantine prototypes. Either the genre itself was mixed (the chronicle, if we are to accept it as a distinct genre), or it could draw on both native and imported verbal traditions, as in the case of the military tale (Josephus Flavius). Here, too, belong two works, which, although highly artistic, are difficult to define in terms of genre: the *Molenie Daniila Zatočnika* and the *Igor' Tale*. The first of these deliberately mixes Slavonic and native prosody,[46] and in general appears to be a parodistic combination of popular and learned styles. In works of this third group, where the scribe was relatively untrammeled by either tradition, he was free to use his own artistic taste and imagination, drawing on the linguistic and poetic resources of both worlds; it is here that we find the widest range of vernacular and Slavonic forms and the most sophisticated attempts at combining them into a new codified style appropriate to these new genres. Nor is it surprising if we find an occasional awkward spot or *temnoe mesto* in *Daniil* or the *Igor' Tale*, any more than we are surprised at the infelicities of a Pastor Gregory some centuries later. This third, mixed group of genres was the sociolinguistic workshop within which the disruptions caused by the advent of Christianity began to be worked out, a workshop in which the opposing extremes of native and imported forms could gradually intermingle and converge (in the same way, at a later date, it was new, nontraditional genres—diplomatic reports, poetry and drama, history and social commentary, novels and short stories—that pro-

---

[45] And Svjatopolk ... sent for Boris, saying, "I wish to make peace with you...." And Svjatopolk arrived in Vyšegorod at night.... *PVL, s.a.* 1015.

[46] K. F. Taranovskij, "Formy obščeslavjanskogo i cerkovnoslavjanskogo stixa v drevnerusskoj literature XI–XIII vv.," *American Contributions to the Sixth International Congress of Slavists, Prague, August 7–13,* vol. 1: *Linguistic Contributions,* ed. Henry Kučera (The Hague–Paris, 1968), 377–394.

vided the workshop for Western European and Slavic elements to be amalgamated into what we now know as contemporary standard Russian). The growth of this third group was interrupted, as we know, by the events of the Second South Slavic Influence.

Although the details vary from one period to another, the general lines of the social history of Russian are clear: new social situations require (or permit) the development of new genres; these, in turn, require their own, new functional styles, and these new functional styles permit the harmonious combination of elements which would have been incongruous in more established genres. Form and function tend toward equilibrium, which can, however, prevail only until the next new social situation evokes a repetition of this dialectic change.

THE IMPACT OF ECCLESIASTIC CULTURE
ON OLD RUSSIAN LITERARY TECHNIQUES

RICCARDO PICCHIO

Russian scholars of the Soviet period are to be given credit for broadly investigating and reappraising many previously neglected aspects of the "old literature" (tenth to seventeenth century) of their country. In the last fifty years, Soviet specialists have established most of the interpretative schemes currently applied to the literary civilization of Rus' and Muscovy.[1] Old and new prejudices have been dispelled. Many old works have been reevaluated not merely as cultural documents but as samples of verbal art. Their ideological messages, formal characteristics, and manuscript transmission have been investigated against the proper historical background. In this way, the production, growth, and eventual decline of what can be considered an autonomous literary system have been outlined with sufficient clarity. Perhaps the valuable *History of Russian Literature from the Tenth to the Seventeenth Century*, recently published by a group of scholars under the direction of D. S. Lixačev, offers the most convenient basis for a critical assessment of the *status questionis* in some fields of research that undoubtedly deserve further investigation.[2]

---

[1] Systematic research on Old Russian literature reflecting the Soviet view of cultural history began in the thirties, and gained formal recognition in 1934 when a *Sektor drevnerusskoj literatury* was established within the Institute for Russian Literature at the Soviet Academy of Sciences in Leningrad.

[2] *Istorija russkoj literatury X–XVII vekov*, ed. D. S. Lixačev (Moscow, 1980). This volume was conceived as a textbook for Soviet students. Its critical interest resides mainly in the effort of its five distinguished authors (L. A. Dmitriev, D. S. Lixačev, Ja. S. Lur'e, A. M. Pančenko, and O. V. Tvorogov) to present their views in a unified form, in accordance with both the new historiographic schemes elaborated by D. S. Lixačev and some traditional interpretative schemes of Soviet scholarship. The latest book by A. N. Robinson, *Literatura drevnej Rusi v literaturnom processe srednevekov'ja XI–XIII vv.* (Moscow, 1980), reached me only after I had completed this study. Some of Robinson's interesting remarks can help us evaluate—from a different point of view—certain supranational trends discussed in the present study. This applies in particular to "the Byzantino-Bulgarian-Russian, Czech-Russian, and later Russian-Bulgarian-Serbian literary interconnections" (p. 65). Chapters 3, 6, and 7 of the same book, which deal with the Old Russian epos and its connections with the epic traditions of the European Middle Ages, also present a different angle as to the international connections of Early Russian literature.

An important characteristic of the old literature of Rus' and Muscovy
appears to be its marked dependence on the religious tradition and, more
particularly, the spiritual patterns upheld by the authority of the Church.
Yet the significance of this particular phenomenon is not consistently
emphasized in current scholarship. The above-mentioned *History* lists several typical features of Old Russian literature such as its conventionality (or
ètiketnost', to use Lixačev's term), its tendency to resist innovation and, last
but not least, its patriotic inspiration.[3] The Soviet authors of this *History*,
however, do not attach equal importance to the predominance of church-
inspired themes or the role of ecclesiastic views on the scope and purpose
of writing activity. The main religious sources are mentioned, but their
pattern-establishing function is not considered of decisive relevance.

It seems fair to assume that this attitude is more the result of long-term
habit than the expression of a critical thesis. Until the early twentieth century, modern scholarship regarded most of the medieval and premodern
writing of the Russian lands as patently nonpoetic, although not deprived
of spiritual value, and as nonliterary products of a church-dominated culture. Ecclesiastic tyranny was held responsible for this state of affairs. It
was therefore believed that one had to prove the nonecclesiastic inspiration
of certain Old Russian texts in order to reevaluate their literary significance.

This view has clearly become obsolete. Nevertheless other considerations
contribute to keep alive the prejudice according to which true literature
should be mainly secular in spirit. One may wonder, in particular, whether
the emergence in eighteenth-century Russia of a new notion of "literature"
(*belles lettres*) in opposition to old-fashioned and bookish "writing" (*pis'-
mennost'*, or *knižnost'*) produced a conceptual dichotomy so deeply assimilated as to survive subsequent changes in critical thought.[4]

At present, the role that Christian doctrine, biblical and patristic models
and, in general, church culture played in the old literature of the Eastern

---

[3] Lixačev, *Istorija*, 3–7.
[4] The need for a new and "real" literature was a pervasive theme in the years that preceded
Peter the Great's cultural revolution. True literature was considered a symbol of progress by
both the Russians and their Western critics. Certain ideological schemes were then elaborated
in part as a response to Western accusations. The Czech Jesuit Georgius David, a biased but acute critic of *Slavia rossica*, observed in 1690 that Russian monks "ebrietati sunt
plerique deditissimi, praeter legere aliud nihil scient." In his opinion, "Ingenia Moscorum
capacia sunt omnis disciplinae, sed inculta et sylvestria, idque ob defectum instructionis ac
studiorum, quod emendari non potest, nisi eo studia literaria inducantur." See Georgius
David, *Status modernus Magnae Russiae seu Moscoviae* (1690), edited with introduction and
explanatory index by A. V. Florovskij (London–The Hague–Paris, 1966), 92, 100. In spite of
its angry rejection of all remarks of this kind, a portion of the modern Russian intelligentsia
seems to have retained some opinions and prejudices of those years.

Slavs is increasingly gaining recognition. However, it is not generally accepted practice to consider ecclesiastic culture as a dominant source of inspiration for Old Russian writers. This reluctance should be put aside. It seems evident that the true meaning of many Old Russian works is very difficult to grasp for the modern reader without sufficient command of the sacred texts or at least a Bible on his desk, plus an adequate collection of biblical and patristic reference books at hand. Obviously it does not matter whether the modern reader is a believer, an atheist, an agnostic, or a differently oriented modern man. He is not supposed to accept or reject the messages of old writing, but simply to investigate a particular aspect of a remarkable literary heritage.

It is assumed that the majority of scholars agree on the latter point. The problem, therefore, seems to be more technical than ideological. To solve it requires the training of a new generation of specialists in medieval Slavic literature, scholars who can systematically search the old texts, looking for direct or indirect references to doctrinary and scriptural literature, borrowings and calques from official and apocryphal Christian texts, imitations of the ecclesiastic style, and any other similarly marked material.[5]

As a preliminary contribution to this badly needed enterprise, this article offers a discussion of the impact that ecclesiastic culture seems to have had on the literary techniques of Old Russian writers.

An appraisal of what is currently defined as Old Russian literature depends to a considerable extent on how the qualifier *Old Russian* is perceived. It is generally known that this is a conventional term which should not be taken literally. To maintain that the spiritual heritage in question can be ascribed to either a bygone "pre-Russian" civilization or to a modern East Slavic community of nations is a moderate way of avoiding patriotic confrontations. To get to the core of the problem, it seems more important to ascertain to what extent national (i.e., local) and/or supranational ideas might have affected, in different periods of time, the cultural milieu out of which "Old Russian" works were brought forth.

It is obviously an exaggeration to claim that national and patriotic feelings did not have any relevant part in the life of medieval Christendom. Medieval national ideas, however, differed from those of our age in so many ways that it is necessary to define their character and role in each

---

[5] In his lucid first chapter of *Istorija,* O. V. Tvorogov reminds Soviet students of the paramount importance of both the Bible and the works of the Church Fathers for the study of Old Russian literature. He provides his readers not only with a concise description of the content of that sacred corpus but also with a valuable survey of the diffusion of patristic literature in Kievan Rus' (pp. 39–43).

particular situation under examination. In the case of both the Eastern and the Balkan Slavs, it seems proper to emphasize the existence of a type of "national" self-awareness that was ethnic political, and religious at the same time. Allegiance to the political code of the Russian (or "Rusian"), Bulgarian, or Serbian land was not at odds with the awareness of belonging to a larger spiritual community which comprised all the followers of the Orthodox Slavic faith. Orthodox Slavs shared a sort of religious patriotism in accordance with the medieval notions of *nationes et confessiones.*[6] This terminological dyad implies both a distinction and a dialectic interrelationship. As to the spiritual community of Balkan and Eastern Slavs, the term *Orthodox Slavdom* (*Slavia orthodoxa*) defines its essence with sufficient precision. This term is accepted in current scholarship in spite of certain reservations and corrections submitted in the last two decades. It does not imply any belief in the existence of fixed territorial boundaries, nor does it suggest any underevaluation of the role played by local traditions, ethnic or political particularism, and even ecclesiastic autonomies.[7]

Thus, our study of "Old Russian literature" cannot consider only one environment. Even if one accepts the idea of an "Old Russian" cultural unity consistently overcoming the centrifugal tendencies of local East Slavic civilizations, it appears that the spiritual history of the Russian lands—

[6] See my study "Questione della lingua e Slavia cirillometodiana," in *Studi sulla Questione della lingua presso gli Slavi,* ed. R. Picchio (Rome, 1972), 7–120, esp. 10–13.

[7] I submitted my definition of *Slavia orthodoxa* for the first time twenty-four years ago (*Ricerche Slavistiche* 6 [1958]: 103–118). The discussion subsequently conducted by various eminent scholars on this concept has helped me redefine it in a more precise way. The remarks of D. S. Lixačev (*TODRL* 17 [1961]: 675–678), C. Backvis (*Revue belge de philologie et d'histoire* 40, no. 3 [1961]: 864–887), I. S. Dujčev (*TODRL* 18 [1962]: 552–568), L. Moszyński (*Rocznik Slawistyczny* 24 [1963]: 153–154), Dj. Trifunović (*Prilozi za književnost, jezik, istoriju i folklor* 38, nos. 1–2 [1972]: 143–144), and H. Birnbaum (in his *On Medieval and Renaissance Slavic Writing* [The Hague–Paris, 1974], 13–40) have been particularly stimulating. Cf. my "Questione della lingua" (see n. 6), 11–12. There has been some doubt as to the way in which the Latin term *Slavia orthodoxa* should be rendered in modern languages. A. M. Pančenko, for example, uses the formula *ortodoksaľnoe pravoslavie* (*Russkaja sillabičeskaja poèzija XVII–XVIII vv.*, Biblioteka poèta, boľšaja serija [Leningrad, 1970], 21, 24). D. S. Lixačev prefers more analytic definitions such as *Pravoslavnyj jugo-vostok Evropy* (*Razvitie russkoj literatury* [Leningrad, 1973], 112–113). Occasionally, however, he refers to *Slavia orthodoxa* as *Pravoslavnoe slavjanstvo* (ibid., p. 38). In my opinion, terminological formulae such as the English *Orthodox Slavdom* or the Russian *Pravoslavnoe slavjanstvo* are perfectly adequate to render the idea of an "obširnaja obščaja literatura i obščij literaturno-cerkovnyj jazyk" (ibid., 38) in accordance with the historiographic scheme I submitted in my 1963 article, "A proposito della Slavia ortodossa e della comunità linguistica slava ecclesiastica," *Ricerche Slavistiche* 11 (1963): 105–127. In 1970 the formula *Slavia orthodoxa* was used as the title of a collection of studies by I. Dujčev, including his discussion of precisely my presentation of this term and concept (I. Dujčev, *Slavia orthodoxa: Collected Studies in the History of the Slavic Middle Ages,* preface by I. Ševčenko [London, 1970]).

during their peculiar and long-lasting "Middle Ages" (until the eighteenth century)—cannot be isolated from that of the supranational community of Orthodox Slavdom.

It is important at this point to note that no historiographic formula can reflect historical truth in all its complexities. Whatever terminological cliché one may use, its meaning can prove adequate only within the limits of a preestablished conceptual convention. What really counts is the historian's ability to use conceptual formulae in accordance with their accepted semantic limitations. With reference to my particular research, the term *Old Russian* can be used as a qualifier expressing a connection with that portion of the Slavic world (*Slavia*) that we may call *Slavia rossica*. It is hoped that one can still rely on the ideological neutrality of Latin formulae of this kind. By stating that *Slavia rossica*, from the religious and cultural point of view, was a part of *Slavia orthodoxa*, I hope to express the idea of a twofold cultural allegiance with acceptable conciseness.

It is essential to the purpose of this study to determine who in old *Slavia rossica* might have had the power to establish the principles and the practical rules that governed the art of writing. One may argue that various literary techniques could have resulted from the merging experiences and the competition of different centers. In reality, such a democratic process—even if its possible impact should not be completely disregarded—did not have any decisive effect on Old Russian tradition. Apparently, it was precisely the limited range of innovative trends that made possible the continuity and unity of that tradition.[8]

The overall picture of Old Russian literary civilization that one can draw from the available corpus of texts is that of a literate minority obeying ecclesiastic rules and providing from its own ranks the kernel of both the authorial body and the reading public. Monasteries and churches were the main places where the Old Russian literary game was performed. In order to understand the rules of that game,[9] a modern reader should let his

---

[8] Cf. N. K. Gudzij, *Istorija drevnej russkoj literatury,* 7th ed. (Moscow, 1966), 12; Lixačev, *Istorija* (see n. 2), 449. According to D. Čiževskij, *History of Russian Literature from the Eleventh Century to the End of the Baroque* (The Hague, 1962), "the geographical-political criterion is fully significant only in later literary development, namely in the transfer of the centre of literary life from Kiev and the rest of the Ukrainian region, to the North and North-East, to the Great-Russian area" (p. 146).

[9] On the "rules of the game," see R. Picchio, "Principles of Comparative Slavic-Romance Literary History," in *American Contributions to the Eighth International Congress of Slavists, Zagreb and Ljubljana, September 3–9, 1978,* vol. 2: *Literature,* ed. V. Terras (Columbus, Ohio, 1978), 630–643, and id., *Études littéraires slavo-romanes,* Studia Historica et Philologica, vol. 6, Sectio Slavoromanica, no. 3 (Florence, 1978).

historical memory revisit those places. To do so, he should have at his disposal detailed descriptions or critical reconstructions of all centers where ecclesiastic literacy may have flourished. A literary-minded topography of Old Russian ecclesiastic culture may well represent a serious task for future scholarship.

On the basis of what is known, it seems reasonable to assume that the power of establishing principles and practical rules for literary activity belonged almost exclusively to the clergy. The secular power of medieval princes and other dignitaries could affect, and occasionally even direct, the activity of ecclesiatic writers, but it would not challenge their technical monopoly on the actual production of written texts. This consideration leads me to believe that the acceptance of certain rules and methods for the art of writing depended mostly on the same authoritative bodies that regulated the work, morals, and doctrinary obedience of monks and priests.

Monks and priests were more aware than anybody else of the cultural unity of Orthodox Slavdom. Even in periods marked by the stagnation of political and commercial exchanges, the few monks and priests who traveled outside the Russian lands or were visited by their spiritual brothers from the Balkan Slavic and Byzantine regions would keep abreast of the regulations of the Orthodox Church. Ecclesiastic vigilance was necessary to prevent and battle deviations from the official doctrine. No other power could preserve the spiritual unity of Orthodox Slavdom better than that of the Church. And no other field of social activity, from the ecclesiastic viewpoint, was more sensitive than that of the written expression and communication.

Given this situation, it is fair to conclude that any equivalent of what one calls today "theory of literature" could only be regulated by ecclesiastic bodies. True, one may wonder whether there was any real theory of literature in Old Rus' and Muscovy. The answer to this question cannot be based on mere speculation. The only way to find out whether Old Russian texts were or were not produced in accordance with established rules is to analyze these texts. If an examination of the literary corpus that has come down to us indicates that Old Russian writers consistently complied with theoretical and practical principles, then one must consider the ecclesiastic establishment as the most likely source of theoretical regulation. By definition, no theory of literature could be conceived apart from the unity of the Orthodox doctrine. This doctrine was meant to be universal and was supposed to govern human behavior in both ecclesiastic and secular life, because both were part of the universal Church.

The actual impact of ecclesiastic regulations on the literary craft of Old Russian writers depended to a great extent on the characteristics of the language they used. Much more so than literary theory, this aspect of the question has attracted modern scholars of different orientations. Current studies recognize the decisive role played by the literary medium common to all Orthodox Slavs and dependent on Church Slavic grammatical and stylistic patterns. These studies confirm the existence of a "Church Slavic linguistic community" until at least the late seventeenth century, paralleling the historical function of the cutural community of *Slavia orthodoxa.*

The best-known aspect of the Orthodox Slavic language question is represented by recurrent attempts to restore the "purity" of the sacred medium into which it was claimed that the Slavic Scripture had originally been translated. In practice, every "revision of the books" (*ispravlenie knig,* according to the formula provided almost a century ago by P. A. Syrku) expressed the concern of a vigilant ecclesiastic authority to keep under control any possible deviation from the "true word." The external history of Orthodox Slavic letters, that is, their changing status within Eastern Christianity, may be outlined on the basis of the discussions that developed on the dignity and norm of the Slavonic (*slověnьskyi*) language. From Xrabr to Evtimij and Kostenečki, from Smotrickij to Avvakum and, in a sense, until the time of Trediakovskij and Lomonosov, one of the main issues in the literary history of Orthodox Slavdom, including *Slavia rossica,* remained that of "correct writing."[10] Before the eighteenth century, no one would even think of tackling such a delicate matter without taking into account its theoretical formulation in the Orthodox tradition. The ecclesiastic authority was beyond discussion.

Thus, if one agrees that the ecclesiastic establishment was the main source of norms regulating the "correct" (i.e., consistent with the "right doctrine") use of the linguistic medium, why should one not assume that the same type of power was wielded by the same religious body in the field of the theory of literature? This consideration seems to be well-founded. At first glance, however, it may create perplexity among Slavic medievalists. Is it proper, some of them may ask, to reduce typically Old Russian, Old Serbian, Old and Middle Bulgarian texts to the common denominator of a pan-Orthodox Slavic theory and practice of literature?

Undoubtedly there is a danger that one may replace one exaggeration— that is, the ideological particularism of the national-patriotic schools—

---

[10] Cf. R. Picchiô, "Introduction à une étude comparée de la Question de la langue chez les Slaves," *Études littéraires slavo-romanes* (see n. 9), 159–180.

with another exaggeration in the opposite direction. This can only happen,
however, if one fails to emphasize the equal importance of each aspect of
the twofold cultural allegiance described above. Neither of the two main
components of Orthodox Slavic literary civilization, namely, the supranational and the national, should be overemphasized at the expense of the
other.

There seems to be a parallel development of the normative activities
affecting the linguistic medium of Orthodox Slavic literature on the one
hand and those affecting rhetoric and poetics on the other. The more the
language was revised and codified according to conservative and puristic
principles—as in the case of the pan-Orthodox movement traditionally
referred to as the Second South Slavic Influence—the more the rhetorical
sophistication of the ecclesiastic style became apparent. Understandably,
some local scribes would see this sort of restoration of linguistic orthodoxy
as an imposition. Their response to certain linguistic expressions, which
they perceived as foreign or artificial, reflected their attachment to developing local traditions. The same, or at least a similar, process may have
characterized the encounters of established themes and stylemes with local
motives, imagery, and narrative habits. To describe and thoroughly evaluate the development of these interrelations, rejections, and compromises
would be tantamount to writing a new type of literary history. Apparently,
no one at present can successfully carry out this enterprise. There is, however, a growing consensus among scholars of the need for preparatory
studies. D. S. Lixačev's book, the *Poetics of Old Russian Literature,* has
greatly contributed to making Slavists aware of this crucial problem.[11]

It has frequently been stated that our understanding of Old Russian literary
techniques is hampered by the lack of old treatises dealing systematically
with the medieval Slavic theory of literature. The few documents advanced
to prove the contrary, such as the Slavic version of Georgios Choiroboskos'
treatise on figures (Περὶ τρόπων ποιητικῶν)[12] have mitigated, but not eliminated, this negative impression. One may wonder, however, whether the

[11] D. S. Lixačev, *Poètika drevnerusskoj literatury,* 2nd ed. (Leningrad, 1971). Lixačev's
research is based on the assumption that "v literaturax pravoslavnogo slavjanstva možno na-
bljudať obščie smeny stilja, obščie umstvennye tečenija, postojannyj obmen proizvedenijami i
rukopisjami" (p. 7). As to the significance of these supranational trends for the study of the
so-called Second South Slavic Influence, see M. Iovine, *The History and Historiography of the
Second South Slavic Influence* (Ann Arbor: University Microfilms, 1979).
[12] Both the Greek text and the Slavic translation are published and commented on in
J. Besharov, *Imagery of the Igor' Tale in the Light of Byzantino-Slavic Poetic Theory* (Leiden,
1956).

real difficulty resides not in the alleged theoretical inadequacy of the
Orthodox Slavic literary civilization, but rather in scholars' improperly
defining the terms of the problem.

Why should one believe *a priori* that in Old Rus' the theory of literature
was conceived of as an autonomous discipline? And if it was not considered
an autonomous discipline, why should we be surprised that no autonomous
Old Russian theoretical treatise, corresponding to Western treatises on
poetics and rhetoric, has come down to us?

Given the ecclesiastic monopoly on writing techniques, it is fair to
assume that the Christian Orthodox dogmatic teaching itself, in its indivisi-
ble unity, was the functional equivalent of what we now call "theory of
literature." The purpose of any practical guidance provided by the religious
establishment could only be that of implementing the supreme law of the
"right doctrine" or *orthodoxy.* If this general principle was accepted (and
one can hardly see how monks and priests could reject it), no separation of
the technical principles (*xitrosti*) from their theoretical foundations (*učenie*)
was admissible. With regard to the general theory of Orthodox Slavic verbal expression, this point has been illustrated by Harvey Goldblatt's
exhaustive analysis of Kostenečki's treatise *On the Letters.*[13] The systematic
investigation of other Orthodox Slavic texts, in particular those of the
Rusian area, may provide an adequate documentation of the validity of this
very principle in the fields of rhetoric and poetics.

Before beginning the complete investigation of the theoretical statements
contained in many Orthodox Slavic works concerning literary activity, it
seems advisable to concentrate on some of the oldest literary documents
preserved in the Russian area. Both the *Izbornik of 1073* and the *Izbornik of
1076* deserve particular attention.

Concerning the *Izbornik of 1073*, its paramount importance for the entire
Orthodox Slavic community has been recently reasserted by scholars
reflecting both Russian and Bulgarian points of view.[14] Its dependence on
Byzantine models has also been emphasized, along with the necessity of
studying its functional features against a broader background. For the
purpose of this study, it is the portion of this miscellaneous codex containing Choiroboskos' treatise that interests us most. This treatise deals with
figures of speech (τρόποι), that is, with the technical use (*xitrosti*) of the

---

[13] H. Goldblatt, "Orthography and Orthodoxy: Constantine Kostenečki's Treatise on the
Letters," Ph.D. diss., Yale, 1977. A revised version of this study is due to appear shortly as vol.
16 of Studia Historica et Philologica (Florence).

[14] *Izbornik Svjatoslava 1073 g., Sbornik statej*, ed. B. A. Rybakov (Moscow, 1977).

literary *ornatus* (cf. below). It does not provide any particularly marked theological or philosophical guidance. Nevertheless, it is worth noting that, as shown by E. È. Granstrem and L. S. Kovtun, most of its examples are taken from Homer and the Bible.[15] This justifies Justinia Besharov's attempt to establish a connection between the rhetorical tradition represented by this document on the one hand and the formal complexities of the *Igor'* *Tale* on the other.[16] Even more important, however, appears to be the treatise's appurtenance to the Greco-Christian tradition. Its abidance by, or at least its reputed nonopposition to, the general tradition of Christian eloquence is implicitly proved by its insertion into an official volume dedicated to Orthodox princes (Simeon and Svjatoslav) by their ecclesiastic entourage.

It seems therefore advisable to evaluate this treatise, *O obrazěxъ*, on the basis of its contextual function rather than as a rhetorical work *per se*. A solid basis for this analysis has been established by L. P. Grjazina and N. A. Ščerbačeva.[17] In the *Izbornik of 1073*, Choiroboskos' discussion of *obrazi* is preceded by two fragments from the works of Maximus the Confessor.[18] The second of these fragments is entitled *Togože o jedinenii jako po desjati byvaet obraz sъjedinenija* (By the same [Maximus], On union: how the form of union takes place in ten ways). The problem discussed in this section represents a crucial aspect of what may be considered the semiotics of Christian (in this case, anti-Monothelitic) gnoseology. In its Slavic wording, Maximus' classification of the *obrazi* 'forms, ways', in which perceivable things can be reduced to unity, reads as follows:

> Vъ jedineniixsja rastojaštiixsja priobъšteno jestь tečenie, sъjedinenije že naričesja. Imьže vъ jedino sъkupljatisja vestьmъ po desjati že obrazъ. Naričajetьsja sъjedinenije po sǫštijǫ, po vъsoblenijǫ, po ljubvi, po složenijǫ, po pričetanijǫ, po rastvoru, po izmutu, po sъlьjanijǫ, po sypanijǫ, po pakysъkuplenijǫ.[19]

[15] E. È. Granstrem and L. S. Kovtun, "Poètičeskie terminy v Izbornike 1073 g. i razvitie ix v russkoj tradicii (analiz traktata Georgija Xirovoskova)," in *Izbornik Svjatoslava 1073 g.* (see n. 14), 99–108.

[16] Besharov, *Imagery of the Igor' Tale* (see n. 12).

[17] L. P. Grjazina and N. A. Ščerbačeva, "K tekstologii Izbornika 1073 g. (po rukopisjam Gosudarstvennoj biblioteki SSSR im. V. I. Lenina)," in *Izbornik Svjatoslava 1073 g.* (see n. 14), 55–89.

[18] Fols. 236r and v, 237r and v, corresponding to nos. 103 and 104 of the Cyrillic listing of chapters in the MS. Cf. the still unreplaced monumental facsimile edition, *Izbornik velikago knjazja Svjatoslava Jaroslaviča 1073 goda, iždiveniem člena učreditelja Obščestva ljubitelej drevnej pis'mennosti Timofeja Savviča Morozova* (St. Petersburg, 1880).

[19] "In [all substances] that show mutual contrast (ἐναντίωσιν), while tending to unite, there is a common trend which is defined as union (ἕνωσις). Through it, substances are reduced to

Is there any connection between the *obrazi* discussed by Choiroboskos in the section of the *Izbornik* that immediately follows? If the connection were based on homonymy, and the *obrazi sъjedinenija* (forms, aspects, or "figures" of the unification of perception) were actually something completely unrelated to the *tvorъčestii obrazi*[20] 'poetic figures' of rhetoric, one would have to believe that Choiroboskos' treatise was inserted in this book by chance. It does not seem probable, however, that a merely homonymous relation could mislead the compilers of such an important, richly illuminated and official collection which was presented to a Kiev prince by the dignitaries of his Church. The real connection between these texts appears to be more subtle. Both types of *obrazi* refer to a complex theory of signs, the foundation of which is to be found in the teaching of the Church. If this consideration is well founded, one must conclude that in the context of this *Izbornik,* Choiroboskos' treatise represents an example of verbal technique (*xitrost'*), the use of which is dependent on the sacred teaching (*učenie*) of the Christian tradition.

At the beginning of the *Izbornik of 1076*, there is a brief text entitled *Slovo někojego kalugera o čь[tenii] knigъ* (A sermon by a certain monk on the reading of books).[21] The text's significance for the history of Early Slavic education has not escaped the attention of scholars. Nevertheless the real meaning of the message conveyed by this symbolic monk has not been elucidated in a satisfactory way. N. P. Popov believed that the whole book was compiled for the benefit of secular readers. He also maintained that the reading discussed in this initial chapter was "la lecture domestique, dans le privé."[22] If this were true, this text would prove the existence of a sizable public of secular readers. Even more important, it would reflect the Church's particular concern for these readers' personal and private education. A closer examination of this *Slovo*, however, leads to a different conclusion.

---

unity in ten ways. Union is defined according to essence (κατ' οὐσίαν), hypostasis (καθ' ὑπόστασιν), intercourse (κατὰ σχέσιν), apposition (κατὰ παράθεσιν), co-augmentation (κατὰ ἁρμονίαν), mixture (κατὰ κράσιν), infusion (κατὰ φύσιν), confusion (κατὰ σύγχυσιν), heaping (κατὰ σωμερείαν), coalescence (κατὰ συναλοιφὴν)." The Greek equivalents are taken from Maximus' *On Definitions of Distinctions* (Περὶ ὅρων διάστολων) according to F. Combefis's edition, *S. P. N. Maximi Confessoris opera omnia,* vol. 2, contained in *PG* 91: 115–116, cols. 211–217.

[20] *Izbornik,* ed. Morozov (see n. 18), fol. 237r: "Tvorъčьstii obrazi sǫtь k̄z (27)"; cf. Besharov, *Imagery of the Igor' Tale* (see n. 12), 4–5: "Ποιητικοὶ τρόποι εἰσιν κζ" (There are twenty-seven poetical figures).

[21] *Izbornik 1076 goda,* ed. V. S. Golyšenko, V. F. Dubrovina, V. G. Dem'janov, and G. F. Nefedov (Moscow, 1965), 151–158.

[22] N. P. Popov, "L'Izbornik de 1076, dit de Svjatoslav, comme monument littéraire," *Revue des études slaves* 14 (1934): 5–25.

The entire text can be seen as a didactic illustration of the motif "studying continually the Law of the Lord," as elaborated in Ps. 119 (118). Selected citations from this psalm form the conceptual and compositional skeleton of the *kaluger*'s instruction. Even if the psalm's universal message could be addressed to any believer, it seems reasonable to assume that its presentation in this particular context was intended to urge monks to study the sacred books with inspired zeal.[23]

The text is carefully reproduced, with an apparatus, in the *Izbornik*'s 1965 edition. Our reading may be made easier by a translation that implies a certain degree of textual interpretation:

> It is a good thing, brothers, to honor books, all the more so for a Christian. *"Blessed are they"*—it is written—*"who search out his testimonies: they will diligently seek him with the whole heart"* (Ps. 119 [118]:2). Why does he [the psalmist] say *"who search out his testimonies"*? When you read books, do not be anxious to go through the pages quickly in order to get to another chapter, but understand what those books and letters mean, turning back even three times to a single chapter. It is written: *"I have hidden your words in my heart, that I might not sin against you"* (Ps. 119 [118]:11). Not only does he say *"With my lips I have declared ..."* (Ps. 119 [118]:13), but also *"In my heart I have hidden [your words], that I might not sin against you."* The one who correctly understands the Scriptures is righteous through them. And I state that the bridle provides guidance and restraint for the horse; the books [provide guidance and restraint] for the righteous man. One cannot assemble a ship without nails, nor can the righteous man do without the honor of books. In the same way that a prisoner thinks of his parents, the righteous man honors books. A weapon is the ornament of the warrior; and the winds [the ornament] of the ship. Similarly, the honoring of books [is an ornament] for the righteous man. *"Open my eyes*—it is written—*"so that I perceive wondrous things from your law"* (Ps. 119 [118]:18). This means that the eyes are the thinking of the heart. And then: *"Hide not your commandments from me"* (Ps. 119 [118]:19). You must understand that *"hide"* does not mean 'from the eyes,' but from the mind and the heart. This is why he [the psalmist] blamed those who did not study, saying: *"Cursed are they that turn aside from your commandments"* (Ps. 119 [118]:21). Thereupon he praised himself, saying; *"How sweet are your words, more so than honey to my mouth"* (Ps. 119 [118]:103), and *"the law of your mouth is better to me than thousands of gold*

---

[23] Because this *Slovo* offers a moral teaching by commenting on a scriptural text, inserts scriptural material into the comment so abundantly that the resulting text reads like a paraphrase, and appears to address members of a community, it can be termed a ὁμιλία in the original sense of the word, i.e., a *social* discourse, to be performed at *home*. In this case, however, by *home* is meant a monastery, with no possible reference to *la lecture domestique,* as Popov understood it. The spiritual model for homilies intended to proclaim a truth by commenting on scriptural passages was offered by Jesus, who commented on Isaiah in the Nazareth synagogue (Luke 4:16–20).

and silver" (Ps. 119 [118]:72). Then he sang, saying: "*I will exult because of your words as one that finds much spoil*" (Ps. 119 [118]:162). He called "*spoil*" the words of God, saying: "*I who am so unworthy* have found such a gift, namely, *to learn from your words all day and night*" (cf. Ps. 119 [118]: 114,97,55,62). Thus, brothers, let us meditate and listen with thoughtful ears so that we may grasp the strength and teaching of the Holy Books. You should listen to the lives of Saint Basil and Saint John Chrysostom and Saint Cyril the Philosopher and many other saints, which begin by saying about them that from their young years they applied themselves to the study of the Holy Books, so that they were moved to do good deeds. You can see that the first incentive to good deeds is the teaching of the Holy Books because, brothers, through them we are spurred to follow the path of their lives and deeds, and we can continuously learn the words of the books, doing their will as they command, *so that we may deserve eternal life* (cf. Matt. 19:16; Luke 10:25; 18:18, John 5:39). For ever, Amen.[24]

This text deserves particular attention because it contains one of the oldest, if not *the* oldest, literary manifesto of Orthodox Slavic civilization. Its significance for the study of the early Slavic "theory of literature" can hardly be overestimated. That its inspiration is not only religious but also strictly ecclesiastic should be evident to any attentive reader. The symbolic voice of the "certain monk" echoes that of the psalmist, in full harmony with Ps. 119 (118). One should not read this text without referring to the whole context provided by that psalm.

The main exegetical-didactic theme of the *Slovo* is that the words of God should be received not merely through the *eyes* (or the ears)—an attitude expressed by mechanical and superficial reading—but through their profound reception in the depths of the *heart*. As any good teacher, the acting voice of this text wants to convince its audience that slow reading is the foundation of scholarship. However, this scholastic precept alone was not sufficient. Monks and priests were invested with a higher mission. The essence of priesthood, and of ascetic monasticism in particular, was dependent on the continuous presence of God's inspiration. Slow reading was meant as a spiritual exercise.

If one refers mentally to the entire text of the psalm-model, the crucial message expounded in this *Slovo* appears to be stressed also by other verses of Ps. 119 (118), which became formulaic models in Orthodox Slavic literature. This applies, for example, to Ps. 119 (118):131 ("I open my mouth, panting eagerly for your commandments") and to Ps. 119 (118):169 ("... let your word endow me with perception").

[24] The translation of biblical quotes is based on *The Oxford Annotated Bible*, Revised Standard Edition (New York, 1962), and *The Septuagint Version of the Old Testament*, with an English translation by Sir L. L. Brenton (London).

The message conveyed by this sermon in a remarkably concise and apparently stylized form makes one wonder whether, and to what extent, it might belong to a didactic corpus already established in the Slavic tradition. Its significance for the early codification of the Orthodox Slavic theory of literature resides in its regarding inspired *words* as carriers of truth. In particular, this text states that careful reading is important because it enables the reader to "continuously learn the words of the books" (*da těmi ... i poučaimъ sę vъinu knižьnyimъ slovesьmъ*). One can interpret this statement as the formulation of a particular Christian theory of imitation concerning the language of literature. The readers of sacred books would assimilate the books' language (*knižьnaja slovesa*) and combine the learning with the imitation of a selected corpus of exemplary works. This corpus, as presented in this sermon, included Basil, Chrysostom, and Cyril the Philosopher.

The models for imitation, therefore, were representative of what one may call a Greco-Slavic paideia. Whether the "Life of Saint Cyril the Philosopher" mentioned here was actually the textual prototype of the Slavic *Vita Constantini* that has come down to us in much later codices is a debatable question. In any case, the fact remains that the models selected for the edification of the *Izbornik*'s readers reflect a Greco-Slavic symbiosis. This circumstance leads us inevitably to consider the *Sermon by a Certain Monk on the Reading of Books* against the Bulgarian background of its earlier version(s).

As recently reasserted by B. St. Angelov, D. Angelov, E. Georgiev, and P. Dinekov, both *Izborniki Svjatoslava* are typical expressions of the literary civilization that flourished in tenth-century "Simeonian" Bulgaria.[25] Their significant role in the Russian lands indicates that the formation of an early supranational literary system in Orthodox Slavdom depended on a *translatio studiorum*, ostensibly connected with missionary activity. Besides reflecting the typically Byzantino-Bulgarian interest in the compilation of sylloges, the *Izbornik of 1076* shares with Old Bulgarian collections a monastic emphasis on literary (i.e., connected with letters) activity as a form of prayer. An interesting parallel can be established between the *Sermon by a Certain Monk on the Reading of Books* on the one hand, which forms the preface to the whole *Izbornik,* and the *Alphabetic Prayer (Azbučna*

[25] B. St. Angelov, "Poxvala carju Simeonu," in *Izbornik Svjatoslava 1073* (see n. 14), 247–256; D. Angelov, "Sbornik Simeona i otraženie v nem duxovnyx interesov bolgarskogo obščestva," ibid., 256–263; È. I. Georgiev, "K voprosu o vozniknovenii i sostaviteljax Izbornika Simeona-Svjatoslava, izvestnogo po rukopisi 1073 g.," ibid., 263–272; P. D. Dinekov, "Značenie Izbornika Simeona-Svjatoslava 1073 g. v razvitii bolgarskoj literatury," ibid., 272–279.

molitva) on the other, which opens the tenth-century Bulgarian *Didactic Gospel* (*Učitelno evangelie*).

K. Kuev has correctly pointed out that the first line of the Old Bulgarian *Alphabetic Prayer*—Azъ slovomь simъ moljǫ sę bogu" (With this prayer, I pray to God)—contains "the most essential chord in the whole hymnic gamut." With these first words, according to Kuev, the Prayer's author "addresses himself to God with humility, and begs Him to send the Holy Spirit to him, to help him in his enterprise."[26]In fact, this initial statement, which is developed in the subsequent lines, marks the Prayer's leitmotif: "Gospoda [sic] duxa posli živǫštajego ... Silǫ prijęti i mǫdrostь u tebe ... Xeruvьskǫ mi myslь i umъ daždь ..." (O Lord, send the Living Spirit ... That I might receive power and wisdom from Thee ... Grant me angelic reasoning and insight). The author of the *Alphabetic Prayer* seeks an Orthodox understanding of the mystery of the Trinity and an angelic, that is, theologically perfect, wisdom: "O, čьstnaja, prěsvętaja troice / pečalь mojǫ na radostь prěloži / cělomǫdrьno da načьnǫ pьsati / čjudesa tvoja prědivьnaja ʒělo / šestькrilatyxъ silǫ vъspriimъ" (O revered, most Holy Trinity, turn my sorrow to joy, that I shall write down with wisdom Thy most wondrous miracles, having received the power of the seraphim). By using this inspired "general wisdom," he hopes, more specifically, "to follow in the Teachers' footsteps": "Šьstvuja nyně po slědu učitelju / imeni jeju i dělu posléduję" (Setting out now in the footsteps of the [two] Teachers, I shall follow them in name and deed).

If one interprets—as seems reasonable—the reference to the "Teachers" (*učiteli*) as a marked allusion to Cyril and Methodius,[27] a parallel can be established with the type of Greco-Slavic paideia presented in the *Sermon by a Certain Monk on the Reading of Books*. This connection suggests that, at the beginning of the Slavic tradition, there was an established way of justifying literary activity in accordance with the teaching of the Church. We can reduce its conceptual foundation to the following points: (1) the human use of words, that is, verbal art as applied to both reading and writing, can serve the purpose of carrying a true message only if God's inspiration helps; (2) the language of the sacred books is the supreme linguistic model; (3) a corpus of models should include the work of Cyril the Philosopher as well as that of Methodius.

There is no reason to take the latter point too literally. One can think of a Cyrillo-Methodian tradition that comprised various works of the disciples

---

[26] K. Kuev, *Azbučnata molitva v slavjanskite literaturi* (Sofia, 1974), 127.
[27] Ibid., 38–40.

and followers of Cyril and Methodius. This consideration is supported by the extant historical data concerning the *translatio studiorum* from Bulgaria to the lands of Rus', especially after the fall of the last portion of the First Bulgarian Empire in 1018.[28]

The existence of a literary corpus of Bulgarian origin that supposedly affected the establishment of literary norms in Kievan Rus' can be postulated also on the basis of formal elements. Besides using similar formulae such as "Šьstvuja nyně po sledu učitelju / imeni jeju i dělu poslěduję" (*Alphabetic Prayer*) and "podvigněmъ sę na putь žitija ixъ" (Let us move onto the path of their life) (*Sermon of a Certain Monk*),[29] the two texts examined above may depend on a common rhetorical model. Such a model might well be Ps. 119 (118). This psalm emphasizes the motive of word-giving inspiration. With regard to its formal characteristics, it is important to note that it represents a celebrated example of *alphabetic* (acrostic) poetry. Ps. 119 (118) was always very popular. It provided the literati of Christian monasticism with a unique spiritual code. The author of the *Alphabetic Prayer* too must have regarded it as a supreme model.

It is hoped that further research will confirm the main conclusions that can be drawn from these preliminary considerations. It appears that from its very beginning, literary activity in Old Rus' was governed by some general principles. These principles concerned the essence of verbal communication, the purpose of reading and writing, and the selection of models for imitation. It seems appropriate to consider these conceptual guidelines as part of a theoretical system basically under ecclesiastic control.

In order to define the theoretical foundations of Orthodox Slavic literature, it might be advisable to have recourse to terms other than *poetic* and/or *rhetoric*, which have acquired a marked meaning, especially in the post-humanistic culture of the West. Although these terms can be useful in the

---

[28] In recent years, the decisive contribution of Old Bulgarian literature to the formation of a supranational tradition common to Southern and Eastern Slavdom has won general recognition among Soviet scholars. D. S. Lixačev has defined old Bulgarian literature as a *literatura-posrednica*, or an "intermediary literature" that codified the Slavic patrimony produced first in Moravia and Bohemia and then in Bulgaria, Serbia and Rus' (Lixačev, *Razvitie russkoj literatury* [see n. 7], 23–44). This very fitting label is also used by O. V. Tvorogov in *Istorija* (see n. 2), 38–39. One may add, however, that the "intermediary" role played by Old Bulgarian literature was not its only achievement. It was during the First Bulgarian Empire that the very foundation of an Orthodox Slavic literary system was laid by Old Bulgarian writers. One may also speak of Old Bulgarian literature as the first "classical" or "pattern-establishing" literary civilization of the Orthodox Slavs.

[29] Cf. the text of the *Alphabetic Prayer* established by K. Kuev in his *Azbučnata molitva* (see n. 26), 170–171.

preliminary stages of our research (because they suggest parallels and equivalences), they become inadequate when one tries to detect the intrinsic features of the Old Russian literary system.

On the basis of the considerations presented above, it seems more appropriate to speak of a *literary doctrine*. In this terminological formula, the qualifier *literary* refers to only a section of the general *doxa*, that is, the official view of the Church. Consequently, the main emphasis must be placed on the governing "right doctrine" or *orthodoxy,* not on "literature." Writing activity could not be governed by purely literary laws because it was not justified by its own pragmatic functions, but by its dependence on higher truths.

If this interpretation of the cultural atmosphere in which book writing developed in the Russian lands is correct, one may wonder whether it does not confirm the pessimistic views of old and new detractors of Old Russian literature. How could any poetic spirit express itself, one may ask, in a society where independent expression could be regarded as a sin? A full-fledged discussion of this delicate point would result in a general evaluation of Russian spiritual history well beyond the limits of "Old Russian literature." It appears, however, that indiscriminate rejection of the Old Russian literary heritage can only spring from superficial and biased approaches.

One should bear in mind that many literary masterpieces were produced in theocratically minded societies long before the formation of Orthodox Slavdom. Even if one acknowledges that Old Russian literature developed in conditions remarkably different from those in which the literary civilization of Western Christianity flourished during the same medieval centuries, one should not overemphasize its singularity.[30] Long before the flourishing of troubadours, trouvères, and Minnesänger, before Chrétien de Troyes, Gottfried von Strassburg, and other significant poets up to the golden age of Dante, Petrarch, Boccaccio and Chaucer, the so-called dark ages had elaborated long-lasting intellectual and poetic models. Cultural environments dominated by ecclesiastic establishments had given birth, for example, to Venantius Fortunatus, Isidore of Seville, Gregory of Tours, the Venerable Bede, Alcuin, Paul the Deacon, Theodulf of Orleans, Hrabanus Maurus, Gottschalk of Fulda, Liutprand of Cremona, and Pietro Damiani. In principle, "ecclesiastic tyranny" cannot be considered as something necessarily unfavorable to the development of verbal art in either the Greco-Byzantine or the Latin world.

---

[30] Lixačev has pointed out that "ot"edinennost' drevnej russkoj literatury—mif XIX v." (*Poètika drevnerusskoj literatury* [see n. 11], 10).

Once again, it is appropriate to warn against the risk of replacing old exaggerations with new ones. To acknowledge the leading role of a Christian Orthodox literary doctrine in old *Slavia rossica* should by no means lead one to deny or minimize the importance of other cultural components. Political particularism, competitions regarding church jurisdictions, ethnic rivalries, social and economic conflicts, and differences in education and intellectual aspirations, including secular-minded trends, were present in Old Rus' and Muscovy as in any other part of the Christian world. Hence the variety of styles, the continuous adaptation of thematic motives, the free textual elaboration of traditional works, the spreading of apocryphal and dissident currents in spite of many recurrent attempts at restoring ideal norms of universal truth.[31]

The main purpose of the literary doctrine was to provide models for imitation. The way in which this imitation was practiced by authors, adapters, translators, and compilers depended on a number of circumstances. One may describe the historical development of the Old Russian literary system by singling out dynamic patterns that resulted from the creative imitation of the generative models codified by the governing literary doctrine.[32]

Apparently, the norms elaborated by the ecclesiastic establishment were implemented most effectively with regard to subject matter. The thematic range was necessarily narrowed by the practical needs of a literary market under church control. No wonder, then, that only a few main types of literary activity—such as chronicle writing, homiletics, and hagiography—characterized the literary landscape of *Slavia rossica* until the dawn of the modern age. Each of these main types permitted the proliferation of subtypes. This is the case, for example, with chronicle writing because its thematic unity depended on an extremely broad view of human events against the all-embracing background of earthly history.

Nevertheless, thematic limitation remained a very important feature of Orthodox Slavic literature in general, and of the old literature of the Russian lands in particular. One can hardly minimize the absence, for example, of the rich gamut of erotic motives that characterizes the medieval literary civilization of Western Europe.

Should one therefore assume that the church-inspired literary doctrine of Orthodox Slavdom had only a limiting and, in the final analysis, negative

[31] Lixačev, *Istorija* (see n. 2), 448–451.
[32] See R. Picchio, "Models and Patterns in the Literary Tradition of Medieval Orthodox Slavdom," in *American Contributions to the Seventh International Congress of Slavists, Warsaw ... 1973,* vol. 2: *Literature and Folklore,* ed. V. Terras (The Hague–Paris, 1973), 439–467.

impact on verbal art? If one insisted on judging it almost exclusively on the basis of its thematic range, the answer might well be yes.

However, a completely different picture emerges from a systematic investigation of the stylistic devices, compositional methods, sound structures, and other formal techniques used by generations of pious writers and continuously readapted by scribe-redactors. Indeed, one may maintain that it was precisely because of an accepted thematic limitation that the essence of writing activity gradually became identified with the skill of elaborating, rephrasing, and reshaping traditional textual materials.

One may even go so far as to say that Orthodox Slavic doctrine was forced to focus on *how* continuously to rephrase a previously established *what*. Notwithstanding often repeated statements to the contrary, it seems that the study of Old Russian literature should concentrate even more on literary techniques and the elaboration of *formal structures* than on thematic motives.

The same considerations that discourage the use of general terms such as *poetics* and *rhetoric* require one to be cautious when applying the particular notion of *literary genre* to Old Russian literature.[33] Such caution is justified by the scarcity of critical data even more than by theoretical doubts as to the criteria one should use to classify Old Russian works.

If one follows the classical definitions of genres according to the *ways* in which literary texts can be produced, no satisfactory conclusion can be reached precisely because there are no adequate studies of the many *ways* in which the same subject matter was treated by Old Russian writers. The current classifications of works according to categories such as chronicles, sermons, or lives of saints suggest that the entire Old Russian tradition is reducible either to the all-embracing genre of prose or to those of history and eloquence. Nor can one rely on structural schemes. No classification of functional codes is possible unless the sets of rules that governed the Old Russian literary system are defined. By equating chronicles, sermons, and hagiography with "genres," one may lose sight of the crucial interconnections of themes and forms. No thematic classification would prove useful if it were contradicted by a parallel assessment of the writers' various choices of formal devices.[34]

---

[33] Currently, discussions on this subject are largely based on D. S. Lixačev's paper "Zarož-denie i razvitie žanrov drevnerusskoj literatury," in *Slavjanskie literatury, VII Meždunarodnyj s"ezd slavistov, Varšava, avgust 1973 g., Doklady sovetskoj delegacii* (Moscow, 1973), 160–177.

[34] Ever since Plato's classical definition of the τύποι of literary activity according to either their ethical approach or the degree of their mimesis, an invariant of theoretical thought has been the rhetoricians' concern for the *way* in which verbal messages are conveyed rather than

Thus, it seems that Slavists still have a long way to go before the formal characteristics of Old Russian literature are clarified. Neither historical analogies with Western literary theory nor the establishment of abstract structures can lead to a better understanding of how the Old Russian literary system might have worked. The only way to find out how Old Russian literary techniques were practiced is to investigate them empirically, on the basis of textual data.

Another major source of uncertainty is presented by the complex ways in which preexisting textual materials were used by Old Russian authors, compilers, and scribes. Current scholarship devotes particular attention to this problem. In this, as well as in other fields of Old Russian studies, it is the challenging work of D. S. Lixačev that offers the main basis for a general discussion.[35] This leading Soviet specialist has emphasized the predominance in Rus' and Muscovy of unprejudiced scriptorial techniques resulting in what can be defined as an *open tradition*.[36] These techniques were based on the idea that scribes could adapt and reshape texts instead of copying them faithfully. Lixačev's conclusions regarding this particular aspect of the problem have been widely accepted. There is no general agreement, however, as to (a) the actual limits of the open tradition, and (b) the methodological conclusions that one should draw concerning the concrete textual-critical study of Old Russian works.

The term *open tradition* describes the handing down of various Old Russian works with no preservation of their full textual identity. Very often, scribes felt free to change words and entire sentences in order to make old texts accessible to new readers. New authors inserted passages taken from other works into their own texts. They paraphrased or reshaped preexisting textual material without identifying or marking these borrowings as citations. Consequently, the techniques of composition and compilation could represent, in a large portion of the Orthodox Slavic tradition, equally acceptable levels of authorship.[37]

---

for the subject matter as such. A valuable discussion of this problem from a modern viewpoint is provided by H. Markiewicz, *Główne problemy wiedzy o literaturze* (Cracow, 1965), 142–173, bibliogr. 170–173. For the history of the debates, see in particular D. S. Garasa, *Los géneros literarios* (Buenos Aires, 1969), bibliogr., 327–337. See also W. V. Ruttkowski, *Die literarischen Gattungen. Reflexionen über eine modifizierte Fundamentalpoetik* (Berne–Munich, 1968), bibliogr., 139–149.

[35] D. S. Lixačev, *Tekstologija. Na materiale russkoj literatury X–XVII vv.* (Moscow–Leningrad, 1962).

[36] See R. Picchio, "Le canzoni epiche russe e la tradizione letteraria," in *Atti del Convegno internazionale sul tema: La poesia epica e la sua formazione* (Rome: Academia dei Lincei, 1970), 467–480; id., "Questione della lingua" (see n. 6), 73.

[37] See R. Picchio, "Compilation and Composition: Two Levels of Authorship in the Orthodox Slavic Tradition," *Cyrillomethodianum* 5 (1981): 1–4.

The true significance of this way of creating new texts by assembling old textual materials cannot be understood without referring to the particular notion of authorship that characterized the Orthodox Slavic tradition. Undoubtedly the widespread disregard for any form of copyright played a decisive role in the development of Old Russian literary techniques. In turn, those techniques depended on a particular conception of literary activity. Once again, one must wonder to what extent a general doctrine of ecclesiastic origin was instrumental in shaping the literary techniques of *Slavia rossica*.

The idea that "true words" were not the individual property of any human was based on the assumption that such words could only come "from above" ("every perfect gift is from above," James 1:17). Technical *xitrosti* were intended to preserve the purity of messages revealed to chosen men. Merely technical expedients could not help anyone utter words of truth. Because of this belief, the image of the *scriba Dei* overshadowed that of the "poet" (ποιητής) or "maker" of literary texts. No wonder that the Orthodox Slavic literary doctrine consistently rejected—for several centuries all over the Balkans and the Russian lands—all "pagan" skills in rhetoric and poetics. To them it opposed the spiritual techniques of impetrating the gift of verbal proficiency through self-humilitation and prayer.

These data indicate that it was the Orthodox Slavic literary doctrine that was largely responsible for a widespread disregard of textual individuality. This consideration, however, does not seem to apply to those texts that enjoyed particular authority. An evaluation of Orthodox Slavic works depends on whether they were or were not marked by an established *traditio auctori* and/or *traditio auctoritatis*.[38] There is no reason to assume that *all* texts were subject to the textual alternations characteristic of the open tradition.

A fruitful discussion of this problem was started by Angiolo Danti (1930–1979).[39] The untimely death of this specialist has deprived us of a

---

[38] R. Picchio, "Questione della lingua" (See n. 6), 13–16.

[39] A. Danti, "Criteri e metodi nell'edizione della *Zadonščina*," in *Annali della Facoltà di Lettere e Filosofia dell'Università degli Studi di Perugia*, vol. 6 (1968–69): 187–220. This article was discussed by Lixačev "Metodika izučenija istorii teksta i problema vzaimootnošenija spiskov i redakcij 'Zadonščiny': Ob issledovanii Andželo Danti," included in his book *"Slovo o polku Igoreve" i kul'tura ego vremeni* (Leningrad, 1978), 278–295. See also A. Danti, "Di un particolare aspetto della tradizione manoscritta antico-russa: testi a duplice redazione e problemi della loro edizione," *Ricerche Slavistiche* 20–21 (1973–1974): 15–44; id., "Per l'edizione della 'Zadonščina'," *Annali dell'Istituto Universitario Orientale di Napoli: Sezione slava*, nos. 18–19 (1974–1975): 163–176; id., "O znaczeniu tekstu krytycznego," *Slavia* 46 (1977): 395–398; id., "Sulla 'Zadonščina' e sulla filologia," *Studi Medievali*, 3-a series, vol. 19, no. 2 (1978): 881–897. A. Danti's last study on the problem of Slavic textual criticism, "Edizione documentaria e edizione

valuable theoretical point of reference in the crucial debate over the
methods of Soviet *tekstologija* and its relationship to the Western schools
of textual criticism. This debate should be continued. As indicated by
Michele Colucci in a recent essay, the methods of Western textual criticism
can be profitable in the study of Old Russian literature.[40] The critical edition of Daniil Zatočnik's *Slovo* and *Molenie*, which Danti and Colucci
published in 1977, represents an example of how the classical methods of
textual criticism can apply to those portions of Old Russian literature not
characterized by an open tradition.[41]

Until the various Old Russian ways of treating and handing down textual
material are thoroughly described, it will be very difficult to understand the
historical development of literary techniques. Even concerning those works
that were continuously edited and rehashed, it is essential to determine
which readings in the existing documentation represent a well definable
textual individuality. If the relationship of the *variae lectiones* to their respective texts remains unclarified and chronologically unmarked, how can one
evaluate them from both the formal and the historical points of view?

Since the result of substantially changing a text can only be the creation
of a different text, the history of *one work* subject to open tradition can be
documented by a sequence of *texts* containing different portions of the
same *textual material*. In this case, the work's continuity is not shown by
the individual texts, but by the *invariance* of their common textual material.
Nevertheless, if one did not establish and properly evaluate the features of
each text, a crucial point of reference in our historical perception would be
lost. It is certainly important not to lose sight of the forest, but let us also
remember that the forest is made up of single trees!

As convincingly shown by Lixačev, one of the best ways to reconstruct
these particular techniques of textual transmission is to study the life-and-
work habits of Old Russian scribes.[42] As members of religious communities,

---

critica," will be included in the forthcoming volume of his selected writings in the series Studia
Historica et Philologica, Sectio Slavica (Florence).

[40] M. Colucci, "'Textual Criticism' versus '*Tekstologija*': The Case of *Daniil Zatočnik.*" MS.

[41] Daniil Zatočnik, *Slovo e Molenie,* Edizione critica a cura di M. Coluci e A. Danti. Studia
Historica et Philologica, vol. 4, Sectio Slavica, no. 2 (Florence, 1977). The results of this important work are not acknowledged by the authors of *Istorija.* Apparently, they have accepted
the policy of consistently ignoring Western contributions to the study of Old Russian literature. Such an attitude, which is certainly disappointing for all their colleagues and friends in
the West, is probably due to the fact that this *Istorija* has been conceived as a manual for
Soviet schools. But why should Russian students ignore the fact that the literary past of their
country is the object of widespread scholarly interest throughout the world? One can only
hope that limitations of this kind will be eliminated in the future.

[42] Lixačev, "Rabota drevnerusskogo knižnika," in his *Tekstologija* (see n. 35), 53–94.

these men were instruments of ecclesiastic power. While their skill was also often used by secular authorities for different purposes, their training never became secular. No less than their use of religious models in the production of new works, their compliance with ecclesiastic rules and traditions in their delicate activity—within a scriptorium or in the isolation of a scribe's cell—deserves to be emphasized.

On the basis of general historical data alone, it is difficult to ascertain how decisive and widespread might have been the impact of ecclesiastic culture on the formation and development of literary techniques in old *Slavia rossica*. What is needed is an analytical inventory of the formal *xitrosti* occurring in Old Russian texts. These *xitrosti* were often concealed and disguised in order to avoid the impression that a writer might rely on them more than on divine inspiration. Nevertheless, emphatically marked *topoi modestiae* such as the one contained in Epifanij Premudryj's often discussed manifesto—"xudъ iměja razumъ i promyslь vredoumenъ, ne byvšu mi vъ Afiněxъ, ... ni filosofia. ni xitrorěčia ne navykoxъ ..., vesь nedouměnia napolnixsja"—should not mislead us.[43] As noted above, *xitrorečie* of the type alluded to by Epifanij might well have been the main practical concern of Old Russian writers.

Even though literary techniques could be neither separated from nor opposed to the guiding principles of literary doctrine, methods aiming at the autonomous description of texts can prove very effective in our research. To produce an inventory of formal devices, one must know the texts' inner structure. Roman Jakobson has proved that one can hardly understand the poetry of grammar without learning the grammar of poetry through the meticulous analysis of textual components.[44] This consideration suggests that one should investigate the formal complexities of Orthodox Slavic texts first. Once an adequate documentation is made available, one may try to interpret the analytical data in a broader context.

It will probably be a long time before an inventory of this kind is completed. It is encouraging to note, however, that at least three crucial topics, namely, (1) the interrelation of a special language of literature and the

---

[43] Having a poor mind and uninsightful reasoning, not having been in Athens ... I have studied neither philosophy nor rhetoric ..., I am completely incapable. *Žitie sv. Stefana Episkopa Permskogo,* publ. V. Družinin; photomechanic reprint with an introduction by D. Čiževskij (The Hague, 1959), 2. On Epifanij's formal devices, see F. D. M. Kitsch, *The Literary Style of Epifanij Premudryj, Pletenie sloves* (Munich, 1976). See also, R. Picchio, "L' 'intreccio delle parole' e gli stili letterari presso gli Slavi ortodossi nel tardo Medio Evo," in *Studi Slavistici in ricordo di Carlo Veridiani,* ed. A. Raffo (Pisa, 1979), 630–643.

[44] R. Jakobson, "Poetry of Grammar and Grammar of Poetry," *Lingua* 21 (1968): 597–609.

codification of stylistic levels, (2) the *ornatus*—or "rhetorical embellishment"—of prose, and (3) the compositional patterns of Old Russian works
are currently the object of growing interest.

Distinguished historians of the Russian language such as Boris Uspenskij, Gerta Hüttl-Folter, and Alexander Issatschenko have used the sociolinguistic notion of *diglossia*, as defined by C. A. Ferguson in 1959, to
describe the relation between Church Slavic and local linguistic habits in
the Russian lands before the eighteenth century.[45]

If one uses the term *diglossia* in reference to a particular aspect of linguistic behavior, namely, the use of different codes depending on the speaker's relation to his or her social environment, its function was certainly
relevant in various cultural milieus of Old Rus'. This concept, however,
does not seem to be equally useful when applied to the intrinsic qualities
of a written literary medium.

The coexistence, in the same language of literature, of Church Slavic and
local (Russian) components can certainly be seen as being dependent on
particular sociolinguistic conditions. The various levels of the written medium, however, did not reproduce a situation of diglossia in the medium itself.

Ferdinand de Saussure's prejudice that a written language does not act as
an autonomous system may be one of the main sources of misunderstanding in this discussion.[46] Against this prejudice, one may maintain that a
written language, whose code is established by literary convention, can
actually function as an autonomous system of signs. To say that it represents nothing but a distorted image of linguistic reality would imply that
the linguistic reality that counts is not the one produced by the message-
carrying function of the medium under examination. Yet, the opposite
seems to be true.

The writer who composes texts in accordance with the sets of rules
proper to a conventional written medium implicitly adheres to a linguistic
reality, the limits of which are established by a community of writers and
readers. Within these limits, a codified written language is governed by its

---

[45] C. A. Ferguson, "Diglossia," *Word* 15 (1959): 325–340; B. A. Uspenskij, "K voprosu o
semantičeskix vzaimootnošenijax sistemno protivopostavlennyx cerkovnoslavjanskix i russkix
form v istorii russkogo jazyka," *Wiener Slavistisches Jahrbuch* 22 (1976): 92–100; G. Hüttl-
Folter, "Diglossia v drevnej Rusi," *Wiener Slavistisches Jahrbuch* 24 (1978): 108–123; A. V.
Issatschenko, "Russian," in *The Slavic Literary Languages: Formation and Development*, ed. A.
M. Schenker, E. Stankiewicz, and M. S. Iovine (New Haven, 1980), 119–142.

[46] For a discussion of Saussure's views on the written language, see R. Picchio, "On Church
Slavonic Isonorms," *Slavic Linguistics and Poetics: Studies for Edward Stankiewicz on his 60th
Birthday (International Journal of Slavic Linguistics and Poetics 25/26)*, ed. K. E. Naylor,
H. I. Aronson, B. J. Darden, A. M. Schenker (Columbus, 1982), 367–378.

own code. This explains why it can be so different from any spoken usage. The more a codified literary medium is capable of expressing its own reality, which depends on its cultural function among writers and readers, the more it acts as a special language. Be that as it may, written representations of noncodified usage do not possess the dignity of a language of literature. Dante was aware of this hierarchy when he defined the difference between Latin and the vulgar tongue by stating that whereas "Latin is perennial and not subject to corruption, the vulgar tongue is unstable and subject to corruption."[47]

The sociolinguistic view of a diglossia governing Old Russian linguistic habits, with special regard to the premodern period, can be used to describe the situation that gave birth to a Russian modern "vulgar tongue" capable of eventually dethroning the old common literary medium of Orthodox Slavdom. Nevertheless, as long as the old language of literature preserved its power and prestige, that situation could only have an external, functionally extralinguistic impact on the accepted written usage.

These considerations lead one to contemplate the norms that governed the literary language of Orthodox Slavdom as part of a general Old Russian corpus of literary techniques under ecclesiastic control. Orthodox writers were not supposed to look at everyday language as a basic term of reference for their literary activity. True models of verbal expression could only come "from above" and were made manifest by the revealed language of the sacred texts. This attitude appears to be in agreement with the general literary doctrine that I am trying to reconstruct. As mentioned earlier, one may attempt to interpret the entire range of literary techniques derived from that doctrine as components of a particular method of Christian *imitatio*. This interpretation, however, cannot be substantiated until more factual data are made available and duly compared.

As regards the codification of the written medium and the regulation of other writing techniques, ecclesiastic control could not affect all things in all places. At first glance, this sort of incomplete censorship may be seen as the major cause for the variety of styles and linguistic levels that characterized Old Russian literature. It would be a mistake, however, to consider as deviations from an allegedly rigid norm any infiltration of "vulgar" forms in the vocabulary, morphology, syntax, and style of the language of literature.

Actually, one can hardly speak of a unified norm in the written language of Orthodox Slavdom. Ecclesiastic culture provided ideal models, but the

---

[47] "Lo latino è perpetuo e non corruttibile, e lo volgare è non stabile e corruttibile," Dante Alighieri, *Il Convivio*, Edizione critica a cura di M. Simonelli (Bologna, 1966), 11 (*Conv.* I, V: 7–8).

actual use of the language of literature depended on normative trends reflecting geographical, cultural, and social differences. "Vulgar" elements could be accepted by various writers either for rhetorical reasons or simply for ensuring that all the readers could understand. As long as the limits of acceptability were established by Orthodox Slavic writers in a way that would not affect the system of the accepted medium, no situation definable as "languages in contact" or "in conflict" could obtain, but only the expansion and enrichment of one language of literature.[48]

This process can be viewed as an equivalent of the open tradition in the scribal treatment of texts. The preservation of the linguistic texture depended on the quality and quantity of textual alterations. The impact of ecclesiastic culture on the techniques that regulated both innovation and restoration was clearly an important conservative factor for several centuries.

The discovery of a hidden patrimony of verbal complexities and rhetorical contrivances in allegedly nonpoetic medieval texts may well mark a turning point in the study of Old Russian literature. The foundations of this critical turnabout were laid by the first generation of the twentieth-century literary avant-garde. Contemporary scholarship is confronted with the challenging task of producing an interpretative synthesis based on both the descriptive methods of formal and structural analysis and the historical-philological work carried out by many outstanding positivistic-minded investigators of the nineteenth century.

A considerable number of twentieth-century scholars—such as V. Peretc, V. V. Vinogradov, V. P. Adrianova-Peretc, N. S. Trubetzkoy, R. Jakobson, D. Čiževskij, I. P. Eremin, N. K. Gudzij, Ad. Stender-Petersen, L. A. Dmitriev, D. S. Lixačev, Ja. S. Lur'e, A. M. Pančenko, O. V. Tvorogov, A N. Robinson, K. Taranovsky, L. I. Sazonova, Ju. K. Begunov, B. A. Uspenskij, and Ju. M. Lotman—have contributed in many and different ways to the reevaluation of Old Russian verbal art. A good deal of research activity in both Europe and the United States has been devoted in recent years to Old Russian and medieval South Slavic formal techniques. Certain principles established on the basis of linguistic and philological observation have provided valuable reference points for further studies. This is the case, for example, with Dean S. Worth's description of *lexico-grammatical parallelism*, Djordje Trifunović's definition of the Old Serbian *rhythmical line*, and Kiril Taranov-

⁴⁸ R. Picchio, "Slave ecclésiastique, slavons et rédactions," in *To Honor Roman Jakobson: Essays on the Occasion of His Seventieth Birthday.* Janua Linguarum, Series Maior, nos. 31–33, vol. 2 (The Hague–Paris, 1967), 1527–1544; "Die historisch-philologische Bedeutung der kirchenslavischen Tradition," *Die Welt der Slaven* 7 (1962): 1–26.

sky's study of the forms of Common Slavic and Church Slavic verse in eleventh to thirteenth-century Old Russian literature.[49] A particularly attractive and fertile field of studies appears to be that of Greco-Slavic interrelations as defined by Roman Jakobson in his programmatic considerations on "The Slavic Response to Byzantine Poetry" and properly discussed by Henrik Birnbaum in his pioneering essay "Toward a Comparative Study of Church Slavic literature."[50]

Before venturing into a more detailed description of the verbal *xitrosti* used by Old Russian writers, it is essential to detect some of the general principles that guided their way of writing. The absence of marked poetic structures and the absolute predominance of prose in Old Russian literature for several centuries have always been a matter of concern for modern investigators. What is particularly puzzling is the fact that the skill of writing in verse was certainly known in *Slavia orthodoxa*. Texts in verse were produced at the very beginning of the Slavic literary tradition. As Trubetzkoy and Jaobson have shown, their survival can be detected in later prose contexts.[51] Moreover, verse techniques were elaborated in the folk tradition.

In the fifties of the eighteenth century, this problem was already seen by V. K. Trediakovskij as the kernel of any discussion on the historical development of literature in the Russian lands. In his essay "Old, Intermediate and New Russian Poetry," he suggested that the ecclesiastic establishment had eliminated the original poetic forms of pre-Christian Russia.[52] This was an audacious view. One wonders to what extent Trediakovskij had to present it in attenuated terms in order to avoid being condemned by the cultural establishment of his time, which was so well represented by

[49] D. Worth, "Lexico-grammatical Parallelism as a Stylistic Feature of the Zadonščina," in *Orbis scriptus. Dmitrij Tschiževskij zum 70. Geburtstag* (Munich, 1966), 953–961; Dj. Trifunović, "Stara srpska crkvena poezija" in *O. Srbljaku. Studije* (Belgrade, 1970), 9–93; K. Taranovskij, "Formy obščeslavjanskogo i cerkovnoslavjanskogo stixa v drevnerusskoj literature XI–XIII vv.," in *American Contributions to the Sixth International Congress of Slavists, Prague, 1968, August 7–13*, vol. 1: *Linguistic Contributions*, ed. H. Kučera (The Hague, 1968), 377–394.

[50] R. Jakobson, "The Slavic Response to Byzantine Poetry," in *Actes du XII Congrès international des études byzantines* (Belgrade, 1964); H. Birnbaum, "Toward a Comparative Study of Church Slavic Literature," in his *On Medieval and Renaissance Slavic Writing: Selected Essays* (The Hague–Paris, 1974), 13–40.

[51] N. S. Trubetzkoy, "Ein altkirchenslavisches Gedicht," *Zeitschrift für slavische Philologie* 2 (1935): 52–54; R. Jakobson, "Stixotvornye citaty v velikomoravskoj agiografii," *Slavistična Revija* 10 (1957): 111–118; id., "Poxvala Konstantina Filosofa Grigoriju Bogoslovu," *Slavia* 39 (1970): 334–361.

[52] V. K. Trediakovskij, *O drevnem, srednem, i novom stixotvorenii rossijskom*, in *Sočinenija*, vol. 2, ed. A. Smirdin (St. Petersburg, 1849), esp. 427–429.

Lomonosov's exaltation of the Slavo-Byzantine heritage. Trediakovskij's main intent was to justify his own reform in the domain of versification by postulating a sort of "classical" antecedent represented by the poetic skill of Slavic pagan priests. This contingent preoccupation may have affected his historical scheme. Nevertheless, his presentation of the basic terms of the problem has not lost its critical spell.

Today, as two hundred years ago, any historian of Old Russian literature cannot help but wonder whether the banishment of verse from literary practice was due to some sort of ecclesiastic censorship. It is reasonable to believe that verse was seen as a form of pagan *xitrorečie*. This conclusion is supported by medieval Slavic statements similar to the one by Epifanij Premudryj cited above as well as by individual condemnations of profane wisdom and skill. Suffice it to mention the case of the twelfth-century rhetorician Kliment Smoljatič and Ivan the Terrible's wicked passion for the performances of court jesters.

When dealing with this and similar problems, it seems advisable to consider not only the passive role played by ecclesiastic culture—that is, its banning certain types of literary activity—but also its possible active participation in the cultural process. Did Orthodox Slavic civilization reject any verbal device and formal embellishment, or did it, for example, approve of certain types of metrical segmentation while outlawing clearly marked verse? Since no theoretical treatise on this subject is available, the best way to proceed appears to be, once again, by analyzing the texts empirically in search of recurrent phenomena that can be reduced to a general principle.

The research that has led to the description of isocolic structures in Orthodox Slavic prose reflects this methodological attitude. The results of this research are very encouraging. The isocolic type of rhythmo-syntactical segmentation appears to be a dominant factor in so many texts that one can speak of a general *isocolic principle.*[53]

What is of particular interest for the investigation of Orthodox Slavic prose is the prevalence of isotonism over isosyllabism. This phenomenon deserves further study. An acceptable explanation of it is offered by the metrical tolerance of isocolic structures. Whereas syllabic segments do not

[53] My first article on this subject was devoted to the *Igor' Tale,* "On the Prosodic Structure of the Igor' Tale," *Slavic and East European Journal* 16 (1972): 147–162. A more comprehensive view on the problem was then submitted in my article "The Isocolic Principle in Old Russian Literature," in *Slavic Poetics: Essays in Honor of Kiril Taranovsky,* ed. R. Jakobson, C. H. van Schooneveld, and D. S. Worth (The Hague–Paris, 1973), 299–331. I have attempted to provide a general assessment of the research up to 1979 in my latest article, "Vǎrxu izokolnite strukturi v srednovekovnata slavjanska proza," *Literaturna misǎl* 24, no. 3 (1980): 75–107.

tolerate extensive textual elaboration, isotonic cola allow the replacement of monosyllabic words with polysyllabic equivalents, without limiting the number of syllables. Since each stressed unit corresponds to a phonic word (i.e., a word plus possible clitics), what counts is the preservation of a very elastic rhythmical structure based on isocola containing the same number of words.

Isocolic structures are an elementary type of rhythmo-syntactic segmentation. This appears to be one of the reasons, although not the only one, for their diffusion throughout Orthodox Slavdom. Texts governed by the parallel distribution of isotonic cola not only were easy to read aloud but could also be easily revised, corrected, expanded, shortened, and inserted in the similarly constructed contexts of other works. Furthermore, one could freely adorn such texts with additional markers such as rhyme, alliteration, phono-semantic cross signals, alternant or framed series, and the like. Recent studies have shown that a great number of such formal variations could easily fit any syntactical structure marked by an isocolic grid. This consideration applies not only to Old Russian works such as the *Slovo* and *Molenie* of Daniil Zatočnik, which has been isocolically scanned by Colucci and Danti,[54] and the *Zadonščina*, which has been isocolically interpreted by Colucci,[55] but also to a number of Glagolitic texts whose isocolic structure has been examined by Edward Hercigonja in his valuable *History of Medieval Croatian Literature*.[56] The role of isocolic structures in the stylistic texture of one of the oldest documents of Old Russian literature has been underlined by Jakobson in his analysis of Ilarion's *Sermon on Law and Grace*.[57]

That isotonic cola are not verse, but verbal figures of a different kind, was clear to Trediakovskij. He used isocolic segmentation in the preface to the 1735 edition of his treatise on versification. However, in the 1752 new version of the same work, he warned his readers that even though "the clauses of the so-called 'rhetorical isocolon' are also divided into almost equal segments, nevertheless these clauses are not verse."[58] This remark

---

[54] Daniil Zatočnik, *"Slovo e Molenie"* (see n. 41), 197–243.

[55] M. Colucci, "È possibile una constitutio textus della 'Zadonščina'?," *Spicilegio moderno* 7 (Imola, 1977), 36-62.

[56] E. Hercigonja, *Srednjovjekovna književnost*, Povijest hrvatske književnosti, no. 2 (Zagreb, 1975), 140–186.

[57] R. O. Jakobson, "Gimn v *Slove* Ilariona *o zakone i blagodati*," in *the Religious World of Russian Culture: Russia and Orthodoxy*, vol. 2, *Essays in Honor of Georges Florovsky*, ed. A. Blane (The Hague–Paris, 1975), 15–16. A valuable example of isocolic reading of texts in connection with the study of compositional patterns is also provided by M. Ziolkowski, "The Discourse of Dmitrij Ivanovič Donskoj," Ph.D. diss., Yale, 1979.

[58] "Ibo členy tak nazyvaemago isokolona retoričeskago takže počitaj opredelennymi čislami padajut; odnako sii členy ne stixi," *Sočinenija* (see n. 52), vol. 1: 123.

indicated that Trediakovskij's new rhetorical rules should not be confused with the traditional patrimony of formal devices of Old Russian literature. From my point of view, the importance of this remark lies in its reference to that older tradition. "Rhetorical isocolon" was clearly an important component of precisely the Old Russian system of literary techniques we want to reconstruct.

One can assume that many other formal devices used by Old Russian writers will be discovered in the future. It is hoped that the comparative evaluation of their function in the general system of Old Russian verbal art will help us reassess our views on the tonic isocolon. What is known suggests that the use of formal devices was not only permitted but was widely encouraged by the Orthodox Slavic literary doctrine. One of the reasons for accepting some of them and rejecting others might have been a widespread tendency to produce linguistically and rhetorically unmarked texts that could freely circulate from one region to another while being subject to frequent corrections and adaptations.

An observation of some major trends in the production and circulation of Old Russian works suggests that whereas thematic motives were subject to doctrinary limitations, formal techniques were frequently used as a sort of malleable clay. This attitude implied the existence of special methods to regulate the marking of thematic motives and their spiritual justification. Otherwise, textual change would have nullified the Church's ideological control, and the essence of "true messages" would not have been conveyed to the reader in thorough observance of the doctrine.

Apparently, an ideologically marked literary technique of this type was used to keep the delicate use of scriptural citations and references under control. By definition, the textual material taken from the Bible or other sacred writings, such as those of the Church Fathers, represented the language of truth, as opposed to the imperfect human language of the post-Babel age. Only by following the spiritual torch of divinely marked words could human writers cast some light on the otherwise blind labyrinth of their verbal constructions.

These were permanent motives in the Orthodox Slavic tradition in accordance with dominant themes of the Christian teaching. However, the intensity of their impact on literary techniques changed during the eight centuries of Orthodox Slavic medieval history depending on local or general trends, the relations between each Slavic region and the Byzantine Church, and the rising or falling power of political institutions.

At present the history of these changes can barely be outlined. Tentatively, however, a very general historiographic scheme for the Russian lands can be drawn (subject to all kinds of revision and correction), comprising three main periods or phases of development. The first period is dominated by the role of monastic-scriptorial centers which asserted the supreme validity of the Christian law for both religious and political ethics, in the spirit of missionary preaching. The second period can be characterized by the spreading of Hesychast trends and by their adaptation to local situations in the spirit of rising anti-West feelings. The third and last period, which lasted through the seventeenth century, focuses on the role of a state-dominated Church or, more precisely, the role of a Church that became part of the state and was dominated by its own political interests.

By studying the dependence of the literary doctrine on the changing interpretation of the ecclesiastic doctrine in its entirety, one may draw conclusions concerning the changes that occurred in the practice of literary techniques. It must be emphasized, however, that these remarks can only help define the general terms of a very complex historiographic problem. More precise interpretations must be deferred until detailed data are properly evaluated and put into a clearer context.

Throughout the long history of Orthodox Slavic literature, a permanent technique was apparently that of organizing texts in such a way that the "true words" contained in scriptural citations could help the reader grasp the higher meaning of each message. Functionally, this technique did not pertain to the *ornatus* of the text, but rather to its composition.

The more one investigates the complexities of Old Russian literature, the more it becomes clear that it was largely dominated by a semantic system based on the distinction between, and combination of, levels of meaning that corresponded to the senses of the Scripture. As in the Bible, which was regarded as the supreme model for imitation, a narrative was often supposed to convey a twofold message, namely, a spiritual message to be interpreted as the proclamation of a universal truth beyond the limits of any contingent event, and a historical message which described concrete earthly situations. These two levels of meaning were equally true. They could not be confused nor separated from each other.

To make sure that the reader would not concentrate on the historical meaning alone and miss the spiritual sense of a written message—which, unfortunately, seems to be the case with most of our current interpretations of Orthodox Slavic texts—particular compositional devices were employed. The use of especially marked thematic clues seems to be the most important among them.

A thematic clue consisted of scriptural references occurring in a compositionally marked place, namely, at the beginning of the exposition or direct narrative. This means that a thematic clue would be placed immediately after any introductory part of the text or, in the absence of an introduction, at the very beginning of the text. This compositional expedient was clearly intended to help the reader recognize especially important "words of truth" and use them to interpret the text's higher meaning. More particularly, a thematic clue was meant to fill the semantic gap between the spiritual and the historical levels of meaning.[59]

The sacred words emphasized by the compositional device described above called the reader's attention to another context, namely, that of a biblical or patristic book. It was that other context that functioned as a higher referent. By referring to it, the reader could translate any historical account into terms of universal truth. The exegetical motive signaled by the thematic clue was then developed throughout the text as a twofold semantic leitmotif.

Since the study of this revealing technique began a few years ago, the regularity of its use has been consistently confirmed. New light has been cast on the interpretation of a number of texts. Ilarion's *Sermon on Law and Grace* appears to be semantically governed by its initial reference to John 1:9–17. The higher meaning of the *Legend, Passion, and Eulogy of the Holy Martyrs Boris and Gleb* is also made clear, this time by a citation from Ps. 111 (112):2–3, which occurs in the work's first lines. The mixed texture of the *Discourse on the Life and Death of Grand Duke Dmitrij Ivanovič* is marked by two thematic clues, based on Ps. 91 (92):12 and 2 Cor. 6:16, respectively, which establish the leitmotifs of two distinct narratives.[60] The puzzling story of Igor' Svjatoslavič in the *Igor' Tale* becomes clear if one grasps its higher meaning as revealed by the thematic clue referring to Deut. 2:30.[61] H. Goldblatt has demonstrated the semantic dependence of Kostenečki's *Treatise* on a thematic clue that refers to both Matt. 10:16 and the *Physiologus*.[62] More recently, Alda Kossova has pointed out that Nestor's *Žitie prepodobnogo Feodosija Pečerskogo* is semantically governed by a thematic clue consisting of a set of references to Isa. 49:1, Jer. 1:15–16, Gal. 1:15–16, and Matt. 5:14–16.[63]

---

[59] R. Picchio, "The Function of Biblical Thematic Clues in the Literary Code of Slavia Orthodoxa," *Slavica Hierosolymitana, Slavic Studies of the Hebrew University*, no. 1, ed. L. Fleishman, O. Ronen, and D. Segal (Jerusalem, 1977), 1–31.

[60] Ibid.

[61] R. Picchio, "Notes on the Text of the Igor' Tale," *Harvard Ukrainian Studies* 2 (1978): 393–422.

[62] H. Goldblatt, "Orthography and Orthodoxy" (see n. 13), 270–276.

[63] A. Giambelluca Kossova, "Per una lettura analitica del *Žitie prepodobnago Feodosija Pečerskago* di Nestore," *Ricerche Slavistiche* 27–28 (1980–1981), in press.

More than any other known *xitrost'*,[64] this sophisticated use of a Christian device of literary exegesis can help us understand how consistent yet subtle was the influence of ecclesiastic culture on Old Russian literary techniques.

A complete inventory of Old Russian techniques and their assessment as expressions of a literary civilization apparently dependent on ecclesiastic models may lead to a substantial revision of current historiographic schemes. Such a revision should not imply indiscriminate rejection of their interpretations. This essay is meant to call the attention of Slavists to important aspects of the Old Russian literary heritage which have been insufficiently investigated in the past. It suggests that a different emphasis should balance our evaluation of that heritage. As stated in the preceding pages, my purpose is certainly not to replace old exaggerations with new exaggerations in an opposite direction. There is no doubt that even in a church-dominated society secular culture could play a significant role in many ways. One should attempt to interpret the history of Old Russian civilization not only as the expression of various oppositions and conflicts but also as the result of merging trends of different origin.

---

[64] The compositional techniques of Orthodox Slavic writers were cleary influenced by certain rhetorical schemes of late-classical and Byzantine origin, which were gradually assimilated by Eastern Christianity. A solid contribution to the study of models of this type is represented by J. Alissandratos's recent book, *Medieval Slavic and Patristic Eulogies*, Studia Historica et Philologica, vol. 14, Sectio Slavica, no. 6 (Florence, 1982).

ON THE RHETORICAL STYLE OF
SERAPION VLADIMIRSKIJ

RALPH BOGERT

Introduction

On the last page of his monographic study about Serapion of Vladimir, E. V. Petuxov gives an answer to the question: What is it that causes the sermons of Serapion to stand out from the vast number of other works belonging to the same genre?

> Samyj sklad poučenij dyšet takoju originaľnosťju i siloj, kotorye soveršenno neobyčny boľšinstvu drugix drevne-russkix proizvedenij v oblasti cerkovnoj propovedi.[1]

In this way Petuxov leaves the investigation of the organic character or make-up of Serapion's sermons to later students, for nowhere does he treat the functional structure of the persuasive aspects of composition—the rhetorical stance—of these works.

It is as a literary historian that Petuxov sees his objective in dealing with Serapion's legacy. He concerns himself with the groundwork of scholarship: he edits, orders, and publishes the texts most definitely attributable to Serapion, commenting superficially on the subject matter they contain.[2] This is not to say, however, that he does not deal at length with the topics of Serapion's addresses. Almost three-fifths of Petuxov's monograph investigates the theme of a single sermon: the persecution of sorcerers by the people and the Church's condemnation of such folk superstition. But

---

[1] E. V. Petuxov, *Serapion Vladimirskij, russkij propovednik XIII veka* (St. Petersburg, 1888), 213.

[2] Petuxov (ibid., 1) cites the only two chronicle references to Serapion, which tell that in 1274 he was brought from his position as archimandrite of the Kievan Cave Monastery to Vladimir, where he served as bishop until his death in 1275. Petuxov further considers in detail the question of the time and place of composition and delivery of Serapion's five sermons, weighing the facts given in historical documents against the preacher's frequent allusions to contemporary events, e.g., the Kievan earthquake in 1230 (sermon one), the second Tatar invasion in 1237 (two), the great famine of 1271 (four), the devastation of Durazzo on the Adriatic in 1273 (five). Sermons one through four are designated according to their order in the *Zlataja cep'*; the fifth is from the *Paisievskij sbornik* (see the Appendix to ibid., III–IV).

Petuxov takes a surface view in his study. He attempts to put Serapion's total literary activity into a broad cultural perspective and to trace the historical and social context of that activity. Indeed, he does not address Serapion's "originality" or "power" in terms of specific, observed phenomena in the texts he so diligently edits. It is ironic that, for Petuxov, once the sermons have been carefully lifted from the manuscripts and shaped into final, publishable form, they suddenly become much less significant as texts than as pretexts. The results are closer to the allegorical interpretation of a piece of literature as a historically valid artifact than to the analytical investigation of the sermons as viably purposeful units of language.

The trend toward the extrinsic criticism of Serapion's literary production was inherited by later scholars. Michel Gorlin responds to Petuxov's study by criticizing his method of dating the sermons.[3] Petuxov had determined that only the first of Serapion's sermons was composed in Kiev. Gorlin reconsiders the five sermons in view of the way in which they reflect known contemporary historical events and concludes that Serapion, known as the "bishop of Vladimir," could only have composed one of the extant sermons, his last, in that city. For Gorlin, Serapion remains a Kievan preacher, but he comes to this conclusion in a relational way, considering history as *found* in, rather than as *functioning* in, Serapion's work. Only in passing does he refer to the importance of studying the intrinsic elements of the inherited literary conventions that may have been instrumental in determining the substance of the work itself: "L'influence byzantine a été déjà relevée par Petuchov ... mais elle mériterait une étude plus approfondie."[4]

N. K. Gudzij continues the line of historical criticism.[5] On the basis of the chronicles, he refutes Gorlin's suppositions and affirms Petuxov's original classification of Serapion's sermons, asserting that Serapion's Kievan heritage would not have been at all out of place in the North and that the content of most of his sermons was integrally connected with the life of Vladimir-Suzdal' Rus'.

A later scholar, V. A. Kolobanov, takes a slightly different tack in studying Old Russian homiletic literature. He attempts to determine the authorship of an anonymous medieval sermon on the basis of its stylistic affinities

---

[3] M. Gorlin, "Sérapion de Vladimir, prédicateur de Kiev," *Revue des études slaves* 24 (1948): 21–28.

[4] Ibid., 25.

[5] N. K. Gudzij, "Gde i kogda protekala literaturnaja dejatel'nost' Serapiona Vladimirskogo?" *IOLJa* 11 (Sept.–Oct. 1952): 450–456.

with Serapion's works.[6] Although his comparative textological analysis is far from comprehensive, his article is indicative of a revived interest in the fruitfulness of structural criticism, albeit incorporated into the traditional historical approach to Serapion's sermons. Yet in another place, Kolobanov reverts to the established genre of Serapion scholarship.[7] He moves away from the patterns and style of the sermons to focus on how they reflect historical personalities and social relations of their times. In this latter respect, it is interesting that Kolobanov shows a preference for the three sermons dealing thematically with the Tatar invasion of southern Russia. These sermons (especially the ones on "the merciless heathen" and "on omens") seem to contain material most easily usable by students of the social sciences and most often included in the standard anthologies of Russian medieval literature.

The two sermons ostensibly dealing with folk customs and superstitions (numbers four and five, according to Petuxov's classification) have been neglected by Soviet scholars, who have preferred the seemingly more politically tendentious sermons. True, from the point of view of a nonaesthetic literary treatment of Serapion's homiletic style, these latter sermons appear to be more immediately palatable. Even Petuxov, who certainly did not suffer under the same pressures as his modern-day countrymen—pressures demanding unswerving allegiance to the idea of always showing the common weal in a favorable light—and who did not hesitate to consider the weakness of the people in order to point out the strength of Serapion as a religious figure—even Petuxov chose to concentrate on general external topics rather than on internally organized themes. It seems that Serapion's most literally popular sermons have traditionally been the most unpopular among scholars.

In passing over the fourth sermon, the Soviet scholars seem to have missed an easy opportunity to interpret the persecution of witches as a manifestation of class conflict. It alone of all the sermons would lend itself to the kind of tendentious interpretation based on political and historical factors at which Soviet scholarship seems particularly adept.[8] This is all the more so because Serapion does not simply tell the people not to fear or kill witches and to believe in God's power to punish instead; he also adds that

[6] V. A. Kolobanov, "O Serapione Vladimirskom kak vozmožnom avtore 'Poučenija k popom,'" *TODRL* 14 (1958): 159–162.

[7] V. A. Kolobanov, "Obličenie knjažeskix meždousobij v poučenijax Serapiona Vladimirskogo," *TODRL* 17 (1961): 329–333.

[8] R. Zguta gives an example of this kind of Soviet sociological bias in his article "The Pagan Priests of Early Russia: Some New Insights," *Slavic Review* 33 (1974): 260.

they must not kill one another out of blind fear or superstition (a condemnation of internecine strife). In fact, he condones killing if it is done according to social law (thereby approving the subjugation of the individual to the
masses). Moreover, he cites David, a plain citizen of peasant stock, as the
paragon, the judicious *bogatyr'* of the Old Testament, whose virtue Serapion's listeners are to emulate. Potentially at least, there seems to be
abundant material here for a traditional socio-allegorical interpretation of
the sermon.

The intent of the present study, however, is to analyze the rhetorical style
used in this fourth sermon. The preceding survey of scholarship on this
subject indicates the need for such an approach. Previous investigators
have looked at these sermons as just so much food for ethical consumption
and digestion. In following such a non-language-oriented approach, they
have disregarded the *mode* of the sermon. In earlier studies, the aesthetic,
personal relationships between the orator and his individual listener have
not been examined, even though this last great preacher from Old Kiev
speaks to the events of his times and the concerns of his compatriots with a
rhythmical urgency perhaps unequaled in Rusian homiletic art. And it is on
the level of speaker-audience interaction that one can most viably delineate
the primary intent of Serapion's oratory: persuasion. The aim of the following descriptive analysis is to examine the objective facts of what Petuxov
subjectively calls the "originality" and "power" with which Serapion's style
"breathes." Here, the sermon will be characterized in terms of specific,
functioning rhetorical techniques. (For the full text of the sermon, see the
end of this essay. In the analysis below, line numbers to the sermon will be
cited in parentheses.)

Descriptive Rhetorical Analysis

Several characteristics of a typical rhetorical exordium are evident in the
very first statement of the sermon:

> Malъ čaŝ poradovaxsja o vasъ, čaâ, vidja vašju ljubovь i poslušanie kъ našei
> xudosti, i mnjaxъ, jako uže utverdistesja i s radostiju primlete bžŝtvenoe
> pisanie, na sveî nečŝtivyxъ ne xodite i na sedališti gubiteî ne sede.

The general, overall purpose here is to inspire a positive feeling of confi-
dence. The speaker aims a compliment at his audience. The intent of such a
statement is to win trust (comprobatio). The speaker underscores his harmonious relations with his listeners by establishing a lexical affinity with
them. The first member of this rhetorical device pertains to the orator

(*poradovaxsja*); the second, to the audience (*s radostiju*). This common feeling is stressed even more by the possessive pronoun-adjective (3).[9] If we look at the sentence from a more specific, personal point of view, we see that the orator has already captured the attention of his listeners by the simple means of direct address. Apostrophic elements here include the use of a personal pronoun and the immediate metaphorical naming (or renaming) of the listeners: *čada*. Serapion thus isolates and emphasizes a symbolic relationship based on expected familiar connections between speaker and listener.[10] The spiritual father is clearly speaking to his charges from a position of authority. In this way, Serapion effectively delimits the relationship between speaker and audience by employing a technique of metonymic reduction. It is significant that he defines who his hearers are at once. He is speaking to an audience of commoners for whom he is morally, but not officially, responsible.[11] Their needs as listeners will determine for him the tone of the diction, the style of the figurative language, and the manner of exposition of the ideas to follow.

The opening statement also illustrates the careful attention Serapion pays to syntax. These lines contain syntactical parallelisms characteristic of paratactically coordinated clauses:

poradovaxsja ...
i mjaxъ ...

Each of these contains a hypotactically subordinate clause, the first of which is introduced by a verbal adverb (*vidja*); the second, by a conjunction (*jako*). The apparently conscious effort to balance these diverse syntactic elements will be discussed below within the context of the next notable rhetorical figures.

Lines four and five contain a direct quotation of an approved authority (apomnemonysis). It is a scriptural passage taken from Ps. 1:1, which in Church Slavonic translation reads:

Blžnъ mužь iže ne ide na svetъ nečtivyxъ
i na puti grešnyxъ ne stanetь
i na sedališti gubitelь ne šde.[12]

---

[9] The text used here is taken from the appendix to Petuxov's monograph on Serapion. I have transliterated it *de verbo ad verbum,* as edited, without attempting orthographical normalization. A tittle ⁻ indicates numbers or abbreviated words (often having a sacred character) in the original Cyrillic text; a circumflex marks letters elevated above the line.

[10] J. Besharov, *Imagery of the Igor' Tale in the Light of Byzantino-Slavic Poetic Theory* (Leiden, 1956), 64.

[11] Were Serapion speaking to the clergy instead of to the laity, he would have had to mention his ecclesiastical rank at the outset. See Kolobanov, "O Serapione Vladimirskom" (see n. 6), 160.

[12] *Psaltir'* (Moscow: Sinodal'naja biblioteka, 1296), no. 235, pp. 2 v-3. Cited by Petuxov in Appendix to *Serapion Vladimirskij,* 11.

Serapion has preserved the negative syntactical parallelisms but has abbreviated the statement by omitting the second clause. What is the purpose of this biblical quotation? It might appear that there is excessive thematic repetition (pleonasmus) here: to "walk in the counsel of the ungodly" seems to be only a paraphrase of "sitting in the seat of the scornful." Yet if Serapion truly intended to produce a dazzling pleonastic effect at this point in his sermon, he could have simply quoted the verse verbatim, thereby reproducing three syntactically parallel coordinate clauses beginning with like negative anaphoric constructions:

> iže ne ide
> i ne stanetь
> i ne ŝde

A natural delaying, retarding device (commoratio) was available to the speaker, had he wanted to use it. Instead, Serapion refrains from expanding his opening statement further.

Though the theme of the sermon has not been stated explicitly up to this point, the manner in which the apomnemonysis is handled indicates what is to follow. Serapion's subsequent argument and theme are implicit in what he cites from the Bible, as well as in what he chooses to omit: "na sveî nečŝtivyxъ ne xodite" implies the attitude of one who *follows* impure, profane forces, while "na sedališti gubiteî ne sedite" refers to a posture of judging (here scornfully), thus of *condemning* unjustly. The speaker is concerned with acts ungodly in both a passive and an active sense.

The second main rhetorical division of the oration (explicatio, the statement of theme) begins with a direct charge addressed to the audience (categoria, direct accusation):

> *A*   Aže ešte poganьskaĝ obyčaja *deržiteŝ*:
>   volxvo(va)niju *verujeî*
>
> *B*   *i požigaeî* ogneḿ nevinyja čĺvky
>   *i navodite* na vsь mirъ i grad̂ ubiistvo

The initial part (*A*) of the accusatory statement is characterized by two syntactically parallel direct object/verb inversions. The separate, complementary elements in this relationship are distinguished by use of dieresis: the objects have been divided into genus (*poganьskaĝ obyčaja*) and species (*volxvo(va)niju*) in order to amplify and qualify. Stylistically, the second part (*B*) of this statement is a mirror-image of the first (*A*). The previous syntactically parallel clausulae are now complemented by two coordinate clauses defined by lexical and syntactical anaphora, and the direct objects are at the *ends* of the lines. There is another kind of reversal as well. The initial type of dieresis (genus to species) is inverted: species (*burning*) goes to genus (*murder*). This passage as a whole represents not only a quantitative, syntactic chiasmus but also a qualitative, semantic exchange. Serapion begins by mentioning pagan custom in general and concludes by naming a sin central to Christianity: murder.

Early in the sermon we already see Serapion's ability to exploit rhetorical devices in a well-balanced, diverse way in order to have a direct, personal effect on his listeners. He goes to some length to expand his statement of accusation, for it contains the specific theme he will treat in the main, argumentative section of his talk. In part *B* of the explicatio, Serapion interpolates adverbial modifiers in a syntactically parallel fashion. The phrase *požigaeĭ ognem̂* is a genuine pleonasmus: the noun is semantically, but not rhetorically, superfluous. And the expression *na vsь mirъ i grad̂* contains a form of exoche, the singling out of a particular (here, *grad*) after the naming of a group or larger entity that would include it. The preacher stresses the *nature* of the particular pagan practice he deplores by means of pleonasmus. The diction is emphatic. We can hear the rise of the voice on *ognem*. With exoche the locale of this practice is singled out; the accusation is brought home to the listeners in a particularly personal way. The town is, of course, not only part of the whole world; it is the home of Serapion's audience. Also, seen as an emblematic trope of substitution, *grad* functions metonymically: murder is brought upon the town, a generalized concept closely associated with the listeners—the townspeople.[13] In this figure Serapion has expanded a relation on the basis of contiguity.

A personalized restatement of the categoria immediately follows (8–10). But the argument proper begins here, too. Functionally, these lines effect a transition from the charge laid against the listeners to the subsequent persuasion supporting it:

---

[13] In the light of Choiroboskos' treatise on tropes and figures as it is interpreted in the Svjatoslav Codex of 1073, this appears to be a typical use of metonymy (*otъimenie*)—the substitution of the habitat for the inhabitants:

> otъimene eže estь jegda otъ odrъžaštiixъ odrъžimaja otъimene naričemъ po rečenuumu nakažetesja vsi sudjaštei zemli rekъše suštiimъ vъ zemi *ili otъ živuštiixъ ideže živutь* (Metonymy occurs when instead of the possessors we name the possession. According to the saying "Be instructed, ye judges of the earth," that is to say: those on the earth. Instead of the inhabitants, there is their habitat.).

For a thorough presentation of Choiroboskos' treatise, see Besharov's study (see n. 10), which contains both the Greek and the Old Slavonic text (cited here), as well as a modern English translation by Milman Parry.

A 1. ašte kto i ne pričastisja ubiistvu,
2. no vsonьmi byvъ vъ edinoi mysli,
3. ubiica že byŝ;

B 1. ili mogai pomošti,
2. a ne pomože,
3. aki samъ ubiti poveleî ē.

These two thematically parallel statements begin on a note of personal address to the members of the audience (interrogative pronoun). Each of the coordinate phrases emphasizes the conditions under which an individual would be culpable. The conditions favor a broad interpretation of the divine law of the Christian constitution. Serapion makes it clear that one may be guilty simply by doing nothing to prevent evil.

This passage holds still another example of the speaker's predilection for rhetorical symmetry. The first statement (*A*) presents the claim that whether one participates in murder or not, he is as guilty as the murderer if he lends his tacit consent. The stress falls on the harm one may do through *passivity*. The syntactic units are

1. a negative subordinate clause;
2. a positive subordinate clause;
3. a principal clause stating that one suffers the condition of a murderer.

The second statement (*B*) is the structural isomer of the first. Here, if one is able to help but does not, he is in the same moral category as the person who orders the murder. Ser„apion is antithetically accenting the *active* benevolence one should manifest. The syntactic units are the counterparts to those above:

1. a positive subordinate clause;
2. a negative subordinate clause;
3. a principal conclusion to the effect that one has actively committed murder.

The speaker has thematically dilated the scripturally suggested ideas, while at the same time he has paraphrased them in figuratively neutral, concrete terms: criminal passivity—following in the way, or counsel, of murderers—takes place in a congregation (*sveî → vsonьmi*); criminal activity—the act of judging who is to die—becomes personal involvement in ordering a murder (*sedališti gubiteî ... sedite → ubiti poveleî ē*). These lines, then, clearly illustrate Serapion's inclination to balance his phrases externally as well as internally. The apomnemonysis is a prime example. The biblical lines have been edited to fit into the comprobatio. As oral works incorporated into a traditional body of writing, psalms provide a basis for studying the poetics of the context in which they appear. It has been observed that stylistic symmetry is a characteristic trait of the Old Testament psalms.[14] This potentially complex interplay of syntactic elements is carried even further in the final parallel lines of the explicatio, where symmetry is realized in the opposition of two semantically equivalent sentences and in the chiastic arrangement of their subordinate members:

	A	*B*	
	(subordinate/antiphrasis)	(subordinate/phrasis)	
1	ašte kto i ne pričastisja ubiistvu,	ili mogai pomošti,	1
	(principal/metaphor)	(principal/simile)	
3	ubiica že byŝ;	aki samъ ubiti poveleî ē.	3
	(subordinate/phrasis)	(subordinate/antiphrasis)	
2	no vsonьmi byvъ vъ edinoi mysli,	a ne pomože,	2

The rhetorical key to providing variation with conformity, to maintaining the clear line of exposition so fundamental to oratory, is inherent in the parallel construction. The implicit is rendered explicit as the metaphor (*A*3) is immediately backed by a simile (*B*3).[15] This does not appear to be the kind of veiled figurative language that would require such overt explication. Yet Serapion constructs his statements with obvious care. He reiterates the earlier dual posture of the person in the psalm who was involved with evil. The position of the subject as seen in the first principal clause (*A*) is static. He is a follower, one among many. Conversely, the posture of the subject in the second clause (*B*) is dynamic. He acts. He alone is judge. It is interesting and, perhaps, not accidental that Serapion has singled out Scripture relating to a man from the people who is to become a singular person. The psalm brings to mind David, the Robin Hood of the Old Testament, a true folk figure who becomes a charismatic (rather than messianic) leader. He will soon reappear as an important referent in the persuasive core of the sermon.

[14] D. S. Lixačev, *Poètika drevnerusskoj literatury,* 2nd ed. (Leningrad, 1971), 186. In studying the poetics of the Psalms, the writer distinguishes this device from repetition (old content, same form, different words) and parallelism (new content, same form, different words): "Stilističeskuju simmetriju otličaet to, čto ona [...] dvaždy govorit ob odnom i tom že [...] no v drugoj forme, drugimi slovami" (old content, new form, different words).
[15] Besharov, *Imagery of the Igor' Tale* (see n. 10), 70.

The main body of the sermon consists of setting forth the arguments in defense and refutation of the charge (amplificatio/refutatio, 10–50). This section begins with a barrage of four rhetorical questions (10, 12, 15, 17). The initial hypophora leads to its answer: the second question, with its subordinate clause (*aže semu veruete*), contains a demonstrative pronoun, the logical antecedent of which is located in the preceding question. The unique construction of this first hypophora relieves the complex symmetry of the hypotactic statement it follows. At once the ear catches retarding, simplifying mechanisms. Coordinative conjunctions regulate the separate synonymic elements. The listeners hear two pairs of coordinate clauses presented simultaneously. The beginning is emphasized by lexical, syntactic, and semantic repetition (commoratio): *Oî kotoryx̂ knigъ ... oî kixъ pisanii* ... Other parallelisms in the second half of the question are accomplished by word repetition in succeeding clauses (conduplicatio): *volxvovaniemь*. There is significance in the manner in which Serapion conceives the apprehending of the written word. He is addressing a lay congregation, a group of listeners whose access to information generally (not only at the moment of this address) is the spoken word: they "hear" from the books. In contrast, the churchman stresses the fact that he has *read* the Word. At this point he appears to be falling back onto his status as one who can and has seen and read (and just quoted) the Scriptures.

The second question (12–13) reflects the logic at the heart of the argument. The hypothetical propositions are

1. People should worship what they believe in.
2. People believe in sorcerers.
3. Therefore, people should worship sorcerers.

The major premise is only theologically valid. There is no attempt to handle the theme of the speech psychologically or sociologically. Serapion's theology does not try to deny the actual existence of sorcery as manifest evil. In fact, he affirms its presence in the world. Rather, he attempts to illustrate the assimilation of what he conceives to be a pagan custom into a larger Christian ontology. He proceeds by rhetorical means to press upon his audience as *individuals* the fact that the effects of sorcery will cease if each of his listeners ceases to practice the pagan custom, a manifest belief in the power of witchcraft. Serapion does not dispute the existence of sorcerers; he only tries to undermine their basis of power. Murder, which is prohibited, may be blessedly transformed into permissible killing if it is motivated by an authoritarian, theocratic urge. It is this *direct* relation of the people to God that is most important to Serapion.

In his monograph, Petuxov studies the origins of sorcery in Russia in the light of its treatment by the Eastern Church, the clergy and Serapion.[16] In contrast to the situation in Western Europe—where, under the penumbra of chiliastic fervor, religious leaders protesting an institutionalized "process" of persecution (the *Hexenprozesse* that resulted from the episcopal inquisitions) chastised a narrow elite (the educated and civil judges) through the medium of writing (antitheological treatises and heretical manifestos)[17]—in medieval Russia the clergy voiced its social concerns by addressing the illiterate masses directly.[18] Practical reasons of persuasive oral communication dictate, in Serapion's case, that the arguments must be simplified and attuned to the ears of the folk congregation. Here Cicero's definition of rhetoric is appropriate to the spoken moment: "Ars dicendi accomodate ad persuadendum." It is innovative redundancy, rather than tight logic, that carries the thrust of the speech. Though Petuxov considers the historical sources in depth, he never comes to terms with the fundamental reasons for the ambivalent attitude Serapion manifests toward the folk and their atavistic practices. However, if one takes into account the disruptive emotional and social atmosphere of the thirteenth century when Serapion composed and delivered this sermon, it seems very probable that in formulating these lines he was more occupied with the live exigencies of their performance than with the erudite consistency of their logic. Yet it is not simply a case of determining the extent to which the absolute validity of content suffers at the expense of form. On certain points the speaker must have striven intentionally toward an umbrageous presentation of his feelings for his congregation. And instead of detracting from the oral presentation, this may have enhanced it. Thus, in one place Serapion openly assails his audience by suggesting that they are still pagans (the "custom," 6), then later he goes on to declare that their mutual enemy is a heathen (47). And he does not hesitate to associate himself directly with his listeners: their common bond is their faith and nationality. (First person plural references in the text indicate the speaker and his audience share the same misery, sins, heathen enemy [Mongols], salvation, spiritual enemy [*vrag*], and God.) In spite of the inconsistent manner in which Serapion defines the relations between man and God—now with "love" (1) and "joy" (3), now with the coldness of blind faith (22–23)—he does adhere to a rhetorical consistency: the logic of the sermon is subordinated to the primary goal of dissuading the listeners form their unorthodox acts.

[16] Petuxov, *Serapion Vladimirskij* (see n. 1), 55–167.
[17] N. Cohn, *The Pursuit of the Millennium* (Fairlawn, New Jersey, 1957), 170–174.
[18] Petuxov, *Serapion Vladimirskij*, 131.

The orator goes on to saturate his interrogative attack with ironic urging. There is a kind of irony in the Socratic sense, as he temporarily feigns ignorance in the argument and assumes, for a moment, the stance of those he accuses in order to belittle their beliefs. This technique is coupled with an emphatic series of commands addressed to the listeners in the second person (*moliteŝ ... čtite ... prinosite*) and complemented by third person imperatives based on nature imagery to which the audience would be readily sensitive:

> atь ... doždь puštajutь,
> teplo privodjatь,
> zemli ploditi veljatь!

Serapion rushes along from question to question, resisting any temptation to insert a retarding pleonasmus (*ognem* is conspicuously absent here, 13). Two more rhetorical questions appear (15–18). They complement one another; the answer to each is strongly implied (erotesis):

> se vьlxvove li *stvoriša*?   [no]
> Ašte ne Bъ li *stroite svoju tvorь....*?   [yes]

The juxtaposition is one of semantically negative parallelisms with the implied answers equally antithetical. Yet these units are syntactically parallel and are even held in alignment by a conscious attempt to repeat words from the same root (polyptoton). Through a variety of devices, the object of Christian worship is inextricably bound up with the witch doctors of folk belief. The speaker simultaneously sets forth arguments for his opponents' view (amplificatio) and confutes them (refutatio). This is why the first of these two questions issues from the most contemporary, topical, concrete fact mentioned in the sermon (Ears would certainly prick up at the reference to the famine, 15.),[19] while the second question presents the abstract, theological tenet fundamental to Serapion's persuasive argument:

> za greŝ naŝ tomja

This seemingly incidental hypotactic addition deftly appends multiple aspects of the speaker's countertheme (mortal sin, divine punishment, personal moral responsibility) to his rhetorical thrust. It is a sermonic épée.

The argument is now shifted in earnest to the basis of personal authority:

> Vide ā oî bžŝtvnago napisanьja

<hr/>

[19] Ibid., 32–33.

The preacher's reliance on his own stature becomes a persuasive device. Offering his own experience as confirmation, he asserts the veracity of his opinions (martyria). The mode of perceiving the Holy Scriptures seems to be amphibolic. The speaker expresses his relationship to them by simultaneously drawing attention to the central mark of distinction of a learned church man, the quality of his special power—the ability to *see* script—and, more obliquely, by implying more than is said (the rhetorical *emphasis*) in order to connote the act of acquiring knowledge from the Scriptures. We see a similar verbal distinction later in the sermon, where David's authoritative wisdom (ability to judge, *Straxoṁ b̃iṁ sudjaše*) is semantically parallel with his divinely inspired in*sight* (*d͞xmь s͞tmь vidjaše*).

The oblique form of the statement beginning in line 21 brings with it a sort of recapitulation, a culmination of the preceding logical argument:

> Bū popuštьšju, besi destvujutь; popuštaetь Bъ, iže kto ixъ boitsja; a iže kto veru tverdu deržitь k Bū, s togo čarodeici ne mogutь.

In this passage Serapion employs a common summarizing device. By referring to generally accepted principles, those of the Old Testament, he confirms the initial comment of the passage (apodixis).[20] The opening statement says that God is omnipotent and that demons function by His consent. The general principles that follow this hold that the demons are God's agents for testing man's faith. Up to this point in the sermon, Serapion has been intent on discrediting the devils and sorcerers and increasing the stature of God. And here we find the doctrine of free will, of individual sin, encapsulated.

From the standpoint of stylistic structure, one of the most noticeable features of this passage is the use of the dative absolute. The presence of such a causal adverbial phrase precisely at this point in the sermon serves several purposes.

(1) The switch to an infrequently used grammatical case enables the speaker to make his point in a concise and unusual way (anthypallage). This is the only use of the dative absolute in the text; Serapion feels it necessary to rephrase this statement in semantically neutral language (*popuštaetь Bъ*).

(2) It is likely that this unique construction would have sounded "bookish." It is probably more closely associated with manuscript and chronicle

---

[20] An analogous apodixis would be:
> Be not deceived; God is not mocked:
> for whatsoever a man soweth,
> that shall he also reap.   (Gal. 6:7)

(written) tradition of ecclesiastic literature than with the oral, homiletic (spoken) tradition.[21] Such usage is not out of place here, since Serapion has just stressed his familiarity with the Holy Writing (18).

(3) The conciseness of this apodixis has the almost aphoristic quality of biblical quotation. It is close to a short, pithy statement of a general truth, condensing into memorable form a common experience (aphorismus, the wisdom of a group of men):

> Eže bo ašte seetъ čelovekъ,
> tožde i požnetъ.

Yet here we see Serapion's own, original formulation (apothegm, the wisdom of one man):

> kto verŭ tverdŭ deržĭtь k Bū,
> s togo čarodeici ne mogutь.

Certain features of this maxim illustrate the speaker's conscious attempt to be original, yet succinct: *veru tverdu* seems to be a locus communis placed here for emphatic and, possibly, metrical reasons; the omission of the verb at the very end of the phrase (ellipsis) has an abbreviating effect. The folk proverb also exhibits these characteristics, as well as others: it often has two clauses of similar metrical quality and/or number of syllables, or, as in the examples above, it is composed of a longer line of regular cadence, followed by a shorter line with fewer syllables and less metrical stress; rhyme at the end of the hemistiches is common; a thematically important word may be located at the caesura; a subordinate clause is introduced by a conjunctive word, then comes a principal clause introduced by a substantivized pronoun.[22] On the nonstructural, semantic level, the proverb metaphorizes an obvious truth from the welter of folk beliefs that give birth to it. Its effectiveness

---

[21] Erich Auerbach (*Mimesis* [New York, 1957], 62) points out this basic distinction between the word of the eye and the word of the ear in speaking of certain biblical passages:

> In all of these instances, there is, instead of the causal or at least temporal hypotaxis which we should expect in classical Latin (with ablative absolute or participial construction) a parataxis with *et*; and this procedure, far from weakening the interdependence of the two events, brings it out most emphatically; just as in English it is more dramatically effective to say: He opened his eyes and was struck ... than; when he opened his eyes, or: Upon opening his eyes, he was struck ...

The point here, of course, is not that Serapion is removed by hypotaxis from any emotional appeal to his audience, but that he is shifting his persuasive powers over to the logical, authoritative mode of cool, classical, causal, temporal style.

[22] S. G. Lazutin, "Nekotorye voprosy stixotvornoj formy russkix poslovic," *Iz istorii russkoj narodnoj poèzii* 12 (1971): 135–146.

depends on the percipient's ability to make an immediate association within this familiar social framework. Serapion takes care to put his apothegm into the right context. He is careful to imply that the God of whom he speaks is antithetical to the sorceresses operating in this world. It is certain that the success of his statement hinges on word patterns and diction used up to this point in the sermon, for nowhere has he baldly stated that sorcery is nonexistent or that it is "bad." Instead, he has attacked it on grounds of its general ineffectiveness. Taken from this context, his statement would be absurd to members of a quasi-pagan society whose sorcerers were believed to be in league with the gods. They would logically expect to hear something like, "The sorcerers can do everything for those who believe firmly in the gods."[23]

This passage, then, is the logical culmination, the apex, of the initial theological argument, for there is a drop in tone and style in the very next statement.

The orator now interrupts the logical discourse and allows an open intrusion of his personal attitude. As we immediately hear, this signals a new, different kind of appeal to authority. Serapion has just previously deferred to his own authority with a cool reference to his stature as an officer of the Church learned in the Scriptures. He now appeals emotionally to the traditional authority of a personality central to these Scriptures—David. The speaker becomes personally involved with his listeners. In two brief, uncompounded statements (23–24) he uses: personal pronoun; apostrophe, imperative; a personal, almost exclamatory reference to his own feelings (a kind of ecphonesis: *Pečalenъ estъ*); and a single, degrading word that emotionally summarizes the listeners' actions he has discussed (meiosis: *bezumъi*).

The passage on David (25–30) exemplifies Serapion's method of citing the authority of a biblical figure as a technique of argument (commemoratio). There seems to be a conscious effort to vary terminology. As a new idea and a biblical reference are introduced and Serapion begins an analogy

---

[23] An analogy may be found in the statement: "If you can't take the heat, stay in the kitchen." If we judge this literally on the basis of our own social context, it seems that some foreign situation is being described, where the stove is not located in the kitchen. However, once we are told that this is a playful reversal of the proverbial formula popularized by President Truman ("If you can't stand the heat, get out of the kitchen") uttered at a recent symposium entitled "Husbands, Sons, and Lovers: Masculinity and the Changing Woman," then we understand that we are hearing a particular display of stylistic cleverness pretending to formulate a contemporary apothegm. (The statement cited was attributed to Betty Friedan, author of *The Feminine Mystique*, by Shana Alexander in "No Person's Land," *Newsweek*, 18 March 1974, 43.)

(David : evil : Jerusalem : : *čada* : *gladi* : *grad*), a phrase is expanded (hendiadys): the contents are stated, then restated through paraphrasis (*oî bezakonnyxъ člvkъ / vsja tvorjaštaja bezakonie*), metaphrasis (*grad ocestiti / grad gŝnь čŝtъ tvorjaše*), and antonomasia (specification of quality or, here, office: *Dvdъ prrkъ i cŝrь*). This section illustrates well Serapion's love of repetition, parallelism, and *symmetria*. Twice he specifies general antecedents by elaborating their consequences: first, a general statement that David rid the city of evil men (27); then, a second general statement (phrased as erotesis, 28–29), followed by three phrases, each beginning with an adverbial modifier and ending with the same rhythmic verbal construction (29–30).

As he did in the beginning, Serapion again moves from the biblical referent to contemporary circumstances: he now considers the manner in which his audience judges. This will be a thematic counterpart to the lines on David. The contrasting emphatic particle (*Vy že*) marks the shift from past to present. The parallels are readily perceptible in the presence of grammatical and thematic anaphora:

David	audience
ovexъ ...	inyi ...
inixъ ...	iny(i) ...
inix že ...	a inyi ...

Another trait of Serapion's negative parallelisms is the amplification through synonymia and paraphrase:

David	audience
po pravde otvetъ dajaše	po pravde ne sudte

The discussion of superstition and the comparison of it with canon law motivated by reference to David ends with the longest rhetorical question in the sermon (37–41). Erotesis is employed to lead to a conclusive answer (yes), which affirms the dogmatic, nonheretical view of evil. It is simply a matter of persuading the listener that the Christian devil, because he owes his existence to the will of God, will always outwit those who superstitiously believe in "false" devils.

Serapion concludes the central argumentative portion of his sermon with a methodical retelling of past events. A review of the unique rhetorical aspects of this enumeratio will reveal how it functions persuasively. The initial general statement (41–42) is followed by a characteristic trait of Serapion's exhortatory method: specific examples are offered immediately. The history of divine wrath is traced in a chronological catalogue. The list proceeds from a reference to an antediluvian event (42–43) to the Roman conquest of Judea and the capture of Jerusalem (46). There is then a shift to events contemporary with the audience. Certain stylistic effects are calculated to convey dynamically the paralleling of facts from the point of view of era (ancient and medieval), experience (historical and contemporary), and significance (sacred and profane).

The separate clauses of this section are put into a semantically climactic order (auxesis). The sketch of the punishments visited upon mankind begins with an event that took place in what, even to the most naive of Serapion's listeners, must have seemed to be a prehistorical, somewhat mythological era—the time of the "giants"—and builds in a chronological crescendo to the present. The nonverbal, telegraphic phrasing of the separate events (achieved through parallel ellipses) facilitates the immediate and direct comprehension of the information conveyed. This is a kind of incantatory chain. Transition from the biblical misfortunes to those experienced by the Russian audience is effected rhetorically by hypophora (47), the answer to which contains a second, shorter catalogue of troubles; and semantically by synecdoche, where one pagan stands for the whole invading Mongol army (*Pri našem že jazyce*) in thirteenth-century Russia, just as a single general, Titus, signifies the entire Roman Seventh Legion.

The sources of the facts alluded to by Serapion have been investigated historiographically.[24] Almost all the events in the catalogue of calamities except the first and last are traced to scriptural references. The punishment of the giants specifically by fire is not canonical; this seems to indicate that Serapion had been exposed to a tradition of Byzantine apocryphal writing influenced by folk sources at least as ancient as Greek mythology.[25] However, it is less important here to trace the precise source of a traditional oral element that penetrated a later literary tradition than to discuss the way it is used. Moreover, the association of an earthquake with the fall of Jerusalem (46) is neither scriptural nor convincingly traceable to any sources that might have influenced Serapion.[26] It is evident from the general thematic intent of the sermon, as well as from the specific manner in which the sermonizer interpretatively treats his scriptural source material (such as the quotation from Psalms), that the "facts" he presents are justified primarily on grounds of rhetorical effectiveness, not historical veracity. Petuxov is aware of at least two lines of literary influence upon Serapion—on the one

---

[24] Petuxov, *Serapion Vladimirskij*, 178ff.
[25] Ibid., 184.
[26] Ibid., 180–181.

hand, the didactic, ecclesiastical sermons of Saint John Chrysostom, and on the other, the historical, nationalistic writings of Josephus Flavius, especially his *Antiquities*.[27] The first is the coryphaeus of Greek and Russian homiletic tradition; the second, a prime mover in the development of the genealogical biography of a people. In the first, Serapion inherited a κοινὸς τόπος for listing the punishments of man's sins from the creation of the world; in the second, he had a precedent for recounting the life of a people from its origin (Genesis) to its war of survival (the Jewish Revolt), a national history that began with a double destruction: once by fire and again by water.

The ostensible topic of his sermon is the persecution of witches by the masses. The actual ethical dogma of such superstitious activity, as described by Serapion, is far from complete. One is not sure that all suspected witches were first tried by water and then, if found guilty, executed by fire. It is clear here, though, that both water and fire were important to the beliefs of the people. These elements were associated with deities (such as those that lived in the water and pronounced judgment on the accused) and with the punishment of sins. But no matter to what extent the mention of fire and water may have been calculated to have an effect on the folk psyche in the scheme of Serapion's eschatological rundown, grammatical necessities of rhetoric did not permit the omission of the first instrument of punishment (*ognem*): the incantatory symmetry of the catalogue is maintained from start to finish.

The mention of an earthquake associated with the fall of a town belonging to the faithful and the persecuted is necessitated by the rhetorical effect the speaker intends to have on his audience. Serapion's goal at this point in the sermon is to create in the mind of the listener a palpable connection between the current state of affairs in Russia and happenings described in the Scriptures. The speaker's powers of imaginative association are extremely active. He develops tropes based not so much on visuality as on tactility. Historically, the fall of Jerusalem is associated with Titus' conquest, but here there is the additional element of the earthquake occurring before the city falls (46). The movement of the earth is a kind of sign of divine displeasure, and, though it is grammatically another instrument of punishment, it also seems to be a veiled form of pathetic fallacy. Thematically, the quake anticipates the shift to events contemporary with the listeners and actually experienced by them. The order of natural calamities in medieval Russia corresponds to the order in the biblical *enumeratio*: the earthquakes come at the end. These lines are tightly organized:

[27] Ibid., 181–182.

pri Tite plenenьemь; potom že trjasenьemь zemli i padenьemь graḏ

The spacing of the verbal nouns, as well as the similarity of sound achieved by identical grammatical cases (homoitopton), is intended to produce an effect of finality and immediacy. The corresponding line across the fulcrum of the hypophora, though no less self-conscious, shows a fresh rhythm:

Rati, g(l)adi, morove i trusi

A final notable characteristic of the structure of this passage is seen in the allusions to God framing it. The first and last statements (41–42, 49–50) present indirect invocations of a supreme deity whose power and authority are extolled and impressed upon the audience:

Slyšaste oî Bā kaznь
Se že vse oî Bā byvaetь

The change in tense is significant. A brief consideration of the artistic use of time is worthwhile. There is an interplay between past and present. In the minds of the listeners, ancient events have the weight of history, tradition, and authority on their side. In a sense, they occur outside the time of those who are hearing about them, and so, they are "eternal." As specific events, the episodes from biblical history to which Serapion refers belong to the past, but as prototypes of present events, they are felt to be close in time. Lixačev recognizes this when he considers aspects of eternity in homiletic literature:

Vetxozavetnye i novozavetnye sobytija zanimajut soveršenno osoboe mesto v sisteme vremeni srednevekovogo soznanija. Xotja oni otnosjatsja k prošlomu, no v kakom-to otnošenii oni odnovremenno javljajutsja i faktami nastojaščego.[28]

There is a sense of the contemporaneous impact of history. Conversely, recently experienced events are affected when they are juxtaposed with historical ones. They are interpreted through (and interpolated into) a universal presentation of history basic to the *Weltanschauung* of the Old Testament;[29] and so, they may be read as symbolic recurrences of significant past events. They have been "prefigured" (*trus* vis-à-vis *trjasenьe*, figuram implere). They have acquired an abstract and therefore timeless significance. Here Serapion alludes to the suprametaphor of his sermon when, in the generalization at the climax of his argument, he specifies the real theme

[28] Lixačev, *Poètika* (see n. 14), 307.
[29] Auerbach, *Mimesis* (see n. 21), 13–14.

at its heart: ... *i simъ namъ spŝnie zdevaet.* Misfortune, suffering, the experience of evil *are* salvation. Lixačev plainly sees this philosophical implication of the stylistics of time:

> Sobytija svjaščennoj istorii pridajut smysl sobytijam, soveršajuščimsja v nastojaščem, oni ob"jasnjajut sostojanie vselennoj i položenie čelovečestva otnositeljno boga. Sobytija èti soveršilis' pod znakom "večnosti" i poètomu prodolžajut suščestvovať i vnov' soveršaťsja. Spasenie čelovečestva, naprimer, —èto večnyj akt....[30]

According to Serapion, salvation is to be taken at face value as good in and of itself. It is not the dogma, but the feeling of salvation that he orates. He appeals to the movable emotions of his audience by offering a view of the general *quality* of salvation. With this in mind, we hear the rhythmic beat at the close of the refutatio; the phrases are vividly paralleled by the emotive use of anaphora:

> *Se že* vse oî Bā byvaetь,
> i *simъ* namъ spŝnie zdevaet.

The most immediate antecedent of these indefinite demonstratives is, of course, the collection of ancient and modern punishments. Yet in a broader sense, the reference is to the fundamental metaphorical mechanism of the sermon. The more general, basic antecedent is to be found in the totality of the foregoing argumentative section of the sermon: one is to have true faith in God. This is affirmed by belief in and adherence to His Scriptures, wherein lies the knowledge of God. This knowledge is conceived of and expressed as rational sense (*razum*), understanding. And the process of understanding is metaphorized as a visual operation—*seeing*. All words and phrases employing the root of mental apprehension (*um*), as well as all individual instances of its metaphorization, are germane to a grasp of Serapion's suprametaphor. They will be discussed in detail below as the final lines of the talk are analyzed.

The next section of the sermon (50–62) takes the form of a rhetorical denouement, offering release from the forensic tone of comparison, contention, and refutation that characterized the polemical discussion preceding it. In fact, this last section corresponds to the final part of a classical oration. It is more than a review of the previous arguments: it is an impassioned summary (peroratio). In his presentation of the general aspects of oral exposition, R. Lanham outlines the most traditional components of the narrative structure, or "arrangement" (L. *dispositio*, Gk. λέξις) of an

[30] Lixačev, *Poètika* (see n. 14), 308.

oration.[31] In the light of that writer's discussion, the ideas in Serapion's sermon seem to unfold in a very common direction.

First, the speaker tries to "establish a specific controllable relation to the audience": the authority of father over son (1). Next, he "seems to take ... [his] ... opponent's arguments into account (paraphrase his weak ones, distort his strong ones)": the sorcerers should be worshiped so they will prevent natural calamities (13-15); water is a lifeless substance and so cannot be used as an agent to come to a decision about a man's life (34-41). Then, the speaker "dilates" his "own good reasons": God's omnipotence, His all-encompassing divine plan for salvation (41-50). Finally, he "offers a loaded summary before ... [he] ... stops": here, in the peroratio, Serapion returns to the emotive rhetorical technique of the exordium. Once again he establishes himself as a man of trust (the shepherd's concern for guidance and protection of his sheep) and plays on the emotions of the audience. The opening emphatic adverb (Nyne že) marks a conscious shift of the address from the removed rational plane of Scripture and history to the immediate presence and time of the listener. We now find stylistic echoes of the exordium and explicatio. The speaker draws attention to his personal involvement(molju) by directly personalizing the address (vy). This apostrophe is reinforced strongly by the third and final battery of imperatives with which Serapion has laced his speech (pokaiteŝ i ne buåte ... pritecete).

A key trope, a simile, follows (51-52). It is the only instance of an explicit, poetically condensed comparison in the text (pepoeemenon):

i ne buåte otsele aki trostь, vetromь koleblema.

This line shows Serapion's fine sense of language. On the thematic level, the figurative energy of the concrete image—a reed swaying in the wind—flows directly back to the specific references to movement at the end of the catalogue of punishments: trostь → trusi → trjasenьe. Such association is reinforced by phonic similarities, rhetorical features to which Serapion, as a man who more than once spoke to the common people, would not have been at all insensitive.

The language of the simile belongs to the class of agrarian phenomena (14, 15, 19) and would have been easily perceived by an audience preoccupied with natural forces. To some extent the syntax is structured to keep the figure simple. The lack of descriptive modifiers, together with the use of an economical participial construction to qualify, rather than a relative clause, preserves a simplicity and terseness characteristic of folk similes and seems to fit in with the generally nonpictorial, tactile orientation of much

---

[31] R. A. Lanham, Handlist of Rhetorical Terms (Berkeley–Los Angeles, 1969), 112–113.

of the other key imagery (see above).[32] This points to the basic dialectic set up in the metaphorical language of the sermon.

The actions and folk beliefs that Serapion reproaches are described as physically, externally sensible to man; or as lacking a certain quality; or as unstable. The established religion, conversely, is characterized in terms of man's internal life, his mental sensitivity, and by stability:

Folk (heretical)	Church (canonical)
ognь	utverdistesja
bezumьe	vera tverda
bezakonije	svjatъ duxъ
voda	umъ
bezdušnoje estьstvo	razumъ božьstvьnъ
trusi	krepkodušьe
trostь	srъdьce
strastь	utroba

Throughout, these two metaphorical systems are related in a consistent way. The primary premise is that pagan life is inferior to the Orthodox one. This is worked out in the sermon in such a way as to demonstrate the relationship between deity and visuality. There is a progression from *divine visuality* (*primlete bžŝtvenoe pisanie*) at the beginning (3), where the faithful sees an abstract sign of God (writing), to *visual divinity* (*ašte ... bija sveta ne uzrite*) at the end (60), where the true believer is said to catch sight of a concrete manifestation of God (light). The verb used throughout to show Serapion's interaction with the Scriptures is *to see*. In contrast to this, it is implied that other senses, especially forms of folk oral communication, are inferior. The following example of meiosis (used to belittle the *vehicle*, not the substance, of popular beliefs) illustrates this dialectical tension between the instability of oral "tale" and the permanence of written "law": *No ašte uslyšite čto basni člvčŝkyxъ, kъ bžŝtvenomu pisaniju pritecete ...*

---

[32] Lixačev (*Poètika* [see n. 14], 193–194), comments on this "nonvisuality" of similes in Old Russian literature:

V protivopoložnosť literature novogo vremeni v russkoj srednevekovoj literature sravnenij, osnovannyx na zriteľnom sxodstve, nemnogo. V nej gorazdo boľše, čem v literature novogo vremeni, sravnenij, podčerkivajuščix osjazateľnoe sxodstvo, sxodstvo vkusovoe, obonjateľnoe, svjazannyx s oščuščeniem materiala, s čuvstvom muskuľnogo naprjaženija.

He cites some very "tactile" examples: "xolop dobr podoben esť nožu ostru; xolop že zol podoben esť nožu bez končatu"; "surovomu služiti, jako skljanicu bljusti na mramore."

RALPH BOGERT

If one examines Serapion's specific use of a reed for the simile, it is apparent that the choice is not accidental. The reed which grows in water reminds us of the earlier references to water—all are negative. Not only was water the means whereby God destroyed all life on earth but, in the particular thematic context of the sermon, water contained, for the audience, the power to decide, to judge. As far as judging witches was concerned, it was their "law," their scripture, and was therefore the habitat of whatever water demons were at the bottom of it all. Very subtly Serapion succeeds in associating the listeners with weak reeds standing in "soulless" water. His use of the images is tightly structured, as he exploits a specific biblical passage (1 Kings 14:15) in which reed(s) and idolatry are linked:

> I nakažetъ gŝdь b͞gъ iĩlja, î pokolebletъ imi, jakože kolebletsja trostь vetromъ na vode. I izorvetъ iĩlja oî vysoty zemli b͞lgija seja, juže dalъ estь oc͞emъ ixъ, i proženetъ ja oî obonu stranu, poneže sotvoriša sebe kapišta prognevajušte gŝda.[33]

It is indicative of the orator's attitude toward his audience that the deprecatory term (*basni*) is taken from the realm of folk creation. The contention between man and God was elaborately presented in the main body of the argument on all three levels of man's rational existence as the Greeks conceived them. Superstitious beliefs in witchcraft have been refuted on the *aesthetic* level (man in relation to himself alone: he simply refuses to fear *unseen* reasons for material discomfort and instead keeps faith in God's protection, 10–23), on the *ethical* level (man in relation to other men: he does not persecute others according to his own arbitrary whims, but instead follows God's system of justice, 23–41), and on the *metaphysical* level (man in relation to the universe: he does not despair in a world of cruel and arbitrary chance, but sees his role in God's predetermined plan for salvation, 41–50). From the point of view of Judaic tradition, these levels correspond respectively to the three kinds of relationships between man and God as reflected in and modulated by the Old Testament: God's Word is simultaneously (1) personal covenant, (2) social law, and (3) world history. Serapion has argued that the people alone are incapable of devising and organizing such a divine plan. Now, in the emotionally charged peroratio, he accomplishes a neat release from this detailed argumentation with a direct formulaic juxtaposition of the human and the divine:

> basni člvčškyxъ, kъ bžŝtvenomu pisaniju

[33] *Biblija sireč' knigi vetxago i novago zaveta po jazyku slavensku ...* (Moscow: Ostrožskaja tipografija, 1663).

The inversion places semantic stress on the epithets and causes a kind of chiastic opposition of clauses.

The contrasting verbs of motion (*pritecete, ôîxodiî*) represent an effort to oppose man and Devil in relation to God and possibly appeal to the folk sense of graphic representation: Holy Scripture now becomes part of a larger, metonymic relationship. The people can only really "flee" to God's Word by seeking refuge in the Church. Once this concrete envisualization of the Scriptures is established, it is not difficult to understand the rest of the metaphorical process in this complex sentence (52–55). What the Devil sees is the reason (*razum*) or spiritual fortitude (*krepkodušье*) of the people who have just fled to the Church. In concrete terms, he is looking at the overt symbols of faith. The directional verbs of motion, in fact, support the belief commonly expressed in folk literature that the Devil and the Cross are mutually antagonistic. Indeed, Serapion does not hesitate to consider himself like the folk that comprise his audience. This is clearly implied by the use of a (first-) personalized antonomastic formula:

vragъ našь dьjavolъ

Serapion follows his own suggestion: fleeing to the Bible very naturally suggests going to the Cross, thus, by extension of this synecdoche, to the Church, a place the Devil is sure to shun. Such gently directed association is aided by an aural clue, repetition of a verbal root: *pritecete* ⟵⟶ *tekuštaja*.

The speaker now begins to signal the end of the sermon by repeating motifs from its beginning. In both places he apprehends his congregation visually; he mentions love and piety; and he underscores a relationship of authority and endearment between himself and the people: the patriarchal position at the outset is transformed at the end into one based on a respect for knowledge, such as the speaker's close connection with the Scriptures. The intimate associations of the head of a family with its members become those of a protective guide, a spiritual teacher with his followers. The "children" are now "sheep."

The urgent tone of the final message of the sermon is further supported by economizing devices: the emotional outcry (ecphonesis—*ašte by mi moštno koegoždo vaŝ napolniti srдce i utrobu razuma Бestvenago!*); rhythmically condensed synonyms with similar endings (homoioteleulon—*nakazaja vy i vrazumljaja, nastavlja(ja)*); intensifying understatement (litotes—*Obida bo mi nemala naležitь*); a condensed form of rhetorical question (erotesis) containing a brief metaphorical paraphrase of allegorical imagery taken from the Gospels (Matt. 10). Serapion concludes this last device of the peroratio with as little ambiguity as possible. He leaves his hearers with an explicit explanation of the metaphorical subsitution: (antapodosis—*kako ā uteŝjuŝ, aŝte koemu vasъ udeetъ zly(i) volkъ-dъjavolъ?*).

Conclusion

In concluding his monograph with the rather tantalizing suggestion that the real originality of Serapion's sermons lies locked in their structural constitution (*sklad*), Petuxov issues an indirect call for further study of that orator. In fact, he goes on to specify what he believes to be the essential significance of his works. As literary creations they are important

> po tomu, kakoj absoljutnoj cennosti idei zaključajut oni i naskoľko blago-tvorno mogut vlijať na um i čuvstvo togo obŝčestva, k kotoromu obra-ŝčajutsja.[34]

The aim of this study has been to investigate the way in which Serapion strives to influence the collective audience he addresses with his values and ideas and in what ways his mode of expression is governed by what he conceives to be the nature of his listeners' minds and feelings. We have seen that the structure of the sermon examined has been largely determined by the conscious effort to balance delicately the practical necessities of *transmitting* a particular set of beliefs with the ideological necessities of *holding* them. The rhetorical process of popular communication is in a state of highly creative equilibrium with the logical process of learned communication.

The style and individuality of Serapion's sermons was determined largely by the class of homiletic literature to which they belonged. Serapion chose to speak not on ecclesiastical life (monasteries, monks, the church hierarchy and organization), but on secular life (towns, people). His audience was composed not of his peers, but of his neighbors. Serapion was also free in his thematic treatment of the topic chosen, since, instead of having to meet the obligations of speaking on the occasion of a church commemorative service or a holiday, he must have decided himself what it was necessary to speak about. He spoke as an individual and could speak his own mind. It is for this reason that Serapion was able to avoid and, indeed, would have considered as inappropriate, both the intricacies of debate (the judicial, or forensic, branch of rhetoric—γένος δικανικόν), and the excesses of praise (the epideictic, or commemorative, branch of rhetoric—γένος πανηγυρικόν). His goal was to move the people, not to tears but to *action* (or, in the circumstances of our sermon here, to refrain from action) of a certain sort.

---

[34] Petuxov, *Serapion Vladimirskij* (see n. 1), 213.

His specific techniques of doing this are outgrowths of his efforts to exploit the people's common sense by appealing to their sense of the common: he asks them to use their eyes; then he draws motifs and moments from the experiential realm of their everyday lives with the purpose of imposing from above a higher order. It is an order they can only seem to see with their mind's eye.

Because Serapion's sermon presents arguments that are contemplatable on the folk level, there is no need for the showy, pictorial, demonstrative style typical of an epideictic address. The sparsity of epithets, for example, is very noticeable in Serapion; the ones that are used are mostly denotative, not connotative. And though Serapion is present in a very personal way, his emotional intrusion is only temporary. It serves as a kind of dramatic relief from the cerebral aspects of the argument and is never sustained for more than a very few lines at a time. In sum, one senses that Serapion is never carried away by his rhetorical skill, but is in full control of each statement.

It is possible to synthesize the results of the preceding analytical observations. Serapion realizes his exhortative intentions by concentrating on two main methods of rhetorical argument: redundancy and consistency. Both of these would be particularly effective in persuading a nonliterate folk audience. Redundancy, as we have seen, takes such forms as chiastic, parallel, synonymic, pleonastic, anaphoric, and paratactic constructions. This method is balanced by techniques of consistency. These include auxetic, dieretic, synecdochical, apodictic, antonomastic, and hypotactic devices. Thus, Serapion carefully alternates between qualitative, sequential modes and quantitative, causal ones. From the beginning to the end of the sermon, the listener is led on both vertically and horizontally; Serapion defines his argument by expansion and by limitation. The passage listing the punishments of divine wrath illustrates several features of both of these methods. Here Serapion endeavors to fill in lacunae, to augment, to supplement, to establish a continuous connection of events. He attempts to create an aura of rational, sequential plausibility around a theological concept that is superficially illogical: he strives to prove rhetorically that destruction leads to salvation!

Serapion was a highly literate man for his time and place, but most of his listeners probably were not. They would, therefore, have responded most easily to ideas from a highly developed literary tradition if they were presented in emotionally dynamic, immediately graspable terms. The style of delivery Serapion used was a millennium old and Byzantine; the meaning of his words was topical and intended for the ears of a largely unschooled

Slavic people. As an orator, his task was to key the medium to the message. To the extent that he succeeded, the points he strove to make seem to be intentionally "inherent" in the substance of his oratory. Consequently, each new turn of a phrase in the sermon we have examined here reveals another aspect of that calculated spontaneity which the skillful orator must exploit in order to capture, dazzle, and persuade his audience.

Text: "Poučenie prepodobnago Serapiona"

.Poučňe p̄rpd̂bngo Serapiona.

Malъ čaŝ poradovaxsja o vasъ, čad̂, vidja vašju ljubovь i poslušanie kъ našei xudosti, i mnjaxъ, jako uže utverdi-

antiphrasis**
(vъspjatьslovije) stesja i s radostiju primlete bžštvenoe pisanie, na svet̂ nečštivyxъ ne xodite i na sedališti gubitel̂ ne sedite.   5

Aže ešte poganьskaĝ obyčaja deržiteŝ: volxvo(va)niju veruet̂

pleonasmus
(izobilije) i požigaet̂ ognem̂ nevinyja čĺvky i navodite na vsь mirъ i grad̂

exoche
(izdrjadije) ubiistvo; ašte kto i ne pričastisja ubiistvu, no vsonьmi

metonymy
(otъimenije) byvъ vъ edinoi mysli, ubiica že byŝ; ili mogai pomošti, a ne pomože, aki samъ ubiti povelel̂ ē. Ôi kotoryx̂ knigъ ili 10

epanalepsis
(porečenije) oî kixъ pisanii se slyšaste, jako volxvovaniemь gladi byvajutь na zemli i paky volxvovaniemь žita umnožajutьŝ? To aže semu

irony
(poruganije) veruete, to čemu požigaete ja? moliteŝ i čtite ja, dary it prinosite imъ; atь strojatь mirъ, doždь puštajutь, teplo privodjatь, zemli ploditi veljatь! Se nyne po ḡ. leî žitu roda neŝ 15 ne tokmo v Rusь, no v Latene: se vъlxvove li stvoriša? Ašte ne Bē li stroite svoju tvorь, jako že xošteî, za grex̂ naŝ

syllepsis
(sъnjatije) tomja? Vide ā oî bžštvnago napisanьja, jako čarodeici i čarodeica besy destvujutь na rod̂ čĺvkmъ i nadъ skotomъ i potvoriti mogutь; nadъ timi deistvujutь, i imъ verujutь. 20

Bū popuštьšju, besi destvujutь; popuštaetь Bъ, iže kto ixъ boitsja; a iže kto veru tverdu deržitь k Bū, s togo

ellipsis
(nestatъk) čarodeici ne mogutь. Pečalenъ esmь o vašemь bezumьi; molju vy, oîstupite delъ poganьskyxъ. Ašte xoštete grad̂ ocestiti oî bezakonnyxъ čĺvkъ, radjusja tomu; oceštaite, jako Dv̄dъ 25 pr̄rkъ i cšrь potrebljaše oî grad̂ Eršlma vsja tvorjaštaja bezakonie:

antonomasia
(vyimenimĕstьstvo) ovexъ ubitiemь, inixъ zatočeniem̂, inix že temnicami; vsegda grad̂ gŝnь čŝtъ tvorjaše oî grex̂. Kto bo takъ be sud̂, jakože

comprobatio*
apomnemonysis
dieresis

chiasmus

hypophora
conduplicatio
commoratio

erotesis

polyptoton

martyria

emphasis

apodixis

anthypallage

apothegm

meiosis

hendiadys

commemoratio

paraphrasis

metaphrasis

---

* The terms in the right margin have been designated according to classical usage; most of them may be found in R. Lanham, *Handbook of Rhetorical Terms.*

** The left margin shows terminology found in Choiroboskos' *Treatise.* Each term is followed by the Old Russian equivalent (in parentheses) taken from the *Izbornik Svjatoslava* of 1073.

D͞vdъ? Straxoṁ бiṁ sudjaše, d͞mь s͞tmъ vidjaše i po pravde
otvetъ dajaše. Vy že k̃ osuždaetь na s͞mrtь, sami strŝti 30

erotesis
synonymia

ispolni sušte? I po pravde ne sud̂te: inyi po vražьde tvoritь,
iny(i) gorkago togo pribytka žadaja, a inyi uma ne
ispolnenъ; tolko žadaetь ubiti, pograbiti, a eže a čto
ubiti, a togo ne vestь. Pravila bž̂stvenago povelevajutь

litotes

mnogymi posluxъ osud̂ti na s͞mrtь č͞lvka. Vy že vodu 35
posluxomь postaviste i g͞lte: ašte utapati načnetь,
nepovinna estь; ašte li poplovetь, volxvovь ē. Ne možet

dialogismus

erotesis

li dijavolъ, vidja vaše maloverьe, poderžati, da ne pogruzitsja,
daby vъvrešti vъ d̃šьgubьstvo; jako, ostavlьše poslušьstvo
бotvorenago č͞lvka, idoste kъ bezdušnu estьstvu—k vode 40
prijastь poslušьstvo na prognevanьe бie? Slyšaste o͡i B͞a
kaznь posylaemu na zemlju o͡i pervyxъ rod̃: do potopa na

ellipsis

gyganty ognemь, pri potope vodoju, pri Sodome žjupolomъ,

enumeratio
auxesis

pri Faraone i͡ ju kaznii, pri Xananiixъ šeršenmi, kamenьemь
ognenymь sъ nbŝi; pri sudьjaẍ ratьmi; pri D͞vde moromь; pri 45
Tite plenenьemь; potom že trjasenьemь zemli i padenьemь
grad̃. Pri našeṁ že jazyce čego ne videxoṁ? Rati, g(l)adi, morove

homoitopton

i trusi; konečnoe, eže predani byxoṁ inoplemennikomь ne

hypophora

tokmo na s͞mrtь i na plenenьe, no i na gorkuju rabotu. Se že

synecdoche
figuram implere

vse o͡i B͞a byvaetь, i simъ namъ spŝnie zdevaet. Nyne že, 50

pepoeemenon
(sъtvorenije)
antonomasia

molju vy, za prednee bezumьe pokaiteŝ i ne bud̂te otsele
aki trostь, vetromь koleblema. Na ašte uslyšite čto basni

simile

člov̂čŝkyxъ, kъ bž̂stvenomu pisaniju pritecete, da vragъ našь

meiosis

dьjavolъ, videvъ vaŝ razuṁ, krepkod̃šьe, i ne vъzmožetь ponuditi
vy na grexъ, no posramlenъ o͡ixodit̂. Vižju vy bo velikoju 55
ljubovьju tekuštaja vъ c͞rkvь i stojašta z govenьemь; temže, ašte
by mi moštno koegoždo vaŝ napolniti srd̂ce i utrobu razuma
бestvenago! No ne utružjusja nakazaja vy i vrazumljaja,

ecphonesis

homoioteleuton

metaphora
(prĕvodъ)

nastavlja(ja). Obida bo mi nemala naležitь, ašte vy takoja
žizni ne polučite i бija sveta ne uzrite; ne možet bo 60

litotes

pastuxъ utešatiŝ, vidja ovci o͡i volka rasxyšteni, to kako
ā utešjuŝ, ašte koemu vasъ udeetь zly(i) volkъ-dьjavolъ?
No pominajušte si našju ljubovь, o vašemь spŝenii

erotesis

potštiteŝ ugoditi stvoršemu ny B͞u, emyže lepo vsjaka
slav̂ čŝtь. 65

Translation: "Sermon of Serapion the Venerable"[35]

Exordium

I have recently come to rejoice over you, my children,
seeing your love and obedience toward our lowly state.

And I thought that you had already become steadfast in your ways
and had joyfully received the Divine Scripture,
that you were not walking in the counsel of the profane
nor sitting in the seats of murderers.

Explicatio

But you are still clinging to a pagan custom:
you believe in witchcraft,
and you are burning innocent people with fire
and bringing murder to all the world and to the town.

For whoever is of like mind with others in assembly—
even though he doesn't take part in murder—is a murderer himself.
Moreover, whoever is able to help the victim, but does not,
is as guilty as the one who ordered the murder.

Amplificatio/Refutatio

From which books or from which scriptures have you heard
that famines occur on earth because of witchcraft and,
what's more, that grain propagates because of witchcraft?

If you *do* believe this is so, then why do you burn them?
Worship and honor them! And bring them gifts!
Let them govern the world, make it rain, bring the warm weather,
and command the earth to bear fruit!

There has been no grain crop for three years now,
not only in Russia, but in the West, too.
Have witches caused this?

Now, doesn't God govern his creation as He wishes,
punishing us for our sins?

I have seen from the Holy Scripture how sorcerers
and sorceresses cause demons to work on mankind and on livestock,
and how they are able to bewitch them.
They work upon those who believe in them.

It is by God's permission that demons do their work.
God allows those who will to fear demons,
but sorcerers can do nothing to the one who keeps firm faith in God.

I am grieved at your senselessness.
I beseech you, quit your pagan ways.
If you want to cleanse the town of lawless men, I am glad.

Purge the town as the king and prophet David
rid the town of Jerusalem of all those who were behaving lawlessly:
some he condemned to death;
others he sent to confinement;
still others he imprisoned.
He always made the Lord's city clean of sins.
For who was ever such a judge as David?

---

[35] This is a free translation intended to convey the general sense of the sermon. No attempt has been made to reproduce the syntax or the rhythm of the original text or to reflect lexical and grammatical irregularities.

He judged with the fear of God;
he saw by the light of the Holy Spirit;
and he passed down judgments according to the truth.

How dare *you* condemn someone to death,
when you are yourselves full of bias?
You are not judging according to the truth!
One of you does it out of animosity;
another does it while longing for that bitter profit;
and another, out of his head, only wants to kill, to plunder,
yet he knows neither whom nor why he wants to kill.

The rules of divine law decree that a person be condemned to
death by means of many pieces of evidence.
But you have taken water as your evidence and have said;
"If she begins to sink she is innocent;
if she floats she is one of the pagan magicians."

Can't the Devil, seeing your lack of faith and wishing to
imperil her life, hold her up so that she won't sink?
For, having put aside the testimony of man, who was created
by the hand of God,
you would go to dead matter—to water—to find your testimony
and risk the wrath of God?

You have heard of the punishment cast upon the earth by God
from the first generations:
Before the flood there was punishment by fire sent upon the giants;
In the time of the flood, He sent punishment by water;
In the time of Sodom, by burning sulphur;
In the time of Pharoah, by the ten plagues;
In the time of the Canaanites, by hornets and burning stones
from Heaven;
In the time of the judges, by wars;
In the time fo David, by pestilence;
In the time of Titus, by captivity,
and then an earthquake and the fall of the city.

In the time of our heathen invader, what have we not seen?
Wars, famines, earthquakes;
and finally, we have seen how we have been
delivered to the foreigners,
not only unto death and captivity,
but also into bitter enslavement.
All this comes from God,
and in this way He brings about our salvation.

Peroratio

And now, I beseech you:
Repent for your former senselessness,
and henceforth do not be like reeds shaken with the wind.
Instead, if you hear any stories told by men, turn to the Holy Scripture,
so that our enemy the Devil, seeing your good sense,
your spiritual strength,
will not be able to force you into sin,
but instead will go away in shame.

For I see you flowing into church with great love
and standing devotedly.
If it thus were only possible for me to somehow fill your hearts
and inner being with divine reason!

But I will not grow tired of instructing you, of making you
listen to reason, of teaching you.
Because it is no small shame for me,
if you do not accept such a life,
if you do not see the light of God.

For a shepherd cannot console himself
if he sees his sheep carried off by a wolf.
So how am I to be consoled if an evil wolf-devil gets to one of you?

Epilogus

And now, remembering our love for you, hasten for the sake of
your salvation unto the God who created us,
Unto God, who deserves every glorious honor.

SOURCES

Choiroboskos, George.
"Choeroboscus' Treatise on Tropes and Figures in the Svjatoslav Codex of 1073." J. Besharov, *Imagery of the Igor' Tale.* Leiden, 1956, 106–112.
"On Figures of Speech in Poetry," J. Besharov, *Imagery of the Igor' Tale,* Leiden, 1956, 4–43.

Serapion of Vladimir.
"Iz slov i poučenij Serapiona. Iz Zlatoj cepi (po rukopisi v biblioteke Troickoj lavry)." *Istoričeskaja xristomatija cerkovno-slavjanskogo i drevne-russkogo jazykov.* Edited by F. Buslaev. Moscow, 1861, 493–498, 504–513.
"Poučenija Serapiona Vladimirskogo (Po rukopisi 'Zlataja cep" isx. XIV veka)." Edited by E. V. Petuxov. Appendix to E. V. Petuxov, *Serapion Vladimirskij, russkij propovednik XIII veka.* St. Petersburg, 1888.

THE FUNCTION OF WORD-WEAVING IN THE STRUCTURE OF EPIPHANIUS' *LIFE OF SAINT STEPHEN, BISHOP OF PERM'*

JOSTEIN BØRTNES

The works of D. S. Lixačev on early Russian literature have compelled scholars to reevaluate the style of Epiphanius the Wise, his *pletenie sloves*, "word-weaving" or "word-braiding." What scholars like Ključevskij and Golubinskij had discarded as mere artifice and empty verbosity, Lixačev singled out as the most significant development in Russian literature towards the end of the fourteenth and the beginning of the fifteenth centuries. Lixačev sees in word-weaving the characteristic features of a new and expressive style, a verbal display of the writer's highly strung emotions. In Epiphanius' *Life of Saint Stephen, Bishop of Perm'*[1] the author "writes at an elevated, emotional pitch, he is in a state of enthusiasm and excitement, he speaks at the top of his voice, and this creates the emotional atmosphere which is essential to his way of stimulating Christian feelings, his devotion to Christian values."[2]

Lixačev's definition of word-weaving would seem to be based on the assumption that certain forms are analogous to particular feelings and may therefore convey a specific emotional experience. This assumption is reinforced by a comparison between Epiphanius' hagiographical style and the style of contemporary icon painting, in which Lixačev finds the same emotional exaltation reflected in the shimmering strokes of the Novgorod masters.

Although it is not possible to revert to a negative assessment of word-weaving after Lixačev's studies, his one-sided emphasis on the emotional aspect of its meaning has left us with a number of unresolved problems. His interpretations of Epiphanius' style rely on empathy rather than on analysis, and like other definitions of poetry as the language of the emotions, Lixačev's also runs the danger of ignoring structure. Both icon

---

[1] All quotations from the *Life of Saint Stephen* refer to the edition by V. G. Družinin (Moscow, 1897), page numbers given in parentheses.

[2] D. S. Lixačev, *Čelovek v literature drevnej Rusi* (Moscow, 1958), 75.

painting and hagiography are highly conventional art forms, in which meaning is the result of a careful selection and combination of traditional elements into new configurations, and one might rightly ask if Lixačev has not gone too far in stressing the significance of word-weaving as an expression of emotional excitement at the expense of its conventional aspect.

Lixačev's interpretation of this style has, however, given rise to a series of investigations into the historical development of its conventions,[3] and we now know that Epiphanius' word-weaving represents the Russian variant of a common Slavonic style, which seems to go back to the *vitae* of Serbian princes and bishops, written in the thirteenth and fourteenth centuries. In the last analysis, this style can be traced to Greek models, and the very term *pletenie sloves* is a calque from the Greek, found in the Slavonic translations of early Byzantine hymns, where it means "praise," and is used in both Serbian and Bulgarian literature before Epiphanius introduced it into his *Life of Saint Stephen*. Today the term *word-weaving* is no longer used to refer only to the style of Epiphanius the Wise but also denotes a mode of writing found in all the Orthodox Slavonic literatures. The most recent studies of Epiphanius' *Life of Saint Stephen* have explicitly analyzed its style as a variant of this common code and have tried to work out its individual characteristics. Our knowledge of the conventions has made it possible to go back to Lixačev's expressionist theory and try to look at the possible interdependence of expression and convention, and to define the function of word-weaving in the context and structure of the *Life of Saint Stephen*. In doing so, I shall attempt to work out the structural dominant of the *vita*, the principle that determines Epiphanius' selection and combination of elements from the common stylistic code.

The Stylistic Dominant of the *Vita*

Verbal art, like all discourse, involves two fundamental operations: *selection*, based on the principle of similarity (and contrast), and *combination*, based on the principle of contiguity (and distance). According to Roman

---

[3] E.g., V. Mošin, "O perodizacii russko-južnoslavjanskix literaturnyx svjazej X–XV vv.," *TODRL* 19 (1963): 28–106; M. Mulić, "Srpsko 'pletenije sloves' do 14. stoljeća," *Radovi zavoda za slavensku filologiju* 5 (1963): 117–129; id., "Pletenije sloves i hesihazam," *Radovi zavoda za slavensku filologiju* 7 (1965): 141–156; id., "Serbskie agiografy XIII–XIV vv. i osobennosti ix stilja," *TODRL* 23 (1968): 127–142; J. Børtnes, *Det gammelrussiske helgenvita: Dikterisk egenart og historisk betydning* (Oslo, 1975); H. Birnbaum, "Serbian Models in the Literature and Literary Language of Medieval Russia," *Slavic and East European Journal* 23 (1979): 1–13; F. C. M. Kitch, *The Literary Style of Epifanij Premudryj: Pletenie Sloves*, Slavistische Beiträge, no. 96 (Munich, 1976).

Jakobson, the first of these processes finds its most condensed expression in metaphor, the second in metonymy.[4] And it is in manipulating these two modes of connection, *similarity* and *contiguity*, that the individual poet or a literary school will exhibit their stylistic dominant. Either the metaphoric or the metonymic principle may prevail. In trying to apply this bipolar theory to an analysis of the *Life of Saint Stephen*, it may be useful to bear in mind the primacy of the metaphoric process in Kievan hagiography, as we know it through, for instance, Nestor's *Life of Saint Theodosius.*[5]

The rhetorical devices that seem to predominate in word-weaving are alliterations and assonances, etymological figures (long sequences of words from the same root in different forms, or the same form with different roots), an accumulation of synonyms, comparisons, antitheses, periphrases, and a large number of quotations from other texts, above all from the Bible, where the Old Testament, and especially the Psalms, are quoted noticeably more often than the books of the New Testament.

Even in purely quantitative terms, the biblical quotations form a salient feature in the style of the *vita.* F. Wigzell (F. C. M. Kitch) has identified 340 quotations from the Bible.[6] In accordance with what is usual for the genre, Epiphanius' quotations from the Bible and other sacred scriptures have either been incorporated into his own discourse or mounted into the text in a way that marks them off from the narrative. In the latter case they are introduced with the help of stereotyped formulas that indicate the source: "as the prophet Isaiah said of old," "as the Apostle says," "and John Chrysostom said," and so on. The quotations occur separately or in tirades. An example of the latter is the introduction to the chapter "On the Calling and Conversion of Many Nations" (64f.), a tirade consisting of 46 quotations from the Psalms, 2 from Jeremiah, 1 from Isaiah, 1 from Micah, another from Isaiah, 1 from Zechariah, and finally 7 more from Isaiah.

Epiphanius' predilection for the Old Testament, especially for the Psalms, is striking. They account for half the number of quotations. This predominance of quotations from the Old Testament over those from the New, and the absolute preponderance of the Psalms over the other books of the Bible, form one of the most important characteristics that Epiphanius' writing has in common with thirteenth- and fourteenth-century word-

[4] R. Jakobson, "Two Aspects of Language and Two Types of Aphasic Disturbances," in R. Jakobson and M. Halle, *Fundamentals of Language*, Janua Linguarum, no. 1 (The Hague, 1956), 55–82.

[5] J. Børtnes, "Frame Technique in Nestor's Life of St. Theodosius," *Scando-Slavica* 13 (1967): 5–16; id., "Hagiographical Transformation in the Old Russian Lives of Saints," *Scando-Slavica* 18 (1972): 5–12; id., *Det gammelrussiske helgenvita* (see n. 3).

[6] Kitch, *Literary Style of Epifanij Premudryj* (see n. 3), 132.

weaving in Serbian hagiography. Historically this may be explained by the fact that the Psalms were part of the daily worship in the monasteries. The Serbian hagiographers quoted above all from the texts they knew by heart, either because these texts were obligatory reading or because they heard them read out during the services at different times of the day.[7]

It is easy to show that Epiphanius also quotes the Bible from memory, and not verbatim. Kitch has convincingly shown that he even transforms the quotations to fit the meaning of the passages into which they are integrated.[8] But this gives us no grounds for presuming that he was being unusually bold or free in his treatment of the texts. If he has altered them "despite medieval man's fear of even the least alteration of the Bible,"[9] it merely shows that on this point Epiphanius does not differ from other medieval authors. It is, in fact, a general characteristic of these biblical quotations that their form is not normally textual, but shaped to fit the writer's own exposition. This Erwin Panofsky has demonstrated in his analysis of Abbot Suger's biblical quotations; they are not copied verbatim either, but adapted to the abbot's own context:

> This does not mean that Suger deliberately "falsifies" the Bible ... Like all medieval writers he quoted from memory and failed to make a sharp distinction between the text and his personal interpretation....[10]

The interaction between quotation and narration in the *Life of Saint Stephen* shows above all that the quotations have not been mounted mechanically into the *vita*. They have been woven into the narrative in the course of an active, creative writing process.

The extensive use of biblical quotations by Epiphanius and the South Slavonic word-weavers indicates that these quotations must have had a particularly important function in their works. The Psalms and other texts from which these authors quote gave them not only a lofty vocabulary and a poetic diction but also a pattern for building up single lexical units into wider contexts. It was especially from their reading of the Psalms that the word-weavers learned to fuse individual components into a higher unity. The Psalms provided them also with a stock of expressive images and comparisons which were transmitted to the lives of their heroes.

[7] St. Stanojević and D. Glumac, *Sv. Pismo u našim starim spomenicima* (Belgrade, 1932), xxiii.
[8] Kitch, *Literary Style of Epifanij Premudryj* (see n. 3), 131ff.
[9] F. Vigzell, "Citaty iz knig svjaščennogo pisanija v sočinenijax Epifanija Premudrogo," *TODRL* 26 (1971): 242f.
[10] E. Panofsky, *Meaning in the Visual Arts* (New York, 1955), 124.

In his characterization of Domentijan's style, V. Mošin has convincingly traced its separate devices and their combination back to the Psalms.[11] The quotations already contain all the images and periphrastic expressions, similes and antitheses, semantic and morphological parallelisms that distinguish his style throughout. These stylistic devices are used to give the discourse emotional color, the particular feature of word-weaving that Lixačev has emphasized.

The tropes and figures of psalmic poetry that give Serbian word-weaving its special character are also typical of the *Life of Saint Stephen*. Repetition of the same root with different suffixes occurs frequently, either as derivation (paregmenon):

> obyčai bo estь vdovamъ novoovdověv'šimъ plakatisę gorko vdovьstva svoego (93);
> prošu u tebe prošenia věrno prosęšču mi (98);[12]

or as inflection (polyptoton):

> napadajušče, napadaxu na nь sъ jarostiju, i sъ gněvomъ i sъ voplemъ, jako ubiti i pogubiti xotęšče (25).[13]

Both figures associate words that are formally similar and semantically contiguous.

The words may also be aligned on the basis of a formal similarity, a similarity on the signans level, not accompanied by a corresponding semantic similarity. The outcome is a kind of pun, in which the formal similarity of the components forms a contrast to their semantic dissimilarity:

> ne povelě mi mučiti, no učiti ... ni povelě kazniti, no nakazati (56).[14]

The asymmetry between signatum (meaning) and signans (form) falls short of our expectations and creates a semantic tension in the text. This play on similarity and contrast between meaning and form also underlies Epiphanius' synonymous couplings, either in pairs

> zělo želaše i veľmi xotęše (8); vozdivisę zělo, i čjudisę veľmi (14); bez' bojazni i bezъ užasti (37);[15]

---

[11] Mošin, "O periodizacii" (see n. 3), 88ff.
[12] For it is the habit of newly widowed widows to weep bitterly over their widowhood; I ask for your asking by my asking faithfully.
[13] Attacking, they attacked him with fury, and with anger, and with clamor, wanting to kill and destroy him.
[14] He did not order me to torture, but to teach ... nor did he order (me) to execute, but to instruct.
[15] They very much wanted and greatly wished; they were very astonished and greatly surprised; without fear and without horror.

or in sequences, as in the following anaphoric repetition:

edinъ [čṛьnecь složiȋ,] ... edinъ kalogerъ, edinъ mniẋ, edinъ inokъ (72).[16]

M. Mulić is inclined to trace this particular sequence back to a similar tirade in Domentijan's *Life of Saint Stephen* (= Stephen Nemanja).[17] A special variant of Epiphanius' synonymous couplings is his explanatory juxtapositions of Greek and Russian words (homoioptoton):

xerotonisanie, rekše rukopoloženie sščenstva (17);
dev'toronomia, rek'še vo v'torozakonii (46);
anafema da budetь, rek'še da budetь proklętъ (84).[18]

Antithesis, the juxtaposition of two components in a pair, where the one negates the other, is also one of Epiphanius' characteristic figures:

ne bo ōt mādrosti, no ōt grubosti (4); i něstь mira v nixъ, no raz'glasie (30).[19]

The antitheses, too, may be concatenated, as in the following example, clearly modeled on Ps. 115, where Epiphanius goes on to weave and couple the antitheses to form anaphoric sequences in a rhetorical arabesque:

Kumiri vaši, drevo sušče bezdušno, děla rǫkъ člčeskъ,
usta imuȋ, i ne gljuȋ:
uši imuȋ, i ne slyšatь,
oči imuȋ, i ne uzręȋ,
nozdri imuȋ, i ne obonęjutь,
rucě imuȋ, i ne osęzajuȋ,
nozě imutь, i ne poiduȋ, i ne xodęȋ, i ne stupajutь ni s města, i ne vozglasęȋ,
gortanmi svoimi, i ne njuxajuȋ nozdręmi svoimi, ni žertvъ prinosimyẋ priimajutь, ni pijutъ ni jaduȋ (28f.).[20]

In this tirade the semantic contiguity between the components is combined with a formal equivalence between their verbal predicates in the first part of each line, whereas in the second part of the line it is the anaphoric

---

[16] One black brother composed it ... one *kalogeros*, one *monachos*, one monk.
[17] Mulić, "Serbskie agiografy" (see n. 3), 140.
[18] Cheirotonia, that is, ordination; Deuteronomy that is, the Second Law [i.e., the fifth book of the Pentateuch]; anathema be he, that is, be he condemned.
[19] And not from prudence, but from ignorance; and there is no peace among them, but discord.
[20] Your idols are lifeless wood, the work of men's hands, they have mouths, and speak not, they have ears and hear not, they have eyes and see not, they have nostrils, and smell not, they have hands, and feel not, they have feet, and walk not; and cannot move, and leave not their place, and do not speak through their throats, and do not smell through their nostrils, nor do they receive the offerings brought to them, nor do they eat or drink.

repetition of the conjunction *i* 'and' that creates formal equivalence between the components, while semantic contiguity is retained.

The interchange of figures gives the discourse a varying rhythm; the tempo increases or decreases, rises towards a climax, or prepares the transition to a fresh theme. The main device to create rhythm is the syntactic similarity between the individual components of the tirade, the isocola, which are linked up anaphorically, through repetition of the same initial word; epiphorically, through repetition of the same word at the end, or by the aid of flectional rhyme (homoioteleuton).

At the same time, the above tirade is an example if distributio, the breaking down of a composite concept or object into its component parts. Here it is the idols of the Permians that are itemized. This figure of speech is one of the most important in the *Life of Saint Stephen*. It may have either a concretionary function, as in the passage cited, where the concretized object is subsequently negated and thereby annihilated, or it may serve a dematerializing, abstractive objective. In each case the figure is based on the principle of contiguity.

Another instance of concretionary distributio is Epiphanius' manner of describing land and people, for example, in the paragraph about the land of the Permians:

A se imena městomъ i stranamь, i zemlęm i inojazyčnikomъ, živuščimь vъkrugъ okolo Pefmi: Dvinęne. Ustьjužane. Viležane. Vyčežane. Pěnežane. Južane. Syrьęne. Galičęne. Vętčane. Lopь. Korěla. Jugra. Pečera. Goguliči. Samoědь. Pefŧasy. Permь Velikaa, glemaa Čjusovaa. Rěka edina, eiže imę Vym̄ si obьxodęščię, vsju zemlju Permьskuju i vnide v' Vyčegdu. Rěka že drugaa imenemь Vyčegda: si isxodęščia iz' zemlę Permьskia i šestvujušči kъ sěverněi straně, i svoim̄ ustiemъ vnide vъ Dvinu, [niže] grada Ustjuga za m̄'. popriščь. | Rěkaz̄ tretiaę naricaemaa Vętka. jaže tečetь sъ druguju stranu Pefmi i ... (9).[21]

Further we have the enumeration of various methods the Permians used in their attempts to kill the saint:

... sъ drekolmi, i s posoxy, i oslopy, i s velikimi urazy, inogda že s' sokyrami, inogda že strělami strělęjušče, ovogda že solomu okolo tebe zapalęjušče, i

---

[21] And these are the names of the places and countries and lands and barbarians living around Perm': the Dvina people, the Ustjug people, the Vilija people, the Vyčegda people, and Pinega people, the Jug people, the Syrjans, the people of Galič, the Vjatka people, the Lapps, the Carelians, the Obugians, the Pečora people, the Gogulič people, the Samoyeds, the Pertasians, the Great Perm', called Čusovaja. A river, whose name is Vym, it encircles the entire Permian land and flows into the Vyčegda. For Vyčegda is another river: it flows from the Permian land towards the north and into the Dvina 40 miles below the city of Ustjug. A third river is called Vjatka, which flows on the other side of Perm', and ...

simъ sъžešči tę xotęšče, i mnogymi obrazy umŕtviti tę myslęšče. No Gb̄ Bḡъ Sps̄ъ sps̄e tę svoimi sudbami ... (103).[22]

An example of abstractive segmentation, or distributio, is the periphrastic description of Stephen in the concluding encomium. The figure of the saint is detached from the action of the story, and his deeds are transformed into timeless and generalized ideas of what he is—a nominal characterization in which a whole string of predicates is invoked and made to stand synecdochically for the man. Gradually, however, the totality of the figure is lost in this segmentation, until it finally defies all description. The tirade opens with a dubitatio of a traditional kind—*quo te domine dicam, nescio*[23]—and weaves the saint's qualities together in a catalogue of virtues that forms a stylistic climax in the *vita*:

No čto tę nareku, o eps̄pe,
ili čto tę imenuju,
ili čim' tę prizovu,
i kako tę provĕščaju,
ili čim' tę mĕnju,
ili čto ti priglašu,
kako poxvalju,
kako počtu, kako ublẕju, kako rezložu, i kako xvalu ti sъpletu? tĕm že, čto tę nareku prork̄a li, jako prorč̄eskaa prorečenia protolkovalъ esi, i gadania prork̄ъ ujęsnilъ esi, i posredĕ ljudii nevĕrnyxъ i nevĕgl̄snyx jako prork̄ъ imъ bylъ esi; aps̄la li tę imenuju, jako aps̄lkoe dĕlo sъtvorilъ esi, i ravno aps̄lom ravno obrazujęsę podvizasę, stopamъ aps̄lkym poslĕduję; zakonodavca li tę prizovu ili zakonopoložnika, imže ljudemъ bezakonnymъ zakonъ dalъ esi, i ne byvšu u nixъ zakonu, vĕru im̄ ustavilъ esi, i zakonъ položilъ esi; krs̄tlę li tę provĕščaju, jako krs̄tilъ esi ljudi mnogy, gręduščaa k tebĕ na krščenie, propovĕdnika li tę proglašu, poněž, jako biričъ na torgu kliča, tako i ty vъ języcĕxъ velegl̄sno propovĕdalъ esi slovo bẕie; evaḡlista li tę nareku ili blḡovĕstnika, im'že blḡovĕstilъ esi v' mirĕ sto̅e | evaḡlie xvo̅, i dĕlo blḡovĕstnika sotvorilъ esi; stĺ̄ę li tę imenuju, eĺma že boĺšii arxierei, i starĕišii stĺ̄ъ, ss̄čenniky postavlęa vъ svoei zemli, nad̄ pročimi ss̄čenniky bylъ esi; uč̄tlę li tę prozovu, jako učiteĺsky naučilъ esi jazykъ zabluždъšii, ili nevĕrnyę v' vĕru privede, i čĺ̄ky nevĕglasy sušča; da čto tę pročee nazovu strs̄oterp'ca li ili mč̄ika, jako mč̄ičesky voleju vdalsę esi v ruky ljudemъ, svĕrĕpĕjuščimъ na muku, i, jako ovca posredĕ voĺkъ, derznulъ esi na strs̄ti, i na terpĕnie, i na mučenie ... (102f.).[24]

---

[22] With cudgels, and with poles, and sticks, and with big clubs, and sometimes with axes, sometimes shooting with arrows, at other times putting fire around you, wishing to burn you to death, and they sought to kill you in many ways. But the Lord, God the Savior, saved you through his will....

[23] G. S. Hafner, *Studien zur altserbischen dynastischen Historiographie*, Südosteuropäische Arbeiten, no. 62 (Munich, 1964), 98.

[24] But what shall I call you, O bishop,
    or how shall I name you,

This encomiastic catalogue is built on the same scheme as the eulogy of Stephen Nemanja in the *Life* that Stephen Prvovenčani wrote of his father; it also has, as A. V. Solov'ev pointed out,[25] another parallel in *Slovo o žitii i o prestavlenii velikago knjazja Dmitria Ivanoviča, carja Rusьskago.* A shorter variant is found in Saint Sava's *Life* of his father.[26] In early Russian literature there is an example where the same scheme is used by Cyril of Turov (second half of the twelfth century), in *Slovo o sьnjatii tela Xristova s kresta.* It occurs here in his eulogy to Joseph of Arimathea. The variants differ in their degree of embellishment. Those of Sava and Cyril are plainer than those of Epiphanius and Stephen. But there can be no doubt that they all have a common basic scheme.

The abstractive distributio in the example above dissolves Stephen's character into an indefinite series of qualities, each of which will warrant inclusion in a particular heroic category. In this way enumeration approaches comparison, as a kind of similarity is presupposed between Stephen and the various heroic ideals he is seen in relation to. Nevertheless, this figure of speech is predominantly metonymic, primarily decomposing the totality into its component synecdochic parts.

---

or how shall I address you,
and how shall I announce you,
or how shall I mention you,
or how shall I invoke you,
how do I praise, how do I honor, how do I argue,
and how do I weave your praise? By calling you a prophet?—for you have interpreted the prophecies of the Prophets, and explained their forecasts, and among the infidel and ignorant people you were like a prophet to them; shall I call you an apostle?—for you have done an apostle's work, and struggling to become equal to the Apostles, you have followed in their footsteps; shall I invoke you as legislator or as the founder of the law?—for you have given the law to lawless people, and because they had no law, you set up a creed for them and founded their law; shall I announce you as the baptist?—for you have baptized many people, who came to you for their baptism; shall I proclaim you a preacher?—since like a herald shouting in the marketplace you have loudly preached the word of God among the heathens; shall I call you an evangelist or a bringer of good news?—for you have brought them the Holy Gospel of Christ in peace, and done the work of an evangelist; shall I call you a prelate?—insofar as you are a great *archiereus* and senior priest, ordaining priests in your land, you were above other priests; shall I address you as a teacher?—for you have taught a bewildered people like a true teacher, brought the ignorant infidels to the faith; and I could further call you a sufferer or a martyr, for with a martyr's will you gave yourself into the hands of people who in their fury wanted to torture you, and like a sheep among wolves you had the courage to face suffering and martyrdom....

[25] A. V. Solov'ev, "Epifanij Premudryj kak avtor 'Slova o žitii i prestavlenii velikago knjazja Dmitrija Ivanoviča, carja russkago,'" *TODRL* 17 (1961): 85–106.

[26] V. Ćorović, *Spisi sv. Save,* Zbornik za istoriju, jezik i književnost srpskog naroda, vol. 1, bk. 17, pt. 1 (Belgrade, 1928), 5–16, 160.

However, direct comparison is not an alien quality in the *Life of Saint Stephen*. Epiphanius employs both quite brief comparisons of individual components and elaborate allegories and examples. By the same token, pure metaphors, in which the conjunction of comparison is left out and one component represents the other, are rare.

The second component in Epiphanius' comparisons is usually a direct quotation from the Bible, especially from the Psalms. The few metaphors to be found are also traceable to the Bible, and like the comparisons, they belong to the traditional stock of hagiographical tropes. Life on earth is in its transience—*aky rěčnaa bystrina, ili aky travnyi cvēt*[27]—an allusion to Ps. 90 (89):4–6, which is subsequently combined with a direct quotation from 1 Pet. 1:24, a variation of the same flower image, introduced by "apslu gljušču."[28] The attempts by the heathens to kill Stephen are represented in direct parallel to Ps. 117 (118):12, through the introductory formula, "Dvdvo slovo gljuščee,"[29] which leads from narration to quotation:

vsi jazyci ob'šedše, obidoša mę jako p'čely sot,
i razgorěšasę jako ognь v ternii (20).[30]

Even in his rendering of the shaman Pam's speech, Epiphanius paraphrases the Psalms in comparisons such as the following:

pred licem moim priiti ne ster'pęt, no jako voskъ protivu plameni veliku pribli-
živsę i istaet, neželi slovesy sъprětisę so mnoju smějut ... (44)[31]

(cf. Ps. 67 [68]:2); when Stephen lets the shaman go, the latter runs off "jako elenь" (57) 'like a deer' (cf. Isa. 35:6).

The comparison may be extended, the second component acquiring the character of an image, as in the account of Saint Stephen's life in the monastery, where it becomes a variation on Ps. 1:3:

i byst jako drevo plodovito nasaženo pri isxodiščix vod, i často napaęemo razumomъ bžstvenyx pisanii, i ottudu prorastaa greznъ dobroděteli, i pro-cvětaa vidy blgovolenia, těmъ i plod svoi dastь vъ vremę svoe. Kyja že plody, plody dxovnye, iže Pavelъ apslъ isčitaetъ, glę: bratie, plod dxovnyi estь: ljuby, radostь, mirъ, dol'goter'pěnie, věra, krotostь, vъzderžanie i pročaa ... (6).[32]

[27] Like the river's flood, or like the flower of the grass.

[28] As the apostle says.

[29] As the word of David says.

[30] All nations compassed me about, they compassed me about like a swarm of bees and burned like the fire of thorns.

[31] They dare not appear before me, but as wax melteth when it comes near a great fire, nor do they dare to dispute with me.

[32] And he was like a tree full of fruit that is planted by the rivers of water, and is often drenched by the knowledge of the Divine Scriptures and thus brings forth the grapes of virtue

Interpretation of metaphor, as in this case, is characteristic of the *Life of Saint Stephen*. The tendency is in the direction of the combined metaphor, where the two components are juxtaposed:

Sego radi ubo vъzljublenʹne, prepoęši istinoju čresla svoę krěpko, aky xrabryi voinъ Xv̄ъ, vobronisę vъ vse oružie b̄stvenoe, obui nozě na ugotovanie b̄gověstovania věry, oblecysę vъ bronę pravdy, priimi že i ščī̄ věry, i šlemъ sp̄senia, i mečь dx̄ovnyi, eže estь gl̄ъ b̄žii (15).[33]

The combined metaphors—"the breastplate of righteousness"; "the shield of faith"; "the helmet of salvation"—equate the two terms by help of a genitive relationship, in which the meaning of one component is transferred to the other, or the metaphors are created by means of an adjective and explained in a relative clause: "the spiritual sword, which is the word of God."

The passage is taken from Bishop Gerasim's exhortation to Saint Stephen before his departure for Perm', and elucidates an inner spiritual reality by means of a traditional imagery. The individual metaphors are strung together loosely and may be viewed separately or as a whole. The principle is the same as in the previous passage, where the saint's intellectual growth is conveyed through a comparison with the image of the growing tree, taken from the Psalms. Another instance of this allegorical representation of a spiritual situation is the author's description of his own sinfulness, at the end of the *vita*:

Uvyi mni, kto me plamenь ugasitъ, kto mi tmu prosvětitъ, se bo v' bezakonii začatъ esmь, i bezakonia moa umnožišasę zělo, i bezakonia moę volnaxъ prilagaju morʹskyxъ, pomyšlenia že vъ jalicaxъ protivnyx' mi větrъ; uvy mně, kako skončaju moe žitie | kako preplovu se more velikoe i prostrannoe, šir̄šeesę, [pečalnoe, mnogomutnoe, nestoęšče, smętuščesę]; kako preprovožu d̄ševnuju mi lodiju promežu volnami sverěpymi, kako izbudu trevolnenia strastei, ljutě pogružajusę vъ glubině zolъ, i zělo potoplęęsę v' bez'dně grěxov-něi; uvyi mně, volnuęsę posrědě pučiny žitiiskago morę, i kako postignu v' tišinu umilenia, i kako doidu vъ pristanišče pokaania ... (101).[34]

---

and the flowers of divine delight and also bears fruit in due time. And what fruits, the spiritual fruits which the Apostle Paul enumerates, saying: brethren, the spiritual fruit is: love, joy, peace, longsuffering, faith, meekness, temperance, etc....

[33] Therefore, my beloved ones, gird your loins fast with the truth, like the bold soldier of Christ, don the divine armor and shoe many with the preparation of the gospel of faith, take on the breastplate of righteousness, receive the shield of faith, and the helmet of salvation, and the spiritual sword, which is the word of God.

[34] Woe is me, who will extinguish the flame for me, who will illuminate the darkness for me?—for I am conceived in sin and my sins have greatly increased, and I compare my sins to the waves of the sea and my good intentions to small boats against the headwind. Woe is me,

The hagiographer's equation of his own life with a voyage, in this extended ship metaphor, varies a *topos* that is not ultimately traceable to the Bible, but to classical rhetoric. In the *Life of Saint Stephen* it must be seen in connection with the distribution in the Middle Ages of this topos, not as an indication of Epiphanius' familiarity with classical rhetoric, as has been suggested.

To the category of expanded comparison belongs also the drawing of parallels between Stephen's mission and biblical analogies, in order to bring out his historical significance. The device is used even from the beginning of the *vita*. Epiphanius here describes the situation of the Permians at the time when the saint started his mission, comparing them to the hired workers in the biblical parable, whom their master employed "at the eleventh hour." This parable is at the same time a key to understanding Epiphanius' use of parallels:

> podobno estь | crstvo nbsnoe člku domovitu, iže izide rano izoutra naimovatь dělatelę v' vinograd svoi. I smolvi s nimi po srebreniku na dnъ. I išed vъ g časъ vidě drugyę stoęšča prazdny, i těm reče: idite i vy v' vinograd moi, i šedše dělaite, i eže budet vъ pravdu damъ vamъ. Oni že idoša. Paky že vъ šestuju i devętuju godinu sъtvori takožde. Vъ edinu že na desęt godinu obrěte drugya stoęšča prazdny, i reče im: čto zdě stoite vesь dnъ prazdny, per'męne, niktož li vas ne najalъ? Oniže otvěščavše, glaša emu: jako nikto že nasъ ne najalъ, rekše niktož nas ne naučilъ věrě krstienьstěi, niktož nasъ ne prosvětilъ stymъ krščeniemъ, nikto že nas ne v'velъ v razumnyi vinogradъ, rek'še v zakonъ Gnъ (12).[35]

Analysis of the most characteristic stylistic features of the *vita* shows that Epiphanius builds up his text by means of various kinds of parallel constructions which activate its language with regard to sounds, morphological

---

how shall I end my life, how shall I cross this great and extensive sea?—wide, gloomy, troubled, unstable, unruly; how shall I steer the ship of my spirit through the furious waves, how shall I be saved from the storm of the passions?—grievously I sink into the deep of evil, vehemently drowning in the abyss of sinfulness, woe is me, storm-tossed in the middle of the ocean of terrestrial life, how shall I reach the calm of humility, and how shall I arrive at the haven of repentance....

[35] The Kingdom of Heaven is like unto a man that is a householder, who went out early in the morning to hire laborers into his vineyard. And he agreed with them for a penny a day. Anu he went out about the third hour, and saw others standing idle, and he said unto them: Go ye also into my vineyard, and whatsoever is right I will give you. And they went. Again he went out about the sixth and ninth hour, and did likewise. And about the eleventh hour he found others standing idle, and saith unto them: Why stand you there all the day idle, Permians, has no one hired you? And they answered, saying unto him: Because no men has hired us, meaning no one has taught us the Christian faith, no one has illuminated us through the holy baptism, no one has led us into the vineyard of knowledge, that is the Law of the Lord.

and syntactical categories and classes of words, as well as larger thematic entities. The correspondences between word-weaving and the poetry of the Bible make it natural to link the historical growth of this style with the development of an Orthodox Slav liturgical poetry based on Greek models. Epiphanius' style has even been thought to derive directly from the *akathistos*-hymns of the fourteenth-century Hesychast patriarchs, Isidoros, Kallistos, and Philotheos.[36] The similarities between Epiphanius' word-weaving and the word-weaving of the Serbian princely *vitae*, however, point in another direction. They indicate that Epiphanius' style represents a late phase in the development of an original panegyrical hagiography in Slavonic literature, modeled on the sublime hagiographical genre in Byzantine literature, where, as early as the eleventh and twelfth centuries it had displaced the older, narrative *vita*. At the same time as the saintly *vita* became a sublime genre, the anecdotal narrative was replaced by a more objective account. The hagiographer no longer addressed a circle of initiates, or a closed monastic community, but the common reader and listener.[37] The lofty style that evolved in Byzantine hagiography represents a combination of stylistic devices of the Bible, especially those of the Old Testament, with the encomiastic style of Hellenistic rhetoric.[38]

In the Serbian princely *vitae*, the heroes are juxtaposed with the heroes of biblical and Byzantine history. The principle of parallelism is used to integrate them into a wider historical context. That it has the same function in the *Life of Saint Stephen* is shown in the parallel created by Epiphanius between the Permians and the hired workers of the biblical parable. Epiphanius' account of the heathens of Perm' is at this point woven into the biblical quotation, so that they are equated with the last unit in the sequence of parallel components: the workers who came "at the eleventh hour." Characteristically, the relations of equivalence, based on the principle of similarity, are not in themselves the dominant feature in this passage; they are merely a prerequisite for the allegorical representation of the Permian people as a link in a chronological chain, as part of a larger whole. Epiphanius' use of quotations from the Bible is determined by his endeavors to create a significant context for his hero. The concatenation of parallel links in series or sequences is part of a process in which the contiguity principle is preponderant. The enumeration of lands and peoples surrounding the Permians, and the breaking down of objects and concepts into

---

[36] R. Mathiesen, "Nota sul genere acatistico e sulla letteratura agiografica slava," *Ricerche slavistiche* 13 (1965): 57–63.

[37] S. V. Poljakova, *Vizantijskie legendy* (Leningrad, 1972), 266ff.

[38] H. Hunger, *Reich der neuen Mitte* (Graz, 1965), 334ff.

synecdochic details, also form part of this process. That is to say, the text is dominated by figures of speech based on metonymic correspondences between the components. This kind of alignment has traditionally been considered a mere accumulation of elements and thus of limited poetic value. It was difficult to see in it any integrative function. But it is not quite as simple as this. I shall try to show how Epiphanius' metonymic sequences contribute to the creation of a holy universe around his protagonist.

External Form in the *Vita*

With respect to external form—that is, the division into separate sections— the *Life of Saint Stephen* follows, on the whole, the conventions of the genre. First is an introduction, where the hagiographer introduces himself and his hero to the audience by means of the traditional *topoi*. Then follows the life proper, which starts with the portrayal of the saint's childhood and adolescence in the hometown of Ustjug. The next phase in the life is the account of the years Stephen spent absorbed in studies, after having taken vows at the Grigor'ev Monastery in Rostov. This phase is concluded by his departure for Moscow, where Bishop Gerasim of Kolomna, deputy metropolitan after the death of Alexius, gives him the blessing of the Church to evangelize the Permians. The story of Stephen's journey to Perm', and his work among the heathens, is the central part of the *vita*. It moves from the description of their resistance to the saint and his preaching, on to his victory through the power of the word, and through his gentle character. The apex of this section is the account of Stephen's disputation with the shaman Pam, who tries to stir up the people by urging his compatriots to stick to the faith of their fathers, at the same time reminding them of their brutal exploitation at the hands of the Muscovites:

> Otčьskyx̄ bogov̄ ne ostavlivaite, a žer'tvъ i trebъ ixъ ne zabyvaite, a staryi pošliny ne pokidyvaite, davnyi věry ne pometaite, iže tvoriša otc̄y naši, tako tvorite, mene slušaite, a ne slušaite Stefana, iže novoprišedšago ot Moskvy; [ot̄ Mos'kvy bo] možet li čto dobro byti namъ? ne ot̄tudu li namъ tęžesti byšę, i dani tęžkyę i nasilьstvo, i tivuni i dovodščici i pristavnicy? sego radi, ne slušaite ego, no mene pače poslušaite, dobra vamъ xotęščago. Az' bo esmь rodъ vašъ i edinoę zemlę s vami, i edinъ rodъ i edinoplemenъ, i edino kolěno, edinъ językъ ... (4).[39]

---

[39] Do not abandon the gods of your fathers and do not forget their sacrifices and offerings, and do not give up the old customs and do not throw away the old faith, but do as your fathers did, and listen to me and not to Stephen, this newcomer from Moscow; for what good can there come from Moscow? Have we not had enough of their oppression, and heavy tributes and outrages, and commissioners, and collectors and inspectors? Therefore, do not listen

However, Epiphanius' description of Stephen's mission belies the shaman's words that nothing good can come from Moscow. The saint is seen in contrast to the secular officials. He is coming to Perm' with the Gospel, they to levy taxes. The disputation between the shaman and the saint ends by Stephen challenging his opponent to a trial of strength. They are to walk through the burning fire and to let themselves be carried by the current under the frozen river, from one hole in the ice to another, to prove whose faith is the stronger. The shaman backs out and retreats from the area that Stephen has Christianized. Stephen builds a church for his new community, and translates Greek as well as Russian ecclesiastical books into the written version of the Permian language that he has worked out, so that the Permians could, in accordance with Orthodox tradition, worship in their mother tongue. After this central section of the *vita* follows the account of the saint's return to Moscow and his appointment as bishop of Perm'. During his stay in Moscow he dies, having first foretold his death and given a valedictory speech to his disciples, in accordance with the conventions of the genre.

The story about the saint is enlarged with a number of prayers, instructions, and lamentations, which Epiphanius has inserted into the narrative in the form of static monologues, to use Zubov's term.[40] Even if he also uses dialogue, it is the static monologues that characterize the *Life of Saint Stephen*. It follows that the character drawing is not predominantly dramatic. The characters are described mostly through strings of epithets.

The most original feature of the external form is the conclusion of the *vita*, where the author deviates quite radically from the conventional scheme, which after the saint's death requires the hagiographer to go on to describe his posthumous miracles, ending with a *conclusio* that links up with the exordium. Instead of this traditional ending, the *Life of Saint Stephen* has a coda consisting of three lamentations, (threnoi or *plači*): *Plač' perm'skyx ljudej*; *Plač' cerkvi perm'skij* (where Stephen's Church emerges in the allegorical guise of a mourning widow) and finally, *Plačeve i poxvala inoka spisajušča*. In these lyric outbursts, sorrow over the departed saint is expressed in forms that derive from both the indigenous Russian *plač'* and from the eulogies and lamentations of the Orthodox Church.[41] Nor were

---

to him, but listen rather to me, who wishes you well. I am of your kin and we are one country, and one kin and one tribe, and one clan, one tongue....

[40] V. P. Zubov, "Epifanij Premudryj i Paxomij Serb," *TODRL* 9 (1953): 145–158.

[41] V. P. Adrianova-Peretc, *Očerki poètičeskogo stilja drevnej Rusi* (Moscow, 1947), 162ff.; J. Holthusen, "Epifanij Premudryj und Gregor von Nyssa," *Festschrift für Margarete Woltner zum 70. Geburtstag* (Heidelberg, 1967), 64–82.

similar lamentations unknown to the Serbian word-weavers, although they used them differently. The close of our *vita* thus becomes totally different from the combination of eulogy and accounts of posthumous miracles that conventionally concludes a saint's life, and which emphasizes the mystical, or rather magical, presence, of the saint among the living. To explain this departure from the conventions of the genre, attention has been called to the fact that Stephen had not yet been canonized when the *vita* was written (canonization did not take place until the Council of 1574, under Makarij) and had not performed any posthumous miracles.[42] It would seem natural also to see a link here with early Russian princely *vitae*, which even from the eleventh century have glorifying threnoi of this kind. The authors of these *vitae* occasionally developed their lamentations on the basis of the laconic mention accorded by the chroniclers to the grief of bereaved relatives.[43] In the lives of saints, however, such threnoi are rare, and Epiphanius' use of them is a fresh and original feature in the history of the genre, according to V. O. Ključevskij:

> This original form of eulogy is exclusively Epiphanius' invention: in not a single translated Greek *vita* would he have been able to find anything similar, and not one of the later Russian *vitae* that borrowed a few isolated passages from Epiphanius' eulogy had the courage to reproduce its literary form.[44]

Adrianova-Peretc has subsequently demonstrated that the use of threnoi for the purpose of glorification is not wholly unknown in Greek hagiography.[45] In any event, they may be found in Russian lives of saints after Epiphanius. She has thus modified Ključevskij's enthusiastic contention. Nevertheless, Epiphanius' conclusio in the form of three threnoi must be regarded as an innovation in Russian hagiography.

Time and Space in the *Life of Saint Stephen*

This survey of its external form shows that the *vita* generally conforms to the rules of the genre, while the deviations from the conventional scheme in the shaping of its conclusion are clear proof that we are not here faced with a mechanical imitation. The question will thus be whether Epiphanius' deviation from the scheme has also an intrinsic function in the *vita*, and is not, albeit a historical necessity, merely a poetic contingency. I shall

---

[42] Kitch, *Literary Style of Epifanij Premudryj* (see n. 3), 50.

[43] V. P. Adrianova-Peretc, "Slovo o žitii i o prestavlenii velikogo knjazja Dmitrija Ivanoviča, carja Russkago," *TODRL* 5 (1947): 73–96.

[44] V. O. Ključevskij, *Drevnerusskie žitija svjatyx kak istoričeskij istočnik* (Moscow, 1871), 84.

[45] Adrianova-Peretc, "Slovo o žitii" (see n. 43).

therefore analyze the *vita* with a view to defining its structure and try to find a systematic coherence between its component parts, including the lamentations.

A basic feature of the *Life of Saint Stephen* is the juxtaposition of Epiphanius' own narrative with quotations from other texts. Historical facts and dates are generally rendered in the form of an enumeration of contemporary events, and subsequently, by means of the quotations, related to events in a historical past. For example, Stephen's work in creating an alphabet for the Permians is compared with similar events in the history of the Greek and Slavic languages. Thus the events of the narrative are incorporated in a diachronic sequence.

Accordingly, an analysis of the *vita* may be divided into two stages: first, an examination of the narrative to find the principle for selection and combination of historical facts and dates, geographical information, and similar synchronic elements in the life proper; second, an examination of the function of the quotations to determine the principles for their selection and combination with the narrative.

In Epiphanius' story, the combination of facts and dates into a syntagmatic sequence may be shown in an example taken from the very first section of the life proper:

> Sii pr̄p̄d̄bnyi ot̄c̄ъ našь Stefanъ bě ubo rodomъ rusinъ, ot̄ ję| zyka slovenьska, ot̄ strany polunoščnyę, gl̄emyę Dvinьskia, ot̄ grada, naricaemago Ustьjuga, ot̄ roditelju naročitu, sn̄ъ někoego xol̄jubca, muža věrna xrs̄tiana, imenemъ Simeona, edinago ot̄ klirikъ velikyę sъbornyę cr̄kvi st̄yę Bc̄a, iže na Ustьjuzě, i ot̄ mtr̄e, tako krs̄tiany, naricaemyę Mr̄ia (4).[46]

Through the information given about the saint's origin, his birthplace, and the names and status of parents, his figure is placed in a historical, geographical, and social context. The exposition is dominated by the referential or denotative function of language and is focused on the third person.

A more comprehensive example of a presentation focused on the context is the portrayal of Stephen being tonsured and his stay in the Grigor'ev Monastery in Rostov. The example shows how the factuality in the portrayal of the saint's surroundings is combined with a purely conventional description of his figure by means of hagiographical topoi:

[46] And this our holy father Stephen was Russian by origin, of the Slavic people, of a Northern land, called the land of Dvina, of a city called Ustjug, of distinguished parents, the son of a lover of Christ, a true Christian man called Symeon, one of the clergy of the Great Cathedral of the Holy Mother of God in Ustjug, and of a mother who was also a Christian, called Maria.

Semu pride Bžia ljuby, eže ostaviti ot̄čьstvo i vsę suščaa imĕnia, i prosto rešči, vsĕmi dobrodĕanii ukrašenъ bĕ otrō toi, pospĕvaa vъzrastomь vъ straxъ Bžii, i straxom̄ Bžiimъ | umilivsę, i ešče mlad̄, sę Bḡu da vъ unosti, otrokъ syi ver̄stoju, postrižesę v̄ černьci vъ gradĕ Rostovĕ, u st̄go Grigoria Bḡoslova v̄ manastyri, naricaemĕm̄ v̄ Zatvorĕ, blizъ eps̄kpьi, jako knigy mnogy bęxu tu dovolny sušča emu na potrebu, počitania radi, pri eps̄pĕ rostov̄stĕmь Par̄fenii, ot̄ ruku že ostrižesę nĕkoēg starca, prozvitera sušča, sanomъ ss̄čennika, imenem̄ Mak̄sima igumena, prozviščo Kalina ... (5f.).[47]

The theme of the above paragraph is Stephen's tonsuring, an event accurately defined in time and space. The event is locally defined through the relationship between the monastery, the abbot's domain, and the episcopal residence. It is temporally defined in relation both to the man who was abbot of the monastery and the man who was bishop of Rostov at the time of the event, that is, in relation to the highest ranks of the city's ecclesiastical hierarchy. This means that, first, the event is defined through a relationship of local contiguity. Second, the historical persons are combined in a hierarchical proximity (between the abbot and the bishop) and distance (between Stephen and the other two). The elements related to each other here belong to a different class. But the principle for the combination of elements is the same: the alignment on the signans level corresponds to a semantic contiguity between the components.

The principle of contiguity also dominates the further account of Stephen's life. The story moves on through the depiction of his gradual rise in the hierarchy: the abbot having received his monastic vows, it is the bishop of Rostov who ordains him as a deacon, and the deputy metropolitan, Gerasim of Kolomna, who installs him in his priestly office. In this way the saint's promotion is expressed through the rising ecclesiastical status of his immediate superior. At the same time his preferment is also expressed through a shift in location: the removals from Ustjug to Rostov, from Rostov to Moscow. Thus parallels are established between the ecclesiastical hierarchy and the hierarchy of the cities: metropolitan Moscow ranks higher than diocesan Rostov.

In the paragraphs quoted, the combination of the signantia corresponds to the relations between the signata: hierarchical relations within the

---

[47] Unto him came the love of God, which is to leave the house of one's father and all one's property, and in simple words, this youth was adorned with all virtues, he advanced in age, in the fear of God, and was seized by fear of God, and still being young, giving himself to God in his youth, he was, yet only a boy in years, shorn a monk in the city of Rostov, in the Monastery of the Holy Gregory the Theologian, called "in the Hermitage," near the bishop's residence; for there were many books, enough of what he needed for his reading, under Bishop Parthenius of Rostov, and the boy was tonsured by a certain *starec*, a presbyter, of rank a priest, the abbot Maxim, called Kalin....

Church, between the cities, and between the buildings. We might call this a diagrammatical representation of reality, a representation in which the similarity between the signans and signatum appears "only in respect to the relations of their parts," according to the definition given by Charles S. Peirce.[48] To the extent that Epiphanius is representing a historical reality in the *Life of Saint Stephen*, his mimesis, his representation of reality, is predominantly an "icon of relation."

As soon as we have become aware of the significance of this principle for the structure of this *vita*, we shall find that it determines Epiphanius' story throughout. Even in sections that are thematically very different from those already quoted, the narrative is similarly oriented towards the context, giving expression to an event in the saint's life by combining components from the same semantic field, so that they form contiguous parts of a larger whole. The description of Stephen's linguistic studies is one example. The components are here the saint's three languages. In addition to Russian, he has a command of Greek and also of the language of the Permians. The progress of his studies is illustrated by linking these components in a sequence:

Želaaž bolšago razuma, jako obrazomъ ljubomudria izučisę i grečeskoi gra-motě, i knigy grečeskia izvyče, i dobrě počitaše ę, i prīsno imęše ę u sebe. I běše uměę glāti tremi jazyki; tako že i gramoty tri uměaše, jaž estъ russkyi i grečesky, per'mъskyi, jako zbytisę o sem slovesi onomu, glĵušču, iže rečesę: jako jazyky vъzglĵutъ novy; i paky: iněmi jazyky glāti ustroi. I dobrě obderžaše i pomyslъ, eže iti vъ Per'mъskuju zemlju i učiti ę: togo bo radi i jazykъ per'mъskyi pokušašesę izučiti, i togo radi i gramotu per'mъskuju sotvori, poneže ... (8).[49]

In the latter as in the former examples, the linking up of elements from the same semantic field leads to their semantic and/or grammatical similarity being subordinated to their contiguity relation, so that together they represent extensions in space and time.

The representation of Stephen's life as a number of removals within a geographically limited space lends to the narrative the character of a

---

[48] R. Jakobson, "Quest for the Essence of Language," *Selected Writings*, vol. 2 (The Hague, 1971), 350.
[49] In his desire for more knowledge he also learned Greek as the prototype of wisdom, and studied Greek books, and he read them thoroughly and always kept them with him. And he could speak three languages; and also read and write them, they are Russian, and Greek, and Permian, so that in him the word was fulfilled which says that they shall speak with new tongues, and again: he let them speak with other tongues. And he was strongly seized by the thought of going to the land of Perm' and to teach it, and therefore he undertook to learn the Permian language, and therefore he created a Permian alphabet, because....

travelogue. The saint moves, in the first part of the *vita*, from his home town of Ustjug, on the periphery, to Moscow, which is the center, via Rostov as an intermediate stage. The story about his journey to Perm' takes us back to the periphery and beyond it. Stephen crosses the boundary of the Christian οἰκουμένη on his mission to the heathens, who are converted and grafted onto the Russian Church. His mission decribes an expansion of boundaries in the universe of the *vita* and forms a climax in the story of his life. After this the story takes us back to Moscow, where Stephen's career culminates in his appointment as bishop. Finally, in the narrative part follows the account of his departure from this world.

The accounts of Stephen's journeys are at the same time a story about his gradual perfection and his rise in the hierarchy of the Church. The story of his rise is combined with a description of his itinerary, so that its individual stages correspond to the individual stages in his career and ethical progress. Time and geographical space thus acquire an ethical and religious significance. The hagiographer's system of moral and religious values is projected into Stephen's surroundings, according to the principle of contiguity which underlies the narrative. The first stages of his life represent, all of them, positive values in the ethico-religious system of the *vita*. Heathen Perm' stands for the negative pole of this system. The transformation of the landscape into a reflection of moral and religious values is reinforced by the introduction of conventional symbols. Heathen Perm', the negative pole, is experienced as the equivalent of darkness; Stephen, who represents the positive pole, illuminates the Permians, bringing them the light. The ultimate source of Epiphanius' light symbolism is the quotation from Isa. 9:2: "The people that walked in darkness have seen a great light; they that dwell in the land of the shadow of death, upon them hath light shined" (67).

The horizontalized space axis of the *Life of Saint Stephen* thus becomes an indication of Epiphanius' ideology. Lixačev's and Dane's attempts to interpret the *vita* as an expression of Hesychast mysticism and of the saintly ideal of the Trans-Volga monks is not confirmed by an analysis of its structure.[50] Epiphanius' representation of the saint's perfection as a progress in the hierarchy of the Church, combined with the story of his journeys, is almost the opposite of the teachings of the Trans-Volga monks about withdrawal from the world, and spiritual perfection in mystical contemplation.

---

[50] Lixačev, *Čelovek v literature* (see n. 2); id., *Kul'tura Rusi vremeni Andreja Rubleva i Epifanija Premudrogo* (Moscow, 1962); id., *Razvitie russkoj literatury X–XVII vekov* (Leningrad, 1973); M. M. Dane, "Epiphanius' Image of St. Stefan," *Canadian Slavonic Papers* 5 (1961): 72–86.

It is the horizontal character of the time and space axes in the *vita* and the transmission of the *vita*'s ethico-religious values to this system of coordinates, that determine the representation of Stephen's sanctity. The opposition of good and evil, of holiness and the ungodly, is in the *Life of Saint Stephen* equated with the opposition of "we" and "the others," of the Orthodox Russian Church and the heathens. Saint Stephen's mission does not bring about any fusion of the opposites in a higher unity. It leads to strife among the Permians, who split up into two irreconcilable groups: those who have taken Stephen's creed, and those who, like the shaman Pam, stick to their old religion:

Oni že ubo, slyšavše propovědь věry kr̄stianьskia, ovii xotęxu věrovati i kr̄stitisę, a druziiž ne xotęxu no i xotęščimь vozbranęxu věrovati. Elikož per-věe malo někto oī nix̄ věrovaša i krešćeni byša oī nego, tii často prixoždaxu k nemu i presědęxu pr̄sno emu, sъbesědujušče i sъvъprašajuščesę s nimъ, i povsegda deržaxusę ego, i zělo ego ljublęxu; a iže ne věrovaša, tii ne ljubętь ego i oīběgajutь, i ubiti pomyšlějuī (19).[51]

The discord among the Permians culminates in the story of how the heathens tried to kill Stephen. The conflict between the two groups is resolved in Stephen's disputation with the shaman. Three times Stephen exhorts the other to follow him into the crackling fire to see who has the stronger faith. Frightened by the flames, the heathen priest flinches, and loses. He has revealed his impotence face to face with the new—in the presence of the whole tribe, who hand him over to Stephen, their new leader, demanding that he pronounce the death sentence on the shaman:

vozmi sego i kazni i, jako povinenъ estь kazni, i po našei pošlině dolženъ estь umreti, poneže ... (55).[52]

Stephen refuses to comply with their demands. The pagan law has been superseded by his Christian mercy:

Oīveščav' že Stefanъ i reče imъ: ni ubo da ne budeī tako, i ne budi ruka naša na našem̄ vrazě, ne skoro ruky moea ne| vozložu na nь, ni kaznę pokaznju ego, i sm̄rti ne predamъ ego. Ne posla bo mene X̄s biti, no blḡověstiti ... (56).[53]

[51] But they, hearing the preaching of the Christian faith, some wished to believe and be baptized, whereas others did not want to, and prevented those who wanted to believe. Though at first only a few of them believed and were baptized, these often came to him and sat next to him, and he talked and discussed with them, and they always kept to him and loved him greatly, whereas those who did not believe, love him not and run away and plan to kill him.

[52] Take him and execute him, for he is guilty of death, and according to our custom he must die, for....

[53] Then Stephen answered and said: No, this must not be, and that our hand never be against our enemy, and I will not hastily lay my hand on him, nor execute him, nor deliver him unto death. For Christ has not sent me to punish, but to preach the Gospel....

The shaman is permitted to leave in peace, on condition that he will never more appear in Stephen's congregation. The old leader is ejected from the community where Stephen, the victor, has now taken over his role:

da něstь emu ni časti, ni žrebia s novokrščenymi, ni jasti ni piti s nimi nigdě že, nikogda že, ni v' čem' že sovokuplętisę s nimi. Koe bo pričęstie světu ko ťmě, ili kaę ob'ščina věrnu s nevěrnym? (57)[54]

The conflict of the *vita* is thus resolved through a shift of boundaries between good and evil forces, between the positive and negative fields, without effecting any change in the values themselves. By Stephen's work, the positive field in the ethico-religious space of the *vita* is extended to include Perm', which becomes part of the Orthodox οἰκουμένη. In close conformity with the horizontal space-coordinates in the *Life*, Stephen's sanctification is represented through the account of his work to extend the territory of the Russian Church. Through contiguity and expansion, Stephen's new community has been incorporated into a larger totality.

Historicism in the *Life of Saint Stephen*

By way of introduction, Epiphanius states his task as a eulogy of "the preacher of the faith, Perm''s teacher and the successor of the Apostles" ("propovědnika věrě i učitelę Per'mi, i apslom naslědnika") (3). The aim of his account is to praise the saint's mission as a historical continuation of the Apostles' work in spreading Christianity. Epiphanius sees his protagonist in a diachronic perspective right from the beginning, a perspective that opens up the frame of references in the narrative and sets Stephen in a wider historical context. How then, is this idea of the apostolic successor realized? The question brings us back to the amplifying digressions which are mounted into the narrative, in particular to the quotations from the history of the Church dealing with events similar to those in Epiphanius' own story. A clear instance is the account of Stephen's journey to Perm', in which Epiphanius' narration is juxtaposed with a description of the itineraries of the first Apostles to spread the word of God. In a long and elaborate excursus, Epiphanius enumerates the various journeys that, according to Orthodox tradition, the Apostles made to many countries. The whole excursus is divided into parallel components, one for each Apostle, which are also paralleled with his own account of Stephen's itinerary. The

---

[54] And let him have neither lot nor share with the newly baptized, and let him never either eat or drink with them, nor join them in anything. For what part has light in darkness, or what common cause has the faithful with the infidel?

connection between narrative and quotations is further emphasized by an almost refrain-like repetition of the words "to Perm' they never came," and similar phrases, in the survey of the itineraries of the Apostles:

ne zaxodili sutь apsli v' Per'mьskuju zemlju; ašče i v Permi ne byli suī; a v' Per'miž ne bylъ; Ašče i v' Permi ne uspěša byti … (10f.).[55]

The repetitions refer back from the quotations to Epiphanius' own narrative, where we find a corresponding enumeration of geographical and ethnographical terms as in the quotations. In the interplay between narration and quotations, these terms acquire a poetic function in addition to their denotative reference. However, similarity between the saint and the Apostles, whose successor the saint is, is subordinate to contiguity, their work being inscribed in a historical process of redemption. Stephen's mission to the Permians and their incorporation into the Christian οἰκουμένη acquire hagiographical significance only when, through the quotations, Epiphanius' narrative is set in this historical perspective. The work that the Apostles began Stephen helps to complete through his Christianization of the Permians "at the eleventh hour." The process of redemption of which Stephen's mission is a part, is first introduced through the retelling of the parable of the workers in the vineyard, and this follows immediately on the excursus about the journeys of the Apostles. The parable is, like Epiphanius' version of world history, formed as a sequence of parallel events in time. Its allegorical function in the *vita* is laid bare in Epiphanius' retelling of the last component, where he substitutes the Permians for the workers hired "at the eleventh hour." Stephen's preaching among the Permians enters history at a point corresponding to the "eleventh hour" in the parable of the hired workers, that is, at a time immediately before the consummation of the ages:

v' poslědnęa dñi, vъ skonʻčanie lěī, vo ostatočnaę vremena, na isxoī čisla sed'myę tysęšča lětъ … (13).[56]

Epiphanius dates the conversion of the Permians from the eschatological concept of time of the Middle Ages, which reckoned that the Last Judgment would take place at the end of the seventh millennium, in 1492 A.D., that is, barely a hundred years after Stephen's death.

Analysis of the function of the excurses gradually reveals the model of world history that Epiphanius, by means of the quotations, reflects in his

---

[55] The Apostles had never visited the Permian land; although they had not been in Perm'; but he never was in Perm'; Although they never got as far as Perm'.

[56] In the last days, at the end of time, in the years that remained, at the wane of the seventh millennium.

narrative. The central passage for the decoding of the historical system of
the *vita* is the description of the Church's memorial feasts in the excursus
on the month of March:

Jako se estь martъ | mšcь načalo vsěmъ mšcemъ, iže pervyi narečetsę vъ
mšcexъ, emuž svidetelьstvuet Moisii zakonodavecь, glę: mšcь že vamъ pervy
vъ mšcěxъ da budetь martъ. Da jakože učimi esmy, iže i naučaem'sę javě
načalo bytiju: marta bo mšca načalo bytia; vsę tvarь Bgomъ sotvorena bystь
ot nebytia v' bytie; marta bo načalo zdaniju bystь, marta že mšcь vъ ka' dnь i
pervozdan'ny člkъ rodonačalnikъ Adamъ rukoju bžieju sъzdanъ bystь. Marta
že [mšca] někogda Iilьtestii ljude drevle, jakože i Grigorii Bgoslovъ vešča, ot
zemlę Egipetskia, i ot raboty faraoniťsky izbyša, i morę. Čermnago pučinu ne
mokrymi stopami, jako po suxu pěši šestvovaša. Marta že mšca paky Iilьtęne
v' zemlju obětovan'nuju vnidoša, Ierslmъ sostaviša; marta že mšca paky Iilь-
tomъ pasxu pradnovati po vsę že lěta uderžasę byvati. Martaž mšca i
blgověščenie bystь styę Bca, eže arxagglъ Gavriilъ blgověsti ei, egda Snъ bžii
za naše spsenie s nbse snide i vselisę vъ prečistuju utrobu vestyę Vldčca našeę
Bdca, prsnodvyę. Mria, i bez' sěmeni plotь ot nea vъspriimъ. Martaž mšca i
raspętie Xs voleju preterpě, i smŕtь za nasъ postrada, i vъskrsenie bgolěpno
namъ prazdnovati ustavi. Marta že mšca paky čaemъ vъskršenia mrtvym, i
vtorago prišestvia Xsva i strašnag groznago trepetnago gor'dago, pritranago,
ne obumen'nago, besposulnago vsemirnago suda, egda priidetь sъ slavoju,
xotę suditi živymъ i mrtvym, i vъzdati komuždo po dělomъ ego; emuž slava
vъ věky (23f.).[57]

[57] For the month of March is the beginning of all the months, which is called the first
among months, to which Moses the lawgiver bears witness, saying: let March be the first of
the months. And as we have been taught, let us teach ourselves boldly about the beginning of
Creation: for the month of March is the beginning of Creation; all things created by God were
made out of nothing into something; for the month of March was the beginning of Creation,
and on the 21st of March the first created man and progenitor of mankind, Adam, was
created by the hand of God. In the month of March the people of Israel some time long ago,
as Gregory the Theologian said, were rescued from the land of Egypt and from the slavery of
the Pharaohs, and walked dry-shod through the depths of the Red Sea as if over land. And
again in the month of March the Israelites entered the Promised Land and founded Jerusalem;
and again in the month of March the Passover began to be celebrated every year by the
Israelites. In the month of March was also the Annunciation of the Holy Mother of God,
which the Archangel Gabriel announced to her, when the Son of God for our Salvation came
down from the heavens and dwelt in the pure womb of Our Holy Lady, the Mother of God
and the eternal Virgin Mary, and received flesh from her without seed. In the month of March
Christ voluntarily underwent Crucifixion and suffered death for our sake, and commanded us
to celebrate the Resurrection to the glory of God. Again in the month of March we expect the
Raising of the Dead, and the Second Coming of Christ, and the fearful, terrible, awesome,
trembling, vehement, unwarned, irredeemable Judgment of the world, when he shall come
with glory and judge the living and the dead, and reward every man according to his works;
glory to him in all eternity.

The birth of Christ, his death and resurrection, form in the *Life of Saint Stephen* links in a chronological chain of events which the Church commemorates for their historical significance. The sacramental aspect of the feasts, however, the ritual revelation of the eternal mystery of the divine— *věčněi taině javlenie*—in perceptible images, is absent from our *vita*, which only refers to it, but never represents it.

Within the historical system of the *Life of Saint Stephen*, the sacrificial death of Christ has its function as a historical event which is, as such, unique. This event marks the decisive turning point in the teleological movement, which progresses from the Creation of the World and the Fall of Adam, towards the close of the ages and resurrection on the Day of Judgment. Both at its beginning and at its end, this movement transcends history, while in the interim a transcendent Godhead rules its course through His providence. In the interim between the beginning and the end of the world, God acts through His Prophets, His Son, the Apostles, and their successors. This idea of history is not unique to the *Life of Saint Stephen*. It is central to the teaching of the Christian Church. What makes this linear idea of history special in our *vita* is Epiphanius' use of it as a basic structural principle. In early Russian literature it goes back to Kievan chroniclers. A similar view of history also underlies the thirteenth-century *Life of Alexander Nevsky*. Here "the mystical truths upon which the Christian dogma is founded, the Incarnation and the Resurrection of Christ are simply included in the chain of historical facts."[58] With its linear structure, however, the *Life of Saint Stephen* differs fundamentally from early Kievan saints' lives. The *Life of Saint Theodosius* and the Boris and Gleb legend are based on the idea of the life of the saint as an imitation of the life of Christ. The saints become *imitatores Christi*.

In the *Life of Saint Stephen*, it is the linear idea of history that determines the selection of the quotations and their combination with Epiphanius' narrative. The time-space between beginning, middle, and end in the course of history is replete with quotations by and about the Prophets of the Old Testaments, the Apostles, and their successors. In this connection, the monk Xrabr's tract on the evolution of languages acquires its full significance in the structure of the *vita*. The tract was written pseudonymously by a Bulgarian monk at the end of the ninth, or the beginning of the tenth century. It was originally an apologia for the written language of the Slavs against those who claimed that Greek ought also to be the language of the Slavic Churches. The author of the tract justifies his stand by referring to

[58] G. P. Fedotov, *The Russian Religious Mind*, vol. 1 (New York, 1960), 383.

the fact that the other languages had been created by heathens over many generations, whereas the Slavic language had been molded by one individual, Constantine the Philosopher, who was also a Christian saint. Epiphanius links his story about Saint Stephen's work on a written language for the Permians to this sequence of languages, so that the relationship between narration and quotation becomes the same here as in the story about Stephen's itinerary. Through the parallels between Stephen's work and events and characters referred to in the quotations, Epiphanius assimilates his protagonist to the historical heroes of the Church. But this is not the dominant function of the parallels. Epiphanius' main objective is to establish a relation of contiguity between his own hero and the heroes of the Bible. By juxtaposing his own narrative with texts referring to the history of the Christian Church, he integrates his hero into this historical context.

This integration is, however, only an intermediate stage in Epiphanius' story of Stephen's sanctification. The final aim of the *vita* is to transcend history, to overcome the distance between Stephen and the *Wholly Other*. When Epiphanius tells us about the death of Stephen, the saint's life has become a link in a historical time sequence that is perfective in relation to the author of the frame and his audience. The departure of the saint creates an insuperable cleft between the "I" of the narrator and his audience in the frame, on the one side, and Stephen, on the other. In his threnos the hagiographer laments:

> uže bo mežju nami meža velika sotvorisę, uže mežju nami propastь velika utverdisę ... (101).[59]

At the moment when Epiphanius is about to leave the story of past events for his representation of the present, it becomes clear that the glorification of Stephen has created a distance between his figure and its frame.

Epiphanius and those to whom he addresses his story are outside the *perfectum* of the quotations, into which the saint has been incorporated through Epiphanius' technique of montage, while both he and his audience, the recipients of the message of the *vita*, are left in the transient *nunc* of the frame. The absolute distance between the narrator-situation in the frame and the life proper is a feature which, together with Epiphanius' orientation towards the historical context and the third person, points in the direction of the epic. The epic past is absolute, precisely because it represents a time plane totally different from the time of the narrator and his audience:

[59] Already a great division has been created between us, already a great abyss has been set between us.

The singer and his audience, both immanent in the epic qua genre, are on the same time plane and on the same level of meaning (hierarchical level), but the represented world of the heroes is on a totally different, unattainable level, in respect of time as well as significance, separated by epic distance.[60]

Unlike an author of the folk epic, however—that is, epic poetry dealing with a people's or a nation's traditions about heroes and events from a distant past, as they appear to the poet at his epic distance—Epiphanius glorifies a hero of his own times. Whereas in the exordium the writer emphasizes his own contemporaneity with Stephen, the conclusio consists of a sequence of threnoi which, as we have seen, stress the distance that has arisen between the glorified figure of the saint and the mourners in the frame. In the course of the biography, the figure of Stephen has been shifted from the transient contemporaneous time of the hagiographer onto a heroic, everlasting past, through a representation of his life that both in form and meaning imitates the canonical writings Epiphanius has woven into his own story. This kind of mimesis has the character of stylization. The author adapts his own narrative to the other texts in a way that abolishes the difference between them. The projection of certain figures and events of the present onto an epic past—that is, onto a past that has no connection with the present as part of the continuous flow of time—is typical of "classicistic" movements in art and poetry.[61] These movements seek permanence in an idealized past, which is seen in opposition to both the formless transience of the present and to the future, perceived either as a pure continuation of the present or as an impending catastrophe and destruction, represented in the case of the *Life of Saint Stephen* by the Last Judgment. This projection of figures from the author's own time into an epically perceived, idealized past is characteristic of the *Kunstepos*. In a strongly hierarchical society, representatives of the law and power are already, by virtue of their high position in the hierarchy, shown to be separated from others in a way that recalls epic distance, representing as they do tradition handed down from their forebears. In the poet's own time, it is only elevated figures of this kind, and their actions, that can be represented by means of the epic form. With the aid of various intermediary links and connections, the poet weaves them into the epic tradition of the heroic past.

Against this background one may define the *Life of Saint Stephen* as epic representation of a church prince of the hagiographer's own time,

---

[60] M. M. Baxtin, "Èpos i roman," *Voprosy literatury* 1 (1970): 295–122; reprint in id., *Voprosy literatury i èstetiki* (Moscow, 1973), 447–483.

[61] Ibid.

determined by a "classicist" view of the history of the Orthodox Church. This in turn is interpreted as a divine process of redemption. The intermediary link is the use of the quotations, by which Epiphanius integrates Stephen into the glorified past. The absolute distance created between this heroic past and the author's own time shows that history seen as a God-ordained process from Genesis to the Last Judgment constitutes a self-contained, closed universe in the *vita*. The series of figures and events in this closed universe is distanced from the hagiographer and his audience: it has its own beginning, middle, and end. The figure of the saint acquires its significance precisely in its separation from the author and his audience, in the establishment of this absolute epic distance between the frame and the life proper.

Lyricism in the *Life of Saint Stephen*

The absolute division between narrator-situation and narrative in epic poetry implies a particular epic author-attitude inherent in the genre. This epic author-attitude, which characterizes Epiphanius' representation of the life of his hero, is defined by Baxtin as "the stance of a person speaking about a past unattainable to him, the reverential stance of a descendant."[62] But in the three concluding threnoi, the point of view is no longer that of the epic narrator. In his final lament, Epiphanius takes an admiring upward-looking view towards his hero from the transient here and now of the frame.

The first of the concluding threnoi, in which Epiphanius describes the grief of the Permians over the loss of their bishop, takes the form of the lamentation of the "flock" over its "shepherd" and is distinctive—compared with the next two—for its factual content. It sketches Stephen's significance for the Perm' people, whom he had helped against both Russian colonizers and neighboring enemy tribes. This survey is interspersed with rhetorical elements, which according to Adrianova-Peretc are traditional in early Russian eulogies of holy educators such as, for example, Saint Vladimir, Leontij Rostovskij, and Constantine Muromskij. "The lamentation of the Permians goes together with the type of eulogy addressed to the 'illuminator,' created as early as in the eleventh century by Metropolitan Hilarion and by the author of the *Life of Vladimir I.*"[63] The admixture of an oral Russian *plač'* tradition is noticeable in the lamentation of the Permian Church, which is, as J. Holthusen has shown, an amplified version of

---

[62] Ibid.
[63] Adrianova-Peretc, *Očerki poètičeskogo stilja* (see n. 41), 164.

Gregory of Nyssa's Funeral Oration to Bishop Meletios of Antioch.[64] The oral elements have been integrated into the typical word-weaving style, where the discourse is dominated by biblical phraseology and allusions to biblical prototypes for the Church's lament, to Rachel's, Joseph's, and King David's laments, and to those of other biblical figures. The oral discourse is discernible only in a few formulaic phrases, such as the recurrent *Uvy mne* 'Woe is me'.[65]

In the third and final threnos, Epiphanius' own lament and eulogy, the author no longer cites the laments of others, but bursts into lamentations of his own. This lament, like that of the Permians, gradually becomes a eulogy. Adrianova-Peretc has called attention to an essential feature in the construction of this threnos: Epiphanius moves away from the traditional motifs of oral lamentation for the dead at the same time as the discourse is noticeably shifted in the direction of the author: "the talk is not so much about the deceased as about the sinful author's helplessness."[66]

The opening of the lament is also a remembrance of the time when Stephen was still alive. This recollection of their time together is seen by the author in contrast to the unbridgeable gulf that separates them now. The opposition between the author's here and now and the saint's existence beyond time and space is then developed in the form of an extended comparison, in which the relationship between author and saint is equated with that of the rich man and Lazarus in the parable:

> ty ubo, jako onъ dobryi Lazarь niščii, počivaeši nně, jako v loněxъ Avraam-lixъ, az že okaan'nyi, aky bogatyi onъ plamenemъ pekomъ syi … (101).[67]

Epiphanius uses the parable of the rich man's adversities to elucidate his own spiritual misery. Through the comparison he debases himself and elevates the saint, so that the distance between them is already maximal when he starts his eulogy. From the lowly standpoint he has taken, he addresses the transcendent saint *de profundis.*

A comparison of the three threnoi shows that in spite of mutual differences, they are composed on the same scheme and form variants of the same structure. With their vertical viewpoint *de sotto in su*, they are in clear contrast to the epic structure of the third person narrative describing Stephen's work in the context-oriented life proper. The laments are represented

---

[64] Holthusen, "Epifanij Premudryj und Gregor von Nyssa" (see n. 41).
[65] Cf. Adrianova-Peretc, *Očerki poètičeskogo stilja* (see n. 41), 164; id., "Slovo i žitii" (see n. 43).
[66] Adrianova-Peretc, *Očerki poètičeskogo stilja* (see n. 41), 164.
[67] For you, like the good poor Lazarus, now rest in Abraham's bosom, whereas I, wretched man, am consumed by the flame like the rich man.

in the first person and addressed to the saint in the second person as exclamations of woe on his departure. Gradually they become encomiastic invocations of his absent figure:

Aščēž i umr̄šu ti, aky k' živu k tebě glīju ... (102).[68]

The shift of orientation from the third to the first person in the final threnos means that the discourse has now acquired another structural dominant, different from the third person narrative with its epic thrust. With its focusing on the lamenting subject, the series of threnoi becomes finally an expression of the feelings of the lamenters when faced with the reality of the saint's absence.

The summaries of Stephen's deeds no longer refer primarily to the historical context of the *vita*. Their main function is to generate the emotional outbursts of the bereaved. Stylistically they are dominated by interjections like *O, Uvy mne*—words belonging to that part of speech in which the purely emotive stratum is most clearly felt. The involvement of the emotive function marks the threnoi as belonging to the lyric genre. However, one factor that complicates the lyric structure of the laments is their panegyric passages, in which the lamenters address their words to the absent saint and call him by a *you* that seems to run counter to the lamentations on his departure. The panegyric invocations of Stephen in the threnoi culminate in the author's own concluding eulogy, addressed directly to the glorified figure of the saint, as if Epiphanius wants to bring him back to the level of the frame and overcome the distance between them. Through this shift in point of view, the saint becomes the addressee, the recipient of the message: "But what shall I call you, O Bishop, or how shall I name you, or how shall I address you ...?" After this sequence of invocations follow the "decomposition" passage and the metonymic portrayal of Stephen's character through personification of his individual qualities, in an attempt to make him present in the frame. The passage shows how Epiphanius uses language also in its magic, incantatory function, a function which is "chiefly some kind of conversion of an absent or inanimate 'third person' into an addressee of a conative message."[69] In the laments of the *vita* this magic use of language is, however, subordinate to its emotive function. Starting from the historical life-work of the saint, the hagiographer abstracts and "decomposes" his figure, so that it dissolves and disappears behind the words, in which the referential function is no longer predom-

---

[68] Even if you are dead, I speak to you as to a living man.
[69] R. Jakobson, "Linguistics and Poetics," in *Style in Language*, ed. Th. A. Sebeok (Cambridge, Mass., 1960), 355.

inant. Their main function is now to connote the grief of the lyric first person. The words refer to one another and are woven into ornamental sequences based on lexical proximity and phonemic similarity. Finally, in the discourse, the saint is present merely in the lyric outbursts of the hagiographer grieving at his absence, present in his absence.

Thus Stephen emerges finally in his *vita* as a sign, a symbol of something other. But this other is not the presence of the divine prototype in his figure as we know it from the *Life of Saint Theodosius*. The saintly figure of the *Life of Saint Stephen* is transformed through the laments and the eulogies into an expression of a state of mind. This state of mind belongs to a first person faced with the omnipresent absence of the *Wholly Other*. The concluding transformation of Stephen through a series of rhetorical attempts to determine his figure describes a lyric withdrawal from what is the true theme of this *vita*, namely, the story of Stephen's glorification, until it is no longer the saint's figure that is represented in the words of the hagiographer, but the withdrawal itself, through a sequence of metonymic decomposition. The *you* at which the eulogy is directed transcends all that Epiphanius' words are capable of expressing. The *Wholly Other* can only be expressed in terms of absence, the rapture of the lyric subject in its enthusiasm before the ineffable. The set towards the saint's *you* and the withdrawal in the direction of the lamenters' state of mind seem to have created a situation in which the audience of the frame has been excluded from the exposition. But this is only apparently so. In the capacity of a lyric subject, the lamenter at the end of the *vita* is no longer identical with the author, but with any auditor or reader of the *vita* who makes Epiphanius' words an expression of his own feelings and is carried away by the author's enthusiasm. The emotional integration of the audience into the lyric subject, which takes place through the concluding threnoi of the *vita*, implies that Epiphanius' function is no longer that of the epic narrator, but rather that of the κορυφαῖος whose *I* not only represents his own person but also the others, when he directs his eulogy towards the *Wholly Other*. The reason why Epiphanius, in his final gesture, again turns towards the audience is precisely that he wants to integrate them into his encomium, with an exhortation to take part in a concluding prayer to the *you* that is the infinite Godhead itself, for whom Stephen was once a missionary to the Permians, and with whom he has now become reunited:

... i molju sprosta vsex' vas' ot mala i do velika, jako da sotvorite o mně mĺtvu kъ Bg̅u, jako da mĺtvami vašimi okon'čavaa slovo vozmogu rešči: slava

ti Gĩ sъtvorivšemu vsę; slava ti sъveršitelju Bḡu, slava davšemu naṁ Stefana,
i paky vzemšemu (111).[70]

[70] And now I simply ask all of you, great and small, to pray with me to God, so that I may
finish my account with your prayers, saying: glory to Thee, O Lord, who has created everything, glory to Thee, O God, who has accomplished everything, glory to Thee, who gave us
Stephen and took him back again.

PROBLEMS OF GLOSSALITY
IN NEWLY TRANSLATED PARTS OF
THE GENNADIUS AND OSTROG BIBLES
OF 1499 AND 1580-81

GERD FREIDHOF

Several years have passed since my earlier inquiry into problems of the
Church Slavic language of the Bible on East Slavic soil in the fifteenth
and sixteenth centuries,[1] and I would now like to return to this issue.
There have been no major relevant contributions in the meantime, apart
from E. Wimmer's study of the possible Latin sources of the Gennadius
manuscript.[2]

Though the data and examples are largely the same, this contribution has
a different aim: to describe the linguistic layers and differentiation of those
parts of the Church Slavic Bible that, owing to new translation, must be
considered texts of the fifteenth and sixteenth centuries. I seek to support
the thesis that already in the fifteenth century the largely normalized East
Slavic recension of Church Slavic had been destabilized, that is, that the
diglossic distribution in force on East Slavic soil for a number of centuries
had become unbalanced and indistinct.

This thesis necessitates a discussion of several problems: those of diglossia, of the so-called *literaturnyj jazyk,* and of codification in general. It is
particularly important to consider these in view of some interesting new
theses stated in recent times.[3] Especially useful in the Slavic context is C. A.

Translated from the German by Henrik Birnbaum.

[1] G. Freidhof, *Vergleichende sprachliche Studien zur Gennadius-Bibel (1499) und Ostroger
Bibel (1580/81). Die Bücher Paralipomenon, Esra, Tobias, Judith, Sapientia und Makkabäer,*
Frankfurter Abhandlungen zur Slavistik, no. 21 (Frankfurt am Main, 1972). Cf. also G.
Freidhof, "Zur ersten Übersetzung des 3. Buches der Makkabäer im Ostslavischen," *Slavistische
Studien zum VII. Internationalen Slavistenkongress in Warschau 1973* (Munich, 1973), 75-80.
[2] E. Wimmer, "Zu den katholischen Quellen der Gennadij-Bibel," in *Forschung und Lehre.
Festgruss Joh. Schröpfer 1974* (Hamburg, 1975), 444-458.
[3] I am thinking in particular of A. V. Issatschenko, "Vorgeschichte und Entstehung der
modernen russischen Literatursprache," *Zeitschrift für slavische Philologie 37* (1974): 235-274;
A. V. Issatschenko, *Mythen und Tatsachen über die Entstehung der russischen Literatursprache,*
Veröffentlichungen der Kommission für Linguistik und Kommunikationsforschung, no. 3

Ferguson's diglossia thesis;[4] modified by the results obtained by J. A. Fishman,[5] it will be utilized in this contribution.

It would not suffice to interpret the corpus in question solely in terms of the problems of diglossia, however, since elements from other languages can be ascertained in the texts. Therefore, in the title of this essay, I have used a term that, in my view, takes this into account: namely, *glossality*, which will be defined below.

A few preliminary remarks regarding the Gennadius and Ostrog Bibles (henceforth GB, OB, respectively) will do, since the basic facts are known to the reader. The GB (1499) was the first complete Bible in East Slavic territory. The original manuscript is currently housed in the Moscow Historical Museum (sign. Sin 915). There exist two copies of this manuscript, also kept in the Historical Museum (Sin 21 and Sin 30), one dated 1558 and the other from the sixteenth century (undated). The translation was made under the supervision of the monk and archdeacon Gerasim during the reign of Grand Prince Ivan Vasil'evič and the terms of office of Metropolitan Simon and Archbishop Gennadij at the archbishop's court in Novgorod.[6] Most of the biblical books are not translations in the narrow sense, but corrected reworkings of already existing manuscripts. Translated afresh from the Vulgate were the books of Chronicles (Paralipomenon in the Vulgate), Ezra, Tobias, Judith, Wisdom, and Maccabees I and II. In addition, the first ten chapters of the book of Esther were translated from the Hebrew. The translator from the Vulgate was in all likelihood the Dominican Benjamin, a Croat who had resided in Novgorod since 1491.[7]

The need to produce a complete manuscript of the Bible was twofold: first, the lack of any such text (some of the books of the Bible had never

---

(Vienna, 1975); review of ibid. by H. Birnbaum in *Russian Linguistics* 3 (1976): 167–180; A. V. Isačenko, "Kogda sformirovalsja russkij literaturnyj jazyk?" *Wiener Slavistisches Jahrbuch* 24 (1978): 124–136; F. P. Filin, "Ob istokax russkogo literaturnogo jazyka," *Voprosy jazykoznanija*, 1974, no. 3: 3–13; G. Xjutl'-Vort (Hüttl-Worth), "Spornye problemy izučenija literaturnogo jazyka v drevnerusskij period," *Wiener Slavistisches Jahrbuch* 18 (1973): 29–47; G. Xjutl'-Folter (Hüttl-Folter), "Diglossija v Drevnej Rusi," *Wiener Slavistisches Jahrbuch* 24 (1978): 108–123; D. S. Worth, "On 'Diglossia' in Medieval Russian," *Die Welt der Slaven* 23 (1978): 371–393.

    [4] See in particular Xjutl'-Folter and Worth, where C. A. Ferguson's approach ("Diglossia," *Word* 15 [1959]: 325–340) is critically applied.

    [5] J. A. Fishman, *Sociolinguistics: A Brief Introduction* (Rowley, Mass., 1970), esp. 73ff. Cf. also N. Dittman, *Soziolinguistik. Exemplarische und kritische Darstellung ihrer Theorie, Empirie und Anwendung. Mit kommentierter Bibliographie* (Frankfurt am Main, 1973).

    [6] Cf. Freidhof, *Gennadius-Bibel und Ostroger Bibel* (see n. 1), 12.

    [7] Ibid.

been translated or were no longer known from copies), and second, the confrontation of Orthodoxy with the heresy of the Judaizers, who had access to all the biblical books.

The OB was the first printing of the entire Bible on East Slavic soil. The edition was commissioned by Prince Konstantin Konstantinovič of Ostrog (Ostrih); the printing itself was done by the well-known Moscow printer Ivan Fedorov.[8] Two different final leaves in the preserved copies suggest that there may have been two editions, one of 1580, the other of 1581. The reasons for the new translation and printing can be found in the confrontation between Orthodoxy, Catholicism, and Protestantism, as well as certain heretical movements (Socianists, Antitrinitarians).[9] Ostrog was particularly suited for such an enterprise; its language college (also known as the "Greek-Slavic school") and the circle of scholars at the court of Prince Konstantin included several persons competent for this task. The translation was preceded by a process of collecting manuscripts, including a lost copy of the Gennadius Bible. The text was collated against the Septuagint, from which some books (Esther, Song of Songs, Maccabees III) were translated anew.[10]

Church Slavic was chosen as the language for the OB, even though texts in Belorussian and Ukrainian already existed—for example, the translations of Skaryna (Prague, 1517ff.) and the *Peresopnycja Gospel* (1556–1561). This was because Church Slavic was the traditional language of the Bible and the OB itself served the purpose of a pan-Orthodox universalism. Another reason for this choice of language may have been that no printer knowledgeable in the vernacular was available; the Moscow printer Fedorov had only an incomplete mastery of the popular speech.[11]

We now turn to the problem of definition posed by the title of this contribution—the notion of *glossality*. I am proceeding from the observation that texts that operate on a uniform linguistic level are not the rule. Instead, many texts display internal differentiation. This particularly holds true of texts containing belles-lettres.

I subsume under *internal differentiation* the entire spectrum of diastratic, diatopic, and functional-stylistic variants of a language. It is essential here that we deal with variants of one and the same language, the use of which is determined by the social marking of individuals and situations, by the

---

[8] Ibid., 19.
[9] Ibid., 20.
[10] For further data, see ibid., "Einführung."
[11] Cf. M. Voznjak, *Stare ukrajins'ke pys'menstvo* (Lvov, 1922), 220.

language's spatial, dialectal distribution, and, in the final analysis, by the communicative function of a specific text.[12] Internal differentiation has been called the "architecture" of a language, to be distinguished from its structure. E. Coseriu has this to say: "Within such an architecture, one cannot speak of oppositions, but merely of differences found at various levels. By contrast, the structure of a language refers to oppositions, i.e., direct differences among members of one and the same system or one and the same technique."[13]

In addition to the levels of internal differentiation, elements from other languages can enter a text, such as, for example, Latin, German, or French influences (grammatical or lexical) in a Slavic text. I refer to this phenomenon, which complements internal differentiation, as *external differentiation* of a text.

Both internal and external differentiation deal with levels of linguistic expression of communicative entities. The use of these levels is, as a rule, functionally determined, but this does not necessarily apply to older texts. For the totality of all levels of differentiation observable in one text, I use the term *glossality*. It is always applicable to all texts, regardless of the evolutionary stage of the language or the text itself. However, difficulties occasionally arise when it comes to distinguishing internal from external differentiation. Relevant are differences of opinion among scholars as to whether a linguistic entity X in a language Y belongs to the same language, a closely related language, or merely a dialect of Y. Admittedly, it is increasingly difficult to answer this question for older texts the more they antedate any attempts at codification.[14]

The distinction between internal and external differentiation calls for additional commentary when it comes to East Slavic, owing to the relationship of Church Slavic to various East Slavic languages (functioning as *linguae vernaculae*). Beyond doubt, there is and has always been a difference in rank between Church Slavic—a language artificially patterned on the model of Greek—and the respective vernaculars (Russian, Belorussian, Ukrainian). In this regard, I fully concur with A. V. Issatschenko, whose line of reasoning is quite convincing indeed.[15]

---

[12] In functional-stylistic marking, it is in particular the functions of message (*soobščenie*), social intercourse (*obščenie*), and influence (*vozdejstvie*) that are important. Cf. also V. V. Vinogradov, *Stilistika. Teorija poètičeskoj reči. Poètika* (Moscow, 1963), 5–6. These basic functions remain valid even though modern text and genre linguistics have now devised much more sophisticated criteria of differentiation.

[13] E. Coseriu, *Probleme der strukturellen Semantik* (Tübingen, 1973), 40.

[14] This is with reference to codification as written-grammatical standardization, which is distinct from written-traditional standardization; cf. below.

[15] Cf. Issatschenko, *Mythen und Tatsachen* (see n. 3), 29ff. This opinion had been expressed previously, e.g., by I. S. Uluxanov, *O jazyke drevnej Rusi* (Moscow, 1972), 22.

But does it follow that one of the two languages must belong to internal, the other to external, differentiation? There is no reason to assume any such automatic distribution. Since both languages function as variants (in the sense of Ferguson's diglossia), either one can theoretically display internal differentiation. Peripheral phenomena of the diglossic variant, to the extent that they can be ascertained, are to be considered external differentiation. However, where texts show a synthesis of Church Slavic and Russian traits—a marking that became characteristic of the later Russian standard language—I consider both variants part of internal differentiation. Synthesis does not necessarily mean (quantitative) equilibrium of both variants; one is usually dominant, but the other is so pronounced that it can no longer be considered peripheral in the sense of the Prague School.

The interpretation of the glossality levels of the GB and OB, as well as the inferences for the problems of diglossia, the *literaturnyj jazyk,* and codification, will be preceded here by a description of the various levels of internal and external differentiation in the GB.

The following levels of internal differentiation can be ascertained in the GB: (1) the Church Slavic level; and (b) the Russian level. These are supplemented by levels of external differentiation, which we can also call alien levels: (c) the Serbo-Croatian level; (d) the Czech level; and (e) the Latin level.

Judging from the quantitative distribution, Church Slavic—that is, the form of Church Slavic known on East Slavic soil after the impact of the Second South Slavic Influence—forms the dominant level of internal differentiation in the GB, as shown in my study of 1972. After a considerable delay, this form of Church Slavic was codified in detail for the first time— in Adelphotes (1591), Zizanij (1596), and Smotryc'kyj (1619).[16]

The dominance of Church Slavic is not surprising, even though we are dealing here with new translations from the end of the fifteenth century. Indeed it is merely a modification of the East Slavic tradition that religious texts be written and recited in Church Slavic, the sacred language. This habit was to continue for several centuries—the first translation of the Gospels into Russian did not occur until 1819!

[16] Adelphotes, *Die erste gedruckte griechisch-kirchenslavische Grammatik* (Lvov-Lemberg, 1591; reprint, ed. O. Horbatsch, Specimina philologiae Slavicae, no. 2 [Frankfurt am Main, 1973]); L. Zizanij, *Hrammatika Slovenska* (Vilnius-Wilna, 1596; reprint, ed. G. Freidhof, Specimina philologiae Slavicae, no. 1 [Frankfurt am Main, 1972]); M. Smotryc'kyj, *Hramatiki slavenskija pravilnoe syntagma* (Evje, 1619; reprint, ed. O. Horbatsch, Specimina philologiae Slavicae, no. 4 [Frankfurt am Main, 1974]).

It is therefore interesting to describe not this dominant Church Slavic
level, but those deviations from it that do not agree with the traditional
standards and characteristics of religious texts. With regard to internal differentiation, this means the inclusion of numerous elements of the Russian
lingua vernacula on all levels of grammar (phonology, morphology, syntax)
and lexicon. It is significant that these Russian elements are not limited to a
few isolated instances, attributable to scribal error. This testifies to the fact
that the knowledge of Church Slavic among the Orthodox clergy was no
longer as active as it had been (although passive knowledge of it may have
remained unchanged). I can see three reasons for this:

(1) The influence of the vernacular increasingly extended into spheres
that previously were strictly subject to the diglossic distribution.

(2) In connection with its controversy with the heretics, the clergy felt
obliged to move toward a language accessible to a broader range of believers (and, in particular, toward a simplified syntax). In my view, this trend is
not counter to the absolute requirement of rendering the biblical truth precisely and faithfully. However, it can be taken as an indication of a change
in the practices of biblical translation.

(3) The linguistic affinity between Church Slavic and the *lingua vernacula*
became less and less evident as Russian continued to evolve. The Second
South Slavic Influence must have further enhanced this trend. Consequently, obsolete grammatical phenomena and lexemes had to be replaced
by other, now Russian ones for the sake of improved comprehension. I
propose that this be considered an internal innovation of the East Slavic
sacred language in Russia.

In what follows, I would like to sketch the impact of Russian on the
language of the GB, using some examples. The page numbers (here and
below) refer to my study of 1972, where the references to the folia of the
GB are also listed.

In the phonology of the GB, a Russian influence is evident in the shift of
[e] to [o] (*pošolъ, žonъ, pěvcovъ, starcovъ, dalečo* 75) and in the confusion of
/ě/ with /i/ (*na stině, vъsmotrixъ* 75) and with /e/ (*vesi, umreti* 76).[17] The
impact of Russian becomes particularly apparent in the confusion of /a/
with /e/ and /o/ in unstressed position (*se estъ tlъkovania ego – haec est
interpretatio eius; tvorenia ... razžagaetъ – creatura ... exardescit; veličestva
– maiestas* 77).These confusions are the traces of phonemic mergers in post-

---

[17] Incidentally, the realization of /e/ instead of /ě/ entered Church Slavic pronunciation
only later; cf. B. A. Uspenskij, *Arxaičeskaja sistema cerkovnoslavjanskogo proiznošenija*
(Moscow, 1968), 29ff.

tonic syllables. I do not think, however, that they can be explained entirely as manifestations of early *akan'e*; yet, there can be no doubt that they are due to influence from the spoken language.

In the morphology of the GB, the influence of Russian is clearly exhibited in several categories.[18] These categories can be summarized as follows:

(1) Analogical levelings among the old stem classes, old *o*- and *u*-stems in particular, as well as *i*- and *jo*-stems; loss of the old consonantal stem endings, and the like. These phenomena are not characteristic specifically of the GB; rather, they are general tendencies in the dynamics of Russian Church Slavic. This can be easily seen by comparing the paradigms in the grammars of Adelphotes, Zizanij, and Smotryckyj.

(2) Partial loss of the vocative and its replacement by the nominative.

(3) Restriction of the dual in nominal paradigms. Here, the Latin original was definitely crucial.

(4) Generalization of gender in the nominative and accusative of adjectives.

(5) A preference in the verb for the forms of the perfect and a concomitant reduction in the number of aorist and imperfect forms. Incertitude concerning the correct use of the aorist can be seen in incorrect formations of the type: *vnidoša sutь gradu*; *vьzpiša sutь*; *radovaxomsja esmy* (109).

(6) Formation of the analytical future by means of the copula *budu*.

(7) A decrease in the frequency of dual verb forms and their replacement by those of the plural. Here, too, the Latin original had a supportive influence. The loss of the dual is by no means consistent with what is recorded in the aforementioned Church Slavic grammars.

(8) A tendency to generalize active participles (in *-šči* and *-ši*), which corresponds to the crystallization of gerunds in Russian.

The influence of spoken Russian is also readily discernible in the syntax of the GB. Here, in particular, we note the use of the predicative instrumental (128), a lack of agreement of the predicate with collective animate subjects (130), and the replacement of complex syntactic constructions involving participles (especially when translating an original Latin ablative absolute).[19] One of many examples is *i tě iže sь Ezdrimь běxu dolžee branjaščisja i utruženi / vьzva iuda g()a pomoščnika i voevodu brani byti – at illis, qui cum Esdrin erant, diutius pugnantibus et fatigatis, invocavit Iudas Dominum adiutorem et ducem belli fieri* (142).

---

[18] Cf. Freidhof, *Gennadius-Bibel und Ostroger Bibel* (see n. 1), 82ff.

[19] In principle, however, constructions with the dative absolute are also attested; cf. ibid., 138.

The Russian impact on the vocabulary of the GB has already been ascertained by A. Gorskij and K. Nevostruev, as well as by A. I. Sobolevskij.[20] I have added to their list a large number of further examples. Among the typical lexical Russisms are *kromъ – arx; posadъ – urbs; tetradь – volumen; tamožnikъ – portitor; kremlь – castrum; denьgi – pecunia; ploščadь – area; kostъrъ – turris; semьja – familia; penja – poena; dokuka – vexatio, taedium; dokučiti – fastidire; djadja – patruus; njatecь – mancipium; oblomokъ – fragmentum; krěpostь – arx; talь – obses; kuny – pecunia; toptati – trepidare; kirpičь – later; rubežь – finis; ozimica – hordeum; bakanъ – fucus, stibinus; zakromъ – horreum; tiski – torcularia; parъ – vapor;* and others. It is only of secondary importance that not all of these Russisms are characteristic of the entire Russian language area. Russisms with only limited distribution must also be considered here (cf. the lexeme *kostъrъ*, probably going back to Middle Greek *kastron* or Latin *castrum*, which was limited to the Novgorod-Pskov region). It is not productive to separate out dialectal phenomena within internal differentiation, as long as no attempts at codifying a language—in the sense of establishing a *literaturnyj jazyk*—have been undertaken, or no significant unification of the language in terms of its written-traditional standardization can be observed.

To sum up, a major Russian influence can be seen in the framework of the internal differrentiation of the GB. This influence is considerably greater in biblical texts conceived as genuinely new translations than in those conceived merely as copies to be made for the purpose of correction and language reform. Such also applies to most of the books in the GB, which were compiled according to the latter principle.

The internal differentiation of the GB is matched by an equally interesting external differentiation. Its pronounced character is due to the Latin original and to the translator and his possible use of other existing texts and knowledge of other Slavic languages. In my opinion, it has been proven that a Croat (probably Benjamin) translated the Latin text, utilizing not only his own language but also his knowledge of Czech. He may have used relevant texts in these languages as well. This does not, however, exclude the possibility that additional translators may have been involved, especially considering the Russian component of the manuscript's internal differentiation.

[20] A. Gorskij and K. Nevostruev, *Opisanie slavjanskix rukopisej Moskovskoj Sinodaľnoj biblioteki,* sec. 1: *Svjaščennoe Pisanie* (Moscow, 1855; reprint, ed. R. Aitzetmüller et al., Monumenta linguae Slavicae dialecti veteris. Fontes et dissertationes, vol. 2 [Wiesbaden, 1964]), 1–164, esp. 50, 51, 78, 79, 127; A. I. Sobolevskij, *Perevodnaja literatura Moskovskoj Rusi XIV–XVII vekov* (St. Petersburg, 1903), 256.

Serbo-Croatian—the native tongue of the translator—forms the first level of the external differentiation of the GB. Serbo-Croatian influences can be clearly shown in the areas of morphology and lexicography.

In morphology, we note, in particular, the formation of the first person singular in *mъ* (*sъtvorimъ - faciam*; *piemъ - bibam*; *učtemъ - recenserem*; *blagoslovimъ - benedico* 104), imperfects without morphophonemic alternation (*mogaxu, prixodjaxu, mogaše, xodjaše, izvodjaxu, trudjaxu* 108),[21] and the analytic formation of the negative imperative using *ne mozi* (*ne mozi otъvratiti - noli avertere*; *ne mozi sъmněnia nositi - noli dubium gerere*; *ne mozite byti - nolite esse* 119). With respect to this last phenomenon, the influence of Latin was crucial.

I see Serbo-Croatian influence also in the noun, especially in the confusion of the genitive and locative plural, which was characteristic of earlier Serbian and Croatian texts (*vsi versi goraxъ - omnes vertices montium*; *vъsxody goraxъ - ascensus montium*; *vъ sredi vodaxъ - in medio aquarum* 94). This influence is also likely in the plural of masculine and neuter stems (*domoxъ, ugloxъ, jazykoxъ* 86; *seloxъ, kolenoxъ, vratoxъ* 92). Such endings, however, also occur in other texts throughout all of Slavic territory. Yet, the frequency of such examples supports my suggestion that there was indeed Serbo-Croatian influence in the GB.

The influence of Serbo-Croatian on the vocabulary of the GB has been demonstrated already by Sobolevskij (e.g., *kovačь - faber*; *staja - stabulum*; *nastojati - urgere*; *kraty - vices; polkъ - populus*; *nastavljati - imponere*).[22] Elaborating on his data, I see Serbo-Croatian influence also in the differentiation of *prijatelь - amicus* and *drugъ - socius* and its derivatives, as well as in the lexemes *stanovitъ - securus, obitelь - familia, roženie - natio, rasmotriti* (in the meaning of *disponere*), *ušnica - inauris,* and, possibly, also in *tverdynja - arx, munitio* (146–147).

Czech forms the second level of external differentiation. Thus, I concur with Sobolevskij in his assumption that the Croat Benjamin, before becoming active in Novgorod, had spent some time in the Emaus Monastery (founded in 1347 in Prague by Emperor Charles IV), where Glagolitic writing was common. I shall try to demonstrate this Czech level by noting various phenomena which, however, because of their low frequency, suggest only a peripheral impact.

---

[21] I see no influence here from Middle Bulgarian, even though such forms are attested in Middle Bulgarian texts. Rather, this phenomenon can be seen as part of the Serbo-Croatian influences.

[22] Sobolevskij, *Perevodnaja literatura Moskovskoj Rusi* (see n. 20), 207.

In the morphology of the GB, there are three instances where the dative plural of masculine stems ends in -*umъ* (*filistimumъ* [twice], *kamenarumъ* 84). In fifteenth-century Czech, the monophthongization of /uo/ to /u:/ had already been completed for the most part, even if the orthography of texts from that period still suggests a diphthong.[23]

Another Czech influence is the confusion of the accusative and instrumental singular in some *a*-stem nouns, a phenomenon not explicable in syntactic terms (*edinu ruku svoju tvorjaxu dělo i drugoju deržaxu mečь – una manu sua faciebat opus et altera tenebat gladium* 95). Since such confusion occurs in four places, simple misspelling cannot be assumed. However, owing to the contraction of the instrumental singular ending in *a*-stems from /oju/ to /u:/, the instrumental (-*ú*) and accusative (-*u*) singular endings were differentiated only by quantity, even though the diphthongization of /u:/ to /ou/ had already been completed in many Czech dialects.

I believe that there are two additional morphological and syntactic phenomena that testify to the Czech impact in the language of the GB. The first of these is the frequent use of verb forms of the type *vnidenъ estъ* (*budu, běxъ, byxъ*), unknown to East Slavic, which earlier I explained (116) exclusively on the basis of the Latin text (here we always have deponents of the type *ingressus est*). I now believe, however, that we are dealing here with a secondary Czech influence, since earlier Czech texts also exhibit such formations (probably as calques). They were, however, rejected as inadmissible formations in the first printed Czech grammar of 1533.[24] Nevertheless, a comparison of the biblical texts of 1488 and 1489 shows that these forms did not originate from those texts. In my opinion, this suggests that Benjamin must have been well acquainted with earlier Czech texts, since it cannot be assumed that such forms were usual in the spoken Czech of the period.

Second, I consider the frequent use of genitive absolutes in the GB to be the result of Czech influences.[25] Considering the Latin original, these constructions could not be of Greek origin (cf., for example, *těxъ posmějuščixsja i porugajuščixsja imъ – illis irridentibus et subsannantibus eos* 138). Genitive, as well as dative and instrumental, absolutes are attested in Old Czech texts. The genitive construction, however, shows up primarily in translated texts (most often Gospels).[26]

[23] This is also true of the two Czech Bible prints of 1488 (Prague) and 1489 (Kutná Hora).

[24] B. Optát, P. Gzel, and V. Philomates, *Grammatyka Česká (Die Ausgaben von 1533 und 1588)*, ed. G. Freidhof, Specimina philologiae Slavicae, no. 7 (Frankfurt am Main, 1974), pt. 1, 64a.

[25] Cf. Freidhof, *Gennadius-Bibel und Ostroger Bibel* (see n. 1), 138.

[26] Cf. A. Lamprecht, D. Šlosar, and J. Bauer, *Historický vývoj češtiny* (Prague, 1977), 257.

This influence, too, can be explained only by Benjamin's knowledge of earlier Czech biblical texts, since nothing comparable can be found in colloquial Old Czech. Nor can such constructions be found in the biblical texts of 1488 and 1489 (at least in those parallel passages where the GB uses constructions of this kind). The passage from Chronicles 30:10, quoted earlier, is identical in both Czech printed versions of the Bible: *A oni pak posmiewali se gim a ruhali.*

It is difficult to prove the influence of Czech in the vocabulary of the GB. In all probability, however, the following items are examples of such influence: *kamenarъ, apotekarъ, spica – acies; uživati/užiti – uti; vyšegradъ – arx*[27] (148–150).

To sum up, the phenomena enumerated above clearly show the Czech influence on the language of the GB. Yet, it is equally important to note that this influence is not evident in the earlier biblical texts of 1488 and 1489.

Let us now turn to the third level of external differentiation—the Latinisms of the GB. The Latin influence is crucial to the GB's external differentiation even though it is limited to syntax, the grammatical categories of the verb, and the lexicon (including word formation). Given the typological distance between input and output languages, no impact in phonology and morphology (i.e., inflectional morphology) could be expected. I must limit myself here, however, to a few essential phenomena that clearly demonstrate this influence.

It is typical that the word order of the Latin original is largely retained, in particular, the placement of the verb at the end of the sentence (*myž na vsemoguščago boga iže možetъ i grjaduščixъ na nasъ i vsego světa edinymъ izvoleniemъ gladiti naděemsja – nos autem in omnipotente Domino, qui potest et venientes adversum nos et universum mundum uno nudo delere, confidimus* 141), the pre-position of the possessive genitive (*pokajanija město – paenitentiae locus* 137), and the separation of syntactically close units, that is, of so-called discontinuous constituents (*i mnogixъ prosi ženъ – et multas petivit uxores; žestoky telesnya poterplju bolězni – duros corporis sustineo dolores* 137).

Because of their frequency in the GB, other phenomena of the Church Slavic level must also be attributed to the Latin influence of the protograph.

---

[27] It is impossible to make an unequivocal determination here. *Uživati/užiti* as well as *vyšegradъ* can also reflect the translator's native Serbo-Croatian; *spica* and *apotekarъ* can be explained as Polonisms. This language must be considered a possibility in view of the fact that Benjamin's route from Prague to Novgorod may have taken him through Cracow; cf. Sobolevskij, *Perevodnaja literatura Moskovskoj Rusi* (see n. 20), 256–258.

This applies, for example, to the accusative with the infinitive (*mnjatъ igru byti životъ – aestimaverunt lusum esse vitam* 133) and the rendering of the Latin ablative absolute by an analogous Slavic construction.

The Latin influence is also evident in the grammatical category of tense. Here one can frequently find a one-to-one correspondence in the use of the pluperfect, the analytic forms of the future, the imperfect, and the periphrastic tenses by means of a participle (*bystъ ... sъbirajušči – erat ... congregans; byša drъžašče – fuerant servantes* 115).

This influence is particularly obvious when Latin deponents are rendered: the rendering is either totally incorrect, or it can, at least in part, be explained by the influence of Czech (see above). Here we can quote such examples as *vnidoša sutъ gradu – ingressi sunt civitatem* (109); *vъzpiša sutъ – vociferati sunt* (109); *vnidenъ budu – ingressus fuero* (116); *obraščeni budete – reversi fueritis* (116). The loss of the dual in the verb in many instances may also be attributable to Latin influence, since this phenomenon is atypical for Church Slavic texts of that period.[28]

In the vocabulary of the GB, the Latin influence can be seen in the use of foreign words and in word formation (lexical calques). Among the many foreign words are the following: *avra – abra; gusterna – cisterna; kanselarъ – cansellarius; kirografъ – chirographus; legatъ – legatus; lira – lyra; prepozitъ – praepositus; senofenija – scenopegia; tribunъ – tribunus; triumfati – triumphare; fibula – fibula.*[29] Of the calques, we note *korabljati – navigare; obraščenie – volumen; pervěnšoe – primitia; izbratelnica – electrix; sъpreselenie – commigratio; zemletjažanie – agricultura; vodovozъ – aquaeductus; umodělatelъ – artifex; braninosecъ – belligerator; zlatokuznecъ – aurifex; poletjažatelъ – agricola.*[30] In addition, whole verbal phrases are carried over as loan translations: *složiti mirъ – componere pacem; složiti ženu – coniungere uxorem; sъmněnie nositi – dubium gerere; izbiti mirъ – percutere foedus; gněvъ nositi – igram gerere; životъ nositi – vitam gerere.*[31]

The Latin influence is particularly noticeable wherever passages are not translated, but rather are quoted directly (barbarisms).[32] Such quotations either lack any explanation at all (*senosъ – senos; doktoresъ – doctores; bazimъ – basim*) or they are translated for the reader in marginal glosses (*kastra – castra*, marginal gloss: *ostrogy; tribulasъ – tribulas*, marginal gloss: *katky čimъ zemlju mjagčatъ; ratesъ – rates*, marginal gloss: *ploty*).

---

[28] Concerning this, cf. relevant remarks in the Church Slavic grammars by Adelphotes, Zizanij, and Smotryc'kyj (see n. 16).

[29] Cf. Freidhof, *Gennadius-Bibel und Ostroger Bibel* (see n. 1), 154ff.

[30] Ibid., 160ff.

[31] Ibid., 162.

[32] Ibid., 46ff.

In the preceding discussion, I have shown that the text of the GB is marked by extensive internal and external differentiation. In this respect, one can see a certain parallel with belletristic texts. They, too, utilize, in addition to the *literaturnyj jazyk*, elements of the dialectal and sociolectal levels, on the one hand, and language-external influences, on the other.[33] Yet, this apparent formal agreement between parts of the GB and certain literary texts must be qualified in terms of a major difference: the internal and external differentiation of the GB does not produce a differentiation of the basic functional role (*vozdejstvie, soobščenie, obščenie*), as is the case, of course, with such texts as Hašek's *Švejk*.[34] Regarding the external differentiation of the GB, however, there are parallels with scientific texts as well, since they frequently show foreign influence without modification of the communicative function of the text.

At this point I am, in fact, embarking on a discussion of the problems of the *literaturnyj jazyk*, codification, and diglossia. To begin with, I shall approach the problem by developing a model which will then be applied to the specific question at hand.

Languages in developed and developing societies are, by nature, potentially mixed, characterized by both internal and external differentiation. This is a direct consequence of the historical evolution of language—social and geographic stratification, on the one hand, and linguistic contacts and cultural differences, on the other.[35]

As a result of the summation of all determining factors—particularly psycholinguistic ones, in addition to those listed under (1) below—each individual within society speaks a truly "other language" (idiolect). Communication must therefore be regulated by a standardization process if it is to be kept free of interference. I subdivide this standardization process as follows:

(1) The period of *oral-traditional standardization.* In this period, no written language has as yet been developed. Small groups (clans or tribes, for

---

[33] An excellent example of this is J. Hašek's *Osudy dobrého vojáka Švejka* (Prague, 1921–1923), which exhibits considerable internal as well as external differentiation (*spisovná čeština, hovorová čeština, obecná čeština*, vulgarisms, and dialectisms, on the one hand, and many Germanisms, some Russisms, as well as many quoted sentences from various languages, mostly German, on the other).

[34] See n. 33.

[35] The notion of cultural differences does not imply a value judgment. What I have in mind is the totality of all referents which are of different relevance in two societies, and thus, which also exhibit a different degree of linguistic development. When a language X adjusts to a language Y in terms of the relevance of its referents, this is usually accompanied by external differentiation from Y.

example) influence one another only with respect to the use of their respective idiolects.

(2) The period of *written-traditional standardization*. In this period, the written language exerts a normative influence on the idiolects. The force of the factor setting the norm is proportional to the number of texts. In this way, linguistic phenomena are stabilized and extended. Texts have a stabilizing influence over larger territories (in East Slavic, for example, the areas of Kiev, Novgorod-Pskov, or Moscow, and even extending beyond them).

(3) The period of *written-grammatical standardization*. In this period, language is standardized, codified.[36] The use of language is prescribed, at least in the written domain. Such standardization covers the widest area possible. The more the codified standardization is promoted and controlled, the less leeway there is for the use of variants.[37]

A language created by such codification can be based on one dialect (largely neglecting the characteristics of the other dialects), on the characteristic features of several dialects, thereby unifying them, or an earlier stages of linguistic evolution (Greek, Arabic). In addition, influences from foreign languages must be taken into account (e.g., the Church Slavic element in Russian).

In accordance with Issatschenko,[38] I define the notion of *literaturnyj jazyk* using the combined characteristics of polyvalence, orthographic, grammatical, and lexical standardization, its obligatory use by all members of a given society or nation, and stylistic differentiation.

Supplementing Issatschenko, I would assign clearly higher priority to polyvalence than to the degree of standardization. For I proceed from the assumption that, theoretically, the *literaturnyj jazyk* can also have existed prior to written-grammatical standardization (codification); that is, it can exist whenever some variation (in terms of genres) of writing (*pis'mennost'*) occurs at a time when the language has attained a considerable degree of unification. Using this abstract modeling procedure, I distinguish different levels or forms of the *literaturnyj jazyk*:

(1) The *literaturnyj jazyk* with written-traditional standardization;

(2) the *literaturnyj jazyk* with written-grammatical standardization, without yet having the characteristics of a national standard language; and

---

[36] In the initial stage of the codifying standardization, the qualitative difference in relation to written-traditional standardization can be quite insignificant with regard to individual phenomena as a result of using admissible variants of the written tradition.

[37] In this context, extralinguistic factors are of crucial importance (the birth of a nation with its own national language, language and cultural policies, etc.).

[38] Issatschenko, *Mythen und Tatsachen* (see n. 3), 5.

(3) the *literaturnyj jazyk* with written-grammatical standardization and displaying the characteristics of a national standard language.

The history and evolution of numerous societies suggests that the characteristic of polyvalence in a given *literaturnyj jazyk* is the result of a lengthy process, in the course of which the intrasocial opposition between cultural language (primarily in the area of religion) and ordinary language (*lingua vernacula*) becomes a common language with stylistic differentiation. Following the lead of previous relevant discussions (Ferguson, Hüttl-Folter, Worth), I am using the notion of diglossia. Depending on the specifics of the components participating in it, such diglossia can be realized in quite different ways:

(1) The participating components may belong to different language groups (cf. Latin in Central Europe, e.g., in France, Germany, Poland);

(2) the participating components may belong to one and the same language group (e.g., Church Slavic on East Slavic territory); or

(3) the participating components may belong to one and the same language, with the archaic type being used as cultural language.

It follows that diglossia can be realized in a variety of feature combinations: it can have bilingual (1, 2) or monolingual (3) direction.[39]

The question arises whether the condition of diglossia (which, by definition, does not permit the polyvalence of one of the two components) in itself precludes the possibility of a *literaturnyj jazyk*. In other words, it is possible to interpret one of the two components (variants) of diglossia—or both of them together—as a *literaturnyj jazyk*?[40] Moreover, can it be inferred that the existence of a particular literature at a given time presupposes the existence of a *literaturnyj jazyk* as well?

Issatschenko is correct, I would suggest, in assuming that the existence of a literature (here, Old Russian literature) does not automatically imply the existence of a corresponding *literaturnyj jazyk*.[41] To put it more succinctly: *Diglossia, negatively marked for the polyvalence of both its components, precludes the existence of a literaturnyj jazyk*. To assign the term *literaturnyj jazyk* to the two combined components would be a contradiction in terms, since the duplicity of grammatical and lexical systems could not be brought into agreement with the notion of standardization.

---

[39] I follow Fishman's definition of the term *bilingual* (*Sociolinguistics* [see n. 5], 73ff.), while, at the same time, using it in a somewhat special way. It should further be noted that the concept of diglossia can also imply the presence of more than just two linguistic entities; cf. Fishman, *Sociolinguistics,* 33.

[40] Issatschenko, "Vorgeschichte" (see n. 3), 238ff., rightly rejects Vinogradov's thesis of the presence of two "language types" within one unified "Old Russian" literary language.

[41] Issatschenko, *Mythen und Tatsachen* (see n. 3), 20.

I shall attempt to apply my conceptual framework to the language of the GB for the purpose of assessing its place in the categorial system. The predominant Church Slavic language in the newly translated portions exhibits the characteristic of written-traditional standardization, whereas an extensive written-grammatical standardization cannot yet be ascertained. This latter phenomenon begins only later, with Adelphotes and Zizanij.

In a way, however, it is possible to speak of a transitional stage, since we know of predecessors of written-grammatical standardization. Yet, the pressure for standardization here is not sufficient; earlier handwritten grammatical treatises on the eight parts of speech are still not sufficiently extensive and, moreover, are too faulty in their grammaticalness to satisfy this criterion fully. Also, the prerequisite of being a national standard language does not apply to Church Slavic.

The situation is even less favorable when considering Russian texts from the end of the fifteenth century. Here, we know of no attempts at grammatical standardization; such are recorded only from a considerably later period. The texts themselves (primarily *gramoty,* but also, for example, the *Zadonščina* from the beginning of the fifteenth century, or Afanasij Nikitin's *Xoženie za tri morja*) exhibit many conspicuous local differences in their written-traditional standardization. No stabilizing effect that would indicate an emerging *literaturnyj jazyk* can as yet be discerned.

This state of affairs suggests that the conditions of polyvalence and standardization are not fully met either by Church Slavic or by Russian. Toward the end of the fifteenth century, neither a Church Slavic nor a Russian *literaturnyj jazyk* was in existence. This definition does not preclude, however, that the two components participating in diglossia together fulfill the function of polyvalence; even a textual genre can be marked by various combinations of Church Slavic and Russian.

Also, since the criteria of general, obligatory use, and stylistic differentiation do not yet apply in the fifteenth century, it can be said that the GB is negatively marked with regard to all characteristics applicable to the *literaturnyj jazyk.* Only when it comes to the standardization of the predominant Church Slavic component of the GB can we speak of a rudimentary transition to positive marking.

It would nonetheless be incorrect to underestimate the significance of the language of the GB (in its newly translated portions) for the evolution and crystallization of the Russian *literaturnyj jazyk.* After all, the formation of a *literaturnyj jazyk* is not the result of merely a few decades of development. I would propose, therefore, that the newly translated portions of the GB constitute an essential step toward the *literaturnyj jazyk,* even though they remain an isolated phenomenon for a long time to come. Their significance lies in the fact that a juxtaposition of Church Slavic and Russian (albeit in different quantities) has occurred in a genre normally reserved for Church Slavic only.

I consider this situation a Russification of Church Slavic, without, however, adopting B. O. Unbegaun's thesis that the entire Russian *literaturnyj jazyk* is merely the result of a gradual Russification of Church Slavic.[42] Rather, I am of the opinion that the Russian *literaturnyj jazyk* of a later date cannot be explained as anything but a synthesis, whatever its nature, of Church Slavic and Russian. In the final analysis, we are dealing here with a synthesis of syntheses; this can be observed to various degrees, depending on the particular genre: (1) Russification of Church Slavic texts; (2) Slavonization of Russian texts; (3) purely Russian texts (folk poetry, *gramoty*); or (4) purely Church Slavic texts (of traditional religious content).

Thus, it appears futile to characterize Lomonosov's stance in his *Rossijskaja grammatika* as that of either Russian with Church Slavic elements or of Church Slavic, increasingly Russified over the centuries. The end result is the same: the major share of this grammar points clearly toward the vernacular.

In my opinion, the portion of the GB in question is a text of the greatest importance for that evolution—it is a milestone that overcomes and eliminates the former diglossic distribution.[43] This is so much more the case, since the Russian share of the text is not marked stylistically to set it off against the main body of the text. In other words, we are dealing here with nearly the same state of affairs that exists in contemporary Russian: Church Slavic forms and lexemes are being used functionally and stylistically on an equal footing with those of Russian; the only difference is that today the respective usage follows a semantic complementary distribution.[44]

It should be pointed out once again that, in my opinion, no Church Slavic *literaturnyj jazyk* existed in the sense defined. This is true even when

---

[42] Cf. B. O. Unbegaun, "Le russe littéraire est-il d'origine russe?" *Revue des études slaves* 44 (1965): 19–28; id., "Jazyk russkoj literatury i problemy ego razvitija," *Revue des études slaves* 47 (1968): 129–134; id., "Proisxoždenie russkogo literaturnogo jazyka," *Novyj žurnal* 100 (1970): 306–319.

[43] Whereas, up to the early eighteenth century, Church Slavic could still be considered a language of culture, it functions today only as a language of cult (sacred language); cf. J. Plähn, *Der Gebrauch des Modernen Russischen Kirchenslavisch in der Russischen Kirche* (Hamburg, 1978).

[44] This does not, of course, preclude the stylistic utilization of this difference in the sphere of belles-lettres.

the criterion of standardization is applied less rigorously. I am basing my
assessment on the canon of extant genres, which can be assumed to reflect
the situation of Early Russian literature; the full spectrum of that literature
could not be realized by Church Slavic alone (cf. the *gramoty*). Thus, contrary to Issatschenko, I project the genre canon of present-day Russian
onto the older period (to the extent that the particular genres existed then)
and consider this a fundamental prerequisite for defining the notion of *literaturnyj jazyk*.[45] In this respect, therefore, I concur with Filin's concept,[46]
although I arrive at a different conclusion: an Old Russian literature (or,
more accurately, a literature in the Old and Middle Russian period) did
exist; but, according to my definition, this literature could avail itself not of
two "literary languages" (in complementary distribution), but simply of
two languages that influenced each other—a Church Slavic, cultural, and
cult language on the one hand, and a Russian language, used in factograph-
ic literature, on the other, with this latter language functioning simultaneously as *lingua vernacula*.[47] The existence of literature does *not* imply the
existence of a *literaturnyj jazyk*.

The text of the GB had a major impact on the subsequent biblical tradition
among the Eastern Slavs in the sixteenth century. While the two aforementioned sixteenth-century copies (Sin 21 and Sin 30 of the Moscow Historical Museum) differ only in minor points from the 1499 manuscript[48]—
they therefore have little bearing on the problems discussed here—the
corresponding portions of the OB must be assessed in terms of a further
development of the Russian biblical language, regardless of whether the
ascertainable modifications should be interpreted as progression (in the
sense of standardizing Church Slavic), stagnation, or regression (toward a
unified *literaturnyj jazyk*).

   In judging the glossality levels of the OB, one must first consider a basic
problem pertinent to the distribution of internal versus external differentiation. The place of publication, Ostrog, is located in Ukrainian territory.

---

[45] I cannot accept the term *Gebrauchsliteratur*, explicitly and implicitly used by Issatschenko
(e.g., in "Vorgeschichte" [see n. 3], 236), since it falls squarely within the genre system of
today's *literaturnyj jazyk*.
[46] F. P. Filin, "Ob istokax" (see n. 3), 8f. With Filin, I consider the *Russkaja Pravda* part of
Old Russian literature.
[47] The fiction of a unified Old Russian literary language will not even be discussed here
since it is contradicted by the linguistic data. Issatschenko is right when he refers to it as a
myth (*Mythen und Tatsachen*, 40).
[48] Cf. Gorskij and Nevostruev, *Opisanie* (see n. 20), passim.

This has not, however, resulted in any major Ukrainian impact on the text (see below).

The pan-Orthodox idea, which must be considered the decisive factor for printing the Bible on East Slavic soil, and the related attempt to suppress vernacular elements preclude the possibility of attributing any particular significance to this text with regard to the crystallization of the Ukrainian, or for that matter the Russian, *literaturnyj jazyk*. Considering the intention of the translators and the Moscow printer, Ivan Fedorov, the internal glossality differentiation can, in my opinion, apply here only to the Church Slavic language itself. Not even the Russian language can be regarded as part of the internal differentiation, the Moscow printer and Russian features notwithstanding. The presence of such features can be explained exclusively as having been transferred from the GB, and not as a result of any independent inclusion.[49] Whereas the language of the GB should be viewed as an attempt at modernizing the language of the Bible, the characteristic trait of the OB is, rather, its linguistic purism, a striving to eliminate vernacular elements from the Church Slavic language of the Bible.

Given these considerations, certain differences in the OB's internal and external diffeerentiation become apparent vis-à-vis the GB. For the internal differentiation I consider only Church Slavic. At the same time, the external differentiation of the OB is more complex than that of the GB. Here, I distinguish between two sets of sublevels:

(1) Levels of external differentiation transferred from the GB:
    (a) the Russian level;
    (b) the Serbo-Croatian level;
    (c) the Czech level; and
    (d) the Latin level.
(2) Newly formed levels of external differentiation:
    (e) the Ukrainian level;
    (f) the Czech level; and
    (g) the Greek level.

The purist influence in the OB becomes apparent if one compares the Russian level and the levels of external differentiation in the GB with their counterparts in the OB. Only some striking phenomena will be mentioned here (the page references are again to my 1972 study):

    (a) Elimination of *polnoglasie* forms (*brěgъ, kravy* 69) and word-initial *ro-* and *lo-* (*raznyxъ, lakotъ* 69).

---

[49] This is readily clear from the fact that, for example, in the book of Maccabees III, which did not form part of the GB and therefore had to be translated anew from the Septuagint, there are no Russian elements whatsoever; cf. Freidhof, "Zur ersten Übersetzung" (see n. 1).

(b) Change of word-initial *o-* to *e-* (*eleja, edino* 69).

(c) Elimination of forms reflecting the shift of [e] to [o] (*pošelъ, ženъ* 75).

(d) Reduction of the confusion of /a/ with /e/, on the one hand, and with /o/, on the other (cf. the examples from the GB above).

(e) Replacement of nominative forms in vocative function found in the GB with vocative forms (83).

(f) The frequent alteration of nominative plural forms in the function of the accusative either to the older accusative forms or to the newer genitive forms (*jazyki, vragi, drugovъ* 85).

(g) The reintroduction of *jo*-stem endings in the locative singular in *-i* (*poli* 90).

(h) The elimination of the confusion of genitive and locative plural forms that were explicable by Serbo-Croatian influence (90f., 94).

(i) A tendency to retain *s*-stem endings (93).

(j) The reintroduction of historical palatalizations in the dative and locative singular of *a*-stem nouns wherever they are missing in the GB (*vъ knizě, k rěcě* 94).

(k) The reintroduction of the dual forms in the noun (98).

(l) Consistent elimination of the first person singular in *-mъ* in thematic verbs (undoing original Serbo-Croatian influence, 104).

(m) The use of the third person singular ending in *-tъ* (in the GB, it usually ends in *-tь*, 105).

(n) The modification of most imperfect forms not having morphophonemic alternations (*možaxu, prixoždaxu* 108).

(o) Modification of incorrect aorist forms (*vnidoša sutъ: vnidoša* 109).

(p) A tendency to replace perfect forms with the aorist (110ff.).

(q) The partial replacement of verb forms of the type *vnidenъ esmь* (116).

(r) The reintroduction of the dual forms in the verb (120).

(s) Consistent elimination of the genitive absolute construction (138f.).

(t) The archaization of the vocabulary. The text of the OB is more archaic and uniform (162), even though some elements of the Russian level and of external differentiation encountered in the GB were carried over.

From this selection, it is clear that the translators and the printer of this Bible have thoroughly changed the text of the GB. One cannot blame them for having been inconsistent in their corrections; no comprehensive grammar of standardized Church Slavic was yet available in 1580–81.

Thus, all phenomena of the first set of sublevels regarding the external differentiation of the OB can be attributed to careless checking of the original.[50] The Czech level is the least pronounced; here, only few passages could go through the correcting hands of the translators and the printer (remnants of the type *vnidenъ esmь*; remnants of the confusion of the accusative and instrumental in *a*-stems).

In assessing the newly formed levels of external differentiation, one must first consider the possibility that the workers in the printing shop—who presumably were familiar with the Ukrainian vernacular but less versed in Church Slavic—introduced changes in the printed version that were in disagreement with the texts that had been readied for print by the translators and the master printer.

Among the Ukrainian phenomena we note, in particular, the dispalatalization of /ř/ in the groups /řa/, /řu/, /ři/ (*zvěra, pisaru, korysti* 73), the shift of the cluster /xv/ to /f/ (*volъfovaniemъ* 73), the apocope of word-initial /i-/ (*bě znosja, mušče, z nixъ* 81), new endings in the instrumental and locative plural (*bičami, okoncami* 89; *vrataxъ, znamenijaxъ* 92), and a few lexical items (*vaga, gai, prezъ, radnyj* 164). In general, however, the impact of the colloquial Ukrainian vernacular is quite limited. It is clearly weaker than the Russian impact on the GB; it is even weaker than the Russian component in the OB (carried over from the GB).

Czech influences of the second set of sublevels are entirely restricted to the book of Maccabees III, which had to be translated anew for the OB. As I have shown previously,[51] the translators availed themselves of a Czech Bible, probably from 1577. This, however, is only an influence of a text-critical nature, not one that can be shown to have affected the categories of grammar and lexicon.

It is in the text-critical sphere that one can also demonstrate Greek influence, since the translators had again collated and corrected the text of the GB according to that of the Septuagint.[52] Contrary to the Czech influence, however, the Greek influence is evident also in the vocabulary and grammar. The following foreign words are, among others, pertinent in this context: *vissonъ* – *byssos*; *evnuxъ* – *eunuchos*; *keravnъ* – *keraunos*; *kinira* –

---

[50] We can refrain from a discussion of the first set of sublevels. The difference in comparison to the corresponding levels of the GB is primarily a quantitative one, caused by correction. As suggested above, only a few phenomena were consistently removed (the confusion of genitive and locative plural, formation of false aorists, formation of the 1st person singular of thematic verbs in *-mъ*, genitive absolute constructions).

[51] Freidhof, "Zur ersten Übersetzung" (see n. 1).

[52] This also applies to the many names in the OB that are markedly different from those in the GB; cf. Freidhof, *Gennadius Bibel und Ostroger Bibel* (see n. 1), 55ff.

kinyra; *korъ* – *koros*; *protarxъ* – *prōtarchos*. There are also numerous
calques, such as *veščestvovati* – *pragmonein*; *žrečestvovati* – *ierateuein*;
predpodvižnikъ – *prōtagōnistēs*; *razvolenie* – *diabulion*; *kamenometnica* –
lithobolos; *rododělatelь* – *genesiurgos* (165ff.).

In the grammar of the OB, the Greek impact can be seen in the unequiv-
ocable imitation of word order in periphrastic constructions of the type *esi
ispytua, bě vъzyskaja* (115, all with analogous formations in the Septuagint),
in the use of the accusative with the infinitive (133), and in purpose clauses
of the type (*vъ*) *eže* + infinitive, which Smotryc'kyj subsequently rejected[53]
(*eže vnesti* – *tu eisenegkai*; *vъ eže čestvovati* – *eis to sebesthai* 139).

In summing up the above observations, I proceed from the following two
assumptions:

(1) The newly translated parts of the manuscript of the GB constitute a
text in which the diglossic distribution has basically been suspended.

(2) By contrast, the printed text of the OB shows a language that still
corresponds to the earlier diglossic distribution.

The suspension of the strict diglossic distribution in various texts depends, in my opinion, directly on the intentions prevailing when the particular texts were prepared. The intention of the translator of the GB—that is,
of its newly translated books—was, in addition to the preservation of the
sacred text as such, the creation of a language that would be appropriate
for the confrontation with the heresy of the Judaizers—in other words, a
language not totally alien to the people. I see in this the first attempt on
Russian soil to overcome the incompatibility of Church Slavic and Russian
within the texts of the Bible (cf. similar previous attempts found in the
Belorussian Skaryna translation and the Ukrainian *Peresopnycja Gospel*).
But it must also be stated that, if we disregard the two copies of the GB
made in the sixteenth century, this attempt remained an isolated phenomenon for more than three hundred years.

The intention of the translators of the OB was quite different. Here, it is
primarily a striving for the unity of the Orthodox Church that is significant.
This unity could best be achieved if elements of the various vernacular
languages (Russian, Ukrainian, Belorussian) did not interfere with the traditional language of culture, Church Slavic. Despite occasional innovations, which were soon to provide an important basis for the codifying
grammars of Church Slavic, the characteristic of artificiality (emulating
Greek) retained its full force.

[53] Cf. O. Horbatsch, *Die vier Ausgaben der kirchenslavischen Grammatik von M. Smotryc'kyj*, Frankfurter Abhandlungen zur Slavistik (Wiesbaden, 1964), 11.

THE LANGUAGE SITUATION AND LINGUISTIC CONSCIOUSNESS IN MUSCOVITE RUS':
THE PERCEPTION OF
CHURCH SLAVIC AND RUSSIAN

BORIS A. USPENSKY

In technical linguistic terms, the language situation of Muscovite Rus' must be defined not as Church Slavic–Russian *bilingualism* in the strict, terminological sense of the word, but as Church Slavic–Russian *diglossia*. Diglossia signifies a situation in which two linguistic systems within the framework of a single speech community can coexist, the functions of these two systems being in complementary distribution and thus corresponding to the functions of a single language in an ordinary (nondiglossic) situation.[1] I am referring here to the coexistence of a "bookish" linguistic system tied to a written tradition (and generally associated directly with the sphere of a specific literary culture) and a "nonbookish" system, connected with everyday life. By definition, no social group within a given speech community uses the bookish linguistic system as a means of spoken communication.[2] In the most obvious case, the bookish language functions not only as a literary (written) language but also as a sacred (cult) language, which determines both the specific prestige of this language and the scrupulously observed distance between the literary and the spoken languages; this is exactly the situation in Russia.

Translated from the Russian by Michael S. Flier.

[1] The diagnostic features of diglossia have been defined by C. A. Ferguson ("Diglossia," in *Language in Culture and Society: A Reader in Linguistics and Anthropology,* ed. D. Hymes [New York–Evanston–London, 1964], 429–439). Regarding diglossia in Rus', see especially B. A. Uspenskij, "Èvoljucija ponjatija 'prostorečija' ('prostogo' jazyka) v istorii russkogo literaturnogo jazyka," in *Soveščanie po obščim voprosam dialektologii i istorii jazyka. Tezisy dokladov i soobščenij, Erevan, 2–5 October 1973* (Moscow, 1973); id., "K voprosu o semantičeskix vzaimootnošenijax sistemno protivopostavlennyx cerkovnoslavjanskix i russkix form v istorii russkogo jazyka," *Wiener Slavistisches Jahrbuch* 22 (1976): 92–100; G. Xjutl'-Folter, "Diglossija v Drevnej Rusi," *Wiener Slavistisches Jahrbuch* 24 (1978): 108–123; D. S. Worth, "On 'Diglossia' in Medieval Russia," *Die Welt der Slaven* (1978): 371–393. The limited scope of the present article does not permit a response to Worth's polemical remarks.

[2] Ferguson, "Diglossia," 435.

Zinovij Otenskij views Maksim Grek's fundamental error precisely as that, being a foreigner, he did not make a distinction between bookish and colloquial language: "Mnjaše bo Maksimъ po knižněj rěči u nasъ i obšča rěčь."[3] According to Ludolf's testimony Church Slavic was not used in everyday situations, i.e., it was not a means of spoken communication:

> Sicuti nemo erudite scribere vel disserere potest inter Russos sine ope Slavonicae linguae, ita è contrario nemo domestica & familiaria negotia sola linguâ Slavonicâ expediet.... Adeoque apud illos dicitur, LOQUENDUM EST RUSSICE & SCRIBENDUM EST SLAVONICAE.[4]

Ludolf specifically notes in this regard that the excessive use of Church Slavic in normal speech might elicit a negative reaction in the speech community. Piotr Skarga's attacks on Church Slavic are quite revealing in this context, in view of the fact that—in contrast to Latin and Greek—no one speaks Church Slavic: "No one can fully understand it because there is no nation on earth that would speak it the way it is written in books."[5]

While outside of diglossia a single linguistic system functions normally in various contexts, in a diglossic situation different contexts are correlated with different linguistic systems. It follows from this, incidentally, that a member of a speech community perceives coexisting linguistic systems as a *single language*, while the outside observer (including the linguist) is apt to regard them as two different languages. Thus if we assume a knowledge of what different languages are, diglossia may be defined as the language situation that arises when two different languages are perceived (in the speech community) and function as a single language. It is worth noting that under the conditions of Church Slavic–Russian diglossia there was no specific designation for the spoken (Russian) language. The term *Russian* did not specifically designate the spoken language, but could refer to the bookish (Church Slavic) language as well, functioning in this capacity as a synonym for *Slavonic* (*slovenskij*); by the same token, the term *simple* (*prostoj*) could also be used with reference to the bookish language.[6] The spoken and bookish languages merge in the linguistic consciousness as two varieties

---

[3] For Maksim thought our bookish language also to be the common language. Zinovij [Otenskij], *Istiny pokazanie o novom učenii* (supplement to *Pravoslavnyj sobesednik* [Kazan', 1863], 967.

[4] H. W. Ludolf, *Grammatica Russica* ... (Oxonii, 1696), preface, foll. 1v–2.

[5] Piotr Skarga, *RIB* 7: cols. 485–486.

[6] Uspenskij, "Èvoljucija ponjatija 'prostorečija'" (see n. 1), 218–219; cf. V. V. Vinogradov, *Očerki po istorii russkogo literaturnogo jazyka XVII–XIX vv.*, 2nd ed., rev. and exp. (Moscow, 1938): 35; C. Vasilev, "Der Ausdruck 'einfache Sprache' bei Avvakum und bei den orthodoxen Südslaven. Das Ende des Kirchenslavischen als Literatursprache," *Wiener Slavistisches Jahrbuch* 17 (1972): 295–298.

of one and the same language—correct and incorrect or corrupted—and are therefore referred to by the same name.

Accordingly, diglossia stands in contradistinction to bilingualism, i.e., the coexistence of two languages enjoying equal status and equivalence in function. Bilingualism is a redundant phenomenon (inasmuch as the functions of one language duplicate those of the other), and an essentially transitional one (since normally one would expect the eventual replacement of one language by the other one or their fusion in one form or other). By contrast, diglossia is a very stable situation, characterized by a persistent functional balance (of mutually complementary functions).

The concept of a linguistic norm—and, consequently, of linguistic correctness—is associated exclusively with the bookish language in the diglossic situation. This is expressed primarily in its codification: the nonbookish language cannot, in principle, be codified under these circumstances. Thus the bookish language functions in linguistic consciousness as the codified and standardized variety of the language. The bookish language, unlike its nonbookish counterpart, is explicitly acquired in the process of formal education; therefore only this language is perceived as correct within the speech community, while the nonbookish language is seen as a deviation from the norm, that is, as a violation of correct speech behavior.

Furthermore, by virtue of the very prestige of the bookish language, such a deviation from the norm is actually recognized as not only admissible but even necessary in particular situations.

In Russia, Church Slavic was perceived as beneficent and salvatory. Just as the name of God[7] would be considered salvatory, so also could the language of communication with God be acknowledged as salvatory by its very nature. Ioann Višenskij's pointed remarks along these lines proclaim that Church Slavic is "sacred" and "salvatory," inasmuch as it "is founded, built and protected by the veracity and truth of God."[8] He asserts as well that "he who would be saved and sanctified will receive neither salvation nor sanctification, if he does not find access to the simplicity and truth of the humble Slavonic language."[9] The passionate polemic surrounding Church Slavic both in Southwestern Rus' (the polemic of Ioann Višenskij

---

[7] Cf. the special emphasis on this in the Hesychast movements, including the relatively recent movement of the *imjaslavcy* (name-praisers) or *imjabožcy* (worshipers of God's name).

[8] Ioann Višenskij, *Sočinenija* (Moscow–Leningrad, 1955), 191–194, 197.

[9] I refer to the works of bookmen from Southwestern Rus' in those cases where their statements do not contradict the linguistic consciousness of Muscovite Rus'. The specifics of the language situation in Southwestern Rus' will be discussed further on.

and Piotr Skarga) and Muscovite Rus' (the work of Maksim Grek) is
explained to a certain degree by faith in its miracle-working power.[10] In an
original article on the creation of "Russian" (actually Church Slavic) literacy, which was included in the *Tolkovaja Paleja* but extant in other manuscripts of the fifteenth through seventeenth centuries as well, Russian literacy together with Russian faith is acknowledged to be revealed by God:
"Eže vědomo vsěmъ ljudemъ budi, jako ruskij jazykъ ni otkudu prija věry
svjatyja seja, i gramota ruskaja nikimъ že javъlenna, no tokmo samim
Bogomъ vsederъžitelemъ, Otcemъ i Synomъ i Svjatym Duxomъ";[11] in the
same way, Church Slavic literacy is referred to as "holy," and "divine" in
the *byliny*.[12] In Rus', Church Slavic can be considered even holier than
Greek, since the Greek language was created by pagans while Church
Slavic was created by holy apostles (i.e., by Saints Cyril and Methodius).[13]

Russian bookmen asserted that Church Slavic leads one to God by the
very fact of its being used in appropriate situations. For example, we read
in the preface to the service and prayer book of the archimandrite of the
Trinity Monastery, Dionisij, from the 1630s: "Ašče čelověkъ čtetъ knigi
prijatno (i.e., adhering to the norms of Church Slavic pronunciation), a

---

[10] Cf. P. I. Žiteckij, "O perevodax evangelija na malorusskij jazyk," *IORJaS* 10, no. 4
(1905): 14–15; A. S. Gruševskij, "Iz polemičeskoj literatury konca XVI v. posle vvedenija
unii," *IORJaS* 22, no. 2 (1917): 299–304.

[11] Let it be known to all that the Russian people did not receive this holy faith from anywhere, nor was Russian literacy revealed by anyone, save God Almighty Himself, the Father
and the Son and the Holy Spirit. V. F. Mareš, "Skazanie o slavjanskoj pis'mennosti (po spisku
Puškinskogo doma AN SSSR)," *TODRL* 19 (1963): 174.

[12] A. B. Markov, *Belomorskie byliny* (Moscow, 1901), 256, 269, 297.

[13] Russian writers often appeal to this argument, which goes back to the well-known tract
"On Letters" by the monk Xrabr. See, e.g., *The Life of St. Stephen of Perm'* (ed. G. Kušelev-
Bezborodko, Pamjatniki starinnoj russkoj literatury, no. 4 [St. Petersburg, 1862], 153; cf. O.
Bodjanskij, *O vremeni proisxoždenija slavjanskix pis'men* [Moscow, 1855], lvi, 94–95), the preface to the Greek-Russian and Tatar-Russian dictionaries of the fifteenth and sixteenth centuries (P. Simoni, *Pamjatniki starinnoj russkoj leksikografii po russkim rukopisjam XIII–XVIII
stol.*, sec. 3: *Poloveckij i tatarskij slovariki. Reči tonkoslovija grečeskogo, IORJaS* 13, no. 1
[1908]: 6), as well as Ioann Višenskij (*Sočinenija* [see n. 8], 24) or Archpriest Avvakum (*RIB*
29: col. 475). The fact that Church Slavic books were translated by saints compelled Zinovij
Otenskij (*Istiny pokazanie* [see n. 3], 961, 967) to object to revising the text of the Creed
proposed by Maksim Grek. Cf. the analogous line in the "Tale of Saint Cyril, the Philosopher–Teacher of the Slavonic Language," which is a reworked Bulgarian version of Xrabr's
treatise. It is stated there that if two priests should come together, one Bulgarian and the other
Greek, the liturgy should not be celebrated in Greek, but in Church Slavic alone or in both
languages, "poneže sīa estь blъgarska liturgija, sīь bo mǫžь stavy ǫ" (inasmuch as the Bulgarian liturgy is holy, for a holy man established it) (I. V. Jagić, *Rassuždenija južnoslavjanskoj i
russkoj stariny o cerkovno-slavjanskom jazyke* [Berlin, 1896], 17; K. M. Kuev, *Černorizec
Xrabăr* [Sofia, 1967], 170).

drugii prilěžno slušaetъ, to oba s Bogomъ besědujutъ."[14] Compare Ioann Višenskij's assertion that "the Slavonic language ... by simple, assiduous reading ... leads to God."[15] Therefore, the use of this language in an inappropriate situation may be viewed as pure blasphemy;[16] by the same token, the reverse situation—that is, the use of Russian (the colloquial language)— would be considered inadmissible and blasphemous in a situation calling for the use of Church Slavic. Thus, by virtue of the special prestige of Church Slavic, the use both of a bookish and nonbookish language in an inappropriate situation is in principle—to one degree or another—a blasphemy. But the bookish language is, of course, highly restricted in its use. The practical inevitability of using the colloquial (Russian) language— which is thought of as a form of Church Slavic corrupted in the course of everyday usage—can apparently be regarded in connection with Original Sin: the rejection of colloquial means of expression and a switch to that language which is considered correct (Church Slavic) would suggest an absolute—actually unattainable—rejection of earthly life and the total elimination of those situations not directly associated with the sacral sphere.

One might say that under conditions of diglossia only the bookish language is *normative*, while the use of the nonbookish language appears to be a *normal*, practically common and unavoidable phenomenon.

It is clear that a departure from the norm of correct behavior under conditions of Church Slavic–Russian diglossia is not blasphemous; at the same time, it is inadmissible and blasphemous to mix different levels of behavior, that is, to violate the correlation between speech behavior and the situation. The unacceptability of this kind of noncorrelation can be

[14] If a man reads books correctly, and another listens attentively, then both converse with God. MS GBL coll. 163, no. 183, fol. 2v.

[15] Višenskij, *Sočinenija* (see n. 8), 23. R. C. Mathiesen ("The Inflectional Morphology of the Synodal Church Slavonic Verb," Ph.D. diss., Columbia University, 1972, pp. 77–78, n. 4, p. 82, n. 9) cites evidence of the same kind pertaining to the nineteenth century.

[16] A similar attitude vis-à-vis Church Slavic can still be found in the eighteenth century (i.e., even after the breakdown of diglossia). This is attested, for example, by Sumarokov's report to the Central Policy Chancery dated January 24, 1774. Reporting that his servant had been arrested for some reason, Sumarokov writes: "Even the police administration acknowledged that my servant was innocent, but Captain Baranov cursed at my messenger in Slavonic: 'Čado, čto glagoleši, abie ašče ...' (Child, what are you saying, lest immediately ...) and other things which cannot be found in the chancery vocabulary. Even though my messenger is a state servant and even though he might be mine, it was indecent for the captain to blaspheme (P. Bartenev, ed., *Osmnadcatyj vek. Istoričeskij sbornik*, vol. 3 [Moscow, 1869], 186). Sumarokov sees not only a personal offense but even blasphemy against something sacred in the behavior of the police official, who resorted to using Church Slavic where the chancery style would have been expected.

illustrated both by the impossibility of translating a sacred text into the colloquial language and of translating in the reverse direction, that is, translating a text that presupposes colloquial means of expression into the bookish language.

It follows that under such circumstances, the comical, parodic use of Church Slavic is basically impossible, namely, the use of the bookish for deliberately nonserious, lighthearted purposes. In fact, parody in a literary language is just a case of using the bookish language in an inappropriate situation, which is contrary to the principles of diglossia. It is only natural, therefore, that Old Russian literature—viewed as the sum of texts written in the literary language—was completely ignorant of parody as a literary genre. By the same token, other light literary genres were also by and large unknown: light, comic content was not expressed through the literary language.

It is no accident that we find injunctions in Old Russian penance books against similar usage with proposals for strict punishment: "Li preložilъ esi knižnaja slovesa na xulnoe slovo, ili na koščjunno. opitem[ьi]. 2. lět," "Rekše slovo xulno. li směšno. na svjatyja knigy ... i oborotivъši slovo svjatyxъ knigъ na igry. 2. lět," "Pisanija sv. na koščuny ne primaešь li," and so forth.[17]

This is strikingly different from the Western language situation, in particular, from the function of Latin in the West. Actually, Latin, in contrast to Church Slavic, is fully capable of expressing light subjects, which is clearly reflected in the range of genres of Western literature. Here, even the parody of the cult of the Church (*parodia sacra*) is possible, a parody that could only be considered blasphemous in Russia. This distinction between the attitude towards Latin in the West and Church Slavic in Russia can be explained largely by the fact that Latin became the language of the Church because it had long been the language of civilization. Church Slavic, on the contrary, became the language of civilization precisely because it was the language of the Church. Thus, in the first case, the literary language is assimilated in all its functions, while in the second, a special, prestigious aspect surfaces when the literary language is utilized.[18]

---

[17] If you have turned bookish words into abusive or blasphemous speech, a penance of two years. If you have uttered an abusive or mocking word against the Holy Scriptures ... and have turned the word of the Holy Scriptures into mockery, two years. Nor should you accept the replacement of sacred writings with blasphemous ones. P. S. Smirnov, *Drevnerusskij duxovnik. Issledovanie po istorii cerkovnogo byta. ČOIDR*, 1914, bk. 2, appendix, 142; A. I. Almazov, *Tajnaja ispoved' v pravoslavnoj Vostočnoj cerkvi. Opyt vnešnej istorii. Issledovanie preimuščestvenno po rukopisjam*, vol. 3 (Odessa, 1894), 150, 158, 276, 282.

[18] Cf. B. O. Unbegaun, "The Russian Literary Language: A Comparative View," *Modern Language*, 1973, p. 68.

Parodies in Church Slavic become possible in Muscovite Rus' as more or less neutral, but not consciously blasphemous, texts only under conditions of diglossic disintegration and the changeover from Church Slavic–Russian diglossia to Church Slavic–Russian bilingualism. This occurs when Church Slavic, ultimately under the influence of the West European language situation (which made its way into Great Russian territory via Southwestern Rus') begins to play approximately the same role as Latin in the West.[19] Such texts appear in the territory of Muscovite Rus' only in the seventeenth century, primarily following the Schism (cf. in particular the "Tavern Service" [*Služba kabaku*], which undoubtedly goes back to the Latin "Services for Drunkards," known in the West as early as the thirteenth century); they are a result of the so-called Third South Slavic Influence, that is, the influence of Southwestern Rus' on Muscovite literary culture. This influence brought about a reexamination of the relationship between Church Slavic and Russian and eventually the disintegration of Church Slavic–Russian diglossia. There is direct evidence that texts of this kind could have originally been regarded as blasphemous.[20]

We must keep in mind that, in contrast to Muscovite Rus', Southwestern Rus' had two functioning literary languages which enjoyed equal status; this situation was not one of diglossia, but of bilingualism. The so-called simple (Russian) language (*prosta* or *ruska mova*) appears alongside "Slavonic" (Church Slavic) in the function of a literary language,[21] the relationship

---

[19] Thus Trediakovskij, in his student days at the Slavonic-Greek-Latin Academy (1723–1726), could use Church Slavic as a means of conversation, apparently considering this language a functional equivalent of Latin, i.e., the language of the learned class (see V. K. Trediakovskij, *Sočinenija*, vol. 3 [St. Petersburg, 1849], 649–650). It is characteristic that about the same time, and precisely in the milieu of the Academy, parallel Church Slavic–Russian texts make their appearance for the first time in a Muscovite context; this also testifies to Church Slavic–Russian bilingualism, at least in a learned setting. Cf. the exercise book of a student of the Academy, one Mixail Ivanov, for the years 1726–1728, where we find exercises in translating from Russian into Church Slavic: corresponding texts are arranged in two parallel columns with the headings "simple" and "Slavonic" (MS GPB Vjaz. Q.16, foll. 72–75; Prof. A. Sjöberg, Stockholm, was kind enough to bring this manuscript to my attention). We find here as well translations from Latin into Church Slavic and from Church Slavic into Russian; hence Church Slavic clearly imitates Latin in function.

[20] Cf. a reference to this in the preface to one of the MSS of the "Tavern Service"; V. P. Adrianova-Peretc, *Prazdnik kabackix jaryžek. Parodija-satira vtoroj poloviny XVII veka* (Moscow–Leningrad, 1936), 44–45, 82.

[21] The distinction in the language situation cited here is reflected in the terminological nomenclature. In Muscovite Rus' the term *Russian language* is understood primarily as Church Slavic (*Slavonic*), while in Southwestern Rus' it designates the literary language, as contrasted with Church Slavic. The *simple language* in Southwestern Rus' is a synonym for *Russian*, i.e., as contrasted with *Slavonic*, whereas in Muscovy it may refer to Church Slavic. Today when we speak of the "Russian" language, consciously opposing it to Church Slavic, we are follow-

between these two languages calquing the Latin-Polish bilingualism of
Poland; Church Slavic acts as the functional equivalent of Latin, while the
"simple language" acts as the functional equivalent of the Polish literary
language.[22] Accordingly, the sphere of use for Church Slavic in Southwestern Rus' appears to be directly dependent on the sphere of use for Latin:[23]
specifically, the possibility—and diffusion—of parodic literature in Latin
conditions the corresponding literature in Church Slavic. Consequently, as
a result of the cultural expansion of Southwestern Rus' in the second half of
the seventeenth and the first half of the eighteenth century, Church Slavic–
Russian diglossia in Muscovite territory becomes Church Slavic–Russian
bilingualism, with the Muscovite recension of Church Slavic broadening its
sphere of use in line with the function of Church Slavic in Southwestern
Rus'.[24] Thus, under the influence of the literary-linguistic situation in
Southwestern Rus'—reflecting in turn the West European situation—the
parodic use of Church Slavic becomes possible in Russia proper, namely, in
satirical literature.[25]

---

ing the Southwestern Russian norm of usage, which became generally accepted as a result of
the Third South Slavic Influence.

[22] In his *Diariuš* (first half of the seventeenth century), Afanasij Filipovič emphasized the
identical relationship between "Rusian" and "Slavonic" on the one hand, and between Polish
and Latin on the other. He notes that "Rus[' poľzuetsja] slovenskim i ruskim, a poljaki latin-
skim i polskim jazykom vedlug narodu i potreby literalnoj knig" (Rus' utilizes Slavonic and
Russian, while the Poles utilize Latin and Polish based on popular usage and the literary
requirements of books) (*RIB* 4, no. 1: col. 125).

[23] It is noteworthy that while in Muscovite Rus'—under conditions of diglossia—Church
Slavic was not used for conversation, in Southwestern Rus'—under conditions of bilingualism—it could be used in this capacity: in the fraternity schools, Church Slavic was deliberately
introduced for conversation, actually on the same basis as Latin in Poland (see the regulations
of the Luc'k Fraternity School of 1624, cited in A. S. Arxangeľskij, *Očerki iz istorii zapadno-
russkoj literatury XVI–XVII vv. Bor'ba s katoličestvom i zapadnorusskaja literatura konca XVI–
pervoj poloviny XVII v.*, *ČOIDR*, 1888, bk. 1: 39–40). Meletij Smotrickij, however, in his
grammar of 1619, specifically warns that teachers should refrain from attempts to converse in
the "Slavonic dialect" under threat of punishment (*Grammatiki slavenskija pravilnoe sintagma*
[Evje, 1619], Preface, fol. 3). But the very existence of such a warning provides clear evidence
of this type of practice.

[24] See the developmental scheme proposed in Uspenskij, "Èvoljucija ponjatija 'prostorečija'" (see n. 1); cf. also Mathiesen, "Synodal Church Slavic Verb" (see n. 15), 51–52, 60–61.

[25] In this regard it is interesting that at the end of the seventeenth century, satirical works,
to the extent that they had penetrated the literature, i.e., had begun to be regarded as genuine
literary works, might be perceived in Rus' as translations from Polish, even when they were
purely Russian in origin. Works of this type were marked in the manuscripts with such typical
notations as "vypisano iz polskix knig" (excerpted from Polish books) or "iz krolovskix knig"
(from royal books), and so forth (N. S. Demkova, "Neizdannoe satiričeskoe proizvedenie o
duxovenstve," *TODRL* 21 [1965]: 95).

The relationships of languages coexisting in diglossia are structured differently, on the level of expression (form) and on the level of content (usage, function)—there being a principled lack of isomorphism (i.e., asymmetry).

On the level of expression, the bookish language is *marked* in the linguistic consciousness since it defines the only possible criteria of linguistic correctness for the given speech community, and, accordingly, the norm through whose prism the nonbookish language is perceived. In the same way, the nonbookish lanugage regularly appears to the linguistic consciousness as a deviation from the norm, and not as an independent norm. Hence the relationship between the two languages may be characterized as a *privative* opposition. The bookish language is clearly delineated within its bounds (codified) and is opposed to the nonbookish language as an organized whole to unorganized elements, that is, as information to entropy, culture to nature, civlization to chaos. In these circumstances any significant (nonaccidental) deviation from the linguistic norm automatically transforms a literary text into a nonliterary one. Naturally this promotes the heterogeneity of the nonliterary language, the organic consolidation of the most variegated linguistic elements within the bounds of nonliterary speech. Thus, for example, in Church Slavic–Russian diglossia, Slavonisms rejected in the process of "correcting books" (i.e., forms that corresponded to the *former* linguistic norm) naturally merged in the linguistic consciousness with original Russianisms and were generally perceived as Russianisms.[26] In analogous fashion, even the diverse borrowings from foreign languages (Europeanisms, Turkisms, etc.) may be assigned to the Russian half of the language dichotomy under these circumstances. Their direct assimilation is connected with the nonnormative (uncodified) status of the living, Russian language; Church Slavic, however, was isolated from borrowing, if Hellenisms are not counted.[27]

Thus on the expression plane, the correlation of the languages—bookish and nonbookish—coexisting in diglossia forms a privative opposition. However, the contexts in which these languages are used are in complementary distribution (actually they do not overlap), and thus on the content (functional) plane, the relationship of the given languages is one of mutually

[26] Cf. the treatment of such forms as *rožestvó, Nikóla, Márija,* etc. Because they were opposed to Church Slavic *roždestvó, Nikoláj, Maríja,* such forms were perceived as specifically Russian. Meanwhile, in their own time, they met the Church Slavic normative requirements because they were, in fact, Church Slavic in origin (cf. B. A. Uspenskij, *Iz istorii russkix kanoničeskix imen* (*Istorija udarenij v kanoničeskix imenax sobstvennyx v ix otnošenii k russkim literaturnym i razgovornym formam* [Moscow, 1969], 13–19, 34, 39ff., 185).

[27] Cf. in this regard the eighteenth-century treatment of those Russian words without Church Slavic lexical correspondences, such as *Varangian, Sarmatian* (see n. 55).

exclusive, *equipollent* opposition. Both the bookish and nonbookish languages are thus directly linked with the semiotic key conditioning their use,
that is, with the semantic characteristics inherent in one or another context.
In other words, if the bookish and nonbookish languages, viewed by
themselves in isolation from their function, are opposed on the basis of
correspondence to the linguistic norm (correspondence to the norm is
marked), then the contexts associated with their use turn out to be *mutually*
exclusive, forming two self-contained and relatively independent semantic
spheres: each language is correlated with a self-contained world of situations organized as a semantic whole. This means that a deviation from the
linguistic norm transfers the speech into a different semiotic key, into
another semantic sphere.

The difference between these two semantic spheres is determined in the
last analysis by the nature of the relation of the content to higher reality,
that is, the Divine, which is manifested above all in the correlation of this
context with the sacred sphere or the secular sphere. Furthermore, the
semantic distinction is not on the level of reference, but on the level of
meaning—that is, the meaning of the text as a whole and not its separate
component parts. The utilization of the bookish or nonbookish language is
thus determined not directly by the content expressed, but by the speaker's
relationship to this content, the speaker here representing the speech community. In other words, the difference between the two languages appears
functionally as a modal distinction. It would be incorrect to assume that if
the topic of speech were, for example, angels, Church Slavic would be used,
but if it concerned people, then Russian would be used. In principle, one
and the same world of objects may be described in one way or the other,
depending on the relationship of the speaker to the subject matter. Thus, if
a reflection of the Divine is perceived in people, or if in general some correlation with the sacred sphere is assumed—explicitly or implicitly—then it
is appropriate to use Church Slavic; in the opposite situation, it is appropriate to use Russian.[28] Hence one can encounter in a Church Slavic text,
for example, a rather detailed description of the operation of the digestive
tract, found in the Eulogy of Saint Constantine of Murom, a homiletic
work of the sixteenth century clearly intended for delivery from the pulpit:

I ašče li voprašaete moeja xudosti: povĕždь namъ, ljubimče, počto ny sozy-
vaeši vo obitelь presvjatyja Bogorodica čestnago Eja Blagoveščenija ..., i čto-
li mzda budetъ sristanija našego vo svjatuju obitelь siju? — Ne na plotnoe

[28] When angels are being discussed, it is more natural, of course, to expect the use of
Church Slavic, but this is determined by the very fact that angels belong to the sacred sphere.
In this instance the subject matter predetermines the attitude towards the topic.

veselie sozyvaju vy, no na duxovnoe, ne na zemnoe piršestvo, iděže mjasa i mnogorazličnyja jadi predlagajutsja, jaže vxodjatъ vo usta, a vъ serdce ne vměščaetsja i afedronomъ isxoditъ i motylo imenuetsja, ni vino, ni medъ gortanь veseljaščee, a umъ pomračajuščee i vъ dětorodnyj udъ izlivajuščeesja i potomъ smradomъ vonjajušče, no sozyvaju vy na trapezu duxovnuju.[29]

The correlation with the sacred sphere in the given case is obvious: a carnal meal, which presupposes the *downward* flow of secular food, is juxtaposed here to a spiritual meal, which presupposes the *upward* flow of spiritual food: hence in this context the use of Church Slavic is fully justified.

In the preface to a collection of proverbs compiled in the second half of the seventeenth century (*Povesti ili poslovicy vsenarodnějšyja po alfavitu*), the first known collection of this type, we find the following passage:

Ašče li rečet někto o pisannyx zdě, jako ne sutь pisana zdě ot Božestvennyx pisanij, takovyj da věstь jako pisana mnogaja soglasna Svjatomu pisaniju. točiju bez ukrašenija, kakъ mirstii žiteli prostoju řěčiju govorjat. I v lěpotu ot drevnix sie umyslisja eže v Božestvennaja pisanija ot mirskix pritčej ne vnositi. takože i v mirskija pritči, kotoroe budet sličně eže vnositi ot knig izbrannyx, i pritočnyja stroki. ili mirskija sija pritči Božestvennago pisanija rečeniem pripodobljati. oboja bo. ašče i edin imut razum. no iže svoja města deržat.[30]

Thus one and the same content (*edin razum*) may be expressed both in Church Slavic and in simple speech (*prostaja rečь*): the utilization of one or the other language is determined not by content, but by the general

---

[29] And should you question my unworthiness: tell us, dear one, why do you summon us together in the Monastery of the Annunciation of the Venerable Mother of God ... and what will be our reward for joining together in this holy monastery?—It is not for carnal joy that I summon you, but for spiritual joy; not for an earthly feast, where meats and all kinds of victuals are offered, food that enters through the mouth, but does not find its way into the heart and exits through the anus and is called feces; neither wine nor mead, which gladden the throat, but cloud the mind, and [enter] into the reproductive organ [finally] pouring out and smelling with a bad stench afterwards. Rather I summon you to a spiritual meal. N. Serebrjanskij, "Drevnerusskie knjažeskie žitija (Obzor redakcij i teksty)," *ČOIDR*, 1915, bk. 3: 244, n. 1; cited from a seventeenth-century copy.

[30] And if someone says that what is written here is not from the Divine Scriptures, let him know that there are many things written in accordance with the Holy Scriptures only without embellishment, the way that lay people talk in simple speech. And from time immemorial it has been deemed appropriate not to introduce into the Divine Scriptures such [things] that come from secular tales. So it is also [with introducing things] into secular tales and lines from such tales, which would be similar to the introduction of [something] from selected books. Or [else] these secular tales should be adapted according to the diction of the Divine Scriptures. For both, even though they have one and the same meaning, nonetheless they [each] have their own place. P. Simoni, *Starinnye sborniki russkix poslovic, pogovorov, zagadok i proč. XVII–XIX stoletij*, vol. 1 (St. Petersburg, 1899), 70–71.

semantic parameters of the text; in these circumstances the bookish and nonbookish languages "svoja města deržat."[31]

The possibility of expressing one and the same content in one or the other language in no way justifies the translation from one language to the other in these circumstances: as soon as the content has been expressed one way or the other in a text, the translation from Church Slavic to Russian or Russian to Church Slavic is not allowed—this would destroy the linguistic relationship, that is, the functional opposition of these languages.

As much as the utilization of the bookish language is conditioned by a connection (direct or indirect) with the Divine, so can the opposition of the bookish and nonbookish languages on the content plane basically approximate the opposition "true—false," that is, irregular (nonbookish) speech behavior can be understood as antibehavior. In this regard, the sinfulness in using the colloquial language is naturally associated in general with the sinfulness of everyday, secular life: the former and the latter are both determined by Original Sin.

The specific character of the Russian linguistic, and more broadly, cultural, consciousness consists for the most part in the fact that here—in the functioning of diglossia as a linguistic and cultural mechanism—there exists no zone that is semantically neutral and which does not make reference to the sacred sphere. Hence, an absence of a connection with the sacred, the Divine, basically signifies a connection with its opposite, with the world of the Devil.

Under these circumstances, an incorrect expression (from the point of view of the accepted linguistic norm) can be linked with a *different* content, that is, with *other* information, and not with an absence of information or simple interference during its transmission. Changes on the expression plane can be connected with another *language*, and not with another *code*, the latter presupposing a recoding of one and the same text. When a given word has a direct sacred meaning, the use of the incorrect form can even give it a completely *opposite* (antonymous) meaning. Thus, for instance, the word *angel* improperly pronounced, read out in accordance with the spelling (which reflects Greek orthographic norms but assumes Greek reading rules for the corresponding orthograms) as *aggel* takes on the opposite meaning, signifying a devil (demon), namely, the *fallen* angel; this meaning, in turn, became firmly established in the linguistic norm, that is, entered

---

[31] The need for this clarification becomes urgent during the breaking-down of diglossia, when the number of texts in the nonbookish language increases; what was common knowledge earlier now requires recollection.

into the bookish, Church Slavic language.[32] An entirely analogous situation obtained when the name *Isus* began to be written as *Iisus* as a result of Nikon's literary reforms. The Old Believers began to perceive the new form as the name of another being, not Christ, but the Antichrist,[33] while their opponents, on the contrary, might have thought that the old form *Isus* referred not to Christ, but to some other person.[34] Both sides in this polemic essentially took an identical position in their treatment of deviations from correct spelling, differing only on the question of which spelling was actually the correct one: a distortion of form in both cases was ascribed another meaning. Noteworthy in this regard is the polemical attack on the Petrinic Most Holy Synod of Drunkards and Fools (1705), where the ordination of pretended metropolitans and patriarchs is described as a demonic act; it is reported that the ordination was performed as a church ceremony, but in negation and profanation of God, and during the ceremony, the newly ordained took vows not to God, *Bog*, but to a certain *Bag*.[35] The word *Bag* (a pronunciation with velar fricative is assumed here, thus [bax], analogous to the pronunciation of the word *Bog* [box]), undoubtedly goes back to the name *Bacchus* [baxus], utilized in the Petrinic mock ceremonies; however, this name has obvious similarities to the word *Bog* and is precisely treated as a distorted form of *Bog*, and thus as a name for the Devil.[36] In a similar way, Ivan Timofeev's *Vremennik* refers to the

[32] B. A. Uspenksij, *Arxaičeskaja sistema cerkovnoslavjanskogo proiznošenija (Iz istorii liturgičeskogo proiznošenija v Rossii)*, (Moscow, 1968), 51–53, 78–82; id., "Knižnoe proiznošenie v Rossii (Opyt istoričeskogo issledovanija)," doctoral dissertation, Moscow University, 1971, pp. 330–339, lxxix–lxxxiv. The Church Slavic written form *aggelъ* reflects the orthography of the original Greek form ἄγγελος. As in Greek, it was meant to be read with a nasal (*angelъ*); moreover, the incorrect spelling pronunciation *aggelъ* began to be associated with the opposite content.

[33] P. S. Smirnov, *Vnutrennie voprosy v raskole v XVII veke. Issledovanie iz načaľnoj istorii raskola po vnov' otkrytym pamjatnikam, izdannym i rukopisnym* (St. Petersburg, 1898), 41; Uspenskij, *Iz istorii russkix kanoničeskix imen* (see n. 26), 216.

[34] Dmitrij Rostovskij, *Rozysk o Raskolničeskoj Brynskoj Vere* ... (Moscow, 1755; written in 1709), fol. 18v; cf. *Praščica*, 240 questions from the Old Believers of the D'jakonov Community addressed to Pitirim, archbishop of Nižgorod (1716) and his replies (1719), (St. Petersburg, 1726), answer no. 146.

[35] S. A. Belokurov, *Materialy dlja russkoj istorii* (Moscow, 1888), 539.

[36] The notion that the name of the Devil is a distorted form of God's name is manifested in the dialectal opposition of *Hospoď* (*Gospoď*) and *haspèd*, which is attested in the Ukraine; cf. the popular belief recorded in the district of Kiev: "Soroku sotvoril ne Hospoď, a haspèd" [It was not the Lord who created the magpie but the enemy of God] (D. K. Zelenin, *Opisanie rukopisej Učenogo arxiva Imperatorskogo Russkogo geografičeskogo obščestva*, vols. 1–3 [Petrograd, 1914–1916], 622. The form *haspèd* is apparently a reshaping of the word *aspid* 'viper', motivated by similarity to the word *Hospoď*. Cf. the last section of this essay regarding an analogous treatment of deviation from the linguistic norm in the case of the word *spasibo*, as a truncation of *spasi Bog*, and the form *Sus Xristos*.

pseudo-patriach Ignatij, ordained under the False Dmitrij, not as *patriarx*, but as *fatriarx*.[37] The juxtaposition of the correct and incorrect linguistic forms in this case corresponds to the juxtaposition of the legitimate and illegitimate patriarchs.

Likewise, any deviation from the normative sacred text, perceived as a whole—for example, the distortion of a prayer—can correlate the entire text with the direct opposite meaning, that is, turn it into its opposite. Thus under Patriarch Nikon, the elimination of the word *istinnyj* 'true' from the text of the Creed (in the phrase "I vъ Duxa Svjatogo, Gospoda istinnago i životvorjaščago ..." [And in the Holy Spirit, the true and life-giving Lord]) was perceived by the conservative Old Believer party as clear proof that Nikon's adherents were professing the untrue spirit, the Evil One. In the words of Archpriest Avvakum, Nikon "glagoletъ neistinna Duxa Svjatago" (is saying 'the untrue Holy Spirit') and in Nikon's books "napečatano: 'duxu lukavomu molimsja'" (it is printed, let us pray to the evil spirit); and in another place Avvakum writes: "Vsěхъ eretikovъ otъ věka eresi sobrany v novyja knigi: duxu lukavomu napečatali molitca."[38] One finds the same affirmation in other Old Believer writings as well—for example, "vъ kreščenii novyxъ knigъ vъ molitvě napečatali: molimsja tebě duxъ lukavyj —istinnago izgnavše, lukavago prizyvajutъ i moljatsja."[39] Hence, even minimal deviations from canonical form can be perceived as evidence of heretical content of the text as a whole. Indicative in this sense is the reaction of the Muscovite abbot Iľja and Ivan Nasedka in 1627 to the form *Xristovi* in the *Didactic Gospel* by Kirill Trankvillion Stavroveckij (published in Southwestern Rus' with spelling norms completely different from those to which the Muscovites were accustomed). "Skaži, *protivniče*," the Muscovite bookmen address Kirill Trankvillion, "ot *kogo* ta rěčь: 'sutь slovesa *Xristovi*'? Esli *Xristova*, dlja čego literu pereměnilъ i vměsto aza iže napečatalъ?"[40] The Muscovite perceive the incorrect form as certain proof of Kirill Trankvillion's non-Orthodoxy, that is, as evidence that the given text did not come from God; in Moscow the style used in this book was interpreted as "heretical." The new grammatical forms that appeared in the liturgical texts

---

[37] *RIB* 13: cols. 370, 372.
[38] All the heretics from the age of heresy are gathered together in the new books: it is printed there that one should pray to the evil spirit. *RIB* 39: cols. 413, 729; cf. cols. 739, 749.
[39] Under Baptism in the new books it is printed in the prayer: we pray to thee, o evil spirit—having expelled the true one, they call forth and pray to evil one. Smirnov, *Vnutrennie voprosy* (see n. 33), 5.
[40] Tell me, adversary ... whose speech is this: Are these Christ's words? And if they are Christ's, why have you changed a letter, and written "i" rather than "a"? A. Golubcov, "Sudʹba Evangelija učiteľnogo Kirilla Trankvilliona-Staroveskogo," *ČOIDR* 28, 1890, bk. 4: 552–565.

resulting from the reforms of Patriarch Nikon and his followers were perceived in exactly the same way. In his discussion of such emendations in the
Creed, for example, the emendation "nasъ radi *čelověkъ*" for "nasъ radi
čelověkovъ," "suditi *živymъ* i *mertvymъ*" for "suditi *živyxъ* i *mertvyxъ*,"
"*edinu* svjatuju sobornuju i apostolьskuju cerkovь" for "*edinuju* svjatuju
sobornuju i apostolьskuju cerkovь," and so on—monk Avraamij concludes
in his petition of 1678 (citing works of Maksim Grek and also the *Great
Catechism* of Lavrentij Zizanij): "A otъ sego, bogoslovcy rěša, *velika eresь
vozrastaetъ vъ cerkvi*, jakože Maksimъ vъ 13 glavě pišetъ. Tako že i vъ
knigě Bolьšago Katixisisa pišetъ, jako *edinymъ azbučnymъ slovomъ* eresь
vnositsja ... i podъ anafemu polagaetъ takovaja tvorjaščixъ."[41] Compare
the statement of priest Lazar' regarding the correction of the phrase "vo
věki *věkomъ*" to "vo věki *věkovъ*" in Nikon's books: "Da vъ novyxъ že
knigaxъ napečatano vo vsěxъ molitvaxъ i vo vsěxъ vozglasěxъ: nyně i
prisno i vo věki věkovъ. *I ta rěčь eretičeskaja*."[42] Archpriest Avvakum also
writes about the use of the form *věkovъ* instead of *věkomъ* in the same
phrase: "maloe slovo sie, da veliku eresь soderžitъ";[43] Avvakum speaks in
exactly the same terms about the form *aminъ*, which appears in the texts
corrected under Patriarch Nikon: "vъ staryxъ [knigax] *aminь*, a v novyxъ
aminъ. Maloe bo se slovo veliku eresь soděvaetъ.[44]

Protesting against the Nikonian redaction of the Creed, which deleted
the conjunction *a* in the phrase *roždenna, a ne sotvorenna* 'born, but not
created', Deacon Fedor—an associate of Archpriest Avvakum—wrote:
"Namъ ... vsěmъ pravoslavnymъ xristianamъ podobaetъ umirati za edinъ
azъ, egože okajannyj vragъ vybrosilь izъ Simvola?"[45] This sort of reaction
was certainly characteristic of that time in general, and not exclusively of
the representatives of the conservative Old Believer party. Thus when
Archimandrite Simeon, an adherent of Nikon's reforms, accidentally

[41] And from this, the theologians have said *great heresy arises in the Church*, as Maksim
writes in chapter 13. Likewise it is written in the *Great Catechism* that by one *single letter of
the alphabet* heresy comes into being ... and those doing such things are subject to anathema.
N. I. Subbotin, ed., *Materialy dlja istorii raskola za pervoe vremja ego suščestvovanija*, vol. 7
(Moscow, 1875/1890), 319–320.

[42] And it is printed in the new books, in all the prayers and all the parts of the *lectio
solemnis*: now and forever and for all time. *And these words are heretical*. Ibid., vol. 4, 200.

[43] This letter is a small one, but it contains great heresy. *RIB* 39: col. 465.

[44] *Aminь* is in the old [books], and *aminъ* in the new ones. Thus this small letter creates
great heresy. A. K. Borozdin, *Protopop Avvakum. Očerk iz istorii umstvennoj žizni russkogo
obščestva v XVII veke* (St. Petersburg, 1898), appendixes, 42.

[45] It behooves all of us Orthodox Christians to die for the letter "a" alone, which the
accursed enemy [referring to Patriarch Nikon] has thrown out of the Creed. Subbotin, *Materialy dlja istorii* (see n. 41), vol. 6, 188–189; cf. 11–12.

uttered the old phrase "roždenna, *a ne sotvorena*" at his ordination as a
bishop, Tsar Aleksej Mixajlovič, who was present at the ordination, nearly
stopped the ceremony, that is, was inclined to question its very validity.[46]
Another supporter of Nikon's innovations, the "book-corrector" Evfimij, a
monk of the Čudov Monastery, justifies the need for exact reproduction of
the Menaea text in his work "Concerning the correction of certain erroneous phrases in previously published books of the Menaea" (1690s) as follows: "Eliko bo žitie svjatyxъ lučšee, toliko ixъ i slovesa našixъ lučša
slovesъ i *dějstvitelnějša* sut[ь]."[47] In all these instances the *validity* of the
sacred word is the issue in question, that is, the correspondence to its
sacred reality.

In light of the above, it is entirely natural that the slightest error in the
pronunciation of sacred texts, such as the nondistinction of the letters *e* and
ě, was immediately corrected during the church services (as currently

[46] Ibid., 229–230.
[47] As much as the life of the saints is better, that much are their words also better and more
valid than ours. K. Nikoľskij, *Materialy dlja istorii ispravlenija bogoslužebnyx knig. Ob ispra-
vlenii Ustava cerkovnogo v 1682 godu i mesjačnyx Minej v 1689–1691 gg.*, Obščestvo ljubitelej
drevnej pisʹmennosti. Pamjatniki drevnej pisʹmennosti, no. 114 (St. Petersburg, 1896), 61; on the
authorship of Evfimij, see V. G. Siromaxa, "Jayzkovye predstavlenija knižnikov Moskovskoj
Rusi vtoroj poloviny XVII v. i 'Grammatika' M. Smotrickogo," *Vestnik Moskovskogo universiteta*, ser. 9, *Filologija* (1979), no. 1. Cf. the justification for not permitting any sort of deviation from the canonical form of a sacred text in the Old Believers' *Kerženskie otvety* of 1719
(the replies of the Old Believers of the Dʹjakonov Community to the questions of Archbishop
Pitirim; Andrej Denisov is assumed to be the author of this work. Speaking of changes in the
text, particularly the linguistic changes that provoked the Schism, the Old Believers proclaim:
"Ne divno že ti budi i o somněnii našemъ, eže iměemъ o novopoloženiixъ vašixъ. Ašče bo
svjaščennyj otecъ Spiridonъ, episkopъ Trimifijskij, i ne sterpě edinyja rěči preměnenija, egda
Trifilij episkopъ, uča vъ cerkvi, preměni rěčь evangelьskuju vъ skazanii, juže reče Xristosъ kъ
razslablennomu, *vozmi lože svoe.* Togda svjatyj Spiridonъ razgněvasja na nego i obliči ego
rekъ: ili ty mnišisja lučši byti glagolavšago: *vozmi odrъ svoj,* i to rekъ izběžalъ ot revnosti izъ
cerkvi, revnuja o Xristovomъ slovesi, xitrostiju ritora Trifilija priměnennomъ.... Kolьmi pače
namъ somnitelьno estь o tolikixъ množajšixъ voznovstvovaniixъ, bojaščimsja cerkovnyxъ
zapreščenij, eže priložiti ne preměniti, niže otložiti čto, krepče utveržajuščixъ" (The doubts
that we have concerning your new positions should come as no surprise to you. For even the
holy father Spyridon, bishop of Trimithus, did not tolerate a single change of wording; when
Bishop Triphyllios, while preaching in church, changed the phrase in a story from the Gospels
which Christ said to the paralytic, namely, *take up they bed* [*lože*]. Then the holy Spyridon
became enraged at him and denounced him saying: can you think yourself better than He,
who said *take up thy bed* [*odrъ*]? And having said this, he ran out of the church in a fervor,
fervently caring about the word of Christ that had been changed through the cunning of the
orator, Triphyllios.... As concerns such multitudes of novelties, how much more doubtful is it
for us who fear the injunctions of the Church, which firmly state: what is set down must not
be changed, nor should anything be deleted). *Otvety Aleksandra diakona (na Keržence) podan-
nye nižegorodskomu episkomu Pitirimu v 1719 godu* [The so-called "Kerženec" or "Dʹjakonov"
replies], Nižnij Novgorod (an appendix to the journal *Staroobrjadec* for 1906; reprint of 1720
MS.), 179–180.

happens even now among the Old Believers).[48] In a mid-seventeenth-century orthoepic manual, a selection of typical reading errors, chiefly concerning incorrect stress, ends with the following important conclusion: "Strašno bo estь bratie ne točiju sie rešči, no i *pomysliti* ...";[49] the correlation of incorrect expression with incorrect content comes across with vivid clarity in these words. Compare the same attitude which copyists had towards *misspellings* of sacred texts; see the special "Molitva razrešeniju pisarem" (prayer of scribal absolution) in the Russian *Trebnik* (Prayer Book): "sъgrešix prepisyvaa svjataa i božestvenaa pisania. svjatyx apostolъ i svjatyx otecь. po svoej voli i po svoemu nedorazumiju. a ne jako pisano."[50] The copyist's position was more difficult, however, inasmuch as he was supposed to correct errors in the text being copied.[51] It is noteworthy that a similar attitude towards errors in written or oral speech is not at all characteristic of the Catholic West;[52] an involuntary error there is in no way associated with a distortion of content and thus is not viewed as a sin (cf., incidentally, the etymology of Russian *pogrešnost'* 'error', as derived from *grex* 'sin'). No less indicative in this regard is the difference in attitude towards this problem in Muscovite Rus' and Southwestern Rus'. Thus, in the preface to the 1646 *Trebnik*, Petro Mohyla especially emphasized that any errors or mistakes occurring in the *trebniki* were in no way harmful to our salvation, for they do not affect the number, power, matter, form, and consequences of the holy mysteries: "esli sutь jakovye pogrěšenija, albo pomylki v ... Trebnikaxъ, tye Spaseniju našomu něčogo neškodjat, ponevažь Ličby, Moci, Materii, Formy i Skutkovъ svjatyxъ Tainъ neznasjatъ."[53]

---

[48] A. M. Seliščev, *Zabajkaľskie staroobjradcy. Semejskie* (Irkutsk, 1920), 16; Uspenskij, "Knižnoe proiznošenie" (see n. 32), 45.

[49] It is horrible, brethren, not only to say this, but even to think it. F. Buslaev, *Istoričeskaja xristomatija cerkovnoslavjanskogo i drevnerusskogo jazykov* (Moscow, 1861), col. 1088.

[50] I have sinned in copying the Holy and Divine Scriptures of the Holy Apostles and the Holy Fathers of my own free will and by my misunderstanding, and not as it is written. A. V. Gorskij and I. K. Nevostruev, *Opisanie slavjanskix rukopisej Moskovskoj Sinodaľnoj biblioteki*, sec. 3, pt. 1 (Moscow, 1855–1917), 219; cf. E. Petuxov, *Serapion Vladimirskij, russkij propovednik XIII veka, Zapiski Istoriko-filologičeskogo fakuľteta Imperatorskogo Sankt-Peterburgskogo universita* 17 (St. Petersburg, 1888), 45–46. Almazov, *Tajnaja ispoveď*, vol. 3 (see n. 17), 210, 216; Nikoľskij, "Materialy dlja istorii" (see n. 47), 58–62.

[51] Cf. among the penitential replies at confession: "knigi pisax i ne pravix" (I copied books and did not correct them) (Almazov, *Tajnaja ispoveď*, vol. 3 [see n. 17], 238; Petuxov, *Serapion Vladimirskij* [see n. 50], 45).

[52] See Mathiesen, "The Synodal Church Slavonic Verb" (see n. 15), 48–49.

[53] F. Titov, *Tipografija Kievo-Pečerskoj lavry. Istoričeskij očerk (1601–1616–1916 gg.)*, vol. 1: *(1601–1616–1721 gg.)* (Kiev, 1918), 268, appendixes.

It is clear that not only thought or belief but even designation itself may be seen as heretical.[54] As a matter of principle, form and content are identified, and any deviation from the correct designation may be associated with a change in content—that is, is at any rate not indifferent to the content. Basically, words of the bookish language function in these circumstances just as proper nouns usually function. In fact, proper nouns are precisely those characterized by a direct and unequivocal association of signifier and signified: a change in the form of the noun is usually connected with another referent (content); that is, an altered form is naturally understood as *another* noun.

Thus, in diglossia, in certain situational contexts, a departure from the norm of correct linguistic behavior turns out, in fact, to be justified—such linguistic behavior, in other words, which the members of the speech community themselves qualify as "incorrect." Quite often (in an absolute majority of cases), a speaker is obliged to behave *incorrectly*, from his own personal point of view; it appears to be practically impossible to avoid *erroneous* behavior—only *blasphemous* behavior can be avoided.

Since deviation from the norm in this connection implies a translation into a different semantic sphere, which turns out to be opposite to the sacred sphere, this incorrect speech behavior naturally merges in the linguistic consciousness with antibehavior.

Hence from a certain perspective, the nonbookish Russian language can be joined in its "incorrectness" or erroneousness, sinfulness with such patently un-Orthodox (heretical) languages as, for example, Tatar or Latin; in other words, a deviation from the Church Slavic norm (practically unavoidable and necessary!) can be identified with a kind of antinorm. Russian bookmen could view the living Russian language—which by necessity they would have to use in everyday life—as the originally bookish language spoiled by contamination with Tatar and similarly "impure" languages; according to this view, Russian, unlike Church Slavic, has something substantially in common with these languages: in the words of Fedor Polikarpov, "rěsnota i čistota slavenskaja zasypasja [ot] čužestrannyxъ jazykovъ vъ pepelъ."[55]

---

[54] Cf. Mathiesen, "The Synodal Church Slavonic Verb" (see n. 15), 28.

[55] The truth and purity of Slavonic were turned into ash by the overlay of foreign tongues. F. Polikarpov, *Leksikon trejazyčnyj sireč' rečenij slavenskix, ellinogrečeskix i latinskix sokroviŝče* (Moscow, 1704), preface, fol. 6. There are traces of a similar interpretation even in the eighteenth and the beginning of the nineteenth centuries. Trediakovskij (*Sočinenija* 3: 203) saw one of the basic distinctions between Church Slavic and Russian precisely "in words newly introduced from foreign languages" and considered Russian words that had no lexical equivalent in

Under conditions of diglossia, the bookish Church Slavic language is in general relatively stable (codified and prescriptive), while the colloquial Russian language is constantly changing, becoming ever more removed from the bookish language (without codification, it is not limited in its evolution). Accordingly, the Russian language is considered to have developed from Church Slavic by corruption of the latter. This change in the living language, which produces an ever greater distance between the bookish and nonbookish languages, is associated with the sinfulness of human nature and is ascribed to the work of the Devil; see the special statements concerning the Devil's machinations against the Church Slavic language by such sixteenth-century bookmen as Zinovij Otenskij or Ioann Višenskij.[56]

Noteworthy in this regard is the fact that *Satan can speak Russian in a bookish Church Slavic text*; see, for example, the "Tale of a Certain Divinely Chosen Emperor and the Devil's Flattery" or the Old Believers' "Selections from the Holy Writ Concerning the Antichrist."[57] This is entirely natural from the point of view of the Russian man of letters, who ascribes the corruption of the Church Slavic language—expressed by the tendency "knižnye [reči] narodnymi obesčeščati"[58]—to the guile of the Devil himself. Likewise, in a psalmodic, intoned reading during the church service (*lectio solemnis*), the direct speech of demons may be marked by

---

Church Slavic to be "Varangian" (P. P. Pekarskij, *Istorija Imperatorskoj Akademii nauk v Peterburge*, vol. 2 [St. Petersburg, 1870–1873], 246). And V. N. Tatiščev ("Pis'mo V. N. Tatiščeva k V. K. Trediakovskomu ot 18 fevralja 1736 g.," *Arxiv AN* [1736], ser. 2, inv. 1, no. 206, fol. 94v; also *Izbrannye proizvedenija* [Leningrad, 1979], 96) called such words "Sarmatian," i.e., he also ascribed to them a foreign origin. Likewise D. V. Daškov (Review of "Perevod dvux statej iz Lagarpa ..." by A. S. Šiškov, *Cvetnik* 8 [1810]: 260; also *O legčajšem sposobe vozražať na kritiki* [St. Petersburg, 1911], 31–32) thought that Russian differed from Church Slavic by its borrowing of Tatar and other foreign words.

It is indicative that in Southwestern Rus' in the sixteenth to eighteenth centuries, popular songs could be recorded in the Latin alphabet, but not in Church Slavic Cyrillic, which was associated chiefly with a religious content and, at any rate, the bookish language (A. Je. Kryms'kyj, "Ukrajins'ka mova, zvidkilja vona vzjalasja i jak rozyvalasja," in Ol. Šaxmatov and A. Kryms'kyj, eds., *Narysy z istoriji ukrajins'koji movy ta xrestomatija z pamjatnykiv pis'mens'koji staro-ukrajinščyny XI–XVIII vv.* [Kiev, 1922], 114). Incantations could be recorded in Rus' in the same way since they were contrasted with church prayers (see, e.g., N. Vinogradov, *Zagovory, oberegi, spasiteľnye molitvy i proč.*, pt. 2 [St. Petersburg, 1909], p. 33, no. 23).

[56] Zinovij [Otenskij], *Istiny pokazanie* (see n. 3), 927; Ioann Višenskij, *Sočinenija* (see n. 8), 23, 194.

[57] N. S. Demkova and N. F. Droblenkova, "'Povesť o ubogom čeloveke, kako ot diavola proizveden carem' i ee usť-cilemskaja pererabotka," *TODRL* 21 (Moscow–Leningrad, 1965), 252–258; V. Keľsiev, *Sbornik praviteľstvennyx svedenij o raskoľnikax*, vol. 2 (London, 1860–1862), 251.

[58] To corrupt the bookish [words] with those of common speech. Zinovij [Otenskij], *Istiny pokazanie* (see n. 3), 965.

colloquial intonation, in contrast to the solemn style of the rest of the reading.[59] Finally, the Chaldeans in the "Fiery Furnace Play," performed before the mid-seventeenth-century in the cathedrals of Moscow, Novgorod, Vologda, and other towns, spoke in Russian (in church!) and not in Church Slavic,[60] this being the unique case of utilizing Russian in a church service. This corresponds to the association of the Chaldeans with demons;[61] the speech of the Chaldeans is thus juxtaposed to the speech of the other participants in the "Fiery Furnace Play." Here one might say that the Russian language is united with the Chaldean in its contrast to Church Slavic. It is noteworthy that in the Vologda performance of the "Fiery Furnace Play" the Chaldeans could speak with *jakan'e* (thus the Vologda Chaldeans pronounced "*čego*" *čavo*[62]—*jakan'e* being uncharacteristic of Vologda dialects, i.e., with patent Russianisms, and markedly incorrect Russian at that.

If demonic speech in a Church Slavic text can be endowed with features of colloquial Russian, then in a Russian text proper demons can express themselves in a nonsense glossolalic language, which may be viewed as a special kind of generalization of foreign speech in the linguistic consciousness.[63] In both cases, of course, we are dealing with nothing other than anti-behavior, i.e., Russian speech and glossolalic speech appear to be functionally compatible phenomena.

No less characteristic is the popular notion that the Devil loves to be called *čert* in Russian, but cannot bear the Church Slavic name *bes*[64] A specific relationship to both Church Slavic and Russian clearly comes across in this case, when Church Slavic is associated with the truth of

[59] T. F. Vladyševskaja, "Rannie formy drevnerusskogo pevčeskogo iskusstva," Cand. diss., Art History Institute, Moscow, 1976, p. 90.

[60] Nikoľskij, *Materialy dlja istorii* (see n. 47), 176, 202–204; M. P. Savinov, "Čin Peščnogo dejstva v Vologodskom Sofijskom sobore," *Russkij filologičeskij vestnik*, 1890, no. 1: 47–49, 53; A. Golubcov, *Činovnik Novgorodskogo Sofijskogo sobora* (Moscow, 1899), 63–66, 247–248, note; *Drevnjaja rossijskaja vivliofika*, 2nd ed., vol. 6: 374, 377.

[61] Cf. A. Olearij, *Opisanie putešestvija v Moskoviju i čerez Moskoviju v Persiju i obratno*, ed. and trans. A. M. Lovjagin (St. Petersburg, 1906), 301–303.

[62] Savinov, "Čin Peščnogo dejstva ..." (see n. 60), 47.

[63] Nonsense speech (*zaumnaja reč'*) is generally associated both with demonic speech (cf. the account of the appearance of the demons in Leskov's "Voiteľnica": "*Šurle-murle, šire-mire—kravemir,*—one yells") and with speaking in a foreign language (cf. the account of a conversation between a Russian soldier and a Frenchman in Tolstoj's *War and Peace*: "Sidorov winked and, turning to the Frenchmen, began over and over to mumble incomprehensible words: '*Kari, mala, tafa, safi, muter, kaská,*' he muttered, trying to impart expressive intonations to his voice"). We must also bear in mind that foreigners might have been viewed in Rus' as sorcerers linked to unclean spirits, or even directly identified with demons (see D. K. Zelenin, *Očerki russkoj mifologii*, vol. 1: *Umeršie neestestvennoj smerťju i rusalki* (Prague, 1916), 74–77). Hence features of demonic behavior are regularly ascribed to them.

[64] Zelenin, *Opisanie rukopisej*, vol. 2 (see n. 36), 89.

Christ, and Russian, with the workings of the Evil One (cf. Ioann Višenskij's opinion that the Devil can be combated with the help of Church
Slavic). Among a specific group of Russian speakers such a Russian word
as *spasibo* (a truncation from *spasi Bog* [may God save (you)]) can be perceived as an appeal to the Antichrist in exactly the same way.[65] This, needless to say, is a direct consequence of the distortion of the word *Bog* as an
etymological component of the given word, but the very possibility of a
similar perception in general characterizes the view of Russian as being a
corruption of Church Slavic. A quite similar situation obtains regarding the
vernacular form *Sus Xristos* (= Isus Xristos), which can be perceived as a
demonic form.[66] In one and the other situation, everyday Russian appears
in the linguistic consciousness as the result of sinful corruption of a sacred
language, a corruption which is naturally attributed to the work of Satan.
This is even more significant, since by necessity this language must be used,
for the use of Church Slavic alone in all these cases would constitute
blasphemy!

[65] There is a legend among Old Believers—which I have heard many times—that the heathen shouted *Spasi, Bo!* or even *Spasi, Ba!* (with markedly incorrect *akan'e* pronunciation)
during the baptism of Rus', calling out to the pagan idol that Saint Vladimir had cast down as
it floated down the Dnieper. Thus the component *bo* or *ba* is understood as the name of a
pagan deity, identified with the Antichrist. This is an interesting example of the retrospective
transferral of elements of later religious consciousness to paganism.

[66] D. N. Sadovnikov, *Skazki i predanija Samarskogo kraja* (St. Petersburg, 1884 [*Zapiski
Imperatorskogo Russkogo Geografičeskogo obščestva po otdeleniju ètnografii* 12]), p. 237,
no. 71.

NOTES ON CONTRIBUTORS

HENRIK BIRNBAUM is Professor of Slavic Languages and Literatures at the University of California, Los Angeles. His works include *On Medieval and Renaissance Slavic Writing* (1974), *Lord Novgorod the Great* (1981), and *Essays in Early Slavic Civilization* (1981).

RALPH BOGERT is Assistant Professor of Slavic Languages and Literatures at Harvard University. The primary focus of his research has been medieval Russian and South Slavic culture and society.

JOSTEIN BØRTNES is Docent in Comparative Literature at the University of Oslo, formerly of Cambridge University. His works include *The Old Russian Vita* (in Norwegian, 1975).

NIKOLAI DEJEVSKY is associated with Thomson Professional Publishing Division in London and was formerly affiliated with Oxford University. His works include *Novgorod in the Early Middle Ages: The Rise and Growth of an Urban Community* (1977).

MICHAEL S. FLIER is Professor of Slavic Languages and Literatures at the University of California, Los Angeles. His works include *Aspects of Nominal Determination in Old Church Slavic* (1974).

GERD FREIDHOF is Professor of Slavic Languages and Literatures at the University of Marburg. His works include *Vergleichende sprachliche Studien zur Gennadius-Bibel (1499) und Ostroger Bibel (1580/81)* (1972).

NORMAN INGHAM is Professor of Slavic Languages and Literatures at the University of Chicago. He has done extensive research in early Slavic civilization with special emphasis on the cultural ties between Old Rus' and Bohemia.

JAKOV LURIA is Senior Researcher in the Institute of Russian Literature of the Soviet Academy of Sciences. His works include *Antifeodal'nye eretičeskie dviženija na Rusi XIV–načalo XVI veka* (with N. A. Kazakova, 1955), *Ideologičeskaja bor'ba v russkoj publicistike konca XV–načala XVI veka* (1960), and *Obščerusskie letopisi XIV–XV vv.* (1976).

KONRAD ONASCH is a specialist in theology, Orthodox art, and Russian literature, formerly on the faculty of the University of Halle. His works include *Ikonen* (1961), *Die Ikonenmalerei* (1968), and *Kunst und Liturgie der Ostkirche in Stichworten unter Berücksichtigung der Alten Kirche* (1981).

RICCARDO PICCHIO is Professor of Slavic Languages and Literatures at Yale University. His works include *Storia della letteratura russa antica* (1959) and *L'Europa orientale dal Rinascimento all' età illuministica* (1970).

ANDRZEJ POPPE is Professor of Medieval History at the University of Warsaw. His works include *State and Church in 11th Century Rus'* (in Polish, 1968) and *The Rise of Christian Russia* (1982).

BORIS A. USPENSKY is Professor of Russian at Moscow State University. His works include *Arxaičeskaja sistema cerkovnoslavjanskogo proiznošenija* (1968), *Poètika kompozicii* (1970), and *O semiotike ikony* (1971).

DEAN S. WORTH is Professor of Slavic Languages at the University of California, Los Angeles. His works include *Sofonija's Tale of the Russian-Tatar Battle on the Kulikovo Field* (with Roman Jakobson, 1963) and *On the Structure and History of Russian* (1977).

RUSSELL ZGUTA is Professor of History at the University of Missouri-Columbia. His works include *Russian Minstrels: A History of the Skomorokhi* (1978).

NAME INDEX

Aaron 134
Aaron, sacristan 94, 94n, 95, 95n, 96, 96n, 97
Abel 40, 41, 42, 45, 48, 49, 51
Abraham 168, 169, 169n, 197, 339, 339n
Adalbert, see Vojtěch, Saint
Adam 42, 155, 155n, 334, 334n, 335
Adelphotes 347, 347n, 349, 354n, 358
Afanasij Filipovič 372n
Agapit, monk 60, 60n
Akila, see Aquila
Aksakov, Ivan 23
Aleksej 115, 115n
Aleksej, Archpriest 145, 170n
Aleksej Mixajlovič, Tsar 30, 380
Aleksij (Aleksej), Metropolitan 62, 324
Aleksandr, Deacon 380n
Alexander, Bishop 85
Alexander Nevsky (Aleksandr Nevskij),
   (Grand) Prince 24, 148, 236, 335
Alexius, see Aleksij, Metropolitan
Al-Fergan 162
Alimpij 60
Al-Masudi 239, 240n
Amartol, Georgij, see Hamartolos, George
Ananias 219
Anastas, Bishop 76, 77, 77n
Anastasia, Saint 143n, 146
Anatoli, Jakov 162
Andrej Bogoljubskij, Prince 59
Andrew, the Apostle, Saint 213
Andrew Stratilates, Saint 211
Anna, Saint 210, 212
Anna Jaroslavna, Queen 242
Antonij Pečerskij, the Blessed 57, 57n, 60,
   242
Antonij Rimljanin 212
Aquila 155, 155n, 156
Areios Makedonios 195
Ariana 192n
Aristotle 20, 61, 66
Arkadij 217
Artemij 201n
Aschaneus, Martin 87n
Athanasios of Alexandria, Patriarch 154
Avraam, see Abraham
Avraam Krymskij 162n
Avraamij, monk 379

Avvakum, Archpriest 204, 205, 253, 366n,
   368n, 378, 379, 379n
Azariah 219
Azarin, Simon, monk 65
Barachiah 40
Baranov, Captain 369
Barbara, Saint 34n, 215
Basil, Emperor 77
Basil the Great, Saint 9, 20, 55, 127, 128,
   135n, 188, 217, 220, 259, 260
Basil the New, Saint 36n
Baškin, Matvej 200, 200n, 201
Batu (Batyj), Khan 27, 73, 73n, 74n, 75, 75n
Bede, the Venerable 263
Benedict of Nursia, Saint 54
Benjamin, Dominican 29, 30, 101, 344, 350,
   351, 352, 353, 353n
Blasius, Saint 182, 183, 184, 216, 218
Boccaccio 263
Bogomil 18
Boleslav, Prince 40, 41, 43, 46, 47, 49, 50, 51, 52
Boris, Prince 4, 154
Boris, Saint 33, 33n, 34, 34n, 35, 36, 37, 38, 39,
   39n, 40, 40n, 41, 42, 43, 44, 46, 46n, 47, 47n,
   48, 48n, 50, 51, 52, 53, 180, 180n, 214, 215,
   217, 218, 222, 240n, 242, 245, 245n, 278, 335
Borough, Christopher 153n
Budny, Szymon 201n
Cain 41, 45, 48, 49
Camblak, Grigorij, Metropolitan 13, 14, 15,
   16n, 18, 29, 144
Catherine II, the Great, Empress 203
Charles IV, Emperor 351
Chaucer 263
Choiroboskos, see Georgios Choiroboskos
Chrétien de Troyes 263
Christian 33n, 37, 41
Clement, Saint 214
Constantine I, Emperor 176
Constantine-Cyril, see Cyril, Saint
Constantine Ducas 36n
Constantine of Murom, see Konstantin
   Muromskij
Constantine VII, Porphyrogenitos, Emperor
   77, 240
Constantine, Saint, see Cyril, Saint
Corvinus, Matthias, King 159

John, the Apostle, see John the Evangelist,
Saint
John the Evangelist, Saint 48, 48n, 129n, 192,
194, 194n, 195, 214, 219, 259, 278
John the Almsgiver, Saint, Patriarch 216
John the Baptist (the Forerunner), Saint 142,
182, 184n, 186, 188, 212, 214, 215, 218, 219
John the Compassionate, Saint, 221
John the Theologian, see John the Evangelist,
Saint
John Vladimir, Saint, Prince 33, 33n, 36n, 38,
42, 53
Joseph 339
Joseph of Arimathea 319
Josephus Flavius 160n, 161, 242, 245
Judas 41, 349
Judith 235, 235n, 236n, 343n, 344
Jurij Podyvnikov 115, 115n
Justinian I, Emperor 176
Jurij Ivanovič, Prince 78, 168
Kallistos, Patriarch 24n, 323
Karadžić, Vuk 22
Kiprian, Metropolitan 13, 13n, 14, 15, 17, 18,
29, 134, 134n, 135n, 136n, 138, 140
Kirik 137n
Kirill Belozerskij 25, 66, 67
Kirill, see Cyril, Saint
Kirill Trankvillion Stavroveckij 378, 378n
Kirill Turovskij, Bishop 16, 20, 21, 22, 105,
108, 319
Kliment of Ohrid, Bishop 4, 21
Kliment Smoljatič, Metropolitan 274
Konstantin, boyar 220, 221, 222
Konstantin Filosof, see Cyril, Saint
Konstantin Konstantinovič, Prince 345
Konstantin Muromskij 338, 374
Konstantin of Kostenec (Kostenečki) 15, 16n,
253, 255, 255n, 278
Konstantin of Preslav, Bishop 4
Konstantin the Philosopher, see Konstantin of
Kostenec (Kostenečki)
Kostjantin Porfienitos, see Constantine VII
Porphyrogenitos, Emperor
Kotošixin, Grigorij 112, 112n, 147
Kožma, Presbyter 154, 192
Kožma, see Cosmas, Saint
Kristián, see Christian
Križanić, Juraj 30
Kukuj 211
Kuricyn, Fedor 153, 157, 157n, 158, 158n, 159,
159n, 160, 161, 170n
Kyprianos, see Cyprian, Saint, Bishop

Lazar', priest 379
Lazar, Prince 36n
Lazarus, Saint 128, 129, 129n, 130, 131, 131n,
132, 132n, 133n, 140, 141, 144, 144n, 339,
339n
Leontij Rostovskij 338
Lidmile, see Ludmila, Saint, Princess
Liutprand of Cremona 263
Lomonosov, Mixail 253
Ludmila, Saint, Princess 33, 33n, 34, 37,
37n, 41n, 43, 47n 52, 180, 240
Ludolf, Heinrich (Henricus) Wilhelm 233,
233n, 366, 366n
Luka Židjata, Bishop 243
Luke, Saint 219, 258n
Lysias 20
Maccabees 343n, 344, 345, 361n, 363
Magnus of Orkney, Saint 38, 42
Makarij antioxijskij, see Makarios, Patriarch
Makarij, Archbishop, see Makarij, Metropol-
itan
Makarij, Metropolitan 84n, 89, 89n, 91n, 96n,
99, 100, 100n, 116, 116n, 117, 169n, 202,
202n, 205, 326
Maksim Grek 151, 237, 366, 366n, 368, 368n,
379, 379n
Makarios, patriarch of Antioch 88, 88n
Maksim Kalin, Igumen 328, 328n
Malalas, John 9, 9n, 242
Malyševič, Prokša, boyar 220
Manuel I Komnenos, Emperor 98
Maria (mother of Saint Stephen of Perm')
327, 327n
Martirij, Archbishop 221
Mary of Egypt, Saint 125, 127, 128
Matthew, the Apostle, Saint 259, 278, 303
Maximus the Confessor 256, 257n
Meletios, Bishop 339
Menander 154
Menander Protector 64
Methodios, Patriarch 135n
Methodios of Patara 142
Methodius, Saint 5, 21, 134n, 261, 368
Micah 313
Michael, the Archangel, Saint 184, 184n, 186n,
213, 214, 217, 218, 219
Michael III, Emperor 135n
Mikula, see Nicholas, Saint
Miloneg 219, 219n
Miroška, Posadnik 220
Mitrofan, Bishop 78, 78n, 164n
Mixail, Prince 27